FINANCIAL ACCOUNTING THEORY

Seventh Edition

William R. Scott
University of Waterloo

Toronto

To Mary Ann, Julie, Martha, Kathy, Paul, and Cary

Acquisitions Editor: Megan Farrell
Sponsoring Editor: Kathleen McGill
Marketing Manager: Claire Varley
Program Manager: Madhu Ranadive
Developmental Editor: Rebecca Ryoji
Project Manager: Jessica Hellen
Production Services: Raghavi Khullar, Cenveo® Publisher Services
Permissions Project Manager: Joanne Tang
Text Permissions Research: Anna Waluk, Electronic Publishing Services
Cover Designer: Suzanne Behnke
Cover Image: © demonishen/Fotolia

---

10 9 8 7 6 5 4 3 2 [EB]

Library and Archives Canada Cataloguing in Publication

Scott, William R. (William Robert), 1931-, author
    Financial accounting theory / William R. Scott. – Seventh
edition.

Includes bibliographical references and index.
ISBN 978-0-13-298466-9 (bound)

    1. Accounting—Textbooks. I. Title.

HF5635.S36 2014   657'.044   C2013-906491-5

ISBN 978-0-13-298466-9

Contents

13 Standard Setting: Political Issues 530

Preface

This book began as a series of lesson notes for a financial accounting theory course of the Certified General Accountants' Association of Canada (CGA). The lesson notes grew out of a conviction that we have learned a great deal about the role of financial accounting and reporting in our society from securities markets and information economics-based research conducted over many years, and that financial accounting theory comes into its own when we formally recognize the information asymmetries that pervade business relationships.

The challenge was to organize this large body of research into a unifying framework and to explain it in such a manner that professionally oriented students would both understand and accept it as relevant to the financial accounting environment and ultimately to their own professional careers.

This book seems to have achieved its goals. In addition to being part of the CGA program of professional studies for a number of years, it has been extensively used in financial accounting theory courses at the University of Waterloo, Queen's University, and numerous other universities, both at the senior undergraduate and professional master's levels. I am encouraged by the fact that, by and large, students comprehend the material and, indeed, are likely to object if the instructor follows it too closely in class. This frees up class time to expand coverage of areas of interest to individual instructors and/or to motivate particular topics by means of articles from the financial press and professional and academic literature.

Despite its theoretical orientation, the book does not ignore the institutional structure of financial accounting and standard setting. It features considerable coverage of financial accounting standards. Many important standards, such as fair value accounting, financial instruments, reserve recognition accounting, management discussion and analysis, employee stock options, impairment tests, hedge accounting, derecognition, consolidation, and comprehensive income, are described and critically evaluated. The structure of standard-setting bodies is also described, and the role of structure in helping to engineer the consent necessary for a successful standard is evaluated. While the text discussion concentrates on relating standards to the theoretical framework of the book, the coverage provides students with exposure to the contents of the standards themselves.

I have also used this material in Ph.D. seminars. Here, I concentrate on the research articles that underlie the text discussion. Nevertheless, the students appreciate the framework of the book as a way of putting specific research papers into perspective. Indeed, the book proceeds in large part by selecting important research papers for description and commentary, and provides extensive references to other research papers underlying the text discussion. Assignment of the research papers themselves could be especially useful for instructors who wish to dig into methodological issues that, with some exceptions, are downplayed in the book itself.

This edition continues to orient the coverage of accounting standards to those of the International Accounting Standards Board (IASB). As in previous editions, some coverage of major U.S. accounting standards is also included.

I have retained the outline of the events leading up to the 2007–2008 securities market meltdowns, since these events have raised significant questions about the validity of many economic models, and continue to have significant accounting implications. Ramifications of these events are interwoven throughout the book. For example, one outcome of the meltdowns is severe criticisms of the efficient market hypothesis. Nevertheless, I continue to maintain that investors are, on average, rational and that securities markets, while not fully (semi-strong) efficient, are sufficiently close to efficiency (except during periods of bubble and subsequent liquidity pricing) that the implications of the theory continue to be relevant to financial reporting. Critical evaluation of these various criticisms and arguments is given. Nevertheless, I have moved from Chapter 3 to the Instructor's Manual the lengthy outline of the diversified portfolio investment decision that was included in previous editions, replacing it with a much abbreviated discussion.

The Conceptual Framework retains its role as an important component of this book. As it is further developed, this framework will be an important aspect of the financial accounting environment. Its relationships to the theory developed here are critically evaluated. While extensive discussion of alternate theories of investor behaviour is retained, this book continues to regard the theory of rational investors as important to helping accountants prepare useful financial statement information.

The book continues to maintain that motivating responsible manager behaviour and improving the working of managerial labour markets is an equally important role for financial reporting in a markets-oriented economy as for enabling good investment decisions and improving the working of securities markets.

I have updated references and discussion of recent research articles, revised the exposition as a result of comments received and experience in teaching from earlier editions, and added new problem material. I also continue to suggest optional sections for those who do not wish to delve too deeply into certain topics.

Summary of Major Changes

Below is a comprehensive list of major changes made to the seventh edition of *Financial Accounting Theory*:

- Thorough review of recent academic accounting research, with updated explanations and discussion of important papers added throughout the text. The text represents the current state of academic accounting theory as published in major research journals up to about mid-2013.

- Increased attention to contract theory (replacing positive accounting theory), with Chapter 8 rewritten to fully explain the roles of reliability and conservatism of accounting information in securing efficient corporate governance, borrowing, and stewardship.

- Extensive discussion and evaluation of criticisms of securities market efficiency and investor rationality following the 2007–2008 securities market meltdowns. Much accounting research relies on these concepts. The important assumptions of rational expectations, common knowledge, and market liquidity that underlie market efficiency theory are explained and discussed. The text concludes that relaxation of these assumptions is needed if accountants are to better understand the working of securities markets and the information needs of investors. The text also concludes that accounting-related securities anomalies, typically claimed to result from investor non-rationality, can also be consistent with investor rationality once these assumptions are relaxed. Theoretical and empirical papers supporting these conclusions are outlined (Chapters 4 and 6).

- New and proposed accounting standards, including for financial instruments, derecognition, consolidation, leases, and loan loss provisioning, are described and evaluated. Discussion of the Conceptual Framework is updated throughout the book.

- Discussion of standards convergence and the possibility of U.S. adoption of International Accounting Standards is updated to take recent developments into account (Chapter 13).

- Recent research using sophisticated computer software to evaluate the information content of the written and spoken word is explained and evaluated. The text includes coverage of research papers using this methodology to study the informativeness of Management Discussion and Analysis (Chapter 3) and of executive conference calls (Chapter 11).

- New problem material is added throughout the text, including numerical problems of present value accounting, decision theory, and agency. Other new problems are based on embedded value, earnout contracts, outside directors, bail-in bonds, delegated monitoring, ESO repricing, and Sarbanes-Oxley Act. Discussions and problem materials derived from recent accounting scandals (Groupon, Olympus Corp., and Satyam Computer Services) are also added.

- Discussion of whether information risk is diversifiable, and thus of the extent to which firms benefit from superior accounting disclosure, is updated in the light of recent research (Chapter 12).

- The lengthy explanation of portfolio theory, included in all previous editions, is moved to the Instructor's Manual, replaced by a much shorter explanation of portfolio diversification (Chapter 3).

- Discussion and illustration of Management Discussion and Analysis (Chapter 3) and of Reserve Recognition Accounting (Chapter 2) are updated.

SUPPLEMENTS

Instructor's Solutions Manual

The Instructor's Solutions Manual includes suggested solutions to all the end-of-chapter Questions and Problems. It also offers learning objectives for each chapter and suggests teaching approaches that could be used. In addition, it comments on other issues for consideration, suggests supplementary references, and contains some additional problem material taken from previous text editions. The Instructor's Manual is available in print format and also available for downloading from a password-protected section of Pearson Education Canada's online catalogue (www.pearsoned.ca/highered). Navigate to your book's catalogue page to view a list of supplements that are available. See your local sales representative for details and access.

- **PowerPoint® Lecture Slides** PowerPoint presentations offer a comprehensive selection of slides covering theories and examples presented in the text. They are designed to organize the delivery of content to students and stimulate classroom discussion. The PowerPoint® Lecture Slides are available for downloading from a password-protected section of Pearson Education Canada's online catalogue (www.pearsoned.ca/highered). Navigate to your book's catalogue page to view a list of supplements that are available. See your local sales representative for details and access.

- **CourseSmart for Instructors** CourseSmart goes beyond traditional expectations, providing instant online access to the textbooks and course materials you need at a lower cost for students. And even as students save money, you can save time and hassle with a digital eTextbook that allows you to search for the most relevant content at the very moment you need it. Whether it's evaluating textbooks or creating lecture notes to help students with difficult concepts, CourseSmart can make life a little easier. See how when you visit www.coursesmart.com/instructors.

- **CourseSmart for Students** CourseSmart goes beyond traditional expectations, providing instant, online access to the textbooks and course materials you need at an average savings of 50%. With instant access from any computer and the ability to search your text, you'll find the content you need quickly, no matter where you are. And with online tools like highlighting and note-taking, you can save time and study efficiently. See all the benefits at www.coursesmart.com/students

- **Pearson Custom Library** Create your own textbook by choosing the chapters that best suit your own course needs, increases value for students, and fits your course perfectly. With a minimum enrolment of 25 students, you can begin building your custom text. Visit www.pearsoncustomlibrary.com to get started.

Acknowledgments

I have received a lot of assistance in writing this book. I thank CGA Canada for its encouragement and support over the past years. I acknowledge the financial assistance of the Ontario Chartered Accountants' Chair in Accounting at the University of Waterloo, which enabled teaching relief and other support in the preparation of the original manuscript. Financial support of the School of Business of Queen's University is also gratefully acknowledged.

I extend my thanks and appreciation to the following instructors, who provided formal reviews for this seventh edition:

Hilary Becker, Ph.D., CGA
Carleton University
Sprott School of Business

Carla Carnaghan
University of Lethbridge
Faculty of Management

Roger Collins
Thompson Rivers University
School of Business and Economics

Charles Draimin
Concordia University
John Molson School of Business

Wenxia Ge
University of Manitoba
Asper School of Business

Luo He
Concordia University
John Molson School of Business

Camillo Lento
Lakehead University
Faculty of Business Administration

I also thank numerous colleagues and students for advice and feedback. These include Sati Bandyopadhyay, Jean-Etienne De Bettignies, Phelim Boyle, Dennis Chung, Len Eckel, Haim Falk, Steve Fortin, Irene Gordon, Jennifer Kao, James A. Largay, David Manry, Patricia O'Brien, Bill Richardson, Gordon Richardson, Dean Smith, Dan Thornton, and Mike Welker. Special thanks to Alex Milburn for invaluable assistance in understanding IASB standards, and to Dick VanOfferen for helpful comments and support on all editions of this work.

I thank the large number of researchers whose work underlies this book. As previously mentioned, numerous research papers are described and referenced. However, there are many other worthy papers that I have not referenced. This implies no disrespect or lack of appreciation for the contributions of these authors to financial accounting theory. Rather, it has been simply impossible to include them all, both for reasons of space and the boundaries of my own knowledge.

I am grateful to Carolyn Holden for skilful, timely, and cheerful typing of the original manuscript in the face of numerous revisions, and to Jill Nucci for research assistance.

At Pearson Canada I would like to thank Gary Bennett, Vice-President, Editorial Director; Claudine O'Donnell, Managing Editor, Business Publishing; Megan Farrell, Acquisitions Editor; Kathleen McGill, Sponsoring Editor; Rebecca Ryoji, Developmental Editor; Jessica Hellen, Project Manager; Marg Bukta, Copyeditor; Raghavi Khullar, Production Editor; Proofreader, Sally Glover; and Claire Varley, Marketing Manager.

Finally, I thank my wife and family, who, in many ways, have been involved in the learning process leading to this book.

William Scott

Chapter 1
Introduction

Figure 1.1 Organization of the Book

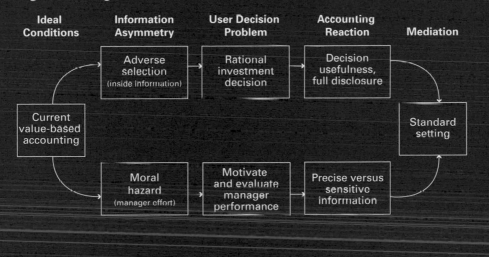

1.1 THE OBJECTIVE OF THIS BOOK

This book is about accounting, not about how to account. It argues that accounting students, having been exposed to the methodology and practice of accounting, need to examine the broader implications of financial accounting for the fair and efficient working of our economy. Our objective is to give the reader a critical awareness of the current financial accounting and reporting environment, taking into account the diverse interests of both external users and management.

1.2 SOME HISTORICAL PERSPECTIVE

Accounting has a long history. Our perspective begins with the double entry bookkeeping system. The first complete description of this system appeared in 1494, authored by Luca Paciolo, an Italian monk/mathematician.[1] Paciolo did not invent this system—it had developed over a long period of time. Segments that developed first included, for example, the collection of an account receivable. "Both sides" of such a transaction were easy to see, since cash and accounts receivable have a physical and/or legal existence, and the increase in cash was equal to the decrease in accounts receivable. The recording of other types of transactions, such as the sale of goods or the incurring of expenses, however, took longer to develop. In the case of a sale, it was obvious that cash or accounts receivable increased, and that goods on hand decreased. But, what about the difference between the selling price and the cost of the goods sold? There is no physical or legal representation of the profit on the sale. For the double entry system to handle transactions such as this, it was necessary to create *abstract* concepts of income and capital. By Paciolo's time, these concepts had developed, and a complete double entry system, quite similar to the one in use today, was in place. The abstract nature of this system, including the properties of capital as the accumulation of income and income as the rate of change of capital,[2] attracted the attention of mathematicians of the time. The "method of Venice," as Paciolo's system was called, was frequently included in mathematics texts in subsequent years.

Following 1494, the double entry system spread throughout Europe. It was in Europe that another sequence of important accounting developments took place. The Dutch East India Company was established in 1602. It was the first company to issue shares with limited liability for all its shareholders. Shares were transferable, and could be traded on the Amsterdam Stock Exchange, also established in 1602. In subsequent years, the concept of a joint stock company, with permanent existence, limited liability, and shares traded on a stock exchange, became an important form of business organization.

Obviously, investors needed financial information about the firms whose shares they were trading. Thus began a long transition for financial accounting, from a system enabling a merchant to control his/her own operations to a system to inform investors who were not involved in the day-to-day operations of the firm. It was in the joint interests of the firm and investors that financial information provided by the firm was trustworthy, thereby laying the groundwork for the development of an auditing profession and government regulation.

In this regard, the English 1844 Companies Act was notable. It was in this Act that the concept of providing an audited balance sheet to shareholders first appeared in the law, although this requirement was dropped in subsequent years[3] and not reinstated until the early 1900s. During the interval, voluntary provision of information was common, but its effectiveness was hampered by a lack of accounting principles. This was demonstrated, for example, in the controversy over whether amortization of capital assets had to be deducted in determining income available for dividends (the English courts ruled it did not).

In the twentieth century, major developments in financial accounting shifted to the United States, which was growing rapidly in economic power. The introduction of a corporate income tax in the United States in 1909 provided a major impetus to income measurement and, as noted by Hatfield (1927, p. 140), was influential in persuading business managers to accept amortization as a deduction from income.

Nevertheless, accounting in the United States continued to be relatively unregulated, with financial reporting and auditing largely voluntary. However, the stock market crash of 1929 and resulting Great Depression led to major changes by the U.S. government. The most noteworthy was the creation of the Securities and Exchange Commission (SEC) by the Securities Act of 1934, with a focus on protecting investors by means of a disclosure-based structure. The Act regulates dealing in the securities of firms that meet certain size tests and whose securities are traded in more than one state. As part of its mandate, the SEC has the responsibility to ensure that investors are supplied with adequate information.

Merino and Neimark (MN; 1982) examined the conditions leading up to the creation of the SEC. In the process, they reported on some of the securities market practices of the 1920s and prior. Apparently, voluntary disclosure was widespread, as also noted by Benston (1973). However, MN claimed that such disclosure was motivated by big business's desire to avoid disclosure regulations that would reduce its monopoly power.

Regulations to enforce disclosure would reduce monopoly power by better enabling potential entrants to identify high-profit industries. Presumably, if voluntary disclosure was adequate, the government would not feel that regulated disclosure was necessary. Thus, informing investors was not the main motivation for disclosure. Instead, investors were "protected" by a "two-tiered" market structure whereby prices were set by knowledgeable insiders, subject to a self-imposed "moral regulation" to control misleading reporting. Unfortunately, moral regulation was not always effective, and MN referred to numerous instances of manipulative financial reporting and other abuses, which were widely believed to be major contributing factors to the 1929 crash.

The 1934 securities legislation, then, can be regarded as a movement away from an avoidance-of-regulation rationale for disclosure toward one supplying better-quality information to investors as a way to control manipulative financial practices.[4]

One of the practices of the 1920s that received criticism was the frequent appraisal and/or overstatement of capital assets, the values of which came crashing down in 1929.[5] A major lesson learned by accountants as a result of the Great Depression was that values are fleeting. The outcome was a strengthening of the historical cost basis of accounting. This basis received its highest expression in the famous Paton and Littleton (1940) monograph *An Introduction to Corporate Accounting Standards*. This document elegantly and persuasively set forth the case for historical cost accounting, based on the concept of the firm as a going concern. This concept justifies important attributes of historical cost accounting, such as waiting to recognize revenue until objective evidence of realization is available, the use of accruals to match realized revenues and the costs of earning those revenues, and the deferral of unrealized gains and losses on the balance sheet until the time comes to match them with revenues. As a result, the income statement shows the current "installment" of the firm's earning power. The income statement replaced the balance sheet as the primary focus of financial reporting.

It is sometimes claimed that the Paton and Littleton monograph was too persuasive, in that it shut out exploration of alternative bases of accounting. However, alternative valuation bases have become more common over the years, to the point where we now have a **mixed measurement system**. Historical cost is still the primary basis of accounting for important asset and liability classes, such as capital assets, inventories, and long-term debt. However, if assets are impaired, they are frequently written down to a lower value. Impairment tests (also called ceiling tests) for capital assets and the lower-of-cost-or-market rule for inventories are examples. Under International Accounting Standards Board (IASB) standards, capital assets can sometimes be written up over cost if their value has increased. Generally speaking, standard setters have moved steadily toward current value alternatives to historical cost accounting over the past number of years.

There are two main current value alternatives to historical cost for assets and liabilities. One is **value-in-use**, such as discounted present value of future cash flows. The other is **fair value**, also called **exit price** or **opportunity cost**, the amount that would be received or paid should the firm dispose of the asset or liability. These valuation bases will be discussed in Chapter 7. When we do not need to distinguish between them, we shall refer to valuations that depart from historical cost as **current values**.

While the historical cost lesson learned by accountants from the Great Depression may be in the process of being forgotten by standard setters, another lesson remains: how to survive in a disclosure-regulated environment. In the United States, for example, the SEC has the power to establish the accounting standards and procedures used by firms under its jurisdiction. If the SEC chose to use this power, the prestige and influence of the accounting profession would be greatly eroded, possibly to the point where financial reporting becomes a process of "manual thumbing," with little basis for professional judgment and little influence on the setting of accounting standards. However, the SEC usually chose to delegate most standard setting to the profession.[6] To retain this delegated authority, however, the accounting profession had to retain the SEC's confidence that it was doing a satisfactory job of creating and maintaining a financial reporting environment that protects and informs investors and encourages **well-working capital markets**— where, by "well-working," we mean markets on which the market values of assets and liabilities equal, or reasonably approximate, their real underlying fundamental values.

Thus began the search for basic accounting concepts, those underlying truths on which the practice of accounting is, or should be, based. This was seen as a way to convince regulators that private sector standard setting bodies were capable of high quality accounting standards. Also, identification of concepts, it was felt, would improve practice by reducing inconsistencies in the choice of accounting policies across firms and enable the accounting for new reporting challenges[7] to be deduced from basic principles rather than developing in an ad hoc and inconsistent way. Despite great effort, however, accountants never did agree on a set of accounting concepts.[8, 9]

As a result of the lack of concepts, accounting theory and research up to the late 1960s consisted largely of *a priori* reasoning as to which accounting concepts and practices were "best." For example, should the effects of changing prices and inflation on financial statements be taken into account, and, if so, how? This debate can be traced back at least as far as the 1920s. Some accountants argued that the current values of specific assets and liabilities held by the firm should be recognized, with the resulting unrealized holding gains and losses included in net income.[10] Other accountants argued that inflation-induced changes in the purchasing power of money should be recognized. During a period of inflation, the firm suffers a purchasing power loss on monetary assets such as cash and accounts receivable, since the amounts of goods and services that can be obtained when they are collected and spent is less than the amounts that could have been obtained when they were created. Conversely, the firm enjoys a purchasing power gain on monetary liabilities such as accounts payable and long-term debt. Separate reporting of these gains and losses would better reflect real firm performance, it was argued. Still other accountants argued that the effects of *both* specific and inflation-induced changes in prices should be taken into account. Others, however, often including firm management, resisted these suggestions. One argument, based in part on experience from the Great Depression, was that measurement of inflation was problematic, and current values were very volatile, so that taking them into account would not necessarily improve the measurement of the firm's (and the manager's) performance.

Nevertheless, standard setters in numerous countries did require some disclosures of the effects of changing prices. For example, in the United States, Financial Accounting Standards Board Statement of Financial Accounting Standards No. 33 (1979) required supplementary disclosure of the effects on earnings of specific and general price level changes for property, plant and equipment, and inventories. This standard was subsequently withdrawn. However, this withdrawal was due more to a reduction of its cost effectiveness as inflation declined in later years than to the debate having been settled.

The basic problem with debates such as how to account for changing prices was that there was little theoretical basis for choosing among the various alternatives, particularly since, as mentioned, accountants were unable to agree on a set of basic accounting concepts.

During this period, however, major developments were taking place in other disciplines. In particular, a theory of rational decision making under uncertainty developed as a branch of statistics. This theory prescribes how individuals may revise their beliefs upon receipt of new information. The theory of efficient securities markets developed in economics and finance, with major implications for the role of information in capital markets. Another development was the Possibility Theorem of Arrow (1963), which demonstrated that, in general, it is not possible to combine differing preferences of individual members of society into a social preference ordering that satisfies reasonable conditions. This implies that there is no such thing as perfect or true accounting concepts, since, for example, investors will prefer different accounting concepts than will managers. Arrow's theorem demonstrates that no set of concepts will be fully satisfactory to both parties. Instead, concepts must be hammered out strategically through negotiation and compromise to the point where both parties are willing to accept them even though they are not perfectly satisfactory to either side. The difficulties that accountants have had in agreeing on basic concepts are thus not surprising. Without a complete set of basic concepts, accounting standards, which, ideally, are derived from the concepts, are subject to the same challenges.

These theories, which began to show up in accounting theory in the latter half of the 1960s, generated the concept of **decision useful** (in place of true) financial statement information. This view of the role of financial reporting first appeared in the American Accounting Association (AAA)[11] monograph *A Statement of Basic Accounting Theory*, in 1966. The joint **Conceptual Framework** of the IASB and the Financial Accounting Standards Board (FASB; 2010), which is the most recent statement of basic accounting concepts, is based on decision usefulness. That is, it states that the objective of financial statements is to provide information to assist investors to make investment decisions. Henceforth, we will usually refer to this document as the Conceptual Framework, or, if the context is clear, the Framework. It is discussed in Section 3.7.

Equally important was the development of the economics of imperfect information, based on a theory of rational decision making. The theory recognizes that some individuals have an information advantage over others. This led to the development of the theory of agency, which has greatly increased our understanding of the legitimate interests of business management in financial reporting and standard setting.

These theories suggest that the answer to which way, if any, to account for changing prices outlined above will be found in the extent to which they lead to good investment decisions. Furthermore, any resolution will have to take the concerns of management into account.

In Canada, the development of financial accounting and reporting has proceeded differently, although the end result is basically similar to that just described. Financial reporting requirements in Canada were laid down in federal and provincial corporations acts, along the lines of the English corporations acts referred to above. The ultimate power to regulate financial reporting rests with the legislatures concerned. However, in 1946, the Committee on Accounting and Auditing Research, now the Accounting Standards Board (AcSB) of the Canadian Institute of Chartered Accountants (CICA), began to issue bulletins on financial accounting issues. These were intended to guide Canadian accountants as to best practices, and did not have force of law. In 1968, these were formalized into the *CICA Handbook*. At first, adherence to these provisions was voluntary but, given their prestigious source, they were difficult to ignore. Over time, the *Handbook* gained recognition as the authoritative statement of Generally Accepted Accounting Principles (GAAP) in Canada. Ultimately, provincial securities commissions and the corporations acts formally recognized this authority. For example, in 1975, for federally regulated companies, the Canada Business Corporations Act required adherence to the *CICA Handbook* to satisfy reporting requirements under the Act. The end result, then, is similar to that in the United States and many other countries, in that the body with ultimate authority to set accounting standards has delegated this function to a private professional body.[12]

Subsequently, several notable events had a major impact on financial accounting and reporting. One such set of events followed from the stock market boom in the late 1990s and its collapse in the early 2000s. During the collapse, share prices of many firms, especially those in the "hi-tech" industry, fell precipitously. For example, while the share price of General Electric Corp., a large U.S. conglomerate firm, fell from a high of about US$55 in August 2000 to a low of about US$21 in October 2002, that of telecommunications firm Nortel Networks fell from a high of about US$82 to a low of 44 cents over the same period.

A contributing factor to the market collapse was the revelation of numerous financial reporting irregularities. Frequently, these involved revenue recognition, which has long been a problem in accounting theory and practice. In a study of 492 U.S. corporations that reported restatements of prior years' incomes during 1995–1999, Palmrose and Scholz (2004) report that revenue restatements were the single most common type of restatement in their sample. In part, this problem is due to the vagueness and generality of revenue recognition criteria. For example, under International Accounting Standard 18 (IAS 18),[13] revenue from the sale of goods can be recognized when the significant risks and rewards of ownership have been transferred to the buyer, the seller loses control over the items, the revenue and related costs can be measured reliably,[14] and collection is reasonably assured. Revenue from services is recognized as the work progresses. Revenue recognition criteria in the United States are broadly consistent with the above, although, at present, they differ somewhat across industries. Revenue can be recognized when it is "realized or realizable" and earned, where earned means the firm has done what it has to do to be entitled to the revenues.[15]

During the boom of the late 1990s, many firms, especially newly established ones with little or no history of profits, attempted to impress investors and enhance their stock prices by reporting a rapidly growing stream of revenue. Subsequently, when the boom collapsed, much recognized revenue proved to be premature and had to be reversed.

Theory in Practice 1.1

In July 2002, Qwest Communications International Inc., a large provider of Internet-based communications services, announced that it was under investigation by the SEC. Its share price immediately fell by 32%. In February 2003, the SEC announced fraud charges against several senior Qwest executives, alleging that they had inflated revenues during 2000 and 2001 in order to meet revenue and earnings projections.

One tactic used was to separate long-term sales of equipment and services into two components. Full revenue was immediately recognized on the equipment component despite the obligation to honour the service component over an extended period. A related tactic was to price services at cost, putting all profit into the equipment component, which, as just mentioned, was immediately recognized as revenue despite a continuing obligation to protect the customer from risk of obsolescence on the equipment "sold." Yet another tactic was to recognize revenue from the sale of fibre-optic cable despite an ability of the purchaser to exchange the cable at a later date. In retrospect, Qwest's revenue recognition practices were premature, to say the least.

In June 2004, the SEC announced settlements with some of the officers charged. One officer, for example, repaid $200,000 of "ill-gotten gains," plus a penalty of $150,000, and agreed to "cease and desist" from any future violations.

Numerous other, even more serious, failures of financial reporting also came to light. Two of these are particularly notable. Enron Corp. was a large U.S. corporation with initial interests in natural gas distribution. Following substantial deregulation of the natural gas market in the United States during the 1980s, Enron successfully expanded its operations to become an intermediary between natural gas producers and users, thereby enabling them to manage their exposures to fluctuating natural gas prices. For example, it offered long-term fixed-price contracts to public utilities and natural gas producers. Subsequently, Enron extended this business model to a variety of other trading activities, including steel, natural gas, electricity, and weather futures. Its stock market performance was dramatic, rising from US$20 in early 1998 to a high of about US$90 per share in September, 2000. To finance this rapid expansion, and support its share price, Enron needed both large amounts of capital and steadily increasing earnings. Meeting these needs was complicated by the fact that its forays into new markets were not always profitable, creating a temptation to disguise losses.[16]

In the face of these challenges, Enron resorted to devious tactics. One tactic was to create various special purpose entities (SPEs). These were limited partnerships formed for specific purposes, and effectively controlled by senior Enron officers. These SPEs were financed largely by Enron's contributions of its own common stock, in return for notes receivable from the SPE. The SPE could then borrow money using the Enron stock as security, and use the borrowed cash to repay its note payable to Enron. In this manner, much of Enron's debt did not appear on its balance sheet—it appeared on the books of the SPEs instead.

In addition, Enron received fees for management and other services supplied to its SPEs, and also investment income. This investment income is particularly worthy of note. By applying current value accounting to its holdings of Enron stock, the SPE included increases in the value of this stock in its income. As an owner of the SPE, Enron included its share of the SPE's income in its own earnings. In effect, Enron was able to include increases in the value of its own stock in its reported earnings! In 2006, financial media, reporting on a five-and-a-half-year jail sentence of Enron's chief accounting officer for his part in the Enron fraud, revealed that $85 million of Enron's 2000 reported operating earnings of $979 million came from this source.

Of course, if the SPEs had been consolidated with Enron's financial statements, as they should have been, the effects of these tactics would disappear. The SPE debt would then have shown on Enron's consolidated balance sheet, fees billed would have been offset against the corresponding expense recorded by the SPE, and Enron's investment in its SPEs would have been deducted from its shareholders' equity.

However, the SPEs were not consolidated, seemingly with the agreement of Enron's auditor. But, in late 2001, Enron announced that it would now consolidate, apparently in response to an inquiry from the SEC. This resulted in an increase in its reported debt of some $628 million, a decrease in its shareholders' equity of $1.1 billion, and large reductions in previously reported earnings. Investors quickly lost all confidence in the company. Its share price fell to almost zero, and it filed for bankruptcy protection in 2001.

A second major abuse involved WorldCom Inc., a large U.S. telecommunications carrier. During the years 1999 to 2002, the company overstated its earnings by about $11 billion. Almost $4 billion of this amount arose from capitalization of network maintenance and other costs that should have been charged to expense as incurred—a tactic that overstated both reported earnings and operating cash flow. Another $3.3 billion of overstatement arose from reductions in the allowance for doubtful accounts. Again, when these abuses came to light, investor confidence collapsed and WorldCom applied for bankruptcy protection in 2002.

These, and numerous other, reporting abuses took place regardless of the fact that the financial statements of the companies involved were audited and certified as being in accordance with GAAP. As a result, public confidence in financial reporting and the working of capital markets was severely shaken.

One result of the reduction of public confidence was increased regulation. The most notable example is the Sarbanes-Oxley Act, passed by the U.S. Congress in 2002. This wide-ranging Act was designed to restore confidence by reducing the probability of accounting horror stories such as those just described. The Act did this by tightening the audit function and improving **corporate governance**, where by corporate governance we mean those policies that align the firm's activities with the interests of its investors and society. For example, creation of an audit committee of the Board of Directors is a corporate governance policy to tighten the audit function by improving communication between the Board and the firm's auditor, particularly where the auditor has concerns about the manager's operation of the firm's accounting and reporting system.

To improve corporate governance, a major provision of Sarbanes-Oxley was to create the Public Company Accounting Oversight Board (PCAOB). This agency has the power to set auditing standards and to inspect and discipline auditors of public companies. The Act also restricts several of the non-audit services offered by auditing firms to their clients, such as information systems and valuation services. Furthermore, the auditor now reports to the audit committee of the client's board of directors, rather than to management. The audit committee must be composed of directors independent of company management. In Canada, the Canadian Public Accountability Board (CPAB), created in 2003 by federal legislation, has a similar role.

Other provisions of Sarbanes-Oxley include a requirement that firms' financial reports shall include "all material correcting adjustments" and disclose all material off-balance-sheet loans and other relations with "unconsolidated entities." Furthermore, the Chief Executive Officer (CEO) and Chief Financial Officer (CFO) must certify that the financial statements present fairly the company's results of operations and financial position. The Act required these two officers, and an independent auditor, to certify the proper operation of the company's internal controls over financial reporting, with deficiencies, and their remediation, publicly reported. (These requirements were relaxed somewhat in 2007.) Similar regulations are in place in Canada, except that officers' certification of internal controls need not be attested to by an independent auditor.

Accounting standard setters also moved to restore public confidence. One move was to tighten the rules surrounding SPEs, so that it was more difficult to avoid their consolidation with the financial statements of the parent entity.

1.3 THE 2007–2008 MARKET MELTDOWNS

Despite these new regulations and standards, however, the use of SPEs did not decline, particularly by financial institutions, where they were frequently called **structured investment vehicles** (SIVs). These vehicles were often created by lenders such as banks, mortgage companies, and other financial institutions to securitize their holdings of mortgages, credit card balances, auto loans, and other financial assets. That is, the institution would transfer large pools of these assets to the SIVs it sponsors. The SIV would pool them into **asset-backed securities** (ABSs)[17]—that is, into tranches of similar credit quality. Thus, a particular ABS would be a tranche of, say, residential mortgages of high quality, another ABS would be of lower quality, etc., down to "subprime" mortgages of lowest quality. These various ABS tranches would then be resold to investors[18] or, particularly for the lowest quality tranche, retained by the SIV and its sponsor to help convince investors that the firm stood behind the investments it sold. As mortgagors made payments, cash flowed to the SIV and on to the tranche holders, after deduction of various fees. Holders of higher-quality (i.e., lower-risk) tranches received a lower return than holders of lower-quality tranches, since they were less subject to defaults by the original mortgage borrowers.

ABSs were highly popular with investors, including many financial institutions, since they offered higher returns than, say, bonds, and were viewed (wrongly, as it turned out) as no riskier than bonds even though the return was higher. In part, this perception of ABS safety was fuelled by a belief that house prices, the ultimate security underlying mortgages, would continue to rise. Perceived safety was also enhanced because of the apparent diversification of **credit risk**, where credit risk is the risk that a party to a financial contract, such as a mortgage, will be unable to meet its financial obligations. This diversification was created by the spreading of credit risk across the large underlying pool of mortgages or other financial assets that backed up ABSs—while some mortgages may go bad, it was felt that these would be a small proportion of the mortgages in the pool. Perceived safety was also reinforced by high-quality ratings from investment rating agencies. Furthermore, investors could customize their investments by buying tranches of the particular risk and return that they desired.

ABSs were frequently further securitized as **collateralized debt obligations** (CDOs), which consisted of tranches of similar quality ABS tranches, a procedure that further increased diversification. Unlike ABSs, CDOs tended to be arranged and sold privately, and often consisted of riskier mortgages or other assets. Henceforth, when it is not necessary to distinguish them, we will refer to these securities collectively as ABSs. To finance the assets purchased from its sponsor, SIVs borrowed money, often by issuing **asset-backed commercial paper** (ABCP).[19] ABCP paid higher interest rates than treasury bills and, like the underlying ABSs, typically received high ratings from investment rating agencies. Thus ABCP was popular with companies and other investors who wanted to invest surplus cash for a short term.

Alternatively, SIVs could retain ABSs rather than sell them on to investors. Since the ABSs generated higher returns than the cost of funds borrowed to acquire them, SIVs became "money machines."

Of course, since it resulted in high leverage, financing holdings of ABSs with borrowed money was a risky strategy for SIVs. The underlying reason is that borrowing and lending were "out of sync." That is, ABSs were long-term investments whereas ABCP borrowings were short term. Despite rising house prices and the inherent diversification of ABSs, some credit losses could still occur, reducing the safety of ABCP and affecting the SIV's ability to roll over maturing ABCP. Consequently, some form of **credit enhancement** of ABSs was often necessary if the SIV was to be able to borrow at a low interest rate. One way to accomplish this was the "**liquidity put**," under which the sponsor agreed to buy back the SIV's asset-backed securities should the market for them collapse. Other enhancements included retention of the lowest-quality tranche by the sponsoring institution, as mentioned above, and various explicit and implicit guarantees to reimburse purchasers for losses.

Also, SIVs could hedge their risk by purchasing **credit default swaps** (CDSs) from some intermediary, such as an insurance company. These were derivative financial instruments that would reimburse the SIV for all or part of credit losses on its ABSs. To obtain this insurance, the CDS purchaser paid a fee (called the spread) to the CDS issuer. The belief that credit losses on the underlying ABSs were protected further increased the confidence of lenders that ABSs and ABCP were low risk.

Note that if an SIV was consolidated into the financial statements of its sponsor, the high SIV leverage would show up on the sponsor's consolidated balance sheet. Despite the apparent safety of ABSs, sponsors would be penalized by the market if their leverage became sufficiently high. This was particularly so for financial institutions, many of which are subject to capital adequacy regulations. Consequently, firms that sponsored SIVs had an incentive to avoid consolidation of their SIVs into their own financial statements. Then, leverage could be further exploited by remaining off-balance sheet.[20]

However, as mentioned, standard setters had moved to tighten up the rules for consolidation of off-balance sheet vehicles. In the United States, FASB Interpretation No. 46(R) (FIN 46; 2003) expanded requirements for consolidation of a particular form of SIVs, called **variable interest entities** (VIEs), and required additional supplementary disclosures by firms with significant interests in VIEs.[21] Variable interests are ownership interests that absorb the expected losses and gains of the VIE—that is, they bear the risks. As noted above, VIEs are thinly capitalized, so that they need to borrow money in order to operate.

Under FIN 46, the primary beneficiary of the VIE (e.g., a bank or other financial institution) must consolidate its financial statements with the VIEs it sponsors. A primary beneficiary was the entity that absorbed a majority of the VIE's expected losses and received a majority of its expected gains. Thus, the primary beneficiary did not need to actually control the VIE (the usual criterion for consolidation) in order for consolidation to be required. It was felt that by mandating consolidation when a sponsor's exposure to their VIEs' risks and returns was significant (thereby bringing VIE assets and liabilities onto their sponsors' balance sheets), the financial reporting for financial institutions, particularly with respect to their overall solvency and capital adequacy, would be improved.

Nevertheless, many sponsors avoided consolidation by creating **expected loss notes** (ELNs). These were securities sold by sponsors to an outside party, under which that party contracted to absorb a majority of a VIE's expected losses and receive a majority of expected net returns. Thus, the holder of the ELN became the primary beneficiary under FIN 46, and consolidation would be with the financial statements of the ELN holder, not with the sponsor. Freed from consolidation, the sponsor could then exploit off-balance sheet VIE leverage as much as it wanted. Typically, the balance of net returns would go to the sponsor. In addition, sponsors would receive fees for various services rendered to VIEs.

Beginning in 2007, this whole structure came crashing down. It had become increasingly apparent that because of lax lending practices to stoke the demand for more and more ABSs to feed leverage profits, many of the mortgages underlying ABSs were unlikely to be repaid—it seems that when mortgage lenders knew that the mortgages they originated would be securitized and sold, they were less careful about evaluating borrowers' credit quality than they would be if they had intended to retain the mortgages. As a result, a major advantage of ABSs from an investor's perspective (diversification of credit risk across many similar assets) turned out to be their greatest weakness: *asset-backed securities lacked transparency*. That is, investors did not know what they contained. This was particularly so for CDOs, which tended not to be publicly traded. As concern about mortgage defaults and housing prices increased, investors were unable to (or neglected to) determine how many mortgages associated with a specific ABS were likely to go bad. Valuing ABSs was particularly difficult due to their complexity. As a result, valuation models based on well-working underlying market variables, which have been used for years to value securities such as options, were not available for ABSs. Instead, valuations were based on projected interest rates and historical default rates. These estimates did not anticipate the high default rates that began to appear.

The rational reaction to growing suspicion about the value of a security is to lower the price offered, or not to buy at all, leading to further declines in market value. The risk of a continuing decline in demand due to skeptical investors' lack of buying is called **liquidity risk**.[22] Note that liquidity risk can result in a market value less than value-in-use. To illustrate the effects of liquidity risk, financial media reported in July 2007 that two mutual funds of Bear Stearns (at the time, a large U.S. investment bank) were suffering severe losses on their large holdings of ABSs. This was followed in August 2007 with a suspension by BNP Paribas, a large France-based bank, of subscriptions to and redemptions of several of its investment funds, on grounds that market values of their holdings of ABSs were impossible to determine. Other U.S. and European financial institutions reported similar problems. In effect, the market for these securities collapsed.

There was another major contributing factor to the market collapse, however. Above, we mentioned that SIVs could purchase CDSs to insure any losses suffered on their ABSs. If so, why did investors lose confidence? The answer lies in **counterparty risk**. As mentioned, many SIVs purchased CDSs to reduce the credit risk of their ABSs. However, as concern about mortgage defaults grew, concern also grew that CDS issuers (i.e., counterparties) would not be able to meet their obligations.

Counterparty risk was greatly enhanced due to a significant CDS feature—it was not necessary for the purchaser of a CDS to own the underlying assets secured by that CDS. Anyone could buy and sell a so-called "naked" CDS that protected against losses on specific reference ABSs by reimbursing for declines in their value. Such a CDS would protect an investor who had no insurable interest in that ABS but wanted to hedge against the possibility of, say, a downturn in the housing market. If the housing market was to deteriorate, the value of ABSs based on that market would also decline. A CDS that pays off if an ABS declines in value would thus increase in value. Thus, in addition to their role in providing insurance, naked CDSs became a vehicle for speculators, since any event that lowered the value of ABS securities would raise the value of CDSs written on those securities.

The demand for CDSs became very high, and their issuance quickly spread from insurance companies to other financial institutions, attracted by the spread that they generated. Indeed, CDSs were often packaged into **synthetic CDOs**—that is, tranches of CDSs, for sale to investors and speculators. As a result, the face value of CDSs written on specific asset-backed securities could be many times their value (estimates ranged as high as five times). Also, like CDOs, CDSs and synthetic CDOs were not traded on an organized exchange, or even settled through clearing houses, where regulations would be in place to standardize, publicize, and protect the integrity of trade transactions. Instead, CDOs were bought and sold privately. These huge amounts of private trading of CDOs and CDSs, combined with the off-balance sheet nature of many VIEs, became part of what was known as the **shadow banking system**. A consequence of shadow banking was that it was difficult to know how many CDSs were outstanding against specific ABSs, except that if a reference ABS was to decline in value, insurance payouts could be huge. For example, the solvency, credit rating, and share price of American International Group, Inc. (AIG), a major U.S. issuer of CDSs, rapidly declined as it became apparent that it was unable to meet its obligations. One reason for this decline was AIG's obligation to post collateral as security to the holders of ABSs it had insured if their market value fell, an obligation that quickly reached $85 billion. In 2008, AIG had to be rescued by the U.S. government to prevent a complete collapse of the financial system. In sum, counterparty risk was a major contributing factor to the ABS market collapse.

Since asset-backed securities often secured ABCP, the ABCP market also was threatened with collapse. Thus SIVs faced several problems simultaneously. They were unable to roll over maturing ABCP from the proceeds of issue of fresh ABCP (no one would buy them due to the collapse of the ABS market), their holdings of ABSs themselves were difficult or impossible to value or sell, and the ability of CDS issuers such as AIG to reimburse losses was doubtful. In the face of this market collapse and severe counterparty risk, SIVs faced either insolvency or the necessity for their sponsors to buy back their impaired assets. For example, the *Financial Times* (November 19, 2008) reported that Citigroup returned the last $17.4 billion of assets of its sponsored SIVs to its balance sheet, recording a writedown of $1.1 billion in the process.

These buybacks had severe consequences, however. Paying for them lowered sponsors' solvency and required writedowns of the "toxic" assets thus acquired. These writedowns were in addition to writedowns of CDSs, and of asset-backed securities held directly by the sponsors. Further writedowns were frequently required as the fair value of these assets continued to deteriorate. Many sponsors failed, raised additional capital at distressed prices, or were rescued by governments, resulting in a major contraction of the financial system. The resulting security market collapse spread to the real economy, leading to worldwide recession, including drastic falls in share prices.

The underlying causes of these catastrophic events, which are rooted in both wealth inequality and global imbalances in consumption, trade, and foreign exchange markets, will be debated by economists and politicians for years. However, blame for the initial collapse of the market for asset-backed securities is usually laid at the feet of lax mortgage lending practices and inadequate regulation. The lack of transparency of the complex financial instruments created by the finance and investment communities was also at fault. Of greater significance for accountants, however, was sponsors' failure to adequately control the risks of excessive leverage in the quest for leverage profits. Firm managers were encouraged/enabled to take on excessive risk since, as described above, financial accounting standards allowed sponsor firms to avoid SIV consolidation, resulting in large amounts of off-balance sheet leverage. Accountants and auditors who allowed this avoidance were arguably meeting the letter of FIN 46 while avoiding its intent.

Another result of the meltdown was severe criticism of fair value accounting, since accounting standards required fair valuation for many financial instruments. Much of this criticism came from financial institutions. They claimed that the requirement to write down the carrying values of financial instruments as fair values fell created huge losses that threatened their capital adequacy ratios and eroded investor confidence. Writedowns were further criticized because inactive markets often meant that fair values had to be estimated by other means. For example, fair value of asset-backed securities could be estimated from the spreads charged by CDS issuers. Since these spreads became very high as underlying ABS values fell, the resulting fair value estimates reflected **liquidity pricing** in the market. Liquidity pricing is an outcome of liquidity risk (see Note 22), under which market value is less than the value-in-use that the institutions felt they would eventually realize if they held these assets to maturity.

Management's concerns about excessive writedowns had some validity. As mentioned above, ABSs lacked transparency. Since investors could not separate the good from the bad, all such securities became suspect. Returning to historical cost accounting, or at least allowing institutions to value these assets using their own internal estimates (i.e., value-in-use), it was claimed, would eliminate these excess writedowns. Of course, allowing firms to use their own internal valuations creates the possibility of manager bias.

Accounting standard setters attempted to hold their ground in the face of these criticisms of fair value. However, faced with threats that governments would step in to override fair value accounting, they did relax some requirements. For example, in October 2008, the IASB and FASB issued similar guidance on how to determine fair value when markets are inactive (i.e., melted down, in terms of our terminology). The guidance was that when market values did not exist and could not be reliably inferred from values of similar items, firms could determine fair value based on value-in-use.

Subsequently, the IASB and FASB embarked on a major reworking of fair value accounting standards, as well as standards on derecognition, consolidation, and revenue recognition. Some of these standards are described in Chapter 7.

Collectively, the events described above raise fundamental questions about the extent of regulation in a markets-based economy. It seems that relatively unregulated capital markets (e.g., the shadow banking system) are subject to catastrophic market failure. This came as a shock to many economists and politicians. The prevailing theory was that markets would always properly price assets, so that regulation could be confined to maintaining an orderly marketplace. Furthermore, it was felt that, in addition to imposing a costly bureaucracy, regulators were inferior to markets in determining what market price should be, and that the consequences of failures by regulators could prove more costly to society than some of the excesses of unfettered markets. These theories, based on underlying economic models of rational investor behaviour and asset pricing, have come under intense criticism following their failure to predict the market meltdowns. Some of these criticisms, and possible responses to them, are discussed later in this book. Market failures have in the past typically led to increased regulation. The question then is, how and to what extent should regulation be increased as a result of this most recent failure? This question is heightened by the globalization of capital markets, which causes the effects of such failures to quickly spread worldwide.

Responses to this most recent failure are still being debated by regulators, economists, and politicians. One response is to require financial institutions to hold increased capital reserves. Of more direct interest in this book is a flurry of new or expanded accounting and disclosure standards. Some of these are outlined in Section 7.5. Another response is to limit or modify the managerial compensation practices of financial institutions, since suspicion arose that existing compensation practices, including large amounts of stock options, contributed to the meltdowns by encouraging managers to indulge in excessive off-balance sheet leverage. This leverage increased the profits, and share prices, of sponsoring institutions but also increased their risk. Yet, for whatever reason, the market had not fully appreciated this risk, bidding up share prices of financial institutions and thus increasing the value of executive stock options. To the extent that stock-based compensation practices encouraged short-run, risk-taking behaviour, they had the opposite effect to their intended purpose, which was to align manager and shareholder interests by encouraging managers' longer-run decision horizons.

Nevertheless, the extent to which additional regulations are desirable is not obvious, since, as mentioned, regulation is costly and also subject to failure. Furthermore, alternative mechanisms to help inhibit market failure, such as the legal system, are available.

In sum, four points relevant to accountants stand out from the events just described. First, financial reporting must be transparent, so that investors can properly value assets and liabilities, and the firms that possess them. With respect to complex financial assets and liabilities, transparency includes full reporting of models used to determine value, disclosure of any repurchase obligations, and explanations of risk exposures and risk-management strategies, including use of credit default swaps. Second, fair value accounting, being based on market value or estimates thereof, may understate value-in-use when markets collapse due to liquidity pricing that results from a severe decline in investor confidence. This leads to management, and even government, objections. It also creates a need for research into the causes of liquidity pricing and how financial reporting may help to control it. Third, off-balance sheet activities should be fully reported, even if not consolidated, since they can encourage excessive risk taking by management. Finally, since accounting standards are a form of regulation, substantial changes to existing standards, including increased disclosures of manager compensation, have taken place.

1.4 EFFICIENT CONTRACTING

Standard setters apparently feel that fair value accounting is the best way to implement the decision usefulness concept that, as described in Section 1.2, developed during the 1960s. For example, we mentioned in Section 1.3 that many financial instruments are valued at fair value. However, the severe criticisms of fair value accounting arising from the security market meltdowns have strengthened an alternative view of financial reporting, namely the **efficient contracting** approach to financial reporting. Efficient contracting argues that the **contracts** that firms enter into (e.g., debt contracts and managerial compensation contracts) create a primary source of demand for accounting information. The role of accounting information is viewed as one of helping to maximize contract efficiency or, more generally, to aid in efficient corporate governance.

Debt and compensation contracts are discussed in later chapters. For now, it is sufficient to note that these contracts usually depend on accounting variables, such as net income. The role of financial reporting for debt and compensation contract purposes is to generate *trust*. Trust is needed if lenders are to be willing to lend to the firm and if shareholders (represented by Boards of Directors) are to be willing to delegate managerial responsibilities to managers. An efficient contract generates this trust at lowest cost. Thus covenants in debt contracts under which, for example, the borrowing firm will not pay dividends if its working capital falls below a specified level, increase lender trust in the security of their loans.

Basing manager compensation on net income increases investor trust by helping to align manager and shareholder interests. That is, net income can be used as a measure of manager performance. Alignment of manager and shareholder interests is the **stewardship** role of financial reporting, one of the oldest concepts in accounting.

Efficient contracting leads to some major accounting policy differences from the measurement approach (i.e., current value accounting) of financial reporting envisaged by standard setters, since trust is compromised to the extent that managers are able to

Theory in Practice 1.2

Serious consequences that can result from lack of conservatism are illustrated by New Century Financial Corp. Formed in 1995, New Century became the second-largest sub-prime mortgage lender in the United States. Its lending was in large part based on automated credit granting programs, and reflected a belief that house prices would continue to rise. Many of these mortgages were securitized and transferred to investors. New Century accounted for these transfers as sales, thereby derecognizing them from its balance sheet. Gross profit was then the difference between the sales revenue received from investors and the cost of the mortgages transferred. Of course, reported earnings should allow for credit losses, since New Century committed to buy back mortgages that became troubled within up to a year after transfer.

In addition, New Century would retain some mortgages for itself (called retained interests), from which it would receive future cash flows. Also, the transfer agreements included the right to service the mortgages, for which New Century charged a fee. The retained interests and servicing rights assets were valued at current value, based on their discounted expected future cash flows. Thus, revenue from retained interests was recognized when the decision to retain was made, and servicing revenue was recognized at the time of mortgage transfer. These policies required numerous estimates and management judgments, especially for retained interests (since a secondary market for these assets did not exist). These policies contrasted with a more conservative policy of recognizing revenues as cash flows from retained interests were received and servicing responsibilities rendered.

The company's share price increased dramatically, to a high of US$64 in 2004. Its reported net income reached $1.4 billion in 2005.

However, through error or design, New Century seriously underestimated the extent of its mortgage buybacks and resulting credit losses. Of $40 billion of mortgages granted in the first three quarters of 2006, it provided only $13.9 million for repurchases. As the number of subprime mortgages in default increased greatly in the fourth quarter of 2006, investor concerns about New Century rose. In particular, the company failed to write down its retained interests as the value of the underlying mortgages decreased. These concerns added to concerns about early revenue recognition from retained interests and servicing. New Century, which was highly levered, was soon unable to borrow money to finance buybacks. In March 2007, it announced that it would no longer accept new mortgage applications. Its shares lost 90% of their value, and the company was delisted from the New York Stock Exchange. In 2007, it filed for bankruptcy protection.

New Century's auditor (KPMG) was drawn into the lawsuits that followed. In 2009, financial media reported a lawsuit of $1 billion, claiming that the auditor had allowed the serious understatement of provisions for buybacks. KPMG denied that it was responsible, claiming that the provisions were deemed adequate at the time, and blaming New Century's failure on the market meltdowns of 2007–2008. Later in 2009 the SEC filed civil fraud charges against three former executives of New Century, seeking damages and return of bonuses. Several other lawsuits followed. In 2010, financial media reported final settlement of a class action lawsuit that included a payment of over $65 million by former company officers and directors, and a payment of $44.75 million by auditor KPMG.

Subsequently, other financial institutions also settled claims for sub-standard mortgage lending. For example, in 2012, Citigroup was fined $158 million for certifying low quality mortgages as eligible for U.S. government mortgage insurance. The fine was to compensate the government for the insurance payouts it had to make when these mortgages went into default. Bank of America was fined $1 billion for similar offences.

manipulate the values of accounting variables used in contracts. One difference is an increased emphasis, relative to current value accounting, on **reliability** of accounting information. Reliability of accounting information benefits lenders by increasing their trust that the firm manager will not take actions that harm their interests (e.g., disguising deteriorating earnings). Reliability also benefits compensation contracting by increasing shareholders' trust that managers cannot cover up poor performance by opportunistically manipulating reported net income and balance sheet values.

The second major difference from the measurement approach is the role of **conservatism** in financial reporting. Under conservatism, unrealized losses from declines in value are recognized when they take place, but gains from increases in value are not recognized until they are realized. Accounting standards include numerous instances of conservatism, such as lower-of-cost-or-market for inventories, and impairment tests for capital assets and many financial instruments.

While both standard setters and adherents to the efficient contracting view recognize that some conservatism is desirable, they differ in the reasons why. Arguably, the standard setters' view is that conservatism reduces the probability of lawsuits that invariably result when firms report major unexpected losses. The contracting view is that conservatism is a vehicle to improve contract efficiency by providing investors, particularly debt investors, with an "early warning system" of financial distress. It also serves a stewardship role by preventing managers from overstating their performance and compensation by recognizing unrealized gains.

In this book, we view the decision useful and efficient contracting roles of financial reporting as equally important. While, as just mentioned, standard setters do see a role for conservatism, they would point out that fair value accounting is, in effect, conservative when fair values fall, but can also serve a useful investor-informing role when fair values rise. Contract theory adherents, however, are more concerned about low reliability of many fair value increases. While they are willing to accept possible low reliability of conservative accounting in order to attain the benefits of contract efficiency and good corporate governance, they argue that low reliability of unrealized fair value gains works against conservatism, contract efficiency, and governance. How to best combine these two important but conflicting roles is a fundamental problem for financial accounting theory. We discuss this problem further in Section 1.10.

1.5 A NOTE ON ETHICAL BEHAVIOUR

The collapse of Enron and WorldCom and subsequent collapse of public confidence, as well as the more recent market meltdowns, raise questions about how to restore and maintain public confidence in financial reporting. One response is increased regulation, including new accounting standards, as just discussed. However, ethical behaviour by accountants and auditors is also required, since numerous accountants designed, were involved in, or at least knew about the various reporting irregularities. Also, the financial statements of the firms involved were certified by their auditors as being in accordance with GAAP. It seems that conforming to GAAP is not sufficient to prevent financial reporting failures.

By ethical behaviour, we mean that accountants and auditors should "do the right thing." In our context, this means that accountants must behave with integrity and independence in putting the public interest ahead of the employer's and client's interests, should these conflict.

It is important to realize that there is a social dimension to integrity and independence. That is, a society depends on shared beliefs and common values. This notion goes back to Thomas Hobbes, a seventeenth-century philosopher and author of *Leviathan*. Hobbes argued that if people acted solely as selfish individuals, society would collapse to the point where force, or the threat of force, would prevail—there would be no cooperative behaviour. He also argued that rules, regulations, and the courts were not enough to restore cooperative behaviour, since no set of rules could possibly anticipate all human interaction. What is needed, in addition, is that people must recognize that it is in their joint interests to cooperate.

The force of Hobbes's arguments can be seen, for example, in the Enron and WorldCom disasters. We have a set of rules governing financial reporting (e.g., GAAP). However, GAAP was not followed and/or was bent so as to conform to its letter but not its intent. Cooperative behaviour broke down because certain individuals behaved in a manner that broke the rules—they did not behave with integrity and independence. This was good for them, at least in the short run, but bad for society. Hobbes's prediction is that increased regulation will not suffice to prevent a repetition of these reporting disasters. What is also needed is ethical behaviour.

Note, however, that there is a time dimension to ethical behaviour. An accountant can act in his/her own self-interest and still behave ethically. This is accomplished by taking a broader view of the consequences of one's actions. For example, suppose that an accountant is instructed to understate a firm's environmental liabilities. In the short run, doing so will benefit the accountant through job retention, promotion, and higher compensation. In the longer run, though, future generations will suffer through increased pollution, shareholders will suffer from reduced share price when the extent of environmental liability becomes known, and investors as a whole will suffer when reduced public confidence in financial reporting lowers the prices of all shares. The accountant will suffer through dismissal, professional discipline or expulsion, and reduced compensation due to reduced stature of all accountants. By taking account of these longer-run costs, the accountant is motivated to behave ethically. In effect, in the longer run, self-interested behaviour and ethical behaviour merge.[23]

In this book, we will often cast our discussion in terms of full disclosure,[24] usefulness of financial statements, cooperative behaviour, and reputation, all of which benefit society. However, in acting so as to meet these desirable characteristics of financial reporting, the accountant is, in effect, acting ethically.

1.6 RULES-BASED VERSUS PRINCIPLES-BASED ACCOUNTING STANDARDS

These longer-run considerations lead directly to the question of rules-based versus principles-based accounting standards. Rules-based standards attempt to lay down detailed rules for how to account. An alternative to detailed rules, however, is for accounting standards to lay down general principles only, and rely on auditor professional judgement to ensure that application of the standards is not misleading. For example, in Section 1.3 we described FASB Interpretation No. 46 (FIN 46). This standard imposed rules for consolidation of variable interest entities, following the abuse by Enron of earlier rules. However, the new rules were in turn circumvented by many financial institutions through the creation of expected loss notes. A principles-based standard for consolidation would require that consolidation be required when failure to do so would be misleading. Thus, if the accountant/auditor felt that excessive financial leverage was otherwise being disguised, he/she would insist on consolidation or, at least, clear supplementary disclosure.

It is often stated that IASB standards are more principles-based than those of the United States.[25] However, Ball (2009) argues that U.S. financial reporting is inherently principles-based, in the sense that the U.S. justice system punishes misleading financial statement reporting even if the financial statements are technically in accordance with GAAP.[26] Ball attributes the rules-based nature of U.S. financial reporting to its high degree of regulation and possible punishment, which produces a "rule-checking" mentality.

Undoubtedly, punishment is a powerful deterrent to fraud. But, the events described in Sections 1.2 and 1.3 demonstrate that the prospect of punishment is not always effective. Furthermore, the serious impacts of the 2007–2008 market meltdowns raise the question of whether the world can afford to wait until the wheels of justice grind to their conclusion. It would be preferable to prevent misleading reporting in the first place.

Principles-based standards are seen as a way to accomplish this, since detailed rules do not seem to work. Of course, professional accounting bodies already encourage principled behaviour, through codes of professional conduct, discipline committees, and the process of standard setting. However, Ball points out that such rules have been widely ignored. Nevertheless, the SEC, in "Study Pursuant to Section 108(d) of the Sarbanes-Oxley Act ... (2003)," recommends that the FASB adopt a principles-based approach to accounting standards. The SEC study is in broad agreement with the FASB's own 2002 "Proposal for a Principles-based Approach to U.S. Standard-setting." Furthermore, a stated goal of the Conceptual Framework introduced in Section 1.2 is to create a foundation for principles-based standards. Without such a foundation, it is unclear just what principles are to be upheld.

It thus seems that the world is moving toward principles-based standards. Yet, even with a strong conceptual framework, such standards will face pressures from managers, and even governments, to bend financial reporting to their wishes. To resist such pressures, auditors and accountants will have to adopt the longer-term view of their responsibilities advocated in Section 1.5.

1.7 THE COMPLEXITY OF INFORMATION IN FINANCIAL ACCOUNTING AND REPORTING

It should now be apparent that the environment of accounting is both very complex and very challenging. It is complex because the product of accounting is information—a powerful and important commodity. The main reason for this complexity is the absence of perfect or true accounting concepts and standards, as discussed in Section 1.2. As a result, individuals will not be unanimous in their reaction to even the same information. For example, a sophisticated investor may prefer the valuation of certain firm assets and liabilities at value-in-use on grounds that this will help to predict future firm performance. Debt investors, such as bondholders, may prefer conservative accounting on grounds that understating assets and earnings protects lenders' interests by making it more difficult for managers to reduce their security by, for example, paying excessive dividends to shareholders. Others may prefer historical cost accounting, perhaps because they feel that current value information is unreliable, or simply because they are used to historical cost information. Furthermore, managers, who will have to report the current values, might react quite negatively. Management typically objects to inclusion of unrealized gains and losses resulting from changes in asset and liability values in net income, arguing that these items introduce excessive volatility into earnings, do not reflect their performance, and should not be included when evaluating the results of their efforts. These arguments may be somewhat self-serving, since part of management's job is to anticipate changes in values and take steps to protect the firm from adverse effects of these changes. For example, management may hedge against increases in prices of raw materials and changes in interest rates. Nevertheless, managements' objections remain, and accountants quickly get caught up in whether reported net income should fulfill a primary role of reporting useful information to equity investors or to debt investors, or to report information that motivates responsible manager performance.

Another reason for the complexity of information is that it does more than affect individual decisions. In affecting decisions it also affects the working of markets, such as securities markets and managerial labour markets. It is important to the efficiency and fairness of the economy itself that these markets work well.

The challenge for financial accountants, then, is to survive and prosper in a complex environment characterized by conflicting preferences of different groups with an interest in financial reporting. This book argues that the prospects for survival and prosperity will be enhanced if accountants have a critical awareness of the impact of financial reporting on investors, managers, and the economy. The alternative to awareness is simply to accept the reporting environment as given. However, this is a very short-term strategy, since environments are constantly changing and evolving.

1.8 THE ROLE OF ACCOUNTING RESEARCH

A book about accounting theory must inevitably draw on accounting research, much of which is contained in academic journals. There are two complementary ways that we can view the role of research. The first is to consider its effects on accounting practice. For example, the essence of the decision usefulness approach that underlies the Conceptual Framework is that investors should be supplied with information to help them make good investment decisions. One has only to compare the current annual report of a public company with a similar report issued in the 1960s and prior to see the tremendous increase in disclosure over the 40 years or so since decision usefulness formally became an important concept in accounting theory.

Yet, this increase in disclosure did not "just happen." It, as outlined in Section 1.2, is based on fundamental research into the theory of investor decision making and the theory of capital markets, which have guided the accountant in what information is useful. Furthermore, as we will see, the theory has been subjected to extensive empirical testing, which has established that, on average, investors use financial accounting information much as the theory predicts.

Independently of whether it affects current practice, however, there is a second important view of the role of research. This is to improve our *understanding* of the accounting environment, which we argued above should not be taken for granted. For example, fundamental research into models of conflict resolution, in particular agency theory models, has improved our understanding of managers' interests in financial reporting, of the role of executive compensation plans in motivating and controlling management's operation of the firm, and of the ways in which such plans use account-ing information. This in turn leads to an improved understanding of managers' interests in accounting policy choice and why they may want to bias or otherwise manipulate reported net income, or, at least, to have some ability to manage the "bottom line." Research such as this enables us to better understand corporate governance issues such as the boundaries of management's legitimate role in financial reporting. It also helps us understand why the accountant is frequently caught between the interests of investors and managers.

In this book, we use both of the above views. Our approach to research is twofold. In some cases, we choose important research papers, describe them intuitively, and explain how they fit into our overall framework of financial accounting theory and practice. In other cases, we briefly refer to research papers on which our discussion is based. The interested reader can refer to the papers to pursue the discussion in greater depth if desired.

1.9 THE IMPORTANCE OF INFORMATION ASYMMETRY

This book is based on information economics. This is a unifying theme that formally recognizes that some parties to business transactions may have an information advantage over others or may take actions that are unobservable to others. When this happens, the economy is said to be characterized by information asymmetry. We shall consider two major types of information asymmetry.

The first is **adverse selection**. For our purposes, adverse selection occurs because some persons, such as firm managers and other insiders, will have better information about the current condition and future prospects of the firm than outside investors. There are various ways that managers and other insiders can exploit their information advantage at the expense of outsiders. For example, managers may behave opportunistically by biasing or otherwise managing the information released to investors, perhaps to increase the value of stock options they hold. They may delay or selectively release information early to selected investors or analysts, enabling insiders, including themselves, to benefit at the expense of ordinary investors. Such tactics are *adverse* (hence the term) to the interests of ordinary investors, since it reduces their ability to make good investment decisions. Then, investors' concerns about the possibility of biased information release and favouritism will make them wary of buying firms' securities, with the result that capital markets will not function as well as they should. We can then think of financial accounting and reporting as a mechanism to control adverse selection by timely and credible conversion of inside information into outside information.

> **Adverse selection** *is a type of information asymmetry whereby one or more parties to a business transaction, or potential transaction, have an information advantage over other parties.*

The second type of information asymmetry is **moral hazard**, which arises when one party to a contractual relationship takes actions that are unobservable to the other contracting parties. Moral hazard exists in many situations. A medical doctor may give a patient a cursory examination. A trustee for a bond issue may shirk his/her duties, to the disadvantage of the bondholders. In our context, moral hazard occurs because of the separation of ownership and control that characterizes most large business entities. It is effectively impossible for shareholders and lenders to observe directly the extent and quality of top manager effort on their behalf. Then, the manager may be tempted to shirk on effort, blaming any deterioration of firm performance on factors beyond his/her control, or biasing reported earnings to cover up. Obviously, if this happens, there are serious implications both for the contracting parties and for the efficient working of the economy. We can then view accounting net income as a measure of managerial performance. This helps to control moral hazard in two complementary ways. First, net income can serve as an input into executive compensation contracts to motivate manager performance. Second, net income can inform the managerial labour market, so that a manager who shirks will suffer a decline in income, reputation, and personal market value in the longer run.

> **Moral hazard** *is a type of information asymmetry whereby one or more parties to a contract can observe their actions in fulfillment of the contract but other parties cannot.*

Note that both adverse selection and moral hazard result from information asymmetry. The difference is that adverse selection involves inside information about matters affecting future firm performance and resulting security returns. Moral hazard involves manager effort—the manager knows how hard he/she is working but investors do not.

1.10 THE FUNDAMENTAL PROBLEM OF FINANCIAL ACCOUNTING THEORY

Given the absence of perfect or true accounting concepts, it turns out that the most useful measure of net income to inform investors—that is, to control adverse selection—need not be the same as the best measure to measure and motivate manager stewardship—that is, to control moral hazard. This was recognized by Gjesdal (1981). Investors' interests are best served by information that enables better investment decisions and better-operating capital markets. Providing it is reasonably reliable, current value accounting fulfils this role, since it provides up-to-date information about assets and liabilities, hence of future firm performance, and reduces the ability of insiders to take advantage of changes in asset and liability values.

Managers' legitimate interests are best served by information that is highly informative about their performance in running the firm, since this enables efficient compensation contracts and better working of managerial labour markets. Fair value accounting can improve reporting on stewardship since, ultimately, the manager is responsible for everything, including current value gains and losses. If the manager cannot earn an acceptable return on the fair value of net assets, these assets (or the manager) should be disposed of.

However, current value accounting can also interfere with reporting on stewardship. Current values are very volatile in their impact on reported earnings, and can even increase earnings volatility beyond the real volatility faced by the firm. Also, unless market values are readily available, current values may be more subject to bias and manipulation by the manager than historical cost-based information. If so, as noted in Section 1.4, contract efficiency is decreased. Both excess volatility and contract efficiency effects reduce the informativeness of earnings about manager stewardship. Thus, from a managerial perspective, a less volatile and more conservative income measure, such as one based on historical cost, or at least a measure that excludes certain unrealized gains, may better fulfil a role of motivating and evaluating managers.

Given that there is only one bottom line, the fundamental problem of financial accounting theory is how to design and implement concepts and standards that best combine the investor-informing and manager performance-evaluating roles for accounting information. In future, we will refer to combining these two roles of financial reporting as the **fundamental problem.**

Some policies require tradeoffs between these roles. For example, as described in Section 1.4, the investor-informing role of financial reporting (i.e., the measurement approach) puts less emphasis on reliability and conservatism than the manager performance-evaluating role envisaged by contract theory. Other policies, such as expanded disclosure, may facilitate both roles. In this regard, a 2008 IASB discussion paper, *"Preliminary Views on Financial Presentation,"* proposed to dichotomize the balance sheet, income statement, and statement of cash flows into separate components for operating, financing, investing, and tax activities. One purpose is to improve investor decision making. However, separate

As a result of the September 11, 2001, terrorist attacks in the United States, numerous companies incurred substantial costs. For example, airlines were unable to fly for two days, and air traffic declined substantially for some time afterward.

The resulting reductions in revenue and profits could hardly be regarded as management's responsibility. Consequently, manager performance would best be measured by earnings *excluding* the costs of these catastrophic events. Yet, from the standpoint of investors who are interested primarily in *future* firm cash flows, earnings *including* these events have greater relevance.

In a 2001 news release, the FASB decided against allowing costs resulting from the attacks to be reported in a separate section of earnings. The FASB had originally considered allowing at least some costs to be reported separately, but came to the conclusion that it would be impos-

sible to reliably separate direct costs resulting from the attack (e.g., airlines' losses of revenue during the two-day shutdown) from operating costs, some of which would be reduced and some which were fixed. Also, some of these costs would be recovered through insurance and government assistance. Consequently, the FASB concluded that all costs resulting from September 11 be included in income from continuing operations, with any government assistance reported as a separate line item.

Thus, separate reporting of earnings best suited to evaluation of manager performance and best suited to investors foundered on concerns about reliability. Nevertheless, from a conceptual standpoint, these events illustrate the fundamental problem. Management performance and prospects for future firm performance are not necessarily best measured by the same net income number.

subtotals for operations and other important manager activities may also improve the reporting on stewardship, assuming responsible allocation by managers into the respective activity components.

Other comprehensive income (OCI) is another approach to reconciling the two roles. A statement of OCI was originally created in the United States by FASB's Statement of Financial Accounting Standards 130 (SFAS 130; 1997), now included in Accounting Standards Codification (ASC) 220-10-45.[27] As mentioned earlier, standard setters have moved increasingly to current value accounting. However, we noted in Section 1.7 that management typically objects to inclusion in net income of unrealized gains and losses resulting from current value accounting. We can view OCI as a compromise to secure manager acceptance of current value standards, since it excludes these gains and losses from net income. Thus OCI includes unrealized current value gains and losses resulting from fair value accounting for securities, foreign currency translation adjustments, changes in some pension expense components, and several other items. As these gains and losses are realized or amortized, they are generally transferred to net income. The sum of net income and other comprehensive income is called **comprehensive income**.

Internationally, IAS 1 imposed a statement of other comprehensive income in 2009. It requires that other comprehensive income be included below net income in a single statement of comprehensive income, or immediately following net income if net income is shown as a separate statement. FASB standards now contain a similar requirement.

The extent to which modifications to the financial statement format will resolve the fundamental problem remains to be seen.

1.11 REGULATION AS A REACTION TO THE FUNDAMENTAL PROBLEM

There are two more basic reactions to the fundamental problem. One is, in effect, to ask, "What problem?" That is, why not keep regulation to the minimum needed to provide a stable environment for trade, resolution of disputes, and punishment for wrongdoing? Then, let market forces determine how much and what kinds of information firms should produce. We can think of investors and other financial statement users as demanders of information and of managers as suppliers. Just as in markets for apples and automobiles, the forces of demand and supply can determine the quantity produced.

This view argues, in effect, that market forces can sufficiently control the adverse selection and moral hazard problems so that investors are protected, and managerial labour markets and securities markets will work reasonably well. Indeed, as we shall see, there is a surprising number of ways for managers to credibly supply information. Furthermore, investors as a group are surprisingly sophisticated in ferreting out the implications of information for future firm performance. Consequently, according to this view, unregulated market prices reasonably reflect firm and manager value.

The second reaction is to turn to regulation to protect investors, on the grounds that information is such a complex and important commodity that market forces alone fail to adequately control the problems of moral hazard and adverse selection. This leads directly to the role of standard setting, which is viewed in this book as a form of regulation that lays down generally accepted accounting concepts and standards.

Of course, consistent with the theorem of Arrow (Section 1.2) and the arguments of Hobbes (Section 1.5), we cannot expect regulation to completely protect investors. Consequently, the rigorous determination of the right amount of regulation is an extremely complex issue of social choice. At the present time, we simply do not know which of the above two reactions to the fundamental problem is on the right track. Certainly, we witness lots of regulation in accounting, and there appears to be no slowing down in the rate at which new standards are coming on line. Consequently, it may seem that society is resolving the question of extent of regulation for us.

Yet, past years witnessed substantial deregulation of major industries such as transportation, telecommunications, financial services, and electric power generation, where deregulation was once thought unthinkable. The reason it is important to question the extent of regulation in accounting is that regulation has a cost—a fact often ignored by standard setters. Again, the answer to the question of whether the benefits of regulation outweigh the costs is not known. However, we shall pursue this issue later in the book.

1.12 THE ORGANIZATION OF THIS BOOK

Figure 1.1 at the beginning of this chapter summarizes how this book operationalizes the framework for the study of financial accounting theory outlined above. There are four main components of the figure, which we outline in turn.

1.12.1 Ideal Conditions

Before considering the problems introduced into accounting by information asymmetry, it is worthwhile to consider what accounting would be like under ideal conditions. This is depicted by the leftmost box of Figure 1.1. By ideal conditions we mean an economy where firms' future cash flows and their probabilities are known. Also, the economy has perfect and complete markets or, equivalently, a lack of information asymmetry and other barriers to fair and efficient working of markets. Such conditions are also called "first best." Then, asset and liability valuation is on the basis of expected present values of future cash flows (i.e., value-in-use). Arbitrage ensures that present values and market values are equal. Investors and managers would have no scope for disagreement over the role of financial reporting and no incentives to call for regulation. Under such conditions, there would be no fundamental problem.

Unfortunately, or perhaps fortunately, ideal conditions do not prevail in practice. Nevertheless, they provide a useful benchmark against which more realistic "second best" accounting conditions can be compared. For example, we will see that there are numerous instances of the actual use of current value-based accounting techniques in financial reporting. Reserve recognition accounting for oil and gas companies is an example. Furthermore, fair value accounting is required for many financial instruments. A study of accounting under ideal conditions is useful not only because practice is moving to increased use of current values, but, more importantly, it helps us to see what the real problems and challenges of current value accounting are when the ideal conditions that it requires do not hold.

1.12.2 Adverse Selection

The top three boxes of Figure 1.1 represent the second component of the framework. This introduces the adverse selection problem. As discussed in Section 1.9, this is the problem of communication from the firm to outside investors. Here, the accounting role is to provide a "level playing field" through full disclosure of useful and cost-effective information to investors and other financial statement users.

To understand how financial accounting can help to control the adverse selection problem, it is desirable to have an appreciation of how investors make decisions. This is because knowledge of investor decision processes is essential if the accountant is to know what information they need. The study of investment decision making is a large topic, since investors undoubtedly make decisions in a variety of ways, ranging from intuition, to "hot tips," to random occurrences such as a sudden need for cash, to sophisticated computer-based models.

The approach we will take in most of this book is to assume that investors are rational on average; that is, the average investor makes decisions so as to maximize his/her expected utility, or satisfaction, from wealth. This theory of rational investment decision has been widely studied. In making the rationality assumption we do not imply that all investors make decisions this way. Indeed, there is increasing recognition that many investors do not behave rationally in the sense of maximizing their expected utility of wealth. We do claim, however, that the theory captures the average behaviour of those investors who want to make informed investment decisions, and this claim is backed up by substantial empirical evidence.

The reporting of information that is useful to rational investors is called the decision usefulness approach. As suggested in Section 1.2, this approach underlies the pronouncements (in particular, the Conceptual Framework) of major standard setting bodies.

1.12.3 Moral Hazard

The bottom three boxes of Figure 1.1 represent the third component of the book. Here, the information asymmetry problem is moral hazard, arising from the unobservability of the manager's effort in running the firm. That is, the manager's decision problem is to decide on how much effort to devote to running the firm on behalf of the shareholders. Since effort is unobservable, the manager may be tempted to shirk on effort. However, since net income reflects manager performance, it operates as an indirect measure of the manager's effort decision. Consequently, the user decision problem is how to design financial reporting to motivate and evaluate manager performance. To be informative about performance, net income should be a precise and sensitive measure of this performance.

1.12.4 Standard Setting

We can now see the source of the fundamental problem more clearly. Current values of assets and liabilities are potentially of greater interest to equity investors than their historical costs since, if markets work reasonably well, current values provide the best available indication of future firm performance and investment returns. However, managers may feel that unrealized gains and losses from adjusting the carrying values of assets and liabilities to current value do not reflect *their own* performance. Accounting standard setters quickly get caught up in mediation between the conflicting preferences of investors and managers. This is depicted by the rightmost box in Figure 1.1.

1.12.5 The Process of Standard Setting

We have pointed out that, in practice, the setting of accounting concepts and standards requires negotiation and compromise. Also, their application must be enforced. We now give a brief description of the structure of accounting standard-setting bodies, to show how these requirements are operationalized.

The International Accounting Standards Board (IASB) The IASB was established in 2001, assuming standard setting responsibility from a predecessor body, the International Accounting Standards Committee. This earlier body was created in 1973 by agreement between accountancy bodies in Australia, Canada, France, Germany, Japan, Mexico, the Netherlands, the United Kingdom and Ireland, and the United States.

The IASB is supported financially by an oversight body, the International Financial Reporting Standards Foundation (IFRS Foundation). As a result, the IASB itself is independent from professional accounting bodies and business organizations in countries that have adopted IASB standards.

The basic objective of the IASB is to develop a single set of high-quality, understandable, and enforceable global accounting standards, now called International Financial Reporting Standards (IFRS). These standards are developed by a board of 16 individuals, most of whom serve on a full-time basis. They must possess technical skills and suitable international business and market experience, and are chosen to represent different world regions.

A majority of 10 of 16 votes is required to pass new standards, a requirement called **super-majority voting**. Super-majority voting decreases the possibility of approval of a standard that is only marginally acceptable to the Board, and also tends to produce a process of negotiation and compromise in the creation of a new standard. Dissenting members will be in a stronger position than they would be if only a simple majority was required and thus are less likely to feel that their views and concerns have been ignored.

In designing standards, the IASB follows **due process**. This includes: broad consultation with interested parties before admitting a topic to the Board's agenda; an investor outreach program; discussion papers, which normally precede exposure drafts of new standards; and assessment of the likely effects of new standards. In 2013, an Accounting Standards Advisory Forum was established, consisting of national standard setting bodies and other bodies with an interest in standard setting, to provide technical advice and feedback.

These various procedures enable interested parties, including management, to react and comment. Public hearings and field tests may also take place. Comments are analyzed and a revised standard is prepared. A statement of basis for conclusions is issued to explain the standard. Representation of diverse constituencies and regions on the Board and super-majority voting also contribute to due process. Post-implementation reviews of new standards are also carried out. Note that following due process is consistent with a need for compromise and negotiation in setting accounting standards.

Many countries, including Canada in 2011, have adopted IASB standards, as has the European Union in 2005. Other adopters include Australia, Israel, Mexico, Russia, South Korea, and many countries in South America and Southeast Asia. Other countries, such as United States, China, Japan, and India, are considering, or are in process of, adoption.

The Financial Accounting Standards Board (FASB) The FASB was established in 1973 to assume from earlier bodies the role of standard setting in the United States. Similar to the IASB, the FASB is supported financially by an oversight body, the Financial Accounting Foundation (FAF).

The FASB's mission is to establish and improve standards of financial accounting and reporting for the guidance and education of the public. To accomplish this, it develops accounting concepts, strives to improve the usefulness of financial reporting, keeps standards current to reflect changes in the business and economic environment, addresses financial reporting deficiencies, improves the understanding of the nature and purpose of information contained in financial reports, and promotes international convergence of accounting standards.

The FASB consists of seven board members, appointed for a maximum of two five-year terms. Collectively, they must have knowledge and experience in investing, accounting, finance, business, education and research; and a concern for investors, other financial statement users, and the public interest. Unlike the IASB, a simple majority vote is required to pass a new standard.

The FASB, like the IASB, is independent of other business and professional organizations. For example, the FASB is distinct from the American Institute of Certified Public Accountants (AICPA), the major American professional accounting body. While the AICPA is one of the sponsoring bodies and endorses FASB standards, many other bodies are also involved in sponsoring the FASB.

In 2002, the FASB established a User Advisory Council. This is a group of over 40 investment professionals that assists the FASB in raising awareness of how investors, analysts, and rating agencies use financial information and how to better design accounting standards to meet their needs.

In setting and updating accounting and reporting concepts and standards, the FASB, like the IASB, places heavy emphasis on due process. Procedures for initiating and adopting new standards are broadly similar to those of the IASB outlined above. Also, the IASB and FASB have been working since 2002 to converge their standards, with substantial progress to date. Convergence is considered further in Section 13.7.1.

The Canadian Accounting Standards Board (AcSB) The AcSB is the Canadian accounting standard setting body. It is authorized by the Board of Governors of the Canadian Institute of Chartered Accountants to publish reports "on its own responsibility," in order to give it a measure of independence from the CICA itself and reduce the possibility of interference in its deliberations. This organizational structure differs from that of the IASB and FASB, which, as mentioned, are independent of related professional organizations.

The AcSB consists of a maximum of nine members, chosen to represent diverse constituencies. Unlike the IASB and FASB, members, with the exception of the Chairperson, serve on a voluntary basis. For publicly accountable enterprises, the *CICA Handbook* now primarily contains IASB standards. To pass a new standard, a super-majority of two-thirds of Board members voting in favour is required.

With its adoption of IASB accounting standards in 2011, the activities of the AcSB have changed somewhat. The Board gives increased attention to special problems of financial reporting for non-publicly accountable enterprises (which do not necessarily report under the same GAAP as publicly traded firms) and to not-for-profit enterprises. Also, the Board will continue to take part in the setting of international standards, through IASB representation and contributions to the development of concepts and new IFRSs.

Securities Commissions If standard setting bodies are to achieve their objectives, financial statements must adhere to GAAP. Adherence to GAAP is accomplished in a variety of ways. Ethical behaviour by managers and accountants is obviously desirable. Also, as we shall see, securities markets and managerial labour markets are important contributors to responsible reporting. When these motivations fail, enforcement takes over. Discipline committees of professional accounting bodies play an important enforcement role, as does the prospect of legal liability for reporting failures.

From our perspective, securities commissions are one of the most important enforcers of accounting standards. Notable among these is the SEC in the United States. Its creation, and its delegation of standard setting to the FASB, were outlined in Section 1.2. However, the SEC also fulfils an important enforcement role, by investigating firms and managers for failures to adhere to GAAP and prosecuting and penalizing them if appropriate. The SEC's reach extends to many Canadian and other foreign firms whose shares are traded in the United States. We shall see several examples of the SEC's enforcement activities in this book.

The SEC also issues accounting standards, mainly for disclosures outside of the financial statements. These include management discussion and analysis, and disclosures of management compensation, which will be discussed in later chapters.

In Canada, securities regulation is a provincial jurisdiction. Consequently, Canada does not at present have a national securities regulator. However, the provincial and territorial securities regulators have created the Canadian Securities Administrators (CSA), a forum to coordinate and harmonize Canadian capital markets regulation. Its mission includes the protection of investors, securing the proper working of capital markets, and reducing risk. One of its regulations is National Instrument NI 52-109, imposing management disclosures of internal control effectiveness similar to those of the Sarbanes-Oxley Act in the United States. Of the provincial securities commissions, the most important is the Ontario Securities Commission (OSC).

The International Organization of Securities Commissions (IOSCO) represents the world's securities regulators, including Canadian regulators and the SEC. It recommends to its members that they use IASB standards, although individual member countries may require reconciliation of IASB standards with their own GAAP. For example, foreign firms that wish to trade their securities in the United States must meet SEC requirements. These include filing financial statements with the SEC either in accordance with IASB GAAP or with U.S. GAAP.[28]

Unlike domestic securities commissions, the IOSCO, hence the IASB, do not have authority to enforce IASB standards. Enforcement is up to the authorities in the respective jurisdictions that adopt these standards.[29] Consequently, analysis of financial statements from foreign jurisdictions should include careful awareness of local customs and business practices, and the legal and other institutional characteristics of those jurisdictions. Research shows that even in the presence of the same set of accounting standards (i.e., IASB standards), the quality of financial reporting varies across countries. Some of this research is discussed in Chapter 13.

1.13 RELEVANCE OF FINANCIAL ACCOUNTING THEORY TO ACCOUNTING PRACTICE

The framework just described provides a way of organizing our study of financial accounting theory. However, this book also recognizes an obligation to convince you that the theory is relevant to accounting practice. This is accomplished in two main ways. First, the various theories and research underlying financial accounting are described and explained in plain language, and their relevance is demonstrated by means of numerous references to accounting practice. For example, Chapter 3 describes how investors may make rational investment decisions, and then goes on to demonstrate that this decision theory underlies the Conceptual Framework. Theory in Practice vignettes, which illustrate the theories more explicitly, are scattered throughout the book. Also, the book contains numerous instances where accounting standards are described and critically evaluated. In addition to enabling you to learn some of the contents of these standards, you can better understand and apply them when you have a grounding in the underlying reasoning on which they are based. The second approach to demonstrating relevance is through assignment problems. A concentrated attempt has been made to select relevant problem material to illustrate, motivate, and extend the concepts.

Recent years have been challenging, even exciting, times for financial accounting theory. We have learned a tremendous amount about the important role of financial accounting in our economy from the information economics research outlined above. If this book enables you to better understand and appreciate this role, it will have attained its objective.

Notes

1. For some information about Paciolo, a translation of his bookkeeping treatise, and a copy of an Italian version, see *Paciolo on Accounting*, by R. Gene Brown and Kenneth S. Johnston (1963).

2. Readers with a mathematical background will recognize these relationships as related to the fundamental theorem of calculus.

3. The dropping of these requirements did not mean that firms should not supply information to shareholders, but that the amount and nature of the information supplied was a matter between the firm and its shareholders. In effect, it was felt that market forces, rather than a legal requirement, were sufficient to motivate information production.

4. Actually, MN posed a much deeper question. Widespread share ownership had long been seen as a way of reconciling increasingly large and powerful corporations with the popular belief in individualism, property rights, and democracy, whereby the "little guy" could take part in the corporate governance process. With the 1929 crash and subsequent revelation of manipulative abuses, a new approach was required that would both restore public confidence in securities markets and be acceptable to powerful corporate interest groups. MN suggest that the creation of the SEC was an embodiment of such a new approach.

5. As an example of one longstanding practice, Montgomery (1912, pp. 191–192) criticized the practice of many firms of valuing capital assets on the basis of appraisals, often using the recorded gains as a source of dividends. A related practice was **watered stock**, under which assets were valued at the par value of stock issued to acquire the assets, when the value of the acquired assets was much lower. For a critical discussion of watered stock, see Hatfield (1927, pp. 208–209). Another practice was the creation of **secret reserves**, under which assets were undervalued and/or liabilities overstated. Then, losses were charged against the reserves (that is, charged against the asset or liability account) rather than to expense, typically without any disclosure to investors. Hatfield (pp. 319–323) also discusses this practice.

    Perhaps surprisingly, however, May (1943, pp. 53–58) discusses the effects of accounting abuses leading up to the 1929 crash, and argues "inadequate or misleading reports played but a relatively unimportant part in causing the catastrophic losses that were sustained."

6. This is not to say that the SEC stands aloof from accounting standards. If it perceives that standards as set by the profession are straying too far from what it wants, the SEC can bring considerable pressure to bear short of taking over the process. In this regard, see Note 7. The SEC reaffirmed its delegation of standard-setting to the FASB in 2003.

7. The controversy over the investment tax credit in the United States provides an excellent example. The 1962 Revenue Act provided firms with a credit against taxes payable of 7% of current investment in capital assets. The controversy was whether to account for the credit as a reduction in current income tax expense or to bring all or part of it into income over the life of the capital assets to which the credit applied. The Accounting Principles Board (the predecessor body to the FASB) issued APB2, requiring the latter alternative. The SEC, however, objected and issued its own standard, allowing greater flexibility in accounting for the credit. The Accounting Principles Board backed down and issued APB4 in 1964 allowing either alternative. The basic problem, as seen by the standard setters, was the lack of a set of basic accounting concepts from which the correct accounting for the credit could be deduced.

8. For a detailed description of the search for basic accounting concepts in the United States from the inception of the SEC to the 1990s, see Storey and Storey (1998).

9. Subsequently, the search for concepts changed to a search for a conceptual framework. This framework is introduced below, and discussed more fully in Section 3.2.

10. IASB standards use the term "profit or loss" rather than "net income." In this book, we will use "net income" or, if the context is clear, "earnings."

11. The American Accounting Association is comprised of academic accountants. It does not have standard setting authority as does the FASB. Nevertheless, professional accountants later picked up on the decision usefulness concept. See American Institute of Certified Public Accountants Study Group on the *Objectives of Financial Statements* (1973), also called the Trueblood Committee Report.

12. The Canada Business Corporations Act in effect confers power on the AcSB to set accounting standards. This is somewhat different from the United States, where the SEC, not the FASB, has ultimate power (see Notes 6 and 7). However, the two situations are similar in that it is the elected governments that have ultimate power over accounting standards. In Canada, this became evident in the "PIP Grant" controversy of 1982. Several large Canadian oil companies disagreed with the deferred recognition of these grants as laid down in the *CICA Handbook*, demanding immediate recognition of the grants in earnings instead. They took their case to the government, which agreed with them. The government threatened legislation to override the provisions of the *Handbook*. The AcSB held its ground and the government eventually backed down. Nevertheless, it was clear where the ultimate power over accounting standards lay. For a detailed account of this controversy, see Crandall (1983).

13. IASB standards are called International Financial Reporting Standards (IFRS), beginning with IFRS 1 (2003). Standards issued prior to that time were called International Accounting Standards (IAS), and, unless replaced, still retain their original titles and authority.

14. In this book, we will often use the word "reliable" in an intuitive sense. That is, reliable information is information that financial statement users can trust. This is the sense in which it is used in this chapter. However, standard setters envisage reliability as a more complex concept. According to the Conceptual Framework, financial statement information should "faithfully represent" what it is intended to represent. That is, there should be a correspondence between the accounting valuation or description of an item and the real item the information represents. The Framework rejects the term *reliability*, explaining that reliability means different things to different people, and the term *faithful representation* reduces ambiguity. In this book, we will usually use the term *reliability* as meaning faithful representation, because the term is shorter and because of its familiarity from past usage. Further discussion of reliability is given in Sections 2.2 and 3.7.1.

15. The IASB and FASB are currently engaged in a joint revenue recognition project, intended to simplify and unify the recognition of revenue. In 2011, the project issued an exposure draft that would require firms to separate distinct performance obligations in contracts with customers (e.g., a machine sold along with a maintenance agreement would contain two such obligations). The total revenue expected from a contract is then allocated to its distinct performance obligations. Revenue is generally recognized when, or as, the customer attains control over the contracted good or service. If the expected cost of meeting a performance obligation greater than one year exceeds its expected revenue, the contract is deemed "onerous," and an expense and associated liability are recognized. The proposed standard also requires extensive supplementary disclosures, such as the assumptions and judgments made in determining expected revenues, when the customer attains control, and when a contract is onerous.

16. For further discussion of Enron's business model, see Healy and Palepu (2003).

17. Asset-backed securities can be backed by several asset types such as mortgages (**mortgage-backed securities**), commercial real estate, credit card debt, student loans, and other receivables.

18. Proceeds of tranche sales could be flowed back to the sponsor to enable it to buy still more mortgages and other financial assets for securitization.

19. SIVs that issued ABCP were called "conduits."

20. This incentive would be reduced to the extent that the market looked through the lack of consolidation and valued the sponsor and its VIEs as one entity. Landsman, Peasnell, and Shakespeare (2008) report evidence that the market did do this. Also, Niu and Richardson (2006) examined the relationship between off-balance sheet financing and the market's evaluation of firm risk. They found that more off-balance sheet financing was associated with higher risk. Both of these studies suggest that, at least to some extent, investors add back off-balance sheet financing to the firm's balance sheet even without consolidation. Despite these findings, avoiding consolidation would be of crucial importance to financial institutions facing capital adequacy regulations.

21. In Canada, Accounting Guideline 15, "Consolidation of Variable Interest Entities" (2004), was similar to FIN 46. Consolidation under IASB standards was governed by Standing Interpretations Committee Interpretation 12, (SIC 12) "Consolidation-Special Purpose Entities" (1998). Since the market meltdown of asset-backed securities originated in the United States, we concentrate on FIN 46 here.

22. The **liquidity** of a security is the extent to which investors can quickly and at reasonable cost buy or sell any quantity of that security without affecting its market price. A **liquid market** is a market composed of liquid securities. The liquidity of a market is a matter of degree.

    Liquidity is a composite of market **depth**—the quantity of a security that investors can buy or sell without affecting its market price—and the **bid–ask spread**—the contemporaneous difference between the buying price and selling price of the security. Both of these components are measures of information asymmetry. The greater that investor concern is about their information disadvantage, the more likely they are to leave the market or, if they stay, the less they are willing to pay relative to the ask price.

    Liquidity risk is thus the risk that market depth and/or bid–ask spread change, thereby changing costs to buy or sell. Certainly, this risk materialized on the downside during the market meltdowns. When this happens, the market is said to be in a state of **liquidity pricing**.

23. This argument derives from the **folk theorem** of game theory. In its simplest form, this theorem states that for a non-cooperative game that is repeated indefinitely, without discounting of future payoffs, a cooperative solution can be attained if the players adopt a rational strategy. In our context, the rational strategy is for the accountant to forgo a short-term gain resulting, say, from bending or violating GAAP to please the client. The accountant will forgo the short-term gain if the strategy of the other players (investors, standard setters, lawmakers, courts) is to sufficiently punish the accountant for deviating from the cooperative strategy. That is, in this broader perspective, the accountant's payoffs are higher if he/she acts cooperatively.

    The folk theorem originated in the 1960s. It is so named because it is not known who established it first. Subsequently, game theorists have strengthened the theorem, for example by deriving conditions under which the theorem can be extended to finite periods, and with some discounting. See Friedman (1986), pp. 103–104. See also Robert Aumann's 2005 Nobel Prize Lecture (http://nobelprize.org/nobel_prizes/economics/laureates/2005/aumann-lecture.html).

    It should be noted, however, that while the folk theorem can produce ethical behaviour, the two mindsets are different. Ethical behaviour is driven by a desire to do the right thing. Folk theorem is driven by a rational calculation by the players that if they deviate from the cooperative solution they will be sufficiently punished.

24. By full disclosure, we do not mean that the financial statements should disclose "everything." This could be very costly, for example, if disclosure revealed valuable information to competitors and/or generated uncertainty about how different individuals or groups might react. Rather, by full disclosure we mean disclosure that does not create a wrong impression. Wrong impressions can be created by, for example, hiding information, delaying its release, biasing valuations, or using overly complex and ambiguous wording.

25. Indeed, the constitution of the IASB commits this body to principles-based standards. While IASB and FASB standards often seem similar, FASB standards are typically accompanied by a mass of detailed underlying rules and guidance, unlike IASB standards.

26. This argument is based on the 1969 court case *U.S. v. Simon*, under which the auditors of Continental Vending Machine Corporation were charged with certifying financial statements that they knew were false. As Ball describes, Continental's balance sheet included an uncollectible account receivable from an affiliated company. Some disclosure was provided in the financial statement notes, and the auditor argued that the financial statements were thus in accordance with GAAP. However, the disclosure was ambiguous. The courts ruled that technical accordance with GAAP was not sufficient to relieve the auditor of liability if the financial statements did not fairly represent financial position.

27. FASB accounting standards are now included in the *Accounting Standards Codification* (ASC; 2009). When we refer to a FASB standard as originally introduced, we denote it by its original title, as is the case here. When we refer to a FASB standard as it currently exists, we will give its ASC reference. Sometimes, we give both.

28. In Canada, IASB-based financial statements of foreign firms are accepted without the need to reconcile to Canadian GAAP, under National Instrument 52-107 (2004) of the CSA. For Canadian firms with shares traded in the United States, the Multi-jurisdictional Disclosure System allows them to file SEC reports using the documents they file in Canada, and vice versa. Canadian firms taking advantage of the Multi-jurisdictional Disclosure System must meet the requirements of the Sarbanes-Oxley Act.

29. However, through its 2002 Multilateral Memorandum of Understanding Concerning Consultation and Cooperation and the Exchange of Information, IOSCO facilitates consultation, cooperation, and the exchange of information for the consistent enforcement of securities regulations.

Chapter 2
Accounting Under Ideal Conditions

Figure 2.1 Organization of Chapter 2

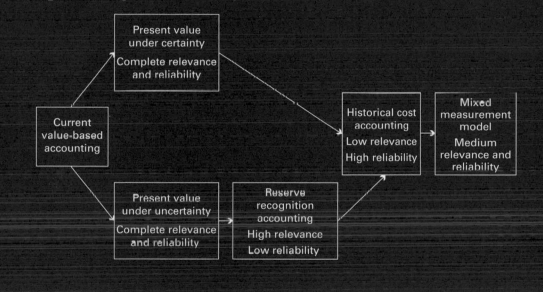

2.1 OVERVIEW

We begin our study of financial accounting theory by considering the present value model. This model provides the utmost in relevant information to financial statement users. In this context, we define *relevant information* as information about the firm's future economic prospects—that is, its dividends, cash flows, and profitability.

Our concern is with the conditions under which relevant financial statements will also be reliable, where reliable information faithfully represents the firm's financial position and results of operations. We will also explore the conditions under which market values of assets and liabilities can serve as indirect measures of present value. This will be the case under ideal conditions (to be defined later). If conditions are not ideal (which is usually the case), fundamental problems are created for asset valuation and income measurement.

Figure 2.1 outlines the organization of this chapter.

2.2 THE PRESENT VALUE MODEL UNDER CERTAINTY

The present value model is widely used in economics and finance and has had considerable impact on accounting over the years. We first consider a simple version of the model under conditions of certainty. By "certainty" we mean that the future cash flows of the firm and the interest rate in the economy are publicly known with certainty. We denote these as **ideal conditions**.

Example 2.1
Illustration of the Present Value Model Under Certainty

Consider P.V. Ltd., a one-asset firm with no liabilities. Assume that the asset will generate end-of-year cash flows of $150 each year for two years and then will have zero value. Assume also that the interest rate in the economy is 10%. Then, at time 0 (the beginning of the first year of the asset's life), the present value of the firm's future cash flows, denoted by PA_0, is

$$PA_0 = \frac{\$150}{1.10} + \frac{\$150}{1.10^2} = \$136.36 + \$123.97 = \$260.33$$

We can then prepare a present value opening balance sheet as follows:

<table>
<tr><td colspan="2" align="center">P.V. Ltd.
Balance Sheet
Time 0</td></tr>
<tr><td>Capital asset, at present value <u>$260.33</u></td><td>Shareholders' equity <u>$260.33</u></td></tr>
</table>

The firm's income statement for year 1 is

<table>
<tr><td colspan="2" align="center">P.V. Ltd.
Income Statement
For Year 1</td></tr>
<tr><td>Accretion of discount</td><td align="right"><u>$26.03</u></td></tr>
</table>

Since future net revenues are capitalized into asset value, net income is simply interest on the opening asset value, just as income from a savings account is interest on the opening account balance.[1] Thus, net income for the year is equal to $PA_0 \times 10\% = \$260.33 \times 10\% = \$26.03$. This amount is called **accretion of discount**. The term arises because the stream of cash receipts is one year closer at the end of the year than it was at the beginning.[2]

At the end of year 1, the present value of the remaining cash flows from the firm's asset is

$$PA_1 = \frac{\$150}{1.10} = \$136.36$$

Then, the end-of-year-1 balance sheet is

P.V. Ltd.
Balance Sheet
End of Year 1

Financial Asset		Shareholders' Equity	
Cash	$150.00	Opening value	$260.33
Capital asset, at present value	136.36	Net income	26.03
	$286.36		$286.36

This assumes that the firm pays no dividend. A dividend can be easily incorporated by reducing cash and shareholders' equity by the amount of the dividend.

Note the following points about Example 2.1:

1. The net book value of the capital asset at any year-end is equal to its present value, or value-in-use (see the discussion of value in use in Section 1.2), where value-in-use is here determined as the present value of the future cash flows from that asset, discounted at 10%.

2. The $26.03 accretion of discount is also referred to as *ex ante*, or expected net income, since, at time 0, the firm expects to earn $26.03. Of course, since all conditions are known with certainty, the expected net income will equal the *ex post*, or realized net income.

3. **Relevant** financial statement information gives information to investors about the firm's future economic prospects. The information in Example 2.1 is entirely relevant. To see this, note first that, fundamentally, economic prospects are defined by the firm's stream of future dividends—it is dividends that provide a payoff to investors, the present value of which serves to establish firm value.

   Then, it might seem that the firm's dividend policy will affect its value, since the timing of dividends will affect their present value. However, under ideal conditions, this is not the case, due to **dividend irrelevancy.**

   To see why dividend policy does not matter under ideal conditions, note that as long as investors can invest any dividends they receive at the *same rate* of return as the firm earns on cash flows *not* paid in dividends, the present value of an investor's overall interest in the firm is independent of the timing of dividends. This holds in our example since there is only one interest rate in the economy. In effect, the firm's cash flows establish the size of the "pot" that is ultimately available to investors, and it does not matter if this pot is distributed sooner or later. If it is distributed during the current year, investors can earn 10% on the distributions. If it is distributed in a subsequent year, the firm earns 10% on amounts not distributed, but this accrues to investors through an increase in the value of their investment. The present value to the investor is the same either way.

Under dividend irrelevancy, cash flows are just as relevant as dividends, because cash flows establish the firm's dividend-paying ability. As a result, the financial statements under Example 2.1 are entirely relevant.

4. As an accountant, you might be wondering why the firm's net income seems to play no role in firm valuation. This is quite true—it doesn't, under ideal conditions. The reason is that future cash flows are known and hence can be discounted to provide balance sheet valuations. Net income is then perfectly predictable, being simply accretion of discount as pointed out above. In effect, under ideal conditions, the balance sheet contains all the relevant information and the income statement contains none.[3] Even though net income is "true and correct," it conveys no information because investors can always figure it out by multiplying the opening balance sheet value by the interest rate. To put this another way, there is no information in the current net income that helps investors predict future economic prospects of the firm. These are already known to investors, and capitalized into asset valuation, by assumption. This is an important point, and we shall return to it later. For now, suffice it to say that when ideal conditions do not hold, the income statement assumes a much more significant role.

5. **Reliable** financial statement information faithfully represents what it is intended to represent (see Chapter 1, Note 14). For example, the balance sheet valuation of capital assets and resulting amortization would not be reliable if operating expenses are capitalized, as in the case of WorldCom described in Section 1.2. Nor would the valuation of long-term debt be reliable if some debt is off balance sheet, as it was in the case of many financial institutions leading up to the 2007–2008 market melt-downs described in Section 1.3.

The information in Example 2.1 is entirely reliable, since we have assumed that future cash flows and the interest rate are known with certainty. Then, balance sheet valuations faithfully represent the real underlying assets and liabilities of the firm. Any attempt by management to hide assets and liabilities, or bias inputs into the present value calculations, and any calculation errors, would be immediately discovered since the various inputs are publicly known.

6. Under the ideal conditions of future cash flows known with certainty and the economy's risk-free interest rate given, the present value of an asset or liability will equal its market value. In terms of the different versions of current value accounting

outlined in Section 1.2, value in use and fair value (exit value) are equal. To see this, consider the following argument: Given an interest rate of 10%, no one would be willing to pay more than $260.33 for P.V.'s asset at time 0—if they did, they would be earning less than 10%. Also, the owners of the asset would not sell it for less than $260.33—if offered less than $260.33, they would be better off to retain it and earn 10%. If they needed the money they could borrow at 10% against the asset as security. Thus, the only possible equilibrium market price is $260.33. This argument is a simple example of the principle of **arbitrage**. If market prices for identical goods and services are such that it is possible to make a profit by simply buying in one market and selling in another, these are called arbitrage profits. However, it seems reasonable to expect that, if future cash flows and the risk-free rate are publicly known, the scramble of self-interested individuals to make these quick profits would eliminate any price discrepancies.[4]

7. As P.V. Ltd. owns only one asset and has no liabilities, the firm's market value would also be $260.33 at time 0, being the sum of the financial assets[5] and the present value of future cash receipts from the capital asset. Thus, the total market value of P.V.'s shares outstanding would be $260.33. In more general terms, if a firm has more than one asset, the market value of the firm would be the sum of the value of its financial assets plus the present value of the joint future receipts from its capital assets, including intangibles, less the present value of any liabilities. At points in time after time 0, the firm's market value continues to equal the sum of its financial assets plus capital assets, net of liabilities. Note, however, that dividend policy affects the amount of financial assets. To the extent that the firm does not pay out all of its profits in dividends, its market value will include the return on reinvested assets. Question 1, at the end of this chapter, illustrates this point. See also the discussion of dividend irrelevancy above.

2.2.1 Summary

The purpose of Example 2.1 is to demonstrate that under the ideal conditions of future cash flows known with certainty and a given interest rate in the economy, it is possible to prepare completely relevant and reliable financial statements. The process of arbitrage ensures that the market value of an asset equals the present value of its future cash flows. The market value of the firm is then the value of its net financial assets plus the value of its capital assets (less other liabilities).

2.3 THE PRESENT VALUE MODEL UNDER UNCERTAINTY

It is instructive to extend the present value model to the presence of uncertainty. With one major exception, the concepts carry over from Example 2.1.

Example 2.2
Illustration of the Present Value Model Under Uncertainty

Let us continue Example 2.1, taking into account that the economy can be in a "bad" state or a "good" state during each year. If it is in the bad state, end-of-year cash flows will be $100 for the year. If it is in the good state, however, end-of-year cash flows will be $200 for the year.

Assume that during each year the bad state and the good state each occur with probability 0.5. Our assumption that state probabilities are the same each year implies that the state realizations are independent. That is, the state realization in year 1 does not affect the probabilities[6] of state realization in year 2.

Uncertain future events that affect firm performance, such as the state of the economy, are called **states of nature**, or **states** for short. Thus, the states in this example are for each year:

> **State 1** Economy is bad (low firm performance of $100).

> **State 2** Economy is good (high firm performance of $200).

Note that no one can control which of the states is realized—this is why they are called states of *nature*. Other examples of states that affect cash flows are weather, government policies, strikes by suppliers, equipment breakdowns, etc. In any realistic situation there will be a large number of possible states. However, our two-state example is sufficient to convey the idea—states of nature are a conceptual device to model those uncertain, uncontrollable future events whose realizations affect the cash flows of the firm.

While at time 0 no one knows which state will occur, we assume that the set of possible states is publicly known and complete. That is, every possible event that can affect cash flows is known to everyone, and everyone knows that everyone knows.[7] Thus, while no one knows for sure which state will occur, it is known that whatever state does happen must be an element of the set. Furthermore, we assume that the state realization is publicly observable—everyone will know which state actually happens. Finally, we assume that the state probabilities are **objective** and publicly known. That is, everyone has the same state probabilities. By objective we mean that if we imagine a long-run sequence of repetitions of our two-period economy, the bad state will occur with relative frequency 0.5 (or whatever other state probability we were to assume). Think by analogy of rolling a pair of fair dice. We know that the probability of a seven, say, is 1/6, and that if we were to roll the dice a large number of times a seven would appear with relative frequency 1/6. Thus, 1/6 is an objective probability of rolling seven, just as 0.5 is an objective probability that the economy is in a good state this period and that firm performance will thus be high. Note that an implication of objective probabilities here is that any particular outcome tells us nothing about what the state probabilities are—these are already known by assumption. Thus, the probability of a seven on the next roll of the dice remains at 1/6, just as the probability of the good state remains at 0.5 in this example, regardless of the state realization this period.

These assumptions extend the concept of ideal conditions, also called "first-best" conditions, to take uncertainty into account. To summarize,[8]

> **Ideal conditions** under uncertainty are characterized by (1) a given, fixed interest rate at which the firm's future cash flows are discounted, (2) a complete and publicly known set of states of nature, (3) state probabilities objective and publicly known, and (4) state realization publicly observable.

Another way to think about ideal conditions is that they are similar to conditions of certainty except that future cash flows are known *conditionally* on the states of nature. That is, *if* state 1 happens, then firm performance will be low, with cash flows of $100, etc. We will assume that P.V. Ltd.'s future cash flows are discounted at 10%.

Be sure you realize that while investors know the set of possible states of nature and their probabilities, they do not know which state will actually occur (or has already occurred, such as the state of the economy, but this is not known until period end). The risk arising from not knowing which state of nature will happen is called **estimation risk**. More generally, estimation risk arises when a decision maker is uncertain about the values of underlying parameters affecting his/her decision, such as, in this example, the state of the economy.

Given these ideal conditions, we can now calculate the **expected present value** of P.V.'s future cash flows at time 0:

$$PA_0 = 0.5\left(\frac{\$100}{1.10} + \frac{\$200}{1.10}\right) + 0.5\left(\frac{\$100}{1.10^2} + \frac{\$200}{1.10^2}\right)$$

$$= (0.5 \times \$272.73) + (0.5 \times \$247.93)$$

$$= \$136.36 + \$123.97$$

$$= \$260.33$$

We can then prepare P.V.'s opening balance sheet as follows:

P.V. Ltd.			
Balance Sheet			
Time 0			
Capital asset, at expected present value	$260.33	Shareholders' equity	$260.33

It is worthwhile to ask whether the time 0 market value of the asset, and hence of the firm, would be $260.33, as per the balance sheet. It is tempting to answer yes, since this is the firm's expected value given dividend irrelevance. But uncertainty introduces an additional consideration not present in the certainty model of Section 2.2. This is that investors may be averse to risk. While the *expected* value of the firm is $260.33 at time 0, it is shown below that the expected value of the firm at the *end* of year 1 will be $236.36 or $336.36, depending on whether the bad state or the good state happens in that year. Ask yourself whether you would be indifferent between having $260.33 in your pocket or a 50/50 gamble of $236.36 or $336.36. The present value of the 50/50 gamble is

$$PA_0 = 0.5 \times \frac{\$236.36}{1.10} + 0.5 \times \frac{\$336.36}{1.10}$$

$$= (0.5 \times \$214.87) + (0.5 \times \$305.78)$$

$$= \$107.44 + \$152.89$$

$$= \$260.33$$

the same as the sure thing. But, most people would prefer the sure thing, because it is less risky. Then, the market value of the firm will be less than $260.33, since to the extent that investors are collectively risk averse they will value the risky firm at less than its present value. In this chapter, we will ignore this complication by assuming that investors are risk neutral. That is, they are indifferent between the sure thing and the 50/50 gamble above. Then, the firm's market value will be $260.33 at time 0. This assumption of risk-neutral investors will be relaxed later, since accountants have a role to play in informing investors about the firm's riskiness as well as its expected value. The concept of a risk-averse investor is introduced in Section 3.4 and the impact of risk on firm valuation is shown in Section 4.5. For now, suffice it to say that the expected value of future cash flows or, more generally, future firm performance, is relevant for investors irrespective of their attitudes to risk.

Given risk-neutral valuation, the arbitrage principle will ensure that the market value of the firm's asset, and of the firm itself, is $260.33. The arbitrage principle would still hold if investors were averse to risk but the market value would be driven to an amount less than $260.33.

To return to the example, accretion of discount is now based on *expected* net income for year 1, calculated as $0.10 \times \$260.33 = \$26.03$.

The major difference between the uncertainty and certainty cases is that *expected net income and realized net income need not be the same under uncertainty*. To analyze this further, assume that the year 1 state realization is a bad economy. Thus *realized* cash flows in year 1 are $100, whereas *expected* cash flows were $0.5 \times 100 + 0.5 \times 200 = \$150$. Realized net income is then the sum of expected net income plus the difference between expected and actual cash flows, as per the following income statement:

The negative $50 of unexpected cash flows results in a $50 "shock" to earnings for the year. The negative $50 earnings shock is called **abnormal earnings**, or, equivalently,

---

P.V. Ltd.
Income Statement
(bad economy)
Year 1

Accretion of discount (0.10 × $260.33)		$26.03
Less: Abnormal earnings, as a result of bad-state realization:		
Expected cash flows (0.5 × $100 + 0.5 × $200)	$150.00	
Actual cash flows	100.00	50.00
Net loss		$23.97

---

unexpected earnings, since it reduces expected earnings of $26.03 to a loss of $23.97. Under uncertainty, net income consists of *expected* net income plus or minus abnormal earnings for the year.[9]

Now, at the end of year 1, the expected present value of the remaining cash flows from the asset is

$$PA_1 = 0.5\left(\frac{\$100}{1.10} + \frac{\$200}{1.10}\right) = \$136.36$$

The year-end balance sheet is as follows:

P.V. Ltd.
Balance Sheet
(bad economy)
End of Year 1

Financial Asset		Shareholders' Equity	
Cash	$100.00	Opening value	$260.33
Capital Asset			
End of year value	136.36	Net loss	23.97
	$236.36		$236.36

Again, arbitrage ensures that the market value of the asset is $136.36 and of the firm is $236.36 at time 1. We continue the assumption that the firm pays no dividend. Ideal conditions ensure that it makes no difference whether the firm pays a dividend or not, as in the certainty case. In other words, dividend irrelevancy continues to hold. Question 4 pursues this point.

It should be noted that in our example abnormal earnings do not **persist**. That is, their effect dissipates completely in the year in which they occur. In general, this need not be the case. For example, if the bad-state realization was due to, say, a market meltdown that affected economic activity, the abnormal effect on earnings may persist for several periods. We ignore this possibility here to keep the example simple. However, we will return to the concept of persistence in Chapters 5 and 6.

Now, let's consider the accounting if the state realization is a good economy. The year 1 income statement is as follows:

P.V. Ltd.
Income Statement
(good economy)
Year 1

Accretion of discount	$26.03
Add: Abnormal earnings, as a result of good-state realization ($200 − $150)	50.00
Net income	$76.03

The abnormal earnings of $50 is the difference between actual and expected cash flows for year 1, and these abnormal earnings increase expected earnings of $26.03 up to a profit of $76.03.

At the end of year 1, the present value of the remaining cash flows is still $136.36. The year-end balance sheet is as follows:

P.V. Ltd.
Balance Sheet
(good economy)
End of Year 1

Financial Asset		**Shareholders' Equity**	
Cash	$200.00	Opening value	$260.33
Capital Asset		**Net income**	76.03
End of year value	136.36		
	$336.36		$336.36

Again, arbitrage ensures that the firm's market value at time 1 will be $336.36, given risk-neutral investors.

Note the following points about Example 2.2:

1. It continues to be the case that financial statement information is both completely relevant and completely reliable. Relevance holds because balance sheet values are based on expected future cash flows, and dividend irrelevancy holds. Reliability holds because ideal conditions ensure that present value calculations faithfully represent the firm's expected future cash flows.

   Note that financial statement reliability and **volatility** are different concepts. While present value calculations are reliable under ideal conditions, net income and balance sheet values are volatile since end-of-period present values depend on which state is realized. This volatility is demonstrated by abnormal earnings in our example, where net income varied from −$23.97 to +$76.03 under bad and good economy realizations respectively, leading to the ending firm value of $236.36 or $336.36. Thus, the investor bears risk even when the financial statements are completely reliable.[10]

2. Like the certainty case, there are still two ways of calculating balance sheet current values: We can calculate expected present values directly or we can use market values. Under ideal conditions, arbitrage forces the two ways to yield identical results. Thus, as in Example 2.1, value in use and fair value are equal.

3. Despite the fact that expected and realized net income need not be equal, the income statement still has no information content when abnormal earnings do not persist. Investors have sufficient information to calculate for themselves what realized net

income will be, once they know the current year's state realization. This calculation is programmable and no accounting policy decisions are needed. We can now say that net income is predictable *conditional on* the state of nature.

4. At the risk of getting ahead of ourselves, let us see how the income statement can have information content. For this, we need only relax the assumption that state probabilities are objective. This puts us into the realm of **subjective probabilities**, which are formally introduced in Chapter 3. Then, investors no longer have "ready-made" state probabilities available to them for purposes of calculating expected future firm performance. Rather, they must assess these probabilities themselves, using whatever information is available. There is no longer any guarantee that in a long-run sequence of repetitions of the two-period economy, the bad and good states will occur with the same relative frequencies as the probabilities assigned by the investor. The reason, of course, is that individuals are limited in their knowledge and forecasting ability. Note that if state probabilities are subjective, so are the resulting expected values. That is, the value of the firm is also subjective.

Subjective probabilities are a more reasonable assumption than objective probabilities, because the future performance of a business entity is much more complex and difficult to predict than a simple roll of fair dice. Since investors know that their predictions are subject to error, they will be alert for information sources that enable them to revise their probability assessments. The income statement is one such source. When state probabilities are subjective, the income statement can provide information about what these probabilities are. For example, observing a net income of $76.03 this year in Example 2.2 may cause you to increase your probability of the good state in future years. This would increase your expectation of future firm cash flows and profitability.

If this argument is unclear to you, return to the analogy of rolling dice, but now assume that you do not know whether the dice are fair. What is your probability of rolling a seven? Obviously, this probability is no longer objective, and you must assess it on the basis of whatever information and prior experience you have. However, rolling the dice (analogous to observing the income statement) provides information, and after a few rolls you should have a better idea whether their true state is fair or not fair. For example, if you rolled five times and a seven came up each time, you would probably want to increase from 1/6 your subjective probability of rolling a seven. Just as improved knowledge of the true state of the dice will help you to predict future rolls, improved knowledge of the true state of the firm will help you to predict future firm performance and investment returns. In Chapter 3 we will show how investors can use financial statement information to revise their subjective probabilities of future firm performance.

2.3.1 Summary

The purpose of Example 2.2 is to extend the present value model to formally incorporate uncertainty, using the concepts of states of nature and objective probabilities. The definition of ideal conditions must be extended to include a complete and publicly known set of states of nature, with future cash flows known *conditionally* on state realization. Also, ideal conditions now specify objective state probabilities and publicly observable state realization. The logic of the present value model under certainty then carries over, except that market values are based on *expected* cash flows, assuming investors are risk neutral.

The major difference between the certainty and uncertainty cases is that *expected* and *realized* net income need no longer be the same under uncertainty, and the difference is called abnormal earnings. Nevertheless, financial statements based on expected present values continue to be both relevant and reliable. They are relevant because they are based on expected future cash flows. They are reliable because financial statement values faithfully represent these expected future cash flows and, in each case, management omission, error, and bias are not possible. All of these conclusions are independent of the firm's dividend policy, since dividend irrelevancy continues to hold.

2.4 EXAMPLES OF PRESENT VALUE ACCOUNTING

2.4.1 Embedded Value

By now, you probably want to point out that the real world is *not* characterized by ideal conditions. This is quite true. As an example of some of the complexities of present value accounting when ideal conditions do not hold, consider Theory in Practice 2.1.

Theory in Practice 2.1

Some insurance companies voluntarily report **embedded value** as supplementary information. This is a form of present value accounting that values the company's insurance business in force at discounted present value of policy amounts to be collected, net of costs (i.e., value in use). These costs consist of income taxes, and a charge for the capital the company is required to hold as a reserve for policy commitments. The discount rate to compute present value is based on a risk-free rate plus a risk premium. Embedded value does not include the present value of expected future business. Thus it is not a full current valuation of the business. Nevertheless, by providing an estimate of the present value of business actually in force, it does provide highly relevant information.

Since insurance policies typically extend well into the future, embedded value requires many assumptions, including for discount rates, investment conditions, and life expectancies. Many of these assumptions are based on actuarial calculations.

The table below is adapted from the embedded value information of Manulife Financial Corporation, a large Canada-based multinational provider of insurance and related financial services. Manulife's common shareholders' equity as per its December 31, 2011, balance sheet was $22,402 million. Its financial statements are prepared in accordance with IASB GAAP. The market value of a Manulife common share was $11.20 on January 3, 2012, rising to $13.96 in late March, 2012, and then falling off. Manulife's new business of $1,086 million is down from 2010, when new business was $1,841 million. The question then is, why is Manulife's share price less than its embedded value?

Serafeim (2011) studied a worldwide sample of 350 insurance companies over the period 1991–2009, of which 93 disclosed embedded value. He reported a lower bid–ask spread (see Chapter 1, Note 22) for shares of firms reporting embedded value information than for firms that did not report this information. This implies greater investor confidence in the overall quality of these firms' financial reporting (i.e., less information asymmetry between the firm and investors). However, this result held only for firms for which an outside auditor or consultant certified the calculations, and was particularly strong for firms that belonged to the CFO Forum, an insurance industry group with objectives that include promotion of transparent reporting. There is no mention in Manulife's annual report that its embedded value information is certified by an outside party, or of CFO membership. Thus, investor concern about reliability could at least partially explain Manulife's lower share price.

Manulife Financial Corporation Annual Report, 2011 Embedded Value	
Embedded value, January 1, 2011 (millions)	$39,303
Interest on embedded value (i.e., accretion of discount)	2,808
Net present value of new business during the year	1,086
Experience variances and other changes in actuarial assumptions	(5,041)
Discount rate changes	(2,416)
Favourable changes in exchange rates	1,171
Dividends and other capital movements	(846)
Embedded value, December 31, 2011	$36,065
Embedded value per share	$ 20.02

2.4.2 Reserve Recognition Accounting

To further illustrate present value accounting, we now consider **reserve recognition accounting** (RRA) for oil and gas companies. RRA is of interest because it provides sufficient information to prepare a present value-based income statement, for comparison with the statement in Example 2.2.

Reserve recognition accounting requires supplemental disclosure of present value, discounted at 10%, of a firm's proved oil and gas reserves (called the **standardized measure**), plus a statement explaining changes in the standardized measure during the year.

At present, IASB standards do not include disclosure requirements for oil and gas reserves. In Canada, CSA National Instrument (NI) 51-101 requires extensive supplementary reserves disclosure. However, these requirements do not include reserve recognition accounting. Consequently, we turn to the United States' reserve recognition standard

ASC 932.[11] As mentioned, this standard provides sufficient information to enable calculation of a present value-based income statement, as well as an asset value.

The intent of ASC 932, presumably, is to provide investors with more relevant information about future cash flows than that contained in conventional historical cost-based financial statements. Oil and gas companies, it can be argued, particularly need to give this type of supplementary disclosure because the historical cost of oil and gas properties may bear little relationship to their value.

It can hardly be said that oil and gas companies operate under conditions of certainty. Consequently, we consider ASC 932 in relation to our present value model under uncertainty, which was illustrated in Example 2.2. Consider first Table 2.1, from the 2012 SEC Annual Information Form 40-F of Husky Energy Inc., a large Canada-based multinational corporation with operations in Canada, the United States, China, Indonesia, and Greenland. Its shares are traded on the Toronto Stock Exchange. Note that the undiscounted future net cash flows are shown, and also the present value of these cash flows, discounted at 10%. When estimating future cash flows, ASC 932 requires that the present value calculations use average oil and gas prices during the past year (as opposed to prices expected to be in effect when the reserves are lifted and sold). ASC 932 does not require disclosure of states of nature and their probabilities, only the end results of the expectation calculation.

Standardized Measure of Discounted Future Net Cash Flows Relating to Proved Oil and Gas Reserves (unaudited)

Husky gives the following information to accompany its standardized measure: "The following information has been developed utilizing procedures prescribed by FASB

Table 2.1 Husky Energy Inc. Standardized Measure of Discounted Future Net Cash Flows Relating to Proved Oil and Gas Reserves

Standardized Measure (unaudited) ($ millions)	Canada[1]			International[1]			Total[1]		
	2012	2011	2010	2012	2011	2010	2012	2011	2010
Future Cash Inflows	43,058	50,824	40,840	5,850	1,510	1,582	48,908	52,334	42,422
Future Production Costs	15,803	18,342	14,682	1,099	503	576	16,902	18,845	15,258
Future Development Costs	8,138	7,932	7,605	1,293	161	182	9,431	8,093	7,787
Future Income Taxes	4,724	6,286	4,752	670	282	255	5,394	6,568	5,007
Future Net Cash Flows	14,393	18,264	13,801	2,788	564	570	17,181	18,828	14,371
Annual 10% Discount Factor	5,747	8,217	6,010	724	199	216	6,471	8,416	6,226
Standardized Measure of Discounted Future Net Cash Flows	8,646	10,047	7,791	2,064	365	354	10,710	10,412	8,145

[1] The schedules above are calculated using year average prices and year-end costs, statutory income tax rates and existing proved oil and gas reserves for 2010, 2011 and 2012. The value of exploration properties and probable reserves, future exploration costs, future change in oil and gas prices and in production and development costs are excluded.

Source: Reprinted by permission of Husky Energy Inc.

Accounting Standards Codification 932, "Extractive Activities—Oil and Gas" and based on crude oil and natural gas reserve and production volumes estimated by the Company's reserves evaluation staff. It may be useful for certain comparison purposes, but should not be solely relied upon in evaluating Husky or its performance. Further, information contained in the following table should not be considered as representative of realistic assessments of future cash flows, nor should the standardized measure of discounted future net cash flows be viewed as representative of the current value of Husky's reserves.

The future cash flows presented below are based on average sales prices and cost rates, and statutory income tax rates in existence as of the date of the projections. It is expected that material revisions to some estimates of crude oil and natural gas reserves may occur in the future, development and production of the reserves may occur in periods other than those assumed, and actual prices realized and costs incurred may vary significantly from those used.

Management does not rely upon the following information in making investment and operating decisions. Such decisions are based upon a wide range of factors, including estimates of probable as well as proved reserves, and varying price and cost assumptions considered more representative of a range of possible economic conditions that may be anticipated."

This disclosure seems to conform fairly well to our theoretical Example 2.2. The $10,710 million total present value is the amount that would appear on Husky's December 31, 2012, present value-based balance sheet for the asset "proved oil and gas reserves" if one was prepared on this basis. It corresponds to the $136.36 valuation of the capital asset at time 1 in Example 2.2. It should be noted, however, that the 10% discount rate used by Husky is not the single known rate in the economy. Rather, this rate is mandated by ASC 932, presumably for comparability across firms. Also, as mentioned, the figures apply only to proved reserves and not all of Husky's reserve assets.

Table 2.2 gives changes in the standardized measure. To understand this statement of changes, we prepare in Table 2.3 an income statement in the same format as the income statement for P.V. Ltd. in Example 2.2.

Check each of the numbers in Table 2.3 from the original Husky statements in Tables 2.1 and 2.2.[12]

The changes in estimates of ($4,556) million in Table 2.3 should be considered carefully. Note, in particular, that there are a number of changes, including revisions of quantities, prices, timing, and costs, as well as related income taxes. Note also that the amounts are quite material, netting out to over four times expected net income. The number and magnitude of these changes are the main differences between our Example 2.2, which assumed ideal conditions, and the "real world" environment in which Husky operates.

Note that the accretion of discount is not 10% of beginning-of-year present value, as it was in Example 2.2. ASC 932 does not require disclosure of how this amount is calculated. Its failure to agree with its theoretical counterpart derives from the various changes to estimates during the year, which impact the calculations. Nevertheless, the concept of accretion of discount as expected net income for the year remains.

Table 2.2 Husky Energy Inc. Changes in Standardized Measure of Discounted Future Net Cash Flows Relating to Proved Oil and Gas Reserves

($ millions)	Canada[1]			International[1]			Total[1]		
	2012	2011	2010	2012	2011	2010	2012	2011	2010
Present Value at January 1	10,047	7,791	6,522	365	354	270	10,412	8,145	6,792
Sales and Transfers, net of Production Costs	(3,538)	(4,239)	(3,129)	(235)	(216)	(227)	(3,773)	(4,455)	(3,356)
Net Change in Sales and Transfer Prices, net of Development and Production Costs	(1,353)	3,281	2,982	(15)	266	99	(1,368)	3,547	3,081
Development Cost Incurred that Reduced Future Development Costs	3,093	2,500	2,697	733	7	6	3,826	2,507	2,703
Changes in Estimated Future Development Costs	(2,234)	(1,921)	(2,639)	(1,551)	26	(1)	(3,785)	(1,895)	(2,640)
Extensions, Discoveries and Improved Recovery, net of Related Costs	937	1,601	1,235	2,774	10	169	3,711	1,611	1,404
Revisions of Quantity Estimates	(460)	156	(68)	426	(47)	43	(34)	109	(25)
Accretion of Discount	1,194	908	911	(101)	55	39	1,093	963	950
Sale of Reserves in Place	(12)	(28)	(4)	—	(59)	—	(12)	(87)	(4)
Purchase of Reserves in Place	9	1,096	247	—	—	—	9	1,096	247
Changes in Timing of Future Net Cash Flows and Other	320	(358)	(579)	(4)	(20)	—	316	(378)	(579)
Net Change in Income Taxes	643	(740)	(384)	(328)	(11)	(44)	315	(751)	(428)
Net Increase (Decrease)	(1,401)	2,256	1,269	1,699	11	84	298	2,267	1,353
Present Value at December 31	8,646	10,047	7,791	2,064	365	354	10,710	10,412	8,145

[1] The schedules above are calculated using year-end average prices and year-end costs, statutory income tax rates and existing proved oil and gas reserves for 2010, 2011, and 2012. The value of exploration properties and probable reserves, future exploration costs, future changes in oil and gas prices, and production and development costs are excluded.

Source: Reprinted by permission of Husky Energy Inc.

In sum, the procedures used by Husky to account for the results of its oil and gas operations under RRA seem to conform to the theoretical present value model under uncertainty, except that it is necessary to make material changes to previous estimates.

2.4.3 Critique of RRA

ASC 932 contains several provisions to mitigate reliability concerns. As mentioned, only proved reserves are included, average oil and gas price for the year is used rather than prices expected when the reserves are lifted and sold, and the interest rate is specified as 10%. However, these provisions reduce relevance, since the extent to which the resulting

Table 2.3 Husky Energy Inc. Income Statement for 2012 from Proved Oil and Gas Reserves (millions of dollars)

Expected net income—accretion of discount		$1,093
Abnormal earnings		
Net present value of additional reserves added during year		3,711
Unexpected items—changes in estimates		
Net changes in sales and transfer prices, net of production and development costs	$(1,368)	
Revisions of quantity estimates	(34)	
Changes in timing of net future cash flows	316	
Changes in estimated future development costs	(3,785)	
Net changes in income taxes	315	(4,556)
Net income from proved oil and gas reserves		$ 248

Source: Reprinted by permission of Husky Energy Inc.

present value predicts future cash flows and their risk is reduced. Thus, while RRA is more relevant than historical costs of proved reserves, it is by no means completely relevant.

Nevertheless, reliability concerns remain.[13] RRA is not a complete representation since it applies only to proved reserves. The concept of proved reserves is itself a matter of judgment, since "proved" essentially means "reasonable certainty" of recovery under current economic, operating, and regulatory conditions. Due to the imprecision of the proved reserves concept, RRA estimates are also subject to bias (see Theory in Practice 2.2 below). Also, estimates are subject to error, as evidenced by the substantial adjustments to previous estimates in Table 2.3 above. Thus, the extent to which the present value calculations faithfully represent actual reserves is open to question.

Consistent with these relevance and reliability considerations, oil company managers, in particular, tend to regard RRA with reservation and suspicion. As an example, Husky's management states (see Table 2.1) that its RRA information should not be solely relied on when evaluating Husky or its performance, is not a realistic measure of future cash flows and the value of the company's reserves, and is not relied upon for internal decision making. Also, the reader is warned that substantial changes to some estimates may be made in future.

One might ask why Husky reports under ASC 932, a U.S. standard. However, since the company has investors residing in the United States, it is subject to SEC requirements. Also, many other multinational oil companies report RRA information, and Husky likely wants to appeal to a broader spectrum of investors than those in North America. The company also reports considerable additional reserves information (not reproduced).

While it is clear that management is cautious about RRA, this does not necessarily mean that it does not provide useful information to investors. As mentioned, RRA is more relevant than historical cost information and steps are taken to mitigate reliability

Table 2.4 Husky Energy Inc. Results of Operations for Producing Activities[1] (unaudited)

($ millions)	Year Ended December 31, 2011		
	Canada	International	Total
Revenues, net of Royalties	5,367	264	5,631
Production and Operating Expenses	1,798	31	1,829
Depreciation, Depletion, Amortization, & Impairment	2,093	11	2,104
Exploration & Evaluation Expenses	305	45	350
Earnings Before Taxes	1,170	177	1,347
Income Taxes	339	51	391
Results of Operations	831	126	956

[1] The costs in this schedule exclude corporate overhead, interest expense and other operating costs, which are not directly related to producing activities.

Source: Reprinted by permission of Husky Energy Inc.

concerns, so it has the potential to be useful. To see the potential for usefulness, compare the present value-based 2012 net income from Table 2.3 with Husky's historical cost-based earnings from oil and gas[14] in Table 2.4.

Comparison of net income under the two bases is complicated by the fact that the present value calculations relate only to proved reserves. However, let us take the $956 million profit from operations for 2012 in Table 2.4 as the historical cost analogue of the $248 million present value–based 2012 net income in Table 2.3. Since oil- and gas-production revenue recorded under historical cost accounting obviously originates from proved reserves, and since corporate overhead, interest expense, and other operating costs are excluded from both RRA and the operating results in Table 2.4 (see Note 1 to table), the two measures should be reasonably comparable.

We see that the present value–based earnings are $708 million lower than their historical cost-based counterpart. What accounts for the difference? The difference can be explained in terms of revenue and cost recognition. Valuation of proved reserves at present value implies revenue recognition as reserves are proved, thus explaining the $3,711 million increase in RRA net income from additional reserves proved in the year. Under historical cost accounting, revenues are not recognized until reserves are lifted and sold.

Also, gains and losses resulting from changes in estimates enter into RRA net income as these estimates change. For example, as can be seen from Table 2.3, the increase in estimated future development costs of $3,785 million works against the $3,711 million reserve quantity increase in its effect on RRA net income. These, and the other items in Table 2.2, are not included in historical cost-based earnings. In effect, under RRA, revenues, gains, and losses are recorded "sooner" than under historical cost accounting. Thus, RRA does provide some relevant information.

The difference between the two income measures can also be explained by different bases of asset valuation. Under RRA, oil and gas assets are valued at expected present value (i.e., value in use), not at historical cost. If proved reserves were valued on Husky's balance sheet at present value of $10,710 million, this value would be $708 million lower than a comparable historical cost value. The balance sheet would still balance, since the lower RRA asset valuation will equal the lower RRA retained earnings. In effect, asset valuation and revenue recognition are two sides of the same coin.

If RRA does convey useful information to investors, we should observe some share price reaction to the release of RRA information. Empirical evidence on the usefulness of RRA is reviewed in Chapter 5. For now, suffice it to say that evidence of usefulness is mixed, at best.

Given questions about usefulness, questions about relevance and reliability, and management's concerns, what is the basic problem of RRA? The basic problem is that Husky does not operate under the ideal conditions of Examples 2.1 and 2.2. Consider the difficulties that Husky's managers and accountants face in applying ideal conditions. First, interest rates in the economy are not fixed, although ASC 932 deals with this by requiring a fixed, given rate of 10% for the discounting. Second, the set of states of nature affecting the amounts, prices, and timing of future production is much larger than the simple two-state set of Example 2.2, due to the complex environment in which oil and gas companies operate. ASC 932 reduces some of this complexity by requiring that reserves be valued at the average oil and gas market price for the year. However, proved reserve quantity states, and the timing of their extraction, are still needed to arrive at the standardized measure.

Theory in Practice 2.2

The reliability issues surrounding reserve estimates are illustrated by the case of Royal Dutch Shell. Long a respected company, Shell's reputation suffered a severe blow when, in January 2004, it reduced its "proved" reserves by 20%, reclassifying them as "probable." This was followed by several smaller reductions. Apparently, the company had been overstating its proved reserves as far back as 1997 to disguise falling behind its competitors in replacing its reserves. Such overstatements were enabled by relatively vague SEC rules at the time (which Shell purported to follow) that required reasonable certainty of recovery to classify reserves as proved. Also, the reserve quantities were unaudited.

This scandal resulted in the dismissals of Shell's chairman and head of exploration and development and a preliminary fine by the SEC of US$150 million, and led to a major drop in Shell's share price as investors revised downward their probabilities of Shell's future performance. The relevance of Shell's reserve information was overwhelmed by low reliability introduced by manager bias.

In 2008, Shell announced an agreement to distribute approximately $80 million to U.S. investors in settlement of their claims for damages, plus an additional $120 million to be distributed through the SEC. In 2009, it agreed to pay US$389 million to non-U.S. investors.

A third problem is more fundamental. Objective state probabilities of proved reserve amounts and timing are not available. Consequently, subjective state probabilities need to be assessed by Husky's engineers and accountants, with the result that the standardized measure is itself a subjective estimate. In effect, it is difficult to apply present value accounting when the ideal conditions it requires do not hold.

Because of these difficulties in applying ideal conditions, the reliability of RRA information is compromised. It is not that estimates of expected future cash flows cannot be made. After all, RRA is on line. Rather, lacking objective probabilities, the complex environment in which oil companies operate renders it effectively impossible to prepare estimates that are completely accurate and unaffected by subsequent events. Thus, consistent with Husky management's reservations, these estimates become subject to errors and possible bias that threaten reliability to the point where the benefit of increased relevance is also threatened. The important point is that, without ideal conditions, complete relevance and reliability are no longer jointly attainable. One must be traded off against the other.

2.4.4 Summary of RRA

RRA represents a valiant attempt to convey relevant information to investors. On the surface, the present value information conforms quite closely to the theoretical present value model under uncertainty. If one digs deeper, however, serious problems of estimation are revealed. This is because oil and gas companies do not operate under the ideal conditions assumed by the theoretical model. As a result, reserve information loses reliability, as evidenced by the need for substantial annual revisions and possible bias, as it gains relevance. It seems necessary to trade off these two desirable information qualities.

2.5 HISTORICAL COST ACCOUNTING REVISITED

2.5.1 Comparison of Different Measurement Bases

To this point, we have mainly considered ideal conditions, which lead to a present value (i.e., value in use) version of current value accounting. But, as we outlined in Section 1.2, present-day accounting practice can be described as a mixed measurement model. While, over the past number of years, standard setters have introduced numerous current value-based standards, current value accounting runs into volatility and reliability issues, as our discussions of embedded value and RRA in Section 2.4 demonstrate. These issues raise questions about the extent to which current value accounting will replace historical cost. Consequently, we now consider these two measurement bases in relation to important accounting concepts.

Relevance Versus Reliability Relevance and reliability are important characteristics of accounting information. As we concluded in the previous section, it is necessary to trade them off. However, different measurement bases imply different tradeoffs. Historical cost accounting is relatively reliable since the cost of an asset or liability to a firm is usually a verifiable number that is less subject to errors of estimation and bias than are present value calculations. However, historical costs may be low in relevance. While cost may equal current value at date of acquisition, this equality will soon be lost as current values change over time. Consequently, the relevance of current value accounting generally exceeds that of historical cost. But the need for estimates when conditions are not ideal opens current value accounting up to problems of reliability.

Revenue Recognition As discussed in Section 1.2, the timing of revenue recognition is controversial. We can also characterize accounting measurement bases in terms of revenue recognition. Recall that for each basis of asset and liability measurement there is an associated basis of revenue recognition. In Section 2.4.3, we demonstrated this for RRA. Valuing proved reserves at current value (i.e., the standardized measure) implies revenue recognition as reserves are proved, since future expected revenues are capitalized into the proved reserves valuation. More generally, current valuation of assets and liabilities implies revenue recognition as changes in current value occur. Under historical cost, valuation of inventories at cost and accounts receivable at selling price implies revenue recognition as inventory is sold. Thus current value accounting implies earlier revenue recognition than under historical cost.

Recognition Lag This same ordering of measurement bases appears in the concept of recognition lag, which is the extent to which the timing of revenue recognition lags behind changes in real economic value. Current value accounting has little recognition lag, since changes in economic value are recognized as they occur. Historical cost accounting has greater recognition lag. As just pointed out, revenue is not recognized until increases in inventory value are validated, usually through realization as sales. As a result, revenue recognition under historical cost lags increases in the economic value of inventory.

Matching of Costs and Revenues Finally, we consider the matching of costs and revenues. As already pointed out, matching is primarily associated with historical cost accounting, since net income under historical cost accounting is a result of the matching of realized revenues with the costs of earning them. This is accomplished through accruals. As you know, common examples of accruals include accounts receivable and payable, allowance for bad debts, amortization, provisions for warranty costs, etc. In all cases, these accruals "smooth out" cash flows so as to allocate cash flows over the periods to which they relate. There is little matching under current value accounting, since, as mentioned, net income is then an explanation of how current values of assets and liabilities have changed during the period. Matching is not required for this since value changes in assets and liabilities are driven by market forces and the firm's response to these forces.

It is important to note that while historical cost matching is reasonably reliable, it is not completely so. To see this, consider the amortization of capital assets. The matching principle requires deduction of amortization of capital assets from revenue for the period to arrive at net income. Yet, the principle does not state how much amortization should be accrued except for a vague indication that it should be systematic and rational. For example, under IAS 16, amortization should be charged systematically over the asset's useful life and reflect the pattern of benefit consumption. However, since useful life and pattern of benefit consumption are largely subjective estimates, there is no unique way to match costs and revenues.[15]

As a result of this vagueness, the door is open to a variety of amortization methods, such as straight-line, declining-balance, and so on. This complicates the comparability of profitability across firms, because the investor must ascertain the amortization methods firms are using before making comparisons. Vagueness also reduces reliability, since firm managers have room to manage their reported profitability through choice of amortization method and useful life, or through changes to these policies.

2.5.2 Conclusion

Characterizations of measurement bases in terms of relevance and reliability, revenue recognition, recognition lag, and matching are basically similar, and we shall use them interchangeably in this book. Thus, to say that historical cost accounting is low in relevance but reasonably reliable also is to say that the accountant waits until objective evidence is available before recognizing revenue, that historical cost lags in recognizing changes in asset and liability values, and that historical cost is a process of matching. Historical cost and current value accounting adopt different tradeoffs between these characteristics.

2.6 THE NON-EXISTENCE OF TRUE NET INCOME

To prepare a complete set of financial statements on a current value basis, it is necessary to value *all* of the firm's assets and liabilities this way, with net income explaining the change in the firm's current value during the period (before capital transactions such as dividends). Yet, we saw with RRA that severe problems arise when we try to apply a present value approach to even a single type of asset. These problems would be compounded if the approach were incorporated into the financial statements proper[16] and extended to all other assets and liabilities.

This leads to an important and interesting conclusion, namely that under the real-world conditions in which accounting operates, *net income does not exist as a well-defined economic construct*. As evidence, simply consider Husky's RRA net income of $248 million in Table 2.3. How can we take this as well-defined, or "true," income when we know that next year there will be another flock of unanticipated changes to the estimates that underlie the 2012 income calculation?

A basic problem is the lack of objective state probabilities. With objective probabilities, present values of assets and liabilities correctly reflect the uncertainty facing the firm, since present values then take into account all possible future events and their probabilities. In this case, accounting information is completely relevant as well as completely reliable, and true economic income exists.

The equality of present values and market values under ideal conditions suggests an indirect approach to true economic income—base the income calculation on changes in market values rather than present values. However, this approach runs into the problem that market values need not exist for all firm assets and liabilities, a condition known as **incomplete markets**. For example, while there may be a market price for a barrel of crude oil, what is the market value of an oil company's reserves? In the face of uncertainties over quantities, prices, and lifting costs, an attempt to establish their market value runs into the same estimation problems as RRA. As a result, a ready market value is not available. If market values are not available for all firm assets and liabilities, an income measure based on changes in market values is not possible. Beaver and Demski (1979) give formal arguments to show that income is not well defined when markets are incomplete.[17]

You may be bothered by the claim that true net income does not exist. Should we devote our careers to measuring something that doesn't exist? However, we should be glad of the impossibility of ideal conditions. If they existed, no one would need accountants! As discussed in Examples 2.1 and 2.2, net income has no information content when conditions are ideal. The present value calculations and related income measurement could then be programmed in advance. All that is needed is the set of states, their probabilities, and knowledge of which state is realized, and accountants would not be needed for this. Thus, we can say of income measurement, "If we can solve it, we don't need it."

This lack of a theoretically correct concept of income is what makes accounting both frustrating and fascinating at the same time. It is frustrating because of the difficulty of agreeing on accounting policies. Different users will typically want different tradeoffs between relevance and reliability. As a result, there are often several ways of accounting for the same thing. It is fascinating because the lack of a well-defined concept of net income means that a great deal of *judgment* must go into the process of asset valuation and income measurement. It is judgment that makes accounting valuable and, indeed, provides the very basis of a profession.

2.7 CONCLUSION TO ACCOUNTING UNDER IDEAL CONDITIONS

Instead of dwelling on questions of existence of net income, accountants have turned their efforts to making financial statements more useful. We now proceed to study decision usefulness.

Questions and Problems

1. Prepare the income statement for year 2 and the balance sheet at the end of year 2 for P.V. Ltd. in Example 2.1 under the assumption that P.V. Ltd. pays no dividends.

2. Show that an owner of P.V. Ltd. in Example 2.1 would not care whether P.V. Ltd. paid any dividend at the end of year 1. State precisely why this is the case.

3. Explain why expected net income is also called "accretion of discount."

4. Show that an owner of P.V. Ltd. in Example 2.2 would not care whether P.V. Ltd. paid any dividend at the end of year 1. Assume that the good-economy state was realized in year 1.

5. Two well-known models of firm value are the dividend discount model and the discounted cash flow model. Under ideal conditions, each model gives the same result.

   In Example 2.2, assume that P.V. Ltd. pays no dividends over its life, until a liquidating dividend is paid at the end of year 2 consisting of its cash on hand at that time.

   ### Required
   Verify that the market value of P.V. Ltd. at time 0 based on the expected present value of its future dividend equals $260.33, equal to P.V.'s market value based on expected future cash flows.

6. A simple example of the difference between ideal and non-ideal conditions is the rolling of a die.

   ### Required
   a. Calculate the expected value of a single roll of a fair die.
   b. Now suppose that you are unsure whether the die is fair. How would you then calculate the expected value of a single roll?
   c. Continuing part b, now roll the die four times. You obtain 6, 4, 1, 3. Does this information affect your belief that the die is fair? Explain.

7. Explain why, under ideal conditions, there is no need to make estimates when calculating expected present value.

8. Explain why estimates are required to calculate expected present value when conditions are not ideal. (CGA-Canada)

9. Do you think that the market value of an oil and gas firm will be affected when RRA information is presented in addition to historical cost-based earnings from oil- and gas-producing activities? Explain why or why not.

10. Explain why, under non-ideal conditions, it is necessary to trade off relevance and reliability when estimating future cash flows. Define relevance and reliability as part of your answer.

11. Why do you think oil company managers express severe reservations about RRA?

12. The text discussion of RRA is primarily in terms of the relevance and reliability of the asset valuation of oil and gas reserves. RRA can also be evaluated in terms of the criteria for revenue recognition. Under IAS 18, revenue from the sale of goods is recognized when the significant risks and rewards of ownership have been transferred to the buyer, the

seller loses control over the items, the revenue and related costs can be measured reliably, and collection is reasonably assured.

Required

a. At what point in their operating cycle do most industrial and retail firms regard revenue as having been earned (i.e., realized)? Use the IAS 18 revenue recognition criteria above to explain why.

b. Suppose that X Ltd. is an oil and gas producer. X Ltd. uses RRA on its books and prepares its financial statements on this basis. When (i.e., at what point in the operating cycle) is revenue recognized under RRA? Does this point meet the criteria for revenue recognition for sale of goods as given in IAS 18? Explain why or why not.

13. Inventory is another asset for which there is a variety of ways to account under historical cost accounting, including first-in, first-out; last-in, first-out; average cost; etc.

Required

a. How would inventory manufactured but not yet sold be accounted for under ideal conditions? In your answer, consider both balance sheet and revenue recognition approaches.

b. Give reasons why inventory is usually accounted for on a historical cost basis. Is accounting on this basis completely reliable? Why?

14. A retail firm has just made a sale. However, it values its account receivable at the cost of the merchandise sold, rather than at the amount owing from the customer. What basis of revenue recognition does this practice imply? Under what conditions might a retail firm value accounts receivable this way?

15. Sure Corp. operates under ideal conditions of certainty. It acquired its sole asset on January 1, 2015. The asset will yield $600 cash at the end of each year from 2015 to 2017, inclusive, after which it will have no market value and no disposal costs. The interest rate in the economy is 6%. Purchase of the asset was financed by the issuance of common shares. Sure Corp. will pay a dividend of $50 at the end of 2015 and 2016.

Required

a. Prepare a balance sheet for Sure Corp. at the end of 2015 and an income statement for the year ended December 31, 2015.

b. Prepare a balance sheet for Sure Corp. as at the end of 2016 and an income statement for the year ended December 31, 2016.

c. Under ideal conditions, what is the relationship between present value (i.e., value in use) and market value (i.e., fair value)? Why? Under the real conditions in which accountants operate, to what extent do market values provide a way to implement fair value accounting? Explain.

d. Under real conditions, present value calculations tend to be of low reliability. Why? Does this mean that present value-based accounting for assets and liabilities is not decision useful? Explain.

Note: In the following two problems, the capital asset is financed in part by means of interest-bearing bonds. This is not illustrated in the text.

16. P Ltd. operates under ideal conditions of certainty. It has just bought a capital asset for $3,100, which will generate $1,210 cash flow at the end of one year and $2,000 at the end of the second year. At that time, the asset will be useless in operations and P Ltd. plans to go out of business. The asset will have a known salvage value of $420 at the end of the second year. The interest rate in the economy is constant at 10% per annum.

P Ltd. finances the asset by issuing $605 par value of 12% coupon bonds to yield 10%. Interest is payable at the end of the first and second years, at which time the bonds mature. The balance of the cost of the asset is financed by the issuance of common shares.

Required

a. Prepare the present value-based balance sheet at the end of the first year and an income statement for the year. P Ltd. plans to pay no dividends in this year.

b. Give two reasons why ideal conditions are unlikely to hold.

c. If ideal conditions do not hold, but present value-based financial statements are prepared anyway, is net income likely to be the same as you calculated in part **a**? Explain why or why not.

17. North Ltd. plans to manufacture cross-country skiing equipment. Its cash flows are highly dependent on the winter weather. North operates under ideal conditions of uncertainty. On August 1, 2015, the beginning of its first year in business, North acquires equipment to be used in its operations. The equipment will last two years, at which time its salvage value will be zero. The company finances the equipment by means of a $500 bank loan at 3% interest, with the balance financed by issuing common shares.

North's annual net cash flows will be $900 if the weather is snowy and $300 if it is not snowy. Assume that cash flows are received at year-end. In each year, the objective probability that the weather is snowy is 0.7 and 0.3 that it is not snowy. The interest rate in the economy is 3% in both years.

North Ltd. will pay a dividend of $50 at the end of each year of operation.

Required

a. In the 2015–2016 skiing season, the weather is snowy. Prepare a balance sheet at July 31, 2016, the end of North Ltd.'s first year of operations, and an income statement for the year.

b. What timing of revenue recognition is implicit in the income statement you have prepared in part **a**? When ideal conditions do not hold, is this timing of revenue recognition relevant? Is it reliable? Explain.

c. Assume that North Ltd. paid the present value you calculated in part **a** for its equipment. Calculate North's net income for the year ended July 31, 2016, on a historical cost basis, assuming that equipment is amortized on a straight line basis. Under the more realistic assumption that ideal conditions do not hold, which measure of net income—present value basis or historical cost basis—is most relevant? Which is most reliable? Why?

18. Electro Ltd. has just commenced operations under ideal conditions of uncertainty. Its cash flows will depend crucially on the state of the economy. On January 1, 2015, the company acquired plant and equipment that will last two years, with zero salvage value. Electro financed the plant and equipment purchase by issuing common shares.

In 2015, net cash flows will be $900 if the state of the economy is good and $600 if it is poor. In 2016, cash flows will rise to $1,200 if the economy is good and remain at $600 if it is bad. Cash flows are received at year-end. In each year, the probability that the economy is good is 0.6. The interest rate in the economy is 3% in both years.

Electro pays a dividend of $60 at the end of 2016.

Required

a. How much did Electro Ltd. pay for its plant and equipment on January 1, 2015?

b. In 2015, the economy is good. Prepare a balance sheet at the end of 2015 and an income statement for 2015.

c. In North America, most property, plant, and equipment is accounted for under historical cost accounting, rather than at current value as above? Suggest why.

19. QC Ltd. operates under ideal conditions of uncertainty. On January 1, 2015, it purchased a capital asset that will last for two full years and then will be retired with zero salvage. The purchase price was financed with an issue of common stock. QC Ltd. plans to pay no dividends until after the end of 2016. The interest rate in the economy is 6%.

QC Ltd. is certain that net cash flow from its only asset will be $100 in 2015. However, net cash flow in 2016 is uncertain. Net cash flows in 2016 will be $200 (the high state) with objective probability 0.60 and $50 (the low state) with objective probability 0.40. All cash flows are received at their respective year-ends. At the end of year 2 it becomes known that the high state is realized.

Required

a. How much did QC Ltd. pay for its capital asset at the beginning of 2015? Show calculations.

b. Prepare, in good form, an income statement for QC Ltd. for the *second year* of operations—that is, 2016.

c. Prepare, in good form, a balance sheet for QC Ltd. at the end of 2016 (before any dividend payments).

Note: In the following problem, state probabilities are not independent over time. Part **b** requires calculations not illustrated in the text.

20. Conditional Ltd. operates under ideal conditions of uncertainty. It has just purchased a new machine, at a cost of $3,575.10, paid for entirely from the proceeds of a stock issue. The interest rate in the economy is 8%. The machine is expected to last for two years, after which time it will have zero salvage value.

The new machine is an experimental model, and its suitability for use in Conditional's operations is not completely known. Conditional assesses a 0.75 probability that there will be a major machine failure during the first year of operation, and a 0.25 probability that the machine will operate as planned. If there is a major failure, cash flow for the year will be $1,000. If the machine operates as planned, cash flow will be $3,000 for the year. If there is no major failure in the first year, the probability of a major failure in the second year, and resulting cash flows of $1,000, falls to 0.60. If there is no major failure in the second year, cash flows for that year will again be $3,000. However, if there is a major failure in the first year, the lessons learned from correcting it will result in only a 0.10 probability of failure in the second year.

It turns out that there is no major failure in the first year.

Required

a. Verify that the cost of $3,575.10 for the machine is correct.

b. Prepare an income statement for year 1.

c. Prepare a balance sheet at the end of the first year.

Note: The next problem contains calculations not illustrated in the text.

21. On January 1, 2015, ABC Ltd. started its business by purchasing a productive oil well. The proved oil reserves from the well are expected to generate $7,000 cash flow at the end of 2015, $6,000 at the end of 2016, and $5,000 at the end of 2017. Net sales is gross revenues less production costs. Net sales equals cash flows. On January 1, 2018, the oil well is expected to be dry, with no environmental liabilities. The management of ABC Ltd. wishes to prepare financial statements on a present value basis with an interest rate of 10%. The following information is known about the well at the end of 2015.

■ Actual cash flows in 2015 amounted to $6,500—that is, $500 less than expected.

■ Changes in estimates: Due to improved recovery (of oil from the well), end of year cash flows for 2016 and 2017 are estimated to be $6,500 and $6,000 respectively.

Required

a. Prepare the income statement of ABC Ltd. for 2015 from its proved oil reserves.

b. Managements of some firms have expressed serious concerns about the reliability of present value information for oil and gas companies. Outline two of these concerns.

22. The following supplemental RRA information is taken from the 2015 annual report of HL Oil & Gas Ltd.

HL Oil & Gas Ltd. Statement of Changes in Standardized Measure Year Ended December 31, 2015	
Present value, January 1, 2015	$6,500
Sales of oil and gas, net of production costs	(2,000)
Changes in prices of oil and gas, net of changes in production costs	1,200
Extensions and discoveries of proved reserves, net	1,500
Accretion of discount	700
Revisions to quantity estimates	(200)
Present value, December 31, 2015	$7,700

Required

a. Prepare an income statement for 2015 on an RRA basis.

b. Use the concepts of relevance and reliability to explain why the standardized measure is not applied to unproved reserves in RRA.

c. Explain why present value calculations for oil and gas reserves lay down a mandatory 10% discount rate. What is an advantage and disadvantage to requiring all firms to use a common discount rate?

23. The following RRA information is taken from the December 31, 2015, annual report of FX Energy, Inc.

FX Energy, Inc.
Changes in the Standardized Measure of Discounted Future Cash Flows
Year Ended December 31, 2015
($ thousands)

Present value at January 1, 2015	$5,460
Sales of oil produced, net of production costs	(1,172)
Net changes in prices and production costs	(159)
Extensions and discoveries, net of future costs	2,511
Changes in estimated future development costs	(53)
Revisions in previous quantity estimates	(31)
Accretion of discount	546
Changes in rates of production and other	116
Present value at December 31, 2011	$7,218

Required

a. Prepare an RRA income statement for FX Energy for 2015.

b. FX Energy reports elsewhere in its annual report an (historical cost-based) operating loss from exploration and production for 2015 of $5,245. While this amount may exclude certain administrative cost allocations, take this operating loss as a reasonable historical cost-based analogue of the RRA income you calculated in part **a**. Explain why RRA income for 2015 is different from the $5,245 loss under historical cost.

c. The standardized measure is applied only to proved reserves under RRA, using average oil and gas prices for the year. Explain why.

d. RRA mandates a discount rate of 10% for the RRA present value calculations, rather than allowing each firm to choose its own rate. Why? Can you see any disadvantages to mandating a common discount rate?

Note: The item "extensions and discoveries, net of future costs" represents additional reserves proved during the year. The item "changes in rates of production and other" represents changes in timing of extraction relative to the timing that was expected at the beginning of 2015.

24. The following RRA information is taken from the 2015 annual report of Moonglo Energy Inc.

Balance of proved reserves: beginning of year	$1,070
Sales, net of production costs	(456)
Sales of reserves in place	(4)
Accretion of discount	125
Extensions and discoveries, net of related costs	162
Development costs incurred in year	629
Changes in estimates	134
Balance of proved reserves: end of year	$1,660

Required

a. Prepare 2015 income statements for Moonglo on an RRA basis.

b. Moonglo reports a profit on its 2015 oil and gas operations, on a historical cost basis, of $173. Explain (in words only) why this profit differs from the RRA income you calculated in part **a**.

c. Which income number (RRA or historical cost basis) is more relevant? Which is more reliable? Explain why.

25. Revenue recognition is a major accounting challenge. Most industrial and retail firms recognize revenue as earned at the point of sale. More generally, according to IAS 18, revenue from the sale of goods should be recognized when the significant risks and rewards of ownership have been transferred to the buyer, the seller loses control over the items, the revenue and related costs can be measured reliably, and collection is reasonably assured. Revenue from services and long-term contracts can be recognized as the work progresses.

It is often not clear just when these general criteria are met. For example, revenue recognition at point of sale may be a reasonable tradeoff between relevance and reliability in most cases. However, relevance is increased (and reliability decreased) if revenue is recognized earlier than point of sale.

Furthermore, revenue recognition policy may be used by firms to impress investors. For example, firms with no earnings history (e.g., startup firms) and firms that are incurring significant losses or declines in earnings have an incentive to record revenue as early as possible, so as to improve, at least temporarily, the appearance of their financial statements.

Consider the case of Lucent Technologies Inc. (now called Alcatel-Lucent). In December 2000, Lucent restated its revenue for its fiscal year ended September 30, 2000, reducing the amounts (in millions) originally reported as follows:

The vendor financing component of the restatement represents previously unrecorded credits granted by Lucent to customers, to help them finance purchases of Lucent products. That is, the customer sales were originally recorded gross, rather than net, of the credits. The distribution partners' component represents product

Vendor financing	$199
Partial shipments	28
Distribution partners	452
Total	$679

shipped to firms with which Lucent did not deal at arm's length, but which was not resold by these firms at year-end. These firms included certain distributors in which Lucent had an ownership interest. The practice of overshipping to distributors is called "stuffing the channels."

In its 2000 annual report, Lucent reported net income of $1,219 million, compared to $4,789 million for 1999 and $1,065 million for 1998.

Despite these December, 2000 adjustments, on May 17, 2004, the SEC announced charges against Lucent and several of its officers for overstating revenues by $1,148 million in 2000 in order to meet sales targets. The company's share price fell by 5.5% on that day. Tactics used, the SEC claimed, included the granting of improper credits to customers to encourage them to buy company products, and invoicing sales to customers that were subject to renegotiation in subsequent periods.

Subsequently, Lucent paid a fine of $25 million for "lack of cooperation." In addition, the company, and some of the executives charged, settled the allegations by paying penalties, without admitting or denying guilt.[18]

Required

a. What is the most relevant point of revenue recognition? The most reliable? Explain. In your answer, consider manufacturing firms, oil and gas exploration firms, retail firms, and firms with long-term contracts.

b. Explain whether or not you feel that Lucent's original recognition of the $679 million of items listed above as revenue was consistent with revenue recognition criteria? While Lucent was a U.S. company, assume that U.S. revenue recognition criteria are similar to the IASB criteria given in the question. In your answer, consider the tradeoff between relevance and reliability.

c. What additional revenue recognition questions arise when the vendor has an ownership interest in the customer?

26. Refer to the revenue recognition practices of Qwest Communications outlined in Theory in Practice 1.1.

Required

a. Use the concept of relevance to argue that firms should record revenue as earned as early as possible in their operating cycles. Was Qwest's revenue recognition policy relevant? Explain.

b. Use the concept of reliability to argue that firms should wait until the significant risks and rewards of ownership are transferred to the buyer, and there is reasonable assurance of collection, before recording revenue. Was Qwest's revenue recognition policy reliable? Explain.

c. When is revenue recognized under ideal conditions? Why?

27. Refer to Theory in Practice 2.1 relating to the embedded value of Manulife Financial's common shares.

    Required

    a. Prepare an income statement for Manulife on an embedded value basis for 2011. Use a format similar to the format used in Table 2.3.

    b. Serafeim (2011) reported lower information asymmetry for insurance companies that report embedded value, compared with companies that do not report this information. However, this lower information asymmetry held only for firms that employed an outside auditor to review the calculations and was particularly strong for firms that also belonged to the CFO forum. Why would information asymmetry be lower for such firms?

    c. Suggest reasons why Manulife's common share market value ($11.20) is so much less than its embedded value per share ($20.02).

28. National Instrument 51-101 of the Canadian Securities Administrators, effective September 30, 2003, lays down disclosure requirements for Canadian oil and gas firms. These requirements include:

    ■ Proved reserve quantities, defined as reserves that can be estimated with a high degree of certainty (operationalized as at least 90% probability) to be recoverable

    ■ Probable reserve quantities, defined as additional reserves such that there is at least a 50% probability that the amounts actually recovered will exceed the sum of estimated proved and probable reserves

    ■ Future net revenues from proved reserves and changes therein, discounted at 10% and undiscounted, using

      i. year-end prices and costs

      ii. forecasted prices and costs

    ■ Future net revenues from probable reserves, discounted at 5%, 10%, 15%, and 20%, and undiscounted, using forecasted prices and costs

      In addition, reserves data must be verified by an independent qualified reserves evaluator or auditor and reviewed by the board of directors.

    Required

    a. Evaluate the relevance of National Instrument 51-101 disclosures in comparison to those of RRA. In your answer, include consideration of whether or not discounting expected future receipts at various rates (rather than at 10% as per RRA) adds to relevance.

    b. Evaluate the reliability of National Instrument 51-101 disclosures in comparison to those of RRA.

    c. In their National Instrument 51-101 disclosures, firms include a disclaimer to the effect that estimated future net revenues contained in their disclosures do not necessarily represent the fair market value of the company's reserves. They also claim that there is no assurance that the forecast price and cost assumptions contained in the disclosures will be attained, and that variances could be material. Give reasons why the companies give these disclaimers.

29. "A theoretically correct measure of income does not exist in the real world in which accountants must operate."

Required

a. What is meant by the phrase "a theoretically correct measure of income"?

b. Why does a theoretically correct measure of income not exist in the real world?

c. Outline the different tradeoffs between relevance and reliability under historical cost accounting and current value accounting. Consider both situations where reasonably well-working market values exist (see definition of well-working markets in Section 1.2) and do not exist.

Notes

1. Net income for year 1 can also be calculated in a more familiar format as:

Cash flow (i.e., sales)	$150.00
Amortization expense	123.97
Net income	$ 26.03

Amortization expense is calculated as $260.33 - $136.36 = $123.97; that is, it equals the decline in the present value of the future receipts from the asset over the year. This way of calculating amortization differs from the way that accountants usually calculate it. Nevertheless, it is the appropriate approach under the ideal conditions of this example—namely, future cash flows known with certainty and a fixed risk-free interest rate.

We view this approach to measuring income under ideal conditions as less instructive than the accretion of discount approach illustrated in the example. It creates the impression that revenue is recognized as sales are made. However, since future net revenues are capitalized into asset value, as explained in the example, revenue is, in effect, recognized when assets are acquired. Calculating amortization on a present value basis forces net income to be the same under either format.

2. Yet another way to calculate income, familiar from introductory accounting, is to calculate the change in balance sheet net assets for the year, adjusted for capital transactions. In this example, we have:

$$\text{Net income} = \$286.36 - \$260.33 - \$0 = \$26.03$$

where capital transactions during the period are zero. Thus, knowing the present values of all assets and liabilities at the beginning and end of the period enables one to calculate present value-based net income.

3. This argument can be turned around. We could argue that if the firm's future income statements were known with certainty, in conjunction with the interest rate, then they would contain all relevant information and the balance sheet could be easily deduced. In effect, each statement contains all the information needed for the other. We view the balance sheet as more fundamental under ideal conditions, however.

4. As another example of arbitrage, assume a share of ABC Ltd. is selling in Toronto for $10, and the same share is selling in New York for $10.50 (in Canadian dollars). Ignoring commissions, ABC shares could be purchased on the Toronto market for $10 and sold in New York for $10.50, for a profit of $0.50 per share. However, share price will quickly rise in Toronto because of greater demand, and will just as quickly fall in New York because of greater supply. This change in the supply/demand relationship will bring the market prices into equality in the two markets.

5. Here, the only financial item is cash. Generally, financial assets are assets whose values are fixed in terms of money, such as accounts receivable and investments with a fixed face value, such as bonds. Certain other assets, such as investments in shares, are also regarded as financial assets if a ready market value is available. Financial liabilities, such as accounts payable, bank loans, and bonds issued, are defined similarly.

6. The independence assumption is not crucial to the example. With slight added complexity we could allow for conditional probabilities, where the probability of state realization in year 2 depends on the state realization in year 1. For example, if the good state happened in year 1, this might increase the probability that the good state would also happen in year 2. See Problem 20. The important point for ideal conditions to hold, however, is that if probabilities will change over time, the pattern of changes is publicly known.

7. This is an example of **common knowledge**. That is, everyone knows the set of states of nature, everyone knows that everyone knows, everyone knows that everyone knows that everyone knows, etc. This assumption is often made in economic and accounting models. Further discussion of common knowledge is given in Sections 4.5.2 and 6.5.2.

8. Somewhat weaker conditions than these would be sufficient to give a first-best economy. Our purpose here, however, is only to give a set of conditions sufficient to ensure that net income is well defined and without information content.

9. We can also calculate net income as

Cash flow (sales)	$100.00
Amortization expense ($260.33 − $136.36)	123.97
Net loss	$ 23.97

See Note 1 for reasons why we prefer the net income format used in the example. Calculating amortization on an *expected* present value basis forces net income to be the same under either format.

10. Of course, if investors are risk neutral, this risk will not matter to them. However, under more realistic conditions, which we will introduce later, risk does matter. Note that the firm can use hedging to reduce this volatility.

11. A more precise reference is ASC 932-235-50. The IASB is currently considering new guidelines for extractive industries. Given the unsettled state of these standards, we proceed in terms of the U.S. standard here.

12. As is the case in Examples 2.1 and 2.2, we can also prepare an income statement in a more conventional format:

Cash flow from operations (sales in year = 3,773 + 12 − 9)	$3,776
Development costs incurred in year	(3,826)
Amortization "expense" (increase in present value of proved reserves during the year) (10,710 − 10,412)	298
Net income from proved oil and gas reserves	$ 248

The $3,826 of development costs incurred during the year is not a change in estimates. It represents the expenditure of some of the development costs allowed for in the beginning-of-year present value.

The selection of items from the statement of changes may seem arbitrary. Notice however, that with the exception of amortization, all the items of the above income statement involve cash flows. In the income statement in the body of the text, none of the items are cash flows.

See also Notes 1 and 8.

13. Note that these changes in estimates contain two components. One component derives from state realization. As illustrated in Example 2.2, state realization introduces volatility into earnings. The second component derives from changes in estimates of cash flow amounts. Under ideal conditions, there are no such errors of estimation. Since ASC 932 does not require disclosure of the states of nature affecting its future cash flow estimates, and which states actually happened, we cannot separate changes in estimates into these two components. The significance of such a separation is that while state realizations generate volatility, they do not reduce reliability. Consequently, attributing all changes in estimates to errors, as we do in our discussion, tends to understate RRA reliability.

14. ASC 392 also requires the reporting of historical cost-based results of operations for oil- and gas-producing activities.

15. For an extensive discussion of the balance sheet versus income statement approaches, and the inability of the income statement approach to resolve the question of how to match costs and revenues, see Storey and Storey (1998).

16. Strictly speaking, the term "financial statements" includes the notes to the statements. When we refer to disclosure within the financial statements themselves, we will use the term "financial statements proper." Thus, if a firm values an asset at current value in its accounts and reports the resulting number on the balance sheet, it reports current value in the financial statements proper. If it discloses current value only in a note, this would be reported in the financial statements but not in the financial statements proper.

17. For a counterargument, see Ohlson (1987).

18. The significance of not admitting or denying guilt is that, while guilty penalties are paid to the government, third parties who may wish to recover damages must prove guilt. Not admitting or denying guilt reduces the expected amount of any such lawsuits.

Chapter 3

The Decision Usefulness Approach to Financial Reporting

Figure 3.1 Organization of Chapter 3

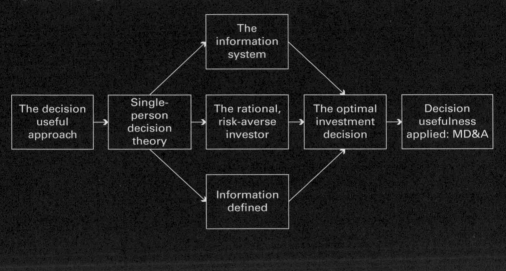

3.1 OVERVIEW

In Chapter 2, we concluded that the present value model faces some severe problems in practice. It is doubtful that a complete set of financial statements on this basis is feasible. This inability to value the whole firm on a present value or market value basis means that a theoretically well-defined concept of net income does not exist in the complex real world in which accountants operate.

Nevertheless, all accountants agree that financial statements should be useful. This leads to an important concept in accounting: **decision usefulness**—that is, the ability of financial accounting information to help users make good decisions. To properly understand this concept, we need to consider other theories (that is, other than the present value model) from economics and finance. This is because we cannot make financial statements more useful until we know what "usefulness" means. We also need a precise definition of information. Decision theories and capital market theories assist in conceptualizing the meaning of useful financial statement information.

The main purpose of this chapter is to introduce you to one of these theories—namely, the theory of rational decision making—and to discuss its relevance to accounting. Figure 3.1 outlines the organization of this chapter.

3.2 THE DECISION USEFULNESS APPROACH

As we can infer from Section 2.6, the decision usefulness approach to accounting theory takes the view that "if we can't prepare theoretically correct financial statements, at least we can try to make financial statements more useful." First enunciated in 1966,[1] and reinforced by the influential 1973 report of the Trueblood Commission,[2] this simple observation has had major implications for accounting theory and practice. In particular, we must now pay much closer attention than we did in Chapter 2 to financial statement users and their decision needs, since under non-ideal conditions it is not possible to read the value of the firm directly from the financial statements.

Decision usefulness is contrasted with another view of the role of financial reporting: stewardship, whereby the role is to report on management's success, or lack thereof, in managing the firm's resources. This role is more past-oriented than the role of helping investors predict future firm performance that we discussed in Chapter 2. Of course, motivating manager performance is also future-oriented in the sense that knowing that past and current performance is monitored will, hopefully, encourage managers to plan for the future. We regard each role as equally important. In this chapter, we begin our discussion of decision usefulness. Discussion of the second role begins in Chapter 8.

In adopting the decision usefulness approach, two major questions must be addressed. First, who are the users of financial statements? Clearly, there are many users. It is helpful to categorize them into broad groups, such as equity and debt investors, managers, unions, standard setters, and governments. These groups are called **constituencies** of accounting.

Second, what are the decision problems of financial statement users? By understanding these decision problems, accountants will be better prepared to meet the information needs of the various constituencies. Financial statements can then be prepared with these information needs in mind. In other words, tailoring financial statement information to the specific needs of the users of those statements will lead to improved decision making. In this way, the financial statements are made more *useful*.

Of course, determining the specific decision needs of users is by no means an obvious process. For example, what information does an investor need to make a rational decision about whether to buy or sell certain shares or debt? Would this decision be helped or hindered by current value accounting? Would it be helped by conservative accounting?

In the face of difficult questions like these, accountants have turned to various theories in economics and finance for assistance. The theory of rational decision making, decision theory for short, is a good place to begin to understand how individuals may make rational decisions under uncertainty.

The theory enables us to appreciate the concept of information, which enables decision makers to update their subjective beliefs about future payoffs from their decisions.

It also helps us to understand the concept of investment risk, and how risk can be at least partially controlled through a strategy of portfolio diversification.

Decision theory is important to accountants because it underlies pronouncements of accounting standard setters. For example, an examination of the Conceptual Framework, introduced in Section 1.2, shows that decision theory lurks under the surface. We examine the Framework more fully in Section 3.7. In particular, the Framework adopts the decision needs of investors as the major purpose of financial reporting. Consequently, an understanding of theories of decision and investment enables a deeper understanding of the pronouncements themselves.

3.2.1 Summary

Accountants have adopted a decision usefulness approach to financial reporting as a reaction to the impossibility of preparing theoretically correct financial statements. However, the decision usefulness approach leads to the problem of identifying the users of financial statements and the information they need to make good decisions. Accountants have decided that investors are a major constituency of users and have turned to various theories in economics and finance—in particular, to theories of decision and investment—to understand the type of financial statement information investors need.

3.3 SINGLE-PERSON DECISION THEORY

Single-person decision theory takes the viewpoint of an individual who must make a decision under conditions of uncertainty.[3] It recognizes that state probabilities are no longer objective, as they are under ideal conditions, and sets out a formal procedure whereby the individual can make the best decision by selecting from a set of alternative actions. This procedure allows additional information to be obtained to revise the decision maker's subjective assessment of the probabilities of what might happen after the decision is made (i.e., the probabilities of states of nature). Decision theory is relevant to accounting because financial statements provide additional information that is useful for many decisions, as illustrated in Example 3.1.

3.3.1 Decision Theory Applied

Example 3.1
A Typical Investment Decision

Bill Cautious has $10,000 to invest for one period. He has narrowed down his choice to two investments: Buy shares of X Ltd. at current market price, or buy government bonds yielding $2^1/_4$%. We will denote the act of buying the shares by a_1, and the bonds by a_2.

If he buys the shares, Bill faces risk.[4] That is, the future performance of X Ltd. is not known when Bill makes his decision. In the face of this risk, he defines two states of nature:

State 1: X Ltd. future performance high
State 2: X Ltd. future performance low

We can think of X Ltd.'s future performance in terms of its future dividends, cash flows, or earnings, all of which affect the end-of-period market value of its shares. Here, we view current financial statement information as a predictor of future firm performance, however future performance is defined.

X Ltd.'s share price will reflect investor expectations of its future performance. Assume that if X Ltd. is in state 1, Bill's net return on the X shares will be $1,600, where net return is calculated as:

Net return = End-of-period share price + Dividends in period − Original investment

If X Ltd. is in state 2, assume that Bill's net return will be zero.

If Bill buys the bonds, he receives interest of $225 next period, regardless of the state of nature. That is, the bond investment is treated as riskless.

The amounts to be received from a decision are called **payoffs**, which we can summarize by a payoff table, as shown in Table 3.1.

Now consider the state probabilities. Bill subjectively assesses the probability of state 1 (the high-performance state) as $P(H) = 0.30$. The probability of state 2 is then $P(L) = 0.70$. These subjective probabilities incorporate all that Bill knows about X Ltd. to this point in time. They are called **prior probabilities**. He could base these probabilities on an analysis of X Ltd.'s past financial statements on the assumption that past performance will persist,

Table 3.1 Payoff Table for Decision Theory Example 3.1

Act	State High	Low
a_1 (buy shares)	$1,600	$ 0
a_2 (buy bonds)	$ 225	$225

plus other news to date about the company. In addition, he could consider the state of the economy, changes in competition, the quality of X Ltd. management, past research success, and any other factors that affect future firm performance. He could also study the current market price of X Ltd. shares. If share price is low, for example, it could indicate an unfavourable market evaluation of X's future prospects, which could cause Bill to lower his prior probability of the high state.

Bill is risk averse. Let us assume that the amount of utility, or satisfaction, he derives from a payoff is equal to the square root of the amount of the payoff.[5] Thus, if he receives a payoff of $1,600, his utility is 40. This assumption of risk aversion is not necessary to our example. We could just as easily assume Bill was risk neutral and evaluate the expected dollar amounts of the various payoffs. However, investors are generally risk averse, so we will work in utilities rather than dollars. Section 3.4 considers risk aversion in greater detail.

A complete evaluation of the utility of an act requires Bill to evaluate any effects of his decision on others. Here, however, Bill's decision is relatively self-contained. That is, whether he buys the shares or the bonds will have little or no effect on anyone else.

Figure 3.2 Decision Tree for Bill's Choice

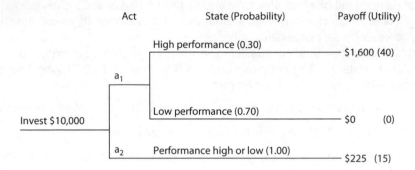

Consequently, we evaluate his utility in terms of its effect on his own wealth. In other decision problems, for example, whether to buy the shares of a firm that is a heavy polluter, Bill may reduce the utility of his payoffs to recognize the adverse social effects of a decision to buy.

Bill is a small enough investor that his buy and sell decisions do not affect market price (in economic terms he is a price taker). He also leaves out of his decision other events that could affect his payoff but are deemed so unlikely that they are not worth considering. For example, an earthquake could seriously affect X Ltd.'s operations. However, since earthquakes are a rare event in X Ltd.'s areas of operation, Bill ignores this possibility. This is called "cutting the decision tree down to size."

Figure 3.2 gives a decision tree diagram for this decision problem. The numbers in parentheses in the middle column of the figure are the probabilities of the states, the second column from the right shows the dollar amounts of the payoffs, and the rightmost column gives Bill's utility for each amount.

The decision theory tells us that, if he must decide now, Bill should choose the act with the highest expected utility. We will denote the expected utility of act a_1 by $EU(a_1)$, and so on.

$$EU(a_1) = (0.30 \times 40) + (0.70 \times 0) = 12$$
$$EU(a_2) = 1.00 \times 15 = 15$$

Therefore, it appears that Bill should choose a_2 and buy the bonds.[6]

However, Bill has another alternative: to obtain *more information* before deciding. Accordingly, let's assume that he decides to become more informed. The annual report of X Ltd. is to be released within the next few days, and Bill decides to wait for it, since it provides readily available evidence about the state of the firm. When the annual report comes, Bill notes that net income is quite high and the firm's net current assets and debt–equity ratio are improved from last year. In effect, the current financial statements show "good news" (GN).

On the basis of extensive experience in financial statement preparation and analysis and his familiarity with GAAP, Bill knows that if X Ltd. really is a high-state firm, there is an 80% probability that the current year's financial statements will show GN and 20% probability that they will show bad news (BN). Denote these conditional probabilities by

Prob(GN|H) = 0.80 and Prob(BN|H) = 0.20, respectively. Note that even if the firm is in the high state, there is still a 20% probability that the financial statements show BN. This is because accounting standards do not generate complete relevance and reliability. For example, the 20% value of P(BN|H) may be due to a tradeoff between relevance and reliability. For example, if the firm is research-intensive, writing off research costs may force reported earnings down, creating an impression of BN even though the research will benefit future periods. Also, accounting standards attempt to prevent premature revenue recognition. Then, expected profit from a major new X Ltd. contract may not be included in current earnings for reasons of reliability, even though it is relevant information about future payoffs. Alternatively, BN may be reported by a high-state firm to disguise high profits. Such firms may wish to smooth earnings to a sustainable level, or reduce the probability of attracting competitors or increased regulation. Since accounting standards give firms some flexibility to choose different accounting policies, such behaviour need not violate GAAP.

Bill also knows that if X Ltd. is a low-state firm, it is still possible that the financial statements show GN. For example, X Ltd. management may choose accounting policies to hide its low state, or at least delay investor awareness of lower profits. This could be accomplished, for example, by understating bad debts expense, or by reducing discretionary expenditures such as research and advertising. Assume that if X Ltd. really is in a low state, the probability that the current year's financial statements will show GN is 10%, giving a 90% probability that they will show BN. Denote these conditional probabilities by P(GN|L) = 0.10 and P(BN|L) = 0.90, respectively.

Now, armed with the GN evidence from the current financial statements and the above conditional probabilities, Bill can use **Bayes' theorem** to calculate his **posterior state probabilities** (that is, posterior to the financial statement evidence). The posterior probability of the high-performance state is:

$$P(H|GN) = \frac{P(H)\,P(GN|H)}{P(H)\,P(GN|H) + P(L)\,P(GN|L)}$$

$$= \frac{0.30 \times 0.80}{(0.30 \times 0.80) + (0.70 \times 0.10)}$$

$$= 0.77$$

where:

P(H|GN) is the (posterior) probability of the high state, given the good news financial statement.

P(H) is the prior probability of the high state.

P(GN|H) is the probability that the financial statements show good news given, that the firm is in the high state.

P(L) is the prior probability of the low state.

P(GN|L) is the probability that the financial statements show good news given, that the firm is in the low state.

Then, Bill's posterior probability P(L|GN) of X Ltd. being in the low-performance state is 1.00 − 0.77 = 0.23. Recall that if the state is high, the payoff from Bill's share investment will be high ($1,600), and if it is low, the payoff will be low ($0).

Bill can now calculate the expected utility of each act on the basis of his posterior probabilities:

$$EU(a_1|GN) = (0.77 \times 40) + (0.23 \times 0) = 30.8$$
$$EU(a_2|GN) = 1.00 \times 15 = 15$$

Thus, the GN current financial statement information has caused Bill's optimal decision to change to a_1—he should buy the shares of X Ltd.

3.3.2 The Information System

It is important to understand why financial statement information is useful. To be useful, it must help predict future investment returns. Under non-ideal conditions, the financial statements do not show expected future firm performance directly. Nevertheless, financial statements will still be useful to investors to the extent that the good or bad news they contain will persist into the future. Think of a progression, from current good or bad news in the financial statements to future expected firm performance to future expected investment returns.

To return to our example, the good news was that current earnings and solvency were high. This information enabled Bill to predict high future X Ltd. performance with probability 0.77, and this is also the probability of the high payoff on his investment. Of course, information is a double edged sword. Had the financial statements contained bad news, Bill's probability of high payoff would have been lowered just as surely as it was raised by good news.

We conclude that financial statements can still be useful to investors even though they do not report directly on future cash flows by means of present value-based calculations. Here, it is the lack of ideal conditions that gives the financial statements their information content—recall that there was really no information in net income in Examples 2.1 and 2.2. While Examples 2.2 and 3.1 both allow for uncertainty, the fundamental difference between them is that state probabilities were objective in Example 2.2 but subjective in Example 3.1. This opens a role for information to help the decision maker update subjective state probabilities and predict investment returns.

The heart of the linkage between current financial statement information and future firm performance is the conditional probabilities (also called likelihoods) given in Table 3.2.

Table 3.2 Information System for Decision Theory Example 3.1

		Current Financial Statement Evidence	
		GN	BN
	High	0.80	0.20
State			
	Low	0.10	0.90

That is, $P(GN|H) = 0.80$, $P(BN|H) = 0.20$, etc. Taken together, these probabilities are called an **information system**, which is summarized in Table 3.2. Note that the probabilities add to 1 *across* the table. The 0.80 and 0.90 probabilities are called main diagonal probabilities; the others are called off-main diagonal probabilities.

> An *information system specifies, conditional on each state of nature, the objective*[7] *probability of each possible financial statement evidence item.*

Note that financial statements are not perfect, or "true"—this would be the case only under ideal conditions. Given the underlying GAAP, there is a 20% probability in our example that even if X Ltd. is in the high state its financial statements would show BN, and a 10% probability that if it is in the low state the financial statements would show GN. These error probabilities reflect both the relevance/reliability tradeoff inherent in GAAP and the average flexibility allowed by GAAP for management to manage the financial statements for its own purposes.[8]

The weakening of the relationship between current financial statement information and future firm performance due to these error probabilities is sometimes described as **noise** or as low **earnings quality** in the financial statements. Nevertheless, an information system is **informative** if it changes the decision maker's prior probabilities, thereby potentially affecting his/her decision. For cases of fully informative and non-informative information systems, see Question 1 at the end of this chapter.

It should also be noted that the information system concept is decision specific. The system in Table 3.2 is geared to a decision whether or not to buy a firm's shares. Other decisions would involve a different table. For example, a decision to evaluate manager stewardship could define states of nature as "high manager stewardship" or "low manager stewardship." The analysis of the financial statements would then be oriented to investigating the extent to which net income reflects the quality of manager ability and performance, with different information system probabilities.

Financial statements that are highly informative, and the information system that underlies them, are often called **transparent, precise**, or **high quality**, since they convey lots of information to investors. While informativeness is the more primitive concept, we shall also use the other terms, particularly in relation to earnings, since various measures of earnings informativeness are used to evaluate the usefulness of reported net income.

Information system and informativeness concepts are helpful in thinking about changes in GAAP. For example, suppose a new accounting standard required X Ltd. to switch to value in use from historical cost for its capital asset. The resulting increase in relevance would increase the main diagonal probabilities of the information system and lower the off-main diagonal ones, since value in use is a better predictor of future firm performance than historical cost. However, switching to value in use would also decrease reliability. Value in use has to be estimated, creating the possibility of error and manager bias. This would have the opposite effect on the information system probabilities. Thus, a move to value in use accounting will increase informativeness only if its greater relevance outweighs the decrease in reliability.

However, if it were possible to increase relevance without sacrificing reliability or vice versa, the result would be to increase financial statement usefulness. One way to accomplish this would be to present supplementary information, such as RRA (Section 2.4), or management discussion and analysis (discussed below). These increase relevance for investors who want to incorporate supplemental information into their decisions while retaining the somewhat greater reliability of the financial statements proper.

Informativeness also depends on the extent to which financial reporting is conservative. Recall from our discussion in Section 1.4 that conservate accounting recognizes unrealized losses, but not unrealized gains, as they take place. That is, the accountant waits to record gains until there is objective evidence of their realization, but records unrealized losses by writing assets down (or liabilities up) when a loss in value occurs. Recognition of unrealized losses but not unrealized gains raises the information system probability of BN/low state relative to the probability of GN/high state, assuming reasonable reliability. Other examples of conservatism, such as expensing research costs currently, have a similar effect. Table 3.2 includes some conservatism, since the BN/low state probability (0.90) is greater than the GN/high state (0.80).

The concept of informativeness of an information system is useful in understanding the role of information in decision making. The higher the main diagonal probabilities relative to the off-main diagonal ones, the more informative the system or, equivalently, the lower is estimation risk (introduced in Section 2.3), since a more informative system reduces risk by enabling better predictions of states of nature and ultimate payoffs. Consequently, the more informative an information system, the more decision useful it is. In an investment context, these payoffs are returns on investments.

While thinking of financial statements as a table of conditional probabilities may take some getting used to, the information system is one of the most powerful and useful concepts in financial accounting theory. This is because it captures the information content of financial statements, thereby determining their usefulness for decision making. Furthermore, many practical accounting problems can be framed in terms of their impact on the information system. For example, we pointed out above that if a move to value in use accounting for capital assets is to be decision useful, the increase in relevance (which increases the main diagonal probabilities) must outweigh any decrease in reliability (which decreases them). Similar reasoning can be applied to other new or proposed accounting standards. Standards requiring fair value accounting for financial instruments, for example, are subject to similar tradeoffs. Since most financial reporting debates can be cast in terms of relevance versus reliability, the information system provides a useful framework for thinking about effects of these debates on decision usefulness.

How does Bill know what the information system probabilities are? One response is simply to *assume* they are known. We made this assumption in Example 3.1 and Table 3.2. This is an example of **rational expectations**—investors are assumed to quickly form accurate estimates of unknown, underlying parameters—in this case, the information system probabilities.[9] This assumption is common in much theoretical economics and accounting research.

As a practical matter, one approach to forming accurate estimates is by sampling. Bill could take a sample of recent financial statements of X Ltd. and similar firms, possibly including previous periods' statements as well, recording the number of times GN is followed by high performance, and similarly for BN. If GAAP does not change over the sample period, these frequencies will equal the probabilities in Table 3.2, for a large enough sample.[10]

A different approach to evaluating information system informativeness was taken by Easton and Zmijewski (EZ; 1989). They examined Value Line analysts' revisions of future quarterly earnings forecasts following the GN or BN in firms' current quarterly earnings. That is, analysts are viewed as rational investors who use financial statement earnings information to revise their beliefs about future firm performance, similar to Bill Cautious in Example 3.1. Future quarterly earnings are analogous to the states of nature in Table 3.2 (Value Line predicts future firm performance in terms of earnings), and the GN or BN in current quarterly earnings constitutes the financial statement evidence in that table. Value Line provides forecasts for a large number of firms, and these forecasts are revised quarterly.

For a sample of 150 large U.S. corporations followed by Value Line over the period 1975–1980, EZ found that for every $1 of GN or BN in reported earnings, the Value Line analysts increased or decreased next quarter's earnings forecast by about 34 cents on average. This implies that the information systems underlying the sample firms' financial statements are informative—that is, analysts use current financial statement information to revise their beliefs about future firm performance. EZ called the effect of current

Theory in Practice 3.1

Decision theory methods are finding applications in several areas other than accounting. Consider, for example, the evaluation of new medical discoveries. Suppose that a drug company has developed a new, expensive test for a deadly disease. It has administered the test to a sample of persons and has compiled the test's success rates (correct identification of persons who do and do not have the disease) and failure rates (incorrect identification). The success rates correspond to the main diagonal probabilities of the information system in Table 3.2, and the failure rates correspond to the off-main diagonal probabilities. The higher the main diagonal probabilities relative to off-main diagonal, the better the test discriminates (i.e., predicts future

performance) between persons who do and do not have the disease.

The company is now trying to decide whether to proceed with marketing the test. Commercial success will be assured if the test is demanded by a large number of people. That is, the test will be popular if persons with low prior probability of having the disease (i.e., most persons) will want to take it. The drug company uses Bayes' theorem to calculate the posterior probability of having the disease for a person with an assumed low prior probability. If it finds the posterior probability to be high (indicating that the test discriminates very well), such persons will be likely to want to take the expensive test. Consequently, the drug company may decide to proceed.

financial statement information on analysts' next quarter earnings forecast a "revision coefficient." This coefficient is a proxy for the average earnings quality of their sample firms; in other words, it reflects the magnitude of the information system probabilities.

EZ also found that the higher a firm's revision coefficient is (recall that the 34 cents above is an average), the stronger was the effect of the GN or BN in current earnings on the market price of the firm's shares. This is consistent with investors accepting the analysts' evaluation of the information system, bidding share price up or down more strongly the higher the quality of the system.

EZ's results suggest that quarterly earnings are decision useful, consistent with the decision theory model of Example 3.1. Empirical studies of the response of share price to financial statement information are considered in greater detail in Chapter 5.

3.3.3 Information Defined

Decision theory and the concept of informativeness give us a precise way to define information:

Information is evidence that has the potential to affect an individual's decision.

Notice that this is an *ex ante* definition. We would hardly expect an individual to gather evidence if he/she didn't expect to learn enough so as to possibly affect a decision. Bayes' theorem is simply a device to process what has been learned. The crucial requirement for evidence to constitute information is that for at least some evidence that might be received, beliefs will be sufficiently affected that the optimal decision will change.

Note that, like the information system, the information definition is decision specific. Thus information needed for good investment decisions will in general differ from information needed to evaluate manager stewardship. Also, the definition is individual specific. As pointed out in Section 1.7, individuals may differ in their reaction to the same information, even for similar decisions. Their prior probabilities and utilities may differ, so that posterior probabilities, and hence their investment decisions, may differ even when confronted with the same evidence.

The definition of information should really be interpreted net of cost. An information source may have the potential to affect an individual's decision but, if it is too costly, it is not information since it will not be used. It can be argued, however, that financial statements are a cost-effective information source (at least for investors, who do not pay for their preparation) since they are readily available and reasonably well understood by investors.

Finally, it should be emphasized that an individual's receipt of information and subsequent belief revision is really a continuous process. We can think of the individual as using Bayes' theorem every time a new information item comes along. Example 3.1 concentrated on belief revision following receipt of the annual report, but obviously there are many other information sources, such as analyst forecasts, quarterly reports, media, websites, speeches and announcements, statistical reports, etc., that can also affect decisions. Thus, the accountant faces competition. Hopefully, by supplying useful tradeoffs between relevance and reliability, financial statements will continue their role as an important source of information.

3.3.4 Summary

Decision theory is important because it helps us to understand why information is such a powerful commodity—it can affect the actions taken by investors. Accountants, who prepare much of the information required by investors, need to understand this powerful role.

3.4 THE RATIONAL, RISK-AVERSE INVESTOR

In decision theory, the concept of a rational individual simply means that in making decisions, the chosen act is the one that yields the highest expected utility.[11] This implies that the individual may search for additional information relating to the decision, using it to revise state probabilities by means of Bayes' theorem.

We emphasize that the decision theory described above is a *model* of rational decision making. Whether individuals actually make decisions this way is difficult to say. Nevertheless, in thinking about questions of decision usefulness, it is helpful to assume that they do. As we will discuss in Section 6.2, we do not mean to imply that all individuals make decisions as the theory suggests, but only that the theory captures the *average* behaviour of investors who want to make good investment decisions. Alternatively, we can argue that if investors want to make good decisions this is how they *should* proceed. If individuals do not make decisions in some rational, predictable manner it is difficult for accountants, or anyone else, to know what information they find useful. At any rate, implications of the theory have been subjected to much empirical testing, as we shall see in Chapter 5. To the extent that predictions of the theory are confirmed empirically, our confidence that the decision theory model is a reasonable one is strengthened.

It is also usually assumed that rational investors are risk averse.[12] To see the intuition underlying this concept, think of yourself as an investor who is asked to flip a fair coin with your university or college instructor—suppose the coin is a penny. You would probably be willing to flip for pennies, if for no other reason than to humour the instructor. If the ante were raised, you would probably be willing to flip for dimes, quarters, even dollars. However, there would come a point where you would refuse—say, flipping for $100,000. (If you didn't refuse, the instructor would.)

Remind yourself that the expected payoff of flipping a fair coin is zero, regardless of the amount at stake, since you have a 50% chance of winning and a 50% chance of losing

Figure 3.3 Risk-Averse Utility Function

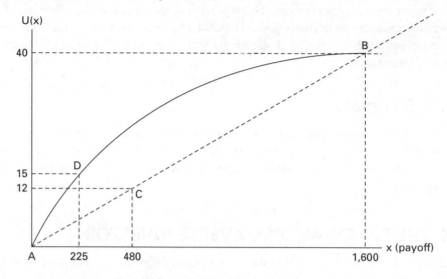

in all cases. Thus, your increasing nervousness as the stakes are raised means that another effect, beyond the expected value of the gamble, is operating. This is risk aversion.

Note also that risk averse individuals trade off expected return and risk. For example, if the coin was biased in your favour—say you have a 75% chance of winning—you would probably be willing to flip for higher stakes than if the coin was fair. In effect, you are now willing to bear more risk in exchange for a higher expected value—the expected payoff of your gamble is now $0.50 per dollar rather than 0.

To model risk aversion, decision theorists use the device of a utility function, which relates payoff amounts to the decision-maker's utility for those amounts.

To portray a utility function, consider Figure 3.3. The solid line shows the utility function of Bill Cautious in Example 3.1. Bill's utility function is

$$U(x) = \sqrt{x}, x \geq 0$$

where x is the amount of the payoff. Note that the utility function of a risk-averse individual is concave.

Based on his prior probabilities, Bill's expected payoff for act a_1 is $(0.3 \times \$1,600) + (0.7 \times \$0) = \$480$. The expected *utility* of the payoff is at point C on the dotted line joining A and B. This expected utility of $(0.3 \times 40) + (0.7 \times 0) = 12$ is less than the utility of 15 for the risk-free investment at point D on Figure 3.3. Consequently, Bill's rational decision is to choose the risk-free investment, if he were to act on the basis of his prior probabilities. This is the case even though the expected payoff of the risky investment ($480) is greater than the risk-free payoff ($225). This demonstrates that Bill is averse to risk.

To see how Bill's decision may change if the risky investment were less risky, assume that the possible payoffs are now $200 (with probability 0.7) and $1,133.33

Figure 3.4 Risk-Neutral Utility Function

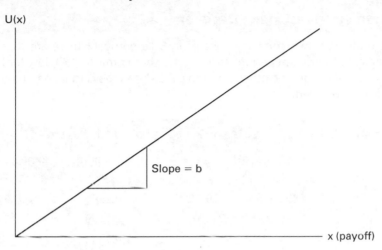

(with probability 0.3) instead of the earlier $0 and $1,600. You should verify that the expected payoff is still $480 but the expected utility rises to 20.[13] Then Bill's rational decision is to buy the risky investment. The reduction in risk raises expected utility, even though the expected payoff has not changed.

Despite the intuitive appeal of risk aversion, it is sometimes assumed that decision makers are risk neutral. This means that they evaluate risky investments strictly in terms of expected payoff—risk itself does not matter per se. We made this assumption in Example 2.2. Figure 3.4 shows the utility function of a risk-neutral decision maker. A typical risk-neutral utility function is $U(x) = bx$, where b is the slope of the line. Here, utility is simply a linear function of the payoff.

Risk neutrality may be a reasonable assumption when the payoffs are small. However, risk aversion is the more realistic assumption in most cases. The concept of risk aversion is important to accountants, because it means that investors need information concerning the risk, as well as the expected value, of future returns.

3.5 THE PRINCIPLE OF PORTFOLIO DIVERSIFICATION

It turns out that Bill can do better than investing all of his $10,000 in X Ltd. in Example 3.1. He can increase his utility by adopting a strategy of **portfolio diversification**. To illustrate, assume that he carries out an analysis of Y Ltd. similar to that for X Ltd. The result is that he expects $5,000 invested in Y Ltd. shares would produce a net return of $993.50 with posterior probability 0.6, and $50 with probability 0.4. Bill decides to **diversify** by investing $5,000 in each company. Note that the same total amount is invested, but that it is now distributed over two securities.

Example 3.2
A Diversified Investment Decision

Since there are now two company's shares in Bill's portfolio, there are four states of nature—namely, future firm performance high for both firms (Hi, Hi), low for both firms (Lo, Lo), or one firm high, the other low. Table 3.3 shows the calculation of the expected payoff for this investment.

Table 3.3 Expected Payoff for X Ltd. and Y Ltd. Portfolio

State	Payoff	Probability	Expected Payoff
Hi, Hi	$800 + $993.50 = $1,793.50	0.5000	$ 897
Hi, Lo	$800 + $50 = 850.00	0.2500	212
Lo, Hi	$0 + $993.50 = 993.50	0.1169	116
Lo, Lo	$0 + $50 = 50.00	0.1331	7
		1.0000	$1,232

Consistent with Example 3.1, $5,000 invested in X Ltd. shares will yield a net return of $800 if its high state happens. If the high state for Y happens, return is $993.50. This gives a Hi, Hi payoff of $1,793.50. The other payoffs are calculated similarly. Note that, to facilitate comparison, the Y Ltd. payoffs and probabilities are chosen so that the expected return of the portfolio is the same as that of an investment of $10,000 in X Ltd. as per Example 3.1 (0.77 × $1,600 + 0.23 × $0 = $1,232).

In any economy, there are states of nature, also called factors, which affect the returns of *all* shares, such as levels of interest rates, foreign exchange rates, the level of economic activity, and so on. These are called **market-wide** or **economy-wide factors**. Their presence means that if the return on one share is high, it is more likely that the returns on most other companies' shares in the economy will also be high—more likely, that is, than would be the case if the returns on shares were independent. Assume that Bill assesses the probability of the state realization (Hi, Hi) as 0.5000, as shown in the table. This probability is greater than the (0.77 × 0.60 =) 0.4620 probability of (Hi, Hi) that would obtain under independence, to reflect these underlying common factors.

Similar reasoning applies to the last row of Table 3.3 with a (Lo, Lo) payoff probability assessed as 0.1331, greater than the (0.23 × 0.40 =) 0.0920 that would obtain under independence. Similar to the reasoning for high returns, if market-wide state realizations work toward low returns (e.g., if the economy is performing poorly), then the probability that both shares realize low payoffs is greater than what would be expected if returns were independent.

Of course, while share returns may covary due to common factors, this covariance is not perfect. It is still possible that one firm realizes a high return and another a low return—witness the two middle rows of Table 3.3. This is because, in addition to economy-wide factors, there are also **firm-specific factors** that affect the return of one firm only. Examples include the quality of a firm's management, new patents, strikes, machine breakdowns, and so on. Thus, the second row of the table represents a situation where firm A realizes a high return (due, for example, to a new invention it has just patented) and firm B realizes a low return (due, for example, to a critical machine failure in its assembly line). Bill assesses the probability of this Hi, Lo outcome as 0.2500. Similar reasoning applies to the third row.[14] We can now calculate Bill's expected utility from this diversification strategy.

$$EU(P) = 0.5\sqrt{1,793.50} + 0.25\sqrt{850} + 0.1169\sqrt{993.50} + 0.1331\sqrt{50}$$
$$= 0.5 \times 42.35 + 0.25 \times 29.15 + 0.1169 \times 31.52 + 0.1331 \times 7.07$$
$$= 21.18 + 7.29 + 3.68 + 0.94$$
$$= 33.09$$

where EU(P) denotes the expected utility of the portfolio. Since this is greater than the expected utility of the bond investment (15), Bill continues to take the risky investment. Even though the amount invested ($10,000) and expected payoff ($1,232) are the same, the diversification strategy has increased Bill's expected utility to 33.09 from 30.80. The reason is that firm-specific risks (also called **idiosyncratic risks**) tend to cancel out. If Bill held only shares of X Ltd., he would bear all of its idiosyncratic risk. With diversification, he bears half of it and half of that of Y Ltd. The possibility of a high return for X and a low return for Y, and vice versa, reduces total idiosyncratic risk. Since Bill is risk averse, his expected utility rises.

If a two-security portfolio decreases firm-specific risk, a three-security portfolio should decrease it even more, and so on. This is true[15] (although expected utility increases at a decreasing rate, implying that most of the benefits of diversification can be attained with relatively few securities). It follows that if there is no cost to investing, Bill should fully diversify by buying all available securities. This is called **holding the market portfolio.**

3.6 INCREASING THE DECISION USEFULNESS OF FINANCIAL REPORTING

3.6.1 Introduction

In this section, we outline and illustrate **management discussion and analysis** (MD&A). This is a standard that requires firms to provide a narrative explanation of company operations to assist investors to interpret the firm's financial statements.

While of interest in its own right, this standard also provides an important illustration of how the amount of useful information in the public domain can be increased. While all public companies provide MD&A, there is some latitude in the extent to which they meet the letter of its disclosure requirements. For example, while some firms may provide what is mainly "boilerplate" and/or a rehash of information already available from the financial statements, others may go beyond the minimum requirements by releasing more extensive information.

3.6.2 Objectives of Management Discussion and Analysis

Objectives of MD&A Our coverage of MD&A is based on the requirements of National Instrument 51-102 of the OSC, as of 2012. Through the Canadian Securities Administrators, harmonized MD&A regulations now apply across Canada. Similar requirements are laid down in other jurisdictions, such as that of the SEC in the United States. In 2010, the IASB issued *Management Commentary*, a practice statement for MD&A, which is broadly consistent with Canadian and U.S. MD&A requirements. Since adoption of the Management Commentary guidelines is voluntary, we will concentrate on NI 51-102 here. MD&A is a narrative explanation, through the eyes of management, of company performance, financial condition, risks, and future prospects. It is to be written in language that investors are able to understand. Forward-looking information is encouraged.

Its objectives include:

- Help current and prospective investors understand the financial statements.
- Discuss information not fully reflected in the financial statements.
- Discuss important trends and risks, including those affecting future performance.
- Provide information about the quality, and potential variability, of earnings and cash flow, to help investors determine if past performance is indicative of future performance.
- Provide information about credit ratings.

To implement these objectives, specific disclosure requirements include:

- Discuss the firm's ability to meet short- and long-term liquidity needs.
- Discuss important commitments and off balance sheet arrangements.
- Explain and discuss trends, risks, and uncertainties that are expected to affect future performance. Explain needed changes to forward-looking information previously provided that is now known to be in error because of subsequent developments. Discuss financial instruments and associated risks.

Several aspects of these requirements should be noted:

- The MD&A standard has a clear forward-looking orientation. For example, known trends affecting future performance should be discussed. This orientation is consistent with Example 3.1, which asserts investors' primary interest in predicting future firm performance. Also, the concept of an information system is implicit in the MD&A standard. As discussed in Section 3.3.2, the information system specifies the probabilistic relationship between current financial statement evidence and future firm performance. By including discussion of trends and risks, the connection between current information and future firm performance is tightened up by adding MD&A to financial reporting. That is, the main diagonal probabilities of the information system are increased. This is recognized in the standard's objective of helping investors to determine if past firm performance is indicative of future performance.

Also consistent with its future orientation, the standard tilts toward relevance in the relevance/reliability tradeoff. That is, there is less need to wait until objective evidence is available than in the financial statements. However, MD&A does not completely ignore reliability considerations. For example, NI 51-102 requires that the firm's MD&A be approved by its board of directors. Presumably, this is to reduce the probability of manager manipulation and bias. Also, the firm is required to discuss any needed changes to forward-looking information provided in previous MD&A that is now known to be in error as a result of further developments. These requirements help with reliability since the manager knows that errors or biases in estimates will likely have to be explained later.

■ The MD&A standard seems reasonably consistent with the theory of rational investor decision making. For example, it emphasizes full disclosure and recognizes that investors need forward-looking information and information about risk. Note, however, that the emphasis is on firm-specific risk disclosure. Yet, as we discussed in Section 3.5, much of this risk can be diversified away. Nevertheless, the disclosures should help to reduce investors' information asymmetry.

With this background in mind, we now illustrate some of these considerations by means of an actual MD&A.

3.6.3 An Example of MD&A Disclosure

Exhibit 3.1 reproduces portions of MD&A from the 2012 *Annual Report* of Canadian Tire Corporation, Limited, including most of its risk management discussion. Canadian Tire is a large Canadian retail organization, with a network of outlets across the country, supported by financial services including credit cards, banking services, and insurance. Its 2012 Annual Report won the CICA Consumer Products Corporate Reporting Award.

Canadian Tire's MD&A begins with an overview of the business (only a summary is reproduced here), then describes its strategic objectives for 2013 in detail. Notice in particular that specific activities to achieve each of these objectives are given. Notice also the candid discussion of the firm's five-year financial aspirations plan, including reasons why some of the plan's objectives have not yet been attained.

The firm also provides extensive discussion of current operating and financing activities. Performance and risks of major divisions are also discussed. These disclosures are not reproduced here.

With respect to its discussion of risk management, note the variety of risks Canadian Tire faces. These range from operating risks, to changes in business relationships, to changes in competitive environment, to natural disasters, to changing technology, to legal risks of failure to meet all applicable regulations. Also faced are various financial risks such as credit risk, financial reporting errors, changes in foreign exchange, and interest rates. Notice, in particular, the disclosures of the strategies used by the company to control these risks.

Exhibit 3.1
MD&A Extracts, from 2012 Annual Report, Canadian Tire Corporation, Limited

2.1 Overview of the business

Canadian Tire Corporation, Limited, through a network of more than 1,700 retail outlets and gas bars, offers products and services that prepare Canadians for the jobs and joys of everyday living in Canada. The core retail business spans categories with solutions for Living, Fixing & Playing, Automotive, Apparel and Sporting Goods. The retail businesses are supported and strengthened by the Financial Services business, which offers products and services including credit cards, in-store financing, product warranties, retail deposits, insurance, and Canadian Tire Home Services.

5.0 Strategic objectives

5.1 Strategic objectives and initiatives

While meeting the needs of the jobs and joys of everyday living in Canada, the Company has focused its retail businesses and financial services business to support growth and productivity improvements in order to achieve the five-year financial aspirations outlined in 2010 (see section 5.2 for financial aspirations). Underlying the growth and productivity initiatives in 2012 were four strategic objectives that are key to sustained future growth:

1. **Strengthen core retail**
   Achieve growth in CTR through a customer-centric approach
2. **Align all business units to reinforce the core**
   Operate as "one company"
3. **Build a high-performing organization**
   Establish a corporate culture of continuous improvement
4. **Create new platforms for growth**
   Identify and evaluate new growth opportunities

5.1.2 Objectives for 2013

1. Strengthen core retail	
2013 Objectives	**2013 Key activities**
Continue rollout of new-concept CTR stores	• Complete at least 50 Smart store projects • Open one new Small Market store and one Small Market replacement store • Pilot new-concept CTR Express store • Develop next new CTR store concept

Continue to execute strategies to deliver an enhanced in-store customer experience at CTR	• Deliver product locator software and training to more than 100 stores • Deliver enhanced tires training to 350 stores • Continue to roll out a comprehensive merchandising and marketing strategy in the Living category, with 400 stores converted by the end of 2013 • Improve automotive service CSI scores by 200 basis points (bps)

2. Align all business units to reinforce the core

2013 Objectives	2013 Key activities
Design and implement an enhanced loyalty program, employ customer-centric retailing and integrate with existing marketing programs	• Continue to learn from and evolve first phase of CTR loyalty offering and identify markets for expansion of program in 2014 • Continue to design target offerings to customers, based on loyalty customer shopping data • Support first phase of new loyalty program at eight gas bars in Nova Scotia
Expand e-commerce and investigate cross-business integration opportunities	• Continue with design of an integrated online/digital experience across various retail banners • Expand e-commerce offering • Launch digital catalogue
Continue to enhance store networks to drive an enhanced customer experience	• Continue Mark's network expansion, including three new stores, nine replacements/expansions and 32 stores rebranded to the new Mark's format, for a total of 203 converted locations nationwide by the end of 2013 • Add or upgrade 20 Petroleum sites, including six new locations, five rebranded locations and nine replacement or retrofit projects; included in the total are three 400/401 series highway sites • Convert approximately eight existing PartSource stores to Super Satellite format
Drive growth in the Retail segment with the Integration and development of FGL Sports	• Complete banner rationalization program by end of Q1 2013 • Complete 39 FGL Sports store network projects, including 27 new Sport Chek and Atmosphere stores, two Sport Chek flagship stores, five replacement stores and five expansions
Expand Financial Services through continued growth of portfolio of services and managed growth of receivables	• Continue to identify and provide alternate financing methods and support to Home Services customer transactions • Continue to market and promote new in-store offerings, including deferred financing, installment payments and new account acquisitions

3. Build a high-performing organization	
2013 Objectives	**2013 Key activities**
Advance key productivity and efficiency initiatives (technology and process capabilities) to sustain benefits into the future	• Simplify the flyer process through review of current flyer planning processes to simplify execution and reduce rework while driving flyer performance and productivity • Continue rollout of new line review processes to identify and execute against defined category roles • Evaluate productivity and effectiveness of SKUs within our assortments to assess future benefits • Identify opportunities to implement technology in support of consistent assortment reviews • Streamline supply chain operations to reduce expenses
Drive business sustainability as a business strategy	• Continue to integrate sustainability across the Company's operations, generating both cost avoidance and revenue from business sustainability initiatives • Optimize key sustainability metrics and reporting

5.2 Financial aspirations

The strategic objectives include financial aspirations for the Company over the five-year period ending December 2014. Progress against these goals is reported annually as:

Financial measure	Aspirations over 5-year period to 2014	2012 Performance	Achieved in 2012	2010 to 2012 CAGR Performance	Achieved from 2010 to 2012
CTR retail sales (POS) annual growth	3% to 5%	0.8%	X	1.7%	X
Consolidated EPS annual growth	8% to 10%	6.9%	X[1]	14.3%	√
Retail return on invested capital	10%+	6.7%	X	6.7%[2]	X
Financial Services return on receivables	4.5% to 5.0%	6.8%	√	6.8%[2]	√
Total return to shareholders (TRS) including dividends	10% to 12%	6.8%	X	7.9%	X

[1] Normalized for the Items described In ttie table in section 7.1, consolidated basic EPS growVi was 13.1%.
[2] Retail ROIC end ROR are targets Intended to be achieved at the end of the outlook period, therefore, have been calculated as at the year-end date.

CTR retail sales annual growth

Retail sales grew 0.8% at CTR for the year, which is below the Company's aspiration. Economic uncertainty and a cautious consumer continued to have an impact on many North American retailers throughout 2012 and are reflected in the Company's sales growth. In addition, the impact of increased competition in the marketplace, and the late start to winter in Central Canada, primarily in Ontario and Quebec, negatively affected retail sales at CTR stores.

Consolidated EPS annual growth

Consolidated basic EPS increased 6.9% in the year, which is below the Company's aspiration. However, there were several non-operating items that were included in the Company's results. Normalizing for unusual items listed in the table in section 7.1, basic EPS was up 13.1%.

Retail ROIC

The rolling 12-month retail return on invested capital was 6.67% at the end of 2012, which was below the Company's aspiration. The Company continues to focus on improving the productivity of its capital investments and has made significant advances on many of its strategic growth initiatives, setting a solid foundation for future growth.

Financial Services return on receivables

The Financial Services segment return on receivables exceeded the targeted range of 4.5 to 5.0% in 2012. Strong performance resulted from improved net write-offs, growth in credit charges, modest growth in credit card receivables, prudent expense management and continuation of relatively low funding costs.

Total return to shareholders

Total return to shareholders, including dividends, was 6.8% in the year. While the Company's TRS was below its aspiration, it was largely in line with the TRS of the S&P/TSX Composite Index which was 7.2% in the year.

Note that the above financial aspirations reflect the Company's expectations over the life of the plan period, and individual fiscal years within that period will vary.

11.0 Enterprise risk management

To preserve and enhance shareholder value, the Company approaches the management of risk strategically through its enterprise risk management (ERM) program. The Company's ERM program sets out principles and tools for identifying, evaluating, prioritizing, monitoring, managing and reporting risk effectively and consistently across the Company.

The ERM program provides an integrated approach to managing risks, supporting the Company's strategic objectives. The Company's ERM program is:

- enterprise-wide in scope by providing an understanding of significant risks and the potential impacts across the organization;
- cross-functional in its perspective to provide a consistent discipline for managing risks;
- designed to allow for improved capital allocation decisions to optimize the risk/reward relationship;
- integrated into the strategic and operational planning and reporting processes; and
- designed to incorporate a number of approaches for managing risk, including avoidance, mitigation, insurance and acceptance.

The ERM program continues to further develop upon its framework relative to: risk identification, risk quantification, risk monitoring and risk integration and optimization in consultation with Executive leadership.

11.1 Risk governance

The mandate of the Board of Directors includes overseeing the development of the ERM program, for which the Board has delegated primary responsibility to the Audit Committee. The Audit Committee is responsible for gaining and maintaining reasonable assurance that management:

- appropriately identifies and manages risks;

- has in place a policy that accurately sets out the Company's risk philosophy and the expectations and accountabilities for identifying, assessing, monitoring, managing and reporting on risks ("the ERM policy");

- fully implements and sustains the ERM program in compliance with the ERM policy, and that the ERM policy continues to accurately state the Company's risk philosophy, as well as expectations and accountabilities for managing risks;

- identifies Principal Risks in a timely manner, including those risks relating to or arising from any weaknesses or threats to the Company's business and assumptions underlying the strategic objectives; and

- effectively assesses, monitors and manages Principal Risks in compliance with the ERM policy.

The officer in charge of each banner and corporate function is accountable for effectively managing risks relevant to their respective business areas. The Executive Committee oversees the Company's risk profile and the management of Principal Risks and other enterprise-wide risks. The Executive Committee is also responsible for reviewing and approving, for recommendation to the Board of Directors, the ERM policy, program and specific policies addressing each of the Principal Risks. This risk oversight is conducted under the leadership of the Chief Financial Officer and Executive Vice-President of Finance (CFO) with the support of the Vice-President of Internal Audit Services and Enterprise Risk Management.

The Company's Internal Audit Services (IAS) division also supports the overall risk management program. The primary role of IAS is to assist the Audit Committee in the discharge of its responsibilities relating to risk and uncertainty, financial controls and control deviations, compliance with laws and regulations and compliance with the Company's Code of Business Conduct and Board-approved policies. To this end, IAS is responsible for conducting independent and objective assessments of the effectiveness of risk management, control and governance processes across the Company.

11.2 Principal Risks

A key element of the Company's ERM program is the periodic review, identification and assessment of Principal Risks. The Company defines a Principal Risk as one that, alone or in combination with other interrelated risks, can have a significant adverse impact on Canadian Tire's financial performance, reputation or ability to service its customers and has, in the absence of controls, a credible probability of occurring. These Principal Risks are enterprise-wide in scope and represent strategic, financial and operational risks. Management has completed its formal annual review of its Principal Risks, which has been presented to the Audit Committee and approved by the Board of Directors. Recent changes include:

- the addition of an operations risk to the Company's list of Principal Risks due to the ongoing growth and complexity of Canadian Tire's businesses; and
- changing the name and/or the underlying definition of some of the existing Principal Risks to better align with identification of the source of the risk.

The following table provides a high-level perspective on each of the identified 11 Principal Risks and describes the main strategy that the Company has in place to mitigate the potential impacts of these risks on its business objectives.

Principal Risks	Risk management strategy
Business continuity Risk of an event or a series of events including natural or man-made disasters or other unplanned and/or prolonged business interruptions that: - compromise the safety of the Company's employees or customers; - result in the Company not being able to provide products or services to its customers; - limit or prevent the Company from communicating with its customers, employees, stakeholders and shareholders; or - can result in a significant financial loss and/or damage to the Company's reputation.	The enterprise-wide business continuity program includes disaster recovery and crisis management. Policies, plans and processes require all essential business areas to be able to respond to an event of business interruption or crisis. Furthermore, information systems are periodically tested through disaster recovery plans. In addition, a comprehensive insurance program with a number of carriers provides related coverage.
Consumer lending Canadian Tire Bank's consumer lending portfolio is exposed to credit or default risk arising from CTB's failure or inability to accurately predict the creditworthiness or credit behaviour of its customers in a normal market or under stressed economic conditions, resulting in a significant negative impact to earnings and the availability of financing for the receivables.	Policies and processes are employed to strategically target the quality of our consumer lending portfolio as outlined in section 7.5.2.2. Further information regarding the Company's exposure to consumer lending risk is provided in section 11.3.
Execution of strategy The Company has a number of key initiatives supporting its strategic objectives. Failure to appropriately identify, plan, resource, execute and achieve the full benefits of these initiatives may result in a significant negative impact on the Company's mid-to-long-term success and reputation, including a loss of revenue, market share or investor confidence.	The Company regularly reviews and updates its long-term strategic objectives and identifies the key initiatives therein as being vital to its long-term success. Operating plans set out each year's objectives required as part of the successful longer-term execution of these initiatives. Further details are set out in section 5.0. The Board of Directors receives reports on progress against the operating plan on a quarterly basis and periodic updates on strategic initiatives. The Board of Directors is also engaged in the annual review of the long-term strategy and influences the agenda of strategic initiatives for the following year.

continued

Principal Risks	Risk management strategy
Financial markets Risk associated with fundamental changes in the economic environment or significant events or volatility in the financial markets, resulting in: • tight capital and debt markets and/or high cost of capital and debt such that the Company cannot maintain sufficient capital to absorb unexpected losses and/or to economically acquire and maintain the required funding and capital structure necessary to carry out its strategic plan; • significant volatility in the U.S. dollar/Canadian dollar exchange rate such that there is significant negative impact on the Company's gross margin and product pricing strategies, resulting in reduced sales and, ultimately, in reduced earnings; and • significant volatility in interest rates such that there is a significant negative impact on the Company's net interest expense. In addition, financial markets risk also includes the risk of market exposures due to inappropriate hedging strategies, resulting in a negative impact on earnings.	Various policies and processes support the management of capital and funding risks. The Treasurer and CFO provide oversight on policy compliance. Further details are set out in section 8.1.1. Various financial risk management policies and processes are employed to manage the Company's hedging activities, which are designed to mitigate the Company's exposure to foreign exchange rate volatility and sensitivity to adverse movements in interest rates and the equity markets. Hedge transactions are executed with highly rated financial institutions and are monitored against policy limits and counterparty limits. Further details are set out in sections 8.3 and 11.3.
Financial reporting Risk of restatement and reissue of the Company's financial statements due to failure to adhere to financial accounting and presentation standards and securities regulations relevant to financial reporting, and/or inadequate explanation of the Company's operating performance, financial condition and future prospects, resulting in regulatory sanctions, loss in share value and/or reputational damage.	Policies and processes provide reasonable assurance regarding the reliability of financial reporting and the preparation of financial statements. These processes include monitoring and responding to changing regulations and standards governing accounting and financial presentation. Further details are set out in section 12.0.
Key business relationships Risks associated with the Company having a wide range of key business relationships and affiliations (with such parties as Dealers, agents and franchisees, as well as a limited number of vendors and suppliers) may result in disruption to business operations and financial loss, The scope, complexity, materiality and/or criticality of these key business relationships can potentially affect customer service, procurement, product and service delivery and can result in legal disputes that may have a significant negative impact on the Company's earnings, cost of operations, reputation and brand.	The Company periodically assesses the capabilities, strategic fit and other realized benefits of key business relationships in the context of supporting the overall business strategy. Appropriate governance structures, including policies, processes, contracts, service level agreements and other management activities, are in place to maintain and strengthen the relationships that are critical to the success of the Company's performance and aligned with its overall strategic needs. A key relationship for the Company is with the CTR Dealers. Management of the CTR Dealer relationship is led by officers of the Company with oversight by the Chief Executive Officer (CEO) and Board of Directors.

Principal Risks	Risk management strategy
Legal	Policies address compliance with legislation and regulations. The Legislative Compliance department provides compliance oversight and guidance to the organization. Each of the business units has also established processes for complying with the laws and regulations of most significance to its business activities. The Audit Committee and Governance Committee have an oversight role in this area.
Risk of failure to comply with current and changing laws, regulations or regulatory policies, codes or rules, resulting in negative impact to the Company's reputation, earnings or capital, regulatory relationships or business activities.	
Laws, regulations and regulatory polices referred to include privacy, securities (disclosure and insider trading), environmental, banking, competition, occupational health and safety, product safety, records, and employment.	Further information regarding the Company's exposure to legal risks is provided in section 11.4.
Marketplace	Processes monitor and analyze economic, demographic, consumer behaviour and competitive developments in Canada. The Treasury and Strategic Planning departments have key roles in these processes.
Risk due to fluctuations or fundamental changes in the external business environment, resulting in financial loss. Fluctuations or fundamental shifts in the marketplace could include:	
• economic recession, depression or high inflation affecting consumer spending;	Results are shared with the Company's executives, who are accountable for any necessary amendments to the strategic and operational plans and for ongoing investment decisions.
• changes in the competitive landscape for the retail or financial services sectors affecting the attractiveness of shopping at Canadian Tire's businesses;	
• changes in the domestic or international political environments (including new legislation) affecting the cost of products and/or ability to do business;	
• shifts in the demographics of the Canadian population, reducing the relevance of the products and services offered by the Company;	
• changes in the buying behaviour of consumers, rendering the Company's products and services less attractive; or	
• the introduction of new technologies rendering the Company's products or services as obsolete, which may result in a significant negative impact on the Company's sales, market share, operating margins and/or inability to achieve its strategic objectives.	
Operations	The officer in charge of each banner and corporate function is accountable for providing assurances that policies and processes are adequately designed and operating effectively to support the Company's strategic and performance objectives.
Risk of failure of the Company's business operations and processes (merchandising, supply chain, store networks and financial services) to support its key business objectives. Failed processes in terms of design, integration and/or execution can result in incremental financial expenditures or losses, theft or fraud, damages to assets, poor service delivery, negative customer experiences or regulatory related issues.	

continued

Principal Risks	Risk management strategy
People Risk associated with the Company not being able to attract and retain sufficient and appropriately skilled people who have the expertise (focus, commitment and capability) to support the achievement of the Company's strategic objectives and not being able to address external and/or internal human-resources-related matters.	Various policies and practices address organizational design, employee recruitment programs, succession planning, compensation structures, ongoing training and professional development programs and performance management. The Company's Code of Business Conduct sets out expected ethical behaviour of employees and directors. The Business Conduct Compliance Office offers multiple channels for employees to report breaches, provides interpretations of and training on the Code and monitors investigations and outcomes of potential breaches of the Code.
Technology (including information systems) Technology risks include the failure to: • invest in technology in a manner that supports the Company's ability to achieve its strategic objectives; • operate in a manner so as to ensure that systems and data files are available to support business operations, including customer needs and management requirements; and • secure and protect customer, employee and corporate information from internal threats, external threats and unexpected effects of change, thereby exposing the Company to possible corruption/loss of data, regulatory sanctions, litigation or reputational damage.	Policies, standards and processes address capabilities, performance, availability and security. Security protocols along with corporate information security policies address compliance with information security standards, including those in relation to information belonging to the Company's customers and employees.

Source: Reprinted by permission of Canadian Tire Corporation, Limited.

Canadian Tire's MD&A seems to fully meet the objectives and requirements of the regulations given earlier. Indeed, its disclosures exceed a minimal rehashing of financial statement information and vague references to future prospects. The information provided with respect to control of risks goes well beyond what can be learned from the financial statements themselves. In particular, the discussion is from management's perspective, and contains considerable forward-looking information to assist investors to assess the probabilities of future firm performance.

It is interesting to speculate why some firms go beyond minimal reporting requirements, particularly due to the potential for lawsuits if the forward-looking disclosures are not met. One possibility is that by building investor confidence through reduced information asymmetry, the firm's cost of capital will be reduced. This is discussed further in Chapter 12. Yet another possibility is that a full-disclosure reputation may also affect customer, as well as investor, confidence.

The potentially serious consequences of violating MD&A requirements are illustrated by the case of Kmart Corp., at the time a giant Michigan-based retail chain.

In August 2005, the SEC announced civil charges against the former CEO and CFO of Kmart, including a ban on their serving as officers or directors of public corporations. These charges arose from the summer of 2001, when Kmart acquired excess inventory of approximately US$850 million. This created a serious solvency problem, as Kmart did not have enough cash and bank credit to pay for the overbuy.

To alleviate this solvency crunch, Kmart decided to delay payments to its suppliers, creating serious concerns in the vendor community. Several major suppliers withheld further shipments. Kmart declared bankruptcy in January 2002, resulting in a $4.5 billion loss to shareholders, a loss of many jobs, and losses of retirement savings.

The SEC charges arose out of claimed fraudulent misstatements in Kmart's 2001 MD&A. For example, there was no disclosure of why approximately $570 million of accounts payable were past due, despite MD&A requirements to discuss short- and long-term solvency needs, to discuss asset and liability items, and to explain factors that have caused period-to-period variations, as well as discussing important trends and risks that are expected to affect future performance.

Instead, the company blamed the accounts payable increase on glitches in a system update. It also reported, vaguely, that the $440 million increase in inventory (about a 6% increase) was due to "seasonal inventory fluctuations and actions taken to improve overall in-stock position."

MD&A represents a major step taken by securities commissions to set standards that increase the decision usefulness of financial reporting. The reason why securities commissions become involved in MD&A disclosure regulation, presumably, is that accounting standards relate to the financial statements, whereas the concern of the OSC and other securities regulators is with the disclosures by management contained elsewhere in the annual report—that is, outside the jurisdiction of the financial statements.

3.6.4 Is MD&A Decision Useful?

It is difficult to evaluate the decision usefulness of MD&A, since, while numbers are involved, the discussion consists mainly of words. In contrast, the financial statements themselves are numbers based, and evaluation of their decision usefulness is facilitated by direct comparison with previous periods, other firms, and benchmarks such as return on assets. Also, MD&A suffers from low timeliness, since by the time the firm's annual report becomes publicly available, much financial information has already been released, such as earnings announcements and management conference calls, which usually accompany these announcements. However, with the aid of sophisticated computer software to read and analyze documents, progress in evaluating MD&A decision usefulness is being made.

Here, we outline two such decision usefulness studies. Consider first Theory in Practice 3.3.

Li (2010) studied the "tone" of MD&A. To begin, with the aid of 15 students with accounting knowledge, he manually classified 30,000 randomly selected forward-looking sentences from actual MD&As into positive, negative, and neutral tones. A forward-looking sentence is one that contains words such as "will," "expect," "intend," etc. A positive-tone sentence is one that indicates management optimism about the firm's future, etc.

In terms of our discussion of decision theory in Section 3.3, tones can be thought of as states of nature. The results of this classification were:

Positive tone: 20% of sentences
Negative tone: 40% of sentences
Neutral tone: 40% of sentences

These percentages were used as prior probabilities by Li. That is, if one randomly selects a forward-looking statement from an MD&A, the prior probability is 0.20 that this sentence is of positive tone, etc.

Li's next task was to determine the information system. Consider, for example, the sentences of positive tone. For each word in these 6,000 sentences (i.e., 20% of 30,000), the number of times that a specific word appeared was determined (by computer). Thus, if the word "will" appeared, say, 300 times in the 6,000 positive-tone sentences, the probability of the word "will" conditional on a sentence being of positive tone is 300/6,000 = 0.05. This process was repeated for the negative- and neutral-tone sentences.[16]

The result was a probability for each word conditional on the state of the sentence that word was in. In terms of our information system discussion in Section 3.3.2, the three tones are the states of nature, with each word being an evidence item.

Armed with these prior probabilities and the information system, Li then extracted 13 million forward-looking sentences from all MD&A statements reported in the United States during the period 1994–2007. For each MD&A, he used Bayes' theorem to classify each of its forward-looking sentences into its tone. For example, the posterior probability that a sentence is of positive tone can be calculated from the prior probability of that tone (20%) and the information system probabilities of the words in that sentence conditional on the sentence being positive tone. The same procedure was applied to determine the posterior probability that that sentence is of negative tone, and similarly for neutral tone. The sentence was then classified into that tone with the highest posterior probability. The tone of an MD&A was taken as an average of the tones of the forward-looking sentences it contains.

The end result was a sample of 145,479 quarterly MD&As classified into their tones. Li reports that the most common tone was negative. Since the years covered by his procedure included both the fallout from Enron and related reporting failures, and the beginning of the 2007–2008 market meltdowns, perhaps this result is to be expected.

A question then is, does the tone of its MD&A help to predict a firm's future performance? If so, this suggests decision usefulness of MD&A. Li examined the link between MD&A tone and earnings over the four quarters following release of the MD&A. After controlling for other factors affecting future firm performance, such as current quarter's earnings, stock market performance, etc., Li reported a significant average positive relationship between a firm's tone and its next quarter earnings. That is, if a firm's MD&A

is of negative tone, that firm is likely to report bad news earnings next quarter, and vice versa. This positive relationship persists for the next three quarters, although becoming somewhat weaker. He also reported similar positive relationships between tone and *changes* in next quarters' earnings.

Li also divided his sample into two periods: before 2003, and 2003 and later. He reported little change in MD&A decision usefulness between the periods.

Our second study is by Brown and Tucker (2011). They used computer software that determines the degree of similarity between documents to analyze changes in MD&A wording from one year to the next over the period 1997–2006. They argued that the greater a firm's economic activity during the year, the greater should be the changes in its MD&A wording compared with the previous year if the firm is meeting the spirit of the MD&A guidelines. Otherwise, it is likely that the firm is using boilerplate to minimize its disclosures. Economic activity measures include change in earnings per share, change in solvency, volatility of share return (to capture firm risk), and acquisitions and disposals.

Brown and Tucker extracted 28,142 firm-year MD&As, computing a score for wording change from previous year for each.[17] They found a positive association between the score and their economic activity measures (except for their measure of firm risk), from which they conclude that the average firm meets MD&A requirements.

They then examined the decision usefulness of MD&A, by comparing their disclosure score with their firms' stock returns over a three-day period beginning on the day their MD&A became publicly available. They reported a significant positive relationship, consistent with decision usefulness.[18]

Brown and Tucker also found, however, that financial analysts do not revise their earnings forecasts following a firm's release of its MD&A. They suggested that analysts' forecasts are primarily short term, such as the coming quarter or year, while MD&A, with its forward-looking emphasis, provides longer-term information.

The authors then analyzed their data separately for each year covered by their study. They found a declining trend for both their wording change scores and investor reaction, concluding that this apparent reduction in decision usefulness over time is due both to increasing use of boilerplate and increasing preemption of MD&A information by other information sources. To some extent, this conclusion differs from that of Li (2010), who, as mentioned above, found no change in decision usefulness over time. However, his decision usefulness measure is ability to predict future quarters' earnings, while that of Brown and Tucker is stock market reaction. A possible explanation for the difference is that stock market prices are affected by many factors in addition to net income.

3.6.5 Conclusion

MD&A represents a major step taken by securities commissions to set a standard that goes beyond the requirements of GAAP. The reason why securities commissions become involved in MD&A disclosure regulation, presumably, is that accounting standards relate to the financial statements, whereas the concern of securities regulators is also with the disclosures by management contained elsewhere in the annual report—that is, outside the jurisdiction of the financial statements.

Current research reports evidence that MD&A is decision useful. However, further studies are needed to determine whether this decision usefulness is declining over time.

3.7 THE REACTION OF PROFESSIONAL ACCOUNTING BODIES TO THE DECISION USEFULNESS APPROACH

3.7.1 The Conceptual Framework

Major professional accounting bodies have adopted the decision usefulness approach. For example, according to Chapters 1 and 3 of the IASB/FASB Conceptual Framework (2010), the objective of financial statements is to provide financial information that is "useful to present and potential investors, lenders, and other creditors about providing resources to the entity."[19]

As noted in Section 3.2, this objective, being primarily oriented to investors and other capital providers, does not include specifically the role of financial statements to report on manager stewardship. The Framework does state that investors need information about "how efficiently and effectively the entity's management and governing board... have discharged their responsibilities to use the entity's resources." However, this stewardship objective implies that the same set of statements meant to inform investors about future firm performance also serves to inform investors about manager performance. Obviously, this is true to some extent. However, the fundamental problem (Section 1.10) implies that the best performance measure to inform investors does not in general serve to best monitor and motivate manager performance. Consequently, as Dopuch and Sunder (1980) pointed out some time ago, the ability of the Framework to create a general foundation for accounting standards can be questioned.

We consider management's role in financial reporting beginning with Chapter 8. Until then, we pursue the investment implications of the decision usefulness approach. Note that decision *usefulness* implies that it is the investor who makes the decision, and that the role of financial reporting is to supply useful information for this purpose. This is the essence of the decision usefulness approach that we outlined in Section 3.2. In particular, the Framework implies that it is not the accountant's role to make investors' decisions for them.

A variety of constituencies are included in the Framework's general objective, namely present and potential investors, lenders, and other creditors. These constituencies are referred to in the Framework as **primary users**. Their use of financial information is oriented to making investment decisions. By recognizing a responsibility to report to all capital providers, the Framework adopts an **entity view** of financial reporting. That is, financial reports reflect the perspective of the firm as a whole, rather than simply that of the entity's shareholders.[20]

The question then arises, what types of information do capital providers need? The Framework states that the primary user group needs information about the "amount, timing and uncertainty" of the firm's future cash flows. This is consistent with our discussion of investor needs in Section 3.2–3.7. In particular, the reference to uncertainty implies that investors are assumed to be risk averse—as we pointed out in Section 3.4. If they were risk neutral they would not care about uncertainty.

Thus, we see that the primary decision addressed in the Framework is the investment decision in firms' shares or debt. Specifically, cash flows are *payoffs*, similar to those in the payoff table (Table 3.1) of Example 3.1. These investment decisions apply to potential investors as well as present ones. This means that financial statements must communicate useful information to the market, not just to existing investors in the firm.

Note also that the information objective is future oriented—it calls for information about "future" payoffs from investments. While the terms are somewhat different from those used in our earlier discussion of the investment decision, the Framework clearly implies that investors need future-oriented information. More specifically, this is information that helps them to assess the expected returns and risk of their investments.

How can financial statements be useful in predicting future returns? For this, it is necessary to establish some linkage between current firm performance and future prospects. Without such linkage, the decision-oriented objectives of the Framework would not be attainable.

We can see the linkage clearly, however, by drawing on the decision theory model. In particular, refer to the information system (Table 3.2) for Example 3.1. Table 3.2 provides a probabilistic relationship between current financial statement information (GN or BN) and the future-oriented states of nature (high or low performance), that will determine future investment payoffs. In effect, current financial statement information and future returns are linked via the conditional probabilities of the information system.

Consistent with the information system linkage, the Framework states (comment in brackets added):

> Consequently, existing and potential investors, lenders and other creditors need information to help them assess the prospects for future net cash inflows to an entity.... Information about a reporting entity's past [including current] financial performance...is usually helpful in predicting the entity's future returns on its economic resources.

These arguments enable the Framework to maintain that even though the financial statements report on current firm financial position and performance, this information can be useful to forward-looking investors.

Recall that under historical cost accounting, the income statement is the primary financial statement (Section 2.5.1). The Framework restores the importance of the balance sheet (comments in brackets added):

> Both types of information [i.e., balance sheet and income statement] provide useful input for decisions about providing resources to an entity.

The Framework also states that the income statement provides:

> ...information about the effects of transactions...that change a reporting entity's economic resources and claims [i.e., the balance sheet].

Defining income as the effect of transactions on the balance sheet suggests that the Framework views the balance sheet as primary.

Consistent with this changed view, the Framework envisages a different role for accruals than their matching role under historical cost accounting:

> Accrual accounting depicts the effects of transactions and other events and circumstances on a reporting entity's economic resources and claims in the periods in which those effects occur, even if the resulting cash receipts and payments occur in a different period.

In effect, the role of accruals is to include the effects of transactions on the firm's balance sheet in the periods in which those effects occur, even if the resulting cash receipts and payments occur in a different period. For example, accounts receivable, less an allowance for doubtful accounts (both are accruals) anticipates on the balance sheet the net cash proceeds to be received in future periods. While current net income includes this net amount, the primary role of the accrual is not viewed as matching costs (bad debt expense) with sales revenue. Rather, it is to provide relevant balance sheet information about the net future proceeds from accounts receivable.

The Framework also states:

> ...information about a reporting entity's economic resources and claims and changes in its economic resources and claims during a period provides a better basis for assessing the entity's past and future performance than information solely about cash receipts and payments during that period

In other words, the financial statements enable a better prediction of future cash flows than current cash flows themselves. This may seem surprising. Nevertheless, several researchers, for example, Kim and Kross (2005), support this statement empirically. For a large sample of U.S. firms taken over the period 1974–2000, they reported that the ability of current earnings to predict next period's operating cash flows exceeds that of current operating cash flows.

The Framework goes on to consider the characteristics that are necessary if financial statement information is to be useful for investor decision making. This is another crucial and delicate aspect of the whole conceptual framework: How can financial statement information be presented so as to be of maximum use to investors in predicting future returns? Once again, the answer lies in the concepts of relevance and reliability, which the Framework regards as fundamental characteristics of useful financial statements.

In Chapter 2, we defined relevant financial statements as those that give information to investors about the firm's future economic prospects. The Framework definition is consistent with ours:

> *Relevant financial information is capable of making a difference in the decisions made by users....*

Clearly, if information helps investors to evaluate future economic prospects, it can make a difference in users' decisions. The definition is also consistent with the definition of information in decision theory. Recall that information is that which has the potential to change individual decisions. In effect, evidence is not really information unless it is capable of affecting user decisions. This role of information is consistent with our use of Bayes' theorem in Example 3.1. By providing a vehicle for investors to update their prior beliefs about relevant states of nature following receipt of new information, Bayes' theorem models how information "is capable of making a difference" in user decisions.

Reliability is another desirable information characteristic. In Section 2.2, we defined reliable information as information that faithfully represents what it is intended to represent (see also Chapter 1, Note 14). The Framework definition is equivalent to ours:

> *To be useful, financial information...must faithfully represent the phenomena that it purports to represent.*

The Framework goes on to point out that to be a faithful representation, information must be complete (i.e., nothing in the valuation or description of an item that affects its faithful representation is left out), free from material error, and neutral, where neutral information is free from any bias that may affect its interpretation by the user.

The Framework does not specifically state that relevance and reliability have to be traded off. Given our conclusion in Section 2.4.4 that a tradeoff is necessary, this may seem surprising. However, the Framework does state:

> *Information must be both relevant and faithfully represented if it is to be useful.... First, identify an economic phenomenon that has the potential to be useful to users of the reporting entity's financial information. Second, identify the type of information about that phenomenon that would be most relevant if it is available and can be faithfully represented. Third, determine whether that information is available and can be faithfully represented. If so, the process of satisfying the fundamental qualitative characteristics ends at that point. If not, the process is repeated with the next most relevant type of information.*

This view implies a hurdle rate for reliability. If the hurdle is not met, relevance is reduced until faithful representation can be attained. This leaves open the unfortunate possibility that the most relevant information, combined with a level of representational faithfulness slightly less than the hurdle, has greater decision usefulness than less relevant but faithfully represented information.

However, a relevance/reliability tradeoff is implicit in this statement since repeating the process with "the next most relevant type of information" in order to attain the hurdle level of reliability clearly indicates that if reliability increases then relevance must decrease. Indeed, the existence of a tradeoff can be empirically demonstrated. For example, Bandyopadhyay, Chen, Huang, and Jha BCHJ; 2010, using a large sample of U.S. firms, measured the relevance of net income by its ability to predict future cash flow, and reliability of net income by its persistence—that is, by its ability to predict future net income.[21]

Based on these measures, BCHJ found that relevance of net income increased over their sample period (1973–2005) and that reliability decreased, clearly implying a tradeoff. BCHJ attributed these findings to increasing conservatism over the period. Conservatism increases relevance since recording writedowns currently anticipates lower cash flows in future. Conservatism decreases reliability to the extent that writedowns are subject to error and possible manager bias.

The Framework goes on to explore other desirable characteristics (called enhancing characteristics in the Framework) of useful financial statement information. One of these is **timeliness**, which is best thought of as a constraint on relevance. That is, as new events come along, a delay in information release reduces its ability to predict future cash flows.

Other desirable enhancing characteristics are comparability, verifiability, and understandability. Despite the presence of numerous impairment tests in accounting standards, as noted in Section 1.4, the Framework does not at present recognize conservatism (called prudence in the Framework) as a desirable characteristic.

It is interesting to note that the Framework states that financial reporting should include management's explanations to enable users to understand financial reports. As noted in Section 3.6, MD&A is a securities commission standard. Whether or not this Framework statement indicates a move by standard setters to include MD&A within the scope of their responsibility remains to be seen.

In 2013, the IASB issued a Discussion Paper for completion of its Conceptual Framework. Included are proposals to revise definitions of assets and liabilities. For example, the proposed asset definition is an economic resource controlled by the firm as a result of past events, and that is capable of generating inflows of benefits. This contrasts with the existing asset definition, under which an asset is essentially an expected flow of benefits. That is, under the proposed definition, the resource itself is the asset, not its expected flow of benefits. Notice that this revision is consistent with the balance sheet orientation of Chapter 1 of the Framework, as discussed earlier in this section.

The Discussion Paper goes on to consider other Framework components, such as criteria for recognizing and derecognizing assets and liabilities, measurement (i.e., historical cost v. fair value v. value in use), and other comprehensive income.

While it is premature to predict the final Framework contents, the Paper does give insights into the FASB's thinking going forward. For example, it concludes that a single measurement basis (e.g., fair value) is unlikely to provide the most relevant information for users. Rather, for assets used in the business, such as property, plant, and equipment, historical cost (subject to impairment testing) may provide more relevant information about future cash flows. This may suggest a slight backing off from the fair value orientation that, as we shall see, characterizes many current IASB standards.

3.7.2 Summary

The Framework develops the characteristics that accounting information should have in order to be useful. In essence, accounting information should provide an informative information system that links current financial statements with future state realizations and payoffs. To be useful for investment decision purposes, the financial statements need not involve a direct prediction of future firm payoffs. Rather, if the information has certain desirable characteristics, such as relevance and reliability, it can be a useful input to help investors form their own predictions of these payoffs. For maximum usefulness, the accountant must seek an appropriate tradeoff between these characteristics.

3.8 CONCLUSIONS ON DECISION USEFULNESS

Following from the pioneering ASOBAT and Trueblood Committee reports, the decision usefulness approach to financial reporting implies that accountants need to understand the decision problems of financial statement users. Single-person decision theory and its application to the portfolio investment decision provide an understanding of the needs of rational, risk averse investors. This theory tells us that such investors need information to help them assess securities' expected returns and the riskiness of these returns.

Financial statements are an important and cost effective source of information for investors, even though they do not report directly on future investment payoffs. The role of GAAP is to provide an information system that can help investors to predict future firm performance, which, in turn, helps predict future investment returns. To maximize the informativeness of the financial statements, accountants need to find the most useful trade-off between relevance and reliability, while keeping the enhancing characteristics in mind.

Management discussion and analysis (MD&A) represents an attempt to further increase the informativeness of financial reporting. Its future orientation provides increased relevance. The extent to which MD&A is actually found to be decision useful by investors is currently being investigated by accounting researchers.

Major accounting standard-setting bodies such as the IASB and FASB have adopted the decision usefulness approach. This is evidenced by their Conceptual Framework, which shows a clear recognition of the role of financial reporting in providing useful information for investors.

Questions and Problems

1. Refer to Table 3.2, the information system table for Example 3.1. Prepare a similar table for a perfect, or fully informative, information system—that is, an information system that perfectly reveals the true state of nature. Do the same for a non-informative information system—one that reveals nothing about the true state.

   Use the probabilities from the two tables you have prepared to revise state probabilities by means of Bayes' theorem, using the prior probabilities and GN message given in Example 3.1. Comment on the results.

2. What would the utility function of a risk-taking investor look like? What sort of portfolio would such an individual be likely to invest in? What information would the investor need?

3. An investor's utility function is

$$U_i(a) = 3\bar{x} - \frac{1}{2}\sigma_x^2$$

   Act a_1 has $\bar{x} = 0.88$, $\sigma_x^2 = 0.512$, yielding $U_i(a_1) = 2.384$. Act a_2 has $\bar{x} = 0.80$.

   What σ_x^2 would this act require to yield the same utility as a_1? Explain the result using the concepts of risk and expected return.

4. The Conceptual Framework states:

   Accrual accounting depicts the effects of transactions and other events and circumstances on a reporting entity's economic resources and claims in the periods in which those effects occur, even if the resulting cash receipts and payments occur in a different period. This is important because information about a reporting entity's economic resources and claims and changes in its economic resources and claims during a period provides a better basis for assessing the entity's past and future performance than information solely about cash receipts and payments during that period.

   Why do you think the standard setters argue that information about earnings based on accrual accounting provides a better prediction of the firm's present and continuing ability to generate cash flows than information limited solely to cash receipts and payments during the period?

5. In Section 3.7.1, the text refers to the study of Kim and Cross, who reported that the ability of current earnings to predict next period's operating cash flows exceeds the ability of current operating cash flows to predict next period's operating cash flows. Give an explanation for this result.

6. Give some reasons why the off-main diagonal probabilities of an information system such as that depicted in Table 3.2 are non-zero. Use the concepts of relevance and reliability in your answer. Explain why an information system is more useful the lower the off-main diagonal probabilities are.

7. Decision usefulness is an important accounting concept.

   Required

   a. State the decision usefulness approach to accounting theory.
   b. What two questions arise once the decision usefulness approach is adopted?

c. What primary constituency of financial statement users has been adopted by the Conceptual Framework as a guide to the reporting of decision useful financial information? What information does this constituency need according to the Framework?

d. What characteristics does financial accounting information need if it is to be useful to the constituency identified in part **c**?

e. Explain why information about the riskiness of securities is useful to investors.

8. Mr. Smart is an investor with $15,000 to invest. He has narrowed his choice down to two possible investments:

- Mutual fund
- Common shares in Buyme Corporation

Figure 3.5 gives a decision tree for Mr. Smart's situation. Mr. Smart is risk averse. The amount of utility he derives from a payoff is

$$\text{Utility} = 2\ln(\text{payoff})$$

where "ln" denotes natural logarithm.

Because of a planned major purchase, Mr. Smart intends to sell his investment one year later. The payoffs represent the proceeds from the sale of the investment and receipt of any dividends, net of the initial investment. The probabilities on Figure 3.5 represent Mr. Smart's prior probabilities about the state of the economy (good or bad) over the coming year.

Required

a. Calculate Mr. Smart's expected utility for each action, and indicate which action he would choose if he acted on the basis of his prior information.

b. Now, suppose Mr. Smart decides that he would like to obtain more information about the state of the economy rather than simply accepting that it is just as likely to be good as bad. He decides to take a sample of current annual reports of major corporations.

Figure 3.5 Decision Tree for Mr. Smart's Problem

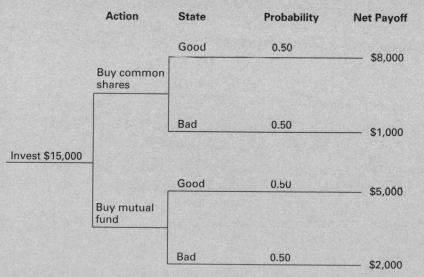

Every annual report shows that its firm is doing well, with increased profits over the previous year. The probability that there would be such healthy profits if the state of the economy actually was good is 0.75. The probability of such healthy profits is only 0.10 if the state of the economy actually was bad.

Use Bayes' theorem to calculate Mr. Smart's posterior probabilities of the high and low states of the economy. Will he change his decision?

Note: Round your calculations to two decimal places.

9. John Save plans to invest $5,000 in one of the following instruments:

■ Bonds of J Ltd., yielding 12% (a_1)
■ Canada Savings Bonds, yielding 8% (a_2)

On the basis of his knowledge of current economic conditions and the outlook for the industry of J Ltd., John assesses the prior probability that J Ltd. will go bankrupt as 0.05. If this happens, John will lose both principal and interest and receive no money at the end of the year. If J Ltd. does not go bankrupt, John plans to sell the bonds, plus interest, at the end of one year.

John assesses the probability that the Canada Savings Bonds will fail to pay off as zero. John also plans to sell these, plus interest, one year later.

John is risk averse and decides to choose the investment that yields the highest expected utility. Assume that John's utility for an amount of $x is given by $\sqrt{x}$, where x is the *gross* payoff.

Required

a. On the basis of his prior probabilities, which investment should John choose?
b. Rather than choosing on the basis of his prior probabilities, assume that John decides to analyze the current financial statements of J Ltd. These financial statements can look "good" (G) or "bad" (B). After his analysis, John realizes that the statements look good. On the basis of his extensive understanding of financial statement analysis, he knows that the probability that the financial statements would look good given that the firm was actually heading for bankruptcy is 0.10:

$$\text{Prob}(G|S_1) = 0.10$$

where S_1 denotes the state of heading for bankruptcy.

Similarly, John knows that

$$\text{Prob}(G|S_2) = 0.80$$

where S_2 denotes the state of not heading for bankruptcy.

Which investment should John now take? Explain why. Use Bayes' theorem.

10. "It is possible to reduce risk in a portfolio by diversification."

Required

a. Do you agree with this statement? Explain why or why not.
b. Can the risk of a portfolio be reduced to zero by diversification? Explain.

11. Marie has $1,000 that she wishes to invest for one year. She has narrowed her choices down to one of the following two actions:

a_1: Buy bonds of Risky Mining Ltd. These pay 14.4% interest, unless Risky goes bankrupt, in which case Marie will lose her principal and interest.

a_2: Buy savings bonds, paying 6.4% interest.

Marie assesses her prior probability of Risky Mining Ltd. going bankrupt as 0.40. The savings bonds will pay off regardless of whether Risky goes bankrupt or not. Marie's utility for money is given by the square root of the amount of her *gross* payoff. That is, if she buys the savings bonds her gross payoff is $1,064, etc. Marie is a rational decision maker.

Required

a. Based on her prior probabilities, which action should Marie take? Show your calculations.

b. Before making a final decision, Marie decides she needs more information. She obtains Risky Mining's current financial statements and examines its debt–equity ratio. This ratio can be either "HI" or "LO." Upon calculating the ratio, Marie observes that it is LO. On the basis of her prior experience in bond investments, Marie knows the following conditional probabilities:

Future State	Debt-to-Equity Ratio	
	LO	HI
NB (Not Bankrupt)	0.50	0.50
B (Bankrupt)	0.05	0.95

Which action should Marie now take? Show your calculations, taken to two decimal places.

c. A new accounting standard requires that Risky Mining Ltd.'s pension liabilities must now be measured in the financial statements at their expected discounted present values (i.e., value in use), instead of the previous pay-as-you-go accounting under which pension expense was based on amounts paid out for pensions during the period with no balance sheet liability recorded.

Evaluate (in words only) the likely impact of the new standard on the main diagonal probabilities of the information system in part **b.**

12. Lucas has $2,000 that he wishes to invest for one year. He has narrowed his choices down to one of the following two actions:

a_1: Buy bonds of X Ltd., a company that has a very high debt–equity ratio. These bonds pay 8% interest, unless X defaults, in which case Lucas will receive no interest but will recover his principal.

a_2: Buy Government Savings Bonds, paying 3% interest.

Lucas assesses his prior probability of X Ltd. defaulting as 0.45, and of the savings bonds defaulting as zero. His utility for money is given by the square root of the amount of his net payoff. That is, if he buys the savings bonds his net payoff is $60, yielding utility of $\sqrt{60} = 7.75$, etc. Lucas is a rational decision maker.

Required

a. Based on his prior probabilities, which action should Lucas take? Show your calculations.

b. Before making a final decision, Lucas decides he needs more information. He obtains X Ltd's current financial statements and examines its times-interest-earned ratio. This ratio can be either "HI" or "LO." Upon calculating the ratio, Lucas observes that it is HI. On the basis of his prior experience in bond investments, Lucas knows the following conditional probabilities:

	Times Interest Earned Ratio	
Future State	**LO**	**HI**
ND (no default)	0.40	0.60
D (default)	0.10	0.90

Which action should Lucas now take? Show your calculations, taken to two decimal places.

c. An accounting standard allows X Ltd. to value its property, plant, and equipment at fair value providing this can be done reliably. The company plans to adopt this option, since it will reduce its debt–equity ratio.

Evaluate (in words only) the likely impact of this adoption on the main diagonal probabilities of the information system in part **b**.

13. Ajay is a rational, risk averse investor with $5,000 to invest for one year. He has decided to invest this amount in a high-technology firm and has narrowed his choice down to either AB Ltd. or XY Ltd. AB is a highly speculative firm with good prospects but no established products. XY is a well-established firm with stable performance. The payoffs (net of amount invested) for each firm depend on its next year's performance, as follows:

		Return	
		AB Ltd.	**XY Ltd.**
	High	$1,089	$324
Next Year's Performance			
	Low	$ 0	$196

For each firm, Ajay assesses prior probabilities of 0.5 for each of the high- and low-performance states. His utility for his investment return is equal to the square root of the amount of net payoff received.

Required

a. On the basis of his prior probabilities, should Ajay invest in AB Ltd., (a_1), or XY Ltd. (a_2)? Show calculations.

b. XY Ltd. has just released its annual report. Ajay decides to analyze it before investing. His analysis shows "good news" (GN). He consults Al, an expert in financial reporting standards who is quite critical of the quality of current GAAP. Al advises that, based on current GAAP, the information system for firms' annual reports is as follows:

		Financial Statement Information	
		GN	BN
Next Year's Performance	High	0.6	0.4
	Low	0.5	0.5

The annual report of AB Ltd. is not due for some time, and nothing else has happened to cause Ajay to change his prior probabilities of AB's next year performance. Which investment should Ajay make now? Show calculations.

c. Concerned by several recent financial reporting failures, the accounting standard setters decide to act. They quickly introduce several new accounting standards, including tighter controls over revenue recognition and greater conservatism in asset valuation. Also, the securities commission introduces new corporate governance regulations and restrictions on the ability of auditors to engage in non-audit services for their clients. Al advises Ajay that the information system for annual reports following these new standards and regulations is as follows:

		Financial Statement Information	
		GN	BN
Next Year's Performance	High	0.8	0.2
	Low	0.2	0.8

Al advises Ajay to ignore the information system in part **b** and instead use this one to revise his prior probabilities of XY Ltd.'s next year's performance based on the GN in its annual report. AB Ltd. still has not reported and Ajay's prior probabilities of its performance are unchanged. Which act should Ajay now take? Show calculations.

14. You are an expert on financial statement analysis and the quality of financial reporting, with extensive experience in rational investing. You determine that the current quality of financial reporting is summarized in the following information system:

The states of nature refer to future performance of CG Ltd., of which you are a shareholder. GN (good news) and BN (bad news) summarize the information content of current financial statements.

CG Ltd. has just released its quarterly financial report. You analyze this report, and decide that it shows GN. Your decision problem is to sell your shares now (a_1) or hold them for another quarter (a_2).

		Financial Statement Information	
		GN	BN
State of Nature	High	0.8	0.2
	Low	0.1	0.9

Your prior probability of the high state is 0.7. The current market value of your CG Ltd. shares is $81. If CG is in the high state, you are sure that your shares will be worth $100 if you sell at the end of the next quarter. If CG is in the low state, you are sure that your shares will then be worth $36. You are risk averse, with utility equal to the square root of your sale proceeds.

Required

a. What information is included in your prior probabilities? Are they subjective or objective? Why?

b. Are the information system probabilities subjective or objective? What determines these probabilities?

c. Should you sell or hold your CG shares? Show calculations.

15. Bill plans to invest $50,000 in the shares of Company Q (act a_1) or the same amount in shares of Company W (act a_2) for 1 year.

Bill, who is a rational investor, identifies two states of nature:

State H: The company expects high future cash flows.

State L: The company expects low future cash flows.

On the basis of his information to date about each firm, Bill assesses the following subjective prior state probabilities (i.e., the same probabilities for each company):

State H: 0.8

State L: 0.2

The following is the payoff table for these two investments. Payoffs are net of (i.e., they exclude) the original investment.

Bill is risk averse, with utility equal to the square root of the amount of net payoff received.

Required

a. On the basis of his prior probabilities, which act should Bill take? Show calculations.

b. Instead of acting now, Bill decides to obtain more information by careful reading of each company's Management Discussion and Analysis (MD&A), from their latest annual reports. He plans to focus on their discussions of risks and uncertainties, in conjunction with their discussions of future prospects. He knows that careful evaluation of the quality of these discussions will provide inside evidence of the companies' future cash flow expectations. That is, companies with high expectations will tend to provide better disclosure.

Act		State	
		H	L
	a_1	$5,000	$2,000
	a_2	$5,250	$1,000

Bill knows, however, that MD&A is not a perfect predictor. Some firms that expect high future performance may disguise their optimism by poor disclosure to reduce the probability that new competitors will be attracted to the industry.

Conversely, some firms that expect low future performance may provide excellent disclosure. They do this to reduce investor concerns that the firm may be trying to hide poor performance, thereby reducing the "hit" to their share price when the poor performance prospects become known.

Bill, who is an expert on GAAP and current MD&A guidelines, knows that these possibilities are summarized by the following information system.

		Current MD&A Evidence	
		Good disclosure	Poor disclosure
State	H	0.8	0.2
	L	0.3	0.7

Upon reading the current MD&As, Bill finds that Company Q has good disclosure and Company W has poor disclosure.

Which act, a_1 or a_2, should Bill take now? Show calculations.

c. Bill tells you about his decision. You respond by suggesting that he should perhaps have bought some of both Company Q and Company W shares. Explain why you make this suggestion. Calculations not required.

16. Sonja, a rational investor, has $2,000 to invest for one year while she completes her professional accounting designation. She is contemplating investing the full amount in shares of Northern Oil & Gas Ltd. (a_1) or in a risk-free government bond yielding an annual return of 3.2% (a_2).

Sonja identifies two states of nature:
State H: Northern has high future cash flow.
State L: Northern has low future cash flow.

On the basis of her prior information about Northern, Sonja assesses the following subjective prior state probabilities:

State H: 0.4
State L: 0.6

The following is the payoff table for these two investments. Payoffs from Northern shares include dividends and estimated capital gain for the year. Capital gain is based on the average analyst forecast for Northern's share price. Payoffs are net of (i.e., they exclude) the original investment.

		State	
		H	L
	a_1	$484	$25
Act			
	a_2	$64	$64

The investor is risk averse, with utility equal to the square root of the net dollar payoff.

Required

a. On the basis of her prior probabilities, which act should Sonja take? Show calculations.

b. Instead of acting now, Sonja decides to obtain more information about Northern by reading its annual report. She knows that financial statements are based on a mixed measurement model. Also, she is a student of financial accounting theory, and estimates the quality of financial statements prepared according to these standards by the following information system:

		Current Annual Report Evidence	
		Good	Bad
	H	0.7	0.3
State			
	L	0.1	0.9

Good evidence means that a company reports profits that are higher than the average analyst forecast. Bad evidence means that the company's profits are less than forecast.
Upon reading the current annual report, Sonja finds it is good. Which act should Sonja take now? Show calculations.

c. After buying the Northern shares, Sonja is disappointed to note that the market price of its shares begins to fall, despite the good news in its earnings report. She now suspects that the good news in Northern's financial statements was not as good as she originally believed. Is this possible? Give reasons why or why not.

17. The following problem is designed to encourage your consideration of Bayes' theorem. It shows how unaided judgment about probabilities can often be far off the mark. The problem is adapted from one appearing in an article in *The Economist*, "Getting the goat," February 20, 1999, p. 72. This article discusses how people who guess at probabilities can frequently be wrong:

A disease is present in the population at the rate of one person per thousand. A test for the disease becomes available. The drug company that is marketing the test randomly selects you to take the test. You agree, and the test results are positive. If the disease is present, the test always shows a positive result. However, the test has a 5% probability of showing a positive result when in fact the disease is not present. What is the probability that you have the disease?

Notes

1. As mentioned in Section 1.2, decision usefulness was the focus of the 1966 AAA monograph, *A Statement of Basic Accounting Theory (ASOBAT)*.

2. The Trueblood Commission was a study group of the American Institute of Certified Public Accountants, which, in its 1973 report, *Objectives of Financial Statements*, accepted the decision usefulness approach of *ASOBAT*. The significance of this acceptance is that the AICPA is a professional accounting body, whereas the AAA is an association of academics.

3. For a formal development of the concepts of decision theory, including utility theory, the information system, and the value of information, see Laffont (1989), especially Chapters 1, 2, and 4. See also Demski (1972), especially Chapters 1 to 3. For an excellent intuitive development of the theory, see Raiffa (1968).

4. Some theorists distinguish between risk and uncertainty. When the underlying parameters generating a random outcome are known, the decision maker faces risk. When the parameters are not known, he/she faces uncertainty. Thus, when flipping a fair coin, the decision maker faces risk. If the coin is not known to be fair, he/she faces uncertainty.

   We do not use this distinction in this text, and use risk and uncertainty interchangeably. We do distinguish, however, between objective and subjective probabilities. If we did distinguish between risk and uncertainty, an investor faces risk if the probabilities of the outcome are objective (i.e., ideal conditions), and faces uncertainty if they are subjective (actual conditions).

5. For a risk averse investor, the riskier an investment, the higher must be its expected return to compensate. This implies that Bill's utility is a concave function, such as the square root, of the payoff. We define utility here in terms of the net payoff. Conceptually, utility should be defined in terms of the investor's total wealth. However, we opt for the simplest presentation in this example. Note also that the payoff for square root utility must be positive. If a negative (net) payoff is possible, we could work with gross payoffs or assume some other measure of utility, such as the log of the payoff.

6. A possible alternative would be to diversify—that is, buy some of each type of security. We will rule this out for now by assuming that the brokerage fees for buying small amounts are prohibitive. Diversification is briefly considered in Section 3.5.

7. While the decision maker's prior and posterior probabilities are subjective, the information system probabilities are usually assumed to be objective in decision theory. For the distinction between objective and subjective probabilities, see the discussion in Example 2.2. However, see also Note 9.

8. While, as noted in Section 3.3.1, the information system probabilities depend on GAAP, GAAP affects different firms differently. For example, since research costs are expensed under GAAP, reported earnings of a research intensive firm are forced down relative to those of a firm that conducts no research. Thus, the same amount of reported earnings have different implications for future firm performance for the two firms, leading to different information system probabilities. Also managers can choose different accounting policies within GAAP, or even in violation of GAAP. For example, a manager may choose accounting policies to maximize reported earnings, perhaps to enhance his/her reputation. Another manager, concerned about potential competition, may choose accounting policies to lower reported earnings. Again, their firms' information system probabilities will differ even though they are both subject to the same GAAP.

Thus, when we say that information system probabilities depend on GAAP, it should be realized that these probabilities incorporate the effects of differences in accounting across industries and in the quality of the firm's corporate governance, which affects the extent to which managers may opportunistically manage the financial statements for their own purposes.

9. The rational expectations assumption need not be interpreted as literally true. It can be interpreted as the end result (in this case, the correct values of information system probabilities) as individuals learn the unknown parameter values through experience, assuming these values stay constant. Also, a rational expectations assumption with respect to the information system is not necessary. Bill could asses a joint prior probability distribution on the states of nature and the information system probabilities, where the state of nature is interpreted as the mean of the distribution of future firm performance, and the information system is interpreted as the variance. Observation of X Ltd.'s financial statements over time can then be interpreted as a sample providing information about both mean and variance. With each observation, Bill updates his prior probabilities of both. Our assumption that the information system is known is primarily for simplicity.

10. As discussed in Note 8, care must be taken in classifying firms as GN or BN, since firms differ in their characteristics, such as industry and accounting policies used. In addition to research intensity, other innate characteristics relevant to classifying firms as GN or BN include size, capital structure, volatility of environment, and the presence of intangibles.

11. Strictly speaking, choosing the act that maximizes expected utility is a *consequence* of rationality, not rationality itself. Savage (1954) defines a set of axioms of rational behaviour under uncertainty with subjective probabilities. If an individual behaves according to these axioms, it can be shown that that individual will prefer one act to another if and only if its expected utility is higher than the other, where the expectation is with respect to the individual's subjective state probabilities. See, for example, Laffont (1989, pp. 14–17) for a demonstration.

12. For a formal development and analysis of risk aversion, see Pratt (1964), or Laffont (1989), Chapter 2.

13. The expected payoff is

$$(0.7 \times \$200) + (0.3 \times \$1{,}133.33) = \$480$$

Expected utility is

$$(0.7 \times \sqrt{200}\,) + (0.3 \times \sqrt{1{,}133.33} = (0.7 \times 14.14) + (0.3 \times 33.66)$$
$$= 9.90 + 10.10$$
$$= 20$$

14. Since the presence of economy-wide factors increases the probabilities of (Hi, Hi) and (Lo, Lo) relative to independence, the probabilities for these high/low payoff realizations must therefore decrease relative to independence, as shown in the table.

15. This is subject to the condition that none of the securities' returns is perfectly correlated. If they were, this would be the same as buying more of the same security.

16. The sample size is so large that these conditional probabilities are almost certainly objective, as assumed by Bayes' theorem—see Note 7.

17. The score is adjusted for MD&A length, since longer documents have a higher probability that the same word will reappear.

18. While statistically significant, the magnitude of investor reaction is small relative to other financial information, such as earnings. Note, however, that due to MD&A's lack of timeliness, other financial information, such as earnings announcements and management conference calls, is available, thereby reducing investor reaction to MD&A itself.

19. Statement of Financial Accounting Concepts No. 1 (1978) (SFAC1), the original conceptual framework, is also consistent with the decision usefulness approach. A difference from the IASB/FASB Framework, however, is its use of the term "rational" decisions, providing additional linkage with the theory of rational decision making. Removal of the term "rational" in the joint Framework is presumably due to theory and evidence suggesting that individuals may not be as fully "rational" as the theory assumes. We shall review this theory and evidence in Chapter 6.

20. The entity view contrasts with the **proprietorship view,** under which the income statement is geared to the firm's common shareholders.

21. The authors point out that to the extent current net income is unreliable, it contains errors and biases. These errors and biases will reverse in future periods, thereby reducing the correlation between current and future net incomes. That is, current earnings do not persist if they are unreliable.

Chapter 4
Efficient Securities Markets

Figure 4.1 Organization of Chapter 4

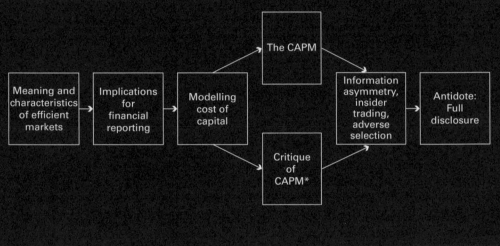

4.1 OVERVIEW

In this chapter, we consider the implications of rational investor behaviour for securities markets. The theory of efficient securities markets predicts that the security prices that result have some appealing properties. In essence, these prices "fully reflect" the collective knowledge and information-processing expertise of investors. The process by which prices do this is complex and not fully understood. Nevertheless, the general outlines of the process are easy to see, and we shall concentrate on these.

Securities market efficiency has important implications for financial accounting. One implication is that it leads directly to the concept of *full disclosure*. Efficiency implies that it is the information content of disclosure, not the form or location of disclosure itself, that is valued by the market. If so, information can be released as easily in notes and supplementary disclosures as in the financial statements proper. The theory also affects how the accountant should think about reporting on firm risk.

In efficient markets theory, accounting is viewed as being in competition with other information sources such as news media, financial analysts, and even market price itself. As a vehicle for informing investors, accounting will survive only if it is useful, timely, and cost effective relative to other sources.

Efficient securities market theory also alerts us to the primary reason for the existence of accounting, namely information asymmetry. When some persons have inside information, the adverse selection problem arises, leading to pressure to find mechanisms, such as financial reporting, by which investors with information disadvantage are protected from possible exploitation by the better informed. Efficient securities market theory is a good place to start when considering the effects on security prices when investors are concerned about inside information. We can then think of accounting as a mechanism to enable communication of useful information from inside the firm to outside. In addition to enabling better investor decisions, this has social benefits through better working securities markets.

As mentioned in Section 1.2, accounting theorists began to realize the importance of securities market efficiency in the late 1960s. Since that time, the theory has guided much accounting research and has had major implications for accounting practice. While, in this chapter, we outline the properties of a fully efficient securities market and their implications for accountants, it should be emphasized that efficiency is a *model* of how a securities market operates. Like any model, it does not capture the full complexity of such a market. Thus, the relevant question is *the degree of efficiency*—that is, how close are actual markets to the full efficiency ideal? Indeed, past years have seen numerous questions about whether the average investor, whose behaviour underlies market efficiency, is as rational as the model assumes, and increasing evidence questioning market efficiency itself. These questions have heightened following the 2007–2008 market meltdowns (Section 1.3).

Alternate theories of how securities markets operate are examined in Chapter 6, where we conclude that while actual securities markets are not fully efficient, they are generally close enough that accountants can be guided by efficiency implications and the rational decision theory underlying them. We also conclude that to the extent securities markets are not fully efficient, this further increases the importance of financial reporting. Despite these conclusions, it is apparent that securities markets can depart substantially from efficiency in periods of liquidity pricing, such as during the 2007–2008 market meltdowns. We discuss liquidity pricing in Chapter 7.

Figure 4.1 outlines the organization of this chapter.

4.2 EFFICIENT SECURITIES MARKETS

4.2.1 The Meaning of Efficiency

In Chapter 3, we studied the optimal investment decisions of a rational investor. Now consider what happens when this rationality describes the average[1] behaviour of all investors interacting in a securities market. Our interest is in the characteristics of the market prices of securities traded in the market and how these prices are affected by new information.

If information were free, it is apparent that investors would want to take advantage of it. For instance, under the ideal conditions of Example 2.2, investors would want to know which state of nature was realized, since this affects the future share price and dividends of the firm. By assumption, information is free under ideal conditions since state realization is publicly observable. Thus, all investors would use this information, and the process of arbitrage, under which investors would quickly buy or sell securities that did not fully reflect this information, ensures that the market value of the firm then adjusts to reflect the revised cash flow expectations that result, as illustrated in Example 2.2.

Unfortunately, information is not free under non-ideal conditions. Investors have to decide how much accounting expertise and information to acquire, and then to form their own subjective estimates of firms' future performance. Furthermore, these estimates will need revision as new information comes along. Each investor then faces a cost–benefit tradeoff with respect to how much information to gather. There is a variety of relevant information sources—the financial press, tips from friends and associates, changes in economic conditions, advice from analysts and advisors, etc. We can think of rational investors as continuously revising their subjective state probabilities as such information is received. From our standpoint, a major source of cost effective information is careful analysis of quarterly and annual reports. Probability revision arising from financial statement information was illustrated in Example 3.1.

At least some investors spend considerable time and money to use these information sources to guide their investment decisions. Such expert investors are called **informed**. Bill Cautious, in Example 3.1, is an example of such an investor.

It should be apparent that informed investors will want to move *quickly* upon receipt of new information. If they do not, other investors will get there first, and the market value of the security in question will adjust so as to reduce or eliminate the benefit of the new information.

When a sufficient number of investors behave this way, the market becomes efficient. There are several definitions of an efficient securities market. The definition that we shall use here is the semi-strong form, from Fama (1970).

> An *efficient securities market* is one where the prices of securities traded on that market at all times fully reflect all information that is publicly known about those securities.

This form of efficiency contrasts with **strong form efficiency**, under which security prices reflect *all* information, not just information that is publicly available. As a practical matter, it is unlikely that a share price could reflect strong form efficiency, due to the high cost of eliminating all inside information. In future, when we refer to market efficiency, we mean semi-strong efficiency.

Four points about efficiency are particularly noteworthy. First, market prices are efficient with respect to *publicly known* information. Thus, the definition does not rule out the possibility of inside information. Persons who possess inside information, in effect, know more than the market. If they wish to take advantage of their inside information, insiders may be able to earn excess profits on their investments at the expense of outsiders. This is because the market prices of these investments, reflecting only outside or publicly available information, do not incorporate the knowledge that insiders possess. Not every insider is "bad," of course. Some managers may seek ways to credibly communicate their inside information to the market, perhaps to bolster their firms' share price and their reputations. Nevertheless, investors will still be worried about the *possibility* of insider trading.

A second, related point is that market efficiency is a *relative* concept. The market is efficient relative to a stock of publicly available information. There is nothing in the definition to suggest that the market is omniscient and that market prices always reflect real underlying value. For example, during the months leading up to the 2007–2008 market meltdowns, market prices of asset-backed securities and the firms that issued them seriously overstated their real value in retrospect. The important question for semi-strong efficiency, however, is whether securities prices reflected *publicly available* information leading up to the meltdown.

The definition of efficiency does imply, however, that once new or corrected information becomes publicly available, the market price will quickly adjust to it. This adjustment occurs because rational investors will scramble to revise their beliefs about future performance as soon as new information, from whatever source, becomes known. As a result, the expected returns and risk of their existing portfolios will change and they will enter the market to restore their optimal risk–return tradeoffs. The resulting buy/sell decisions will quickly change security prices to fully reflect the new information.

A third implication is that investing is a **fair game** if the market is efficient. This means that investors cannot expect to earn excess returns on a security, or portfolio of securities, over and above the normal expected return on that security or portfolio, where the normal expected return allows for risk. One way to establish a normal return benchmark is by means of a capital asset pricing model, as will be illustrated in Section 4.5.

Finally, given market efficiency, a security's market price should fluctuate randomly over time. That is, there should be no serial correlation of share returns. Thus, if a firm reports good news today, its share price should rise to reflect this news the same day. If, in the absence of any further news, its price continues to rise during succeeding days, this is evidence of inefficiency. The reason why price fluctuations are random is that anything about firm value that can be *expected*, such as the seasonal nature of its business, the retirement of its chief executive, or the expected profit on a major new contract, will be fully reflected in its security price by the efficient market as soon as the expectation is formed. That is, the market's expectation of the effect of such events on the value of the firm is on average *unbiased*. The only reason that prices will change again is if some relevant but *unexpected* information comes along. By definition, unexpected events occur randomly. For example, an accident may change the expected profit on a contract, and the firm's share price will quickly respond to reflect this random event. Thus, if we examine the time series formed by the sequence of price changes for a particular security, this series should fluctuate randomly over time. A time series that exhibits such serially uncorrelated behaviour is sometimes called a **random walk**.[2]

4.2.2 How Do Market Prices Fully Reflect All Available Information?

We now consider *how* market prices can fully reflect all available information. This process is by no means obvious. As described previously, rational, informed investors will demand information about securities. However, there is no guarantee that even rational individuals will react identically to the same information. For example, they may have different prior beliefs. Some may have superior expertise to analyze financial statement information. In a sense, the decision theory model is like an automobile. It provides a vehicle to process information, but nothing guarantees that everyone's driving habits are identical or that they all take the same route to a destination.

As a result, it is quite likely that different investors will react to the same information differently, even though they all proceed rationally. Yet, investors interact in a market, each making buy/sell decisions about various securities. Since the market price of a security is the result of the demand for and supply of the security by investors, how can the market price fully reflect all available information when the individuals making the demand and supply decisions are different?

An interesting insight into this question can be gained from an example in Beaver (1981, p. 162, Table 6-1). The example relates to forecasting the results of football games. The *Chicago Daily News*, during 1966–1968, printed weekly the predictions of each of its sports staff as to who would win that weekend's college football games. Table 4.1, taken from Beaver, summarizes the outcomes of these predictions.

Table 4.1 Forecasting Outcomes of Football Games

	1966	1967	1968
Total forecasters (including consensus)	15	15	16
Total forecasts made per forecaster	180	220	219
Rank of consensus*	1 (tie)	2	2
Median rank of forecasters	8	8	8.5
Rank of best forecasters:			
J. Carmichael (1966)	1 (tie)	8	16
D. Nightingale (1966)	1 (tie)	11	5
A. Biondo (1967)	7	1	6
H. Duck (1968)	8	10	1

*When all three years are combined, the consensus outperforms every one of the forecasters (that is, ranks first).

Source: William H. Beaver, *Financial Reporting: An Accounting Revolution*® 1981, p. 162, Table 6-1. Reprinted by permission of Prentice-Hall Inc., Upper Saddle River, New Jersey. Data are from "Here's How Our Staff Picks 'Em," as published in the *Chicago Sun-Times*. Courtesy of Chicago Sun-Times.

Note the following points from Table 4.1. First, there were a number of different forecasters (15 or 16) and a large number of forecasts were made (619 over the three years). Second, no one individual forecaster dominated in terms of forecasting ability. The best forecasters in 1966 were well down the list in subsequent years, and vice versa. Third, note the consistent performance of the consensus forecast. The consensus forecast was also published weekly by the *Chicago Daily News* and, for each game, consisted of the team favoured to win by the majority of those forecasting. It is clear that the consensus forecast has a quality that transcends the forecasting ability of the individual forecasters from which the consensus is derived.

To translate the example into a securities market context, we can think of the forecasters as investors in a security and the forecasts as their various buy/sell decisions. The consensus forecast is analogous to the market price, since it is a type of average of the various individual forecasting decisions.

Theory in Practice 4.1

Prof. Burton Malkiel, in his 1973 book *A Random Walk Down Wall Street*, argued that randomly throwing darts at a list of shares traded on the New York Stock Exchange would earn just as high a return as the returns earned by professional money managers. His argument drew on efficient markets theory, which predicts that, since share price always fully reflects all publicly available information, there are no "bargain" stocks (i.e., investing is a fair game). Then, professional money managers cannot do better than a strategy of random stock choice.

During the 1990s, *The Wall Street Journal* tested this argument. It sponsored a monthly series of contests, whereby four investment analysts each picked a favoured stock. The return on each stock over the next six months was tallied and compared with the return on a randomly chosen stock for the same period. For the first 100 contests, the pros earned an average six-month return of 10.9% while the darts earned a 4.5% return. The average six-month return of the Dow Jones index was 6.8%.

When asked to explain these results, Prof. Malkiel defended the efficiency theory, arguing that the results could be explained by risk differences—if the pros picked riskier than average stocks, we would expect them to earn higher returns over time. He also pointed out that stock market performance during the 1990s was driven by very large firms. But, since there are many more relatively small firms on the market than large firms, the probability that a randomly thrown dart would pick a small firm was quite high. Also, as investors learned of the stocks picked by the pros they would revise upward their opinions of these stocks. The resulting increase in demand would raise their prices and returns relative to the randomly chosen stocks.

While not mentioned by Malkiel, it is also possible that the pros had access to inside information. Regulation FD of the SEC, which prohibits managers from disclosing information to analysts before disclosing it to the general public, did not come into effect until 2000. Regulation FD is discussed in Section 13.4.

The rationale behind the example is not hard to see. It appears that the differences in forecasting ability of individual forecasters tend to cancel out when the consensus is formed, leaving a "market price" that outperforms the ability of any of the market participants.

Of course, just because a consensus forecast outperforms individual forecasters of football games does not by itself mean that the same phenomenon carries over to security prices. Essentially, what is required is that investors' estimates of security values must on average be unbiased. That is, the market does not systematically misinterpret the valuation implications of a stock of information, but rather puts a valuation on securities that is correct or unbiased. As mentioned, this does not mean that any individual investor will necessarily be correct, but it does mean that *on average* the market uses all available information. This averaging process underlies the term "fully reflects" in the definition of securities market efficiency given earlier.

It should be emphasized that this argument assumes that individual decisions are independent, so that individual differences cancel out in their effect on price. If this is not the case, efficiency arguments break down.[3] Thus, if our football forecasters got together to work out and agree on a consensus forecast, their forecasts would not be independent if they reflected the views of, say, a dominant and persuasive member of the group. Similarly, if a sufficient number of investors were to display a collective bias in their reaction to new information about a firm, the resulting share price would be biased. For example, a firm may have reported a pattern of increasing earnings. If investors expect future earnings growth to continue simply because of growth in the past, share price **momentum** may develop. Then, share prices may be "too high," being driven by past price increases rather than by rational evaluation of information by independent investors. We will return to this point in Chapter 6, where we discuss whether securities markets are fully efficient.

4.2.3 Summary

In an efficient securities market, prices fully reflect all available information, and the price changes on such a market will behave randomly over time. Efficiency is defined relative to a stock of information. If this stock of information is incomplete, say due to inside information, or wrong, then security prices will be wrong. Thus, market efficiency does not guarantee that security prices fully reflect real firm value. It does suggest, however, that prices are unbiased relative to publicly available information and will react quickly to new or revised information.

The quantity and quality of publicly available information will be enhanced by timely reporting and full disclosure. However, individual investors may have different prior beliefs and/or may interpret the same information differently. Nevertheless, roughly speaking, we can think of these differences as averaging out, so that the market price has superior quality to the quality of the information processing of the individuals trading on the market. This argument assumes, however, that investors evaluate new information independently.

4.3 IMPLICATIONS OF EFFICIENT SECURITIES MARKETS FOR FINANCIAL REPORTING

4.3.1 Implications

An early examination of the reporting implications of efficient securities markets appeared in an article by W. H. Beaver, "What Should Be the FASB's Objectives?" (1973). Beaver was writing to explain to practicing accountants some of the implications of what was, at the time, a new theory. Here, we will outline Beaver's arguments.

According to Beaver, the first major implication is that accounting policies adopted by firms do not affect their security prices, as long as these policies have no differential cash flow effects, the particular policies used are disclosed, and sufficient information is given so that the reader can convert across different policies. Thus, Beaver would regard accounting policy choices such as, say, straight-line versus declining balance amortization of capital assets as having only "paper" effects. The policy chosen will affect reported net income, but will not directly affect future cash flows and dividends. In particular, the amount of income tax the firm must pay will not be affected by its amortization policy choice since tax departments have their own ways of allowing many deductions from income, independent of how the firm accounts for them on its books. If investors are interested in future cash flows and dividends and their impact on security returns, and if choosing between accounting policies does not directly influence these variables, the firm's choice between accounting policies should not matter.

The efficient market argument is that as long as firms disclose their selected policy and any additional information needed to convert from one method to another, the market can see through to the ultimate cash flow and dividend implications regardless of which accounting policy is actually used for reporting. In effect, the efficient market is not "fooled" by differing accounting policies when comparing different firms' securities. This suggests that management should not care about which particular accounting policies they use as long as those policies have no direct cash flow effects.

We thus see that full disclosure extends to disclosure of the firm's accounting policies. This is recognized by standard setters. For example, IAS 1 states that a complete set of financial statements includes disclosure of accounting policies.

A second implication follows—namely, efficient securities markets go hand in hand with full disclosure. If a firm's management possesses relevant information about the firm and if this can be disclosed at little or no cost, management should then disclose this information on a timely basis unless it is certain that the information is already known to investors from other sources. More generally, management should develop and report information about the firm as long as the benefits to investors exceed the costs. The reasons are twofold. First, market efficiency implies that investors will use all available information about the firm as they strive to improve their predictions of future returns, so that additional information will not be wasted. Second, the more information a firm discloses about itself, the greater is investors' confidence in the working of the securities market, since there is less inside information to worry about.

Third, market efficiency implies that firms should not be overly concerned about the naïve investor—that is, financial statement information need not be presented in a manner so simple that everyone can understand it. The reasoning, from Fama (1970), is that if *enough* investors understand the disclosed information, the market price of a firm's shares is the same as it would be if all investors understood it. This is because informed investors will engage in buy/sell decisions on the basis of the disclosed information, moving the market price toward its efficient level. Also, naïve investors can hire their own experts, such as financial analysts or investment fund managers, to interpret the information for them, or can mimic the buy/sell decisions of informed investors. As a result, any information advantage that informed investors have is quickly arbitraged away. In other words, naïve investors can trust the efficient market to price securities so that they always reflect all that is publicly known about the firms that have issued them, even though these investors may not have complete knowledge and understanding themselves. This is referred to as investors being **price-protected** by the efficient market.

Since Beaver's paper, accountants have recognized that there is a variety of reasons for trading securities. For example, some investors may make a rational decision to rely on market price as a good indicator of future payoffs, rather than incur the costs of becoming informed. Others may trade for a variety of non-portfolio reasons—perhaps an unexpected need for cash has arisen. Consequently, "naïve" may not be the best word to describe uninformed investors. This is considered further in Section 4.4.

A final implication is that accountants are in competition with other providers of information, such as websites and other media, disclosures by management, and various financial institutions. That is, belief revision is a continuous process, as pointed out in Section 3.3.3. Thus, if accountants do not provide useful, cost-effective information, the role of the accounting function will decline over time as other information sources take over—accountants have no inherent right to survive in the competitive marketplace for information. However, survival will be more likely if accountants recognize that the ultimate responsibility of their profession is to society. This longer-run point of view is encouraged by standards that promote useful information, by penalties for individuals who abuse public trust for short-term gain, and by encouragement of ethical behaviour.

Beaver's paper was published in 1973. It illustrates the early enthusiasm of accounting theorists for efficient securities markets. It also highlights the concept of decision usefulness that underlies the Conceptual Framework, discussed in Section 3.7.

4.3.2 Summary

Beaver argued that securities market efficiency has several implications for financial reporting. First, managers and accountants should not be concerned about which accounting policies firms use unless different accounting policies have direct cash flow effects. Many accounting policy alternatives, about which accountants have argued long and hard, do not have such cash flow effects. Second, firms should disclose as much information about themselves as is cost effective—the fact of disclosure and not the form it takes is what is important. The efficient market will prefer the least costly form of disclosure, other things equal. One can argue, however, that financial statements are a cost-effective disclosure medium. Third, firms need not be concerned about the naïve investor when choosing disclosure policies and formats. Such persons are price-protected, because efficient security prices fully reflect all that is publicly known about those securities. Furthermore, there is a variety of media, including websites, management disclosures, and financial institutions, whereby investors can take advantage of sophisticated information without needing to fully understand it themselves. Finally, the efficient market is interested in useful information from any source, not just accounting reports.

4.4 THE INFORMATIVENESS OF PRICE

4.4.1 A Logical Inconsistency

The careful reader may have noticed an inconsistency in our discussion of efficient securities markets to this point. Recall that efficiency implies that the market price of a security at all times fully reflects all that is publicly known about that security. What is it that drives market price to have this "fully reflects" characteristic? It is the actions of informed investors, who are always striving to obtain and process information so as to make good buy/sell decisions.

However, by our definition of market efficiency, all available information is already reflected in market price. In this regard, we can apply the concept of informativeness to share price (in addition to applying it to net income as in Chapter 3). Thus, under market efficiency, share price is **fully informative**.[1] Since information acquisition is costly, and investors could not expect to beat the market when the market price already reflects all publicly known information, an implication of fully informative share prices is that investors would stop gathering information and rely on market price as the best indicator of future security returns. For example, a simple decision rule would be to buy and hold a diversified investment portfolio, changing its composition only if the risk–return tradeoff of the portfolio gets out of line.

The logical inconsistency, then, is that if prices fully reflect available information, there is no motivation for investors to acquire information; hence, prices will not fully reflect available information. In terms of football forecasting, the forecasters would stop putting effort into their forecasts because they couldn't beat the consensus forecast, but then the consensus forecast would lose its superior forecasting ability.

This has potentially serious implications for accounting theory, since a lack of equilibrium makes it problematic whether financial statement information is useful to investors. What is the purpose of costly financial statement analysis if the market instantaneously reflects all the information in the statements?

Technically speaking, the problem here is that stable equilibrium prices do not exist if share prices are fully informative, as shown by Grossman (1976). What would happen is that fully informative share prices would collapse as investors stopped gathering information. But, once share prices stopped reflecting all available information, investors would realize it was worthwhile to gather information so that share prices would quickly become fully informative again, and the process would continue over time with share prices oscillating wildly.

Since we do not usually observe share prices behaving this way, modifications to the theory are needed. A common way out of the inconsistency is to recognize that there are other sources of demand and supply for securities than the buy/sell decisions of rational, informed investors. For example, people may buy or sell securities for a variety of unpredictable reasons—they may decide to retire early, they may need money to pay gambling debts, they may have received a "hot tip," etc. Such persons are called **noise traders**. Their buy/sell decisions will affect a security's market price, but the decisions come at random—they are not based on a rational evaluation of information.

To illustrate how market price is affected by the presence of noise trading, suppose that a rational investor observes a security's price to be higher than he/she had expected, based on all the information currently possessed by that investor. Now, our investor knows that other rational investors also have their own information about the security and that this information may well be more favourable. These other investors may be buying and driving up the security's price. As a result, our investor is inclined to raise his/her expectation of the security's value. While the investor does not know what information other investors have, it is rational to believe that the information is favourable and this may be what is driving up the security's price.

However, our investor also knows that the higher than expected security price may simply be due to noise trading. Perhaps someone has temporarily invested a large cash windfall in a randomly chosen portfolio of securities, including the security in question. If so, our investor would *not* want to increase his/her expectation of the security's value. Since each scenario is possible, the investor will increase his/her expectation of the security's value, but to an amount *less than* the security's current market price. That is, the rational investor responds by putting some weight on each possibility. In effect, the current share price conveys *some* information about share value but not *all* information, as in the fully informative case.

For our purposes, an important point to note is that rational investors now have an incentive to update their beliefs by gathering more information, as we illustrated in Example 3.1. If they can find out which explanation is the correct one, this can quickly be turned into a profitable investment opportunity. For example, if further investigation reveals that the firm is undervalued, the investor will buy. If, instead, investigation reveals that the share price is temporarily high due to noise trading, the investor will sell or sell short. The efforts of investors to do this will then drive the share price toward its efficient value. Presumably, at least some of this additional information will come from analysis of financial statements.

Investor behaviour such as this is another example of rational expectations—the investor correctly figures out how much weight to put on the possibility that the share price reflects noise trading and how much on the possibility that other investors have better information. Security prices are said to be **partially informative** in the presence of noise trading and rational expectations. Note that market prices are still efficient in the presence of noise trading, but in an *expected value* sense, given that noise has expectation zero. That is, the investor expects *a priori* that a security's market price fully reflects all publicly available information, but, *ex post*, further investigation may reveal that this is not the case.

The extent to which investors gather additional information depends on a number of factors, such as how informative price is, the quality of financial statement information, and the costs of analysis and interpretation. These factors lead to empirical predictions about how security market prices respond to financial statement information. For example, we might expect that price will be more informative for large firms, since they are more "in the news" than small firms, hence their market price will incorporate considerable information. This reduces the ability of financial statements to add to what is already known about such firms. Thus, we would predict that security prices respond less to financial statement information for large firms than for small firms.

Furthermore, note that firm management has an incentive to cater to the desire of investors to ferret out information. For example, management may have inside information that leads it to believe the firm is undervalued. To correct this, management may engage in **voluntary disclosure**—that is, disclosure of information beyond the minimum requirement of GAAP and other reporting standards. Such disclosure can have credibility, even if unaudited, since legal liability and reputation damage impose discipline on managers' reporting decisions. Unfortunately, there are limitations on voluntary disclosure, not only because the legal system and reputation concerns may be unable to completely enforce credibility but because management will not want to reveal information that would give away competitive advantage.

However, voluntary disclosure is much more complex and subtle than simply disclosing information. Management can signal inside information by its choice of accounting policies and, indeed, by the nature and extent of voluntary disclosure itself. The rational investor will thus look carefully at what the manager *does* in terms of accounting policy choice and disclosure. For example, instead of directly revealing good news about a secret research program, a firm that feels it is undervalued could choose very conservative accounting policies. This reveals inside information about the firm's future performance since management would not likely adopt conservative policies unless it felt that future cash flows and earnings would be high enough to absorb the resulting conservative "hit." Even though they may not know what the specific inside information is, rational investors would respond to these conservative policies by bidding up the firm's share price. This means that there are potential rewards to investors, and analysts, for careful and complete analyses of firms' annual reports. Such analyses may identify mispricing and can quickly be turned into profitable investment decisions.

Also, an increase in the quality of financial statement disclosure, other things equal, should lead investors to increase their utilization of financial statement information relative to price. For example, the requirement by securities commissions that firms include management discussion and analysis (MD&A) in their annual reports may increase the decision usefulness of annual reports. Annual reports should have higher information content with MD&A than without it. As we discussed in Section 3.6.4, evidence on the decision usefulness of MD&A is beginning to appear.

We conclude that the term "fully reflects" in the efficient securities market definition has to be interpreted with care. It does not mean that security prices are fully informative with respect to available information at all points in time. Indeed, if it did, this would have adverse implications for the usefulness of financial statements. Rather, security prices are *partially* informative. Partial informativeness reflects a tension between the level of informativeness that remains in the presence of noise traders, and the ability of investors and analysts to identify mispriced securities through private information search, such as analysis of the financial statements proper, supplementary disclosures, accounting policy choice, the nature and extent of voluntary disclosure, and, indeed, of all other available information. With this interpretation in mind, it is important to point out that the implications of security market efficiency as outlined by Beaver in Section 4.3 continue to apply. In particular, the importance of full disclosure remains.

4.4.2 Summary

While the ability of a market price to *average out* individual differences in information processing, as we saw in the football forecasting example, is on the right track, the process of price formation in securities markets is much more complex than this. Through consideration of ways that rational investors can become more informed by careful analysis of managers' disclosure decisions, and by allowing for noise trading, accountants are better able to understand the role of information in price. The presence of noise traders does not necessarily mean that the efficient securities market concept that share prices "fully reflect" information is invalid, but rather that this concept must be interpreted with care.

Improved understanding of the process of price formation leads to empirical predictions of how security prices respond to accounting information and, ultimately, enables accountants to prepare more useful financial statements.

4.5 A MODEL OF COST OF CAPITAL

4.5.1 A Capital Asset Pricing Model

We are now in a position to formalize the relationship between the efficient market price of a security, its risk, and the expected rate of return on that security. We shall do so by means of the well-known Sharpe-Lintner capital asset pricing model (CAPM; Sharpe, 1964; Lintner, 1965).

First, we need some preliminaries. Define R_{jt}, the net rate of return on the shares of firm j for time period t, as

$$R_{jt} = \frac{P_{jt} + D_{jt} - P_{j, t-1}}{P_{j, t-1}} = \frac{P_{jt} + D_{jt}}{P_{j, t-1}} - 1 \qquad (4.1)$$

where:

P_{jt} is the market price of firm j's shares at the end of period t.

D_{jt} is dividends paid by firm j during period t.

$P_{j, t-1}$ is the market price of firm j's shares at the beginning of period t.

This is the return concept used in Examples 3.1 and 3.2. It is a *net* rate of return, given that the opening market price is subtracted in the numerator. We can also define a *gross rate of return* as $1 + R_{jt}$, where

$$1 + R_{jt} = \frac{P_{jt} + D_{jt}}{P_{j, t-1}}$$

Since the only difference between the two rates of return concepts is the 1, we can use them interchangeably. In fact, to conform to common practice, we will usually refer to both net and gross rates of return as simply **returns**.

We can think of returns as either *ex post* or *ex ante*. Ex post, we are at the end of period t and looking back to calculate the return actually realized during the period, as in Equation 4.1. Alternatively, we can stand at the beginning of period t (i.e., at time t − 1) and think of an *ex ante* or expected return as

$$E(R_{jt}) = \frac{E(P_{jt} + D_{jt})}{P_{j, t-1}} - 1 \qquad (4.2)$$

That is, the expected return for period t is based on the expected price at the end of the period plus any dividends expected during the period, divided by the current price. Note how this formula reflects securities market efficiency. That is, the expected price fully reflects all publicly available information at time t − 1.

Now, consider an economy with a large number of rational, risk-averse investors. Assume that there is a risk-free asset in the economy, with return R_f for period t. Assume also that the security market is efficient and transaction costs are zero. Then, the Sharpe-Lintner CAPM shows that

$$E(R_{jt}) = R_f(1 - \beta_j) + \beta_j E(R_{Mt}) \qquad (4.3)$$

where β_j is the beta of share j and $E(R_{Mt})$ is the expected return on the market portfolio for period t.

Beta is defined as

$$\beta_j = \frac{\text{Cov}(j, M)}{\text{Var}(M)}$$

where Cov(j,M) is the covariance between the return on share j and the return on the market portfolio. This covariance measures the degree to which the return of share j changes as the return on the market changes. For example, a high-beta stock undergoes wide swings in returns relative to the market return. Shares of airlines and aircraft manufacturers are examples, since these industries are sensitive to the state of the economy. Fast food firms and electric utilities would be low beta, since demand for their products is less affected by the level of economic activity. Thus beta captures that portion of a stock's risk that is due to economy-wide factors. This risk is called **systematic risk**.

Var(M) is the variance of the return on the market. It is a standardization device to make betas more comparable. For example, to the extent that the variances of Canadian, U.S., European, and other stock exchanges are different, dividing by an exchange's variance aids in comparing firms' systematic risks.

Note that the model is in terms of the market's *expected* returns. Equation 4.3 states that at the beginning of period t, firm j's expected return for the period equals a constant $R_f(1 - \beta_j)$ plus another constant β_j times the expected return on the market portfolio. $E(R_{jt})$ can also be interpreted as the firm's cost of equity capital, since it represents the expected return demanded by the market on that firm's shares.

Strictly speaking, markets do not have expectations—individuals do. One way to think of the market's expectations is that the price of a share behaves *as if* the market holds a certain expectation about its future performance. More fundamentally, the market price of a share includes an average of the expectations of all informed investors, much like the consensus forecast in the Beaver football example (Section 4.2.2) includes an average expectation of the forecasters.

It is not difficult to see the intuition of the model. Since rational investors will fully diversify when transaction costs are zero, the only risk measure in the formula is β_j. Firm-specific risk does not affect share price because it disappears in fully diversified portfolios. Also, note that the higher is β_j the higher is expected return, other things equal.[5] This is consistent with risk aversion, since risk-averse investors will require a higher expected return to compensate for higher risk.

Note also the role of the current market price $P_{j,t-1}$ in the model. The return demanded by the market on share j for period t—that is, $E(R_{jt})$ in Equation 4.3—is a function only of R_f, R_{Mt}, and β_j. The current market price of firm j does not appear. However, in Equation 4.2, given expected end-of-period price P_{jt} and dividends D_{jt}, we see that $P_{j,t-1}$ in the denominator will adjust so that the right hand side of Equation 4.2 equals $E(R_{jt})$. That is, a share's current price will adjust so that its expected return equals the return demanded by the market for that share as given by Equation 4.3.

We can now see how new information affects firm j's share price. Suppose that at time $t - 1$ (now) some new firm-specific information comes along that raises investors' expectations of P_{jt} (and possibly also of D_{jt}), without affecting R_f, β_j, or $E(R_{Mt})$. This will throw Equation 4.2 out of balance, since $E(R_{jt})$ from Equation 4.3 does not change. Thus, $P_{j,t-1}$, the current price, must rise to restore equality. This, of course, is consistent with market efficiency, which states that the market price of a security will react immediately to new information.

For our purposes, there are three main uses for the CAPM formula. First, it brings out clearly how share prices depend on investors' expectations of future share price and dividends. If these expectations change (the numerator of Equation 4.2), current price $P_{j,t-1}$ (the denominator) will immediately change to reflect these new expectations.

For a given change in expectations, and given R_f and $E(R_{Mt})$, the amount of the change in current price depends only on the share's beta. To put this another way, the larger the change in expectations, the larger the change in price, other things equal.

Second, by reverting to an *ex post* view of returns, the CAPM provides us with a way of separating the realized return on a share into expected and unexpected components. To see this, consider the following version of the model, where we are now at the end of period t and looking back:

$$R_{jt} = \alpha_j + \beta_j R_{Mt} + \epsilon_{jt} \tag{4.4}$$

This version of CAPM is called the **market model**. It explains the realized return R_{jt} on a firm's shares by decomposing it into the beginning-of-period *expected* return $(\alpha_j + \beta_j R_{Mt})$ and the *unexpected* or **abnormal**[6] return ϵ_{jt}. The expected return comes from the CAPM, with $\alpha_j = R_f(1 - \beta_j)$. The ϵ_{jt} captures the impact on R_{jt} of all those events during period t that were not expected at the beginning of the period. By definition in an efficient market, $E(\epsilon_{jt}) = 0$, since new information comes along randomly. But, in any period t the *realized* value of ϵ_{jt} need not be zero. Its realized value will depend on just what information did come along. Thus, the market model enables an *ex post* separation of the realized return R_{jt} into expected and unexpected or abnormal components.

Third, the market model provides a convenient way for researchers and analysts to estimate a stock's beta. Notice that the market model is presented in the form of a regression equation. By obtaining a recent sample of past data on R_{jt} and R_{Mt}, the coefficients of the regression model can be estimated by least-squares regression. If we assume that the market is able to form unbiased expectations of R_{Mt} (so that R_{Mt} is a good proxy for $E(R_{Mt})$, which is unobservable), and if we assume that β_j is stationary over time, then the coefficient of R_{Mt} from least-squares regression is a good estimate[7] of β_j. Furthermore, the reasonableness of the estimation can be checked by comparing the estimated coefficient α_j with $R_f(1 - \beta_j)$—the two should be similar.

As we will see in Chapter 5, much empirical research in accounting has required an accurate estimate of beta, and we will return to its estimation in Section 7.12.1. For now, it is important to realize that the CAPM provides an important and useful way to model the market's expectation of a share's returns and a firm's cost of capital. Also, it shows clearly how new information affects current share price.

4.5.2 Critique of the Capital Asset Pricing Model*

For later reference, we now consider several underlying assumptions of the CAPM. It is instructive to consider these here because the CAPM is an example of the type

---

*This section can be omitted with little lack of continuity.

of mathematical economic model that has received harsh criticism for failure to predict the share mispricing and subsequent 2007–2008 market meltdowns described in Section 1.3. Consideration of these assumptions will help us to better understand these criticisms.

First, the CAPM assumes rational expectations. That is, investors are assumed to know stocks' betas, which can be thought of as unknown underlying decision parameters. As a practical matter, these may not be accurately known, creating a source of estimation risk for the investor (recall from Section 2.3 that we define estimation risk as the risk that arises from not knowing the true value of underlying parameters affecting a decision). For example, as described above, the market model can be used to estimate beta. However, this estimate is unlikely to be completely accurate, especially if only a few periods of data are available for the estimation. Also, a firm's beta may change. Then, investors must go through a learning process of evidence gathering and belief revision before an accurate estimate of its new value is obtained. This learning process may take some time, during which shares may be mispriced relative to their real efficient market value. To the extent this estimation risk is not diversified away (in a diversified portfolio, overestimates of beta for some shares may be offset by underestimates for others), investors will demand a higher return than the CAPM, to compensate for this additional risk.

Second, the CAPM does not consider that the securities market may contain rational investors with different levels of sophistication. Granted, our earlier discussions have distinguished between informed investors and noise traders. However, in reality, securities markets contain more than one class of rational investor. Contrary to this reality, the CAPM assumes **common knowledge**. That is, not only does everyone know β_j but everyone knows that everyone knows β_j, etc. The significance of the common knowledge assumption is that the CAPM then rules out the possibility that some investors (e.g., hedge funds) will be better informed than others (e.g., ordinary rational investors). If so, the more sophisticated investors may feel that ordinary investors, with an inferior knowledge of β_j, will make incorrect investment decisions. These better informed investors will then take advantage of the share mispricing that results, rather than making the diversified investment decisions that underlie the CAPM.

Third, as mentioned, the CAPM assumes that transaction costs of buying and selling securities are zero. That is, it assumes perfectly liquid markets. Recall (Chapter 1, Note 22) that a liquid market is a market in which investors can quickly and at reasonable cost buy or sell any number of securities at the current market price. Obviously, investors favour markets with high levels of liquidity.

Realistically, however, markets are not perfectly liquid—there are always costs of buying and selling shares, such as brokerage fees and the bid–ask spread. Also, depending on the degree of liquidity, large transactions may themselves affect price. Furthermore, market liquidity can vary over time, creating liquidity risk. This risk became apparent during the 2007–2008 security market meltdowns (Section 1.3), when liquidity pricing arose.

Finally, the CAPM assumes investor rationality. This assumption has long been questioned, and we consider it in detail in Chapter 6.

If economic modelling of the role of information in capital markets is to recover from the criticisms that have been made against it, it will be necessary to defend investor rationality, or develop models to combine rational and non-rational behaviour. Also, more realistic models, which relax assumptions of rational expectations, common knowledge, and perfect market liquidity, will have to be developed. Some models of these types are described in Chapter 6.

4.5.3 Summary

Despite these various concerns, the CAPM is a good starting point to understand the role of information in capital markets. Its assumption of diversified investors is consistent with many investment strategies, and it continues to be used by firms and researchers to estimate the cost of capital.

4.6 INFORMATION ASYMMETRY

4.6.1 A Closer Look at Information Asymmetry

In this section, we take a closer look at the notion of "publicly available" information in the efficient securities market definition. This leads directly to what is undoubtedly the most important concept of financial accounting theory—*information asymmetry*. As mentioned in Section 1.9, there are two major types of information asymmetry: adverse selection and moral hazard. Investor concern about adverse selection arises when one type of participant in the market (insiders, for example) knows something about the asset being traded that another type of participant (ordinary investors) does not know. Investor concern about moral hazard arises because manager effort in running the firm is typically unobservable, creating the possibility that the manager may shirk on effort.

These two types of information asymmetry create additional sources of estimation risk for the investor. With adverse selection, the unknown parameter is the honesty of the insider. With moral hazard, the unknown parameter is the extent of manager shirking. In the face of information asymmetry, outside investors will protect themselves by bidding down the price of securities by the expected amount of their losses at the hands of persons with an information advantage, thereby increasing firms' cost of capital. It is unlikely that this estimation risk is fully diversifiable, since investors are much more likely to lose than to gain from adverse selection and moral hazard. Indeed we will see numerous cases where firms benefit from reducing estimation risk by, for example, superior disclosure[8].

Our more detailed consideration of moral hazard begins in Chapter 9. Here, we primarily consider adverse selection.

First, note that information asymmetry is an important reason for market incompleteness (Section 2.6). That is, in extreme cases, a market may collapse or fail to develop in the first place as a result of information asymmetry. To illustrate, consider the market for insurance policies. Assuming you are risk averse, you may wish to buy insurance against the possibility of failing to attain your university or college degree or professional accounting designation. You would be better off with such a policy, at least if the cost was fair. Serious illness or accident may prevent your completion of the course of studies, and you could eliminate this risk if you had a policy that reimbursed you for your loss of the present value of the increased future income that would follow the attainment of your degree or designation.

However, offering such a policy would create severe difficulties for the insurance company. One difficulty is that people who are sick would flock to enroll in educational programs (a version of the adverse selection problem because people whose health is adverse to the insurance company's best interests self-select themselves to buy insurance). Then, when their illness leads to their failure, they could collect on their policies and still enjoy the monetary fruits of a degree.

Another problem is that if you owned such a policy, you would probably shirk your studies, even if you were perfectly healthy. Why put in all the time and effort to complete your course of studies when, by merely failing, you could receive equivalent compensation from your insurance policy? This is a version of the moral hazard problem, since only you know how hard you are working. Then, you are tempted to cheat the company by shirking your studies. Note that requiring a medical certificate would not be of much use here, because of the difficulty in establishing that it was the illness that led to the failure.

As a result, no insurance company would sell you a policy that would reimburse you for your full income loss if you failed to attain your degree. The problem is information asymmetry. You have a major information advantage over the company, because the company can only observe whether you fail, not whether your illness, accident, or shirking caused you to fail.

Faced with information disadvantages of this magnitude, the company responds by not writing insurance policies of the type described, contributing to market incompleteness.

In other cases, information asymmetry is not so severe as to prevent the market from developing. Nevertheless, the market does not work as well as it might. This situation was studied by Akerlof (1970). An example of a market characterized by adverse selection is the used car market. The owner of a car will know more about its true condition, and hence its future stream of benefits, than would a potential buyer. This creates an adverse selection problem because the owner may try to take advantage of this inside information by bringing a "**lemon**" to market, hoping to get more than it is worth from an unsuspecting buyer. However, buyers will be aware of this temptation and, since they don't have the information to distinguish between lemons and good cars, will lower the price they are willing to pay for any used car, a process called **pooling**. In effect, the market price of a used car reflects the average quality of used cars on the market. As a result, many cars—the good ones—will have a market value that is less than the real value of their future stream of benefits, and vice versa for bad cars. The arbitrage effect, whereby cars of similar service potential must sell for similar prices, operates less effectively when it is difficult to know exactly what the service potential of a used car is. Thus, owners of good cars are less likely to bring them to market. This is another source of market incompleteness—a market can exist but be incomplete in the sense that purchasers cannot always buy a used car of the exact type and condition they want.

We can also think of this pooling process from a risk perspective. The buyer of a used car faces estimation risk since he/she does not know the true underlying state of a used car.

Note that since sellers have an incentive to bring lemons to market, while owners of good cars know they will receive less than the expected value of their cars' future services, the average quality of used cars on the market will deteriorate over time, to the point where the market collapses. However, there is a variety of regulatory and voluntary devices that markets use to reduce the effects of adverse selection and resulting estimation risk. Thus, used car markets are characterized by safety certificates, repair records, warranties, test drives, dealers who attempt to establish a good reputation, and so on. With respect to our insurance example above, insurance markets feature devices such as medical examinations for life and health insurance, co-insurance and deductible clauses for fire insurance, and premium reductions for good driving records. However, because they are costly, these various disclosure devices do not completely eliminate the problems. Nevertheless, they may be sufficiently effective to at least allow used car and some insurance markets to operate, albeit not as well as they would in the absence of information asymmetry.

We can think of the seller of a used car as analogous to an insider in a stock market context. Then, it should be apparent that securities markets are also subject to the lemons problem. With adverse selection, outside investors face estimation risk because they do not know as much as insiders about the firm's real future performance prospects. Here, as mentioned, the underlying unknown parameter is the honesty of insiders, who are tempted to exploit their information advantage. Then, as in the case of used cars, market prices will reflect outside investors' expected losses at the hands of insiders. For example, company insiders may delay the release of bad news, possibly engaging in insider trading by selling shares before the news becomes publicly known. They will thus make a profit at the expense of outside investors who have bought shares in the interim. Alternatively, if the inside information is good news, insiders may make a profit by buying before the good news becomes publicly known, again at the expense of outsiders who may have sold shares in the interim. Thus, outside investors making buy or sell decisions face an expectation of loss whether the inside information is good or bad[9].

Notice that, unlike for used cars, investors may diversify at least some estimation risk arising from inside information, since firms differ in the integrity of their insiders. Thus, for some firms, investor losses at the hands of insiders may be more than expected while losses may be less than expected for others.

Nevertheless, while share prices will reflect average investor losses at the hands of insiders, individual firms that wish to do so can reduce inside information about themselves, and thus their cost of capital, by superior disclosure, much like the seller of a used car may receive a higher price if he/she makes maintenance records available to the purchaser.

Inside information as a source of estimation risk also applies to the CAPM as introduced Section 4.5.1. That is, the CAPM does not allow for the effects of inside information.[10] Then, as just discussed, share prices will reflect investors' expected losses at the hands of insiders, in which case the CAPM will understate cost of capital.

To appreciate the potential of inside information to concern investors, consider the study by Jagolinzer, Larcker, and Taylor (JLT; 2011). They studied a sample of 260 U.S. firms with **blackout policies**, which restrict firm insiders from buying or selling company shares during periods when they are particularly likely to possess inside information. For example, a typical policy prohibits insider trading for a period of several weeks prior to and shortly after a quarterly earnings announcement.

Over the period June 2003 to December 2005, there were 7,856 insider stock sales and purchases in JLT's sample. Perhaps surprisingly, 24% of these trades took place *within* blackout periods.

JLT also report that 80% of their sample firms require their general legal counsel to approve insider trades. Presumably, this is to protect the insider and the firm from the possible consequences of violating insider trading regulations, which may penalize insiders who take advantage of non-public information to earn trading profits.

For firms with no general counsel approval, JLT report that insiders earned an average excess return of 3.6 % during the 180-day period following their purchase and sale transactions outside the blackout zone (i.e.,7.2% per annum). For trades within blackout periods, the average excess return was 10.8 %, or 21.6% per annum. This suggests that, given the opportunity, insiders do exploit their information advantage.

However, when general counsel approval was required, these abnormal profits were effectively eliminated. JLT conclude that general counsel approval is a more effective corporate governance device than blackout periods per se. Nevertheless, the excess returns without legal counsel approval, particularly during the blackout periods, warrants considerable investor uncertainty about the extent of insider trading.

4.6.2 Fundamental Value

In this section, we consider the difference between the efficient market price of a share and its **fundamental value**.

> *The fundamental value of a share is the value it would have in an efficient market if there is no inside information. That is, all existing information about the share is publicly available.*[11]

Fundamental value is a theoretical ideal. We would not expect that inside information can be completely eliminated. It may not be cost effective for a firm to directly reveal strategic information about research in process or plans for a takeover bid, for example.

The steps taken by governments and accounting bodies to restore public confidence following the market collapses outlined in Sections 1.2 and 1.3 can be regarded as attempts to reduce estimation risk arising from inside information, by improving financial reporting informativeness, thereby increasing the average quality of publicly available information or, equivalently, moving share prices closer to fundamental value. The 2002 Sarbanes-Oxley Act is a prominent example. Also, we will describe in Section 7.5.2 some of the new standards introduced following the 2007–2008 market meltdowns to control off balance sheet liabilities and securitized financial instruments. Many of these steps involve improved disclosure to expand the set of information that is publicly available, and reduce investor concern about incorrect or misleading information coming from insiders. Thus, we can think of financial reporting as a device to increase the average quality of publicly available information so as to reduce investor concerns about adverse selection and its resulting estimation risk. This improves the working of securities markets and reduces incompleteness, thereby benefitting ordinary investors. Figure 4.2 illustrates this role.

The outer circle of the figure depicts the firm's fundamental value. The inner circle depicts the information underlying the efficient market price of the share, being all publicly available information.[12] The difference between the inner and outer circle depicts inside information. The role of financial reporting is to convert inside information into outside information, thereby enlarging the inner circle. As mentioned, the inner circle cannot fully reach the outside, since the cost of eliminating all inside information would be astronomic.

We will refer to markets where the inner circle is "large" relative to the outside circle as markets that **work well**. If an improvement in financial reporting increases the stock of

Figure 4.2 Role of Financial Reporting in an Efficient Market

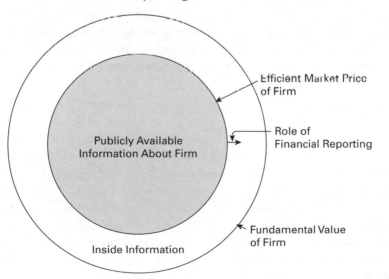

publicly available information and/or increases investor confidence in that information, we shall say that the market **works better**.

Market collapse, as in the cases of Enron, WorldCom, and, more recently, many financial institutions, will take place if investors realize that much of the information in the inner circle is not useful—that is, it overstates the value of the firm and, as a result, share price is too high. If investor concern is serious enough, liquidity pricing ensues. Then, the inner circle collapses, taking share price with it.

Research by Maffett (2012) supports the argument that higher quality financial reporting can benefit investors. Maffet distinguished between ordinary and sophisticated investors, where sophisticated investors are investors with sufficient expertise and resources to develop their own private information about future firm performance that is superior to that of ordinary investors. We can view sophisticated investors as insiders in Figure 4.2.

Based on a sample of 42,930 mutual funds (his proxy for sophisticated investors) from 42 countries over the period 1999–2009, and 43,290 firms in these countries, Maffet found on average, a negative association between the ability of mutual funds to earn positive abnormal returns on a firm's shares and the financial reporting quality of that firm.[13] This suggests that sophisticated investors can develop an information advantage over ordinary investors by developing their own private information, and that this information advantage is larger the lower is the amount of public information released by the firm in its financial statements.[14] These abnormal returns are at the expense of ordinary investors, since share price will already have risen by the time the inside information of the sophisticated investors becomes publicly known. If so, securities markets would work better, and ordinary investors would benefit, with higher quality reporting.

Maffett also estimated country-level financial reporting quality[15] for the countries in his sample. He found that the ability of mutual funds to earn abnormal returns on shares of firms with low quality reporting is reduced as overall financial reporting quality in that firm's country increases. As he pointed out, this suggests that improvements in a country's accounting standards and corporate governance can reduce the information disadvantage of ordinary investors. This point will become relevant when we discuss in Chapter 13 the potential benefits to a country from adopting IASB accounting standards.

4.6.3 Summary

Under ideal conditions, the firm's market value fully reflects *all* information, with no reduction due to estimation risk. That is, price equals fundamental value. When conditions are not ideal, inside information exists. Then, market value fully reflects all *publicly available* information, if security markets are (semi-strong) efficient. This "fully reflects" characteristic of market value includes a reduction due to (non-diversifiable) estimation risk.

The difference between fundamental value and efficient market price is due to inside information. Full and timely disclosure will reduce inside information, so that securities markets work better. Since eliminating all inside information is too costly, however, some insider information advantage and estimation risk will remain.

4.7 THE SOCIAL SIGNIFICANCE OF SECURITIES MARKETS THAT WORK WELL

In a capitalist economy, securities markets are the primary vehicle whereby capital is raised and allocated to competing investment needs. Consequently, it is socially desirable that these markets work well—that is, if share prices are close to fundamental value. Then, firms will invest in capital projects until the marginal profitability of further investment equals the marginal cost, thereby creating an efficient capital allocation. Markets will work well to the extent that investors trust managers and other insiders, that is, if their concerns about adverse selection are controlled. Of course, this is what society wants, since investment capital is in scarce supply. Social welfare will be enhanced if scarce capital goes to the most productive alternatives.

However, as mentioned, security prices do not fully reflect fundamental value in the presence of inside information. Ordinary investors will be aware of the estimation risk resulting from adverse selection and insider trading. Then, a lemons phenomenon comes into play. Investors recognize that the market is not a "level playing field" and either withdraw from the market or lower the amount they are willing to pay for any security. As a result, firms with high quality investment projects will not receive a high price for their securities, and they will underinvest relative to the socially efficient level. A related problem is that if too many investors withdraw, the market becomes **thin** or, equivalently, it loses **depth**, where depth is the number of shares that investors can buy or sell without affecting the market price (see Chapter 1, Note 22). When depth is low, potential investors may not be able to buy or sell all they want of a security at the market price, which further hampers investment.

Empirical evidence on the importance of markets that work well for efficient capital allocation is provided by Wurgler (2000). He estimated the efficiency of capital allocation for 65 countries over the years 1963–1995 and found that countries with more firm-specific information incorporated into share prices (relative to industry- and economy-wide information, which affects all share prices) enjoy greater capital allocation efficiency.[16] Note that more firm-specific information incorporated into share prices is just another way of saying that the market is working better, or, equivalently, that there is less inside information.

One might then ask, how does firm-specific information become incorporated into share prices? An answer is through high quality reporting. Then, share price will better reflect future firm performance. In terms of Figure 4.2, share price will be closer to fundamental firm value.

The effect of reporting quality on capital allocation was studied by Francis, Huang, Khurana, and Pereira (FHKP; 2009). They began with the premise that firms in all countries want to take advantage of new global growth opportunities (e.g., cellphones). However, a firm's ability to do so is constrained by its ability to obtain financing. They then argued that, other things equal, it is easier to obtain financing the higher the quality of financial reporting in their country.

To test this argument, FHKP predicted that if two countries have similar high quality reporting, the growth rates by industry in each country should be similar (i.e., highly correlated) if reporting quality is a significant determinant of capital availability. If reporting quality is low in one or both countries, growth rate correlation is predicted to be lower, since the ability to obtain financing for growth then depends more on other factors (e.g., level of economic development, capital inflows), which differ across countries.

FHKP studied a sample of industry growth rates from 37 countries over the period 1980–1990. They measured a country's reporting quality in several ways (e.g., audit quality, synchronicity—see Note 15) and, after controlling for other factors affecting financing of growth, report results consistent with their predictions.

Of course, developed capitalist economies have a variety of mechanisms for promoting reporting quality. One such approach is regulation. Thus, we witness government securities commissions, as outlined in Section 1.12.5. These agencies create and/or enforce regulations that, for example, set accounting standards, control insider trading, and promote timely disclosure of significant events, with penalties for violation. If such regulation is effective, estimation risk resulting from inside information is reduced. Investors will then remove firms from the lemons category and, as a result, will be willing to pay higher prices for securities than they otherwise would.

However, the market can provide **incentives** for individual firms to release inside information over and above that required by regulation. Just as a used car dealer who develops a reputation for honesty and fair dealing will enjoy higher sales prices, a firm with a credible policy of full disclosure beyond the regulatory minimum may enjoy higher share prices and lower cost of capital. This is because full disclosure reduces investors' concerns about inside information.

Obviously, regulations and market incentives are not mutually exclusive—we witness both in our economy. Regulation is like a "stick" and requires penalties to enforce it. The need for regulation will be reduced, however, to the extent that "carrots," such as improved reputation, higher share price, and lower cost of capital, operate to motivate full disclosure. In both cases, the economy benefits since security prices are closer to fundamental firm value. A study by Biddle, Hilary, and Verdi (BHV; 2009) illustrates the potential of carrots (i.e., the benefits to a firm of high quality disclosure) to improve investment efficiency. They pointed out, as we have above, that inside information creates a lemons problem that raises firms' costs of capital, leading to underinvestment relative to the socially efficient level. They also pointed out that overinvestment will result if managers use firm size (i.e., overinvestment) as a vehicle to increase their reputation and compensation.

Based on a large sample of U.S. firms over the period 1993–2005, and several measures of reporting quality, BHV reported evidence that high quality reporting reduces both underinvestment and overinvestment.[17] This suggests that reporting quality is an important contributor to investment efficiency in the economy.

We conclude that the social benefits of securities markets that work reasonably well will be attained if the following two conditions are met:

- All useful information is publicly available, at least up to the ability of penalties and incentives to cost effectively motivate high quality reporting.
- Securities market prices are efficient relative to publicly available information.

4.8 CONCLUSIONS ON EFFICIENT SECURITIES MARKETS

Rational investor behaviour underlies efficient securities market theory. However, it is not necessary that all investors react to information the same way. What is required is that individual differences cancel out such that security prices correctly reflect publicly available information. Thus the model of a rational investor, and the efficient securities market prices that result, represent the behaviour of an *average* investor, not necessarily that of any particular individual.

Implications of efficient securities markets for accountants include full disclosure. This includes disclosure of accounting policies since the market will ignore differences in policies that do not have cash flow effects, provided it knows what policies are used. Other implications include lack of concern for naïve investors since they are price protected by the efficient market price, and that accountants must provide useful information if they are to survive in the competitive information market.

Market efficiency contains a logical contradiction, since if market prices always correctly reflect all publicly available information, no one has an incentive to gather (costly) information, in which case prices would quickly lose their efficient quality. To rescue the theory, theorists have introduced the concept of noise traders.

Despite full disclosure, there will always be some inside information, creating an information disadvantage for investors who react by discounting share prices for their expected losses at the hands of insiders. Accountants can minimize this disadvantage by encouraging decision useful standards and encouraging firms to disclose as much information as is cost effective. In so doing, security prices approach fundamental value as closely as possible. This benefits both investors and firms, and improves the allocation of scarce capital in the economy.

Models, such as the CAPM, that assume investor rationality and efficient securities markets have come under severe criticism lately. They are accused of not predicting the 2007–2008 security market meltdowns. To recover from these criticisms, models may need to become more realistic, by amalgamating behavioural models of investor behaviour and/or relaxing underlying assumptions of perfectly liquid markets, rational expectations, and common knowledge.

Despite these criticisms, there exists a great deal of empirical evidence consistent with average investor rationality and market efficiency. In the next chapter, we will review some of this evidence.

Questions and Problems

1. Two firms, of the same size and risk, release their annual reports on the same day. It turns out that they each report the same amount of net income. Following the release, the share price of one firm rose strongly while the other rose hardly at all.

Explain how it is possible for the market to react positively to one firm's annual report and hardly at all to the other when the firms are similar in size, risk, and reported profitability.

2. Shares of firm A and firm B are traded on an efficient market. The two firms are similar in their operations, are of the same size and risk, and are growing rapidly. They both report the same net income. However, you see in the financial statement notes that firm A uses declining balance amortization for capital assets, while firm B uses straight-line amortization.

Which firm's shares should sell at the higher price–earnings ratio, all other things being equal? Explain.

3. Using the concept of information asymmetry, answer the following questions:

a. You observe that used cars sold by new car dealers sell for a higher price, for models of same make, year, and condition, than used cars sold by used car dealers. Why?

b. Why would a fire insurance policy contain a $1,500 deductible provision?

c. Why would a life insurance company require a medical examination before approving applications for new policies?

d. A firm plans to raise additional capital by means of a new issue of common shares. Before doing so, it hires a well-known investment house to help design and market the issue, and also switches auditors from a small, local firm to a "Big Four" firm. Why? (CGA-Canada)

4. To what extent might the financial press provide a relevant source of information for investors? Would this information source conflict with or complement financial statement information? Explain.

5. On January 21, 1993, *The Wall Street Journal* reported that General Electric Co.'s fourth-quarter 1992 earnings rose 6.2% to $1.34 billion or $1.57 a share, setting a new record and bringing the earnings for 1992 to $4.73 billion or $5.51 a share. After adjusting for low-persistence items, 1992 earnings from continuing operations were up about 10% from the previous year.

The *Journal* also reported that forecasts made by analysts averaged $1.61 per share for the fourth quarter of 1992, and from $5.50 to $5.60 per share for the whole year. One analyst was quoted as saying that 1992 "wasn't a bad year for GE" despite the downturn in the stock market on the day of the earnings announcement.

Yet, on the same day the fourth-quarter earnings were announced, General Electric Co.'s stock price fell $1.50 to $82.625 on the New York Stock Exchange.

Required

a. Give three reasons to explain why this could happen.

b. Use the Sharpe-Lintner CAPM (Equations 4.2 and 4.3) to explain how the new information caused the current price to fall. Calculations are not required.

6. The IASB/FASB Framework (Section 3.7.1) includes comparability as an enhancing characteristic of financial information. If securities markets are efficient, give an argument why lack of comparability of a firm's accounting policies with other firms should not affect its share price. Give an argument why its share price may be affected by lack of comparability.

7. On February 27, 2007, Laurentian Bank of Canada released results for its first quarter, ending on January 31, 2007. It reported profit of 74 cents per share (70 cents per share before a non-recurring gain). Analysts' estimates of profit for the quarter were 65 cents per share. For the same quarter of the previous year, profit was 59 cents per share. Total revenue increased 6%. The bank announced a quarterly dividend of 29 cents per share, unchanged from the two previous quarters. The CFO of Laurentian stated that its loan exposure to struggling forestry and manufacturing firms was better, although there was still room for improvement.

   Laurentian's shares are traded on the S&P/TSX exchange. The TSX index rose 5 points on February 27, closing at 13,040.11. Laurentian's share price fell 34 cents for the day, to $30.71.

   ### Required

   Why did Laurentian's share price fall? Assume efficient securities markets, and consider both economy-wide and firm-specific factors in your answer.

8. Concept Ltd. is a listed public company. It is in a volatile industry. The market price of its shares is highly sensitive to its earnings. The company's annual meeting is to be held soon and the president is concerned, expecting to be attacked strongly by a dissident group of shareholders.

   One issue the dissidents are expected to focus on is the company's amortization policy. They will claim that the annual declining balance amortization charges are excessive—that the company's conservative amortization policy seriously understates annual earnings per share, causing the shares' market price to be artificially low. Threats have even been made of suing management and the board of directors to "recover the resulting loss in market value, relative to shareholders in companies with less conservative amortization policies, suffered by Concept's shareholders."

   The president has asked you to help prepare a defence against the expected attack on the company's amortization policy.

   ### Required

   Write a memo summarizing how you would recommend the president respond to this attack.

9. The article "GM to Take Charge of $20.8-Billion" here reproduced from *The Globe and Mail* (February 2, 1993) describes the potential impact of SFAS 106, "Accounting for Postretirement Benefits Other Than Pensions," on General Motors and Ford. SFAS 106 was a 1990 FASB accounting standard that required firms to accrue a liability for estimated retirement benefits, such as health care. Previously, such costs were accounted for on a pay as you go basis, under which the expense for the year equalled the cash paid out for retiree benefits during the year.

   From the article, General Motors planned to record a liability of $20.8 billion, reducing its shareholders' equity from $27.8 billion to $7 billion, about a 75% reduction.

GM to Take Charge of $20.8-Billion

Atlanta—General Motors Corp. will take a $20.8-billion (U.S.) charge against 1992 earnings to account for a new way of estimating retiree health care costs, the auto maker's directors decided yesterday.

The charge, which will not affect the struggling auto maker's cash flow, will leave GM with the largest annual loss of any U.S. corporation, eclipsing the company's 1991 loss of $4.45-billion, which was a record at that time.

Including accounting changes, other charges and losses on its North American operations, GM's 1992 loss could approach $23-billion.

The $20.8-billion is a non-cash charge. It reduces GM's net worth to about $7-billion, still sufficient to pay stock dividends under the laws of Delaware, where GM is incorporated.

Separately, GM said it would take a $744-million fourth-quarter restructuring charge for its National Car Rental Systems business. In a recent U.S. Securities and Exchange Commission filing, GM estimated that charge at about $300-million.

The accounting change, required by the Financial Accounting Standards Board of all publicly traded U.S. companies, has had a major effect on each of the Big Three U.S. auto makers.

Ford Motor Co. said it would take a $7.5-billion charge against 1992 earnings to account for the change. Chrysler Corp. said it has not decided whether to take its $4.7-billion charge as a lump sum in the first quarter or spread it over 20 years, as the standard allows.

GM had estimated its charge for adopting the new accounting standard at $16-billion to $24-billion. The $20.8-billion actual charge includes its workers, GM Hughes Electronics Corp. and its financial subsidiary, General Motors Acceptance Corp.

The company's EDS Corp. subsidiary does not pay health benefits, so it was exempt.

Source: "General Motors to Take Charge of $20.8-Billion," *The Globe and Mail*, February 2, 1993. Reprinted by permission of The Associated Press.

Required

Describe and explain how you would expect the efficient securities market to react to this information. Include in your answer reasons why share price might fall and why it might rise.

10. You have just obtained inside information about a firm that employs you and in which you own shares. The information is that the current quarter's earnings will be substantially below forecast. Should you sell your shares before the bad news becomes publicly known? Outline arguments for and against this temptation.

11. A major reason for the rarity of formal financial forecasts in annual reports is the possibility of lawsuits if the forecast is not met, particularly in the United States. On November 17, 1995, *The Wall Street Journal* reported that the SEC was supporting a bill before the U.S. Senate to provide protection from legal liability resulting from forecasts, providing that "meaningful cautionary statements" accompanied the forecast.

Required

a. If firms are discouraged from providing financial forecasts by the prospect of litigation, how could this lead to a negative impact on the working of securities markets? Can you give an argument that a litigious environment might actually improve the working of securities markets?

b. Explain how the passage of a bill such as that mentioned above might benefit investors.

c. Explain how passage might benefit firms.

12. Refer to Theory in Practice 4.1 in Section 4.2.2.

Required

a. Use efficient securities market theory to explain how "dart throwing" may be a desirable investment strategy.

b. Explain Prof. Malkiel's argument that risk differences may be driving the superior average returns earned by the pros and the Dow Jones index. How would you determine whether risk differences were affecting the results?

c. Explain another possible reason, not mentioned by Prof. Malkiel, for the superior returns earned by the pros.

13. For companies with no history of positive earnings, such as startup companies, growth of revenues provides an alternative performance measure and indicator of possible future earning power. This is particularly the case if the new company incurs high R&D costs, advertising, and other startup expenditures that delay the advent of profitability. Without positive reported earnings, such companies may inflate reported revenues to impress investors. In an article in *The Globe and Mail*, December 30, 2000, Janet McFarland discusses some of these practices. They include

■ recognizing full revenue even though products or systems can be returned, or when there are future obligations such as servicing the products and systems sold

■ recording revenue on long-term contracts in advance of billings to the customer (billings may be delayed as a form of vendor financing to the customer, a practice frequently used to attract business from cash-short firms)

■ recording revenue from gross sales when the company is an agent rather than a principal

Examples of such practices include Imax Corp., which reported the (discounted) full amounts of minimum royalties due under 10-year or more leases of its theatre systems. While, at the time, this was in accordance with GAAP for long-term leases, it left Imax open to the possibility that customers might default on payments due in future. Other examples include JetForm Corp., which recognized revenue from consulting contracts on the percentage-of-completion method, although amounts billed to customers were less. Bid.Com, a firm that conducted online auctions as agent for the seller, included the purchase price, rather than its commission on the purchase, as revenue.

One of the problems surrounding reporting of revenue is that while a firm's revenue recognition policy must be disclosed, the disclosure standards are vague. Thus, companies typically stated that revenue is recognized as goods are shipped or services rendered, or that revenues on long-term contracts are recognized on a percentage-of-completion basis. These statements are sufficiently general that practices such as the above may be unknown to the market.

Required

a. To what extent can revenue growth substitute for net income as a predictor of future earning power? Explain. Use efficient securities market concepts in your answer, and consider the requirement under GAAP for immediate writeoff of research and startup costs.

b. Use the concept of relevance to defend the revenue recognition policies outlined above.

c. Use the concept of reliability to criticize the revenue recognition policies outlined above.

d. To the extent that investors are aware of the possible use of revenue recognition policies that overstate revenues (even though, for a specific firm, they may not know the extent to which that firm is using such policies), what is the effect on the operation of the capital market? Explain. A good answer will draw on the concept of an information system.

14. Zhang (2005) examined revenue recognition practices in the software industry. Software firms derive revenue from software licensing and post-contract customer support. In both cases, the point in time when the significant risks and rewards of ownership have been transferred to the buyer, the seller loses control over the items, and the revenue and related costs can be measured reliably is unclear. Also unclear is whether collection is reasonably assured. Consequently, there is scope for alternative revenue recognition practices in the industry.

With respect to licensing, one alternative is to recognize revenue when the licensing contract is signed (early recognition). Another is to wait until the software is delivered to the customer, consistent with the usual sale basis of revenue recognition (late recognition). With respect to post-contract customer support, alternatives are to recognize revenue when contracts are signed (early recognition) or recognize revenue ratably over the term of the contract (late recognition).

Zhang examined a sample of 122 firms over the period 1987–1997, of which 22 firms were early recognizers and 93 were late. He measured the relevance of a firm's quarterly revenue by its association with its share returns for the quarter. Given securities market efficiency, the revenues of early recognizers should be more highly associated with their share returns than the revenues of late recognizers. Zhang reported significant statistical evidence consistent with this expectation.

Zhang measured the reliability of revenue information by examining the cash flows from quarter end accounts receivable collected over the following two quarters. Recall that in Section 3.7.1 we pointed out the role of accruals in anticipating future cash flows. Here, the accrual in question is the allowance for doubtful accounts. Thus, the closer the amounts of cash collections are over these following two quarters to opening *net* accounts receivable, the more reliable the revenue information is. Zhang found that the reliability of revenue information measured this way was significantly less for early recognizers than for late recognizers.

Combination of these two findings suggests that relevance and reliability must be traded off, since the greater relevance of early revenue recognition is accompanied by reduced reliability.

Required

a. Explain why securities market efficiency implies that revenues of early recognizers should be more highly associated with their share returns than revenues of late recognizers. In your answer, assume that information about licensing contracts becomes public information when the contract is signed.

b. Explain why the closer cash collections are for the following two quarters to opening accounts receivable, the more reliable revenue information is.

c. Do Zhang's findings imply that early revenue recognition for licensing contracts has the potential to be decision useful for investors? Use the concept of an information system (in particular, the effects of relevance and reliability on the main diagonal probabilities) in your answer.

15. What implications does estimation risk have for the working of securities markets, and for social welfare, in a capitalist economy? Explain how estimation risk can be reduced in our economy. Can estimation risk be eliminated?

Notes

1. All investors in the market need not behave rationally. All that is required is that behaviour is rational on average.

2. More generally, the random fluctuation could be about a trend line. For example, the price of a security may have an upward trend over time.

3. This phenomenon, that the collective judgments of a large group can be surprisingly accurate, has been documented in numerous contexts. Surowiecki (2004) gives four conditions needed for the effect to operate: diversity of information, independence, decentralization, and aggregation. Arguably, all of these conditions are present in a securities market.

4. In Section 3.3.2, we applied the term "informative" to the information system. An informative information system enables the decision maker to revise his/her prior probabilities. In that context, a *fully* informative information system perfectly reveals the state of nature (see Question 1 of Chapter 3). In the context of this chapter, "fully informative" applies to share price rather than to an information system, but the reasoning is similar—a fully informative share price always fully reflects all publicly available information. Note that if share price is fully informative, the information system formed by financial statements is non-informative: It reveals nothing new to investors about the firm since, given market efficiency, share price already reflects all the information contained in those statements. Hence the logical inconsistency: If we view financial statements as a message about future firm performance, and if share prices are fully informative, no one would use financial statements. But, if no one used financial statements, share prices would no longer be fully informative with respect to the information contained in those statements. For a formal analysis of these arguments, see Huang and Litzenberger (1988), Sections 9.8–9.10.

5. This requires that $E(R_{Mt}) > R_f$. This is reasonable, however, since the market return is risky. The excess of the expected return on the market over the risk-free rate is called the **equity risk premium**.

6. This abnormal return should not be confused with abnormal earnings like those of P.V. Ltd. in Example 2.2. While the idea of differing from expectations is the same, abnormal security return here refers to a *market* return, whereas abnormal earnings refer to *accounting* net income.

7. Actual return may differ from expected return for many reasons, including changes in the market's expectation of future cash flows and changes in discount rates. If the sample average actual return is to be a good proxy for the market's expected return, these reasons must average out to zero. Otherwise, actual return is a biased estimate of expected return.

   Given that actual return is a reasonable estimate of expected return, estimating beta by least-squares regression is not inconsistent with the formula for beta given below Equation 4.3. The regression approach merely provides a convenient framework to carry out the estimation. To see this, note the definition of the coefficient of an independent variable in a regression model; it is the amount of change in the dependent variable (R_{jt}) for a unit change in the independent variable (R_{Mt}). This is exactly the definition of beta. As explained above, beta measures the strength of the variation in a security's return as the market return varies.

8. The actual amount of loss or gain is a random variable. The lower the mean of this random variable, the more will investors bid down share price. However, actual gains or losses will be randomly distributed about this mean. It is possible that this remaining estimation risk is diversifiable. The

extent to which estimation risk is diversifiable is currently an unanswered question in financial accounting. This is considered further in Section 12.9.3.

9. If the insider trades affect share price, as it could if the market is imperfect (e.g., not completely liquid), investors may be able to infer inside information from the effect of the trade on market price. However, as discussed in Section 4.4.1, the presence of noise traders means that such inferences cannot be perfect. Thus, some estimation risk remains.

10. The CAPM can be extended to incorporate estimation risk. The model of Lambert, Leuz, and Verrecchia (2007) is reviewed in Section 12.9.1.

11. Fundamental value can also be interpreted as value under strong form market efficiency.

12. If insiders release false or misleading information about fundamental value, and the market accepts this information, the efficient market price circle could be *outside* the fundamental value circle in Figure 4.2. Such a situation is consistent with the valuation of shares of Enron, WorldCom, and many financial firms leading up to the 2007–2008 market meltdowns, as described in Chapter 1. Nevertheless, the role of financial reporting, to convert inside information into outside information, remains. Unfortunately, it seems that the auditors of the affected companies did not completely fulfill this role.

13. Mafffet uses the concept of **opacity** to measure financial reporting quality, where opacity is defined as "the unavailability of firm-specific information to those outside publicly traded firms." In effect, it is a negative measure of reporting quality.

    Maffet measures opacity of a firm's reporting by number of analysts following the firm, analyst forecast accuracy, the extent to which analyst forecasts differ, lack of a Big 5 auditor, and extent of income smoothing.

14. Maffett points out that it is possible that the costs of developing inside information may exceed the abnormal returns. However, he presents evidence that this is unlikely.

15. Maffett measures country-level reporting quality by the quality of its disclosure regulations and the quality of its corporate governance. He also includes a measure of media penetration in the country, on grounds that the better the development and quality of a country's media is, the less difficult it is for investors to find inside information.

16. Wurgler estimates a country's efficiency of capital allocation by the relationship between its growth in investment and its growth in output; more output from a unit of growth in investment implies higher capital allocation efficiency. He estimates the amount of firm-specific information in a country's share prices by their **synchronicity** (the extent to which share prices move together)—less synchronicity or, equivalently, less co-movement between share prices, implies more firm-specific information relative to industry- and economy-wide information. In obtaining his result, Wurgler controls for shareholder minority rights and extent of state ownership in the economy, which also affect capital allocation efficiency.

17. BHV measured investment by the sum of capital investment, acquisitions, and R&D. They classified their sample firms into categories of low cash and high leverage (likely to underinvest) and high cash and low leverage (likely to overinvest). They found that for low cash/high leverage firms, higher reporting quality was associated with less underinvestment, while for high cash/low leverage firms, higher reporting quality was associated with less overinvestment.

    As an additional test, BHV examined their sample firms' growth opportunities (proxied by sales growth). A firm's rate of growth creates an *expected* level of investment, since growth and investment go hand in hand. For sample firms with actual investment lower than expected (i.e., underinvestment firms), BHV report that higher reporting quality was associated with less underinvestment. For firms with actual investment higher than expected, higher reporting quality was associated with less overinvestment. These results are consistent with the results of their cash-/leverage-based tests.

Chapter 5

The Value Relevance of
Accounting Information

Figure 5.1 Organization of Chapter 5

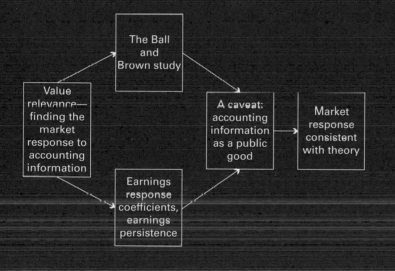

5.1 OVERVIEW

There is a saying that "the proof of the pudding is in the eating." If the efficient markets theory and the decision theories underlying it are reasonable descriptions of reality on average, we should observe the market values of securities responding in predictable ways to new information.

This leads to an examination of empirical research in accounting. Despite the difficulties of designing experiments to test the implications of decision usefulness, accounting research has established that security market prices do respond to accounting information. When security prices respond in this manner, we say that accounting information has **value relevance**. The first significant evidence of this security market reaction to earnings announcements was provided by Ball and Brown in 1968. Since then, a large number of empirical studies have documented additional aspects of value relevance.

On the basis of these studies, it does seem that accounting information is useful to investors in helping them estimate the expected values and risks of security returns. One has only to contemplate the use of Bayes' theorem in Example 3.1 to see that if accounting information did not have information content, there would be no revision of beliefs upon receipt, hence no triggering of buy/sell decisions. Without buy/sell decisions, there would be no trading volume or price changes. In essence, information is useful if it leads investors to change their beliefs and actions. Furthermore, the degree of usefulness for investors can be measured by the extent of volume or price change following release of the information.

The value relevance approach takes the view that investors want to make *their own* predictions of future security returns (instead of having financial statements do it for them, as under ideal conditions) and are capable of "gobbling up" all useful information in this regard. Value relevance also implies that empirical research can help accountants to further increase usefulness by letting market response guide them as to which information is and is not valued by investors.

One must be careful, however, when equating usefulness with the extent of security price change. While investors, and accountants, may benefit from useful information, it does *not* follow that *society* will necessarily be better off. Information is a very complex commodity, and its private and social values are not the same. One reason is *cost*. Financial statement users do not generally pay directly for this information. As a result, they may find information useful even though it costs society more (e.g., in the form of higher product prices to help firms pay for generating and reporting the information) than the increased usefulness is worth. Furthermore, information affects people differently, requiring complex cost–benefit tradeoffs to balance the competing interests of different constituencies.

These social considerations do not invalidate value relevance. Accountants can still strive to improve their competitive position in the information marketplace by providing more useful information. And it is still true that securities markets will work better to allocate scarce capital if security prices provide good indicators of investment opportunities and future firm performance. However, what accountants cannot do is claim that the best accounting policy is the one that produces the greatest market response.

Figure 5.1 outlines the organization of this chapter.

5.2 OUTLINE OF THE RESEARCH PROBLEM

5.2.1 Reasons for Market Response

We begin by reviewing the reasons why the market price of a firm's shares may respond to financial statement information. For most of this chapter we will confine financial statement information to reported net income. The information content of net income is a topic that has received extensive empirical investigation. Information content of other financial statement components will be discussed in Section 5.6 and in Chapter 7.

Consider the following predictions about investor behaviour in response to financial statement information:

1. Investors have prior beliefs about a firm's future performance—that is, its dividends, cash flows, and/or earnings, which affect the expected returns and risk of the firm's securities. These prior beliefs will be based on all available information, including market price up to just prior to the release of the firm's current net income. Even if they are based on publicly available information, these prior beliefs need not all be the same because investors will differ in the amount of information they have obtained and the extent to which they become informed.

2. Upon release of the current period's net income, some investors will quickly decide to become more informed by analyzing the income number. For example, if net income is high, or higher than expected, this may be good news. If so, investors would revise upward their beliefs about future firm performance. Other investors, who perhaps had overly high prior beliefs of what current net income should be, might interpret the same net income number as bad news.

3. Investors who have revised their beliefs about future firm performance upward will be inclined to buy the firm's shares at their current market price, and vice versa for those who have revised their beliefs downward. Investors' evaluations of the riskiness of these shares may also be revised.

4. We would expect to observe the volume of shares traded to increase when the firm reports its net income. Furthermore, this volume should be greater the greater are the differences in investors' prior beliefs about future firm performance, and in their interpretations of the current financial information.[1] If the investors who interpret reported net income as good news (and hence have increased their expectations of future performance) outweigh those who interpret it as bad news, we would expect to observe an increase in the market price of the firm's shares, and vice versa.

Beaver (1968), in a well-known study, examined trading volume reaction. He found a dramatic increase in volume during the week of release of earnings announcements. Further details of Beaver's findings are included in Question 9 of this chapter. In the balance of this chapter we will concentrate on market price reaction. Market price reaction may provide a stronger test of decision usefulness than volume reaction. For example, the model of Kim and Verrecchia (1997) suggests that volume is noisier than price change as a measure of the decision usefulness of financial statement information.

You will recognize that the preceding predictions follow the decision theory and efficient markets theory of Chapters 3 and 4 quite closely. If these theories are to have relevance to accountants, their predictions should be borne out empirically. An empirical researcher could test these predictions by obtaining a sample of firms that issue annual reports and investigating whether the volume and price reactions to good or bad news in earnings occur as the theories lead us to believe. This is not as easy as it might seem, however, for a number of reasons, as we will discuss next.

5.2.2 Finding the Market Response

1. Efficient markets theory implies that the market will react quickly to new information. As a result, it is important to know *when* the current year's reported net income first became publicly known. If the researcher looks for volume and price effects even a few days too late, no effects may be observed even though they had existed.

Researchers have solved this problem by using the date the firm's net income was reported in the financial media such as *The Wall Street Journal*. More recently, many firms announce earnings information at a news conference or in a conference call. If the market is going to react, it should do so in a **narrow window** of a few days surrounding these dates.

2. The good or bad news in reported net income is usually evaluated relative to what investors *expected*. If a firm reported net income of, say, $2 million, and this was what investors had expected (from quarterly reports, speeches by company officials, analysts' predictions, forward-looking information in MD&A and, indeed, in the share price itself), there would hardly be much information content in reported net income. Investors' prior beliefs would have already been revised to reflect the earlier information. Things would be different, however, if investors had expected $2 million and reported net income was $3 million. This good news would trigger rapid belief revision about the future performance of the firm. This means that researchers must obtain a proxy for what investors expected net income to be. These proxies are usually based on previous earnings or analyst earnings forecasts.

3. There are always many events taking place that affect a firm's share volume and price. This means that a market response to reported net income can be hard to find. For example, suppose a firm released its current year's net income, containing good news, on the same day the government announced a substantial increase in the deficit. Such a public announcement would probably affect prices of all or most securities on the market, which in turn might swamp the price impact of the firm's earnings release. Thus, it is desirable to separate the impacts of market-wide and firm-specific factors on share returns.

5.2.3 Separating Market-Wide and Firm-Specific Factors

As described in Section 4.5, the market model is widely used to *ex post* separate market-wide and firm-specific factors that affect security returns. Figure 5.2 gives a graphical illustration of the market model for firm j for period t, where we take the length of the period as one day. Longer time periods, such as a week, month, or year, and even shorter periods, are also used by researchers.

The figure shows the relationship between the return on firm j's shares and the return on the market portfolio (proxied, for example, by the Dow Jones Industrial Average index or the S&P/TSX Composite index).

Figure 5.2 Separating Market-Wide and Firm-Specific Security Returns Using the Market Model

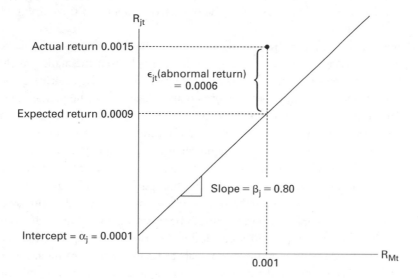

Consider the equation of the market model, repeated here from Section 4.5 (Equation 4.4):

$$R_{jt} = \alpha_j + \beta_j R_{Mt} + \epsilon_{jt}$$

As described in Section 4.5, the researcher will obtain past data on R_{jt} and R_{Mt} and use regression analysis to estimate the coefficients of the model. Suppose this yields $\alpha_j = 0.0001$ and $\beta_j = 0.80$, as shown in the figure.[2]

Now, armed with this estimate of the market model for firm j, the researcher can consult the financial media to find the day of the firm's current earnings announcement. Call this "day 0." Suppose that for day 0 the return on the Dow Jones Industrial index was 0.001.[3] Then the estimated market model for firm j is used to predict the return on firm j's shares for this day. As shown in Figure 5.2, this expected return[4] is 0.0009. Now assume that the *actual* return on firm j's shares for day 0 is 0.0015. Then the difference between actual and expected returns is 0.0006 (that is, $\epsilon_{jt} = 0.0006$ for this day). This 0.0006 is an estimate of the abnormal, or firm-specific, return on firm j's shares for that day.[5] This abnormal return is also interpreted as the rate of return on firm j's shares for day 0 *after removing* the influence of market-wide factors. Note that this interpretation is consistent with Example 3.2, where we distinguished between market-wide and firm-specific factors. The present procedure provides an operational way to make this separation.

5.2.4 Comparing Returns and Income

The empirical researcher can now compare the abnormal share return on day 0 as calculated above with the unexpected component of the firm's current reported net income. If this unexpected net income is good news (that is, a positive unexpected net income) then, given reasonable securities market efficiency, a positive abnormal share return constitutes evidence that investors on average are reacting favourably to the unexpected good news in earnings. A similar line of reasoning applies if the current earnings announcement is bad news.

To increase the power of the investigation, the researcher may wish to also examine a few days on either side of day 0. It is possible, for example, that the market might learn of the good or bad earnings news a day or two early. Conversely, positive or negative abnormal returns may continue for a day or two after day 0 while the market digests the information, although market efficiency implies that any excess returns should die out quickly. Consequently, the summing of abnormal returns for a three-to-five-day narrow window around day 0 seems more reasonable than examining day 0 only. It also helps protect against the possibility that the announcement date of current earnings may not be a completely accurate estimate of the date of their public availability.

If positive and negative abnormal returns surrounding good or bad earnings news are found to hold across a sample of firms, the researcher may conclude that predictions based on the decision theory and efficient securities market theory are supported. This would in turn support the decision usefulness approach to financial accounting and reporting, because, if investors did not find the reported net income information useful, a market response would hardly be observed.

Of course, this methodology is not foolproof—a number of assumptions and estimations have to be made along the way. One complication is that other firm-specific information frequently comes along around the time of a firm's earnings announcement. For example, if firm j announced a stock split or a change in its dividend on the same day that it released its current earnings, it would be hard to know if a market response was due to one or the other. However, researchers can cope with this by removing such firms from the sample.

Another complication is the estimation of a firm's beta, needed to separate market-wide and firm-specific returns as in Figure 5.2. As mentioned, this estimation is usually based on a regression analysis of past data using the market model. Then, the estimated beta is the slope of the regression line. However, as we will discuss in Section 6.2.3, a firm's beta may change over time, for example as the firm changes its operations and/or its capital structure. If the estimated beta is different from the true beta, this affects the calculation of abnormal return, possibly biasing the results of the investigation.

There is a variety of ways to cope with this complication. For example, it may be possible to get a "second opinion" on beta by estimating it from financial statement information rather than from market data. (This is considered in Section 7.12.1.) Alternatively, beta may be estimated from a period after the earnings announcement and compared with the estimate from a period before the announcement.

Also, there are ways to separate market-wide and firm-specific returns that ignore beta. For example, we can estimate firm-specific returns by the difference between firm j's stock return during period 0 and the average return on its shares over some prior period. Or, we can take the difference between firm j's return during period 0 and the return on the market portfolio for the same period. Alternatively, as in Easton and Harris (1991), we can simply work with total share returns and not factor out market-wide returns at all.

The rationale for these simpler procedures is that there is no guarantee that the market model adequately captures the real process generating share returns—see our discussion in Section 4.5.2. To the extent that the market model does not fully capture reality, its use may introduce more error in estimating beta and abnormal returns than it reduces by removing market-wide returns and controlling for risk. A further complication is that there is a variety of market portfolio return indices available, of which the Dow Jones Industrial Average is only one. Which one should be used?

These issues were examined by Brown and Warner (1980) in a simulation study. Despite modelling and measurement problems such as those just mentioned, Brown and Warner concluded that, for monthly return windows, the market model-based procedure outlined in Section 5.2.3 performed reasonably well relative to the above alternatives. Consequently, this is the procedure we will concentrate on.

Using this procedure, it does appear that the market reacts to earnings information much as the theories predict. We will now review the first significant evidence and interpretation of this reaction, the famous 1968 Ball and Brown study.

5.3 THE BALL AND BROWN STUDY

5.3.1 Methodology and Findings

In 1968, Ball and Brown (BB) began a tradition of empirical capital markets research in accounting that continues to this day. They were the first to provide convincing scientific evidence that firms' share returns respond to the information content of financial statements—that is, that financial statements have value relevance. This type of research is called an **event study**, since it studies the narrow window securities market reaction to a specific event, in this case, a firm's release of its current net income. A review of the BB paper is worthwhile because its basic methodology, and adaptations and extensions of it, are still used. Their paper continues to provide guidance, as well as encouragement, to those who wish to better understand the decision usefulness of financial reporting.

BB examined a sample of 261 New York Stock Exchange (NYSE) firms over nine years from 1957 to 1965. They concentrated on the information content of earnings, to the exclusion of other potentially informative financial statement components such as solvency and capital structure. One reason for this, as mentioned earlier, was that earnings for NYSE firms were typically announced in the media prior to actual release of the annual report so that it was relatively easy to estimate when the information first became publicly available.

BB's first task was to measure the information content of earnings—that is, whether reported earnings were greater than what the market had expected (GN) or less than expected (BN). Of course, this requires a proxy for the market's expectation. One proxy they used was last year's actual earnings, from which it follows that unexpected earnings is simply the change in earnings.[6] Thus, firms with earnings higher than last year's were classified as GN, and firms with earnings lower than last year's were classified as BN.

The next task was to evaluate the market return on the shares of the sample firms near the time of each earnings announcement. This was done according to the abnormal returns procedure illustrated in Figure 5.2. The only difference was that BB measured share returns over a month-long return window (daily returns were not available on databases in 1968).

Analogously to Figure 5.2, suppose that firm j reported its 1957 earnings in February 1958, and that these earnings were GN. Suppose also that the return on the NYSE market portfolio in February 1958 was 0.001, yielding an expected firm j return of 0.0009. BB would then calculate the actual return on firm j shares for February 1958. Suppose this was 0.0015, yielding an abnormal return for February of 0.0006. Since firm j's 1957 earnings were reported in February 1958 and since its shares earned 0.0006 over and above the market in this month, one might suspect that the reason for the positive abnormal return was that investors were reacting favourably to the GN information in earnings.

The question then was, was this pattern repeated across the sample? The answer was yes. If we take all the GN earnings announcements in the sample (there were 1,231), the *average* abnormal security market return in the month of earnings release was strongly positive. Conversely, the average abnormal return for the 1,109 bad news earnings announcements in the sample was strongly negative. This provides substantial evidence that the market did respond to the good or bad news in earnings during a narrow window consisting of the month of earnings announcement release.

An interesting and important aspect of the BB study was that they repeated their abnormal security market returns calculation for a **wide window** consisting of each of the 11 months prior to and the six months following the month of earnings release (month 0). BB calculated average abnormal returns for each month of this 18-month window. The results are shown in Figure 5.3, taken from BB.

The upper part of Figure 5.3 shows cumulative average abnormal returns for the GN earnings announcement firms in the sample; the bottom part shows the same for the BN announcement firms. As can be seen, the GN firms strongly outperformed the total sample (the total sample approximates the market-wide return), and the BN firms strongly underperformed, over the 11-month period leading up to the month of earnings release.

5.3.2 Causation Versus Association

Note that the monthly returns are *cumulative* in Figure 5.3. While there was a substantial increase (for GN) and decrease (for BN) in average abnormal returns in the narrow window consisting of month 0, as described above, Figure 5.3 suggests that the market began to *anticipate* the GN or BN as much as a year earlier, with the result that returns accumulated steadily over the period. As can be seen, if an investor could have bought the shares of all GN firms one year before the good news was released and held them until the end of the month of release, there would have been an extra return of more than 5% over and

Figure 5.3 Abnormal Returns for GN and BN Firms

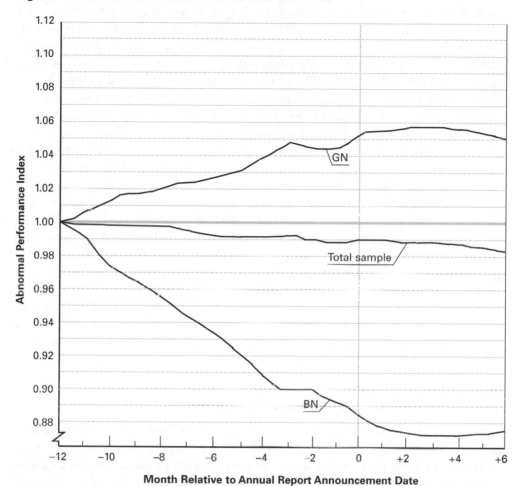

Month Relative to Annual Report Announcement Date

Source: Ray Ball and P. Brown, "An Empirical Evaluation of Accounting Income Numbers," *Journal of Accounting Research* (Autumn 1968), p. 169. Reproduced with permission of John Wiley & Sons Ltd.

above the market-wide return. Similarly, an abnormal loss of over 9% would have been incurred on a portfolio of BN firms bought one year before the bad news was released.[7]

   This leads to an important distinction between narrow and wide window studies. If a security market reaction to accounting information is observed during a narrow window of a few days (or, in the case of BB, a month) surrounding an earnings announcement, it can be argued that the accounting information is the *cause* of the market reaction. The reason is that during a narrow window there are relatively few firm-specific events other than net income to affect share returns. Also, if other events do occur, such as stock splits or dividend announcements, the affected firms can be removed from the sample, as mentioned. Thus, a narrow window relationship between security returns and accounting information suggests that accounting disclosures are the *source* of new information to investors.[8]

Evaluation of security returns over a wide window, however, opens them up to a host of other events that affect share price. For example, a firm may have discovered new oil and gas reserves, be engaged in promising R&D projects, or have rising sales and market share. As the market learns this information from more timely sources, such as media articles, firm announcements, conditions in the economy and industry, quarterly reports, and insider buying (for GN) and selling (BN), share price would begin to rise. This reflects the partly informative nature of security prices since, in an efficient market, security prices reflect all available information, not just accounting information. Thus, firms that in a real sense are doing well should have much of the effect on their share prices anticipated by the market before the GN appears in the financial statements. That is, because of recognition lag, *prices lead earnings* over a wide window.[9] Thus the most that can be argued for wide windows is that net income and returns are *associated*. That is, it is the real, underlying, economic performance of the firm that generates the association, since both share price and (with a lag) net income reflect real performance.

Clearly, this effect was taking place in the BB study. A glance at Figure 5.3 reveals that while there was a significant increase (GN firms) and decrease (BN) in cumulative annual return during month 0, as noted earlier, most of the information in net income was anticipated prior to month 0. In fact, BB estimated that, on average, 85%–90% of the information in annual earnings was already built into share price by the time annual earnings were announced. Nevertheless, the narrow window results remain; the market did not anticipate all the information in net income, thereby supporting both the decision and efficient markets theories and the value relevance of accounting information.[10]

5.3.3 Outcomes of the BB Study

One of the most important outcomes of BB was that it opened up a large number of additional usefulness issues. A logical next step is to ask whether the *magnitude* of unexpected earnings is related to the *magnitude* of the security market response—recall that BB's analysis was based only on the *sign* of unexpected earnings. That is, the information content of earnings in BB's study was classified only into GN or BN, a fairly coarse measure.

The question of magnitude of response was investigated, for example, by Beaver, Clarke, and Wright (BCW) in 1979. They examined a sample of 276 NYSE firms with December 31 year ends, over the 10-year period from 1965 to 1974. For each sample firm, for each year of the sample period, they estimated the unexpected earnings changes. They then used the market model procedure described in Sections 4.5.1 and 5.2.3 to estimate the abnormal security returns associated with these unexpected earnings changes.

Upon comparison of unexpected earnings changes with abnormal security returns, BCW found that the greater the change in unexpected earnings, the greater the security market response. This result is consistent with the CAPM and decision usefulness, since the larger are unexpected earnings changes the more investors on average will revise their estimates of future firm performance and resulting returns from their investments, other things equal.[11]

Also, accounting researchers have studied securities market response to net income on other stock exchanges, in other countries, and for quarterly earnings reports, with similar results. The approach has been applied to study market response to the information contained in new accounting standards, auditor changes, etc. Here, however, we will concentrate on what is probably the most important extension of BB, earnings response coefficients. This line of research asks a different question than does BCW—namely, for a *given* amount of unexpected earnings, is the security market response greater for some firms than for others?

5.4 EARNINGS RESPONSE COEFFICIENTS

Recall that the abnormal securities market returns identified by BB were *averages*—that is, they showed that on average their GN firms enjoyed positive abnormal returns, and their BN firms showed negative ones. Of course, an average can conceal wide variation about the average. Thus, it is likely that some firms' abnormal returns were well above average and others' were well below.

This raises the question of *why* the market might respond more strongly to the good or bad news in earnings for some firms than for others. If answers to this question can be found, accountants can improve their understanding of how accounting information is useful to investors. This, in turn, could lead to the preparation of more useful financial statements.

Consequently, one of the most important directions that empirical financial accounting research took following the BB study was the identification and explanation of differential market response to earnings information. This is called earnings response coefficient (ERC) research.[12]

> An **earnings response coefficient** *measures the extent of a security's abnormal market return in response to the unexpected component of reported earnings of the firm issuing that security.*

That is, to calculate an ERC, divide abnormal share return (for the window surrounding the date of earnings release) by unexpected earnings for the period. This measures the abnormal return per dollar of abnormal earnings, enabling comparisons of ERCs across firms and over time.

5.4.1 Reasons for Differential Market Response

A number of reasons can be suggested for differential market response to reported earnings. We will review these in turn.

Beta The riskier the sequence of a firm's future expected returns is, the lower its value will be to a risk-averse investor, other things equal. For a diversified investor, the relevant risk measure of a security is its beta, explained in Section 4.5. Since investors look to current earnings as an indicator of future firm performance and share returns, the riskier these future returns are, the lower investors' reactions to a given amount of unexpected earnings will be, leading to a higher cost of capital.

To illustrate, think of a risk-averse, rational investor whose utility increases in the expected value and decreases in the risk of the return on his/her portfolio. Suppose that the investor, upon becoming aware that a firm has just released GN earnings information, revises upward the expected rate of return on the firm's shares and decides to buy more. However, if this security has a high beta, this will increase portfolio risk.[13] Since the investor trades off risk and return, the high beta acts as a brake on the investor's demand for the GN security. Since all rational, risk-averse, informed investors will think this way, the demand for the GN firm's shares will be lower the higher its beta is, other things equal. Of course, lower demand implies a lower increase in market price and share return in response to the GN, hence, a lower ERC.

Empirical evidence of a lower ERC for higher-beta securities was found by Collins and Kothari (1989) and by Easton and Zmijewski (1989).

Capital Structure For highly levered firms, an increase, say, in earnings (before interest) adds strength and safety to bonds and other outstanding debt, so that much of the good news in earnings goes to the debtholders rather than the shareholders. Thus, the ERC for a highly levered firm should be lower than that of a firm with little or no debt, other things equal.

Empirical evidence of a lower ERC for more highly levered firms was reported by Dhaliwal, Lee, and Fargher (1991).

Earnings Quality Recall from Section 3.3.2 that we define the quality (i.e., the informativeness) of earnings by the magnitude of the main diagonal probabilities of the associated information system. The higher these probabilities, the higher we would expect the ERC to be, since investors are better able to infer future firm performance from current performance.

As a practical matter, measurement of earnings quality is less clear, since information system probabilities are not directly observable and a sampling approach runs into problems of sampling error. An indirect approach, discussed in Section 3.3.2, is to infer earnings quality by the magnitude of analysts' earnings forecast revisions following earnings announcements. However, this just raises the question of *why* analysts revise their forecasts more for some firms than others.

Fortunately, several other measures of earnings quality are available. Here we consider two such measures. The first is **earnings persistence**. We would expect that the ERC will be higher the more the good or bad news in current earnings is expected to persist into the future, since current earnings then provide a better indication of future firm performance. Thus, if current GN is due to operating efficiencies, the successful introduction of a new product or cost-cutting by management, the ERC should be higher than if the GN was due to, say, an unanticipated gain on disposal of plant and equipment. In the latter case, the firm's market value increases dollar-for-dollar with the amount of the gain, since there is little reason to expect the unusual gain to recur. With improved operations, the revenue increases or cost savings will persist to benefit future income statements as well, so the ERC should be higher.

Evidence that ERCs are higher the higher the persistence of unexpected current earnings changes was presented by Kormendi and Lipe (1987), whose measure of persistence was the extent to which earnings changes of the past two years continued into the current year—the greater the influence of the past two years' earnings changes on the current year's earnings change, the greater the persistence of these previous earnings.

Li (2011) proposed a related approach to measuring persistence. He argued that a firm's capital and labour investment decisions reflect management's inside information about the firm's longer-term earnings prospects. That is, a rational manager will only invest capital and labour in positive expected value projects.[14] If so, the strength of the relationship between changes in capital expenditures and changes in earnings is a measure of earnings quality. Since longer-term earnings and earnings persistence are similar concepts, Li's approach enables an alternate earnings persistence estimate.

Based on a sample of firms over the period 1952–2004, Li documented a positive relationship between changes in capital expenditures and changes in earnings, and that this relationship is correlated with earnings persistence, consistent with his arguments. These results hold after controlling for other measures of earnings quality.

Persistence is a challenging and useful concept. One reason, advanced by Ramakrishnan and Thomas (RT; 1991), is that different components of net income may have different persistence. For example, suppose that in the same year in which a firm successfully introduces a new product it also reports a gain on disposal of plant and equipment. Then, the persistence of earnings is a weighted average of the differing persistence of the components of earnings. RT distinguish three types of earnings events:

- Permanent, expected to persist indefinitely
- Transitory, affecting earnings in the current year but not future years
- Price-irrelevant, persistence of zero

The ERCs per dollar of unexpected earnings for these are $(1 + R_f)/R_f$ (where R_f is the risk-free rate of interest), 1, and 0, respectively.[15]

In effect, there are three ERCs, all of which may be present in the same income statement. RT suggest that instead of trying to estimate an average ERC, investors should attempt to identify the three types separately and assign different ERCs to each. In so doing, they can identify the firm's permanent, or persistent, earning power.

To understand the ERC for permanent earnings, note that it can be written as $1 + 1/R_f$. Thus, under ideal conditions, the market response to $1 of permanent earnings consists of the current year's installment of $1 plus the present value of the perpetuity of future installments[16] of $1/R_f$. Writing the ERC this way also shows that when earnings persist beyond the current year, the magnitude of the ERC varies inversely with the interest rate.

Another aspect of ERCs is that earnings persistence can depend on the firm's accounting policies. For example, suppose that a firm uses fair value accounting for a capital asset[17], and that the fair value of the asset increases by $100. Assume that the increase results from an increase in the price of the product produced by the asset. Then, assuming that changes in fair value are included in net income, the net income for the period will include the unrealized asset price increase of $100. Since unexpected changes in value occur randomly, by definition, the market will not expect the $100 to persist. Thus, its ERC is 1.

Suppose, instead, that the firm uses historical cost accounting for the asset and that the annual increase in contribution margin is $9.09. Then there will be only $9.09 of GN in earnings this year. The reason, of course, is that under historical cost accounting the $100 increase in current value is brought into income only as it is realized. The efficient market will recognize that the current $9.09 GN is only the "first installment."[18] If it regards the value increase as permanent and $R_f = 10\%$, the ERC will be 11 (1.10/0.10).

Zero-persistence income statement components can result from the choice of accounting policy. Suppose, for example, that a firm capitalizes a large amount of organization costs. This could result in GN on the current income statement, which is freed of the costs because of their capitalization. However, assuming the organization costs have no salvage value, the market would not react to the "GN"; that is, its persistence, as measured by the ERC, is zero.

ERC s can be negative. Suppose that a firm writes off research costs currently in accordance with GAAP. This could produce BN in current earnings. However, to the extent the market perceives the research costs as having future value, it would react positively to this BN so that persistence, as measured by the ERC, is negative.

A second dimension of earnings quality is **accruals quality**. This approach was proposed by Dechow and Dichev (DD; 2002). They pointed out that net income is composed of

$$\text{Net income} = \text{Cash flow from operations} \pm \text{Net accruals}$$

where net accruals include changes in non-cash working capital accounts such as receivables, allowance for doubtful accounts, inventories, accounts payable, etc., as well as amortization expense. The manager has considerable control over the amounts and timing of accruals. If the manager uses this control over accruals to influence the amount of reported net income, they are called **discretionary accruals**. DD, in effect, argued that the greater discretionary accruals are relative to cash flows, the more likely it is that those accruals contain a substantial discretionary component, leading to lower earnings quality. They then argued that earnings quality depends primarily on the quality of working capital accruals, since cash flow from operations is relatively less subject to errors and manager bias, and therefore is of reasonably high quality to start with.

To measure accrual quality, DD suggested that to the extent current period working capital accruals show up as cash flows next period, those accruals are of high quality. This is consistent with the Conceptual Framework, discussed in Section 3.7.1, where the role of accruals is envisaged as one of anticipating future cash flows. Thus, if accounts receivable at the end of the current period are $1,000 less an allowance for doubtful accounts of $100, and if $900 is collected next period, then the accounts receivable and doubtful accounts accruals are of high quality since they match perfectly with the cash subsequently collected. However, if only $800 is subsequently collected, the accruals are of lower quality since there has been an error in their estimation or, perhaps, deliberate misstatement by management so as to increase current reported net income.

A similar argument applies to last period's accruals. Suppose, for example, that accounts receivable last period were $700, less an allowance for doubtful accounts of $60, and that they realized $600 in the current period. This lowers the quality of current accruals and earnings since current bad debts expense includes the $40 under provision, which really belongs to last period.

To test this concept of accrual quality, DD suggested estimating the following regression equation:

$$\Delta WC_t = b_0 + b_1 CFO_{t-1} + b_2 CFO_t + b_3 CFO_{t+1} + \varepsilon_t \qquad (5.1)$$

where ΔWC_t is the change in net non-cash working capital for the firm in question for period t—that is, working capital accruals. For example, in our illustration above, if accounts receivable and allowance for doubtful accounts are the only non-cash working capital items, working capital has increased by $\Delta WC_t =$ $260 (i.e., $900 − $640) in period t. This is an accrual because net income includes this amount (assuming the firm recognizes income at point of sale) but it has not yet been received in cash.

CFO_{t-1} is cash flow from operations in period t − 1, etc., b_0, b_1, and b_2 are constants to be estimated, and ε_t is the residual error term—that is, the portion of total accruals not explained by cash from operations.

For a specific firm, Equation (5.1) is estimated using data from several recent periods. Accrual quality, hence earnings quality, is based on the variability of the ε_t residuals— that is, high ε_t variability indicates a poor match between current accruals ΔWC_t and actual operating cash flow realizations.

Evidence that firms' ERCs and share prices respond positively to accrual quality as measured by this procedure is reported by Francis, LaFond, Olsson, and Schipper (2005) and Ecker, Francis, Kim, Olsson, and Schipper (2006).[19, 20]

Growth Opportunities The GN or BN in current earnings may suggest future growth prospects for the firm, and hence a higher ERC. One might think that since financial statements still contain a considerable historical cost component, net income really cannot say much about the future growth of the firm. However, this is not necessarily the case. Suppose that current net income reveals unexpectedly high profitability for some of the firm's recent investment projects. This may indicate to the market that the firm will enjoy strong growth in the future. One reason, of course, is that to the extent the high profitability persists, the future profits will increase the firm's assets. In addition, success with current projects may suggest to the market that this firm is also capable of identifying and implementing additional successful projects in future, so that it becomes labelled as a growth firm. Such firms can easily attract capital, and this is an additional source of growth. Thus, to the extent that current good news in earnings suggests growth opportunities, the ERC will be high.

To illustrate, extend the persistence example above by assuming that the $9.09 of current permanent earnings increase is expected to grow by 5% per year. The present value at 10% of a perpetuity that increases by 5% per year is $1/(0.10 - 0.05) = 20$, which is greater than $1/0.10 = 10$ under no growth. Thus, the ERC is 21 rather than 11, as before.

Evidence that the ERC is higher for firms that the market regards as possessing growth opportunities was shown by Collins and Kothari (1989). They used the ratio of market value of equity to book value of equity as a measure of growth opportunities, the rationale being that the market will be aware of the growth opportunities before they are recognized in net income and will bid up share price accordingly. Collins and Kothari find a positive relationship between this measure and the ERCs of their sample firms.

The ability of financial statements to provide "clues" about future firm performance may seem surprising. However, this supports the Conceptual Framework's contention that "information about an entity's past financial performance is usually helpful in predicting the entity's future returns...."

The Similarity of Investor Expectations Different investors will have different expectations of a firm's next-period earnings, depending on their prior information and the extent of their abilities to evaluate financial statement information. However, these differences will be reduced to the extent that they draw on a common information source, such as analysts' consensus forecasts (e.g., an average of all forecasts), when forming their expectations. Consider a firm's announcement of its current earnings. Depending on their expectations, some investors will regard this information as GN, others as BN; hence, some will be inclined to buy and some to sell. However, to the extent that investors' earnings expectations were "close together," they will put the same interpretation on the news. For example, if most investors base their earnings expectation on the analysts' consensus forecast, and current earnings are less than forecast, they will all regard this as BN and will be inclined to sell rather than buy. Thus, the more similar the earnings expectations the greater the effect of a dollar of abnormal earnings on the share price. In effect, the more precise (i.e., low dispersion) analysts' forecasts are, the more similar are investors' earnings expectations and the greater the ERC, other things equal.[21]

The Informativeness of Price In Section 4.4, we described how share price is partially informative about the future value of the firm. A consequence is that *prices lead earnings*, since market price aggregates all publicly known information about the firm, much of which the accounting system recognizes with a lag. This effect shows up with particular clarity in the Ball and Brown study (see Figure 5.3), where share returns anticipated the GN or BN in earnings beginning as much as 12 months before earnings were released. Consequently, the more informative price is, the less the information content of current accounting earnings will be, other things equal, hence the lower the ERC.

A proxy for the informativeness of price is *firm size*, since larger firms are more in the news. However, after controlling for firm risk and growth, factors that are also affected by firm size, Easton and Zmijewski (1989) found that firm size was not a significant explanatory variable for the ERC. Collins and Kothari (1989) dealt with size by moving the wide window over which security returns were measured earlier in time for large firms, on the grounds that share price is more informative for such firms. They found that this substantially improved the relationship between changes in earnings and security returns, since a more informative share price implies that the market anticipates changes in earning power sooner. However, once this time shifting was done, size appeared to have no explanatory power for the ERC. Thus, while the theory is clear that informativeness of share price affects the ERC, an empirical proxy for informativeness of price is less clear.

5.4.2 Implications of ERC Research

Why should accountants be interested in the market's response to financial accounting information? Essentially, the reason is that improved understanding of market response suggests ways that they can further improve the decision usefulness of financial statements. For example, empirical evidence of a positive relationship between ERC and earnings quality suggests that higher earnings quality is valued by equity investors.

Also, the finding that ERCs are lower for highly levered firms supports arguments to expand disclosure of the nature and magnitude of financial instruments, including those that are off balance sheet. If the relative size of a firm's liabilities affects the market's response to net income, then it is desirable that all liabilities be disclosed. Recall from Section 1.3 that the off balance sheet liabilities of financial institutions were a contributing factor to the 2007–2008 market meltdowns.

The importance of growth opportunities to investors suggests, for example, the desirability of disclosure of segment information (Section 12.10), since profitability information by segments would better enable investors to isolate the profitable, and unprofitable, operations of the firm. Also, MD&A enables the firm to communicate its growth prospects, as illustrated in Section 3.6.

Finally, the importance of earnings persistence to the ERC means that disclosure of the *components* of net income is useful for investors. Lots of detail in the income statement, in the balance sheet, and in supplemental information helps investors interpret the persistence of the current earnings number. This argument is supported by Jones and Smith (2011), who studied the persistence of unusual and non-recurring gains and losses (termed **special items** by the authors), based on a sample of U.S. companies over the period 1986–2005. They reported that special items persist on average for at least five years.[22]

Jones and Smith also examined the persistence of other comprehensive income (OCI; Section 1.10). They reported that OCI items are transitory, persisting on average for only one year.

Another reason for the importance of full disclosure of low persistence items is that their reporting is surprisingly complex, despite the seeming simplicity of the concept of persistence. For example, under FASB standards (ASC 225-20-45), an **extraordinary item** is a realized gain or loss that is both unusual and infrequent. Thus, classification of a gain or loss as an extraordinary item is subject to manager judgment. While classification of gains and losses into OCI, being governed by ASC 225, is less subject to judgment, these gains and losses are unrealized, complicating the evaluation of their persistence.

Further adding to complexity, low persistence items appear in different sections of the income statement. Extraordinary items under FASB standards are shown, net of tax, below income from continuing operations. Other low persistence items, such as unrealized gains and losses from fair valuing certain securities, are included in OCI.

Disclosure also varies between IASB and FASB standards. IAS 1 prohibits the use of the term "extraordinary items" to describe low persistence gains and losses. It requires separate disclosure in the income statement, or in the notes, of material writedowns and any reversals thereof, restructuring provisions and any reversals, gains and losses on disposals, and other low persistence items. Also, like FASB, other low persistence items appear in OCI.

Given these complexities, it is perhaps not surprising if reporting of low persistence items is subject to abuse. In this regard, McVay (2006) reported evidence of **classification shifting**. That is, in large samples of U.S. firms over the period 1989–2002, she found that firms reporting large income-decreasing extraordinary items, such as restructuring charges and lawsuits, tend to report lower than expected core expenses (cost of goods sold plus selling, general, and administrative expenses). The reason, according to McVay, is that managers increase the amount of the special items by allocating core expenses to them (e.g., allocating continuing costs of legal department into cost of lawsuits). Notice that since core expenses are expected by investors to be of high persistence while special items are not, the result is to increase the apparent persistence of net income. McVay reported evidence consistent with this interpretation.

The research of Jones and Smith, and McVay, highlights the argument made by Ramakrishnan and Thomas: Since income statement items vary widely in persistence, full disclosure is necessary if investors are to be able to evaluate overall earnings persistence.

5.4.3 Measuring Investors' Earnings Expectations

As mentioned previously, researchers must obtain a proxy for expected earnings, since an efficient market will react to only that portion of an earnings announcement that it did not expect. If a reasonable proxy is not obtained, the researcher may fail to identify a market reaction when one exists, or may incorrectly conclude that a market reaction exists when it does not. Thus, obtaining a reasonable estimate of earnings expectations is a crucial component of value relevance research.

Under the ideal conditions of Example 2.2, expected earnings is simply accretion of discount on opening firm value. When conditions are not ideal, however, earnings expectations are more complex. One approach is to project the time series formed by the firm's past reported net incomes—that is, to base future expectations on past performance.

A reasonable projection, however, depends on earnings persistence. To see this, consider the extremes of 100% persistent earnings and zero persistent earnings. If earnings are completely persistent, expected earnings for the current year are just last year's actual earnings. Then, unexpected earnings are estimated as the *change* from last year. This approach was used by Ball and Brown, as described in Section 5.3. If earnings are of zero persistence, then there is no information in last year's earnings about future earnings, and all of current earnings are unexpected. That is, unexpected earnings are equal to the *level* of current year's earnings. This approach was used by Bill Cautious in Example 3.1.

Which extreme is closer to the truth? This can be evaluated by the degree of correlation between security returns and the estimate of unexpected earnings, a question examined by Easton and Harris (1991). Using regression analysis of a large sample of U.S. firms over the period 1969–1986, they documented a correlation between one-year security returns and the change in net income, consistent with the approach of Ball and Brown. However, there was an even stronger correlation between returns and the level of net income. Furthermore, when both earnings changes and levels were used, the two variables combined did a significantly better job of predicting returns than either variable separately. These results suggest that the truth is somewhere in the middle; that is, both changes in and levels of net income are components of the market's earnings expectations, where the relative weights on the two components depend on earnings persistence.

The foregoing discussion is based solely on a time series approach, however. Another source of earnings expectations is analysts' forecasts. These are now widely available for most large firms. If analysts' forecasts are more accurate than time series forecasts, they provide a better estimate of earnings expectations, since rational investors will presumably use the most accurate forecasts. Evidence by Brown, Hagerman, Griffin, and Zmijewski (1987), who studied the quarterly forecasting performance of one forecasting organization (Value Line), suggests that analysts outperform time series models in terms of accuracy. O'Brien (1988) also found that analysts' quarterly earnings forecasts were more accurate than time series forecasts. These results are what we would expect, since analysts can bring to bear information beyond that contained in past earnings when making their earnings projections.

When more than one analyst follows the same firm, it seems reasonable to take the consensus, or average, forecast as the proxy for the market's earnings expectation, following the reasoning underlying the football forecasting example of Section 4.2.2. O'Brien pointed out, however, that the age of a forecast has an important effect on its accuracy. She found that the single most recent earnings forecast provided a more accurate earnings prediction in her sample than the average forecast of all analysts following the firm, where the average ignored how old the individual forecasts were. This suggests that the timeliness of a forecast dominates the cancelling-out-of-errors effect of the average forecast.

Despite evidence that analysts' forecasts tend to be more accurate than forecasts based on time series, other evidence (Easton and Sommers, 2007) suggests that analysts' forecasts are optimistically biased, particularly for smaller firms. Nevertheless, recent studies of the information content of earnings tend to base earnings expectations on analysts' forecasts.[23]

Cisco Systems Inc. is a large provider of networking equipment, based in San Jose, California. In August 2004, it released financial results for the quarter ended July 30, 2004. Its revenues increased by 26% over the same quarter of 2003. Its net income for the quarter was $1.4 billion, or 21 cents per share, a 41% increase over the same quarter of 2003, and 5% in excess of the average analysts' forecast of 20 cents.

Yet, Cisco's share price fell almost 18% to $18.29 following the announcement. This fall in price seems contrary to the results of Ball and Brown and subsequent researchers, who have documented a positive market response to good earnings news. However, certain balance sheet and supplemental information was not so favourable. For example, inventory turnover declined to 6.4 from 6.8 times in 2003, gross margin declined slightly, order backlog was down, and, while revenue was growing, its rate of growth appeared to be declining. Also, several analysts commented on an increase in inventories, suggesting lower earnings persistence and accrual quality to the extent these inventories would be slow in selling. Furthermore, Cisco's CEO, commenting on the quarter's results, mentioned that the firm's customers were becoming more cautious about spending.

These negative signals implied low quality and negative persistence for the good earnings news, probably compounded by very similar investor expectations. The result was a negative ERC.

5.4.4 Summary

The value relevance of reported net income can be measured by the extent of security price change or, more specifically, by the magnitude of the security's abnormal market return, around the time the market learns the current net income. This is because rational, informed investors will revise their expectations about future firm performance and share returns on the basis of current earnings information. Revised beliefs trigger buy/sell decisions, as investors move to restore the risk–return tradeoffs in their portfolios to desired levels. If there were no information content in net income there would be no belief revision, no resulting buy/sell decisions, and hence no associated price changes.

For a given amount of unexpected net income, theory predicts that the extent of security price change or abnormal returns depends on factors such as firm size, capital structure, risk, growth prospects, persistence, the similarity of investor expectations, and earnings quality.

Following the pioneering study of Ball and Brown, empirical research has demonstrated a differential market response depending on most of these factors. These empirical results are really quite remarkable. First, they have overcome substantial statistical and experimental design problems. Second, they show that the market is, on average, very sophisticated in its ability to evaluate accounting information. This supports the theory of securities market efficiency and the decision theories that underlie it. Finally, they support the decision usefulness approach to financial reporting. As accountants gain a better understanding of investor response to financial statement information, their ability to provide useful information to investors will further increase.

5.5 A CAVEAT ABOUT THE "BEST" ACCOUNTING POLICY

To this point, we have argued that accountants can be guided by securities market reaction in determining usefulness of financial accounting information. From this, it is tempting to conclude that the best accounting policy is the one that produces the greatest market price response. For example, if net income reported under current value accounting produces a greater market reaction than net income reported under conservative accounting, should current value accounting not be preferred? To some extent, the answer is yes, since, as we have seen in this chapter, security market response is a measure of usefulness to investors.

However, we must be extremely careful about this conclusion. Accountants may be better off to the extent that they provide useful information to investors, but it does not follow that *society* will necessarily be better off.

The reason is that information has characteristics of a **public good**. A public good is a good such that consumption by one person does not destroy it for use by another. Consumption of a **private good**— such as an apple—eliminates its usefulness for other consumers. However, an investor can use the information in an annual report without eliminating its usefulness to other investors. Consequently, suppliers of public goods may have trouble charging for these products, so that we often witness them being supplied by governmental or quasi-governmental agencies—roads and national defence, for example. If a firm tried to charge investors for its annual report, it would probably not attract many customers, because a single annual report, once produced, could be downloaded to many users. Instead, we observe governments through securities legislation and corporations acts, *requiring* firms to issue annual reports.

Of course, firms' annual reports are not "free." Production of annual reports is costly. Other, more significant, costs include the possible disclosure of valuable information to competitors and the possibility that managers' operating decisions will be affected by the amount of information about those decisions that has to be released. For example, managers may curtail plans for expansion if too much information about them has to be disclosed. Investors will eventually pay for these costs through higher product prices and/or lower share prices. Nevertheless, investors perceive annual reports as free, since the extent to which they use them will not affect the product prices they pay. Also, investors may incur costs to inform themselves, either directly by paying to receive the information as soon as possible, or indirectly by paying for analyst or other information services. Nevertheless, the basic "raw material" is perceived as free, and investors will do what any other rational consumer will do when prices are low—consume more of it. As a result, *investors may perceive accounting information as useful even though from society's standpoint the costs of this information outweigh the benefits to investors.*

Also, as mentioned in Chapter 1, information affects different people differently. Thus, information may be useful to potential investors and competitors, but managers and current shareholders may be harmed by supplying it. As a result, the social value of such information depends both on the benefits to potential investors and competitors and on the costs to managers and shareholders. Such cost–benefit tradeoffs are extremely difficult to make.

Think of information as a commodity, demanded by investors and supplied by firms through accountants. Because of the public-good aspect of information, we cannot rely on the forces of demand and supply to produce the socially "right" or first-best amount of production, as we can for private goods produced under competition. The essential reason is that the price system does not, and probably cannot, operate to charge investors the full costs of the information they use. Consequently, from a social perspective, we cannot rely on the extent of security market response to tell us which accounting policies should be used (or, equivalently, "how much" information to produce). Formal arguments to support this conclusion were given by Gonedes and Dopuch (1974).

The 2007–2008 market meltdowns provide a dramatic illustration of the broader social effects of accounting information. Following the meltdowns, arguments appeared that fair value accounting is pro-cyclical; that is, it increases the magnitude of booms and busts. The argument is that, in good times, fair value accounting inflates earnings. Then, firms are encouraged to expand, and banks (whose earnings are also inflated) are encouraged to lend to support this expansion. An economic boom results. However, when the boom collapses, as it did in 2007–2008, liquidity pricing can result (Section 1.3), in which case the fair values of financial assets fall below their value in use. Then, banks' legal capital is threatened, they stop lending, and the economy falls into recession. By concentrating on providing useful fair value information to investors, standard setters were vulnerable to charges that they ignored these broader social effects. We will return to the question of regulation of information production in Chapters 12 and 13. For now, the point to realize is that it is still true that accountants can be guided by market response to maintain and improve their competitive position as suppliers to the marketplace for information. It is also true that securities markets will work better to the extent that security prices provide good indications of underlying real investment opportunities. However, these social considerations do suggest that, as a general rule, accounting standard-setting bodies should be wary of using the securities market response as a sole guide for their decisions.

5.6 THE VALUE RELEVANCE OF OTHER FINANCIAL STATEMENT INFORMATION

In this section, we depart from our concentration on the information content of net income in order to consider the informativeness of other financial statement components, such as the balance sheet and supplementary information.

Overall, it has been difficult to find direct evidence of usefulness of other financial statement information, unlike the impressive evidence of market reaction to earnings described earlier. For example, the value relevance of RRA (Section 2.4) has received considerable research attention. Despite its relevance, studies by Magliolo (1986) and

Doran, Collins, and Dhaliwal (1988) were unable to find more than a weak market reaction to RRA, although Boone (2002) reported a stronger market reaction to RRA information than to historical cost-based information, and argued that the relatively weak reaction reported by earlier researchers is due to statistical problems in their methodology.

Low reliability is one possible explanation for these mixed results. Another possibility is that RRA is pre-empted by more timely sources of reserves information, such as announcements of discoveries, and analyst forecasts. Also, the point in time that the market first becomes aware of the RRA information is often unclear. For net income, media or conference call reporting of the earnings announcement provides a reasonable event date. However, given the inside nature of oil and gas reserves information and its importance to firm value, analysts and others may work particularly hard to ferret it out in advance of the annual report. If a reasonable event date for the release of other financial statement information cannot be found, return studies must use wide windows, which are open to a large number of influences on price in addition to accounting information.

However, there is an indirect approach to finding evidence of usefulness that links other information to the quality of earnings. To illustrate, suppose that an oil company reports high earnings this year, but supplemental RRA information in the financial statement notes shows that its reserves have declined substantially over the year. An interpretation of this information is that the firm has used up its reserves to increase sales in the short run. If so, the quality of current earnings is reduced, since they contain a non-persistent component that will dissipate if new reserves are not found. Then, the market's anticipation of the bad news in the RRA information may be more easily found in a low ERC than in a direct reaction to the reserve information itself. Conversely, a higher ERC would be expected if reserves had increased.

This approach was generalized by Lev and Thiagarajan (LT; 1993). They identified 12 "fundamentals" used by financial analysts in evaluating earnings quality. For example, one fundamental was the change in inventories, relative to sales. If inventories increase, this may suggest a decline in earnings quality—the firm may be entering a period of low sales, or simply be managing its inventories less effectively. Other fundamentals include change in capital expenditures, order backlog, and, in the case of an oil and gas company, the change in its reserves.

For each firm in their sample, LT calculated a measure of earnings quality by assigning a score of 1 or 0 to each of that firm's 12 fundamentals, then adding the scores. For example, for inventories, a 1 is assigned if that firm's inventories, relative to sales, are down for the year, suggesting higher inventory turnover and earnings quality, and a 0 score is assigned if inventories are up.

When LT added these fundamental scores as an additional explanatory variable in an ERC regression analysis, there was a substantial increase in ability to explain abnormal security returns beyond the explanatory power of current unexpected earnings alone. This suggests that anticipation of balance sheet information, and supplementary information in financial statement notes, shows up in the ERC.

More recently, DeFranco, Wong, and Zhou (2011) conducted a more direct test of the value relevance of information in notes to the financial statements. They examined a sample of large U.S. firms over the period 2002–2007, and reported that share prices responded to financial statement note information in a seven-day narrow window surrounding the firms' 10K reports filed with the SEC[24] (the earliest date on which information in the notes becomes available to the market). Examples of information in the notes include RRA, lease liabilities, underfunded pension costs, off balance sheet securitizations, and improved ability to estimate earnings persistence. Response to this information was after controlling for other information that may also affect share price such as earnings announcements, tone of MD&A (Section 3.6.4), and analyst forecasts.

The authors suggest that this share response is driven by sophisticated investors, such as financial analysts. Consistent with this suggestion, they reported that the greater the additional information in the notes is relative to the information in net income, the more likely analysts are to issue revised target share prices and the larger these revisions are. Overall, it seems that note information is decision useful to investors and that analyst forecast revisions are a vehicle whereby note information becomes incorporated into share prices.

5.7 CONCLUSIONS ON VALUE RELEVANCE

The empirical literature in financial accounting is vast, and we have looked only at certain parts of it. Nevertheless, we have seen that, for the most part, the securities market response to reported net income is impressive in terms of its sophistication. Empirical research in this area generally supports the efficient markets theory and underlying decision theories.

However, accountants must ensure that unusual, non-recurring items are fully disclosed, either in the financial statements proper or the notes. Otherwise, investors may overestimate the persistence of current reported earnings.

Until relatively recently, it has been difficult to find evidence of market response to other financial statement information as strong as to earnings information. The extent to which the lack of strong market response to this other information is due to research methodology difficulties, to low reliability, to availability of alternative information sources, or to failure of efficient markets theory itself is not fully understood, although it may be that investors anticipate balance sheet and supplementary information to fine-tune the ERC, rather than using such information directly, and/or are guided by more sophisticated investors, such as financial analysts. To maximize their competitive position as suppliers of information, accountants may use the extent of security market response to various types of accounting information as a guide to its usefulness to investors. This motivates their interest in empirical research on decision usefulness. Furthermore, the more information accountants can move from inside to outside the firm, the better can capital markets guide the flow of scarce investment funds.

Despite these considerations, accountants must be careful of concluding that the accounting policies and disclosures that produce the greatest market response are the best for society. This is due to the public-good nature of accounting information. Investors will not necessarily demand the "right" amount of information, since they do not bear its full costs. These concerns limit the ability of decision usefulness research to guide accounting standard setters.

Much of the research described in this chapter has been oriented to financial statement information containing a significant historical cost component. While finding value relevance in historical cost-based earnings is encouraging, standard setters have moved increasingly to current value accounting-based financial statements, which have potential to capture more of the information affecting firm value that becomes available during the year. Historical cost-based financial statements capture this information only with a lag. Presumably, standard setters feel that current value accounting will further increase value relevance. In the next chapter, we explore possible reasons for this move.

Questions and Problems

1. Explain what is meant by the value relevance of accounting information. Does it rely on the historical cost basis of accounting?

2. Refer to the separation of market-wide and firm-specific (i.e., abnormal) security returns as shown in Figure 5.2. Which factors could reduce the accuracy of the estimate of firm-specific returns?

3. Is the market's anticipation of the GN/BN in earnings during 12 months prior to the month of release of the earnings release, as Ball and Brown found in Figure 5.3, consistent with a correlation or a causation argument for the effect of accounting information on abnormal stock returns? Explain. With which argument is the market response during month 0 most consistent? Explain.

4. Give examples of components of net income with
   a. High persistence
   b. Persistence of 1
   c. Persistence of 0

   Assume that the firm uses historical cost accounting.

5. Explain why it is desirable to find the exact time that the market first became aware of an item of accounting information if any security price reaction to this information is to be detected. Can such a time always be found? Explain why or why not. What can researchers do when the exact time the market first became aware of the information cannot be isolated?

6. Is a negative ERC possible? Explain why or why not.

7. A researcher finds evidence of a security price reaction to an item of accounting information during a narrow window of three days surrounding the date of release of this information and claims that it was the accounting information that caused the security price reaction. Another researcher finds evidence of security price reaction to a different item of accounting information during a wide window beginning 12 months prior to the release

of the financial statements containing that item. This researcher does not claim that the accounting information caused the security price reaction but only that the information and the market price reaction were associated.

Explain why one can claim causation for a narrow window but not for a wide window. Which price reaction constitutes the stronger evidence for usefulness of accounting information? Explain.

8. XYZ Ltd. is a large retail company listed on a major stock exchange, and its reported net income for the year ended December 31, 2015, is $5 million. The earnings were announced to the public on March 31, 2016.

Financial analysts had predicted the company's net income for 2015 to be $7 million. The financial analysts' prediction of $7 million net income was in effect up until the release of the 2015 earnings on March 31, 2016.

Assumptions

■ No other news about XYZ Ltd. was released to the public on March 31, 2016.
■ No significant economy-wide events affecting share prices occurred on March 31, 2016.

Required

a. Would you expect a change in price of XYZ Ltd.'s common stock on March 31, 2016? If so, why?

b. Consider the two situations below:

   i. The deviation of forecasted earnings from actual earnings of $2 million is completely accounted for by the closing down of a number of its retail outlets.

   ii. The deviation of the forecasted earnings from actual earnings of $2 million is completely accounted for by a fire in XYZ Ltd.'s largest retail outlet, which had caused the outlet to be closed temporarily for six months.

   In which of these two scenarios would you expect the price change of XYZ Ltd.'s common stock to be greater? Explain.

c. Suppose instead that significant economy-wide events on March 31, 2016 resulted in a major increase in the stock market index. Would this affect your answer in part **a**? Explain.

9. In a classic study, Beaver (1968) examined the trading volume of firms' securities around the time of their earnings announcements. Specifically, he examined 506 annual earnings announcements of 143 non-December 31 year end NYSE firms over the years 1961–1965 inclusive (261 weeks).

For each earnings announcement, Beaver calculated the average daily trading volume (of the shares of the firm making that announcement) for each week of a 17-week window surrounding week 0 (the week in which the earnings announcement was made). For each firm in the sample, he also calculated the average daily trading volume outside its 17-week window. This latter calculation was taken as the normal trading volume for that firm's shares.

For each week in the 17-week window, Beaver averaged the trading volumes over the 506 earnings announcements in the sample. The results are shown in Figure 5.4 below. The dotted line in the figure shows the average normal trading volume outside the 17-week window.

Figure 5.4 Volume Analysis

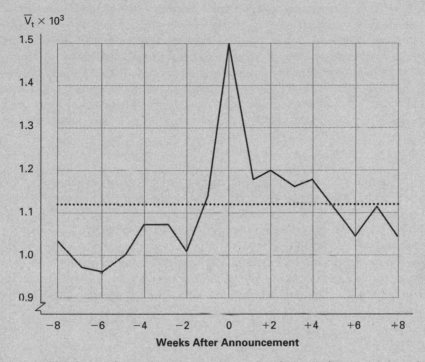

Source: W. Beaver, "The Information Content of Annual Earnings Announcements," *Journal of Accounting Research,* Supplement, 1968: 67–92. Reproduced with permission of John Wiley & Sons Ltd.

As can be seen from the figure, there was a dramatic increase in trading volume, relative to normal, in week 0. Also, volume is below normal during most of the weeks leading up to week 0.

Subsequent research investigates factors affecting the week 0 increase in trading volume, based on the decision theory model of Section 3.3. A key driver of this volume is the extent to which prior beliefs about future firm performance differ across investors. If investors are primarily small, such as Bill Cautious in Example 3.1, their prior probabilities of a firm's future performance will tend to be similar, since small investors are exposed to basically the same public information. Consequently, for a given information system (Table 3.2), their posterior probabilities will also be similar. Lacking investors with different opinions, there is little incentive for investors to trade among themselves, and trading volume will be relatively low.

If investors are primarily institutions, with more resources than small investors and larger share holdings, they will invest more heavily in developing private information about future firm performance. Consequently, their prior probabilities about future performance will differ from those of small investors. Since the institutions are sophisticated, they will be confident in their prior beliefs, so that the earnings announcement will have a relatively low impact. That is, an institution's prior and posterior beliefs about future firm performance will be similar. If we further assume that the various institutions are equally sophisticated, their posterior probabilities will tend to be similar across institutions. Again, there is little incentive for institutions to trade among themselves, and trading volume will also be relatively low.

It follows that trading volume will be highest when the market for a firm's shares consists of both small and institutional investors. Then, differences in investor beliefs (i.e., small versus large investors) about future firm performance are highest, in which case there is a relatively high incentive for trading following an earnings announcement.

In sum, theory predicts that trading volume is an inverted U-shaped function of the proportion of a firm's shares held by institutions. Empirical evidence consistent with this prediction is presented by Ali, Klasa, and Li (2008).

Required

a. Why do you think Beaver found that trading volume increased in week 0?

b. Why do you think Beaver found that trading volume was below normal in the weeks leading up to week 0?

c. Do the findings of Beaver and Ali, Klasa, and Li support the decision usefulness of earnings information? Explain.

d. When trading volume is low surrounding an earnings announcement, does this mean that the change in share price surrounding that announcement will necessarily be low? Explain. Use the degree of decision usefulness of net income in your answer.

10. X Ltd. is a growth firm that uses very conservative accounting policies. Y Ltd. is growing more slowly and uses fair value accounting for its capital assets and related amortization.

Otherwise, X Ltd. and Y Ltd. are quite similar. They are the same size and have similar capital structures and similar betas.

Required

a. Both X Ltd. and Y Ltd. report the same GN in earnings this year. Which firm would you expect to have the greater security market response (ERC) to this good earnings news? Explain.

b. Suppose that X Ltd. had a much higher debt–equity ratio and beta than Y Ltd. Would your answer to part a change? Explain.

11. On the basis of the empirical evidence presented in this chapter and in Chapter 3 (i.e., MD&A, Section 3.6), do you feel the Conceptual Framework (Section 3.7.1) is correct in its claim that the financial statements, which show the effects of current and past firm performance, help investors to assess the amount, timing, and uncertainty of its future cash flows? Explain. In your answer, consider amount, timing, and uncertainty separately.

12. IAS 1 recognizes the need for full disclosure of the components of reported net income. Explain why full disclosure of net income components is important if investors are to properly interpret the implications of current reported net income for future firm performance.

What is classification shifting? Why does classification shifting make it more difficult for investors to predict future firm performance from current reported net income? How could the problem of classification shifting be reduced?

13. Explain why financial statement information has characteristics of a public good. Include a definition of a public good in your answer. What does this imply about using the *extent* of security market reaction to accounting information to guide accountants? To standard setters?

14. You estimate empirically the ERC of firm J as 0.38. Firm K is identical to firm J in terms of size, earning power, persistence of earnings, and risk. Unlike firm J, however, firm K includes a high-quality financial forecast in its MD&A. You estimate firm K's ERC as 0.57. Which firm's net income report appears to be more useful to investors? Explain. Does this mean that all firms should be required to prepare high-quality financial forecasts? Explain.

15. Different bases of accounting, such as current value accounting and historical cost-based accounting, do not affect total earnings over the life of the firm, but only the *timing* of the recognition of those earnings. In effect, over the life of the firm, the firm "earns what it earns," and different bases of accounting will all produce earnings that add up to this total.

   If this is so, then we would expect that the greater the number of time periods over which we aggregate a firm's historical cost earnings, the closer the resulting total will be to economic income; that is, the earnings total that would be produced over the same periods under ideal conditions.

   This was studied by Easton, Harris, and Ohlson (EHO; 1992) and by Warfield and Wild (WW; 1992). EHO proxied economic income by the return on the firm's shares on the securities market. When this return was aggregated over varying periods of time (up to 10 years) and compared with aggregate historical cost-based earnings returns for similar periods, the comparison improved as the time period lengthened. WW studied a similar phenomenon for shorter periods. They found, for example, that the association between economic and accounting income for quarterly time periods was on average about 1/10 of their association for an annual period, consistent with mixed measurement model-based net income lagging behind economic income in its recognition of relevant economic events.

   Required

   a. In Example 2.1, calculate total net income over the two-year life of the firm, assuming that P.V. Ltd. uses historical cost accounting with straight-line amortization for its capital asset, while retaining all other assumptions. Verify that total net income over the life of P.V. Ltd. equals the total economic net income that P.V. Ltd. would report using present value amortization.

   b. Do the same in Example 2.2, assuming that the state realization is bad and good in years 1 and 2 respectively.

   c. Use the fact that accruals reverse to explain why total net income over the two years in parts **a** and **b** above are the same under economic and straight-line amortization. Are these results consistent with the empirical results of EHO and WW outlined above?

   d. If all accounting methods produce the same total net income over a sufficiently long period, why does accounting policy choice and full disclosure matter to investors?

Note: The following problem also draws on material in Chapters 3 and 4.

16. Leo, a rational investor, has $5,000 to invest for one year pending the purchase of a house. He has narrowed his choice down to two investments. One is to invest the full amount in shares of Company X (a_1). The other is to buy risk-free government bonds yielding an annual return of 4.5% (a_2). Company X has little debt and its stock is low-beta.

Leo identifies two states of nature:

State H: Company X performs well.

State L: Company X performs poorly.

Leo searches the Internet for financial information about X Ltd. Based on this evidence, he assesses the following subjective prior state probabilities:

State H: 0.3

State L: 0.7

The following is the payoff table for these two investments. Payoffs from X Ltd. shares consist of dividends and capital gain for the year, based on the average analyst forecast for X Ltd., and are net of the original investment.

		State	
		H	L
	a_1	$2,500	$ 25
Act			
	a_2	$ 225	$225

Leo is risk averse, with utility equal to the square root of the net dollar payoff.

Required

a. On the basis of his prior probabilities, which act should Leo take? Show calculations.

b. Instead of acting now, Leo decides to obtain more information about Company X by consulting a financial advisor. The advisor, who claims to be familiar with GAAP, advises Leo that the quality of X Ltd.'s financial statements prepared under current GAAP can be represented by the following information system:

		Current Annual Report Evidence	
		GOOD	BAD
	H	0.6	0.4
State			
	L	0.2	0.8

Upon reading the X Ltd.'s most recent annual report, the advisor advises Leo that performance is Bad. Which act should Leo take now? Show calculations.

c. Shortly after making his decision in **b**, Leo is surprised to note that the market price of X Ltd. shares rises significantly, despite the bad news in its recent earnings report. He asks the advisor how this could happen. The advisor replies that favourable economy-wide events occurring after the financial statements were issued were the reason for the share price increase. Do you agree? Explain why or why not.

d. Leo suspects that the advisor did not study X Ltd.'s annual report carefully enough, and decides to investigate himself. He turns to theoretical and empirical studies of rational, risk-averse investors and an efficient securities market, and to market response to financial statement information, to help understand why the market seems to have responded positively following X Ltd.'s annual report, even though the financial statements showed bad news. Suggest, and briefly explain, possible reasons for the positive market response.

17. On May 8, 2001, the *Financial Post* reported "The Street Turns Against Canadian Tire." Canadian Tire Corporation, Ltd.'s share price had risen by $0.75 to $24.90 on May 2, 2001, following a news release in which Wayne Sales, president and CEO at the time, said, "We are pleased with our ability to deliver double digit growth...." Canadian Tire's reported earnings of $0.37 per share exceeded analysts' expectations.

The market soon learned, however, that reported earnings included an $8 million one-time gain on sale of certain Canadian Tire assets. Without this gain, earnings were $0.29 per share, 6% below earnings for the same quarter of 2000. Canadian Tire's share price quickly fell back to $22.95.

The *Post* reported that "passing off" a one-time gain as part of operating earnings "didn't fool or impress analysts" and is something they "hoped not to see again."

Required

a. Use efficient securities market theory to explain the rise in Canadian Tire's share price on May 2, 2001, and the rapid subsequent fall in share price.

b. Was Canadian Tire correct in including the $8 million one-time gain in net income? Explain.

c. Evaluate the persistence of Canadian Tire's reported net income of $0.37 per share (no calculations required). Does the fact that Mr. Sales ignored this item in his press release affect your evaluation? Explain why or why not.

18. *The Globe and Mail* reported on Imperial Oil Ltd.'s earnings for the third quarter ended on September 30, 2000, released on October 18, 2000. Net income was a record $374 million, up from $191 million for the same quarter of the previous year. Return on equity was 25.7%, up from 10.1% a year earlier. Earnings for the quarter included a $60 million gain on Imperial's sale of its Cynthia pipeline and other assets. Cash flow for the quarter was $433 million, up from $270 million in the previous year's third quarter. The reported profit of $374 million was in line with analysts' expectations.

On October 18, the TSE oil and gas index rose by 0.6%, as the market anticipated higher prices for oil and gas. Yet, Imperial's share price fell on the day by $1.25, to close at $37.35. *The Globe and Mail* also reported analysts' comments about a widening discount for heavy crude oil relative to light crude. Imperial is Canada's biggest producer of heavy crude. Also, Imperial's production from its oil sands projects declined in the quarter, due to maintenance and temporary production problems.

Required

a. Use the market model to calculate the abnormal return, relative to the TSE oil and gas index, on Imperial Oil's shares for October 18, 2000. Imperial Oil's beta at the time was approximately 0.65. The risk-free interest rate at this time was approximately 0.0002 per day. Note the theoretical relationship $\alpha_j = R_f (1 - \beta_j)$.

b. Is the abnormal decline in Imperial's share price on October 18 consistent with efficient securities market theory? Explain why or why not. Consider earnings persistence in your answer.

19. On October 21, 2004, Abitibi-Consolidated Inc., a large Canadian-based newsprint and groundwood producer, reported net income for its third quarter, 2004, of $182 million. This compares with a net loss for the same quarter of 2003 of $70 million. Sales for the quarter were up, to $1,528 million, and earnings excluding low-persistence items were $82 million. The analyst forecast for the third quarter, 2004, excluding low-persistence items, was a loss of $27 million.

The low-persistence items included a gain of $239 million before tax from foreign exchange conversion. Much of the company's long-term debt is denominated in U.S. dollars. The foreign exchange gain arose because of the rising value of the Canadian dollar, relative to the U.S. dollar, during the quarter.

Comparable figures for the third quarter of 2003 were as follows: sales of $1,340 million, a loss before low-persistence items of $32 million, and foreign exchange conversion gain of $13 million.

There is no mention of R&D costs in the company's third quarter report. Its 2003 annual report mentions R&D only in passing, with reference to forest conservation. Presumably, R&D expenditures are relatively low.

Abitibi-Consolidated's share price rose $0.59 to $7.29 on the Toronto Stock Exchange on October 21, 2004. The S&P/TSX Composite index gained 59 points to close at 8,847 on the same day. According to media reports, the increases were driven by a "red-hot" materials and energy sector (including Abitibi-Consolidated). In a conference call accompanying its third quarter report, Abitibi-Consolidated's CEO complained that investors were too pessimistic about the company. The company's beta, according to Yahoo! Finance, was 0.779. The risk-free interest rate at this time was approximately 0.00020 per day. Note the theoretical relationship $\alpha_j = R_f (1 - \beta_j)$.

Required

a. Evaluate (in words only) the persistence of Abitibi-Consolidated's net income for the third quarter of 2004.

b. Suppose that Abitibi-Consolidated's R&D costs were high. How would this affect earnings persistence?

c. Do you feel that the increase in Abitibi-Consolidated's share price on October 21 was consistent with efficient securities market theory, or do you agree with the CEO? Explain, and show any calculations.

20. On September 13, 2005, the shares of Best Buy Co. fell $5.14 to $45.22 on the New York Stock Exchange, a decline of 10.2%. The decline followed the release of its second quarter 2005 financial results. Best Buy is a large North American retailer of consumer electronics and appliances, with over 700 stores in the United States and Canada, including the Future Shop chain. Best Buy reported earnings of 37 cents per share, compared with 30 cents for the same quarter of 2004. However, its 2005 earnings included an expense for stock-based compensation. If the second quarter of 2004 had included this expense, earnings for that 2004 quarter would have been 26 cents per share. Sales revenue rose 10% for the quarter, including a 3.5% increase in same-store sales. (Same-store

sales, which exclude the effects of new store openings, are a closely watched indicator of retail company performance.) Its gross profit rose to 25.5% of sales from 24.2% a year earlier. In its news release accompanying the financial results, management predicted earnings of 28 to 32 cents per share for its third 2005 quarter. This prediction included the effects of Hurricane Katrina, which, in late August 2005, caused widespread devastation in parts of the southern United States and led to a brief closing of 15 company stores. Management also announced plans to open 86 new stores in the United States and Canada during the fiscal year ending February 25, 2006. While management expressed concerns about the effects of high gasoline prices on consumer spending, it reiterated its guidance that future annual growth in earnings from continuing operations would be about 26%.

Analysts had estimated second quarter 2005 earnings of 38 cents per share, and third quarter earnings of 34 cents.

The New York Stock Exchange Composite Index closed at 7,578.25 on September 13, 2005, and at 7,762.60 on September 12, 2005. Best Buy's stock beta, as per its website, is 1.84. The risk-free interest rate at this time was approximately 0.0001 per day.

Required

a. What percentage return on Best Buy's stock price would you expect on September 13, 2005, strictly as a result of market-wide (i.e., systematic) factors? Use the market model and show your calculations. Note the theoretical relationship $\alpha_j = R_f (1 - \beta_j)$.

b. What was the abnormal return on Best Buy's stock on September 13, 2005? Is this return consistent with securities market efficiency? Explain why or why not.

c. Evaluate (in words only—no calculations required) the persistence of the news (i.e., the increase from 26 cents per share to 37 cents per share) in Best Buy's second quarter 2005 earnings.

21. An article in *The Globe and Mail*, February 16, 2002, reported that IBM used the $300 million proceeds of a sale of one of its business units to reduce operating expenses in its fourth quarter 2001 income statement. This added about 8 cents per share to its fourth quarter earnings. As a result, IBM beat analysts' forecasts by 1 cent per share.

IBM defended its treatment by claiming that buying and selling businesses is a normal business practice, and that most of the sale proceeds related to intellectual property that it had developed. The article quotes a Merrill Lynch analyst as saying, "Our only concern is that the company could have done more to call out the magnitude of the transaction." According to the article, IBM's share price fell by 4% as a result of this news.

While not mentioned in this article, the SEC opened a preliminary inquiry into IBM's accounting practice, expressing concerns that IBM had let it be known that the reason for its higher operating earnings was tight cost controls, rather than the sale proceeds. This inquiry was subsequently dropped, but the SEC issued a bulletin reminding firms to report gains or losses on asset sales separately from operating costs.

Required

Explain why IBM's share price dropped following the Merrill Lynch analyst's comment and the news of the SEC's preliminary inquiry.

22. The methodology used to evaluate the value relevance of financial statement information can also be used to evaluate security market reaction to other events affecting firm value.

For example, on April 30, 2012, financial media reported that Apple Inc. sold $19 billion of bonds of various maturities. The proceeds were to help finance a $100 billion cash return to shareholders, including a share buyback of $60 billion. In this way, Apple was attempting to increase its share price, which had fallen from $705 in September 2012 to $385 in mid-April 2013. Also, Apple was taking advantage of low interest rates in the economy. For example, the interest rate on the 10-year portion of its bond issue was only 2.4%.

Apple's share price increased by 9.02% for the week ended April 30, 2013, closing at $442.78. Its beta at the time, as per Reuters, was .99. Apple's shares trade on the NASDAQ exchange. For the week ended April 30, 2013, the NASDAQ Composite Index closed at 3,328.79, after opening the week at 3,262.21. The U.S. Federal Funds Rate at the time was 0.15% per annum.

Required

a. Did the market for Apple's shares react favourably or unfavourably to the bond issue during the week ended April 30, 2013? Take calculations to four decimal places. Note that α_j in the market model formula is equivalent to $R_f (1 - \beta_j)$ in the CAPM, where R_f is proxied by the weekly Federal Funds Rate.

b. A market analyst at the time was quoted as saying that, generally speaking, it is not wise to buy bonds used to finance a share buyback. Do you agree or disagree? Give reasons.

Notes

1. To the extent that investors have different prior beliefs, their beliefs posterior to the firm's earnings information will differ, generating trading volume. Different *interpretations* of the firm's current earnings information arise when investors have different decision models. For example, some investors may look only at net income. Others may conduct an extensive analysis of earnings components, others may rely on analyst forecasts, etc. Different decision models will also generate different posterior beliefs, again leading to trading volume.

   Trading volume resulting from differences in investors' interpretation of current reported earnings means that they use different information systems. However, this does not invalidate our Example 3.1, where we assumed a single information system capturing the quality of GAAP. Other investors may have more complex systems, to capture other sources of information. For example, we could envisage a four-column information system in Example 3.1, where in addition to the financial statements, the investor may receive a favourable or unfavourable message from a financial analyst, etc. A rational investor using such an information system will likely have different posterior beliefs about future firm performance than Bill Cautious in Example 3.1.

2. As mentioned in Section 4.5, this estimate of α_j should equal $(1 - \beta_j)R_f$, where R_f is the risk-free rate of interest. Here, $\alpha_j = 0.0001$ implies $R_f = 0.0005$ per day for $\beta_j = 0.80$.

3. The market return for day 0 is calculated as follows:

$$R_{M0} = \frac{\text{Level of D / J index, end day 0} + \text{Dividends D / J index, day 0}}{\text{Level of D / J index, beginning day 0}} - 1$$

   Sometimes, because of data problems, the dividends are omitted.

4. Calculated as

$$E(R_{jt}) = a_j + b_j R_{M0}$$
$$= 0.0001 + (0.80 \times 0.001)$$
$$= 0.0009$$

5. Again, this abnormal return should not be confused with abnormal earnings like those of P.V. Ltd. in Example 2.2. While the idea is the same—that is, abnormal is the difference between expected and actual—abnormal return here refers to a *market* return, whereas abnormal earnings refer to *accounting* net income.

6. Other ways to estimate investor expectations are discussed in Section 5.4.3.

7. Note that the loss on bad news firms can be converted into a gain by selling short the shares of the bad news firms.

8. However, even in a narrow window, it is difficult to *prove* that accounting information is the cause of security returns in studies such as these, since controlled experiments are generally not possible. For example, the researchers may have failed to notice that the GN sample firms were export-oriented while the BN firms were concentrated in domestic industries. If, say, a new free trade agreement signed during the narrow window opened up trade opportunities for export-oriented industries but increased import competition for domestic industries, this could also explain the BB results. This is the problem of correlated omitted variables. Thus, event studies depend crucially on the knowledge and skill of the researcher.

   Nevertheless, if additional studies over different time periods, different stock exchanges, and different countries produce similar results, the cumulative body of evidence consistent with the theory provides increasing support for that theory. Some of these additional studies are described later in this chapter.

9. If we widen the window to include the whole life of the firm, the total net income over this period equals income under ideal conditions, since all firm cash flows are then known. On this point, see Problem 15.

10. Event studies such as that of BB are sometimes called *joint* tests of value relevance, investor rationality, and market efficiency.

11. The information system described in Section 3.3.2 contained only two columns: GN and BN. To model the market response to the *magnitude* of GN or BN, we could add more columns, to give, say: VGN (very GN), GN, NO NEWS, BN, VBN. Thus, VGN firms would have very high unexpected earnings, etc. In principle, the information system concept can be extended to any number of information refinements. Our two-column example is only for simplicity.

12. As explained in Section 5.3.2, security price changes in narrow windows are interpreted as caused by accounting information, while, for wide windows, security price changes and accounting information are only associated. Thus the interpretation of a narrow window ERC is different from a wide window ERC. Here we will refer, somewhat loosely, to both types as simply ERCs.

13. In reasonably diversified portfolios, most of the portfolio risk stems from the betas of the securities in the portfolio. Thus, if the investor were to buy more shares of a security whose beta is greater than the average beta of the securities currently in the portfolio, this would raise the average, hence increasing portfolio risk.

14. Li notes that managers may not always make rational investment decisions (e.g., "empire building"). Consistent with this argument, he finds that his results are weaker for firms that are less likely to invest rationally.

15. These are "market value" ERCs, where the market's response to GN or BN is expressed in terms of the abnormal change in share *market value*, rather than the abnormal share *return* as in our ERC definition. To convert a market value ERC to a rate of return ERC, divide it by opening firm value.

16. This ignores riskiness of the future installments, which is appropriate if investors are risk neutral or the permanent earnings are firm-specific.

17. This is allowed by the revaluation option for property, plant, and equipment of IAS 16 (Section 7.3.4).

18. This assumes that the market knows that the increase in market value is $100. Possibly, this would be known from sources other than the financial statements. If not, considerable onus is put on the firm for full disclosure. Perhaps MD&A provides a vehicle for management to reveal this information.

19. However, accrual "quality" is perhaps not the best term for the ε_t residuals. As DD pointed out, they contain a mixture of discretionary and non-discretionary items. For example, firms that have high volatility in their operating and policy environments will experience larger and more frequent inventory writedowns, greater swings in bad debts, and, generally, more accruals with greater estimation errors. Consequently, a careful scrutiny by the investor of firm characteristics and manager strategies and incentives is needed to fully understand whether accrual quality is good or bad.

20. Arguably, these findings imply that higher accrual quality reduces estimation risk, since higher quality reporting reduces investor concerns about the integrity of management and other insiders.

21. For an analysis of conditions under which the ERC is increasing in the precision of analysts' earnings forecasts and how this precision is affected by factors such as the number of analysts forecasting the firm, see Abarbanell, Lanen, and Verrecchia (1995).

22. Jones and Smith define persistence as the extent to which a component of earnings predicts itself. In our discussion of persistence, we have defined it as the extent to which a component of earnings affects current and future earnings. Since the concepts are closely related, we interpret their results in terms of our ERC definition.

23. Subsequent research, however, qualifies these findings somewhat. Hou, van Dijk and Zhang (2012), like Easton and Sommers, found that analysts' forecasts are biased upward on average. However, they also found that while analysts' forecasts are on average more accurate predictors of future earnings than time series-based forecasts, the ERC based on time series forecasts is higher than the ERC based on analysts' forecasts. This latter finding suggests that when predicting future firm performance, investors look to past firm performance at least as much as they look to analysts' forecasts.

24. The 10K is a report filed annually by firms subject to SEC jurisdiction. It contains an overview of the company's business and its financial condition, including the audited financial statements. It is due 60–90 days after the firm's year end.

Chapter 6

The Measurement Approach to Decision Usefulness

Figure 6.1 Organization of Chapter 6

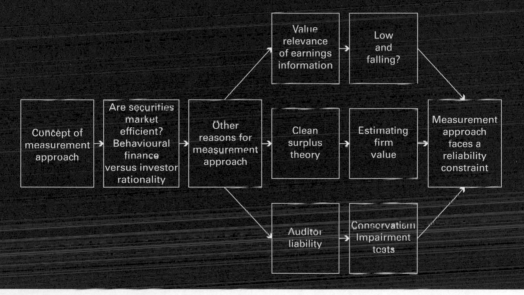

6.1 OVERVIEW

The measurement approach to decision usefulness implies greater usage of current values in the financial statements proper. We define the measurement approach as follows:

> The **measurement approach** to decision usefulness is an approach to financial reporting under which accountants undertake a responsibility to incorporate current values into the financial statements proper, providing that this can be done with reasonable reliability, thereby recognizing an increased obligation to assist investors to predict firm performance and value.

The measurement approach does not invalidate our argument in Section 5.1 that it is the investor's responsibility to make his/her own predictions of future firm performance. Rather, the intent of this approach is to enable better predictions of this performance by means of a more informative information system.

However, as noted in Section 1.4, accountants disagree about the extent to which current value accounting increases informativeness. If a measurement approach is to be useful for investors, increased relevance must outweigh any reduction in reliability. Standard setters must think it does, since they have been moving toward greater use of the measurement approach for many years. This may seem strange, given the problems that techniques such as RRA have experienced. The purpose of this chapter is to suggest and evaluate possible reasons underlying increased emphasis on current values.

One such reason involves investor rationality and securities market efficiency. Despite the impressive results outlined in Chapter 5 in favour of the decision usefulness of reported net income, recent years have seen theory and evidence suggesting that securities markets may not be as efficient as originally believed—recall our statement in Section 4.1 that we view efficiency as a matter of degree, rather than efficient/not efficient.

Our interest in the extent of efficiency arises because lack of efficiency has major implications for accounting, the most basic being whether or not the theory of rational decision making outlined in Chapter 3 underlies average investor behaviour. To the extent that investors are not collectively rational and markets are not fully efficient, reliance on these theories to guide accounting disclosures is threatened. Furthermore, while beta is the only relevant risk measure according to the CAPM, there is evidence that certain accounting variables in addition to beta, such as firm size and book-to-market ratio, significantly improve prediction of share returns compared to beta alone. If so, a measurement approach may improve the ability of financial statements to report on firm risk.

It is apparent that security prices can, at times, depart significantly from their fundamental value. As pointed out in Section 4.2.1, they did so in the bubble leading up to the 2007–2008 securities market meltdown. However, the important question for efficiency is whether securities prices reflect *publicly available* information,[1] not whether they reflect fundamental value. We shall suggest that much information that could have predicted the meltdown, such as the full extent of riskiness of financial institutions' investment strategies, was not in the public domain. If so, market efficiency theory can be defended from the numerous charges levied against it following the meltdown. However, other theory and evidence, drawn largely from behavioural science, also questions market efficiency. We shall argue that much of this evidence can be explained equally well by rational decision theory as by non-rational investor behaviour, and we will conclude that except for periods of liquidity pricing, securities markets are close enough to full efficiency that the theory can serve as a guide to accountants. Furthermore, we shall suggest that the extent of inefficiency and non-rational investor behaviour can be reduced by a measurement approach.

Other reasons for moving toward a measurement approach derive from a low proportion of share price variability explained by historical cost-based net income, from the Ohlson clean surplus theory that provides support for increased measurement, and from the legal liability to which accountants are exposed when firms become financially distressed. Figure 6.1 outlines the organization of this chapter.

6.2 ARE SECURITIES MARKETS FULLY EFFICIENT?

6.2.1 Introduction

In recent years, serious questions have been raised about investor rationality and securities market efficiency. That is, there is evidence that shares are mispriced relative to their efficient market values. Questions of investor rationality and market efficiency are of considerable importance to accountants since, if these questions are valid, the practice of relying on supplementary information in notes and elsewhere to augment the financial statements proper may not be completely effective in conveying useful information to investors. Furthermore, if shares are mispriced, improved financial reporting may be helpful in reducing inefficiencies, thereby enabling securities markets to work better. In the next few subsections we will outline and discuss the major questions that have been raised about market efficiency.

The basic premise of these questions is that average investor behaviour may not correspond to the rational decision theory and investment models outlined in Chapter 3. For example, individuals may have **limited attention**. That is, they may not have the time, inclination, or ability to process all available information. Then, they will concentrate on information that is readily available, such as the "bottom line," and ignore information in notes and elsewhere in the annual report. Furthermore, investors may be biased in their reaction to information, relative to how they should react according to Bayes' theorem. For example, there is evidence that individuals are **conservative** (not to be confused with conservatism in accounting as introduced in Section 1.4) in their reaction to new evidence. Conservative individuals revise their beliefs by *less than* Bayes' theorem implies. That is, they retain excess weight on their prior beliefs.

Psychological theory and evidence also suggests that individuals are often **overconfident**—they overestimate the precision of information they collect themselves. For example, an investor who privately researches a firm may overreact to the evidence he/she obtains. If we equate the individual's self-collected information with prior probabilities in Bayes' theorem, this implies that the overconfident individual will *underreact* to new information that is not self-collected relative to information that is. This underreaction seems to be particularly apparent if the new information, such as an earnings report, is perceived as statistical and abstract.

Another individual characteristic from psychology is **representativeness**. Here, the individual assigns too much weight to evidence that is consistent with the individual's impressions of the population from which the evidence is drawn. Then, situations are viewed as unique, when consideration of past history could yield valuable insights. For example, suppose that a firm's profits have grown strongly for several years. The investor subject to representativeness will assign this firm to the growth firm category, ignoring the fact that true growth firms are a rare event in the economy—the individual assigns too much weight to the recent evidence of earnings growth and not enough to the prior information that the base rate of growth firms in the population is low. This behaviour seems particularly likely if the evidence is salient, anecdotal, or extreme—for example, a firm's earnings growth may be the subject of sensational media articles. Then, the investor overreacts to the evidence, revising his/her beliefs that the firm in question is a growth firm by *more than* prescribed by Bayes' theorem. In effect, the individual takes the evidence of a few years of growth in earnings as *representative* of a growth firm, ignoring the fact that it is quite likely that earnings will revert to normal in the future. If enough investors behave this way, share price will *overreact* to the reported growth in earnings.

Yet another attribute of many individuals is **self-attribution bias**, whereby individuals feel that good decision outcomes are due to their abilities, whereas bad outcomes are due to unfortunate realizations of states of nature, hence not their fault. Suppose that following an overconfident investor's decision to purchase a firm's shares, its share price rises (for whatever reason). Then, the investor's faith in his/her investment ability rises. If share price falls, faith in ability does not fall. If enough investors behave this way, share price **momentum** can develop. That is, reinforced confidence following a rise in share price leads to the purchase of more shares, and share price rises further. Confidence is again reinforced, and the process feeds upon itself; that is, it gains momentum. Daniel, Hirshleifer, and Subrahmanyam (1998) presented a model whereby momentum trading develops when investors are overconfident and self-attribution biased. Daniel and Titman (1999), in an empirical study, reported that over the period 1968–1997 a strategy of buying portfolios of high-momentum shares and short-selling low-momentum ones earned high and persistent abnormal returns (i.e., higher than the return from holding the market portfolio), consistent with the overconfidence and momentum arguments.[2] These various behavioural characteristics are, of course, inconsistent with securities market efficiency and underlying rational decision theory. For example, according to the CAPM, higher returns can be earned only if higher beta risk is borne. Yet Daniel and Titman reported that the average beta risk of their momentum portfolios was less than that of the market portfolio.

Motivated reasoning is a somewhat different behavioural characteristic. Here, individuals accept at face value information that is consistent with their preferences (e.g., good news (GN)). However, if the information is inconsistent with their preferences (BN), it is received with skepticism, and the individual attempts to discredit it.

Motivated reasoning was tested in an experimental study by Hales (2007), using 60 MBA students as subjects. Each subject was provided the same information about a hypothetical firm, including past earnings and several news reports. In this way, all subjects had similar prior information of future firm performance. They were then randomly assigned to long or short positions in the company's shares. Thus, those with a long position stood to gain from GN and lose from BN, and vice versa.

Subjects were also given analyst forecasts of future earnings. Some subjects received GN (i.e., high earnings predicted) and some received BN. Subjects were then asked to give their own predictions of future earnings. They were motivated to predict accurately by means of a small reward that increased as their forecast error decreased.

Motivated reasoning theory predicts that a subject with a long position who receives a BN forecast will be skeptical, and that his/her own forecast will thus be *higher* than that of the analysts. GN information, however, will be accepted at face value, so that analyst and subject forecasts should be similar.[3] Also, the dispersion of forecasts by subjects receiving BN should be relatively high, since individuals will differ in the extent of their skepticism about analyst ability and quality. Subjects who receive GN should exhibit less forecast dispersion, since they are not inclined to be skeptical. Hales reports results consistent with the motivated reasoning predictions.

Hales's research was extended by Han and Tan (2010). They considered managers' earnings forecasts rather than analysts' forecasts, and noted that managers' forecasts are often in the form or ranges of earnings rather than single point forecasts. Drawing on behavioural theory, the authors argued that range forecasts are perceived by investors as more vague and uncertain than point forecasts. They thus predicted that the effects of motivated reasoning will be stronger (i.e., more sceptical) when forecasts are in the form of ranges rather than single points. That is, when an investor holds a long position in a company's shares, his/her own earnings estimate will be higher following receipt of a manager's range forecast rather than a point forecast, and vice versa for a short position.

The authors also argued that investors will perceive GN forecasts as less credible, hence less certain, than BN, since managers have greater incentive to release (and perhaps exaggerate) GN than BN, so that the directional preferences effect will be stronger for GN than for BN further increasing GN scepticism. They thus predicted that when an investor holds a long position and receives a manager's range forecast, his/her own earnings estimate will be higher when the forecast is GN rather than BN.

Han and Tan designed an experiment, using 74 Masters students as subjects, and reported results consistent with their predictions.

These results suggest that behavioural factors can affect investors' reactions to analyst and manager forecasts. This contrasts with decision theory, where the average subject faces, and acts according to, the information system. Then, his/her estimate of future firm performance or its dispersion should not depend on investment position (long or short), the type of forecast received, or whether the forecast contained GN or BN.

As is apparent from the foregoing, behavioural characteristics can produce a wide variety of share price behaviours over time. For example, overconfidence leading to share price momentum implies positive serial correlation of returns while the momentum continues (and negative longer-term correlation as the overconfidence is eventually revealed), whereas representativeness implies negative serial correlation (i.e., share price overreacts to evidence, leading to subsequent price correction as overvaluation is revealed). Also, market reaction to bad news may be delayed as investors subject to motivated reasoning take time to conduct their own evaluations. All of these patterns are contrary to the random walk behaviour of returns under market efficiency.

The study of behavioural-based securities market inefficiencies is called **behavioural finance**, which began with the seminal paper of De Bondt and Thaler (1985). For a comprehensive review of the theory and evidence of behavioural finance, see Hirshleifer (2001). We now review several other questions about efficiency that have been raised in this theory.

6.2.2 Prospect Theory

The prospect theory of Kahneman and Tversky (1979) provides a behavioural-based alternative to rational decision theory, described in Section 3.3. According to prospect theory, an investor considering a risky investment (a "prospect") will separately evaluate prospective gains and losses. This separate evaluation contrasts with decision theory, where investors evaluate decisions in terms of their effects on their total wealth (see Chapter 3, Note 5). Separate evaluation of gains and losses about a reference point is an implication of the psychological concept of **narrow framing**, whereby individuals analyze problems in too isolated a manner as a way of economizing on the mental effort of decision making. This economizing on mental effort may lead to limited attention, as mentioned above. As a result, an individual's utility in prospect theory is defined over deviations from zero for the prospect in question, rather than over total wealth.

Figure 6.2 shows a typical investor utility function under prospect theory.

The investor's utility for gains is assumed to exhibit the familiar risk-averse, concave shape as illustrated in Figure 3.3. However, prospect theory assumes **loss aversion**, a behavioural concept whereby individuals dislike even very small losses. Thus, beginning at the point where the investment starts to lose in value, the investor's rate of utility loss is greater than the rate of utility increase for a gain in value.[4] Indeed, the utility for losses is assumed to be convex rather than concave, so that the investor exhibits risk-taking behaviour with respect to losses. This leads to a **disposition effect**, whereby the investor holds on to losers and sells winners, and, indeed, may even buy more of a loser security.

Figure 6.2 Prospect Theory Utility Function

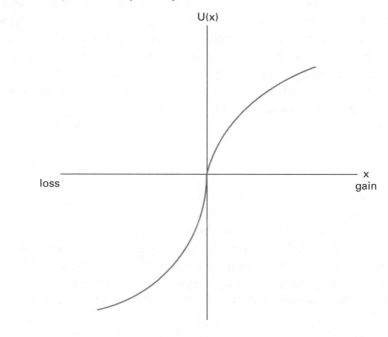

Hossain and List (2009) conducted an experiment in a Chinese high-tech factory. Some workers were told they would receive a bonus of 80 yuan if they met a weekly production target. Others were told that they had actually been awarded the same bonus, but that they would lose it if they did not meet the target.

In both cases, productivity improved, but the improvement was 1% greater in the second case. It seems that the fear of loss had a somewhat stronger effect on productivity than the prospect of gain.

The disposition effect was studied by Shefrin and Statman (1985). They identified a sample of investors whose rational decision was to sell loser securities before the end of the taxation year. They found, however, that the investors tended to avoid selling, consistent with the disposition effect. Theory in Practice 6.1 describes another test of loss aversion.

Prospect theory also assumes that when calculating the expected value of a prospect, individuals under- or overweight their probabilities (i.e., posterior probabilities are less than or greater than those resulting from application of Bayes' theorem). Underweighting probabilities is a ramification of overconfidence. Thus, information not generated by the investor him/herself, such as GN in reported earnings, will be underweighted relative to other evidence. As a result, the individual's posterior probability of the high future performance state may be too low. BN will be underweighted for similar reasons, in which case the posterior probability of low future performance may also be underweighted.

Overweighting probabilities is a ramification of representativeness, whereby individuals tend to overweight current evidence that, for example, a stock's value is about to take off, even though realization of the state "taking off" is a rare event.

These tendencies can lead to "too low" posterior probabilities on states that are likely to happen, and "too high" on states that are unlikely to happen. The posterior probabilities need not sum to one.

The combination of separate evaluation of gains and losses and the weighting of probabilities can lead to a wide variety of "irrational" behaviours. For example, fear of losses may cause investors to stay out of the market even if prospects have positive expected value according to a decision theory calculation. Also, they may underreact to bad news by holding on to "losers" so as to avoid realizing a loss and, as mentioned above, may even buy more of a loser stock, thereby taking on added risk. Thus, under prospect theory, investor behaviour depends in a complex way on payoff probabilities that may differ from those obtained from Bayes' theorem, risk aversion with respect to gains, and risk taking with respect to losses.

A well-known accounting-related test of prospect theory was conducted by Burgstahler and Dichev (BD; 1997). In a large sample of U.S. firms from 1974–1976, these researchers documented that relatively few firms in their sample reported small losses. A relatively large number of firms reported small positive earnings. That is, there is a "gap" just below zero in the distribution of firms' reported earnings. BD interpreted this result as evidence that firms that would otherwise report a small loss manipulate cash flows and accruals to manage their reported earnings upward, so as to instead show small positive earnings.

BD pointed out that this result is consistent with prospect theory. To see why, note again from Figure 6.2 that the rate at which investor utility decreases for small losses is greater than the rate at which it increases for small gains. This implies a relatively strong negative investor reaction to a small reported loss. Managers of firms that would otherwise report a small loss thus have an incentive to avoid this negative investor reaction, and enjoy a positive reaction, by managing reported earnings upward. (Of course, managers of firms with *large* losses have similar incentives, but as the loss increases it becomes more difficult to manage earnings sufficiently to avoid the loss. Also, the incentive to manage earnings upward declines for larger losses since the rate of negative investor reaction is not as great.)

However, BD suggested that their evidence is also consistent with managers behaving rationally. Lenders will demand better terms from firms that report losses, for example. Also, suppliers may cut the firm off or demand immediate payment for goods shipped.

Theory in Practice 6.2

A number of experiments have tested the predictions of prospect theory. In one experiment (Knetsch, 1989), a group of student subjects was each given a chocolate bar and another group each given a mug. While the longevity of the two items (i.e., prospects) differed, they were of equal monetary value. The subjects were then allowed the option of trading with other subjects. For example, a student who had received a chocolate bar but who preferred a mug could exchange with someone who wanted a chocolate bar. Since the two prospects were assigned randomly, rationality predicts that about half of the subjects would trade. However, only about 10% traded.

These results are consistent with prospect theory. This can be seen from Figure 6.2. Since the rate at which investor utility decreases for small losses is greater than the rate at which it increases for small gains, disposing of ("losing") an item already owned creates a larger utility loss than the utility gained by acquiring another item of equal value. As a result, the subjects tended to hold on to the item they had been given.

Subsequent experiments by List (2003) cast these results in a different light, however. List conducted experiments in real markets, rather than in simulated markets with student subjects as above. A distinguishing feature of real markets is that they contain traders with varying degrees of experience. List found that as their experience increased, the behaviour of market participants converged toward that predicted by rational decision theory. He also showed how more experienced traders could buy and sell from less sophisticated ones so as to drive market prices toward their efficient levels.[5] Consequently, List's results tend to support the rational decision theory over prospect theory.

To avoid these consequences, managers have an incentive to avoid reporting losses if possible. Also, firms in a loss position may be eligible for income tax refunds, which could put them into a small profit position even without deliberate earnings management.

BD's interpretation that a gap in reported earnings just below zero indicates earnings management has generated considerable subsequent research, much of which supports BD. For example, Roychowdhury (2006) reported evidence that firms use real earnings management techniques (e.g., cutting advertising) to avoid reporting small losses. However, Durtschi and Easton (2009) concluded that the gap reported by BD may result instead from the statistical methods used by the authors.

The extent to which the BD results support prospect theory thus seems unclear.

6.2.3 Is Beta Dead?

An implication of the CAPM (Section 4.5.1) is that a stock's beta is the sole firm-specific determinant of the expected return on that stock. If the CAPM reasonably captures rational investor behaviour, share returns should be increasing in β_j and should be unaffected by other measures of firm-specific risk, which are diversified away. However, in a large sample of firms traded on major U.S. stock exchanges over the period 1963–1990, Fama and French (1992) found that beta, and thus the CAPM, had little ability to explain stock returns. Instead, they found significant explanatory power for the book-to-market ratio (B/M; ratio of book value of common equity to market value). They also found explanatory power for firm size. Their results suggest that rather than looking to beta as a risk measure, the market acts as if firm risk increases with book-to-market and decreases with firm size.

Fama and French's findings are not necessarily inconsistent with rational investor behaviour. For example, investors may purchase shares of low B/M firms to protect themselves against undiversifiable risk of, say, a downturn in the economy that would lead many firms into financial distress. Purchasing shares of low B/M firms provides such protection since one reason that the market assigns high market value, relative to book value, to a firm is that the firm is unlikely to become financially distressed. The $E(R_{Mt})$ term of the market model (see Section 4.5.1) may not fully capture the risk of financial distress since it is an average across all firms in the market. As a result, rational investors will look to other risk measures, such as the book-to-market ratio (B/M), when making their portfolio decisions.[6]

The Fama and French results do threaten the CAPM, however, since they imply that beta is not an important risk measure. The low explanatory power for beta documented by Fama and French has led some to suggest that beta is "dead."

Somewhat different results are reported by Kothari, Shanken, and Sloan (1995), however. They found that over a longer period of time (1941–1990) beta *was* a significant predictor of return. The B/M also predicted return, but its effect was relatively weak. They attributed the difference between their results and those of Fama and French to differences in methodology and time period studied.

Researchers have generally reacted to these findings by adding B/M and firm size to the market model described in Section 4.5, as additional variables to help explain share return.

Behavioural finance, however, provides a different perspective on the validity of the CAPM and beta. That is, share return behaviour inconsistent with the CAPM is viewed as evidence of market inefficiency. In this regard, Daniel, Hirshleifer, and Subrahmanyam (2001) presented a model that assumes two types of investors—rational and overconfident. Because of rational investors, a stock's beta is positively related to its returns, as in the CAPM. However, overconfident investors overreact to self-collected information. This drives share price too high or low, driving the firm's B/M too low or high. Over time, share price reverts toward its efficient level as the overconfidence is revealed. As a result, both beta and B/M are positively related to future share returns. Thus, in the Daniel, Hirshleifer, and Subrahmanyam model, the positive book-to-market relation to future share returns found by Fama and French is not driven by rational investors protecting themselves against financial distress. Rather, it is driven by overconfidence, a behavioural effect inconsistent with rationality and efficiency.

The status of the CAPM and its implications for beta thus seem unclear. A possible way to rescue beta is to recognize that it may change over time. Our discussion in Section 4.5 assumed that beta was **stationary**. However, changes in interest rates, firms' cost and capital structures, improvements in firms' abilities to manage risk, and development of global markets may affect the relationship between the return on individual firms' shares and the market-wide return, thereby affecting the value of firms' betas. If so, evidence of share return behaviour that appears to conflict with the CAPM could perhaps be explained by shifts in beta.

If betas are non-stationary, rational investors will want to reduce their estimation risk by figuring out when and by how much firms' betas change. This is a difficult question to answer in a timely manner, and different investors will have different opinions. Different estimates of beta introduce differences in investment decisions, even though all investors have access to the same information and proceed rationally with respect to their estimate of what beta is. As a result, additional volatility is introduced into share price behaviour, but beta remains as a variable that explains this behaviour. According to this argument, the CAPM implication that beta is an important risk variable is reinstated, with the proviso that beta is non-stationary. Models that assume rational investor behaviour in the face of non-stationarity[7] are presented by Kurz (1997a and b). Evidence that non-stationarity of beta explains much of the apparent anomalous behaviour of share prices is provided by Ball and Kothari (1989).[8]

From an accounting standpoint, to the extent that beta is not the only relevant firm-specific risk measure, this can only increase the role of financial statements in reporting useful risk information (B/M is an accounting-based variable, for example). Nevertheless, in the face of the mixed evidence reported above, we conclude that beta is not dead. However, it may change over time and may have to "move over" to share its status as a risk measure with accounting-based variables.

6.2.4 Excess Stock Market Volatility

Further questions about securities' market efficiency derive from evidence of excess stock price volatility at the market level. Recall from the CAPM that, holding beta and the risk-free interest rate constant, a change in the expected return on the market portfolio, $E(R_{Mt})$, is the only reason for a change in the expected return of firm j's shares. Shiller (1981) argued that a determinant of $E(R_{Mt})$ is the aggregate expected dividends across all firms in the market—the higher aggregate expected dividends are, the more investors will invest in the market. Other things equal, this increases the demand for shares and drives the stock market index up (and vice versa). Consequently, if the market is efficient, changes in $E(R_{Mt})$ should not exceed changes in aggregate expected dividends.

However, Shiller found that the variability of the stock market index was several times greater than the variability of aggregate dividends. He interpreted this result as evidence of market inefficiency—his prediction, based on the CAPM, that the variability of the stock market should be similar to the variability of dividends was not borne out, and the CAPM assumes market efficiency.

A possible explanation for this apparent inefficiency is that behavioural factors increase stock market volatility. For example, the momentum model of Daniel, Hirshleifer, and Subrahmanyam (2001) implies excess market volatility as share prices overshoot and then fall back. A different argument is made by DeLong, Shleifer, Summers, and Waldmann (1990). They assume a capital market with both rational and positive feedback investors. Positive feedback investors are those who buy in when share price begins to rise, and vice versa. One might expect that rational investors would then sell short, anticipating the share price decline that will follow the price run-up caused by positive feedback buying. However, the authors argued that rational investors anticipate the actions of less sophisticated investors and instead "jump on the bandwagon," to take advantage of the price run-up while it lasts. As a result, there is excess volatility in the market since share prices continue to rise even though these same rational investors believe that share price exceeds its efficient market value.

Another explanation of Shiller's findings, however, is that dividends are largely firm-specific. That is, even for firms with similar earnings, dividends range from zero to a significant proportion of earnings. Consequently, the variability of dividends across firms can be diversified away in large portfolios. If so, we would not expect variability of aggregate dividends to explain much of the variability of the stock market index, since a large firm-specific component of dividends implies that the economy-wide component of dividends is relatively small. For example, Jackson (2009), during the recession following the 2007–2008 market meltdowns, reported ". . . no major dividend cuts this earnings season."

However, other accounting variables than dividends may contain a higher economy-wide component. In this regard, Ball, Sadka, and Sadka (2009) compared the variability of earnings (as opposed to dividends) to the variability of stock market returns. Based on a large sample of firms over the period 1950–2005, they found that a significant proportion of earnings variability is explained by economy-wide factors, in which case earnings variability, unlike that of dividends, cannot be diversified away. Consistent with this, they also found that aggregate earnings and stock market returns are highly correlated, and that earnings variability explains a significant portion of returns variability. In effect, unlike Shiller's result for dividends, the variability of the stock market index does not greatly exceed that of earnings. These results are much more consistent with securities market efficiency than those of Shiller.

6.2.5 Stock Market Bubbles

Stock market bubbles, wherein share prices rise far above fundamental values, represent an extreme case of market volatility. Shiller (2000) investigated bubble behaviour with specific reference to the surge in share prices of technology companies in the United States in the years leading up to 2000. Bubbles, according to Shiller, derive from a combination of biased self-attribution and momentum, positive feedback trading, and "herd" behaviour reinforced by optimistic media predictions of market "experts." These reasons underlie then Federal Reserve Board Chairman Greenspan's famous "irrational exuberance" comment on the stock market in a 1996 speech.

Shiller argued that bubble behaviour can continue for some time and that it is difficult to predict when it will end. Eventually, however, it will burst because of growing beliefs of, say, impending recession or increasing inflation.

It is now generally recognized that security price behaviour leading up to the 2007–2008 market meltdowns was a bubble. Certainly, in the light of subsequent events, the market's apparent ignoring of the riskiness of the investment strategies of many financial institutions caused their share prices to far exceed their fundamental value. However, the development of a bubble does not necessarily contradict market efficiency. Since we define efficiency relative to publicly available information, the relevant question for securities market efficiency is whether or not the information available to investors *at the time* was sufficient to diagnose this riskiness. If it was, behavioural theories such as those mentioned by Shiller are supported, particularly since evidence reported by Niu and Richardson (2006) and Landsman, Peasnell, and Shakespeare (2008; see Chapter 1, Note 20) suggests that at least some information relevant to the impending collapse was in the public domain. Nevertheless, this information may not have been sufficient to counteract the general impression at the time that asset-backed securities were a more efficient way to bear risk, leading investors to bid up the share prices of firms engaged in ABS activities.

6.2.6 Discussion of Securities Market Efficiency Versus Behavioural Finance

Collectively, the behavioural finance theory and evidence discussed in the previous sections raise serious questions about the extent of securities market efficiency and rational investor behaviour. Fama (1998), however, evaluated much of this evidence and concluded that it did not explain the "big picture." That is, while there is evidence of market behaviour inconsistent with efficiency, there is not a unified alternative theory that predicts and integrates the anomalous evidence. For example, Fama pointed out that theory and evidence of overreaction of share prices to information is about as common as underreaction. What is needed to meet Fama's concern is a theory that predicts when the market will overreact and when it will underreact.

This lack of a unified theory may be changing. For example, Barberis, Shleifer, and Vishny (BSV; 1998) drew on the behavioural concept of conservatism to explain under-reaction. That is, conservative investors underweight new evidence relative to their prior information. As a result, share price underreacts, relative to an efficient market reaction, and drifts upward or downward over time as the under/overvaluation becomes apparent from future earnings reports or other sources.

With respect to overreaction, BSV drew on representativeness. Suppose that an investor subject to this characteristic observes a firm's earnings increasing steadily over time. This investor will regard (i.e., represent) this firm as a growth firm, despite the fact that real growth firms are rare. That is, the investor downgrades the prior information of a low population base rate for growth firms. Then, relative to an efficient market, share price overreacts to reported earnings, and continues to increase until, as is likely to happen, an earnings reversal eventually takes place.

Thus, according to these authors, underreaction occurs when new evidence, such as sharply increased earnings this period, comes along on a one-time basis. Overreaction occurs when a longer-term sequence of increased earnings causes investors to assume that growth will continue.

As another example, Hirshleifer and Teoh (2003) presented a model in which some investors are fully rational but others have limited attention, which affects their ability to process publicly available information. Limited attention implies that the *form* of presentation, as opposed simply to its information content, affects investors' interpretations of the information. Then, the market may underreact to supplemental information. For example, consider the difficulty researchers have had in documenting a securities market response to RRA, discussed in Section 2.4. We suggested there that low reliability and availability of alternate reserves information were responsible. Another explanation derives from limited attention. Suppose that the present value of proved reserves has decreased sharply this year. The Hirshleifer and Teoh model predicts that the market will underreact to this information, since investors with limited ability to process information concentrate on reported net income, ignoring the RRA information included in MD&A or the notes. Thus, instead of fully reacting right away, the firm's share price will drift downward as the bad news about reserves becomes apparent over time. Bringing current value accounting for proved reserves into the financial statements proper would make it easier for these investors to realize the implications for future firm performance, speeding up the market reaction.

Empirical support for this argument is provided by Ahmed, Kilic, and Lobo (2006), who studied a sample of U.S. banks that disclosed values of their derivatives as supplemental information prior to the 1998 introduction of SFAS 133, and valued them at fair value in their financial statements proper subsequently. SFAS 133 (now included in ASC 815), like IFRS 9, requires all derivatives to be valued on the balance sheet at fair value (accounting for derivatives is discussed in Section 7.9). They found no significant share price reaction to the value of derivatives disclosed as supplemental information but a significantly positive reaction when disclosed on the balance sheet. This finding contrasts with efficient securities market theory, which predicts that as long as the derivative values are disclosed, and assuming equal reliability, the location of disclosure does not matter.

Thus, by setting out conditions under which different behavioural characteristics lead to overreaction and underreaction, behavioural researchers are responding to Fama's concern.

6.3 EFFICIENT SECURITIES MARKET ANOMALIES

We now consider evidence of market inefficiency that more specifically involves financial accounting information. Recall that the evidence described in Chapter 5 generally supports efficiency and the rational investor behaviour underlying it. There is, however, other evidence suggesting that the market may not respond to accounting information exactly as the efficiency theory predicts. For example, share prices may not fully react to financial statement information right away, so that abnormal security returns continue for some time following the release of the information. Also, it appears that the market may not always extract all the information content from financial statements. In statistical terms, anomalies such as these imply that share returns are serially correlated, whereas, under market efficiency, serial correlation is zero. Cases such as these that appear inconsistent with securities market efficiency are called **efficient securities market anomalies**. We now consider two such anomalies.

Post-Announcement Drift Once a firm's current earnings become known, the information content should be quickly digested by investors and incorporated into the efficient market price. However, it has long been known that this is not exactly what happens. For firms that report good news (GN) in quarterly earnings, their abnormal security returns tend to drift upward for some time following their earnings announcement. Similarly, firms that report bad news (BN) in earnings tend to have their abnormal security returns drift downward for a similar period. This phenomenon is called **post-announcement drift** (PAD). Traces of this behaviour can be seen in the Ball and Brown study reviewed in Section 5.3—see Figure 5.3 and notice that abnormal share returns drift upward and downward for some time following the month of release of GN and BN, respectively.

Bernard and Thomas (BT; 1989) further examined this issue. In a large sample of firms over the period 1974–1986, they documented the presence of PAD in quarterly earnings. Indeed, an investor following a strategy of buying the shares of GN firms and selling short BN on the day of earnings announcement, and holding for 60 days, would have earned an average return of 18% per annum over and above the market-wide return, before transaction costs, in their sample. By GN or BN here, BT mean the difference between current quarterly reported earnings and those of the same quarter last year. These differences are called **quarterly seasonal earnings changes**. The assumption is that investors' expectations of current quarterly earnings are based on those of the same quarter of the previous year.[9]

It seems that, collectively, *investors underestimate the implications of current earnings for future earnings*. As BT pointed out, it is a known fact that quarterly seasonal earnings changes are positively correlated for up to three subsequent quarters. Thus, if a firm reports, say, GN this quarter, in the sense that this quarter's earnings are greater than the same quarter last year, there is a greater than 50% chance that its three subsequent quarters' earnings will also be GN. Rational investors should anticipate this and, as they bid up the price of the firm's shares in response to the *current* GN, they should bid them up some more due to the increased probability of GN in *future* quarters. However, BT's evidence suggests that this does not happen. The implication is that PAD results from investors taking considerable time to figure this out, or at least that they underestimate the magnitude of the correlation (Ball and Bartov, 1996). In terms of the information system given in Table 3.2, BT's results suggest that Bill Cautious evaluates the main diagonal probabilities as less than they really are.[10]

Be sure you see the significance of PAD. If it exists, sophisticated investors could earn arbitrage profits, at least before transaction costs, by modifying the diversified investment strategy described in Section 3.5. For example, an investor could buy GN shares on the day the GN was announced. If he/she could then sell short other companies' shares whose returns were perfectly correlated with the efficient market price changes of the GN shares, the combined portfolio would be riskless—all price changes other than those arising from PAD would cancel out since gains and losses on the GN shares are offset by losses and gains on the short sales shares. Then, the investor will earn a riskless profit as the value of the GN shares drifts upward over future quarters. Furthermore, proceeds from the short sales can be used to buy the GN shares, so little if any capital is required.

The existence of such a "money machine" seems hard to imagine. One would expect that the scramble of investors to exploit a riskless profit opportunity would immediately bid up the prices of GN shares, thereby restoring them to their efficient market value. Yet, the results of BT suggest this does not happen.

Post-announcement drift has generated much subsequent research into the source of the anomaly. One explanation is limited attention, under which investors do not exert the time and effort needed to fully understand the serial correlation of quarterly earnings changes. However, several related explanations have been suggested. For example, Narayanamoorthy (2006) drew on accounting conservatism to argue that the positive correlation between current and next quarters' seasonal earnings changes will be lower for BN firms than for GN firms. This is because with conservatism at least some of the BN is driven by writedowns, which forces future reported earnings up—a writedown of plant and equipment reduces future amortization expense, for example. For such firms, an increase in future earnings works *against* the positive correlation of current and future quarters' seasonal earnings changes, which is at the heart of PAD. GN firms are less likely to have suffered conservative writedowns, so that this effect does not then operate. Thus, given PAD, there should be more profits to be made from investing only in GN firms. Narayanamoorthy showed that a strategy to exploit PAD by investing only in GN firms earned an abnormal return even greater than BT's 18%.

Chordia and Shivakumar (CS; 2005) suggest that investors do not fully incorporate the effects of inflation on firms' future profits into their decisions. They argue that instead of *anticipating* the effects of inflation on future earnings growth, investors seem to wait until the increased or decreased earnings actually show up. Thus share prices drift upward or downward over time, depending on whether the firm benefits or suffers from inflation. Based on a large sample of U.S. firms over the period 1971–2004, CS reported evidence in favour of this argument. They concluded that investor failure to anticipate inflation provides at least a partial explanation for PAD.[11]

Zhang (September, 2008) studied the effect on PAD of the timeliness of analyst forecast revisions following quarterly earnings announcements. Based on a large sample of U.S. firms' quarterly earnings announcements over the period 1996–2002, she found that when analysts quickly revised their forecasts of next-quarter earnings (i.e., within two days of the date of the current quarter's announcement), firms' ERCs were significantly higher and their PAD was lower relative to firms for which analyst forecast revisions were less timely. This suggests that investor response to current-quarter earnings is at least partly based on analysts' forecast revisions, and that PAD is at least partly due to analyst delay in predicting future quarter's earnings.

In a related study, Zhang (2012) pointed out that many managers release a forecast of next quarter's earnings at the same time as they report current quarter's earnings. Based on a large sample of such "bundled" announcements over the period 1997 to 2007, she reported that PAD over the next quarter is significantly reduced when investors (correctly) expect that the manager's forecast is accurate.

The effect of earnings volatility (as opposed to the level of earnings) on PAD was studied by Cao and Narayanamoorthy (CN; 2012). CN argue that earnings of firms with high earnings volatility[12] are less persistent, and thus exhibit lower quarterly seasonal earnings change correlations, than earnings of firms with low earnings volatility. The reason is that, by definition, the greater earnings volatility is, the more earnings change over time, leading to lower persistence and correlations. For a large sample of firms over the period 1987–2008, CN reported significantly lower quarterly earnings persistence and correlations for the high earnings volatility firms in their sample, consistent with their argument. This implies that the higher is earnings volatility the lower is the potential for PAD.

The question then is, is PAD actually lower as earnings volatility increases? CN showed that the answer is no in their sample. This suggests that investors not only underestimate the implications of current earnings for future earnings, as in the original BT study, but they also ignore the impact of earnings volatility.

Market Response to Accruals Sloan (1996), for a large sample of annual earnings announcements over the years 1962–1991, separated reported net income into operating cash flow and accrual components. This can be done by drawing again on the formula:

$$\text{Net income} = \text{Cash flow from operations} \pm \text{Net accruals}$$

Sloan included changes in non-cash working capital accounts such as receivables, allowance for doubtful accounts, inventories, accounts payable, as well as amortization expense, in his net accruals analysis.

Sloan pointed out that accruals are more subject to errors of estimation and possible manager bias than cash flows, and argued that this lower reliability should reduce the association between current accruals and next period's net income. That is, while almost all accruals eventually reverse, accruals subject to error and bias reverse relatively quickly. Operating cash flows, however, result from continuing operations. They are less likely to reverse and are less subject to error and bias. Recall from Section 5.4.1 that persistence is the extent to which the good or bad news in current earnings is expected to continue into the future. Since accruals are less reliable than cash flows and thus tend to reverse quickly, the good or bad news they contain in the current period is less likely to continue into the next period than good or bad news in cash flows. In effect, Sloan argued, the cash flow component of earnings is more persistent than the accrual component.

Sloan examined separately the persistence of the operating cash flows and accruals components of net income for the firms in his sample, and found that next year's reported net income was more highly associated with the operating cash flow component of the current year's income than with the accrual component, supporting his argument of greater cash flow persistence.

If this is the case, we would expect an efficient market to respond more strongly to the GN or BN in earnings the greater is the cash flow component relative to the accrual component in that GN or BN, and vice versa.

Sloan's results suggest that this does not happen. While the market does respond to the GN or BN in earnings, it does not seem to "fine-tune" its response to take into account the cash flow and accruals composition of those earnings. Instead, share returns of high positive accrual firms tended to drift downward over time rather than falling right away, and share returns of low negative accrual firms drifted upward. Sloan designed a simulated investment strategy to exploit the apparent market mispricing. By buying shares of low-accrual firms and short selling shares of high-accrual firms, and holding for one year, he demonstrated a return of 10.4% per annum over and above the market return, before transaction costs.

Sloan's results raise questions about investor rationality and securities market efficiency similar to PAD. It seems that a money machine is available for accruals as well.

As with PAD, researchers continue to try to understand the accruals anomaly. For example, Richardson, Sloan, Soliman, and Tuna (2005) expanded the set of accruals used by Sloan to include all non-cash assets and liabilities. They then classified these accrual components into categories of high, medium, and low reliability (e.g., change in long-term debt is likely to be more reliable than change in net accounts receivable). Based on a large sample of firms over the period 1962–2001, they found that lower reliability accruals were less persistent. They also found that investors appeared to ignore this lower persistence. That is, the less reliable the accrual component, the more investors overestimate earnings persistence, leading to greater share mispricing. An investment strategy to exploit this greater mispricing generated annual abnormal returns, before transaction costs, even stronger than the 10.4% in Sloan's original study,

Since low reliability accruals, by definition, are more subject to manager manipulation, these results suggest that investors do not fully take the possibility of earnings management into account when reacting to reported earnings.

There is also evidence that investors do not fully understand the effects of growth and capital investment on accruals. For example, Zhang (2007) studied a large sample of firms over the period 1964–2003. He documented that high-growth firms tend to generate low stock returns in future years. A likely reason for lower future returns is that managers accept less-profitable projects in a quest for growth for growth's sake. Their ability to do this is aided by the behavioural characteristic of representativeness (Section 6.2.1), under which investors overestimate the continuing performance of growth firms, rewarding such firms with lower cost of capital. Also, as firms grow, their risk tends to decline, further lowering the cost of capital. Since as firms grow their accruals increase (e.g., accounts receivable, inventories),[13] the combination of lower future returns and increasing accruals suggests that the accrual anomaly arises because investors fail to anticipate the lower future earnings of growth firms.

In sum, the anomaly studies outlined to this point suggest that securities markets are not fully efficient and that the inefficiencies are driven by behaviourially biased investors.[14] However, two questions arise. First, why do the anomalies persist over time? The study of Cao and Narayanamoorthy outlined above implies that PAD persists at least to 2008, even though the anomaly was discovered in 1989. One might expect that even behaviourially biased investors would soon realize the existence of a money machine and begin to exploit it. Second, could the anomalies instead be created by rational investors? If so, the theory of investor rationality can be salvaged, even though securities markets may not be fully efficient. We explore these questions in the next two sections.

6.4 LIMITS TO ARBITRAGE[*]

The studies reviewed above suggest several reasons why security market inefficiencies can arise due to behaviourially biased investors. However, once an efficient market anomaly is discovered, should it not die out over time? One might expect that if share mispricing results from behavioural factors, even relatively unsophisticated investors would learn from their mistakes, thereby correcting their biases? One possibility is that the investment environment is extremely complex, made more so by constant change in underlying

---

[*]This section can be omitted with little lack of continuity.

economy parameters. In the face of this complexity, the feedback that investors need to correct their biases is distorted—it is hard to correct one's behaviour when the losses from a behaviourally biased investment decision may be due either to the bias or to changes in the economy since the decision was made. This complexity provides fertile ground for biases to arise and persist.

However, there are other reasons for the persistence of anomalies, called **limits to arbitrage**. These are costs incurred by investors that limit their ability to fully exploit an anomaly and thereby arbitrage it away. We consider two such limits: transaction costs and risk.

Note that persistence of the anomalies because of limits to arbitrage is consistent with average investor rationality. Regardless of whether their persistence is due to behavioural biases or limits to arbitrage, securities markets are not fully efficient. However, the real question is whether this lack of efficiency is, or is not, due to behaviourally biased investors.

Transaction costs include more than brokerage commissions. They may also include the bid–ask spread (see Chapter 1, Note 22), since an arbitrage strategy involves buying shares and selling them later, or selling short and buying back later. Short selling may incur additional costs. Also, if the market is not highly liquid, share price may rise upon purchase, and fall from short sale, creating another cost. Time and effort are also required, including continuous monitoring of earnings announcements, annual reports, and market prices, overcoming any behavioural biases, and development of the required expertise.

In this regard, Ng, Rusticus, and Verdi (NRV; 2008) in a study of the post-announcement drift anomaly, measured transaction costs faced by investors by the bid–ask spread plus commissions. In a large sample study over the period 1988–2005, they found that the abnormal returns to a strategy of buying shares of high GN firms and selling short shares of high BN firms and holding for three months were negative after deducting transaction costs. When the holding period was extended to 12 months, net returns were not necessarily negative but were greatly reduced. NRV also studied those firms in their sample with the highest transaction costs. Shares of the high-transaction costs firms had the highest post-announcement drift, hence the greatest potential for NRV's investment strategy to earn a high return. They found, however, that the net 12-month return from such firms was insignificantly different from zero. These results suggest that transaction costs at least partially constrain investors' abilities to exploit the accruals anomaly—the highest amounts of money left "on the table" are for firms where the money machine is most costly to access.

Another reason to discourage arbitrage investment is **risk** arising from reduced diversification. Note first that a portfolio containing shares for which mispricing exists, such as portfolios designed to exploit the PAD and accruals anomalies, represents a departure from a fully diversified investment strategy. Instead, the investor tries to earn a return greater than that of the market portfolio by investing in shares that he/she perceives as mispriced. As a result of less diversification, firm-specific variance of returns assumes a greater role. That is, an arbitrage investment strategy incurs idiosyncratic risk (Section 3.5).[15]

In our money-machine investment strategy described in Section 6.3, idiosyncratic risk was eliminated, since the investor sold short shares with efficient market price changes perfectly correlated with those of the mispriced shares in his/her portfolio. However, as a practical matter it is difficult, if not impossible, to find such shares. Consequently, idiosyncratic risk remains to limit the arbitrage of rational, risk-averse investors.

Mashruwala, Rajgopal, and Shevlin (2006), who studied the accruals anomaly for a large sample of firms over the period 1975–2000, reported that the highest returns to a strategy of investing in extreme-accrual firms in their sample were concentrated in shares of high idiosyncratic risk—the higher the risk the higher the return demanded by risk-averse investors, thereby putting a brake on arbitrage investing. This finding demonstrates the practical difficulty of eliminating idiosyncratic risk. Mendenhall (2004) reported similar results for the PAD anomaly.

In sum, it seems that transaction costs and idiosyncratic risk provide at least a partial explanation why anomalies such as PAD and accruals have persisted.

To better understand the persistence of anomalies, however, it is necessary to consider more than one type of investor, since investors differ in sophistication and face different levels of transaction costs and risk. In particular, large institutions such as banks, investment houses, insurance companies, and hedge funds possess greater expertise and economies of scale than behaviourally biased or unsophisticated rational investors. As a result, large institutions' transaction costs are relatively low and their expertise in minimizing risk is high. Much anomaly research has studied the extent to which large institutions may arbitrage the anomalies away.

For example, Bartov, Radhakrishnan, and Krinsky (2000) found that PAD is less if a greater proportion of a firm's shares is held by institutions, This implies that institutional investors earn arbitrage profits, thereby eliminating at least some PAD. Ke and Ramalingegowda (2005), who studied a large sample of quarterly earnings announcements over the period 1986–1999, also reported that some institutions earn arbitrage profits by trading to take advantage of PAD. The proportion of their profits from PAD is quite small, however, being dominated by other strategies such as buy and hold or momentum trading.

With respect to the accruals anomaly, Lev and Nissim (2006) studied a large sample of firms over the period 1965–2002. They found that institutional investors trade on the anomaly, indicating that they are aware of it. But similar to the PAD findings of Ke and Ramalingegowada just mentioned, the amount of their trading is quite low, well short of what would be needed to arbitrage the accruals anomaly away. Lev and Nissim pointed out that the firms in their sample tend to be small, young, with relatively low share prices, low dividend yield, and low book-to-market ratios, and argue that these are not investment characteristics favoured by financial institutions.

Battalio, Lerman, Livnat, and Mendenhall (BLLM; 2012) examined stock trade sizes for firms listed on major U.S. exchanges around the dates that their quarterly reports became publically available (this is the earliest date on which actual accrual information becomes publically known). Their study covered the period 1993–1999.[16] They reported that, on average, investors who initiated large-size trades (5,000 shares or more bought or sold) bought shares of GN firms with low accruals and sold holdings of GN firms[17] with high accruals. That is, they did take advantage of the accrual anomaly. BLLM also reported, however, that the volume of trading by large-trade investors was not sufficient to completely bid away the anomaly.

The behaviour of small-trade investors (less than 500 shares bought or sold) was quite different. Consistent with the anomaly, small investors did not respond to accruals at all. BLLM argued that such investors are relatively unsophisticated, and supported this argument with evidence that their trading behaviour is instead driven by factors such as media attention, high trading volume, and extreme one-day returns.[18]

Despite these various anomaly explanations, more recent research suggests that the two anomalies may now have almost disappeared, net of costs. Richardson, Tuna, and Wysocki (2010), using more comprehensive measures of transaction costs and expected risk than previous studies, reported that investment strategies to exploit both anomalies earned effectively zero returns during the period 2003–2008. Green, Hand, and Soliman (2011) studied the returns to exploiting the accrual anomaly during the period 2004–2010 for the 3,000 largest U.S. firms based on market capitalization. As they pointed out, the transaction costs of trading in the shares of large firms will be low relative to smaller firms. Using an investment strategy similar to that of Sloan (Section 6.3), who initially documented the anomaly in 1996, they reported an abnormal return not significantly different from zero over the period 2004–2010. The authors attributed this finding to increased interest in the anomaly by hedge funds that, arguably, enjoy low transaction costs and considerable risk management sophistication.

Overall, it seems that large institutional investors, with low transaction costs and, arguably, sophisticated risk management systems, have increased over time their exploitation of the PAD and accruals anomalies to an extent that the anomalies, net of costs, seem to have largely disappeared. If so, a cost and risk based explanation for the persistence of anomalies is supported.

6.5 A DEFENCE OF AVERAGE INVESTOR RATIONALITY*

6.5.1 Dropping Rational Expectations

A more fundamental question, however, is why the anomalies appear in the first place. Do they necessarily result from behavioural characteristics, as we discussed earlier, or can similar observations be produced if investors are on average rational? If the latter, the theory of rational investor behaviour can be salvaged, even though markets may not be fully efficient.

In theory, share price behaviour similar to that predicted by behavioural finance can be generated by rational investors. This was shown by, for example, Brav and Heaton

---

*This section can be omitted with little lack of continuity.

(2002), who relaxed the rational expectations assumption that investors immediately figure out a change in underlying firm parameters. Instead, they considered how investors may refine their estimates of these parameters over time.[19] To see their argument, suppose that a firm has just reported a substantial increase in earnings. The question then is, has the firm's expected earning power increased, or is this simply noise, such as a one-time blip produced by some low-persistence earnings item or short-run favourable state realization? While careful analysis of the financial statements may help, the rational investor is unlikely to know the answer with complete accuracy, due, for example, to inside information, possibly compounded by poor disclosure. That is, the investor faces estimation risk with respect to the underlying non-stationary firm parameter of expected earning power.

In the face of this estimation risk, the rational investor will revise his/her earning power beliefs by less than if he/she was sure the higher earnings would persist, but by more than if he/she were sure the higher earnings were simply noise. Other rational investors will react similarly. The additional demand will trigger an immediate share price increase. This increase will be less than it would be if investors were certain of the increase in expected earning power, but more than if they knew there was no expected earning power increase. To reduce their estimation risk, investors will watch for additional information. If expected earning power has in fact increased, new information that is on balance favourable will be observed over time. For each information item, investors will revise their expected earning power estimate and will buy additional shares. The firm's share price will drift upward. Notice that this upward drift produces a time pattern of share returns similar to the behavioural concept of conservatism. It is also similar to the upward drift for GN firms' share prices documented in the PAD studies, and for the upward drift of share prices of low-accrual firms.

Conversely, if expected earning power has not increased, unfavourable information will be observed over time. Then, we would expect the share overvaluation to reverse as the overvaluation is revealed. This overreaction to net income produces a time pattern of share returns similar to the behavioural concept of representativeness, and is consistent with PAD for BN firms, and with high-accrual firms.[20]

A related share mispricing argument is given by Lo's **adaptive market hypothesis** (2004). Like Brav and Heaton, Lo dropped the rational expectations assumption that underlies much of the theory of market efficiency. Instead, investors are viewed as **boundedly rational** (Simon, 1955)[21]. That is, when their environment changes (e.g., higher reported firm profits, increased awareness of firm risk), individuals do not react right away. Rather, they adapt to their new environment over time. This produces effects on share returns similar to those predicted by behavioural finance—namely, in our context, underreaction or overreaction to accounting information. It is also consistent with the increasing exploitation by large institutions of the PAD and accrual anomalies over time, as outlined in the previous section.[22]

Empirical evidence consistent with the above arguments is presented by Callen, Khan, and Lu (CKL; 2013), who examined delayed share price reaction to new information, based on a large sample of firms over the period 1981–2006. CKL estimated the delay in price reaction by adding four past market return terms to the market model (Section 4.5.1). To the extent that a share's current market return depends on four previous market returns in addition to the current market return as in the CAPM, this suggests a delay in investor reaction to information. Delay can thus be measured by any increase in the R^2 of the augmented regression over the R^2 of the market model (see Note 32 re R^2). The authors found a significant positive delay on average, suggesting that delay in fully reacting to new information is commonplace. CKL also estimated delay specifically related to accounting information by replacing past market returns with firm-specific returns (Section 5.2.3) in the procedure just described, with similar results. These findings do question full securities market efficiency, since prices appear to react to information with a delay. However, since prices do eventually react, the findings are consistent with our argument above that investors reduce their estimation risk by searching for subsequent information.

CKL then used their estimates of market reaction to information to evaluate how delay relates to accounting quality. Using several quality measures, including the accrual quality measure of Dechow and Dichev (Section 5.4.1), they found that higher accounting quality is significantly associated with lower delay. They also found a significant positive relationship between a firm's delay and its future abnormal share returns, consistent with investors demanding a higher return on shares for which they perceive greater estimation risk. These results are consistent with average investor rationality, even though the existence of delay implies less-than-full market efficiency.

Our argument that rational investors take time to fully interpret earnings announcements is also supported by the empirical results of Zhang (2012) and Zhang (September, 2008) (Section 6.3), who found PAD was significantly reduced when earnings announcements were accompanied by management forecasts that investors perceived as accurate, and when analysts quickly revised their earnings forecasts. This reduction in PAD suggests that credible forecasts help investors to resolve more quickly their uncertainty about future earnings.

6.5.2 Dropping Common Knowledge

As noted in Section 4.5.2, economic models, such as the CAPM, typically assume common knowledge. In the case of the CAPM, not only is each investor assumed to know a stock's beta (a rational expectations assumption) but all investors know that everybody knows beta. This rules out the possibility that some investors may feel that they have superior information about beta. If they do feel they have superior information, investors could invest so as to exploit their better information at the expense of less well-informed investors instead of adopting the rational diversified investment strategy envisioned by the CAPM.

Our Example 3.1 also implicitly assumed common knowledge. Bill Cautious, our rational investor, made his investment decision based only on his own information, without consideration of the possibility that his information might be better or worse than that of others.

However, we have already seen an example of what might happen without a common knowledge assumption. In Section 6.2.4, we cited the paper of DeLong, Shleifer, Summers, and Waldmann (1990), where rational investors, instead of selling shares of firms they felt were overvalued, jumped on the bandwagon to exploit the price runups they believed were caused by momentum investors. When investors make decisions on the basis of their beliefs about the beliefs of others, instead of solely on their beliefs about relevant states of nature, such beliefs are called **higher order beliefs**.

Our interest in higher order beliefs arises because such beliefs by rational investors can produce share price behaviour similar to that predicted by behavioural finance. In this regard, Allen, Morris, and Shin (AMS; 2006) modelled a market composed of overlapping generations of rational, short-term, risk-averse investors. Each generation "lives" for 2 periods. The first generation of investors invests in securities of a risky firm at the beginning of the first period. At the beginning of the second period, they sell their holdings on the market, to enjoy consumption. A new generation of investors takes over by buying these securities on the market, holding for one period, then selling in turn to a third generation, and so on. This process continues for a fixed number of periods, at the end of which the fundamental value of the firm is revealed. We can think of this underlying firm value as the state of nature in this model.

While somewhat artificial, this model of investor behaviour is designed to capture the short-term horizon of many investors, so as to create higher order beliefs.[23]

Share market value at the beginning of the first period is determined by the beliefs about underlying firm value held by the first generation of investors. Share market value at the end of the first period will be determined by the beliefs about underlying firm value held by the second generation of investors, who buy shares at this time from the retiring first generation. Market value at the end of the second period will be determined by the beliefs of the third generation, and so on.

The crucial aspect of this setup is that the each generation of investors, except the last, has higher order beliefs. That is, each generation is interested in share market value at the end of the period, which is determined by the beliefs of the next generation. Thus each generation's investment decision, except the last, is based on what they think the beliefs of the next generation about underlying firm value will be, and not solely on their own beliefs about fundamental firm value. Beliefs about fundamental firm value, which we could label primary beliefs, are not directly relevant except to the last generation. The question then is, how does the market price of the firm's securities behave over time in the presence of these higher order beliefs?

To answer this question, AMS assumed that at the beginning of the first period, investors receive a noisy, unbiased *public* message of fundamental firm value.[24] In our context, we can think of this message as the firm's financial report. Since it is noisy, this public message will generally differ from fundamental value. However, since this is the only information about firm value available at this time, the first investor generation will believe that this will be the beliefs of the second generation. Thus the firm's beginning share price will be based on the public message.

Subsequently, in each generation, each investor acquires a noisy, unbiased, *private* message of firm value. To motivate investors to acquire this additional information, AMS assume the presence of noise traders (see our discussion in Section 4.4.1).

The source of the private messages could be from each investor's more detailed examination of the firm's financial report. Alternatively, it could be from consultations with financial advisors or, in general, from any other private information searches, such as media reports. Then, viewing the public message as prior information about firm value and the private message as additional information, each investor's posterior expectation of firm value is a weighted average of the public and private messages, as in Bayes' theorem (Section 3.3).[25]

Note two aspects of this model. First, since the private signals are unbiased, the average private signal equals fundamental firm value. However, market price at period end will not equal this value due to the continuing influence of the first-period noisy public message in posterior beliefs. Nevertheless, over time, as successive generations continue to receive private signals,[26] the influence of the noisy public message on investors' posterior expectations of firm value declines. In effect, the total information available to each successive generation better and better approximates fundamental firm value. Thus, the market price of the firm's shares converges toward fundamental value over time.

Second, the presence of noise traders introduces additional risk into market prices beyond the risk arising from investors' lack of knowledge of actual firm value. Since investors are risk averse, and since they are primarily interested in the firm's share value at end of period, and only indirectly in actual firm value, this additional risk reduces their demand, thereby slowing the convergence of share price to fundamental value.[27]

This pattern of share price behaviour violates a condition of market efficiency, since security price changes exhibit serial correlation rather than behaving as a random walk. Yet, in the model investors are rational.

The AMS model has a number of implications. Serial correlation of security returns is interpreted by many behavioural finance-based studies, such as the post-announcement drift and accruals anomalies discussed in Section 6.2.6, as evidence of investor non-rationality and market inefficiency. The AMS model provides an alternative theory to explain why market inefficiencies can be consistent with investor rationality.

Another implication of AMS is that if the initial noisy public message is, say, below fundamental firm value, price rises over time. As AMS pointed out, this could precipitate a bubble, since some rational investors may then jump on the bandwagon to exploit share price momentum while it lasts. In addition, other investors (whose private message is bad news) will believe a security is overvalued even though its price keeps rising. This is consistent with claims by some investment professionals that they had predicted the 2007–2008 market meltdowns but were ignored by the market.

Experimental evidence consistent with higher order beliefs is presented by Elliott, Krische, and Peecher (EKP; 2010). They presented a group of 67 experienced financial analysts with financial information about a firm. The firm reports an 11% rate of growth in net income. However, this growth is attained through earnings management. Specifically, the firm has been selling financial assets that have appreciated in value, thereby transferring unrealized gains included in other comprehensive income (see Section 1.10) into realized gains included in net income. At least some unsophisticated investors will be fooled by this tactic, with the result that the firm's shares will be overpriced.

EKP manipulated the transparency of disclosure of this earnings management. In their high transparency setting, other comprehensive income was reported immediately below the net income statement (consistent with current IASB and FASB standards). In their low transparency setting, other comprehensive income was reported as part of a statement of changes in shareholders' equity (allowed at the time by FASB standards), in which case the earnings management was less likely to be detected by unsophisticated investors.[28]

EKP also manipulated the firm's investor base by varying the type of sophisticated investor. Dedicated investors are sophisticated investors with a longer-term investment strategy, with relatively low portfolio turnover and relatively little momentum trading. Transient investors are also sophisticated, but with a short-term investment strategy, characterized by frequent buying and selling, including momentum trading.

In the low transparency earnings management setting, EKP argued that sophisticated investors (both dedicated and transient) are likely to discover the earnings management, but unsophisticated investors are unlikely to discover it. Dedicated investors will likely sell, driving share price down toward the firm's fundamental value and reducing any share mispricing resulting from the firm's earnings management. Transient investors, however, are less likely to sell right away. Instead, they may jump on the bandwagon to exploit the temporary share overpricing resulting from the unsophisticated investors being "fooled" by the earnings management.

In the high transparency setting, EKP argued that unsophisticated investors are now more likely to discover the earnings management. Those who do, having "figured out" the earnings management, may exhibit overconfidence, leading to share price momentum. EKP argued that transient sophisticated investors are then even more likely to jump on the bandwagon and engage in momentum trading, whereas dedicated sophisticated investors are likely to hold or sell.

As a result, EKP predicted that when earnings management becomes more transparent, the analyst subjects will expect greater share mispricing when transient investors have primary influence on share price. This prediction is somewhat surprising since one might expect that more transparent reporting will improve decision making and reduce mispricing. According to EKP, the argument that transparent reporting improves decision making only applies to longer-term investors whose interests lie in fundamental firm value.

When the analysts were asked for their judgment about extent of share mispricing, their answers were, on average, consistent with EKP's arguments. This evidence supports the existence of higher order beliefs, since the analyst subjects' judgments were conditional on their beliefs about the nature of investors (i.e., dedicated or transient) who were driving the share price. If such beliefs did not exist, different types of investors would not affect analysts' judgments.

6.6 SUMMARY RE SECURITIES MARKET INEFFICIENCIES

Figure 6.3 summarizes our discussions to this point about the various arguments surrounding securities market inefficiencies. It adds an inner circle to Figure 4.2, representing the reduced information included in the actual share price when markets are not fully efficient. Then, share price does not incorporate all publicly available information (or incorporates it with bias). Note that the missing and/or biased information under market inefficiency can be favourable or unfavourable. That is, share price can be lower than or greater than the efficient market price.

There are several possible reasons underlying the inefficiency implied by the inner circle. One reason derives from behavioural finance, under which behaviourially biased investors do not take all publicly available information into account in their decisions. A second reason, suggested by Lee (2001), derives from behaviourally biased noise traders, who may drive market price away from the efficient market ideal. Also, the models of Brav and Heaton, Lo, and Allen, Morris, and Shin that retain an assumption of rational (or boundedly rational) investors, attribute the inefficiency to investor learning over time or to higher order beliefs. Regardless of the reason, these inefficiencies add an important role for financial reporting, to reduce inefficiencies by making the mispricing area between the two inner circles as small as possible. High quality reporting fulfills this role. It can help behaviourally biased investors improve their decisions. It can speed up the corrections to mispricing caused by noise trading. It can help rational investors learn over time or, by releasing publicly available information, reduce the effects of higher order beliefs.

Figure 6.3 Roles of Financial Reporting When Securities Market Is Not Fully Efficient

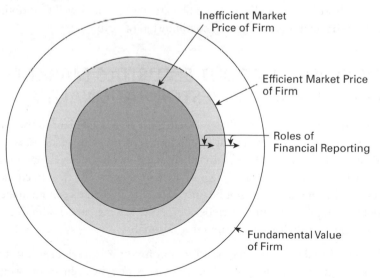

It should now be apparent that recent capital markets research has moved well beyond relatively simple economic models, such as the CAPM, that assume only one type of rational investor in a setting of rational expectations and common knowledge.[29] Arguably, if economic modelling is to recover from the intense criticisms noted in Section 1.3, arising from failure to predict the 2007–2008 security markets meltdowns, it will have to drop rational expectations and common knowledge in favour of closer attention to different types of investors and to how rational investors learn over time. In turn, a better understanding of investor behaviour, and how different investor types interact in a securities market, should enable accountants to improve decision usefulness by "fine tuning" their concepts of full disclosure and transparency. For example, increased usage of current value accounting, or at least moving current values from the financial statement notes into the financial statements proper, can increase decision usefulness to the extent it helps behaviourally biased investors improve their decision making.

These various arguments lead to an interesting possibility, namely that behavioural theories of investment and the theory of rational investment that underlies market efficiency may be moving together. For example, the EKP study reviewed in the previous section displays a combination of rational and behavourial investor characteristics. Brav and Heaton suggested a related argument. Is there a great difference in claiming, on the one hand, that failure of share prices to fully reflect accounting information in a timely manner is due to behavioural characteristics such as conservatism and representativeness, and claiming, on the other hand, that such failures are driven by investor uncertainty about underlying firm parameters? For example, the conservative investor underreacts to current increased earnings. The rational investor, unsure whether or not current increased earnings represent a persistent increase, places some probability on both possibilities. The boundedly rational investor may not immediately conduct the in-depth analysis needed to identify the correct possibility but will learn over time. In each case, the market is not fully efficient. However, the inefficiency can be attributed just as well to rational investor behaviour, to behavioural biases, or to a combination of both.

6.7 CONCLUSIONS ABOUT SECURITIES MARKET EFFICIENCY AND INVESTOR RATIONALITY

With respect to securities market efficiency, efficient or not efficient is the wrong question. Instead, the question is the *extent* of efficiency. In previous sections, we concluded that securities markets are not always fully efficient, based on the development of liquidity pricing following a bubble, and various lags in the convergence of prices to efficient values.

However, while markets may not be fully efficient, arguments can be made that they are reasonably close, except during periods of liquidity pricing, and that market behaviour is reasonably consistent with average investor rationality:

■   Experimental studies supporting non-rational investor behaviour using student subjects leave open the question of whether more experienced investors would behave in a similar manner. To the extent that investors are experienced, it seems hard to believe that security prices do not reasonably reflect available information.

- With respect to the bubble leading up to the 2007–2008 market meltdowns, there is some evidence that the market tried to adjust for off balance sheet risk (see Chapter 1, Note 20). However, available information may not have been sufficient to fully diagnose this risk and overcome a general feeling that asset-backed securities increased the efficiency of risk bearing. This feeling was not overcome until it became apparent that complex financial instruments such as asset-backed securities lacked transparency. Consequently, the underreaction to risk that contributed to the bubble was not necessarily due to market inefficiency, since risk was masked by high ratings from ratings agencies, and inadequate reporting of off balance sheet obligations.[30]

    In this regard, Cheng, Dhaliwal, and Neamtiu (CDN; 2011) studied the ability of investors in asset-backed securities (ABS) to evaluate their riskiness. To a considerable extent, ABS risk depended on the extent to which the banks that issued these securities offered implicit guarantees (see Section 1.3 re credit enhancement of ABSs). Generally, these guarantees were not disclosed.[31] CDN found that the greater the investor uncertainty about the extent of credit enhancement offered by a bank, the greater the bid–ask spread on that bank's stock. Since the bid–ask spread is a measure of the information asymmetry and resulting estimation risk perceived by investors, this is consistent with investors rationally reacting to lack of ABS transparency.

- The evidence of sophisticated response to accounting information described in Chapter 5 suggests considerable efficiency and investor rationality. While the studies described there are now quite old, more recent studies continue to document sophisticated market response to the quality of accounting information. For example, the CDN study just described suggests considerable investor sophistication, which would hardly be observed if investors were on average non-rational.

- As we will describe in Section 7.5.2, standard setters are introducing new standards for derecognition of securitized assets, consolidation, and expanded disclosures. This suggests that they now perceive accounting practices during the bubble to have provided insufficient information. Also, as described by Bitti (2013), major audit oversight agencies worldwide are reconsidering rules to reinforce the objectivity and independence of the auditing profession. Proposals include mandatory re-tendering of audits after a specified number of years, mandatory auditor rotation, joint audits, and increased disclosures by audit committees and/or auditors. These investigations suggest a concern that more responsible auditor reporting could have increased investor awareness of risks leading up to the 2007–2008 market meltdowns.

- As we pointed out in Section 4.2.1, security price changes fluctuate randomly on an efficient market. That is, security returns do not predict unexpected events. The full significance of changes in underlying economic parameters, such as globalization of capital markets, resulting high correlation of market meltdowns worldwide, and the near simultaneity of collapses of markets for housing, asset-backed securities, asset-backed commercial paper, and credit default swaps may not have been predictable leading up to the bubble collapse, even by an efficient market. These events had never happened before. Certainly, market prices reacted rapidly once the full underlying riskiness of firms' operations became apparent.

■ Investor risk aversion may vary over time. Lack of transparency of complex financial instruments, inadequate reporting of off balance sheet obligations, and sudden realization of the high correlation of market meltdowns worldwide, could lead to a widespread increase in aversion to risk. If so, increased risk aversion contributes to the rapid decline in market prices following a bubble burst.

We conclude that while securities prices can depart significantly from efficient market pricing at times, securities markets are generally close enough to full efficiency that accountants, and standard setters, can be guided by the theory, although they will have to recognize that in some cases convergence to efficient prices may take time. The exception to this argument seems to be in periods during liquidity pricing. When liquidity pricing takes hold, investors, including large financial institutions, sell securities because they need the money and/or are fearful that prices will decline even further. This scramble to sell forces fair values of securities below value in use, and below the value they would have if market price reflected all publicly available information. In this regard, IFRS 13 requires that fair value measurement requires an "orderly transaction." This incorporates some flexibility into fair value standards to cope with the possibility of liquidity pricing.

With respect to investor rationality, the question is whether rational or behavioural theories best underlie securities market behaviour. While this question seems to be open, we remind the reader that rationality is an average concept. Undoubtedly, individual investors exhibit many different types of behaviour. The real question is whether these behaviours average out so that security prices are unbiased relative to available information, or whether individual biases are strong enough that securities are mispriced relative to this information.

A strong argument can be made that the rational decision theory model is still the most useful model for accountants to understand investor needs. This argument is based on theoretical arguments that complexity and non-stationarity of underlying earnings quality parameters provides a rational explanation for what is often interpreted as evidence of inefficiency, and on the fact that limits to arbitrage are consistent with rationality—we can hardly expect investors to use more information than is cost-effective to exploit. Higher order beliefs provide additional theory showing how market inefficiencies can develop with rational investors.

However, in the final analysis, it may not matter to accountants whether the rational model or behavioural models are most descriptive of investors, since the action implications are similar. One can argue that by enabling better predictions of future firm performance, bringing current values into the financial statements proper will benefit rational investors. Alternatively, one can argue that helping investors overcome behavioural biases by bringing current values into the financial statements proper will help them to improve their decision making. In either case, a measurement approach may help attain these desirable goals.

6.8 OTHER REASONS SUPPORTING A MEASUREMENT APPROACH

A number of considerations come together to suggest that the decision usefulness of financial reporting may be enhanced by increased attention to measurement. As just discussed, securities markets may not always be as efficient as previously believed. Thus, investors may need more help in assessing probabilities of future firm performance than they obtain from historical cost statements. Also, we shall see that reported net income explains only a small part of the variation of security prices around the date of earnings announcements, and the portion explained may be decreasing.

From a theoretical perspective, Ohlson's clean surplus theory shows that the market value of the firm can be expressed in terms of income statement and balance sheet variables. While the clean surplus theory applies to any basis of accounting, its demonstration that firm value depends on fundamental accounting variables is consistent with a measurement approach.

Finally, increased attention to measurement is supported by more practical considerations. In recent years, auditors have been subjected to major lawsuits. In retrospect, it appears that net asset values of failed firms were seriously overstated. Conservative accounting standards that require one-sided current value-based techniques, such as impairment tests, may help to reduce auditor liability in this regard.

We now review these other considerations in more detail.

6.9 THE LOW VALUE RELEVANCE OF FINANCIAL STATEMENT INFORMATION

In Chapter 5 we saw that empirical accounting research has established that security prices do respond to the information content of net income. The ERC research, in particular, suggests that the market is quite sophisticated in its ability to extract value implications from financial statements. Nevertheless, as we pointed out in Section 5.3.2, Ball and Brown concluded that most of the information in net income was built into share price prior to its announcement date. This conclusion was further investigated by Lev (1989), who pointed out that the market's response to the good or bad news in earnings is really quite small. In fact, he reported that only 2% to 5% of the abnormal variability of narrow-window security returns around the date of release of earnings information can be attributed to earnings itself.[32]

These findings question the value relevance of financial statement information. Value relevance is closely related to the concept of earnings quality, since it uses abnormal changes in share price surrounding earnings releases to measure the extent to which financial statement information assists investors to predict future firm value.

An understanding of value relevance requires an appreciation of the difference between statistical significance and practical significance. Statistics that measure value relevance such as R^2 (see Note 32) and the ERC can be significantly different from zero in a statistical sense, but yet value relevance can be quite small. Thus, we can be quite sure that there *is* a security market response to earnings (as opposed to *no* response), but at the same time we can be disappointed that the response is not larger than it is. To put it another way, suppose that, on average, security prices change by $1 during a narrow window of three or four days around the date of earnings announcements. Then, Lev's point is that only about two to five cents of this change is due to the earnings announcement itself, even after allowing for market-wide price changes during this period.

Subsequently, researchers have studied the trend of value relevance over time. Lev and Zarowin (1999), in a study covering the period 1978–1996, reported a falling R^2 over time. They also reported a falling ERC. A falling ERC is more ominous than a falling R^2, since a falling R^2 is perhaps due to an increased impact over time of other information sources on share price. The ERC, however, is a direct measure of accounting value relevance, regardless of other information sources.

Contrasting evidence, however, is provided by Landsman and Maydew (LM; 2002) for a sample of quarterly earnings announcements over the period 1972–1988. Instead of R^2 and ERC, they measured the information content of quarterly earnings by the abnormal share return (i.e., by the residual of the market model (Section 4.5.1)) over a three-day window surrounding the earnings release date. Recall from Section 5.2.3 that the residual term of the market model measures the firm-specific information content of an earnings announcement. By this measure, LM found that the information content of earnings had *increased* over the period they studied.

This raises the question, How can the R^2 and ERC fall but abnormal share return increase? A reconciliation is suggested by Francis, Schipper, and Vincent (FSV; 2002). They pointed out an increasing tendency for large firms to report other accounting information, such as sales, special items, and forward-looking information, at the same time as they make their earnings announcements. If current earnings news is, say, favourable, we would expect these additional news items to also be favourable, thereby further increasing investors' expectations of future firm performance. Thus, while the share price response to net income as such (measured by R^2 and ERC) may be falling, the response to the earnings announcement taken as a whole (measured by abnormal return) is increasing. FSV examined the three-day abnormal returns to a sample of quarterly earnings announcements containing other information, during the period 1980–1999, and reported results consistent with this argument.

Further evidence on value relevance is reported by Ball and Shivakumar (2008). For a large sample of firms, for each year over the period 1972–2006, they studied the relationship between the total annual return on their sample firms' shares (a measure of the value of all information about a firm coming to market for a year) and the sum of the return on these shares during three-day windows surrounding the firm's quarterly earnings reports (a measure of the value of all information about a firm coming to market around its earnings reports). The R^2s of their regression equations then measure the value of information coming to market at the time of the firms' quarterly reports relative to all information about those firms during the year. They found that on average over all sample firms and years the proportion of total returns explained by earnings announcement-period returns was only about 1.9%. This finding is consistent with earlier studies reporting low value relevance. However, consistent with the results of FSV, the proportion increased substantially in the later years of their study, reaching a maximum of about 7.3% over the period 2004–2006.

Of course, we would never expect net income to explain *all* of a security's abnormal return, except under ideal conditions. Historical cost accounting and conservatism mean that net income lags in recognizing much economically significant information, such as management forecasts, unrecognized intangibles, and increases in current values. We saw this effect in the Ball and Brown study in Section 5.3. Most of the good or bad news in earnings was anticipated by the market in the year leading up to the net income reporting date, leaving relatively little value relevance for net income itself. That is, recognition lag lowers R^2 and ERC by waiting longer than the market before recognizing value-relevant events.

Even if financial statements were the *only* source of information to the market, our discussion of the informativeness of price in Section 4.4, and the resulting need to recognize the presence of noise traders, tells us that accounting information cannot explain all abnormal return variability. Accounting information can also affect investors' perceptions of a firm's risk, possibly affecting its cost of capital. If cost of capital changes, the effects on share price will create abnormal return volatility. Also, non-stationarity of parameters such as beta (Section 6.2.3) and excess volatility introduced by non-rational investors (Section 6.2.4) further increase the amount of share price volatility to be explained.

Nevertheless, a "market share" for net income of only 2% to 7%, depending on how and when measured, seems low, even after the above counterarguments are taken into account. Lev attributed this low share to poor earnings quality. If so, this suggests that earnings quality could be improved by introducing a measurement approach into the financial statements, thereby recognizing value relevant events sooner. At the very least, evidence of low value relevance of earnings suggests that there is still plenty of room for accountants to improve the information content of financial statements for investors.

6.10 OHLSON'S CLEAN SURPLUS THEORY

6.10.1 Three Formulae for Firm Value

The Ohlson **clean surplus theory** provides a framework consistent with the measurement approach, by showing how the market value of the firm can be expressed in terms of fundamental balance sheet and income statement components. The theory assumes ideal conditions in capital markets, including dividend irrelevancy.[33] Nevertheless, it has had some success in explaining and predicting actual firm value. Our outline of the theory is based on a simplified version of Feltham and Ohlson (FO; 1995). The clean surplus theory model is also called the **residual income** model.

Much of the theory has already been included in earlier discussions, particularly Example 2.2 of P.V. Ltd. operating under ideal conditions of uncertainty. You may wish to review Example 2.2 at this time. In this section, we will pull together these earlier discussions and extend the P.V. Ltd. example to allow for earnings persistence. The FO model can be applied to value the firm at any point in time for which financial statements are available. For purposes of illustration, we will apply it at time 1 in Example 2.2—that is, at the end of the first year of operation.

FO pointed out that the fundamental determinant of a firm's value is its dividend stream. Assume, for P.V. Ltd. in Example 2.2, that the bad-economy state was realized in year 1, and recall that P.V. pays no dividends until a liquidating dividend at time 2. Then, the expected present value of dividends at time 1 is just the expected present value of the firm's cash on hand at time 2:

$$PA_1 = \frac{0.5}{1.10}(\$110 + \$100) + \frac{0.5}{1.10}(\$110 + \$200)$$
$$= \$95.45 + \$140.91$$
$$= \$236.36$$

Recall that cash flows per period are $100 if the bad state happens and $200 for the good state. The $110 term inside the brackets represents the $100 cash on hand at time 1 invested at a return of $R_f = 0.10$ in period 2.

Given dividend irrelevancy, P.V.'s market value can also be expressed in terms of its future cash flows. Continuing our assumption that the bad state happened in period 1,

$$PA_1 = \$100 + \left(0.5 \times \frac{\$100}{1.10}\right) + \left(0.5 \times \frac{\$200}{1.10}\right)$$
$$= \$100 + \$45.45 + \$90.91$$
$$= \$236.36$$

where the first term is cash on hand at time 1—that is, the present value of $100 cash is just $100.

The market value of the firm can also be expressed in terms of financial statement variables. FO show that

$$PA_t = BV_t + G_t \tag{6.1}$$

at any time t, where BV_t is the net book value of the firm's assets per the balance sheet and G_t is the expected present value of future abnormal earnings, also called **goodwill**. For this relationship to hold, it is necessary that all items of gain or loss go through the income statement, which is the source of the term "clean surplus" in the theory.

To evaluate goodwill for P.V. Ltd. at time t = 1, look ahead over the remainder of the firm's life (one year in our example).[34] Recall that abnormal earnings are the difference between actual and expected earnings. Using FO's notation, define ox_2 as earnings for year 2 and ox_2^a as abnormal earnings for that year.[35] From Example 2.2, we have:

If the bad state happens for year 2, net income for year 2 is

$$(\$100 \times 0.10) + \$100 - \$136.36 = -\$26.36$$

where the bracketed expression is interest earned on opening cash.

If the good state happens, net income is

$$\$10 + \$200 - \$136.36 = \$73.64$$

Since each state is equally likely, expected net income for year 2 is

$$E\{ox_2\} = (0.5 \times -\$26.36) + (0.5 \times \$73.64) = \$23.64$$

Expected abnormal earnings for year 2, the difference between expected earnings as just calculated and accretion of discount on opening book value, is thus

$$E\{ox_2{}^a\} = \$23.64 - (0.10 \times \$236.36) = \$0$$

Goodwill, the expected present value of future abnormal earnings, is then

$$G_1 = 0/1.10 - 0$$

Thus, for P.V. Ltd. in Example 2.2 with no persistence of abnormal earnings, goodwill is zero. This is because, under ideal conditions, arbitrage ensures that the firm expects to earn only the given interest rate on the opening value of its net assets. As a result, we can read firm value directly from the balance sheet:

$$PA_1 = \$236.36 + \$0$$
$$= \$236.36$$

Zero goodwill represents a special case of the FO model called **unbiased accounting**; that is, all assets and liabilities are valued at current value. When accounting is unbiased, and abnormal earnings do not persist, all of firm value appears on the balance sheet. In effect, the income statement has no information content, as we noted in Example 2.2.

Unbiased accounting represents the extreme of the measurement approach. Of course, as a practical matter, firms do not account for all assets and liabilities this way. For example, if P.V. Ltd. uses historical cost accounting or, more generally, conservative accounting for its capital asset, BV_1 may be biased downward relative to current value. FO call this **biased accounting**. When accounting is biased, the firm has *unrecorded* (i.e., self-developed) goodwill G_t. However, the clean surplus formula (Equation 6.1) for PA_t holds for any basis of accounting, not just unbiased accounting under ideal conditions. To illustrate, suppose that P.V. Ltd. uses straight-line amortization for its capital asset, writing off $\$130.17$ in year 1 and $\$130.16$ in year 2. Note that year 1 present value–based amortization in Example 2.2 is $\$123.97$. Thus, with straight-line amortization, earnings for year 1 and capital assets at the end of year 1 are biased downward relative to their ideal conditions counterparts. We now repeat the calculation of goodwill and firm value at the end of year 1, continuing the assumption of bad state realization for year 1.

With straight-line amortization, expected net income for year 2 is

$$E\{ox_2\} = (\$100 \times 0.10) + 0.5\,(\$100 - \$130.16) + 0.5\,(\$200 - \$130.16) = \$29.84$$

Expected abnormal earnings for year 2 is

$$E\{ox_2{}^a\} = \$29.84 - (0.10 \times \$230.16) = \$6.82$$

where $230.16 is the firm's book value at time 1, being $100 cash plus the capital asset book value on a straight-line basis of $130.16.

Goodwill is then

$$G_1 = \$6.82/1.10 = \$6.20$$

giving firm market value of

$$PA_1 = \$230.16 + \$6.20$$
$$= \$236.36$$

—the same as the unbiased accounting case.

While firm value is the same, the goodwill of $6.20 is unrecorded on the firm's books. This again illustrates the point made in Section 2.5.1 that under historical cost accounting net income lags real economic performance. Here, historical cost-based net income for year 1 is $100 − $130.17 = −$30.17, which is less than the net income of −$23.97 in Example 2.2. Nevertheless, if unrecorded goodwill is correctly valued, the resulting firm value is also correct.

This ability of the FO model to generate the same firm value regardless of the accounting policies used by the firm has an upside and a downside. On the upside, an investor who may wish to use the model to predict firm value does not, in theory, have to be concerned about the firm's choice of accounting policies. If the firm manager biases reported net income upward to improve apparent performance, or biases net income downward by means of conservative accounting, the firm value as calculated by the model is the same.[36] The reason is that changes in unrecorded goodwill induced by accounting policy choice are offset by equal but opposite changes in book values. The downside, however, is that the model can provide no guidance as to which accounting policies *should* be used.

We now see the sense in which the Ohlson clean surplus theory supports the measurement approach. Current value accounting for P.V.'s assets reduces the extent of biased accounting. In doing so, it moves more of the value of the firm onto the balance sheet, thereby reducing the amount of unrecorded goodwill that the investor has to estimate. While in theory the sum of book value and unrecorded goodwill is the same whether or not the firm uses current value accounting, in practice the firm can presumably prepare more accurate estimates of the current values of its assets and liabilities than can the investor. If so, and if the estimates are reasonably reliable, then the decision usefulness of the financial statements is increased, since a greater proportion of firm value can simply be read from the balance sheet. This is particularly so for investors who may not be fully rational, who may benefit from reading the effects of current value changes directly from the financial statements.

*6.10.2 Earnings Persistence

FO then introduced the important concept of *earnings persistence* into the theory. Specifically, they assumed that abnormal earnings are generated according to the following formula:

$$ox_t^a = \omega ox_{t-1}^a + v_{t-1} + \tilde{\epsilon}_t \qquad (6.2)$$

FO call this formula an **earnings dynamic**. The $\tilde{\epsilon}_t$ are the effects of state realization in period t on abnormal earnings, where the "~" indicates that these effects are random, at the beginning of the period. As in Example 2.2, the expected value of state realization is zero and realizations are independent from one period to the next.

The ω is a persistence parameter, where $0 \leq \omega < 1$. For $\omega = 0$, we have the case of Example 2.2; that is, abnormal earnings do not persist. However, $\omega > 0$ is not unreasonable. Often, the effects of state realization in one year will persist into future years. For example, the bad-state realization in year 1 of Example 2.2 may be due to a rise in interest rates, the economic effects of which will likely persist beyond the current year. Then, ω captures the proportion of the $50 abnormal earnings in year 1 that would continue into the following year.

However, note that $\omega < 1$ in the FO model. That is, abnormal earnings of any particular year will die out over time. For example, the effects of a rise in interest rates will eventually dissipate. More generally, forces of competition will eventually eliminate positive, or negative, abnormal earnings at a rate that ultimately depends on the firm's business strategy.

Note also that persistence is related to its empirical counterpart in the ERC research. Recall from Section 5.4.1 that ERCs are higher the greater the persistence in earnings. As we will see in Example 6.1, this is exactly what clean surplus theory predicts—the higher ω is, the greater the impact is of the income statement on firm value.

The term v_{t-1} represents the effect of other information becoming known in year $t - 1$ (i.e., other than the information in year $t - 1$'s abnormal earnings) that affects the abnormal earnings of year t. When accounting is unbiased, $v_{t-1} = 0$. To see this, consider the case of R&D. If R&D were accounted for on a current value basis (i.e., unbiased accounting), then year $t - 1$'s abnormal earnings would include the change in value brought about by R&D activities during that year. Of this change in value, the proportion ω will continue into next year's earnings. That is, if R&D is valued at current value, there is no relevant other information about future earnings from R&D—current earnings includes it all.

When accounting is biased, v_{t-1} assumes a much more important role. Thus, if R&D costs are written off as incurred, year $t - 1$'s abnormal earnings contain no information about future abnormal earnings from R&D activities. As a result, to predict year t's

---

*Section 6.10.2 can be skipped without loss of continuity.

abnormal earnings it is necessary to add in as other information an outside estimate of the abnormal earnings in year t that will result from the R&D activities of year t − 1. That is, v_{t-1} represents next period's earnings from year t − 1's R&D.

In sum, the earnings dynamic models the current year's abnormal earnings as a proportion ω of the previous year's abnormal earnings, plus the effects of other information (if accounting is biased), plus the effects of random state realization.

Finally, note that the theory assumes that the set of possible values of $\tilde{\epsilon}_t$ and their probabilities are known to investors, consistent with ideal conditions. It is also assumed that investors know ω. If these assumptions are relaxed, rational investors will want information about $\tilde{\epsilon}_t$ and ω and can use Bayes' theorem to update their subjective state probabilities. Thus, nothing in the theory conflicts with the role of decision theory that was explained in Chapter 3.

Example 6.1
Present Value Model Under Uncertainty and Persistence

We now extend Example 2.2 to allow for persistence. Continue all the assumptions of that example and add the further assumption $\omega = 0.40$. Since ideal conditions imply unbiased accounting, $v_{t-1} = 0$. Recall that abnormal earnings for year 1 are −$50 or $50, depending on whether the bad state or good state happens. Now, 40% of year 1 abnormal earnings will persist to affect operating earnings in year 2.

Assume that the bad state happens in year 1. (A similar analysis applies if the good state happens.) Then, we calculate P.V.'s market value at time 1. We begin with the formula based on expected future dividends.

$$PA_1 = \frac{0.5}{1.10}[(\$110 - (0.40 \times \$50) + \$100)] + \frac{0.5}{1.10}[(\$110 - (0.40 \times \$50) + \$200)]$$

$$= \left(\frac{0.5}{1.10} \times \$190\right) + \left(\frac{0.5}{1.10} \times \$290\right)$$

$$= \$86.36 \times \$131.82$$

$$= \$218.18$$

Note the effect of persistence: 40% of year 1 abnormal earnings will persist to reduce year 2 cash flows. Otherwise, the calculation is identical with Example 2.2. We see that the effect of persistence of the bad state is to reduce the time 1 firm value by $236.36 − $218.18 = $18.18, which is the present value of the $20 of reduced future cash flows.

Now, moving from the dividends formula to the clean surplus formula for firm value (Equation 6.1), FO used the earnings dynamic equation (Equation 6.2) to show that the firm's goodwill g_t can be expressed in terms of the current year's abnormal earnings, giving a market value of

$$PA_1 = BV_t + (\alpha \times ox_t^a) \tag{6.3}$$

where $\alpha = \omega/(1 + R_f)$ is a capitalization factor.[37] Note, as mentioned above, that the higher the persistence parameter ω is, the higher the impact of current earnings information is on share price PA_t. In our example, for $t = 1$

Cash on hand	$= \$100.00$
Book value of asset, as per Example 2.2	$= \$136.36$
bv_t	$= \$236.36$

This gives

$$PA_1 = bv_t + (\alpha \times ox_t^a)$$

$$= \$236.36 + \left(\frac{0.40}{1.10} \times -\$50 \right)$$

$$= \$236.36 - \$18.18$$

$$= \$218.18$$

which agrees with the market value based on expected future dividends.

The implications of the FO model with persistence are twofold. First, even under ideal conditions, *all the action is no longer on the balance sheet*. The income statement is important too, since it reveals the current year's abnormal earnings, 40% of which will persist into future periods. Thus, we can regard abnormal earnings as 40% persistent in this example.

Second, the formula (Equation 6.2) implies that investors will want information to help them assess persistent earnings, since these are important to the future performance of the firm. Accountants can help in this regard by appropriate classification of items with low persistence. Also, the formula is consistent with the empirical impact of persistence on the ERC as outlined in Section 5.4.1, where we saw that greater persistence is associated with stronger investor reaction to current earnings.[38]

6.10.3 Estimating Firm Value

The FO model can be used to estimate the value of a firm's shares. This can then be compared to the actual market value, to indicate possible over/undervaluation by the market, and to aid in investment decisions. The following example applies the model to Canadian Tire Corporation, Limited. The methodology used in this example is based on the procedures outlined in Lee (1996).

Example 6.2

Example 6.2
Estimating the Value of Common Shares of Canadian
Tire Corporation

From Canadian Tire's 2012 annual report (not reproduced here), we take 2012 net income (NI_{2012}) as $499.2 (all dollar figures are in millions), its book value as $4,409.0 at December 31, 2011, and $4,763.6 at December 30, 2012 (BV_{2012}). This gives Canadian Tire's 2012 return on opening equity (ROE_{2012}) as 0.1132. Somewhat arbitrarily, we assume that this return will continue for the next seven years, after which the return will equal Canadian Tire's cost of capital. We will return to this assumption shortly.

Dividends totalled $101.7 for 2012, giving a dividend payout ratio of 101.7/499.2 = 0.2037. We assume that this ratio will also continue for seven years.

To estimate Canadian Tire's cost of equity capital, we use the CAPM (Section 4.5):

$$E(R_{jt}) = R_f(1 - \beta_j) + \beta_j E(R_{Mt})$$

where firm j is Canadian Tire and t is April, 2013. That is, we assume the market was aware of Canadian Tire's 2012 annual report by that time. $E(R_{jt})$ thus represents the rate of return demanded by the market for Canadian Tire shares at that time or, equivalently, its cost of capital. We take the risk-free rate of interest as $R_f = 0.0125$ per annum, the Canadian bank prime rate in April 2013. To this rate, we add a market risk premium[39] of 5.80% to estimate the expected annual rate of return on the market portfolio as 0.0705. Canadian Tire's beta on the TSX exchange in April 2013 as per Thompson Reuters was 0.66. So, our estimate of the firm's cost of equity capital in April 2013 is

$$E(R_{jt}) = 0.0125(1 - 0.66) + 0.66 \times 0.0705 = 0.0043 + 0.0465 = 0.0508$$

We will take Canadian Tire's cost of capital as 5.1%, and assume that it will stay constant.

Next we evaluate Canadian Tire's unrecorded goodwill. As stated earlier, goodwill is the present value of expected future abnormal earnings, which we evaluate over a seven-year horizon from December 2012. First, we use the clean surplus relation to project end-of-year book values:

$$BV_{2013} = BV_{2012} + NI_{2013} - D_{2013}$$

where D is dividends. Using the relationships $D_t = kNI_t$, where k is the dividend payout ratio, and $NI_t = BV_{t-1} \times ROE$, this becomes

$$
\begin{aligned}
BV_{2013} &= BV_{2012} + (1 - k)NI_{2013} \\
&= BV_{2012}(1 + (1 - k)roe) \\
&= \$4763.6(1 + (0.7963 \times 0.1132)) \\
&= \$4763.6 \times 1.0901 \\
&= \$5,193
\end{aligned}
$$

Similar calculations give

$$BV_{2014} = \$5,661$$
$$BV_{2015} = \$6,171$$

$$BV_{2016} = \$6,727$$
$$BV_{2017} = \$7,333$$
$$BV_{2018} = \$7,994$$

Now abnormal earnings are defined as the difference between actual earnings and accretion of discount. Accretion of discount is cost of capital times opening book value. Actual earnings for a given year are projected as ROE times opening book value. Thus expected abnormal earnings for 2013 are

$$ox^a_{2013} = [ROE - E(R)]BV_{2012}$$
$$= (0.1132 - 0.051) \times \$4,763.6$$
$$= 0.0622 \times \$4,763.6$$
$$= \$296$$

Similar calculations give:

$$ox^a_{2014} = \$323$$
$$ox^a_{2015} = \$352$$
$$ox^a_{2016} = \$384$$
$$ox^a_{2017} = \$418$$
$$ox^a_{2018} = \$456$$
$$ox^a_{2019} = \$497$$

The present value of these abnormal earnings—that is, goodwill, at December 30, 2012, discounted at Canadian Tire's cost of capital, is

$$G_{2012} = \frac{296}{1.051} + \frac{323}{1.051^2} + \frac{352}{1.051^3} + \frac{384}{1.051^4} + \frac{418}{1.051^5} + \frac{456}{1.051^6} + \frac{497}{1.051^7}$$
$$= \$2,207$$

Finally, we add in December 31, 2012, book value (i.e., bv_{2012}):

$$PA_{2012} = \$4,764 + \$2,207$$
$$= \$6,971$$

Canadian Tire had 81,143,767 shares outstanding[40] at the end of 2012, giving an estimated value per share of $85.91.

Canadian Tire's actual share price in mid-April 2013 was around $72, considerably less than our estimate. While one could adjust estimates of the risk-free interest rate, dividend payout ratio, and cost of capital, reasonable changes to these estimates would not affect the calculation significantly. Consequently, the discrepancy between estimated and actual share price in Example 6.2 seems rather large.

A possible explanation of this discrepancy lies with the ROE used in our earnings projections. We have assumed that Canadian Tire's ROE stays constant at 0.1132. Perhaps the market expects that ROE will decrease, due to strong and increasing competition. That is, our estimate may not have fully used all available information. To gain some insight into this possibility, consider analysts' forecasts of Canadian Tire's earnings. We have used only information from the 2012 financial statement in our estimates, whereas analysts can bring considerably more information to bear. Canadian Tire reports earnings per share for 2012 of $6.10, and from Reuters in April 2013, the average of analysts' earnings per share forecasts was $6.70 for 2013 and $7.10 for 2014. These forecasts represent annual earnings increases of 10% and 6%, respectively. This compares with an annual earnings increase of (ROE × (1 − k)) 9% implicit in our 2012 analysis. While this seems reasonably consistent with analysts' earnings forecasts for 2013, it is considerably greater than forecasts for 2014. It seems that analysts are anticipating a decline in profitability.

A related possibility for the discrepancy is the pattern of abnormal earnings. We have assumed that Canadian Tire generates abnormal earnings of 0.1132 − 0.051 = 0.0622 for seven years and zero thereafter. That is, current abnormal earnings are assumed to be completely persistent for seven years and then to immediately fall to zero. Other persistence assumptions are possible. For example, we could assume that current abnormal earnings will persist for only five years. With other assumptions unchanged, this would reduce the estimated share value to $77.42. Alternatively, we could assume a declining abnormal earnings pattern for seven years, consistent with analyst expectations.

In sum, the most likely explanation for the shortfall of market value over our estimate is that the market expects that the rate of Canadian Tire's earnings growth will decline in future below the 9% implicit in our analysis.

Despite discrepancies such as this between the estimated and actual share value, the FO model can be useful for investment decision making. To see how, suppose that you carry out a similar analysis for another firm—call it Firm X—and obtain an estimated share value of $90. Which firm would you sooner invest in if they were both trading at $72? Canadian Tire, with an estimated share value of $85.91, may be the better choice, since it has a lower ratio of model value to actual share value. That is, more of its actual share value is "backed up" by book value and expected abnormal earnings. Indeed, Frankel and Lee (1998), who applied the methodology of Example 6.2 to a large sample of U.S. firms during the period 1977–1992, found that the ratio of estimated market value to actual market value was a good predictor of share returns for two to three years into the future. Thus, for the years following 2012, Frankel and Lee's results suggest that Canadian Tire's share return should outperform that of Firm X.

We conclude that while our procedure to estimate Canadian Tire's share price is on the right track, the market at the time seemed to have considerably lower earnings expectations than ours. This leads to an examination of empirical studies of the ability of the clean surplus approach to predict earnings and share price.

6.10.4 Empirical Studies of the Clean Surplus Model

Clean surplus theory has generated much empirical research. One aspect of this research compares the relative predictive ability of the dividend, cash flow, and residual income models. Recall from Section 6.10.1 that under ideal conditions all three models produce identical valuations. However, when conditions are not ideal, the model that produces the best predictions is an empirical matter. For example, it is argued that the clean surplus model has an advantage because it uses financial statement information, which includes accruals. Since accruals anticipate future cash flows, they, in effect, bring these cash flows forward onto the balance sheet. Thus, to the extent accruals are value relevant, much of the forecasting work is already done. Cash flow and dividend models have "more" to predict, since they must predict total future flows. It is also argued that the clean surplus model is more convenient to apply than the cash flow model. It uses readily available financial statement information and does not have to back cash flows out of accrual accounting-based reports.

Our discussion in Sections 6.10.1 and 6.10.2 assumed that earnings, cash flows, and dividends were known for the complete future of the firm (only two years for P.V. Ltd.). In reality, the life of the firm and its future earnings, cash, and dividend flows are not known. What is usually done when using clean surplus to estimate firm value is to predict earnings for a forecast horizon of a few years into the future, and then estimate a terminal value—that is, the present value of abnormal earnings for all remaining years of the firm's life. A major practical problem in applying all three models is the choice of forecast horizon, and what amount, if any, to assign to the terminal value. Our Canadian Tire estimate used a forecast horizon of seven years, with a terminal value for earnings beyond seven years of zero (that is, expected earnings and cost of capital equal) on the grounds that competitive pressures are expected to eliminate abnormal returns beyond that time. Of course, this zero terminal value assumption is rather arbitrary. Perhaps a better (but still arbitrary) assumption is that Canadian Tire's abnormal earnings would not fall to zero, but rather start to decline after seven years. Then, terminal value is greater than zero, which would increase our value estimate. Indeed, if the firm has opportunities for future growth that outweigh competitive pressures, abnormal earnings will increase, rather than decrease, beyond the forecast horizon, further increasing terminal value.

An alternative terminal value approach is based on analysts' long-range forecasts. In this regard, Courteau, Kao, and Richardson (2001), for a sample of U.S. firms over the period 1992–1996, studied the relative predictive ability of the dividend, cash flow, and clean surplus models, using a five-year forecast horizon. They found that predictions using arbitrary terminal value assumptions, as we did for Canadian Tire, substantially underestimated share market prices. When terminal values were based on analysts' forecasts of share price at the end of year 5, predictions of current share prices were much more accurate. Furthermore, the three models were then roughly equal in their forecasting ability, consistent with our theoretical expectation.

Conservative accounting further complicates the forecast horizon, since it biases downward both book value and reported earnings. In Section 6.10.1, we showed that in theory this does not matter, since abnormal earnings over the life of the firm increase to counteract the bias. As mentioned, however, in actual applications the forecast horizon is shorter than the life of the firm, so that all of the bias is not counteracted. If the terminal value estimate is not increased to recognize this shortfall, firm value estimates will be too low.

A second type of empirical clean surplus research studies the prediction of future earnings, since future earnings over the forecast horizon are a main input into the goodwill estimate. This represents a significant change in emphasis from research under value relevance described in Chapter 5, which studied the association between financial statement information and share returns.

For most large firms, analysts' forecasts provide readily available future earnings estimates (as opposed to our estimates for Canadian Tire based on ROE). However, analysts' forecasts are only as good as the analysts who prepare them. In this regard, Abarbanell and Bushee (1997), in an extension of the approach used by Lev and Thiagarajan (1993) (Section 5.6), showed how certain "fundamental signals" from the current financial statements, such as changes in sales, accounts receivable, inventories, gross margin, and capital expenditure, could improve the prediction of next year's earnings changes. They went on to show that analysts appeared to underuse the fundamental signals when predicting earnings. In a similar vein, Begley and Feltham (2002) added analysts' forecasts and current capital expenditures as other information in the earnings dynamic. They found that this significantly improved prediction of unrecorded goodwill for their sample firms. Overall, these results suggest that analysts' earnings forecasts would benefit from greater attention to the full information potential of financial statements.

Finally, another use of the theory is to estimate a firm's cost of capital. In Example 6.2, note that any four of the five variables—actual share price, book value, expected future earnings, risk-free interest rate, and cost of capital—can be used, in principle, to solve for the other one. The result of solving for cost of capital is called the firm's **implied cost of capital**. Thus, the clean surplus model provides an alternative to the CAPM for cost of capital estimation. Indeed, clean surplus offers some advantages over the CAPM by eliminating the need to estimate beta and the expected return on the market portfolio (see Section 4.5.1).[41]

Of course, the implied cost of capital estimates are only as good as the estimates of future earnings. If these estimates are based on analysts' forecasts, there is evidence (e.g., Easton and Sommers (2007)) that their forecasts are upwardly biased, leading to a possible overstatement of cost of capital.[42] Hou, van Dijk, and Zhang (HVZ; 2012), based on a large sample of firms over the period 1963–2009, also found that analysts' earnings forecasts are positively biased on average.

HVZ proposed an alternate approach to predicting future earnings, based on average firm past financial performance. They reported higher average ERCs based on their approach than ERCs based on analysts' forecasts. This suggests that when predicting future firm performance, the market looks to past firm performance at least as much as it looks to analyst forecasts. The authors suggested that their approach provides a better basis for predicting future firm earnings, hence of implied cost of capital estimation. It seems that the best approach to estimating future earnings is unsettled at the present time—while analysts can bring more information into their earnings forecasts than that contained in financial statements, any biases in their forecasts reduces their forecast accuracy.

6.10.5 Summary

Clean surplus theory has had a major impact on financial accounting theory and research. By demonstrating that firm value can be expressed equally well in terms of financial accounting variables as in terms of dividends or cash flows, it has led to increased research attention to earnings prediction. Much of this research explores how current financial statement information can be used to improve this prediction. Better earnings prediction enables better estimates of unrecorded goodwill, leading to better predictions of firm value and hence better investment decisions.

The theory also leads to a measurement approach, since more current values reported on the balance sheet mean a lower proportion of firm value included in unrecorded goodwill, hence less potential for investor mistakes in estimating this complex component of firm value.

6.11 AUDITORS' LEGAL LIABILITY

Perhaps the main source of pressure for the measurement approach, however, came as a reaction to the spectacular failures of large firms. Many such events have taken place in the United States. During the 1980s and early 1990s, almost 1,300 financial institutions, specifically savings and loan associations, failed. The U.S. government laid out over $125 billion to bail them out.[43] While these failures preceded the Enron and WorldCom financial reporting disasters (see Section 1.2), they remain important because they generated many of the pressures leading to the measurement approach.

The savings and loan debacle began with an inverted yield curve in the late 1970s. That is, short-term interest rates became higher than long-term rates. As a result, the savings and loans had to pay more interest to depositors than they earned from their long-term loans (mainly mortgages). Failure to write these loans down to current value resulted in overstatement of net assets on the audited balance sheets, with resultant overstatements of earnings.

Another tactic to increase reported earnings was **gains trading**, also called "cherry picking." This is a practice that can be employed when investment portfolios are valued on a cost basis (as they typically were at the time) and when at least some securities have risen in value. Then, the firm can realize a gain by selling securities that have risen in value, while continuing to hold securities that have fallen in value. No loss was typically recognized on these latter securities. They continued to be carried at cost on grounds that they would be held to maturity.

Auditors are often under considerable pressure from management, or even politicians, to bend or "stretch" GAAP, so that legal capital requirements, earnings targets, and/or analysts' forecasts will be met. Here, the stretching was to value loan assets at historical cost when their current values were substantially less, and sanctioning gains trading. These were major contributing factors to the savings and loans failures since it enabled the firms to hide their problems from the market, even though their real financial condition continued to deteriorate over time. Eventually, the savings and loans became insolvent, leading to the catastrophic series of failures described above.

But, yielding to such pressure can result in substantial legal liability. For example, an article in *The Wall Street Journal* (March 11, 1994, p. A2) reported lawsuits against the audit firm of Deloitte and Touche totalling $1.85 billion. The charges arose from alleged clean audit opinions issued to savings and loan associations that, in retrospect, were insolvent. The article described a proposed settlement of these lawsuits in excess of $300 million. While considerably less than the amounts at suit, this was the second-largest liability settlement surrounding the savings and loan debacle. (The largest was a $400 million settlement by Ernst and Young for similar charges.)

How can auditors protect themselves against pressures and potential liabilities such as these? One response, of course, is ethical behaviour. Auditors should recognize that the long-run interests of the accounting/auditing profession are served by not yielding to inappropriate pressures to stretch GAAP.

Ethical behaviour, however, can be bolstered by conservative accounting. The lower-of-cost-or-market rule for inventories is a long standing example. This rule is an example of **conditional conservatism**. That is, an economic loss in value has already occurred, although it has not been realized. Conditional conservatism contrasts with another type of conservatism, namely **unconditional conservatism**, under which risky assets are valued at less than current value even though an economic gain or loss has not yet taken place. Examples include recording profitable capital assets at cost even though current value is higher, retaining inventories at historical cost until reliable evidence of realization is obtained, and writing research costs off as incurred. These two types of conservatism are considered further in Section 6.12.

Nevertheless, GAAP did not at the time of the savings and loan failures require recognition of current value decreases for major classes of assets and liabilities if the firm intended to hold them to maturity. Examples include certain financial assets, capital assets, intangibles, and long-term debt. Retention of these items at cost or amortized cost was justified by the going concern assumption of historical cost accounting. But, as mentioned above, overvaluation of net assets was a major criticism of financial reporting following the savings and loan failures.

It seemed that a stronger form of conditional conservatism, requiring an extension of lower-of-cost-or-market thinking, was needed. Standard setters implemented several standards of this nature in the years following the savings and loan debacle, such as impairment tests for capital assets and goodwill. These tests represent a partial application of the measurement approach.[44] If net future cash flows from an asset are less than book value, the asset is written down to its current value. Then, perhaps, the fact that such writedowns are required by GAAP will help auditors resist management pressure to overstate net assets. Furthermore, auditors can reduce their liability exposure by pointing out that, with impairment tests, the financial statements proper incorporated the negative value changes that precede bankruptcy, merger, downsizing, environmental liabilities, etc. Indeed, to the extent negative value changes are inside information, their disclosure via impairment tests informs the market about the existence and magnitude of such changes. Of course, determination of current value requires greater use of estimates and judgment but, because of legal liability, the relevance/reliability tradeoff may have shifted toward greater relevance.

The incidence of conditionally conservative financial reporting in the United States was investigated by Basu (1997). He measured conservatism by the correlation between net income and share returns. Basu argued that an efficient securities market will bid up the share prices of firms that are performing well in economic terms and bid down the prices of firms that are performing poorly. Under conservative accounting, the earnings of firms that are performing well *will not* include the unrealized increases in assets that characterize a firm that is doing well. However, the earnings of firms that are performing poorly *will* include decreases in the values of their assets. It follows that the correlation between share returns and earnings will be higher for firms that are performing poorly than for firms that are performing well. As Basu puts it, earnings are more timely in their recognition of poor performance than of good performance. A stronger net income/share price relationship for poorly performing firms than for firms that are doing well can thus be viewed as evidence of conditionally conservative accounting, assuming securities market efficiency. In a large sample of firms over the years 1963–1990, Basu found a significantly higher net income to share price relationship for firms in his sample that were doing poorly than for firms that were doing well, consistent with his argument.

Using this measurement approach, Basu went on to examine the period 1983–1990. This has been identified as a period of high growth in litigation against auditors and corresponds roughly to the period of the savings and loan failures described above.

He found that conditional conservatism increased in this period relative to earlier periods of low litigation growth. This suggests that standard setters reacted to investor losses and auditors' legal difficulties by increasing conditional conservatism, as in the impairment test standards referred to above. Indeed, the trend to increasing conservatism continued. Ball and Shivakumar (2006) documented increasing conditional conservatism to 2002, a period ending after the Enron and WorldCom failures. Lobo and Zhou (2006) documented an increase in conditionally conservative accounting practices subsequent to the 2002 passage of the Sarbanes-Oxley Act. It seems that investor losses, auditor liability, and severe penalties for managers who overstate earnings reinforce conservative accounting. For more discussion of these litigation- and regulation-based explanations for conservatism, see Watts (2003a and b).

One might reasonably ask, if auditors are penalized for investor losses arising from overstatements, why are they not also penalized for investor losses arising from understatements? Investors also lose from understatements of assets and earnings. If these understatements lead to understated share values, investor losses can arise from sales of undervalued shares. Also, even without sale, understated share prices can lead to investor utility losses if they postpone consumption because they believe they are less wealthy than they really are. Yet, lawsuits arising from overstatements are relatively rare. An answer is that risk-averse investors lose more utility from an understatement than from an overstatement of the same magnitude. Examples 6.3 and 6.4 illustrate this loss asymmetry.

6.12 ASYMMETRY OF INVESTOR LOSSES*

These explanations for conservatism can be supported by the decision theory outlined in Chapter 3. To see this, consider the following examples.

Example 6.3*
Asymmetry of Investor Losses I

Bill Cautious, a rational investor, has an investment in the shares of X Ltd., with current market value of $10,000. He plans to use this amount to live on over the next two years. After that time, he will have graduated and will have a high-paying job. Consequently, he is not concerned right now about planning beyond two years. His goal is to maximize his total utility over this period. For simplicity, we assume that X Ltd. pays no dividends over these two years. Bill is risk averse, with utility in each year equal to the square root of the amount he spends in that year.

It is easy to see that Bill's total utility will be maximized if he spends the same amount each year. Thus, he sells $5,000 of his shares now and plans to sell the remaining $5,000 at the beginning of the second year.[45] Suppose, however, that at the beginning of year 1, certain X Ltd. assets have fallen in value. The loss is unrealized, and the X Ltd. auditor fails to recognize that an impairment loss should be recorded. Consequently, the loss remains as inside information, and the market value of Bill's unsold shares remains at $5,000. The loss becomes realized during year 1, and Bill's remaining shares are worth $3,000 at year-end.

Calculate Bill's utility for the two years, evaluated at the end of year 1:

$$EU^a \text{ (Overstatement)} = \sqrt{5,000} + \sqrt{3,000}$$

$$= 70.71 + 54.77$$

$$= 125.48$$

where EU^a denotes Bill's actual utility, being the utility of the $5,000 he spends in the first year plus the utility to come in year 2 from the sale of his shares for $3,000.[46]

If Bill knew at the beginning of the first year that his wealth was only $8,000, he would plan to spend $4,000 each year. His expected utility would have been

$$EU \text{ (Overstatement)} = \sqrt{4,000} + \sqrt{4,000}$$

$$= 63.25 + 63.25$$

$$= 126.50$$

where EU denotes Bill's utility if he knew the ultimate value of his shares. Thus, Bill loses utility of $126.50 - 125.48 = 1.02$ as a result of an opening $2,000 wealth overstatement.

---

*Examples 6.3 and 6.4 can be skipped without loss of continuity.

---

*Section 6.12 can be skipped without loss of continuity.

Now assume instead that the X Ltd. assets have risen in value by $2,000 at the beginning of year 1. Again, the unrealized gain is not recognized by the auditor at the beginning of year 1, and it remains as inside information. The gain becomes realized during the year, and Bill's shares rise in value to $7,000 at year-end. His actual utility over the two years is

$$EU^a \text{ (Understatement)} = \sqrt{5,000} + \sqrt{7,000}$$

$$= 70.71 + 83.67$$

$$= 154.38$$

Whereas, if Bill had known his wealth was $12,000,

$$EU \text{ (Understatement)} = \sqrt{6,000} + \sqrt{6,000}$$

$$= 77.46 + 77.46$$

$$= 154.92$$

Thus, Bill loses utility of $154.92 - 154.38 = 0.54$ as a result of an opening wealth understatement. Note that even though Bill's total consumption will be $2,000 higher than he had originally expected, he still suffers a loss of utility, since the understatement costs him the opportunity to optimally plan his spending over time.[47]

The main point of the example is that while the amount of misstatement is the same, Bill's loss of utility for an overstatement is almost twice the loss for an understatement of the same amount. The loss arises because Bill misallocates his consumption over time due to errors and bias in reporting his wealth. Bill will be upset in either case, but he is more upset about an overstatement. Consequently, the auditor is more likely to be sued for overstatement errors.[48] For a more formal model to demonstrate this asymmetry, see Scott (1975).

Anticipating the investor's loss asymmetry, the auditor, who wishes to avoid lawsuits, reacts by being conservative. When current value has decreased, writing assets down to current value benefits the investor in our example by avoiding the utility loss of 1.02, thereby decreasing the likelihood of the investor suing the auditor. Regulators, who would also like to see fewer investor losses and lawsuits, will encourage this conservatism with punitive laws for firms and their managers who fail to release bad news in a timely manner, and with new accounting standards such as impairment tests.

This example illustrates **conditional conservatism** since the economic loss in value has already occurred, although it has not been realized at the beginning of year 1. The example suggests a rationale for recognizing the unrealized loss—lower investor losses and less auditor exposure to lawsuits.

In sum, one way that accountants and auditors can bolster ethical behaviour, increase usefulness for investors, and protect themselves against legal liability is to expand conditional conservatism. Note that since conditional conservatism requires measurement of current values, we can regard it as an asymmetric (i.e., one-sided) version of the measurement approach.

Of course, this example raises the question, why not write assets up to current value as well? Recognizing a $2,000 unrealized asset increase at the first of year 1 would have increased Bill's utility by 0.54. While not as great as the utility increase from recognizing a

$2,000 unrealized loss, this move to full fair value accounting would constitute a further improvement in financial statement usefulness. A possible answer is that the auditor may be concerned about the reliability of current values, particularly for current value increases since management usually prefers to report gains than losses and may thus tend to anticipate and/or overstate such gains. The increase in usefulness and decrease in lawsuit exposure from writing assets down may be high enough to outweigh reliability concerns, whereas the benefits from writing assets up may not be. This asymmetry of utility losses, which is driven by the concavity of a risk-averse investor's utility function, creates an investor demand for conservatism, which underlies the litigation and regulation explanations for conservatism outlined in Section 6.11.

Example 6.4
Asymmetry of Investor Losses II

To pursue conservatism further, continue the assumptions above, except that now there has been no change in X Ltd.'s asset value at the beginning of year 1. However, the asset value, and hence Bill's share value, may change in future. Specifically, assume that the auditor expects that at the end of year 1, assets will either have fallen in value by $2,000 or risen in value by $2,000, each with probability of 0.5. What asset value should the auditor report at the beginning of year 1? Specifically, should the assets be reported at their expected value (i.e., fair value) of $10,000?

To answer this question, assume that the auditor wants to maximize financial statement usefulness for Bill. That is, he/she wants to assist Bill to maximize his expected utility of consumption over the two years.[49] Bill's expected utility (EU) at the beginning of the first year is

$$EU = \sqrt{x/2} + 0.5\sqrt{8,000 - x/2} + 0.5\sqrt{12,000 - x/2} \qquad (6.4)$$

where x is the value of wealth that Bill uses for planning purposes, and x/2 is his consumption in the first year. Second-year consumption is either $8,000 minus first-year consumption or $12,000 minus first-year consumption, each with probability 0.5.

Now, if Bill uses x = $10,000, and X Ltd.'s assets are worth $8,000 at year-end, he will suffer a utility loss of 1.02, as calculated in Example 6.3. Similarly, he will lose utility of 0.54 if X Ltd.'s assets turn out to be worth $12,000. Given this loss asymmetry, Bill should base his first-year consumption on a wealth estimate of less than $10,000. In fact, to maximize EU, he should use a wealth estimate of x = $9,400, yielding EU = 140 in Equation 6.4. If Bill uses a wealth estimate of x = $10,000 (i.e., the expected value of his wealth), his EU falls to 139.93.[50]

Anticipating this loss asymmetry, the auditor may value X Ltd. assets at $9,400 at the beginning of year 1, rather than their current value of $10,000. This alerts Bill to use a conservative wealth value for his consumption planning.[51] Also, legal liability is reduced, since auditors are also likely to be sued for failing to anticipate losses (as opposed to Example 6.3, where the auditor is sued for failing to report a loss that has already occurred). Experimental evidence consistent with auditors' greater avoidance of potential overstatements relative to understatements in the presence of litigation risk is reported by Barron, Pratt, and Stice (2001). Example 6.4 provides a rational underpinning to evidence such as this.

This example illustrates **unconditional conservatism**, since the accountant values risky assets at less than current value even though an economic gain or loss has not yet taken place.

It is sometimes claimed that unconditional conservatism is not decision useful since, unlike conditional conservatism, it conveys no direct information about future cash flows, and the downward bias can be adjusted for by investors. However, one must ask why investors would want to fully remove a downward bias since, as just illustrated, a downward bias increases expected utility of consumption. That is, optimally applied, unconditional conservatism conveys information about risk. Given that the auditor has better information about the distribution of future asset values than the investor, the conservative valuation of $9,400 represents the auditor's estimate of the most decision useful value for risk-averse investors who need a wealth estimate for decision making purposes.

In practice, there are several ways that unconditional conservatism is implemented. For example, profitable capital investments are usually valued at historical cost, inventories are retained at historical cost until an increase in value is realized, and amortization expense may run ahead of economic depreciation. Also, historical cost accounting requires certain expenditures on intangibles, such as research costs, to be expensed as incurred. Some of these policies can be justified on grounds of reliability. However, they can also be viewed as a response to an investor/auditor demand for unconditional conservatism.

Unconditional conservatism runs counter to the Conceptual Framework (Section 3.7), which asserts that accounting information should be unbiased. Even conditional conservatism (i.e., impairment tests) creates bias at the financial statement level, since it generates a persistent understatement of the firm's earnings and net asset values relative to their economic values. However, Examples 6.3 and 6.4 demonstrate conditions under which a downward bias increases decision usefulness.

Of course, as an alternative to reporting a single value for an asset, the auditor could report the various possible asset values and their probabilities. In Example 6.4, the $8,000 and $12,000 possible end-of-year 1 values and their probabilities could be reported as supplementary risk information. Then, Bill could pick whatever wealth estimate he wants for planning purposes, rather than rely on a single number based on the financial statements. As a practical matter, however, this would involve overcoming possible manager objections and, for such a report to be credible, would require auditing a large multivariate probability distribution of the current values of all assets and liabilities, complete with covariances. Thus, even though the auditor will have a better estimate of this distribution than the investor, it is more reliable, and almost as relevant, to report conservative net income and balance sheet values instead.[52]

Note that unconditional conservatism preempts conditional conservatism (the lower asset valuation is now, the less there is to write down later). If the X Ltd. asset was valued at the beginning of year 1 at $9,400, as per this example, and a $2,000 loss on the asset is realized in year 1 as per Example 6.3, the writedown would be only $1,400 ($2,000 − $600), since $600 of the loss is buffered by the initial conservative asset valuation. Thus, the utility loss Bill suffers in Example 6.3 is reduced.

The extent of unconditional conservatism can be measured by a firm's market-to-book ratio, since an efficient market will bid up the value of a firm (i.e., the numerator) to recognize publicly available information about investment opportunities, goodwill, and profitable assets. Book value (the denominator), however, does not include these items due to recognition lag, and is further reduced by unconditional conservatism. Thus, following from the previous paragraph, there should be a negative short-run relationship between unconditional conservatism (measured by the market-to-book ratio) and conditional conservatism. Both market-to-book and conditional conservatism may contain error as conservatism measures, though, since they are also affected by matters such as past writedowns, market inefficiencies, and earnings management tactics. However, in a large sample of U.S. firms over the years 1970–2001, Pae, Thornton, and Welker (2005) documented empirically that market-to-book ratio and conditional conservatism did exhibit the predicted short-run negative relationship.[53]

Empirical evidence consistent with the arguments in Examples 6.3 and 6.4 is reported by Skinner (1997). He examined a sample of 221 U.S. lawsuits following the reporting of large negative earnings surprises (i.e., bad news) in quarterly earnings over 1988–1994, relative to quarters from which no lawsuits ensued. Skinner reported that managers were more likely to alert the market to bad news before the quarterly earnings were reported, relative to their tendency to disclose early other types of earnings news. This suggests that early voluntary loss disclosure may be an attempt by managers to discourage the lawsuits that usually follow bad news. However, Skinner found no evidence that early disclosure reduced lawsuits, suggesting that, despite early disclosure, shareholders have a powerful incentive to sue following bad earnings news.

Skinner also reported, however, that early disclosure tended to reduce the *amounts* of lawsuits settlements. Again, this is consistent with our examples, since the earlier the disclosure, the sooner the shareholder can revise his/her consumption decision, thereby reducing the amount of utility loss.

More recently, Shroff, Venkataraman, and Zhang (SVZ; 2013) also drew on the threat of lawsuits as a motivator of conservative reporting. They argued that lawsuits are particularly likely when some event has a *material unfavourable* economic effect on a firm. The question then is, does the effect of this adverse event show up in earnings *sooner* than a *material favourable* economic event? If so, our argument that investor loss asymmetry leads to conditional conservatism is supported.

To identify when a material economic event affects a firm, SVZ identified quarters in which there is a three-day abnormal return on a firm's shares of −10% or more (i.e., a material unfavourable event) or +10% or more (favourable). For a large sample of such firms over the period 1982–2007, SVZ found that, on average, the negative effect on quarterly earnings following a material unfavourable event appears sooner than the positive effect of a material favourable event, consistent with a litigation argument for conditional conservatism.

6.13 CONCLUSIONS ON THE MEASUREMENT APPROACH TO DECISION USEFULNESS

Serious questions have been raised about investor rationality and market efficiency. First, securities markets may not be as fully efficient as had previously been believed, suggesting that behaviourially biased investors might need some help in figuring out the full implications of accounting information for future returns. Behavioural theory suggests that help may be supplied by moving some information, such as current values, from financial statement notes into the financial statements proper.

Nevertheless, we argue that except during periods surrounding liquidity pricing, efficient securities market theory continues to be useful in guiding accountants' reporting and disclosure decisions. Admittedly, however, convergence to an efficient price may take time. A more fundamental question is the extent to which investors are on average rational. We suggest that much security price behaviour that has been used to challenge rationality can also be explained by rational behaviour, once assumptions of rational expectations and common knowledge are relaxed.

With respect to the value relevance of accounting information, a market share of 2% to 7% for net income seems low, suggesting considerable scope to increase its usefulness for investors. In addition, legal liability may force accountants, auditors, and managers to increase conservatism in the financial statements by requiring impairment tests, which we view as an asymmetric version of current value measurement.

The measurement approach is reinforced by the development of the Ohlson clean surplus theory, which emphasizes the fundamental role of financial accounting information in determining firm value. Thus, the clean surplus theory leads naturally to the measurement approach.

Of course, the measurement approach runs into problems of reliability. Consequently, we do not expect this approach to extend to a complete set of financial statements on a current value basis. Rather, the question is one of degree—to what degree will current values supplant costs in financial reporting? Consequently, in the next chapter we review GAAP from a current valuation perspective. There always has been a substantial present value and market value component to the financial statements. But, as we shall see, recent years have witnessed a continuing increase in current value standards.

Questions and Problems

1. Why does a measurement approach to decision usefulness suggest more value relevant information in the financial statements proper, when efficient securities market theory implies that financial statement notes or other disclosure would be just as useful?

2. What will be the impact on relevance, reliability, and decision usefulness of financial statement information resulting from accountants' adoption of a measurement approach?

3. Efficient securities market theory has long been under attack from behavioural finance, which draws on psychological theories of investor behaviour to explain why security prices do not always behave as the economic theories of rational investing and market efficiency predict. These attacks have increased following the 2007–2008 security market meltdowns.

   Required
   a. Give two reasons why prospect theory predicts that security prices will differ from their prices under efficient security markets theory.
   b. Describe two accounting-related efficient securities market anomalies and, for each, explain why it is an anomaly.
   c. The efficient securities market anomalies suggest that investors underreact to the full information content of financial statements. Identify two behavioural characteristics that predict this underreaction and, for each, explain *why* it predicts underreaction.
   d. Should accountants be concerned that the importance of financial reporting may decline if behaviourally biased investors do not use all the information in the financial statements?

4. Explain in your own words what "post-announcement drift" is. Why is this an anomaly for securities market efficiency? Give two behavioural biases that could generate post-announcement drift.

5. Explain in your own words why the market response to accruals, as documented by Sloan (1996), is an anomaly for securities market efficiency.

6. An investor considers two mutual funds. Based on past experience, the first fund has an expected return of 0.08 and a standard deviation of 0.05. The second fund has an expected return of 0.07 and a standard deviation of 0.06. There is no reason to assume that future performance of these funds will differ from past performance. However, the second fund has a guarantee attached that the return in any year will not be negative.

   Required
   a. Which fund would a rational investor be likely to buy according to single-person decision theory?
   b. The investor buys the second fund. Use prospect theory to explain why.

7. Lev, in his article "On the Usefulness of Earnings" (1989), pointed out the low ability of reported net income to explain variations in security prices around the release date of earnings information. Lev attributed this low value relevance of earnings to low earnings quality.

   Required
   a. Define "earnings quality." Relate your answer to the concept of an information system in single-person decision theory.
   b. Suggest reasons why earnings quality may be low.
   c. How might a measurement approach to financial reporting increase earnings quality, and hence the impact of earnings on security prices?

8. It appears that the value relevance of reported earnings, as measured by R^2 or ERC, is low, and possibly falling over time. Use single-person decision theory to explain why the value relevance of reported earnings can be measured by R^2 or ERC. Is it possible for an abnormal share return to increase but R^2 and ERC to fall? Explain.

9. The joint IASB/FASB Framework (Section 3.7) will have significant effects on financial reporting as it is implemented.

Required

a. The Framework drops the word "rational" as a description of investor and creditor decision making. This description appeared in the original 1978 FASB Statement of Financial Accounting Concepts. Instead, in the joint Framework, the objective of financial reporting is to help financial statement users "in making decisions in their capacity as capital providers." Why do you think the word "rational" has been dropped?

b. If investors do not make rational decisions, does this increase or decrease the role of financial reporting in providing useful information to investors? Explain.

c. The joint Framework also states that financial statement users need information about "future cash flows" from their investments. Thus, some linkage between current financial statement information and future cash flows is needed. The concept of an information system provides such a linkage.

What are the effects of relevance and reliability of financial information on the main diagonal probabilities of the information system? Why do these desirable qualities have to be traded off when conditions are not ideal? Define "relevance" and "reliability" as part of your answer.

10. Define two limits to arbitrage, and explain why these might explain the lengthy existence of efficient securities market anomalies such as post-announcement drift and the accruals anomaly.

11. A firm is expected to earn $100 net income for next year, at the end of which time the firm will be wound up. The $100 expected earnings includes gains and losses from disposals of assets and liabilities, and all other winding up costs. The firm's book value at the beginning of the year is $600, and its cost of capital is 12%. What is the firm's estimated market value at the beginning of the year?

   a. $625.00
   b. $672.00
   c. $689.29
   d. $700.00

12. Obtain the most recent annual report of a publicly traded company, and use the procedure outlined in Section 6.10.3 to estimate the value per common share of the company. Compare this value with the company's actual market value per share about three months after the company's year end. Explain any difference. In your explanation, include consideration of possible effects of recognition lag, and justify your assumption about the persistence of abnormal earnings.

13. You are the senior accountant of a large, publicly traded company that is experiencing a decline of business that management feels is temporary. To meet earnings projections given in its previous year's MD&A, management asks you to find an additional $5 million of reported earnings for the current year. After some study, you determine that to increase earnings by this magnitude, it is necessary to recognize additional revenue on contracts in process, even though the contracts are far from completion and it is questionable whether or not any profits will actually be realized. A careful study of accounting standards relating to revenue recognition leads you to the conclusion that to recognize $5 million of profits at this stage would not be in accordance with GAAP. Consequently, the auditors will be expected to object.

You report this to management, but are instructed to proceed anyway. Management assures you that next year's business will be much better and the premature revenue recognition will never be noticed. Furthermore, management is sure it can convince the auditor of this as well.

Required

What will you do in response to this ethical dilemma? Give reasons for and against your decision.

14. Recent years have seen considerable litigation against auditors in the United States. A major source of this litigation arises from the pressure firms feel to meet analysts' earnings expectations. To avoid reporting lower-than-expected earnings, firms sometimes use earnings management techniques, such as premature revenue recognition and other devices, to raise reported net income. To avoid a qualified audit report, the firm may pressure its auditor to "stretch" GAAP. This puts the auditor in a difficult ethical position. The auditor's primary responsibility is to the shareholders. However, it is management that influences the audit committee and pays for auditor appointments. If the auditor does not go along, he or she may lose the audit client, and any non-audit services also provided. Furthermore, he or she will inevitably be drawn into lawsuits when the earnings management becomes known (as is likely, since accruals reverse).

    One can sympathize with company managers for wanting to meet earnings expectations. The market will severely penalize their stock price if they do not. For example, in 1997, Eastman Kodak announced that revenue would not meet expectations due to the high value of the U.S. dollar, and analysts reduced their estimate of first quarter 1997 earnings from $0.90 per share to $0.80. Kodak's share price fell by $9.25 to $79 in heavy trading. Subsequently, Kodak reported earnings per share for the quarter of $0.81, and share price rose $2.25 to $75.37.

    This market reaction has been repeated many times since. An article in *The Wall Street Journal* in April 2000 quoted a prominent investment manager as saying that the market is "overdiscounting" changes in earnings expectations and that it is "reacting too much."

    Required

    a. Why might an auditor be tempted to go along with client pressure to manage reported earnings so as to meet analysts' expectations? What are some of the possible longer-run costs to the auditor if he or she goes along?

    b. To what extent would increased use of a measurement approach to financial reporting reduce auditor exposure to client pressure and lawsuits?

    c. Use concepts from behavioural finance to explain why the market may "overreact" to changes in earnings expectations.

    d. Is the $9.25 reduction in Kodak's share price reported above inconsistent with efficient securities market theory? Use the relationship between change in analysts' earnings estimates and share price change to explain why or why not. Do the same for the subsequent $2.25 increase in share price.

15. The 2007–2008 meltdown of the market for asset-backed securities is often blamed on lax mortgage lending practices, poor risk controls by financial firms, greedy managers, and inadequate regulation. However, the meltdown also has important implications for financial accounting and reporting practice. Give two such implications and, for each one, explain why accountants should be aware of it and take it seriously (see also Section 1.3).

16. In its 2005 annual report, TD Bank Financial Group (TD) reported **economic profit** of $1,062 million. Its calculation of economic profit is summarized as follows (millions of dollars):

Average common shareholders' equity for the year	$14,600
Add back goodwill/intangibles amortized to date	3,213
Average invested capital before goodwill amortization	$17,813
Net income per income statement	$ 2,229
Capital charge at 10.1% per annum, estimated using CAPM	1,799
Economic profit after amortization of intangibles and items of note	430
Amortization of intangibles ($354) and items of note ($278)	632
Economic profit before amortization of intangibles and items of note	$ 1,062

Required

a. What is the relationship between TD's calculation of economic profit and the calculation of firm value using clean surplus theory, illustrated in Example 6.2?

b. Does TD have unrecorded goodwill? Explain why or why not.

c. Amortization of intangibles of $354 million is added back to TD's 2005 GAAP net income of $2,229 for purposes of calculating economic profit, on the grounds that net income before amortization of intangibles better measures bank performance. The goodwill and other intangibles arose because of TD's acquisitions of Canada Trust in 2000 and Banknorth in 2005. Items of note of $278 are also added back. Items of note are defined in the annual report as items that management does not believe are indicative of underlying business performance. They include a charge for legal liability, costs of preferred share redemption, restructuring charge, loss on derivatives, and several related items.

   As an investor in TD Bank shares, do you find economic income more or less useful than reported net income for predicting future bank performance? Explain. Focusing on economic income, do you find economic income before or after adding back amortization of intangibles and items of note to be most useful? Explain.

17. Refer to Theory in Practice vignette 1.2. New Century's accounting policies were severely questioned following the 2007–2008 market meltdowns. KPMG was drawn into the lawsuits that followed New Century's filing for bankruptcy protection.

Required

a. Do you agree with New Century's policy of derecognizing mortgages transferred to investors from its balance sheet, and creating an allowance for credit losses resulting from mortgage buybacks? The alternative would be to retain the mortgages on New Century's books and treat the proceeds received as a liability until the mortgage had to be bought back or the buyback commitment expired. If the latter, then both the mortgage and the liability would then be transferred to income.

b. Do you agree with New Century's policy of valuing its retained interests at their discounted present value? Explain why or why not.

c. Would a more conservative policy for valuing mortgage credit loss provisions for buybacks have reduced the likelihood of lawsuit against the auditor? Explain.

Notes

1. Recall from Section 4.2.1 that we use the semi-strong form of market efficiency. For the distinction between semi-strong efficient market price and fundamental value see Section 4.6.2.

2. It should be noted that Daniel and Titman's investment strategy used hindsight to pick stocks with high and low momentum. The strategy would not be implementable in real time.

3. For subjects with a long position, a relatively low analyst earnings forecast is BN. For a short position, a relatively high forecast is BN, in which case subjects' forecasts should be lower than the analysts'.

4. In mathematical terms, the utility function is continuous but not differentiable at zero.

5. This supports the argument of Fama (1970) (see Section 4.3.1) that a sufficient number of sophisticated investors can drive the efficient market security price.

6. Vassalou (2003), in an empirical study, found that news related to future growth in gross domestic product (a proxy for the risk of an upturn or downturn in the economy) predicted stock returns as well as the book-to-market ratio did. This supports the argument that investors are concerned about the risk of a downturn (or upturn) in the economy, and buy low (or high) B/M firms accordingly.

7. Non-stationarity provides an alternative to noise trading, discussed in Section 4.4.1, for the non-collapse of share prices on an efficient market. When share price parameters, such as beta, are non-stationary, investors will have differing opinions as to whether current share prices reflect their current beta values, and they will trade on the basis of these opinions.

8. While it does not apply directly to beta, further CAPM support is provided by Durnev, Morck, Yeung, and Zarowin (DMYZ; 2003). Recall from Section 4.5 (Equation 4.4) that the residual term ϵ_{jt} of the market model includes the firm-specific portion of share return (whereas the $\alpha_j + \beta_j R_{Mt}$ term captures the market- and industry-wide portion). DMYZ found that the variance of the market model residual is positively related to amounts of future abnormal earnings. Now the variance of ϵ_{jt} can be interpreted as an inverse measure of synchronicity (see Chapter 4, Note 14), since the residual variance captures the amount of firm-specific information, relative to the amount of industry- and economy-wide information, incorporated into share price—relatively more firm-specific information generates a bigger variance, or lower synchronicity. Later (since net income lags in recognizing many relevant events), this information shows up as gains and losses in net income. In effect, consistent with the results of Ball and Brown (Figure 5.3), the market anticipates much of the GN and BN in earnings and capitalizes it into share price before the earnings are reported. This result supports the CAPM and the efficient markets theory on which it is based, because, as originally suggested by Roll (1988), the low ability of the CAPM to explain share returns may be due in part to the large amount of firm-specific information constantly being developed by investors, rather than just to the CAPM leaving out important risk variables. DMYZ found no support for an alternative interpretation of the variance of ϵ_{jt} as simply the result of noise trading or investor limited attention.

9. The magnitude of PAD seems to depend on the earnings expectation construct used by the researcher. Most PAD studies measure the GN or BN in quarterly earnings based on quarterly seasonal earnings changes (a time series approach). However, Livnat and Mendenhall (2006) reported that PAD is significantly greater when GN and BN are measured based on analysts' forecasts. Subsequently, Ayers, Li, and Yeung (2011) analyzed PAD based on quarterly seasonal earnings changes (investor behaviour that they attribute to small investors) separately from PAD based on the difference between reported earnings and analysts' forecasts (which they attribute to large investors). They reported that analyst-based PAD lasts much longer than small investor-based PAD, and attributed the result largely to analyst delay in revising their earnings forecasts following earnings announcements.

10. An alternative possibility is that firms' betas may shift when they announce good or bad earnings news. If the beta shifts were positive for GN firms and negative for BN, this could explain post-announcement drift as simply an artifact of the higher (for GN firms) and lower (for BN) returns that investors would demand to compensate for the changes in risk—as discussed in Section 3.4, investors

trade off risk and return. While BT presented evidence that, following earnings announcements, betas do shift in the manner described above, the magnitude of the shifts is much smaller than what would be required to explain the magnitude of the post-announcement drift.

11. Chordia and Shivakumar (CS) based their argument on the Modigliani and Cohn (1979) inflation illusion hypothesis, which states that common stock investors do not seem to incorporate the effects of inflation levels on the nominal growth rate of firms' earnings. CS pointed out that firms are affected differently by inflation—some firms' earnings benefit and some suffer. The inflation illusion hypothesis predicts that shares of firms that benefit are undervalued, and vice versa.

12. The authors measure earnings volatility by the variance of earnings over the previous eight quarters.

13. This result varies by industry. For example, the accrual increase for retail and manufacturing firms is larger than for service and mining firms.

14. The presence of behaviourially biased investors affects our caveat in Section 5.5, where we pointed out that standard setters could not assume the accounting policy that generates the highest response on an efficient securities market is the best for society. To the extent that high quality financial reporting policies increase security market response by reducing biases, society *does* benefit, since markets work better.

    However, as we will argue in Section 6.5, serial correlation in share prices can also be generated by rational investors. Thus, an answer to the question of the extent to which standard setters can rely on security market response as a guide to standard setting awaits a fuller understanding of why the efficient market anomalies persist. In the meantime, our caveat remains.

15. A related cost of reduced diversification arises from the "Hirschleifer effect" (Hirshleifer, 1971). Prior to the release of public information (e.g., earnings announcements) about investments held by a less–than-fully diversified, risk-averse, investor, he/she faces the risk that the information will be unfavourable, thereby reducing the market value of affected investments. The investor may wish to protect against this risk by increasing diversification prior to the information release. However, if the less-than-fully diversified portfolio is held so as to exploit an anomaly, increasing diversification works against the expected anomaly profits. Thus, continuing to hold creates another risk-related cost of exploitation. For a demonstration of the Hirschleifer effect in a capital markets context, see Ball (2013).

16. BLLM were forced to cut off their study in 1999 since changes in stock exchange practices and investor trading techniques led to unavailability of the data needed for their study after 1999.

17. These large investors did not respond to accruals of BN firms. BLLM argued that large-trade investors are most likely to be sophisticated financial institutions, such as mutual funds. Since the accruals anomaly predicts that share prices of BN firms decline over time, exploitation of the anomaly requires short selling. Financial institutions usually face severe short-selling restrictions.

18. BLLM also reported that investors with trades *between* 500 and 5,000 shares did not respond to the magnitude of accruals either.

19. In our introduction to rational expectations in Section 3.3.2, our interest was in predicting only the *ultimate effect* of new information. Here, we consider the *process* leading to the ultimate effect. This process can be lengthy when firm parameters, such as information system probabilities, are subject to change and investors learn over time, thereby generating the serial correlation of share returns that are often taken as evidence of investor irrationality.

20. A related argument is made by Ng, Rusticus, and Verdi (NRV; 2008), whose study of the impact of transaction costs on PAD was introduced in Section 6.4. NRV assumed that following, say, a GN earnings announcement, subsequent GN or BN comes along randomly. This contrasts with the Brav and Heaton argument, where subsequent news is correlated with the GN or BN in the earnings announcement.

NRV then argued that if subsequent GN comes along sufficient to outweigh transaction costs, arbitrage investors will buy more shares, thereby moving share price upward. However, if BN comes along, they will tend to hold, since they still expect share price to increase and selling now will eliminate this expected profit. Thus, even if subsequent news comes along randomly, share price will drift upward following a GN earnings announcement. A related argument applies if the earnings announcement is BN.

21. Bounded rationality is a theory that is somewhat "in between" the decision theory described in Chapter 3 and the behavioural theories described here. Decision makers do revise state probabilities upon receipt of new information as under decision theory, but for complex problems they "cut the decision tree down to size" by eliminating consideration of states of nature and evidence that, for them, are of marginal importance and/or too costly to evaluate. In our context, this could result in rules of thumb, such as ignoring information in financial statement notes, concentrating instead on the income statement or simply the bottom line, even though they are aware that the rest of the financial statements may contain relevant information. They are sufficiently rational, however, to react to new information over time that supports, or does not support, their initial evaluation.

22. For evidence that barriers to arbitrage explain much of PAD over shorter time horizons, see Chung and Hrazdil (2011).

23. As AMS pointed out, the model could also apply to longer-term investors who may nevertheless buy and sell at short notice so as to manage their consumption over time.

24. AMS assumed that the distribution of firm value is continuous. Then, equality between the amount reported and actual firm value is an event of measure zero. That is, equality can never happen—there will always be some noise.

25. AMS assumed that the distribution of underlying firm value is a normal distribution, in contrast to the two-point distribution used in our illustration of probability revision in Example 3.1. Then, each investor's posterior expectation of firm value is a weighted average of his/her prior expectation of firm value and the private message received, where the weights are the precisions (i.e., reciprocals of the variances) of the prior distribution and the private message, respectively. Thus, the greater the precision of the public message, the greater the weight it has in posterior beliefs, and vice versa.

26. Each generation also knows the history of past share prices.

27. From an accounting perspective, a possible interpretation of the model is that the financial statements should be made less informative, so as to reduce the weighting of the public message in investors' posterior beliefs and speeding the convergence of market price to fundamental value. However, Gao (2008) showed that this interpretation is incorrect. The reason is that less precise (i.e., noisier) financial statements increase the initial expected share mispricing created by the public message. This increase in mispricing outweighs the decrease in mispricing over time.

28. Hirst and Hopkins (1998) presented experimental evidence that information located in shareholders' equity is less likely to be detected by investors. They asked a group of financial analysts to predict the value of a firm that was managing reported net income upward by selling financial instruments that had gained in value (and buying them back later). The effect of this strategy was to transfer unrealized gains from other comprehensive income into net income. U.S. accounting standards at the time allowed changes in other comprehensive income to be reported in a separate statement close to net income, or in a statement of changes in shareholders' equity. Arguably, reporting the transfer out of other comprehensive income is more transparent if reported close to net income rather than buried in changes in shareholders' equity, particularly for investors subject to behavioural biases such as limited attention.

   Hirst and Hopkins found that analysts exposed to the "close to net income" option were better able to diagnose the earnings management than those exposed to the changes in shareholders' equity option. This suggests that greater transparency enables even sophisticated investors (i.e., analysts) to better understand the financial statements.

29. Note that with more than one class of investors, the concept of information asymmetry expands. To this point, we have usually thought of information asymmetry between inside and outside investors. This view of information asymmetry remains. However, we can now also think of information asymmetry between different classes of investors, when one class is better informed than another. In either case, the role of financial reporting to reduce information asymmetry remains.

30. In February 2011, the SEC disclosed that it was investigating a range of banking activities leading up to the meltdowns. One area of investigation was whether investors were properly informed about the procedures used by lending institutions to approve mortgage loans and the resulting low quality of mortgages underlying asset-backed securities. For example, in October, 2012, the SEC filed a fraud lawsuit against Bank of America Corp. of $1 billion for mortgages sold to Fannie Mae and Freddie Mac (agencies of the U.S. government) that were subsequently found to be "toxic." This was in addition to a $1 billion settlement in February 2012 between the Bank and the U.S. Federal Loan Administration, for false claims made when submitting mortgages for insurance.

31. Banks had an incentive to avoid disclosure of implicit guarantees since, if they offered too much protection to investors, the off balance sheet accounting for ABSs would be disallowed. If so, the transfer of ABSs to special purpose vehicles would have to be treated as a secured borrowing, in which case the ABSs and related borrowing liabilities would remain on the bank's balance sheet.

32. R^2 measures the proportion of the variability of the dependent variable on the left side of a regression that is explained by the explanatory variables on the right side. In this case, R squared measures the proportion of abnormal security returns for the sample firms that is explained by unexpected earnings. R squared is thus a measure of the informativeness of earnings.

33. The clean surplus model can be extended to allow for some information asymmetry, although under restrictive conditions. See Feltham and Ohlson (1996).

34. In the FO model, the firm's life is assumed to be infinite.

35. The "o" stands for "operating." If the firm has financial assets, such as cash or securities, these are assumed to earn the risk-free rate of interest. Consequently, financial assets do not contribute to goodwill, which is the ability to earn *abnormal* earnings.

36. The investor may wonder *why* the manager chose these particular accounting policies, however. That is, the manager's choice of accounting policies may itself reveal inside information to the market. Then, it is not completely correct to say that the investor need not be concerned about an accounting policy choice. This is considered in Chapter 11.

37. Our expression for α differs slightly from that of FO. They assumed that the firm has an infinite life, whereas our assumption is that P.V. Ltd. has a two-year life.

38. The persistence parameter ω can be related to the three types of earnings events distinguished by Ramakrishnan and Thomas (RT; 1991) (Section 5.4.1)—namely, permanent, transitory, and price-irrelevant, with ERCs of $(1 + R_f)/R_f$, 1, and 0, respectively. First, consider a $1 permanent abnormal earnings event occurring in year t for a firm with an infinite life. This will increase bv_t, in FO notation, by $1. In addition, ω of this will persist to year t + 1, ω^2 to year t + 2, etc. Thus, the total effect, discounted at the rate R_f, of the $1 of year t abnormal earnings on PA_t—that is, the ERC, is

$$ERC = 1 + \frac{\omega}{1 + R_f} + \frac{\omega^2}{(1 + R_f)^2} + \frac{\omega^3}{(1 + R_f)^3} + \cdots = \frac{1 + R_f}{1 + R_f - \omega}$$

In RT terms, permanent abnormal earnings have an ERC of $(1 + R_f)/R_f$. To express this ERC in terms of ω, we have

$$\frac{1 + R_f}{1 + R_f - \omega} = \frac{1 + R_f}{R_f}$$

which holds for $\omega = 1$.

Thus, permanent abnormal earnings have $\omega = 1$. Note that this is outside the range of ω in the earnings dynamic (Equation 6.2). That is, for an infinite firm horizon the FO model is not defined for permanent earnings.

RT transitory abnormal earnings have an ERC of 1. Thus,

$$\frac{1 + R_f}{1 + R_f - \omega} = 1$$

which holds for $\omega = 0$. Thus, transitory earnings have an ω of zero.

For price-irrelevant abnormal earnings, with ERC of 0, we have

$$\frac{1 + R_f}{1 + R_f - \omega} = 0$$

which is satisfied only in the limit as $\omega \to \pm\infty$. Since this is again outside the allowed range for ω, the FO model is not defined for price-irrelevant abnormal earnings.

39. The market risk premium is the additional return, over and above the risk-free rate, demanded by investors to compensate them for bearing the systematic risk of the market portfolio. The 5.8% estimate of this premium for Canada is taken from Damodaran Online, the webpage of Aswath Damodaran (stern.nyu.edu/~adamodar). The estimate is at January 2013.

40. Canadian Tire Corporation, Limited has two classes of shares outstanding—voting and non-voting, with most of the shares non-voting. For purposes of this example, we combine the two classes.

41. The result of solving the clean surplus model for cost of capital is called an *ex ante* or implied cost of capital since it is based largely on forecasts of future earnings. This contrasts with *ex post* CAPM-based cost of capital estimates, where estimation of the CAPM is based on past data. Thus, the validity of the CAPM for cost of capital estimation requires an assumption that the market on average forms unbiased expectations of expected market returns. If it does, past market returns approximate expected returns for large samples.

42. Also, if markets are not fully efficient, share mispricing will affect the implied cost of capital estimate, since share price will differ from its efficient market value. While the result will be an estimate of the return actually demanded by investors, this differs from the CAPM approach, under which cost of capital is based on what it should be, given investor rationality and, market efficiency, and other assumptions discussed in Section 4.5.2.

43. For further information about the 1980s savings and loan debacle, see Zeff (2003, pp. 272–273), and the references therein.

44. Some accountants deny this statement, arguing that impairment tests are a modified version of historical cost. That is, they regard the written-down value as the new "cost."

45. To verify this, Bill's utility from spending the same amount in each year is

$$\sqrt{5{,}000} + \sqrt{5{,}000} = 70.71 + 70.71 = 141.42$$

Any other spending allocation has lower utility. For example, if he spends $4,500 in year 1 and $5,500 in year 2, his utility is

$$\sqrt{4{,}500} + \sqrt{5{,}500} = 67.08 + 74.16 = 141.24$$

For simplicity, we assume that Bill has zero time preference for consumption. That is, a dollar of spending in year 1 has the same utility as in year 2, and vice versa. We also assume that Bill's utility function in year 2 is not affected by the level of consumption in year 1.

46. Strictly speaking, Bill's second-year utilities should be discounted, since a dollar's worth of consumption next year is worth less than the same consumption today. However, this would complicate the example without changing the point to be made.

47. Basu (1997), described earlier, assumed that the market becomes aware of unrealized gains and losses as they occur from sources other than the financial statements, whereas our example assumes that the auditor misstatements remain as inside information, hence unknown to the market until their existence is later revealed. To the extent that Basu's assumption is valid, the force of our example is reduced. However, Basu's assumption relies heavily on availability of public information about gains and losses from other sources. It also relies on market efficiency with respect to this information. To the extent that inside information remains, our example applies. To argue that the market fully figures out inside information is to deny that inside information exists, to deny that financial statements have information content, and to deny auditor liability.

48. If Bill holds a diversified portfolio, overstatement errors by one firm may cancel out against understatement errors by another. If they do, Bill's wealth at the end of year 1 is correctly stated on average, with no net loss of utility. However, the auditor is not off the hook, since it is unlikely that Bill, or the courts, will forgive one error because the auditor of another firm in his portfolio made an opposite error—we do observe auditor liability for valuation errors. In effect, "two wrongs do not make a right."

49. If the market for audit services is competitive, forces of competition will force auditors to do this. If the market is not competitive, ethical behaviour (Section 1.5) may produce a similar result. Alternatively, consistent with the view adopted here, we can regard the function of the legal system as aligning the interests of auditors and investors.

50. To find the x that maximizes Bill's EU, take the first derivative of Equation 6.4 with respect to x and equate to zero. With some simplification, this yields

$$\frac{\partial EU}{\partial x} = x^{-1/2} - \frac{1}{2}[(16,000 - x)^{-1/2} + (24,000 - x)^{-1/2}] = 0$$

It can be verified that x = 9,400 satisfies this equation. Substitution of x = 9,400 into Equation 6.4 yields EU = 140.

If Bill uses the expected value of his wealth, substituting x = $10,000 into Equation 6.4 yields EU = 139.93.

51. Instead of reporting a conservative valuation, the auditor could report the asset at current value and disclose the conservative valuation in the financial statement notes. However, the auditor may feel that disclosure is not a substitute for recognition in the financial statements proper, due to investor behavioural biases and/or bounded rationality.

52. We say almost as relevant because to report an asset value that exactly maximizes Bill's expected utility, the auditor needs to know Bill's utility function.

53. Since the market-to-book ratio and the Basu measure are both measures of conservatism, a negative relationship between them has led to criticism of the Basu measure, on grounds that two measures of the same construct (i.e., conservatism) should be positively, not negatively, correlated. However, Basu's measure is of conditional conservatism, whereas we regard the market-to-book ratio as primarily a measure of unconditional conservatism. Since these are different conservatism concepts, it is not clear that this criticism is valid. Indeed, as shown by Roychowdhury and Watts (2007), the two measures are positively correlated over longer periods, since the effects of recognition lag decrease as the number of periods is increased.

Chapter 7
Measurement Applications

Figure 7.1 Organization of Chapter 7

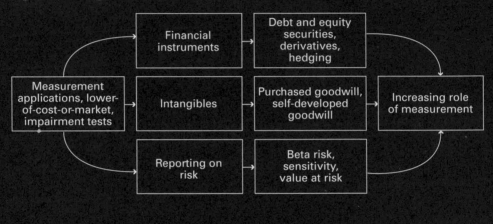

7.1 OVERVIEW

Despite the pressures for a measurement approach discussed in Chapter 6, the movement of accounting practice in this direction encounters some formidable obstacles. The first is reliability. The decision usefulness of current value-based financial statements will be compromised if too much reliability is sacrificed for greater relevance.

Second, management's skepticism about reserve recognition accounting (RRA) that we saw in Section 2.4.3 carries over to current value accounting in general, particularly since the measurement approach implies that current values, and the volatility that accompanies them, are incorporated into the financial statements proper. This skepticism was increased by instances of liquidity pricing during 2007–2008, which seriously eroded the stability of many financial institutions. However, firms do operate in a volatile environment. To the extent that the volatility of current value accounting captures economic reality, one can argue that the financial statements should reflect the real risks facing the firm. Nevertheless, in this and later chapters we shall see reasons why managers may dislike volatile financial statements.

Third, managers, investors, and auditors may prefer conservative accounting to current value accounting in some circumstances. Arguments that conservative accounting can contribute to investor decision making and reduction of auditor liability were given in Sections 6.11 and 6.12. Arguments concerning the role of conservatism in corporate governance will be discussed in Chapter 8.

While these obstacles suggest that extension of current value accounting runs into increasing questions, recent years have seen major new measurement-oriented standards, with more on the horizon. In this chapter, we consider in greater depth the two versions of current value that were introduced in Section 1.2, and review and evaluate some important current value-based standards, including for intangibles. We will also see that the measurement approach extends into reporting on risk.

Figure 7.1 outlines the organization of this chapter.

7.2 CURRENT VALUE ACCOUNTING

7.2.1 Two Versions of Current Value Accounting

Value in Use Value in use can be measured by the discounted present value of cash expected to be received or paid with respect to the use of the asset or liability.[1,2] Present value accounting as illustrated in Examples 2.1 and 2.2 is based on value in use.

Now recall our definition of relevant information—namely, that it informs the investor about the firm's future economic prospects. One might then conclude that value in use is the ultimate in relevance, since it measures the expected cash flows to or from the firm. However, this is subject to a major qualification—value in use depends on how the item is used, and management might change, often strategically, how it intends to use the asset or liability. For example, an impaired capital asset that faces a writedown might instead be put up for sale. This reduces the stigma of a writedown, since any loss on sale would be regarded as of lower persistence. Also, if certain financial assets, currently valued at market value, have fallen in value, management may declare an intent to hold them as a long-term investment, thereby avoiding a writedown. Thus, management intent is a shifting sand upon which to build a measurement approach based on value in use.

Value in use also suffers from problems of reliability, since future cash flows have to be estimated. This exposes the estimates to error and possible manager bias.

Fair Value Fair value accounting is currently governed by IFRS 13, effective in 2013. This standard is substantially the same as accounting standards in the United States (SFAS 157, effective 2007, now ASC 820-10). We shall discuss IFRS 13 here, with the understanding that our discussion also applies to current U.S. fair value rules.

Fair value is defined in IFRS 13 thus:

Fair value is the price that would be received to sell an asset or paid to transfer a liability in an orderly transaction between market participants at the measurement date.

This basis of valuation is also termed **exit price**. Exit price measures the **opportunity cost** to the firm of the intended use of its assets and liabilities. By using them, the firm gives up the opportunity of putting them to their next-best use, which could be to sell them or redeem them at their exit price.

Ideally, fair value is based on the selling price of an asset in a well-working market, or the amount the firm has to pay to dispose of a liability.

However, due to market incompleteness, well-working market prices do not exist for many assets and liabilities. In the face of this difficulty, both standards create a **fair value hierarchy**, consisting of three levels summarized as follows:

- *Level 1*: Assets and liabilities for which a reasonably well-working market price exists.
- *Level 2*: Assets and liabilities for which a market price can be inferred from the market prices of similar items.
- *Level 3*: Assets and liabilities for which a market value cannot be observed or inferred. Then, the firm shall use the best available information about how a market participant holding the asset or liability would value the item.

Note in particular the term "market participant" in Level 3. Level 3 valuation requires the firm to envisage such a prospective purchaser and estimate how much the purchaser would be willing to pay. This amount could be the expected future cash flows of the asset, adjusted for risk, from the purchaser's best use of the item. Note in particular that the concept of value to a prospective purchaser is conceptually different from the concept of value to the firm that owns the asset. However, the firm's own expected cash flows could perhaps be used as a place to start in estimating fair value. In other cases, Level 3 values could perhaps be based on replacement cost, since a prospective purchaser would not pay more.

Extensive supplementary disclosures about how fair values have been determined are required by IFRS 13. However, despite supplementary disclosures, Level 3 valuations, and to a lesser extent Level 2, raise questions about reliability similar to those of value in use, since numerous estimates and management judgments are required.

Nevertheless, Song, Thomas, and Yi (2010), who examined the value relevance of these three levels, based on a 2008 sample of U.S. banks, reported a positive relationship between banks' share prices and reported fair values for all three levels of the hierarchy, with the positive relationship between Levels 1 and 2 assets or liabilities stronger than for Level 3 ones. They also found that as the quality of corporate governance of their sample banks increased, these relationships strengthened. Overall, these results suggest that relevance of fair values of financial instruments outweighs concerns about reliability, even for Level 3, supporting decision usefulness. Note that these results were obtained for 2008—following the 2007–2008 market meltdowns, which, as noted in Section 1.3, raised serious questions about fair value accounting.

7.2.2 Current Value Accounting and the Income Statement

We can also consider current value accounting from a revenue recognition point of view. Value in use recognizes revenues before they are realized, since anticipated future cash flows are capitalized into asset values. Fair value accounting recognizes gains and losses as changes in fair value occur. In effect, fair value accounting, as viewed by standard setters, represents an attempt to increase the forward-looking nature of the income statement, thereby reducing recognition lag and increasing decision usefulness for investors.

Thus, fair value accounting changes the nature of the income statement. Under historical cost accounting, net income is the result of the matching of costs and revenue, with revenue recognized when it is considered to be realized. Some accountants, such as Dichev and Tang (2008), argue in support of historical cost, on grounds that the matching process reduces earnings volatility and improves the ability of investors to predict future earnings. If so, the net income statement assumes greater importance than the balance sheet. This argument is reminiscent of the 1940 Paton and Littleton monograph outlined in Section 1.2. That is, to the extent history repeats itself, historical cost net income represents the current installment of the firm's, and the manager's, realized earnings ability, providing a platform for predicting future earnings.

However, history does not repeat itself exactly. Firms operate in an environment that is constantly changing. Consequently, fair value proponents argue that current values of assets and liabilities provide the most useful indication of the firm's future prospects. This argument is based on Samuelson (1965), who demonstrated that when markets work well (e.g., Level 1 and, to a lesser extent, Level 2), market prices fluctuate randomly. If so, current price is the best predictor of future price. Since asset and liability values are volatile, the income statement will also be volatile. However, this volatility reflects the volatility of the firm's environment, which, current value supporters argue, should not be artificially smoothed.

As a result, under fair value accounting, the balance sheet assumes greater importance, and, consistent with our discussion of the Conceptual Framework in Section 3.7.1, net income is regarded as an explanation of the changes for the period in balance sheet fair values, to help forward-looking investors assess the prospects of future cash flows.

Fair value accounting also improves the ability of net income to report on manager stewardship. We can view the manager as charged with the opportunity cost of net assets used in the business. Assuming reasonable reliability, the manager's performance is then measured by his/her ability to generate a return over and above cost of capital on the opportunity cost of net assets. Otherwise, the firm would be better off to sell the net assets. Thus, under fair value accounting, the income statement assumes the dual role of reporting decision useful information to investors and helping to report on manager stewardship. This expanded stewardship role will increase decision usefulness for those investors who believe that the quality of management is an important indicator of future firm performance.

7.2.3 Summary

Both versions of current value accounting offer increased relevance relative to historical cost accounting. However, they both face problems of reliability. Under value in use, reliability issues arise both because future cash flows usually have to be estimated, and because management may strategically change intended use, hence the future cash flows, of the asset or liability.

Reliability of fair value is high when valuation is based on well-working market values (Level 1 valuation). However, due to market incompleteness, such values may not exist (Level 3). Then, reliability issues also arise for fair values.

Some accountants are sufficiently concerned about reliability that they recommend retaining historical coat accounting as a better relevance–reliability tradeoff. However, there is some empirical evidence supporting value relevance for all levels of the fair value hierarchy.

In the following review of current value-based accounting standards, we shall see that both value in use and fair value approaches are used by standard setters.

7.3 LONGSTANDING MEASUREMENT EXAMPLES

Even though financial statements are based on a mixed measurement model, they contain a substantial current value component. To preface a discussion of more recent measurement-oriented standards, we will review some common, longstanding instances of current value-based measurements.

7.3.1 Accounts Receivable and Payable

For most firms, current accounts receivable (net of allowance for doubtful accounts) and accounts payable are valued at the expected amount of cash to be received or paid. Since the length of time to payment is short, the discount factor is negligible, so that this basis of valuation approximates present value.

7.3.2 Cash Flows Fixed by Contract

There are numerous instances where cash flows are fixed by contract. For example, long-term debt may be valued at the present value of future interest and principal payments, discounted at the **effective interest rate**—that is, the interest rate on the debt established at time of issuance. Then, as long as the firm's borrowing rate does not change, book value equals value in use. Of course, if the interest rate changes, this equality is lost.

Discounting assets and liabilities at their effective rates is called **amortized cost accounting**, under which expected future contractual cash receipts or payments are discounted at the effective interest rate under the contract, and this rate is retained despite changes in relevant interest rates and/or the firm's credit rating. Thus, amortized cost accounting is a version of value in use, discounted at the effective rate rather than the firm's cost of capital. Income or expense for the period is thus interest at the effective rate times opening book value.

As another example of amortized cost accounting, IAS 17 requires finance lease contracts[3] and related leased assets to be initially valued by the lessee at the lower of the fair value of the leased asset or the present value of minimum lease payments, using the interest rate implicit in the lease or the lessee's incremental borrowing rate when the implicit rate is impracticable to determine. The finance expense of the lease for the period is then the opening present value of the lease liability times the interest rate. A problem with this lease accounting is that firms often carefully design lease contracts so that they do not qualify as finance leases. Then, no asset and liability need be recorded. In effect, the lessee obtains financing off balance sheet.

In response, a joint IASB-FASB Exposure Draft (2013) proposes to require capitalization of most lease contracts with a term greater than 12 months. The Draft divides leases into two types. Type A leases cover substantially all of the leased asset's useful life, such as a lease of equipment. The lessee records a liability for the present value of future lease payments, discounted at the interest rate the lessor charges the lessee or, if not determinable, at the lessee's borrowing rate. Amortized cost accounting is applied to this liability. The cost of the leased asset includes this same initial present value, and is depreciated over the lease term.

Type B lease contracts cover less than the asset's useful life, such as a lease of a land and building. Again, amortized cost accounting is applied to the lease liability. However, depreciation of the leased asset is recorded so that the total lease expense (interest on opening lease liability plus depreciation) is the same each period. In effect, lease expense is recorded on a straight-line basis over the lease term.[4]

It thus seems that lease accounting is moving increasingly toward a measurement approach.

7.3.3 The Lower-of-Cost-or-Market Rule

The lower-of-cost-or-market rule, traditionally applied to inventories, is a long-established example of a partial measurement approach. Under IAS 2, when the net realizable value of inventory falls below cost, it is written down to the lower value. If the net realizable value subsequently increases, the inventory may be written up, but not above cost. U.S. GAAP (ASC 330) also includes a lower-of-cost-or-market rule. However, subsequent writeup of written down inventory is not allowed.[5]

The lower-of-cost-or-market rule can be justified in terms of conservatism. It is more difficult to justify in terms of decision usefulness to equity investors, however, since one might think that if current value information is useful, it would be useful when value is greater than cost as well as when it is less than cost, assuming equal reliability. However, as argued in Sections 6.11 and 6.12, conservatism reduces the probability of overstatement errors, and auditors, along with managers, feel with some justification that their exposure to legal liability is greater for an asset overstatement than for an equivalent amount of understatement. Consequently, the rule remains as a partial application of the measurement approach.

7.3.4 Revaluation Option for Property, Plant, and Equipment

While historical cost accounting for property, plant, and equipment is the norm under accounting standards in the United States, IAS 16 allows a **revaluation option**. As an alternative to historical cost, non-financial assets, such as property, plant, and equipment, can be valued at fair value, providing this can be done reliably. Once assets are revalued, fair values must be kept up to date, so as not to differ materially from fair value at the balance sheet date. These revaluations may increase or decrease carrying value. This option constitutes another major example of the measurement approach.

7.3.5 Impairment Test for Property, Plant, and Equipment

Standard setters have imposed an impairment test for most non-financial assets, such as property, plant, and equipment. Impairment tests help protect the auditor from legal liability, and, since they force writedowns of assets that would otherwise be overvalued, they contribute to the increase in conditional conservatism documented by Basu (1997), as discussed in Section 6.11. Like the lower-of-cost-or-market rule, we regard impairment tests as a partial application of the measurement approach in this chapter, since determining the impaired value involves similar problems to determining current value.

Under IAS 36, an impairment loss for assets such as property, plant, and equipment is recognized in net income. The loss is the excess of book value over the **recoverable amount**, where the recoverable amount is the greater of fair value less costs of disposal or value in use.

Impairment losses for assets, other than goodwill, can be reversed if the recoverable amount has increased, but not above the book value the assets would have had if no impairment loss had been recorded.

Under FASB rules, impairment tests are somewhat different. ASC 36-10-35 lays down a two-step procedure. First, it is determined whether the asset is impaired. This is the case if book value exceeds the sum of undiscounted expected future direct net cash flows.[6] If an asset is deemed impaired, it is written down to its fair value.

Under both IASB and FASB standards, impairment losses are charged against current earnings.[7] However, unlike IAS 36, FASB standards do not allow for subsequent reversals of these writedowns. Thus, IAS 36 is somewhat closer to a full measurement approach.

Nevertheless, despite the asymmetric nature of their application, impairment tests represent an important extension of the measurement approach to major classes of assets.

7.3.6 Summary

The above is only a partial listing of current value-based measurements in GAAP. For our purposes, the main point to realize is that a considerable amount of measurement approach is inherent in the mixed measurement model.

These examples, however, understate the extent of measurement in current GAAP. We now turn to a consideration of more recent current value-oriented accounting standards.

7.4 FINANCIAL INSTRUMENTS DEFINED

A **financial instrument** is defined as follows:

A financial instrument is a contract that creates a financial asset of one firm and a financial liability or equity instrument of another firm.

Financial assets and liabilities are defined quite broadly.[8] Thus, a financial asset is

- cash
- an equity instrument of another firm
- a contractual right
    - to receive cash or another financial asset from another firm
    - to exchange financial instruments with another firm under conditions that are potentially favourable

Similarly, a financial liability is any liability that is

- a contractual obligation
    - to deliver cash or another financial asset to another firm, or
    - to exchange financial assets or financial liabilities with another firm under conditions that are potentially unfavourable

Thus, financial assets and liabilities include items such as accounts and notes receivable and payable, debt and equity securities held by the firm, and bonds outstanding. These are referred to as **primary instruments**. Also included are derivative instruments, to be discussed in Section 7.9.

7.5 PRIMARY FINANCIAL INSTRUMENTS

7.5.1 Standard Setters Back Down Somewhat on Fair Value Accounting

Following the 2007–2008 market meltdowns described in Section 1.3, many firms reported fair value writedowns of their financial assets. Since valuations based on market values that suffered from liquidity pricing were obviously very low, writedowns were huge. Since spreads on credit default swaps were wide, attempts to infer market values based on the cost of insurance also produced low valuations. These writedowns were severely criticized by management, who viewed them as excessive. For example, *The Economist* (September 18, 2008) reported a "chorus of criticism" against fair value accounting, including pressure on standard setters by banks, who argued that sound assets had suffered excessive writedowns and that fair value accounting for such assets should be suspended.

Standard setters were thus caught in the position that their standards imposed fair value accounting under an assumption that markets worked well, but markets were clearly not working well. In the face of this difficulty, they introduced some modifications in 2008:

■ The IASB and FASB issued similar guidance on how to determine fair value when markets are inactive (i.e., not working well). The guidance was that when market values did not exist and could not be reliably inferred from values of similar items, firms could determine fair value by using their own assumptions of future cash flows from the assets and liabilities, discounted at a risk-adjusted interest rate. Notice the subtle difference from the wording of Level 3 in the valuation hierarchy of IFRS 13 above. Instead of using assumptions about how a prospective purchaser would value a financial item, firms could use their own assumptions about future cash flows from the item. Of course, this relaxation reduced reliability, since it is possible that managers might bias their value in use estimates for their own purposes. However, the standard setters required extensive supplementary disclosure of how the estimated fair value was determined. Furthermore, the requirement to use a risk-adjusted discount rate in a period of high risk would lower the present value estimates.

The FASB also weakened rules that require certain debt and equity securities to be written down to fair value with losses included in net income. Such writedowns were not required if the decline in value was felt to be temporary and there was a reasonable probability that the company would hold the asset until the temporary decline in value was over.

Theory in Practice 7.1

Deutsche Bank was quick to take advantage of these revisions. In its quarterly report for the period ending September 30, 2008, it reported that it had reclassified loans and receivables from a fair value accounting basis to a cost basis. At September 30, 2008, the reclassified assets were valued in the financial statements on a cost basis at €24.901 billion, whereas their fair value at this date, according to Deutsche Bank, was €23.386 billion. However, Deutsche Bank estimated the future cash flows from these assets at €26 billion. Since this was greater than book value, no writedown was required. This "saving" of a €1.515 billion writedown enabled Deutsche Bank to report a net income for the quarter of €414 million. Upon release of this news, the company's share price increased by almost 18% on the Frankfurt exchange.

- The IASB allowed reclassification of certain financial assets to allow greater consistency with FASB standards, which allowed relaxation of fair value in "rare circumstances." The market meltdowns were deemed such a circumstance. For example, loans and receivables could be valued at cost, even though fair value was lower, as long as their expected future cash flows were greater than cost.

7.5.2 Longer-Run Changes to Fair Value Accounting

The above changes were stopgap measures, due to political pressure from management and regulators. Subsequently, the IASB embarked on a project to replace IAS 39, its previous standard for financial assets and liabilities.

IFRS 9, not effective until at least 2015, is an outcome of this project. Under this standard, financial assets and liabilities are to be recorded on a fair value basis at acquisition. Subsequent valuation of most liabilities is at amortized cost. Subsequent valuation of financial assets is at fair value except for financial assets that pay interest and principal. If the objective of the firm's **business model** is to hold the asset in order to collect this interest and principal, the asset is valued on an amortized cost basis.[9] However, if the asset becomes impaired, it must be written down to its new expected present value, with the loss included in net income. Impairment writedowns are reversed to the extent that the value in use of the asset subsequently increases.

As we noted in Section 7.2.1, present value accounting is subject to the possibility that management may change strategically the intended use of the asset so as to influence the present value. Under IFRS 9, changes in the business model are expected to be rare. In this way, the standard makes it more difficult for management to influence the present value inputs into amortized cost. In effect, valuation based on intent is retained, but the ability of management to change its intent is restricted.

Changes in fair values are generally included in net income. However, for financial assets that are equity investments, the firm may elect at acquisition to include unrealized fair value gains and losses in other comprehensive income unless the asset is intended for resale.

IFRS 13 also requires expanded supplementary disclosures. For example, the particular methods and inputs the firm adopts to determine fair value must be disclosed, particularly for Level 3, so that outside parties can see how fair value has been arrived at. Also, for liabilities, disclosure is required of any credit enhancements (for example, see the discussion of credit enhancements of ABSs in Section 1.3). Additional disclosures are required by IFRS 7, including book values, and fair values if different, of various categories of financial assets and liabilities and their levels in the fair value hierarchy. Disclosures of assumptions used in determining fair values are also required.

Firms may have incentives to shift financial assets between classes. For example, if an asset valued at amortized cost has appreciated in value, transferring it to fair value would enable a gain to be recorded. However, IFRS 9 makes such transfers difficult, since classification of financial assets between the two valuation bases generally requires a change in the firm's business model. As we noted above, such changes are expected to be rare, thereby reducing the probability that management will change valuation bases for strategic reasons.

At time of writing, FASB rules for valuation of debt and equity securities are somewhat different. ASC 320-10 imposes a three-part classification for financial assets:

- **Trading**. These securities are acquired with the intention of reselling. They are valued at fair value, with unrealized gains and losses included in net income.

- **Held to Maturity**. These securities are acquired with the intention that they be held to maturity. They are valued at amortized cost. If their fair value falls below their amortized cost, the securities are written down to their fair value. Unlike IFRS 9, this writedown may not be reversed if the fair value subsequently increases. With few exceptions, sales before maturity of securities intended to be held to maturity cause all remaining securities in this classification to be reclassified as available for sale.

- **Available for sale**. These securities are valued at fair value, with unrealized gains and losses included in other comprehensive income.

Note that the criterion for classifying a security as held to maturity is just what it says—the firm must intend to hold the asset to maturity. This contrasts with IFRS 9, which requires only an intent to hold to collect interest and principal. Since this is a significantly weaker requirement to qualify for amortized cost accounting, we may expect greater use of fair value accounting under FASB standards than under IFRS. It will be interesting to see the extent to which these two bodies converge their financial instruments standards. Convergence would require the FASB to adopt, or the IASB to drop, the business model concept as a condition for amortized cost accounting. Alternatively, both standard setters may compromise by applying the business model concept to only certain types of assets held to collect interest and principal.

Note also that both standards allow certain unrealized fair value gains and losses to be included in other comprehensive income. Since fair values tend to be volatile, the effect is to reduce net income volatility. This is a concession to management who, for reasons to be discussed in Chapters 9 and 10, dislike income volatility.

However, there is another way to reduce net income volatility, which we now consider.

7.5.3 The Fair Value Option

IFRS 9 contains a **fair value option**. At acquisition, the firm can irrevocably designate financial assets and/or financial liabilities that would normally be valued at amortized cost into the fair value category if this reduces a **mismatch,** where a mismatch is earnings volatility in excess of the real volatility facing the firm. Changes in fair value of assets and liabilities designated under the fair value option are included in net income.

Mismatch arises when some assets or liabilities are fair valued but related liabilities or assets are not. For example, suppose that a firm issues bonds to finance the purchase of a portfolio of interest-bearing loans receivable. The bond liability is valued at amortized cost. However, assume that the firm frequently buys and sells the loans in its portfolio. That is, its business model does not require that the loans be held solely to earn interest and principle. Consequently, the loans are valued at fair value. As market interest rates change, the fair value of the bonds payable will rise or fall and the fair value of the loans receivable will fall or rise. Thus, in real terms, the bonds provide a **natural hedge** of the effect of interest rate changes on the loans receivable. However, in accounting terms, if changes in the fair value of the loan assets are included in net income but there is no fair value gain or loss recorded on the bond liability, the volatility of the firm's net income exceeds the real volatility the firm has chosen through its natural hedging activities. This is mismatch.

To reduce the potential for mismatch, the firm could adopt the fair value option for its long-term debt so that "both sides" of the natural hedge are fair-valued, with gains and losses on both included in net income Under IFRS 9, use of the fair value option is restricted. One restriction is that this option is used to reduce a mismatch such as the one just described.

In the United States, ASC 825-10-15 creates a similar fair value option, although it does not restrict choice of this option to mismatch situations. Thus, when market interest rates change, the firm can use the fair value option to record a gain or loss on changes in the fair value of its debt in net income even in the absence of a natural hedge. Theory in Practice 7.2 illustrates this possibility.

Theory in Practice 7.2

While net income under FASB standards may increase due to a decline in the fair value of debt, it can also decrease when fair value increases. Morgan Stanley, a large U.S.-based financial institution, reported long-term debt at the beginning of 2008 of $190.624 billion. In 2008, the company took advantage of the fair value option to fair value its long-term debt. It included a gain from fair-valuing this debt of $10.176 billion in its 2008 net income, enabling it to report income from continuing operations of $2.287 billion before tax. In 2009, however, the market value of Morgan Stanley's debt increased. This led to a loss from an increase in the fair value of debt of $1.5 billion for its first quarter. The company reported a net loss of $177 million for the quarter.

The fair value of a firm's debt can also change due to changes in its own credit risk, even in the absence of a change in market interest rates. If changes in the fair value of debt resulting from changes in the firm's own credit risk are included in net income, the results may seem strange. For example, suppose that a firm receives a downgrade from a credit rating agency. As a result, the fair value of its debt falls in response to the increased credit risk borne by lenders, where credit risk here is the risk that the firm will be unable to meet its contractual liabilities as they come due. The firm could use the fair value option to fair-value its debt, and would thus report a gain in net income as its own credit risk increases.

Two points about this gain should be noted. First, the decline in fair value of debt creates a wealth transfer between constituencies: Shareholders gain through lower economic value of firm debt, and debtholders lose through increased risk of future interest and principal payments. Under the **entity view** of financial reporting adopted by the Conceptual Framework (Section 3.7.1), the income statement is a report of firm performance to all capital providers.[10] Consequently, it is questionable whether a gain to shareholders accompanied by a loss to debtholders represents income of the entity.

Second, an increase in a firm's credit risk is usually accompanied by a decline in the fair value of its assets. Yet, many of these assets, such as the value of R&D or self-developed goodwill, are unrecorded. Other assets, such as property, plant, and equipment, are recorded but usually valued on a cost basis. To the extent that writedowns to fair value of these assets are not recorded, there is no loss to offset the decline in the fair value of debt, creating a mismatch-like situation. Thus, it is again questionable whether a gain to shareholders should be recorded.

The impact of changes in the firm's own credit risk on its share price was studied by Barth, Hodders, and Stubben (2008). For a large sample of U.S. firms over the years 1986–2003, they reported that, as we would expect, the firms' share prices declined following a credit downgrade (and increased following an upgrade). However, share price declines were reduced to the extent that the firms had debt outstanding. This finding is consistent with both securities market efficiency and the wealth transfer argument given above. The authors also reported evidence that if all firm assets (including intangibles) were fair valued, most firms would report a net loss following a downgrade, net of the credit downgrade gain to shareholders. Since, as mentioned, all assets are not fair valued in practice, this finding suggests that if firms' own credit losses are included in net income, most firms would record a gain even if there is a loss in economic terms.

IFRS standards seem largely consistent with our reservations about recording the firm's own credit risk gains and losses in net income. Under IFRS 9, financial liabilities are valued at their amortized cost, in which case no gain would be recorded following a credit downgrade. However, IFRS 9 gives the firm an option to value the financial liabilities at fair value. While a change in fair value is then normally included in net income, the change is included in other comprehensive income if it results from a change in credit risk.[11]

7.5.4 Loan Loss Provisioning*

A second outcome of the IASB project to replace IAS 39 is a proposal to revise the rules for recognizing impairment of financial assets valued at amortized cost, such as loans receivable. The proposal is to include expected credit losses in the calculation of expected future cash flows for loans receivable, a process called **loan loss provisioning**. In effect,

---

*This section can be omitted with little lack of continuity.

credit losses would be recognized "sooner" than under previous impairment standards, under which credit losses were not recorded until an asset became impaired. Loss provisioning proposals are a response to criticisms of the huge impairment writedowns during the 2007–2008 market meltdowns, where expected credit losses may have been building up for some time before the impairment was suddenly recognized.

A 2013 IASB exposure draft, applicable to all financial instruments that are subject to impairment testing, divides financial assets into two groups. One group consists of assets for which there has been a significant increase in credit risk since their acquisition. Such an asset is valued net of a loan loss allowance equal to the discounted expected credit losses from the asset over its remaining life ("lifetime expected credit losses"). The second group consists of assets with no significant increase in credit risk since acquisition. An asset in this group is valued net of a loan loss allowance equal to "12-month expected credit losses," where this amount is calculated as the firm's assessed probability of a default within 12 months times the asset's lifetime expected credit loss.[12]

If an asset is valued based on lifetime expected credit losses and its credit risk subsequently is restored, the original 12-month expected credit losses accounting can be restored.

The important point to note about this proposed accounting is that loan losses are recorded before an actual credit default takes place, thereby responding at least partially to the criticisms mentioned above of huge unexpected loan writedowns during the 2007–2008 market meltdowns.

The FASB proposed loan loss provisioning standard differs somewhat from that of the IASB. The FASB proposes to value all loans based on lifetime expected credit losses; that is, without the 12-month rule of IASB. According to the IASB, deducting a lifetime expected credit loss double-counts expected losses on loans for which there has not been a deterioration in credit risk, since the fair value of the loan at acquisition already prices in expected loan losses at that time.

Loan loss provisioning obviously raises questions about reliability, since it increases the ability of managers to opportunistically manage the loss estimates. However, if done responsibly, it increases relevance since, arguably, management has the best estimate of credit losses. If so, loan loss provisioning improves the ability of investors to predict future firm performance and risk. This interplay between relevance and reliability was examined by Bushman and Williams (BW; 2012), based on a sample of banks from 27 countries over the years 1995–2006. As the authors pointed out, a responsibly managed bank should respond to increased risk of future cash flows by increasing its equity capital to protect against possible insolvency. If the bank does so, its leverage (ratio of debt to equity) should fall. Conversely, if bank risk decreases leverage should increase. This change in leverage alerts investors that the bank's risk has changed.

However, banks face an incentive to report smooth earnings over time, so as to create an image of solidity and low risk. An important vehicle for smoothing earnings is the loan loss provision. To the extent that managers have flexibility to manage this provision, income smoothing should increase. Thus BW used the extent of income smoothing in each sample country as a proxy for the flexibility of banks to manage their loan loss provisions.

BW found that the relationship between leverage and bank risk (measured by asset volatility) in a country weakened as the extent of income smoothing in that country increased. This suggests that bank managers use flexible loan loss provision rules to smooth income. As mentioned, this makes it harder for investors to detect changes in bank risk. In other words, loan loss provisioning is subject to reliability problems.

However, BW also found that the greater the ability of loan loss provisions to accurately predict future loan losses in a country (implying less discretion to manage the loan loss provision), the greater the increase in the relationship between leverage and bank risk. This suggests that in countries with less ability to opportunistically manage earnings, the ability of investors to detect risk changes increases. In other words, loan loss provisioning, if used responsibly, increases relevance.

At time of writing, the final version of this impairment standard is not known, particularly since it is unclear if it will be converged with FASB standards. It will be interesting to see the extent to which the final standard trades off relevance and reliability. Nevertheless, to the extent to which it "speeds up" the recognition of impairment losses, the new standard will represent an important, and hopefully useful, move toward the measurement perspective.

7.5.5 Summary and Conclusions

We conclude that the accounting for financial instruments is an important application of fair value accounting. However, in IFRS 9, the IASB backs off somewhat from fair value, relative to U.S. standards, since it allows increased use of amortized cost accounting of debt securities by introducing the business model concept. The likely result, unless and until the two standard setting bodies converge their standards, is that financial statements prepared under U.S. GAAP will exhibit greater use of fair values for financial instruments than statements prepared under IASB GAAP. Nevertheless, both standard setters take steps to reduce the volatility of net income that fair value accounting creates. These steps include allowing certain unrealized gains and losses to be included in other comprehensive income, and the fair value option. The FASB fair value option is somewhat broader than that of the IFRS, since it is not confined to mismatch situations. However, in the absence of mismatch, it is questionable whether gains from fair valuing debt following a credit downgrade are income of the firm.

Standard setters are also proposing to introduce loan loss provisioning. This would result in recognizing expected credit losses on loan assets sooner than under current standards under which such losses are not recognized until incurred. While it would increase relevance, this proposal raises questions of reliability. The final version of this proposal is not known at the present time.

7.6 FAIR VALUE VERSUS HISTORICAL COST*

As noted in Section 7.2.2, some accountants argue that historical cost accounting is more useful to investors than current value. In this regard, several theoretical models evaluate the relative merits of fair value and historical cost accounting for financial instruments. Allen and Carletti (AC; 2008) presented a model in which banks and insurance firms hold both long-term and short-term financial assets. Should a state of nature happen under which insurance companies cannot pay their claims, they must liquidate, including selling their long-term assets. This generates liquidity pricing since, for investors to be willing to buy the excess supply of long-term assets brought to market, their selling price must fall substantially, at least to the point that their returns are higher than those of the short-term assets. As noted in Section 1.3, liquidity pricing drives market price below value in use.

Under fair value accounting, banks must then write down their long-term asset holdings to the liquidity price, leading to violation of legal capital requirements and technical insolvency, even though on a value in use basis they are solvent. Under historical cost accounting, these writedowns do not occur and banks remain solvent.

The AC model thus predicts that historical cost accounting is socially preferred to fair value, since it avoids the possibility of financial contagion from one industry to another when the industries hold similar assets in common.

However, as Sapra (2008) pointed out, the AC model does not allow for the likelihood that governments will step in to try to contain the contagion, such as investing public money into the banking industry, relaxing legal capital constraints, or buying the excess long-term assets. Also, if the returns on the long-run asset are correlated over time, fair value accounting may serve as an early warning system of impending bank failure, so that governments can step in before the financial system deteriorates to the point where banks become insolvent. The savings and loan debacle (Section 6.11) provides a dramatic example of how historical cost accounting can disguise deteriorating asset value until it is too late, thereby greatly increasing investor losses and the costs of government bailout. Furthermore, standard setters themselves allow some relief from a contagion scenario based on full fair value accounting. As we saw in Section 7.5.2, IFRS 9 and related FASB standards allow certain financial assets to be valued at amortized cost, and certain unrealized gains and losses to be included in other comprehensive income rather than net income. Furthermore, when a market is inactive or non-existent, firms may be able to use their own assumptions to estimate fair value (see Section 7.5.1). To the extent that these assumptions are based on value in use, the liquidity pricing effect is reduced.

Nevertheless, the AC model does help us to see how financial distress can spread across the financial services industry, and to understand why financial firms are usually the strongest opponents of fair value accounting. However, the model seems too strong in its blanket condemnation of fair value accounting.

---

*This section can be omitted with little lack of continuity.

In this regard, a model of Plantin, Sapra, and Shin (PSS; 2008), which we adapt to a liquidity pricing context, shows conditions under which fair value accounting can be bad or good. Their model consists of a large number of financial institutions holding illiquid, longer-term assets, such as loans and asset-backed securities (ABSs). The managers of these firms are assumed to want to maximize reported net income for the year. That is, they have a shorter planning horizon than the duration of their assets. Such a horizon can arise if the manager's compensation depends on net income for the year, and/or if major writedowns threaten legal capital regulations.

The manager's decision at the first of the year is whether to hold the firm's longer-term assets to maturity or sell them during the year at market price.

Suppose first that there is a collapse of investor confidence, leading to a decline in economic activity and falling security prices. Assume that the firm's longer-term assets are valued at fair value. PSS argued that if prices continue to fall, managers expect that at period-end there will be a substantial writedown of these loan assets under fair value accounting. If the assets are sold before period-end there will be a realized loss, but this loss will be less than the loss produced by the period-end fair value writedown if prices continue to fall. Managers, who want to maximize current period earnings and/or avoid falling below regulatory capital limits, will face pressure to sell now

A crucial assumption of PSS is that managers take other managers' actions into account. Knowing that every manager is likely to sell, they all rush to sell right away before market value falls any further. Price quickly falls to below value in use, and we have liquidity pricing.

Since value in use is greater than fair value under liquidity pricing, shareholders would be better off if the loans were held to maturity. However, the manager's fixation on maximizing net income for the year works against this. The result is that under fair value accounting, the market price of illiquid assets is driven to well below their actual worth to the financial institution.

Instead, assume that loans are accounted for under pure historical cost. Then, there is no writedown at year end. This eliminates managers' motivations to sell, encouraging firms to retain their loans and thereby reducing the fall in market value. Thus, under these conditions, historical cost accounting is preferred from the shareholders' perspective.[13]

Suppose instead that investor confidence and economic activity, hence fair values of securities, are high. Under historical cost accounting, managers are motivated to sell loan assets that have increased in value to realize a gain and increase net income for the year (gains trading). Since gains trading is essentially selling the winner securities (high value in use) and holding the losers, this is to the shareholders' longer run disadvantage. Under fair value accounting, there is no motivation to sell, since unrealized gains are included in income. The firm retains its loans and will realize their value at maturity. Then, from the shareholders' perspective, fair value accounting is preferred to historical cost.

Given the assumptions of the model, it thus seems that the choice between historical cost and fair value accounting depends on whether economic conditions are high or low.

Firms that express concerns about fair value accounting should realize that their preferences may change should the state of the economy change.

However, like the AC model, the assumptions of the PSS model should not be taken for granted. In particular, to the extent that managers' decision horizons are lengthened by, for example, large holdings of company stock (to be discussed in Section 10.3), the relative unattractiveness of fair value accounting during periods of low economic conditions could change since managers may then look through short-run losses to longer-term gains. Also, it is important to emphasize that the PSS analysis applies to illiquid assets, for which the act of selling lowers market price. If asset markets are deep, prices will fall less, or not at all, when assets are sold (see Chapter 1, Note 22). It is managers' anticipation of these lower prices, motivating quick sales, that drives much of the inefficiency of fair value accounting in the model. Also, governments may step in to improve economic conditions and investor confidence. Nevertheless, the models' implications that the basis of accounting may affect managers' real decisions, and their predictions that managers and shareholders, particularly those of financial institutions, will complain about fair value accounting when economic conditions are bad seems consistent with the experiences following the 2007–2008 asset-backed security (ABS) market meltdown.

These models have been empirically tested. Bhat, Frankel, and Martin (BFM; 2011) studied the effects of the stopgap modifications to fair value accounting described in Section 7.5.1, which essentially allowed increased use of value in use in place of fair value, on a sample of U.S. banks. Consistent with the theories of AC and PMS outlined above, they found that banks with relatively large holdings of ABSs and in relatively poor financial condition (high loan losses, and close to violating legal capital constraints) did decrease their ABS holdings. They also found that the 2008 fair value relaxations reduced these ABS reductions. They reported that bank share prices responded positively to these relaxations, with banks that had sold the most ABSs enjoying the greatest share price increases.

Interestingly, BFM found that prices of bonds issued by their sample banks did not fall as a result of the favourable effects of the fair value relaxations on shareholders. Since the fair value relaxations allowed greater use of value in use, and since value in use gives managers considerable discretion to influence the valuation of their ABS holdings, it is possible that bank managers would inflate their value in use estimates so as to avoid legal capital violations. If the bond market suspected this, it would likely react negatively and the banks' bond prices would fall. But this did not happen. As Kolasinski (2011) argued, this implies that these fair value relaxations benefitted society. That is, by benefitting shareholders without harming bondholders, the relaxations seem to have generated a net social benefit.

However, somewhat different conclusions were reached by Badertscher, Burks, and Easton (BBE; 2012). They obtained a sample of 150 U.S. banks that were large holders of securities subject to fair value accounting as of June 30, 2006 (i.e., just before the 2007–2008 security market meltdowns), and estimated the total quarterly fair value writedowns relative to total reported quarterly earnings of their sample firms over the period 2004–2008. During 2008, these writedowns reached record amounts. For example, they totalled $8 billion for Q3, 2008. However, BBE pointed out that this was a relatively small component of total net losses reported by their sample banks of $22 billion. This suggests that managers' objections to fair value accounting may have been overdone. The write-down of loans was much larger, being about $43 billion for the quarter. But, since they pay interest and principal, loans are generally accounted for on a value in use basis (subject to impairment writedowns), and thus less subject to manager complaints about fair value accounting.

BBE also studied the effects of fair value writedowns on their banks' regulatory capital positions, reporting only a very small effect. For example, in Q3, 2008, fair value writedowns lowered average capital adequacy by about 3%. For those banks with the weakest capital adequacy (lowest 20% of their sample), the effects were somewhat greater—about an 8% reduction. Again, the effect of bad loan writedowns on regulatory capital was much higher.

BBE also evaluated the predictions of PSS that managers will rush to sell illiquid assets to avoid further losses. Such pro-cyclical selling leads to further liquidity pricing, contributing to a downward spiral of market prices, investor confidence, and economic activity. However, BBE found no evidence of pro-cyclical selling for their sample firms.

Overall, empirical testing of the AC and PSS models show mixed results. Furthermore, the results of BBE suggest that the objections to fair value accounting raised by managers and politicians during the market meltdowns may have been overstated.

7.7 LIQUIDITY RISK AND FINANCIAL REPORTING QUALITY

The responses of standard setters to the 2007–2008 market meltdowns that were outlined in Sections 1.3 and 7.5.1 were largely due to lack of liquidity in securities markets, since lack of liquidity results in markets that do not work well, thereby threatening the well-working market assumption that underlies fair value accounting. Concerns about the transparency of ABSs and of financial reporting itself due to lack of reporting of off balance sheet risk were important contributors to the lack of liquidity, since, as investor concerns grew they reduced buying activity and even left the market. Consequently, costs of buying and selling securities rose dramatically, since the very act of buying and selling on an illiquid market affects the security price.

Acharya and Pedersen (AP; 2005) defined liquidity risk as the uncertainty about what this buying or selling cost will be. The CAPM assumes perfect liquidity, as noted in Section 4.5.2. AP extended the CAPM to model the effect of liquidity risk on cost of capital, showing conditions under which cost of capital increases for firms with high liquidity risk.

This raises the question, can financial reporting help to reduce liquidity risk, hence cost of capital? These questions were examined by Lang and Maffett (LM; 2011), who pointed out that transparent financial reporting increases the amount of publicly-available firm-specific information. The resulting reduction in information asymmetry makes the firm's share price less sensitive to changes in market volatility, since investors are more confident in the value of shares of transparent firms and thus less likely to sell in the face of the uncertainty created by an increase in market volatility. The researchers argued that such effects are particularly likely during severe downturns such as the 2007–2008 market meltdowns.

LM studied a large sample of firms from 37 countries over the period 1996–2008. They used several measures of reporting transparency, including auditor (Big-Five audits are viewed as generating greater transparency than non-Big-Five audits) and analyst forecast accuracy (more accurate forecasts are presumed to result from greater reporting transparency). They found that greater reporting transparency is associated with lower volatility of firms' share liquidity,[14] particularly during periods of crisis, consistent with their argument.

In a related study, Ng (2011) also studied the relationship between financial reporting quality and liquidity risk.[15] He measured reporting quality several ways, including the accruals quality measure of DeChow and Dichev (2002) described in Section 5.4.1. Based on a sample of U.S. stocks over the period 1983–2008, Ng also reported a negative association between reporting quality and liquidity risk.

We conclude that liquidity risk can be a significant contributor to cost of capital, particularly in times of severe market downturns, and that quality financial reporting, by reducing liquidity risk, can help to reduce the adverse effects of liquidity risk on the cost of capital.

7.8 DERECOGNITION AND CONSOLIDATION

Derecognition and consolidation are at the heart of the accounting issues that contributed to the 2007–2008 market meltdowns outlined in Section 1.3. Off balance sheet financing, which concealed much of the risk borne by financial institutions, would not be possible without asset derecognition and subsequent failure to consolidate the off balance sheet entities that held many of the sponsors' derecognized assets. Standard setters have responded to these issues with new rules that attempt to control off balance sheet financing and bring it out into the open.

Accountants have debated the question of asset derecognition for many years. That is, when can an asset be removed from the balance sheet and revenue recognized on the resulting sale? The usual criterion for derecognition is point of sale. For example, inventory sold is derecognized and revenue is recognized based on the sale proceeds. Any risks of the resulting accounts receivable are provided for through estimates of credit losses. Other obligations, such as warranties arising from the sale, are also provided for.

However, many firms do not retain their accounts receivable. Rather, they are securitized (i.e., ABSs) and transferred to another entity. Mortgages receivable can also be securitized and transferred in this manner. Then, the question arises, can these transferred assets be derecognized? The alternative to derecognition is to retain transferred assets on the balance sheet and treat the proceeds received as a **secured borrowing** (i.e., the firm has "borrowed" the proceeds of the transaction, giving the transferred asset as security).

This treatment is appropriate if the transfer is accompanied by so many risks and future obligations that the risks and rewards of ownership have not really been transferred to the buyer.

Firms have an incentive to derecognize, since this can improve their leverage ratios. For example, Niu and Richardson (2006), for a sample of 535 securitizations generated by 103 firms over the period 1997–2003, estimated that the average debt–equity ratio of the firms in their sample would have gone from 5.97 under derecognition to 10.20 had these transfers been accounted for as secured borrowings. The following vignette illustrates a rather creative abuse of derecognition.

Theory in Practice 7.3

A report published in March 2010 by A.R. Valukis, partner of a large U.S. law firm, examined the events leading up to the November 2008 collapse of Lehman Brothers Holdings Inc., a large U.S.-based financial institution. Included in the report was a description of the accounting tactics used by Lehman to improve the appearance of its balance sheet in the quarters leading up to its collapse by derecognizing assets. These tactics, and the auditor's acceptance of them, received wide attention and condemnation in the financial media.

The tactics were based on **repurchase agreements** (repos), a very common and accepted business transaction, whereby a firm that needs cash on a short-term basis pledges collateral assets to a counterparty (e.g., a bank) as security for a cash loan. At the same time, the borrowing firm enters into an agreement with the counterparty to repurchase the collateral assets shortly thereafter, thereby repaying the loan. This agreement, which is essentially a derivative liability, would have little or zero fair value on the firm's books since the repurchase price is close to the amount borrowed and the time to maturity is very short. The borrowing firm pays a fee to the counterparty for this service. This fee would typically be low, since the amount borrowed is secured by the pledged collateral For example, under a **repo 105**, the firm would post collateral assets valued at 105% of the loan amount.

Normally, repos are accounted for as secured borrowings, since the borrower has an obligation to repurchase the transferred assets. The pledged assets remain on the balance sheet and the amount borrowed is shown as a liability.

Lehman's accounting for its repo 105 transactions was different, however. As its financial condition deteriorated due to the 2007–2008 market meltdowns, it entered into large (up to almost $50 billion) repo transactions just prior to its quarter-end dates, pledging various assets, many of which were illiquid, as collateral. Instead of accounting for these as secured borrowings, it recorded the pledge of assets as a sale, thereby derecognizing them from its balance sheet. As a result, no liability for its borrowing appeared. Furthermore, Lehman could use the cash it received to temporarily pay down other liabilities. Shortly after the balance sheet date, the derecognized assets were reacquired, the loan repaid, and, presumably, the paid-down liabilities reinstated. This process was repeated at the next balance sheet date.

This accounting resulted in substantial improvements in Lehman's quarter-end financial statements. To the extent that the pledged assets had declined in fair value, "selling" them at an agreed price avoided large writedowns (the counterparty would be less concerned about fair value since the repurchase agreement would obligate

Lehman to buy the assets back at the same value ascribed to them when pledged. Of greater significance was the effect on Lehman's balance sheets. Its debt–equity ratio was decreased and, given positive shareholders' equity, its assets to debt ratio was increased. In effect, Lehman was able to disguise its deteriorating condition by treating the pledge of assets as a sale.

Lehman was able to account for its pledged assets as a sale because of FASB accounting standards at the time, which stipulated that the repo transaction be treated as a sale unless the repurchase price of the secured assets was within 98%–102% of the amount borrowed. If so, the transaction would be accounted for as a secured borrowing. By pledging 105% or more of the amount borrowed to reacquire the assets, Lehman was able to treat the transaction as a sale. This apparently allowed Lehman's auditor to avoid a qualified audit opinion on the firm's financial statements. The report also indicated that instead of contracting to repurchase the same assets that were pledged, these were retained by the counterparty. Instead, Lehman purchased from the counterparty assets similar in terms of type, maturity, and value. Presumably, this was to reinforce the sale accounting treatment

since the original assets, technically speaking, were not reacquired. Even so, it appears that sale accounting for such a repo transaction would not be allowed in the United States. However, Lehman worked around this difficulty by securing an opinion from a U.K. law firm that sale accounting for such a transaction was legal under U.K. law. Thus Lehman carried out these transactions on the books of its U.K. subsidiary. However, upon consolidation of this subsidiary with the parent firm, the effect was to improve Lehman's consolidated balance sheet as well.

In 2010, the IASB tightened up its accounting standards for repos, by amending IFRS 7 to require the firm to disclose any "disproportionate amount" of repo transactions entered into around the end of the year. In 2013, the FASB proposed to restrict sale accounting for repo transactions. When the transaction requires the firm to repurchase the transferred assets, or similar assets, at a fixed price, they are to be accounted for as secured borrowings. This will move the FASB standards into greater consistency with IASB.

Also in 2010, the U.K. Accountancy and Actuarial Disciplinary Board launched an 18-month investigation into Lehman's auditor's actions. It decided not to penalize the auditor.

Derecognition has attracted increasing attention following abuses leading up to the 2007–2008 market meltdowns. Many financial institutions securitized assets such as mortgages, student loans, and other receivables. The resulting ABSs were then derecognized by selling them to off balance sheet entities and other investors. In retrospect, much of this derecognition was questionable since sponsoring institutions credit-enhanced their transferred securities, thereby retaining some residual liability for the assets they had derecognized. Common forms of credit enhancement included the liquidity put and other explicit and implicit warranties.

The question for standard setters, then, is how much liability for transferred assets can the transferring firm retain and still be allowed to derecognize? Under IAS 39, which was in effect at the time of the meltdowns, "substantially all" the risks and rewards of ownership must be assumed by the transferee if the transfer is to be accounted for as a derecognition. Under FASB standards at the time, the transferring firm must "surrender control" of the transferred assets. As is apparent, these standards left an opening for firms to derecognize even though they retained some liability should the transferee suffer losses on the transferred assets, a liability that would not appear on the firms' balance sheets. In retrospect, this opening was wide enough to create the huge amounts of securities that had to be taken back by sponsoring institutions, as noted in Section 1.3.

Standard setters have now reconsidered derecognition. IFRS 9 allows derecognition when the firm transfers substantially all the risks and rewards of ownership of a financial asset, similar to the earlier IAS 39. However, IFRS 9 contains extensive provisions to try to prevent the off balance sheet abuses leading up to the 2007–2008 market meltdowns. For example, despite transferring the risks and rewards, the firm shall not derecognize a financial asset if it retains control of that asset, such as in repo transactions as described in Theory in Practice 7.3. When a financial asset *is* derecognized, the difference between the book value of the transferred asset and the consideration received is included in net income.

These derecognition requirements have been converged with FASB standards. Thus, U.S. derecognition standards (ASC 860-20) are basically similar to those of IFRS 9.

With respect to consolidation, IFRS 10 requires consolidation when one entity controls another. The question then is, how does one determine if control exists? IFRS 10 attempts to tighten up and clarify the concept of control. It defines control to exist when one entity has rights to the variable returns of another entity and can affect those returns through its power over that entity. Note the two dimensions to this definition—**power and risk**. Power exists when an entity has the power to direct the activities that significantly affect the returns of another. Risk exists because the controlling firm has a variable interest. That is, it shares in the profits and losses (and thus the risks) of the other.[16]

Normally, power exists when one entity has more than half of the voting rights in another. However, under IFRS 10, control can also exist with less than majority voting rights, providing, as just mentioned, that the controlling entity has power to direct the other entity's significant activities. For example, a firm may have a larger block of votes in another entity than any other party (e.g., other voting interests may be widely dispersed), and, in practice, this may be sufficient to control that entity's policies.

Subsequently, the FASB has also tightened the criteria for special purpose entity (SPE) consolidation, with criteria converged with those of IFRS 10 just described. Under ASC 810-10, control can be obtained when the sponsor has the power to direct the activities of the SPE that most significantly impact the SPE's economic performance, and has an obligation to absorb losses or receive benefits from the SPE. Such sponsors are regarded as the primary beneficiary, and thus must consolidate.

New standards also require substantial additional disclosures relating to consolidations and derecognition. IFRS 12 requires, for example, disclosure of "significant judgments" made in determining if the firm has control of another entity. It also requires disclosure of interest in and risks arising from joint arrangements with others and from "unconsolidated structured entities" such as SPEs and variable interest entities (VIEs).

IFRS 7 requires disclosure of assets that have been derecognized but in which the firm has a continuing involvement.

Notice that the power and risk criteria of IFRS 10 and related FASB standards avoid, or at least reduce, the possibility of abuse suffered by FIN 46 of the FASB, where consolidation was required if the sponsor was entitled to a majority of the returns of the SPE. As mentioned, IFRS and FASB standards require consolidation if the controlling entity has both power and risk. Under FIN 46, consolidation required only risk (i.e., entitlement to a majority of returns). As described in Section 1.3, this risk requirement was avoided by the creation of expected loss notes.

The implication of these additional derecognition, consolidation, and disclosure standards is that prior to the market meltdown, investors did not have enough information to fully evaluate off balance sheet activities.[17] Otherwise, why mandate new standards? We conclude that standard setters are working to improve reporting and disclosure, so that accounting practices that contributed to the meltdowns will not recur. However, the extent to which clever individuals devise ways to work around the new standards remains to be seen.

7.9 DERIVATIVE FINANCIAL INSTRUMENTS

7.9.1 Characteristics of Derivatives

Derivative instruments are contracts, the value of which depends on some **underlying** price, interest rate, foreign exchange rate, or other variable. A common example is an option, such as a call option, that gives the holder a right to buy, say, 100 shares of a firm's common stock for $20 each during, or at the end of, some specified period. The notional amount of the contract is $2,000, the number of shares involved times the exercise price. The underlying is the market price of the shares. The higher the market price, the higher the value of the option, other things equal. Other examples of derivatives include futures, forward and swap contracts, interest rate caps and floors, and fixed-rate loan commitments. Generally, these instruments convey a benefit to the holder if there is a favourable movement in the underlying. If the underlying moves unfavourably, there may or may not be a loss to the holder.

A characteristic of derivative instruments is that they generally require or permit settlement in cash—delivery of the asset associated with the underlying need not take place. Thus, the option contract above need not involve the holder actually buying the shares, but only receiving the value of the option in cash at the time of settlement. As another example, suppose a firm needs to borrow a large sum of money in six months' time. It is concerned that interest rates may rise over this period. It buys a bond futures contract giving it the right and obligation to sell government bonds at a specified price on a settlement date six months hence. If interest rates go up, the market value of the underlying bonds goes down, and the value of the futures contract rises to offset the higher borrowing cost. If this contract had to be settled physically, the firm would have to enter the bond market on the settlement date, buy the requisite amount of government bonds, and sell them to the party on the other side of the contract at the contract price to realize the value of the contract. With cash settlement, the firm can simply receive, or pay, cash equal to the value of the contract, thereby saving both sides the costs of physical buying and selling. The ability to settle derivative instruments in cash has contributed to the great increase in their use.

Derivative instruments may or may not require an initial net investment. For example, a firm with, say, an asset on which it receives a variable interest rate may wish to reduce risk by converting this cash flow to a fixed rate. It enters into an interest rate swap contract under which it transfers its variable cash flow to a counterparty in exchange for a fixed cash flow at an agreed interest rate. This requires no cash outlay. In other cases, if an initial cash outlay is required, it is for less than the notional amount of shares times the underlying. In the option example above, if the current share price is, say $18, the cost to the buyer of the option contract will certainly be less than $1,800, the amount that would be required to buy the shares outright. This is reasonable, because the holder of the option will participate in any price increase of the shares only during the option term, not necessarily over the life of the underlying. Other rights of ownership, such as dividends, are also excluded. In our bond futures contract example, the firm could also have protected itself by borrowing now to lock in the current interest rate. But this would require an additional interest cost for six months on the full amount needed.

These three examples illustrate the leverage aspect of derivatives—a lot of protection can be acquired at a relatively low cost. Leverage is another reason for the great increase in the use of derivatives. Of course, leverage is a two-edged sword. If managers use derivatives opportunistically to speculate on the underlying price rather than to manage risk, the amount that can be lost, for a low initial investment, can be very large indeed.[18]

This low initial investment characteristic of derivatives is a reason why accountants have found them difficult to deal with under historical cost accounting. Since there is little or no cost to account for, all or part of the contract is off balance sheet. Then it is difficult, or impossible, for investors to figure out the firm's derivative dealings and exposures from the financial statements proper. Accountants have responded to this difficulty by requiring supplemental disclosure. However, in view of behavioural characteristics such as limited attention, such disclosure may not be completely effective.

In this regard, the accounting for derivative instruments is moved substantially toward a measurement approach under IFRS 9, and ASC 815-10-10 in the United States. These standards require that all derivatives be measured at fair value for balance sheet purposes.

How does one fair-value a derivative? If a derivative is traded on a market that works reasonably well, fair value is measured by its market value. If it is not traded, models of derivative value can be used. To illustrate, consider our example of a call option to purchase 100 shares at $20, where the current market price is $18 per share. Assume that the option can be exercised at the end of two months, and that the firm will pay no dividends.

Assume also that the shares change their price only at the end of each month, and that these price changes follow a random walk (see Section 4.2.1). Specifically, assume that share price will increase each month by $2 with probability 0.5 or decrease by $2 with probability 0.5. This price behaviour is depicted in Figure 7.2.

Figure 7.2 A Simple Option Pricing Model

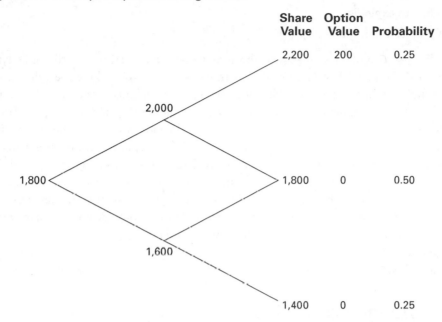

	Share Value	Option Value	Probability
	2,200	200	0.25
	2,000		
1,800	1,800	0	0.50
	1,600		
	1,400	0	0.25

Looking ahead from time 0 (now), at the end of the first month the 100 shares will have a market value of $2,000 with probability 0.5, and a value of $1,600 with probability 0.5. At the end of the second month (the expiry date of the option) their market value will be $2,200 with probability 0.25 (i.e., 0.5 × 0.5), $1,800 with probability 0.5 (0.25 + 0.25) or $1,400 with probability 0.25.

Now the option will be exercised only if the value of the shares is $2,200. Since the exercise price is $20 per share, or $2,000 in total, the value of the option is then $200. For the other two possible share values, the option will not be exercised so that its value is then $0.

The question then is, what is the fair value of the option at time 0, its date of issuance? If we assume that the risk-free interest rate in the economy is zero, this fair value is simply $200 × 0.25 = $50, the expected value of the option at maturity.[19]

Of course, our assumption that the share price changes only at the end of each month is unrealistic. In reality, many share prices change almost continuously. This can be modelled in our example by increasing the number of times that price changes in Figure 7.2 (but holding the time to expiration constant at two months). As the number of times the price changes goes to infinity (i.e., share price varies continuously) the fair value of the option is given by the famous Black-Scholes (1973) option pricing formula,[20] which values the option as a function of the following five variables:[21]

- Current market price of the share—$18
- Variability of return of the share

- Exercise price of option—$20
- Time to expiration
- Risk-free interest rate

The first two of these inputs to the formula are characteristics of the underlying share price. Thus, given values for the last three variables, we see how the value of the option derives from the current market price and return variability of the share. Given the exercise price, the higher the current share price the more valuable is the option. Given the current share price, the lower the exercise price the more valuable is the option. The greater the variability of the price, the more valuable is the option since there is a greater probability that the price will rise by the expiry date (there is also a greater probability that the price will fall but, in that case, the option need not be exercised). Since the Black-Scholes model, other models to value more complex derivative instruments have been developed. Thus, under appropriate conditions, models provide a way to implement the calculations required by fair value accounting standards.

Changes in fair value of derivative instruments are recognized in net income under IFRS 9 and ASC 815-10-35, except for certain hedging contracts, which we now discuss.

7.9.2 Hedge Accounting

Firms issue or acquire financial instruments for a variety of reasons. For example, they may manage their capital structure by means of convertible debt. They may manage their cash flows by issuing zero-coupon debt. Interest rate swaps and bond futures contracts may enable lower financing costs. Perhaps the major reason why firms deal in derivative financial instruments, however, is to help manage risk.[22] In this regard, derivatives help to reduce market incompleteness, since they enable the firm to purchase protection against risks that would otherwise be difficult to control. It is this risk management role of financial instruments that we concentrate on here.

The term "manage risk" is used advisedly. The goal of risk management is to produce a desired level of firm-specific risk, not necessarily to reduce it to zero. Zero risk may be too costly, or not even possible. Indeed, it may not even be desirable, since investors can reduce firm-specific risk for themselves through portfolio diversification.

A variety of derivative financial instruments has been developed to enable firms to better manage risks. Many of these risks are **price risks** (also called market risks), arising from changes in interest rates, commodity prices, and foreign exchange rates. Other risks arise from credit risk. The accounting for these financial instruments involves difficult issues of recognition and valuation.

In Section 7.5.3, we introduced the concept of a natural hedge, under which a changes in the fair value of certain non-derivative liabilities are offset by fair value changes of certain non-derivative assets. Since natural hedges are ultimately a management decision, any evaluation of a firm's susceptibility to risk should also consider natural hedging. In effect, hedging with derivatives takes over where natural hedging leaves off.

The Blackstone Group is a large U.S.-based investment company whose operations include investing in public companies and taking them private. A major component of its earnings from these investments derives from "carried interest." This is a management fee based on a preferential interest in the profits earned by unconsolidated companies in which it has invested. For example, a typical arrangement would be for Blackstone to receive an annual payment of 20% of a company's profits in excess of a hurdle rate of return on equity. These payments could continue for, say, five years, after which Blackstone would plan to sell its interest in the company.

Under historical cost accounting and the equity method of accounting for unconsolidated subsidiaries, carried interest fees would be recorded as revenue each period, if and as they are earned, with the offsetting debit to the investment account. Note, however, that Blackstone's preferential right to receive future fees conditional on a hurdle rate of return on the equity of a firm in which it has invested has option like characteristics, expiring in five years in the above example.

In 2007, Blackstone planned an initial public offering of its stock. In its preliminary prospectus, dated March 22, it revealed that for many of its unconsolidated investments it would use the fair value option to value future carried interest fees on a fair value basis, with the offsetting credit to current earnings. Presumably, an option pricing model, such as Black-Scholes, would be used to determine fair value. If this accounting had been applied in 2006, Blackstone indicated that its 2006 earnings would have increased by $595,205, relative to earnings reported using the equity method of accounting for its unconsolidated investments.

Note that fair value has to be re-evaluated each period. Blackstone pointed out that this could introduce considerable volatility into its reported earnings. It seemed that Blackstone was willing to bear this volatility in order to secure earlier revenue recognition.

Concerns about the reliability of Blackstone's proposed accounting soon appeared in the financial media, despite the greater relevance of this approach. A major source of concern was that since bought-out companies are typically taken private, the amount of public information about them is minimal. This makes it particularly difficult for the market to assess Blackstone's valuation, and puts considerable onus on Blackstone to fully disclose its assumptions in determining fair value. Concern was also expressed that Blackstone could bias its financial results by means of these assumptions.

In its final prospectus, dated June 25, Blackstone changed its mind, announcing that it would not use the fair value option. Instead, it would recognize carried interest quarterly based on its share of non-consolidated companies' quarterly earnings. Nevertheless, this episode illustrates the potential of the fair value option to implement the measurement approach.

In this regard, Guay and Kothari (2003) studied the hedging practices of a sample of U.S. non-financial firms. They found that, on average, the proportions of the sample firms' interest rate, foreign exchange, and commodity price risks hedged with derivatives is quite small relative to risk exposures. One explanation for this result is that managing risk by means of derivatives incurs costs. Also, as mentioned earlier, investors may not want the firm to fully protect against its risks, since they can diversify firm-specific risk themselves. Another explanation, not inconsistent with cost and diversification, is that natural hedging also provides risk protection, so that there is less need for the protection provided by derivatives.

There are different types of hedges. Derivative instruments designated as hedges of recognized assets and liabilities are called **fair value hedges**. The essence of a fair value hedge is that if a firm owns, say, a risky asset or liability, it can hedge this risk by acquiring a **hedging instrument**—some other asset or liability whose value moves in the direction opposite to that of the **hedged item**. Accounting for hedges of transactions that take place entirely within the current period is relatively straightforward. The gain or loss on the hedged item and the loss or gain on the hedging instrument can both be recorded in current net income, which then includes a realized loss or gain only to the extent the hedge is not completely effective. Hedges may not be completely effective because there may not exist a hedging instrument that will completely offset the hedged item's gain or loss. For example, a bank may have trouble finding a perfect hedge for the risk of changing interest rates on its deposit liabilities. The risk resulting from the absence of a perfectly effective hedge is called **basis risk**.

Frequently, however, hedging transactions do not take place entirely within the current period. For example, suppose that during the year a firm, concerned that selling prices might decline, hedges the price risk on its inventory by entering into a forward contract to sell the inventory at its current market price. Thus, the inventory is the hedged item and the forward contract is the hedging instrument. Suppose that, at year-end, the inventory is still on hand and its market price has fallen. As a result, the fair value of the forward contract has risen.

Under IFRS 9 and ASC 815-25, fair value hedges are valued at fair value, with gains and losses resulting from changes in fair value generally included in current net income. The related loss or gain on the hedged item is then also included in current net income. Thus, our firm writes its inventory down to market value and writes the forward contract up, so that net income is affected only to the extent that the hedge is not completely effective. On the balance sheet, the value of the forward contract is added to the inventory. In effect, the firm can avoid the effect on net income of lower-of-cost-or-market and, more generally, impairment tests and other fair value changes, by appropriate hedging strategy.

Firms also may hedge *anticipated* transactions, providing the value of the anticipated transaction can be reliably measured and the transaction is "highly probable." For example, the firm may wish to reduce risk arising from price changes of its future production. Such contracts are called **cash flow hedges**. Firms engage in cash flow hedging for a variety of reasons. Perhaps the most important of these is that reducing the riskiness of future cash flows helps to ensure cash availability for future investment projects, where these are to be financed internally.

Under IFRS 9 and ASC 815-30, cash flow hedging instruments are also fair-valued, with unrealized gains and losses included in other comprehensive income until the hedged transactions affect net income. Then, any accumulated gain or loss is transferred into net income for that period. For example, an oil and gas producer may wish to hedge next period's sales. These cash receipts are risky because of fluctuations in oil and gas prices and, if the oil and gas are sold in foreign markets, fluctuations in foreign exchange rates. Including unrealized gains and losses on cash flow hedges in other comprehensive income reduces mismatch and resulting net income volatility by delaying their effect on net income until the next period, when the anticipated cash flows are realized.[23]

Hedge accounting for fair value and cash flow hedges is beneficial to the firm, since the net income volatility and mismatch resulting from the IFRS 9 requirement that all derivatives be fair valued is reduced. High net income volatility has particularly adverse effects on firms with high debt loads by increasing the probability of financial distress.

As noted above, hedge accounting benefits include deferring recognition of unrealized loss on hedging instruments to other comprehensive income until the hedged transaction takes place (cash flow hedge), and offsetting unrealized gains or losses on the derivative by fair-valuing the hedged item (fair value hedge). In both cases, net income volatility is reduced.

However, the standards lay down a formal procedure if these benefits are to be attained. First, the financial instrument must be eligible for hedging. Most derivatives, and non-derivative financial assets and liabilities valued at fair value, are eligible to be hedging instruments, with gains and losses included in net income. Second, eligible instruments must be **designated** as a hedge at the inception of the hedge, the hedged item identified, and the nature of the risk being hedged documented. Management's documentation should be consistent with the firm's business model; that is, consistent with its established risk management objective and strategy. The rationale is that reported net income would lose reliability if management had the discretion to change its intent and designate a hedging instrument at any time it wanted. For example, faced with a major loss on derivatives held as a speculation, management might want to retroactively designate them as cash flow hedges of forecasted transactions. Then the loss could be excluded from net income, thereby at least delaying its impact.

Another criterion for designation as a hedge is that the derivative instrument must be effective in offsetting changes in the fair value of the hedged item. IFRS 9 and ASC 815 do not lay down a specific method for determining effectiveness. However, hedge effectiveness essentially means that there is a high negative correlation between the fair values of the hedging instrument and the hedged item.[24]

IFRS 7 requires extensive supplementary disclosure of the firm's dealings in derivatives. These include a complete description of the types of hedges the firm has entered into, the financial instruments designated as hedging instruments and their fair values, and the nature of the risks that are hedged.

7.10 CONCLUSIONS ON ACCOUNTING FOR FINANCIAL INSTRUMENTS

Fair value accounting for financial instruments is a prominent example of standard setters' movement toward fair value accounting. However, fair value accounting for financial instruments came under considerable pressure following the 2007–2008 market meltdowns, due to concerns about huge writeoffs of financial assets triggered by falling market prices and, in many cases, lack of existence of prices due to inactive markets. Existing fair value accounting standards were viewed as too complex to cope with the resulting pressures. Standard setters were forced to revise standards to allow increased usage of value in use and amortized cost accounting for financial instruments that the firm intends to hold to maturity. However, this creates concerns about reliability of the resulting valuations. In addition, standard setters have revised standards on derecognition, consolidation, derivatives, and disclosure, since weaknesses in these standards contributed to the market meltdowns in the first place.

7.11 ACCOUNTING FOR INTANGIBLES

7.11.1 Introduction

Intangible assets are capital assets that do not have physical substance, such as patents, trademarks, franchises, good workforce, location, restructurings, information technology, Internet site names, and, more generally, goodwill.

Some intangibles are accounted for much like property, plant, and equipment. If they are purchased or self-developed with reasonable certainty of future net benefits, they are valued at cost and amortized over their useful lives. If they are acquired in a business combination and fair value can be determined reliably, their cost is equal to their fair value at acquisition. Such intangibles are subject to an impairment test. An impairment writedown is required under IAS 36 if the asset's recoverable amount is less than book value, where the recoverable amount is the greater of fair value (net of costs to sell) and value in use. Intangible assets are important assets for many firms and, for some firms, intangibles compose most of firm value. However, their values, and even their costs, are often difficult to establish reliably, particularly if they are self-developed. This is because the costs of intangibles may be spread over many years and, as these costs are incurred, it may not be known whether they will ever produce future net benefits. An example is the costs of R&D, which can lead to many of the intangibles mentioned above. Since it is so difficult to predict future payoffs from these costs, it is not reliably known whether they will be recovered, let alone what their fair value is. As a result, IAS 38 requires that research costs not appear on the balance sheet at all—instead, they are charged to expense as incurred. Costs of developing a product or process resulting from research may be capitalized if the results of the research are technically and commercially feasible and the costs can be measured reliably. In the United States, ASC 730-10-05 requires that R&D costs be written off in the year in which they are incurred. Consequently, self-developed intangibles resulting from the firm's research will usually not appear on the balance sheet at all under U.S. GAAP.

However, it is important to realize that intangibles are "there" even if they are not on the balance sheet. Instead, due to recognition lag, they appear through the income statement. That is, since historical cost accounting waits until value is realized as sales and earnings, the income statement contains the current "installment" of the value of intangibles. If these installments are positive, the firm has goodwill.[25] That is, goodwill exists if the firm earns more than its cost of capital on its net assets, including any separately identified intangibles. This mirrors exactly our procedure in Section 6.10.3, where Canadian Tire's unrecorded goodwill was calculated as the present value of expected future abnormal earnings.

The question then is, should goodwill remain off the balance sheet, with the implication that the income statement reports on it as realized, or should goodwill's fair value be measured and reported on the balance sheet? Reporting the fair value of goodwill has potential for increased decision usefulness, since this may reveal management's inside information about future expected earning power (which is what creates the goodwill), and it is management that has the best information about what this earning power is. But reporting the fair value of goodwill creates serious problems of reliability.

At this point, it is helpful to distinguish between self-developed goodwill and purchased goodwill. We first consider purchased goodwill.

7.11.2 Accounting for Purchased Goodwill

When one firm acquires another in a business combination, the **purchase method** of accounting for the transaction requires that the tangible and identifiable intangible assets and the liabilities of the acquired company be generally valued at their fair values for purposes of the consolidated financial statements. Goodwill is then the difference between the net amount of these fair values and the total purchase price paid by the acquiring company. We illustrate the traditional accounting for purchased goodwill with an example.

Example 7.1
Accounting For Purchased Goodwill

JDN Ltd. is a rapidly expanding "hi-tech" firm. At January 1, 2015, it had 100 shares outstanding, trading at $10. Assume that its balance sheet was as follows:

JDN Ltd. Balance Sheet January 1, 2015			
Capital Assets	$500	Liabilities	$100
		Shareholders' Equity	400
	$500		$500

S Ltd. is also growing rapidly, and is in a business similar to that of JDN. Its balance sheet at January 1, 2015, was as follows:

S Ltd.
Balance Sheet
January 1, 2015

Capital Assets	$300	Liabilities	$140
		Shareholders' Equity	160
	$300		$300

On January 1, 2015, JDN purchases all the 160 outstanding shares of S Ltd. in exchange for 40 shares of JDN's stock valued at $10 each, for a total purchase price of $400. The balance sheet of JDN immediately after the acquisition was:

JDN Ltd.
Balance Sheet (Post-Acquisition)
January 1, 2015

Capital Assets, excluding		Liabilities	$100
Investment in S	$500		
Investment in S	400	Shareholders' Equity	800
	$900		$900

As mentioned, the identifiable assets and liabilities of the purchased company must be valued at their fair values for purposes of preparing a consolidated balance sheet, with any excess of the purchase price over net fair value reflected as goodwill. Assume that at the date of acquisition the fair value of S Ltd.'s capital assets was estimated as $340, and its liabilities as $140. The consolidated balance sheet of JDN and its wholly owned subsidiary S Ltd. at date of acquisition was thus:

JDN Ltd. and Subsidiary
Consolidated Balance Sheet
January 1, 2015

Capital Assets,		Liabilities	$ 240
excluding goodwill	$ 840		
Goodwill	200	Shareholders' Equity	800
	$1040		$1040

Goodwill is determined as the amount paid for S Ltd., $400, less the fair value of net assets acquired, $200.

Traditionally, this goodwill was amortized over its useful life, consistent with the matching concept of historical cost accounting. Management strongly complained about goodwill amortization, however, since it forced down consolidated net income following the acquisition, making it more difficult to convince investors that the acquisition was a successful business strategy. Obviously, management has an incentive to demonstrate, through increased reported earnings, its good business judgment in entering into a business combination.

In response, many managers attempted to circumvent goodwill amortization. One approach was to adopt **pooling of interests** accounting, under which the combination was formally regarded as a merger of equals. Under this accounting, the balance sheets of the merged entities were simply added together. Since no new purchased goodwill was recognized, there was nothing to amortize. Many firms abused this accounting, however, and numerous combinations were accounted for as poolings that did not meet the merger of equals criterion. Pooling of interests was eliminated in the United States by SFAS 141 in 2001 and internationally by IFRS 3 in 2004.

Another approach adopted by management to work around goodwill amortization was to emphasize **pro-forma income** (also called cash income[26] and a variety of other terms), where pro-forma income is net income before goodwill amortization, restructuring charges, and a variety of other items selected by management. Under this tactic, the GAAP income statement itself is not affected. However, pro-forma income is emphasized in earnings announcements, messages to shareholders, MD&A, etc. In this way, management seeks to convince investors that goodwill amortization and other selected items do not matter, in the sense that they are not relevant to the evaluation of the performance of the consolidated entity.

A criticism of pro-forma income was that to the extent management succeeded in convincing investors that this is a better profit measure than GAAP net income, there was less discipline for managers to avoid overpaying in business acquisitions. The excessive goodwill amortization that results from overpaying was simply ignored. Another criticism is that pro-forma earnings may mislead investors, since there are few rules to determine just what items are excluded from GAAP income. This is of particular concern if securities markets are not fully efficient.

Theory in Practice 7.5

As an illustration of pro-forma income, consider the 2000 *Annual Report* of Toronto-Dominion Bank (TD Bank). In its MD&A, TD Bank reported operating cash basis net income of $2,018, $1,472, and $1,183 (all dollar amounts in millions) for 2000, 1999, and 1998, respectively, explaining that these amounts exclude items that are not "part of our normal operations." The bank's reported GAAP net incomes for these three years as per its consolidated income statement were $1,025, $2,981, and $1,138, respectively. For 2000, the difference is due to the after-tax

Cont . . .

effects of $1,203 amortization of goodwill aris- ing from TD Bank's acquisition of Canada Trust in that year, plus $475 of restructuring costs from the same transaction. Clearly, the two earnings sequences give different impressions of TD Bank's operations.

As another illustration, JDS Uniphase Corporation reported a preliminary GAAP net loss for its fiscal year ended June 30, 2001, of $50.558 billion, reportedly the largest loss ever incurred by a North American corporation to that time. This loss included a writedown of pur- chased goodwill of $44.774 billion,[27] in addition to amortization of remaining purchased good- will of $5.475 billion. Nevertheless, in a news announcement accompanying the release of its 2001 preliminary loss, JDS reported a pro-forma profit of $67.4 million.

In response to tactics such as these, standard setters eliminated the amortization of purchased goodwill. This was accomplished by SFAS 142 in 2001 and, under interna- tional standards, by IAS 36 in 2004. These standards constitute a substantial movement toward the measurement approach. Specifically, goodwill is retained on the consolidated balance sheet at its value established at the time of purchase, unless there is evidence of impairment, in which case an impairment test is applied to write goodwill down to its cur- rent value. A goodwill writedown may not be reversed if fair value subsequently increases.

Presumably, elimination of goodwill amortization reduces managers' incentive to emphasize pro-forma income. However, subsequent research suggests that while the aver- age difference between pro-forma and GAAP earnings has declined, the number of firms reporting pro-forma earnings has not (Heflin and Hsu, 2008).

Regardless of its effect on pro-forma reporting, eliminating amortization does not necessarily prevent opportunistic manager behaviour with respect to goodwill, since initial goodwill valuation, and the timing and amount of impairment test writedowns, require judgment. Thus, some ability of management to manage purchased goodwill remains. Concerns such as these are increased because of a great increase over recent years in mergers and acquisitions, with resulting increases in purchased goodwill. In this regard, Muller, Neamtiu, and Riedl (MNR; 2012) reported that during the period 2002–2007 in the United States, the number of firms with purchased goodwill increased by over 50%, with an average annual goodwill growth rate of 17%, over the period. Based on a sample of U.S. firms reporting goodwill impairment writedowns during 2002–2007, MNR found net insider selling by senior managers during a period extending from two years to six months before their firm reported the writedown. The incidence of this selling significantly exceeded that of a control sample of firms that did not report a goodwill writedown. The authors argued that it is not unreasonable for managers to know about impending impair- ment writedowns as much as two years before the impairment writedown is reported. They attributed this delay to goodwill impairment tests usually conducted only annually, plus managers' ability to delay the timing of impairment recognition. This finding is consistent with managers exploiting their inside information about the impending writedown. NMT did not find excess insider selling during the six-month period immediately prior to the writedown, which they attributed to insiders' concerns about legal liability.

7.11.3 Self-Developed Goodwill

Unlike purchased goodwill, no readily identifiable transactions exist to determine the cost of self-developed goodwill. Consequently, costs that may create goodwill, such as R&D, are mostly written off as incurred. Indeed, IAS 38 prohibits the capitalization of internally generated goodwill. As mentioned, any internally generated goodwill shows up instead as abnormal earnings in subsequent income statements. This recognition lag is a major reason why share price responds to earnings announcements, as documented in Chapter 5. The market watches net income carefully for clues as to future earning power.

Nevertheless, the proportion of abnormal share return explained by net income is low, and may be declining over time, as discussed in Section 6.9. There, we outlined the study of Lev and Zarowin (LZ; 1999), who found declining value relevance of earnings over time. Here, we consider LZ's investigation into reasons for this falling market share. They argued that this is due primarily to a failure to account properly for self-developed intangibles.

LZ's argument is easy to see. Consider a firm's current R&D expenditures. Since they are expensed, these costs force reported net income down. However, an efficient market will not penalize the firm for the resulting lower reported earnings to the extent it expects positive results from the R&D, and may even reward it with a higher stock price. Obviously, if the firm's share price responds positively to costs that force current net income down, this will show up as a low association between abnormal share return and net income, and a low, possibly negative, earnings response coefficient (ERC). Furthermore, LZ suggest, most firms' expenditures on self-developed intangibles increase over time, driven by deregulation, innovation, and competition. If so, the low association intensifies. In effect, current accounting for R&D results in a mismatch of the costs of intangibles with the revenues generated by those intangibles. These effects, LZ argued, are a prime contributor to low and declining R^2s and ERCs.

To investigate this argument, LZ examined a sample of U.S. firms with high research intensity—that is, firms whose research costs have grown at an increasing rate. While research is only one intangible, they focused on it on grounds that research is a major contributor to self-developed goodwill. LZ found a significantly lower association between share returns and reported earnings for this sample than for a second sample of firms with low research intensity, consistent with their argument.

The question then is, what might be done to improve the accounting for intangibles? One suggestion made by LZ is for a type of successful efforts accounting for R&D. They proposed that the accumulated costs of an R&D project be capitalized if the project passes a test, such as a working model or a successful clinical trial. LZ argued that while capitalization at this point reduces reliability, it provides a reasonable tradeoff with relevance, and reveals inside information to the market about the firm's R&D efforts. The capitalized costs would then be amortized over their estimated useful life. This proposal can be regarded as an extension of IAS 38, which, as mentioned above, allows development costs to be capitalized once a research project attains technical and financial feasibility.

Clearly, standard setters' reluctance to capitalize research costs is due to concerns about reliability. However, an argument is made by Kanodia, Singh, and Spero (KSS; 2005) that maximizing the value to investors and society of reporting capitalized R&D costs may require some degree of unreliability.

To see KSS's argument, suppose that, contrary to present standards but consistent with LZ's suggestion, the firm capitalizes the costs of research projects as they are expected to be successful, and writes off the costs of unsuccessful projects currently. Assume initially that this separation of successful and unsuccessful R&D is completely reliable. Thus, the market knows exactly the cost of successful R&D.

There are two components of the market's reaction to these successful R&D costs. First, it will react positively to the increased expected profits these costs create. However, the amount invested in R&D also has a signalling effect. That is, the greater the firm's research potential (driven by competent research personnel, superior ability to identify promising research areas, and the expected profitability of future patents resulting from the research), the more it will invest in R&D. While the market will not know the details of this research potential (this is inside information of management), it interprets the amount spent on R&D as a signal of what this research potential is. This creates a second component of the market reaction to R&D cost—the more the firm spends, the higher its potential must be. For both of these reasons, the higher is the capitalized R&D cost, the more the market will bid up the price of the firm's shares.

Now, consider this scenario from management's standpoint. Perceiving the "extra" market reaction to its R&D, management will overinvest in R&D. More precisely, it will push its R&D investment beyond the point where marginal costs equal marginal benefits, thereby reducing future profitability.

Investors, having purchased shares at inflated prices, will soon realize that the firm is not as profitable as they thought, due to the overinvestment in R&D. Thus, they will lower their expectations of R&D profitability. The share price will fall until it reflects actual profitability. However, the firm's R&D overinvestment remains, since these costs have already been incurred. This outcome is called a **fully revealing signalling equilibrium** (Spence, 1974). Firms signal their profitability by their choice of investment level. It is called fully revealing because in a rational expectations equilibrium firms' share prices are consistent with their actual levels of profitability.

Such an outcome is unfortunate, however. Overinvestment is hardly desirable from shareholders' or society's perspective. Notice that it occurs here as a result of the complete reliability of reporting of R&D costs.

Now consider a more realistic scenario, where reporting is not completely reliable. Specifically, some of the firm's capitalized R&D costs will not be profitable, and some written-off costs may be profitable after all.

From an investor's standpoint, lack of knowledge of R&D profitability creates estimation risk.[28] As a result, investors do not bid up the firm's share price in response to reported R&D as much as under complete reliability. Consequently, the firm's incentive to overinvest is reduced. KSS show that as the information asymmetry between shareholders and manager about R&D profitability increases (the manager's inside information advantage about R&D is likely to be quite high) the lower should be reliability if overinvestment in R&D is to be discouraged. We may conclude that, in theory, considerable unreliability in the reporting of R&D costs can be tolerated in situations where management has an incentive to over invest, supporting LZ's suggestion.

7.11.4 The Clean Surplus Model Revisited

Another approach to valuing self-developed goodwill is to use the clean surplus model discussed in Section 6.10. Recall that our valuation of the share value of Canadian Tire Corporation, Limited in Section 6.10.3 resulted in a goodwill estimate of $2,207 million. Perhaps this amount could be formally incorporated into the financial statements as the fair value of Canadian Tire's self-developed goodwill. While we discussed at the time some of the reliability issues surrounding this estimate, if the estimate were to be prepared by management it would convey relevant information about Canadian Tire's expected future earning power.[29]

Alternatively, the clean surplus goodwill calculation could possibly serve as an impairment test for purchased goodwill. If, in the case of Canadian Tire, the book value of its purchased goodwill exceeds $2,207 million, this suggests that purchased goodwill should be written down so as not to exceed this value.[30] Such a procedure, however, clouds the distinction between purchased and self-developed goodwill. For example, the purchased goodwill might be worthless, in which case it should be written down to zero, and the $2,207 million would then be entirely self-developed.[31]

7.11.5 Summary

Accounting for intangibles is the ultimate test of the measurement approach. Application of the measurement approach to accounting for goodwill creates severe reliability problems. These problems may be somewhat mitigated for purchased goodwill, since at least an estimated cost figure is available. Yet, even for purchased goodwill, amortization was essentially arbitrary due to the difficulty of establishing useful life. Furthermore, management disliked being charged for goodwill amortization and took steps to avoid it. Standard setters have moved toward a measurement approach to purchased goodwill by introducing standards to write it down only if there is evidence of impairment. The clean surplus model may provide a framework to structure the estimation of the fair value of goodwill.

When goodwill is self-developed, further reliability problems arise, and standard setters usually react by requiring immediate expensing of the costs of intangibles that underlie self-developed goodwill. However, this creates a mismatch between costs and revenues, and, arguably, is the root cause of low value relevance of reported earnings. A suggestion to improve the accounting for self-developed goodwill is capitalization and amortization of successful research projects.

7.12 REPORTING ON RISK

7.12.1 Beta Risk

The theory underlying the CAPM suggests (Section 4.5) that a stock's beta is the sole firm-specific risk measure for a rational investor's diversified portfolio. We discussed this theory in Section 6.2.3, concluding that despite evidence that other measures may also explain share price, beta remains as an important risk concept.

The usual way to estimate beta is by means of a regression analysis based on the market model. However, as noted in Section 6.2.3, beta is subject to estimation risk, particularly if beta is not stationary. Financial statement information may help here, since beta and certain financial-statement-based risk measures are correlated. Furthermore, these measures can indicate the direction and magnitude of a change in beta sooner than the market model, which would require several periods of new data for reestimation.

Beaver, Kettler, and Scholes (BKS; 1970) were the first to examine formally the relationship between beta and financial-statement-based risk measures. For a sample of 307 New York Stock Exchange firms over two time periods, 1947–1956 and 1957–1965, they used a market model regression analysis to estimate betas for their sample firms for each time period. Then they calculated various financial-statement-based risk measures for the same periods. The correlations between three of these risk measures and betas are shown in Table 7.1.

Dividend payout is the ratio of common share cash dividends to net income. Leverage is the ratio of senior debt securities to total assets. Earnings variability is the standard deviation of the firm's price–earnings ratio over the period.

Table 7.1 Correlation Coefficients Between Accounting Risk Measures and Beta, for Five-Security Portfolios

Accounting Risk Measures	Period 1 1947–56	Period 2 1957–65
Dividend payout	−0.79	−0.50
Leverage	0.41	0.48
Earnings variability	0.90	0.82

Source: Based on BKS, Table 5. Reprinted by permission of the American Accounting Association.

Notice that the signs of the correlations are what we would expect (for example, the higher the dividend payout, the lower the risk, since a firm facing significant risks would likely retain its earnings for protection rather than pay them out) and that most of the correlations are quite high. Furthermore, there is reasonable consistency between periods 1 and 2. Indeed, BKS reported that their most highly correlated accounting variable was a better predictor of a stock's beta than its current beta, supporting our suggestion above that accounting-based risk measures may provide timely indications of shifts in beta.

These correlation results may seem surprising since, *a priori*, it is not obvious why a market-based risk measure has anything to do with accounting variables. However, Hamada (1972) showed that, under ideal conditions, there is a direct relationship between the debt–equity ratio and the beta. Lev (1974) showed a direct relationship, also under ideal conditions, between operating leverage and beta (operating leverage is the ratio of fixed to variable operating costs). BKS's results suggest that these relationships carry over at least in part to non-ideal conditions.

The rationale for these results is not hard to see. The higher a firm's financial and operating leverage, the more it will benefit if business conditions improve and suffer if they deteriorate, since high leverage means a high proportion of fixed costs in the firm's cost structure. Then, earnings are highly affected by changes in the level of activity. The market will be aware of this, and the higher the leverage the more it will bid up share price when business conditions improve, and vice versa. The stock market index will also rise and fall with business conditions. Since beta measures how strongly the firm's share price varies as the market varies, the greater the leverage the higher is beta.

BKS' findings have financial reporting implications. Hamada's study implies that off balance sheet liabilities should be brought onto the balance sheet at current value. Failure to consolidate off balance sheet entities leading up to the 2007–2008 market meltdowns (Section 1.3) and the misuse of repo transactions (Theory in Practice 7.3) are prominent examples of missing liabilities, which new standards described in Section 7.8 are trying to prevent. By including all liabilities on the balance sheet, measurement of the debt component of the debt–equity ratio is improved.

Lev's study implies that firms should separate fixed and variable operating costs, if investors are to infer beta from the financial statements. Surprisingly, financial reporting seems of little help here. Indeed, Ryan (1997) pointed out that absorption cost accounting, which includes fixed operating costs in inventory, actually increases the difficulty of evaluating operating leverage.

7.12.2 Why Do Firms Manage Firm-Specific Risk?

While the BKS results are encouraging, they do not answer the questions of why firms manage their *firm-specific* risk, and why accounting standards require disclosures of firm-specific risks and how they are managed. In other words, if investors diversify their portfolios, is information about firm-specific risk decision useful, since investors can manage this risk for themselves? However, several reasons for managing and reporting on firm-specific risk can be suggested:

- Reporting on the firm's risk management strategies may reduce investor concerns about estimation risk resulting from adverse selection. In this regard, refer to the risk disclosures in Canadian Tire Corp.'s MD&A reproduced in Section 3.6.3, and note that the company gives extensive discussion of how it controls its various risks.

- Firms that are planning large capital expenditures may wish to ensure cash is available when needed. This reason applies particularly to firms that are growing rapidly and to firms that find it expensive to raise external capital. Risk management, such as by hedging, can reduce cash flow risk.

- Managers may use derivatives to speculate, a possibility raised in Section 7.9.2. This is a form of risk management that increases risk rather than reduces it. It may be difficult for investors to diversify speculation risk, since losses can be very large and can threaten the existence of the firm itself. Then, full disclosure of the firm's risk management strategies, the fair values of its various derivatives, and their unrealized gains and losses, is desirable.

- As argued in Sections 6.11 and 6.12, conservative accounting can help reduce legal liability arising from firm losses. However, hedging to manage risk may prevent losses from arising in the first place.

- Yet another reason, to be discussed in Section 10.4.3, is that risk-averse managers whose compensation is based on earnings may use derivatives to reduce the volatility of their compensation.

7.12.3 Stock Market Reaction to Other Risks

In the previous section, we suggested several reasons why firms may wish to manage and report on firm-specific risk despite the theory of diversification, under which investors can reduce or eliminate firm-specific risk. We have already seen in Section 3.6 that MD&A requires a discussion of risks and uncertainties, particularly with respect to downside risk. As pointed out in Section 3.7.1, the Conceptual Framework suggests that accountants' responsibility for full disclosure extends to management's explanations. Since much of MD&A relates to risk management, we may see increasing attention by standard setters to risk reporting in MD&A.

Many of the supplemental disclosures required by IFRS 7 and related FASB standards are risk related. These disclosures include supplementary information about exposures to market, liquidity, and credit risks, and about the firm's risk management policies.

These various motivations for reporting on risk raise the question, does the stock market react to firm risks other than beta? Much of the empirical research in this area relates to interest rate risk of financial institutions. For such firms, financial assets and liabilities comprise most of book value, and it is to financial assets and liabilities that many of the risk-related disclosure standards relate.

Hodder, Hopkins, and Whalen (HHW; 2006) studied interest rate risk for a sample of U.S. banks over the period 1996–2004. They first calculated what they called full fair value (FFV) income for each bank. This earnings measure adds to net income the unrealized gains and losses on all of a bank's financial assets and liabilities. Sources of information for their FFV calculations include other comprehensive income (which reports unrealized gains and losses on certain investments and cash flow hedges), supplementary disclosures, and various filings with regulatory authorities.

HHW then calculated the variance of FFV income. Think of FFV volatility as a measure of a bank's unhedged interest rate risk. HHW found that over their sample period the volatility of FFV income greatly exceeded that of comprehensive income for most of their sample banks. This finding implies that comprehensive income contains only a relatively small amount of information about a bank's interest rate risk. Other sources of interest rate risk not reported on by other comprehensive income include deposit liabilities (not fair valued) and held-to-maturity securities (written down if current value declines, but not subsequently written up under U.S. GAAP). The finding also implies, as in earlier studies, that banks do not fully hedge their interest rate risk (if they did, the volatility of FFV would be much lower, and less than that of comprehensive income).

HHW also found that the additional volatility of FFV income was negatively related to share price, and positively related to cost of capital, after controlling for other factors affecting interest rate risk such as maturity gap, again suggesting that investors are sensitive to firm-specific risk. Indeed, these findings suggest that increased use of fair value accounting, if reasonably reliable, would be decision useful, since it could help investors to better evaluate firm risk.

In this regard, Ahmed, Kilic, and Lobo (AKL; 2011) studied the effects of SFAS 133 (the FASB standard on derivatives in effect at the time, now ASC 815) on the riskiness of a sample of 141 U.S. banks during two years before and two years after its 1998 implementation (SFAS 133 required all derivatives to be fair valued). AKL measured a bank's risk by the interest rate it paid on its bonds (after controlling for other factors affecting interest rate). With respect to derivatives designated as hedges under SFAS 133, the authors reported a significantly greater negative association between extent of hedging and interest rates paid by banks on their bonds post-SFAS 133 relative to pre-SFAS 133. They attributed this reduction in banks' cost of debt capital to increased confidence by bond investors in hedge accounting, resulting from better hedge documentation from SFAS 133's designation requirements, and increased hedge effectiveness.

In sum, evidence of market response to interest rate risk suggests that this risk is not fully hedged by banks and that equity and bond investors do not, or cannot, fully diversify the risk that remains. It does seem, however, that SFAS 133 improved risk reporting. Furthermore, comprehensive income seems ineffective relative to FFV income in reporting on interest rate risk, implying that increased adoption of a measurement approach could convey useful risk information.

We would expect that if other sources of risk than beta were to be useful for investors, it would be for interest rate risk of financial institutions. However, firms in other industries also face price risks, raising the question of whether the market also responds to these. Wong (2000) examined the foreign exchange risk of a sample of 145 manufacturing firms during the period 1994–1996. He found that, for some firms in his sample, share price was sensitive to foreign currency exposure, implying that firms and investors do not fully diversify foreign exchange risk. However, neither the fair value nor the notional amount of firms' foreign exchange derivatives positions explained the magnitude of the sensitivity. One possible explanation is that investors sufficiently diversify their holdings so that they are not sensitive to firms' foreign exchange risks. However, Wong attributed the lack of results to shortcomings of hedging disclosures in annual reports. He recommended more disaggregated disclosures in annual reports of notional amounts, fair values, long and short positions, and maturities by class of instrument. Much of this disclosure is now required.

7.12.4 A Measurement Approach to Risk Reporting

The disclosures discussed in the previous section are primarily oriented to qualitative risk disclosures—they involve the communication of information to help investors to make their own risk evaluations. Much of this risk information is reported as part of MD&A—see our discussion of Canadian Tire's risk disclosures in Section 3.6.3. However, like valuations of assets and liabilities, reporting on risk is also moving toward increased measurement.

Two quantitative measurement techniques are of interest. The first is **sensitivity analysis**, showing the impact on earnings, cash flows, or fair values of financial instruments resulting from changes in price risks—that is, risks arising from possible changes in relevant commodity prices, interest rates, and foreign exchange rates. The second is **value at risk**, being the loss in earnings, cash flows, or fair values resulting from future price changes sufficiently large that they have a specified low probability of occurring. Under IFRS 7, firms are required to report at least one of these measures.

In these risk measures, the firm, rather than investors, prepares the quantitative risk assessments. We would expect that it is the firm that has the most accurate estimates of its own risks. Hence, these latter two risk measures have potential for decision usefulness. Table 7.2 shows a sensitivity disclosure from the 2012 MD&A of Husky Energy Inc. The table shows the impact on earnings of relevant commodity and foreign exchange rate risks.

Table 7.2 shows the effects on Husky's pre-tax earnings and net earnings from changes in certain key variables for 2012. The table shows what the effect would have been on 2012 financial results had the indicated variable increased by the notional amount.

Note that the sensitivities exclude effects of fair value accounting on earnings (Note 1). Presumably, the company believes that unrealized gains and losses resulting

Table 7.2 Husky Energy Inc., Sensitivity Analysis, 2012

Sensitivity Analysis	2012 Average	Increase	Effect on Pre-tax Earnings[1]		Effect on Net Earnings[1]	
			($ millions)	($/share)[2]	($ millions)	($/share)[2]
WTI benchmark crude oil price[3][4]	94.21	U.S.$1.00/bbl	66	0.07	49	0.05
NYMEX benchmark natural gas price[5]	2.79	U.S. $0.20/mmbtu	24	0.02	18	0.02
WTI/Lloyd crude blend differential[6]	62.89	U.S.$1.00/bbl	(16)	(0.02)	(12)	(0.01)
Canadian light oil margins	0.044	Cdn $0.005/litre	16	0.02	12	0.01
Asphalt margins	22.90	Cdn$1.00/bbl	9	0.01	7	0.01
New York Harbor 3:2:1 crack speed[7]	31.36	U.S.$1.00/bbl	53	0.05	34	0.03
Exchange rate (U.S. $ per Cdn $)[3][8]	1.001	U.S. $0.01	(55)	(0.06)	(41)	(0.04)

[1]*Excludes mark to market accounting impacts.*
[2]*Based on 982.2 million common shares outstanding as of December 31, 2012.*
[3]*Does not include gains or losses on inventory.*
[4]*Includes impacts related to Brent-based production.*
[5]*Includes impact of natural gas consumption.*
[6]*Excludes impact on asphalt operations.*
[7]*Relates to U.S. Refining & Marketing.*
[8]*Assumes no foreign exchange gains or losses on U.S. dollar denominated long-term debt and other monetary items, including cash balances.*

Source: Reprinted by permission of Husky Energy Inc.

from mark-to-market accounting are not useful for risk evaluation. Also, it seems that sensitivities exclude the effects of hedging. Thus, according to Table 2, Notes 3 and 8, gains and losses on inventories and foreign exchange rate changes are excluded. This exclusion is reasonable to the extent that these risks are substantially hedged. Lack of additional information about hedging is probably because the extent of Husky's risk management activities varies over time, although it is also possible that the company does not want to reveal sensitive information about hedging strategies.

Sensitivity estimates are subject to relevant range problems. Thus, if the price of oil were to change by, say, $3/bbl, it is unlikely that the impact on earnings would be three times the impact of the $1/bbl change given in the table. Another problem is with co-movements in prices. It is unlikely, for example, that changes in the prices of crude oil and natural gas are independent. Yet, each change estimate holds the other prices constant. Finally, nothing is said about the probabilities of price changes. These would have to be assessed by the investor.

The value at risk approach addresses some of these problems. Consider, for example, a firm's portfolio of financial instruments at year-end. To calculate value at risk, the firm first needs to assess a joint probability distribution of the various price risks that affect the fair value of the portfolio over some holding period—say, one day. This probability distribution is then converted into a probability distribution of the changes in the fair value of the portfolio. The value at risk is then the loss in portfolio fair value that has only a 2.5% (or some other low probability) chance of occurring over the holding period. In effect, a loss greater than the value at risk is a rare event. The approach can also be extended to cash flow and earnings value at risk.

Microsoft Corporation is a well-known user of value at risk. It faces foreign currency, interest rate, commodity, and securities price risks, which it hedges by means of options and other derivatives. Microsoft does not fully hedge these risks; this is likely to be too costly. However, it uses value at risk to estimate its unhedged exposure, and reports the results in its annual report. Presumably, Microsoft adjusts the extent of its hedging activities so as to attain the level of price risk it is willing to bear.

Microsoft's 2012 Annual Report disclosed that there was a 97.5% probability that the loss on its assets subject to interest rate, currency, commodity, and equity price risks would not exceed $292 million over a one-day holding period (thus, only a 2.5% probability of a loss greater than this amount).

Note that a prolonged market decline extending for more than one day could result in a larger loss. Nevertheless, given Microsoft's 2012 reported net income of $16,978 million, the investor would have known that a one-day loss due to price risks of more than 1.7% of earnings is unlikely.

While primarily geared to downside risk, there appears to be no reason why value at risk could not be applied to upside risk as well. Thus, assuming the price distribution is symmetric, Microsoft was unlikely to gain more than $292 million in one day if prices moved in its favour.

A challenging aspect of value at risk, however, is the need to assess the joint price distribution, including correlations between the price risks. Microsoft does this by keeping track of past price changes, "assuming normal market conditions." This can be a formidable task. For example, if there are only, say, 10 price risks faced by a portfolio, then 10 expected values, 10 variances, and 45 correlations need to be estimated. In previous annual reports, Microsoft has indicated it keeps track of 1,000 risks.

Banks also use value at risk as a risk measure for their trading operations, and the variability of a bank's trading securities portfolio can be an important component of its total risk. Liu, Ryan, and Tan (2004) examined the one-day value at risk disclosures of a sample of 17 large U.S. banks over the period 1997–2002. They found that value at risk enabled improved predictions of next-quarter trading income for their sample. This suggests that despite concerns about accuracy, this risk measure has potential to be decision useful.

However, serious problems with measuring value at risk became apparent with the 2007–2008 meltdown of the market for ABSs and credit default swaps. As pointed out in

Section 1.3, financial institutions use credit default swaps to hedge some or all of the risk of their holdings of these financial instruments. As a result, when reporting value at risk, like Microsoft, they included only unhedged risk exposures in their calculations.

Given the severity of the 2007–2008 market meltdowns, however, the spectres of liquidity pricing and counterparty risk emerged. That is, investors refused to buy ABSs due to lack of transparency, and it became apparent that the issuers of credit default swaps did not have the financial resources to pay all the claims against them. This, of course, further lowered the fair value of ABSs, and was a major contributor to the massive writedowns to fair value recorded by holders of these instruments. In effect, the distribution of joint price changes used to estimate value at risk did not include the risks of market meltdown. Microsoft pointed out that its value at risk measure does not include liquidity risks.

This raises the question whether users of value at risk should amend their procedures so as to include liquidity risks in their estimated joint price distributions. Admittedly, this is problematic since liquidity pricing is, hopefully, a rare event. Nevertheless the failure of value at risk to predict the massive writedowns suffered by many firms during 2007–2008 has raised severe criticisms. At the least, firms could give value at risk measures for gross risk exposure as well as unhedged exposure.

7.12.5 Summary

We conclude that information about firm risk, in addition to beta, is valued by the stock market, particularly for financial institutions. This is documented by the reaction of share and bond returns of these institutions to risk exposures and to the impact of hedging on these risks. These findings supplement our conclusion in Chapter 5 that the market exhibits considerable efficiency in its response to financial accounting information, and our arguments in Section 6.7 that securities markets are generally reasonably close to the semi-strong efficiency ideal. Financial reporting has responded to the need for risk disclosure by increased discussion of risks and how they are managed, and by supplementary disclosure of financial instrument information. This enables investors to better evaluate the amounts, timing, and uncertainty of returns on their investments.

Financial reporting also requires the providing to investors of quantitative risk information, such as sensitivity analyses and value at risk. Despite methodological challenges, these represent important steps in moving risk disclosures toward a measurement approach.

7.13 CONCLUSIONS ON MEASUREMENT APPLICATIONS

Reasons for a measurement approach to financial reporting, as discussed in Chapter 6, include the low value relevance of historical cost-based net income, reactions to theory and evidence that securities markets may not be as fully efficient as originally believed, increasing acceptance of a theory that expresses firm value in terms of accounting variables, and auditor legal liability resulting from financial statement overstatements. The combined effect of these factors is consistent with accounting standard setters' conviction that striving for greater relevance (i.e., current value accounting) is worthwhile, even at the cost of some sacrifice of reliability. Current value measurements can be unreliable in the absence of well-working market prices, since they are then subject to considerable manager judgment and possible manipulation.

Nevertheless, there are numerous instances of current values in financial reporting. Many uses involve only partial application of a measurement approach, as in lower-of-cost-or-market and impairment tests, including an impairment test for purchased goodwill. However, even one-sided applications of current value have the potential to be decision useful to the extent they reveal a material change in the firm's financial position and prospects.

However, several standards require fair value measurement, which extend the measurement approach so as to periodically recognize both value increases and decreases. Equity securities and derivative financial instruments are important examples. These fair value standards take steps to reduce the net income volatility that accompanies fair values, including allowing some gains and losses reported in other comprehensive income, and the fair value option. Also, the IASB revaluation option for property, plant, and equipment, if adopted, requires that fair values be kept up to date.

New IASB standards introduced following the 2007–2008 market meltdowns show some backing off from fair value accounting. In particular, assets that, according to the firm's business model, are held so as to earn interest income can be valued at amortized cost rather than fair value (subject to impairment testing). The concept of the firm's business model is intended to control the unreliability that would result if management was free to opportunistically transfer assets between fair value and amortized cost. New standards also require increased supplemental disclosures of firms' financial instruments-related activities. Expanded risk disclosures are also required. Some of this disclosure is quantitative, such as sensitivities and value at risk, thereby moving risk reporting into the measurement approach.

Questions and Problems

1. Accounts receivable are usually valued on the balance sheet at current value—namely, the amount owing from customers less an allowance for uncollectible accounts. Does this violate the historical cost basis of accounting? Explain.

   Note: A good answer will consider the point in the operating cycle at which revenue is realized.

2. A technology company sells a complex computer program. It promises customers that it will provide updates and virus protection for three years from date of sale. The company recognizes 80% of the proceeds of selling the program as revenue, and regards the remaining 20% as an obligation to be extinguished over three years.

The company tentatively plans to report its obligation to service its product as deferred revenue on the balance sheet, recognizing one-third of the obligation as revenue each year, on grounds that this produces the best matching of costs and revenues. However, it consults you before finalizing its policy.

You point out that accounting standards are now primarily based on a measurement approach, and that matching of costs and revenues is not consistent with this approach. Instead, you recommend that the liability be measured at the amount the firm would rationally pay to be relieved of the obligation.

Required

a. How is the 20% of proceeds allocated to the service obligation viewed under historical cost accounting? How would the obligation be viewed under a measurement approach?

b. Suggest one or more ways to determine the amount the firm would rationally pay to be relieved of the obligation.

c. Compare the relevance and reliability of your suggested approach(es) with the matching approach of writing the obligation off over three years.

3. Explain why a firm may not necessarily want to reduce its price risks to zero by entering into hedging transactions.

4. Share prices of many "high-tech" firms are quite volatile relative to the stock market index. In an article in *The Wall Street Journal* (reprinted in *The Globe and Mail*, May 16, 2001, Greg Ip discussed a reason why. He pointed out that high-tech firms have high fixed costs, consisting mainly of R&D driven by rapid technological progress. They also have low variable costs, since the direct production costs of their products tend to be low. In effect, high-tech firms have high operating leverage.

For example, Yahoo Inc. incurred a drop in revenue of 42% in the first quarter of 2001, but its costs barely dropped. It reported an operating loss of $33 million for the quarter, compared to a profit of $87 million in the last quarter of 2000.

Required

a. Use high operating leverage to explain high stock price variability.

b. Use the argument that beta is non-stationary (Section 6.2.3) to explain high stock price volatility.

c. Use the behavioural finance concepts of momentum and bubbles to explain high stock price volatility.

d. Are these three sources of volatility mutually exclusive? Explain.

5. **Note:** This question is based on optional Section 7.5.4 re: loan loss provisioning.

Under IAS 39, the IASB financial instrument standard in effect at the time, loans receivable were valued at amortized cost. That is, valuation was based on expected future receipts from the loan discounted at the effective rate of interest established at loan acquisition. If the loan became impaired (i.e., expected future receipts fell), the loan would be written down to its new expected value, discounted at the original effective rate.

During the 2007–2008 market meltdowns, loan impairment writedowns were criticized for waiting "too long." That is, writedowns were delayed until the financial institution holding the loan decided that impairment had occurred. This often generated huge sudden writedowns, particularly if the impairment had been building up over some considerable period of time prior to the impairment recognition.

Subsequently, in 2009, the IASB proposed to record writedowns sooner. Specifically, a loan loss allowance at the end of each period would be accumulated even if the loan was not impaired, based on expected future credit losses (see Section 7.5.4 for the current state of this proposal).

This proposal did not satisfy the Basel Committee on Banking Supervision, a group of central bankers and financial supervisors from major world economies. The Committee proposed that the IASB should consider providing for credit losses through the business cycle (**dynamic provisioning**). That is, in periods of high economic activity, loan lenders should provide greater-than-expected credit losses when calculating the loan loss allowance. This would create an excess allowance that could be used to absorb greater-than-expected credit losses in periods of low economic activity. The result would be to bolster banks' loan loss protection and smooth reported earnings over the business cycle.

Required

a. Evaluate the relevance of each of the three loan loss policies outlined above.

b. Evaluate the reliability of each policy.

c. Why not require fair value accounting for loans, rather than amortized cost accounting? Consider Levels 1, 2, and 3 of the fair value hierarchy in your answer, and note that most loans are not traded on a market.

6. Refer to Theory in Practice vignette 1.2, concerning the bankruptcy of New Century Financial. New Century had securitized and transferred to investors (i.e., derecognized) many (but not all) of its subprime mortgages, treating the transfers as sales. However, as the 2007–2008 market meltdowns developed, it was forced to repurchase many of these mortgages. Its provisions for credit losses on repurchases proved to be woefully inadequate. The company quickly ran out of cash.

Required

a. Why would a company such as New Century retain an interest in some of the mortgages it originated, rather than selling all of them on to investors via securitization?

b. Why would the company commit to repurchasing delinquent mortgages?

c. Suppose that the derecognition provisions of IFRS 9 and the disclosure provisions of IFRS 7 and 12, outlined in Section 7.8 were in effect from 1995, the date New Century was formed. Could New Century's filing for bankruptcy protection have been avoided? Explain.

7. In a 2010 interview with *The Globe and Mail*,[32] Larry Fink, founder of BlackRock, Inc., one of the world's largest asset management companies, commented on mark-to-market (i.e., fair value) accounting. He acknowledged that it was good for investors since it enabled "a more accurate appraisal" of assets than historical cost accounting and increases "granularity and transparency." However, he claimed that it also "forces investors, analysts, and corporate management to concentrate on quarterly results," discouraging "longer-term corporate thinking."

Required

Do you agree with Mr. Fink? Give reasons why or why not.

8. Barclays Capital is a division of Barclays Bank, a U.K.–based multinational financial institution. On September 16, 2009, Barclays Capital announced a deal to sell US$12.3 billion of "toxic" ABSs and other mortgage-related securities to Protium Finance, a Cayman Islands fund owned by C12 Capital Management Holdings and operating from New York.

The announcement indicated that 45 of Barclays Capital managers would leave the division to manage C12, which would receive $40 million annually from Barclays Capital to manage the portfolio.

Protium is highly levered. Its purchase of the securities is financed by a $12.6 billion 10-year, prime plus 2.75%, loan from Barclays Capital, plus $450 million of loans contributed by two unnamed U.S. and U.K. institutions.

The effect of this deal was to remove $12.3 billion of securities from Barclays' balance sheet, replacing it with a loan receivable. That is, Barclays derecognized these securities. However, they were not derecognized for purposes of reporting to regulators. That is, Barclays' legal capital ratio was not affected by the transaction. Barclays did not explain why the regulator took this position.

Speculation about the motive for this deal quickly appeared in financial media. Reasons included the following:

- *Counterparty Risk.* Most of the financial instruments were insured by CDSs (Section 1.3). However, there was continuing concern in the market about the solvency of insurers following the collapse of AIG in 2008. Fair value of the transferred securities fluctuated daily with fluctuations of the market's assessment of this risk. In particular, should an insurer become financially distressed, fair value of the transferred instruments would plummet, requiring a huge writedown on Barclays' books. Under the announced deal, this risk would be borne by Protium.

- *Earnings Volatility.* By substituting an interest-bearing loan for the transferred securities, Barclays' earnings is freed from the volatility induced by fair-valuing them. It should be noted, however, that if Protium could not collect sufficient cash to pay interest and principal to Barclays, the value of the loan would have to be written down. Thus Barclays retained the ultimate risk of non-repayment of the mortgages underlying the transferred securities, even though it had gotten rid of the short-term fluctuations in fair value.

- *Manager Compensation.* Since the securities in question were transferred to Protium at fair value (they had already been written down from $13.5 to $12.3 billion earlier in 2009), any subsequent increase in fair value would accrue to Protium and C12, not to Barclays. Given that securities markets in 2009 were recovering from the 2007–2008 meltdowns, given the high leverage of Protium, and the large amount of securities involved, even a small increase in fair value would convey a huge increase in wealth to Protium and, presumably, to the 45 former employees now with C12.

In effect, Barclays gave up the prospect of such gains in exchange for lower counterparty risk and earnings volatility. However, since several world leaders at the time were calling for controls on bonuses paid to financial institution managers, suspicion emerged that the deal was really a device to enrich certain Barclays managers through fair value appreciation instead. The extent to which new derecognition standards will discourage such transactions remains to be seen.

Required

a. Would Barclays' derecognition of the $12.3 billion of transferred securities be consistent with IFRS 9 and related FASB standards?

b. Should Protium be consolidated with Barclays for purposes of financial reporting to investors under IFRS 10 and related FASB standards?

c. On September 16, the day of the announcement of the deal, Barclays' share price rose 11 pence sterling to 390, an increase of 2.9%. On the same day, the U.K. FTSE 100 index rose 82 points, to 5,124.10. Barclays' beta, per Yahoo! Finance UK at the time, was 2.1568. Assume that the daily risk-free interest rate was effectively zero. Assume securities markets efficiency. Also assume that no other significant firm-specific information about Barclays became available on September 16. As evidenced by its share price performance, did the market approve or disapprove of this deal? Explain, and show calculations.

9. Should firms be required to fair-value their long-term debt, even in the absence of a mismatch? Outline arguments for and against this suggestion.

10. A firm buys, and designates, an effective forward contract to hedge the price risk of its current stock of inventory. Suppose that the inventory is still on hand at period-end, and that its market value has fallen. Will application of the lower-of-cost-or-market rule to write down the inventory to market affect net income? Explain why or why not.

11. On March 11, 2000, *The Globe and Mail* reported "Ballard losses double." The reference was to Ballard Power Systems Inc., a Canadian developer of fuel cell technology. On March 10, 2000, Ballard reported an operating loss of $26 million for the fourth quarter of 1999, bringing its loss for the year to $75.2 million on revenues of $33.2 million. Its loss for 1998 was $36.2 million on revenues of $25.1 million. The reason for the increased loss in 1999, according to Ballard, was a huge increase in R&D spending for its fuel cell technology.

   On March 10, 2000, Ballard's share price closed at $189 on the Toronto Stock Exchange, up $14 on the day for an increase of 8%.

Required

a. Does the increase in Ballard's share price on March 10, 2000, on the same day that it reported an increased loss, imply a high or low R^2 and ERC for the relationship between the return on Ballard's shares and abnormal earnings? Explain, using the arguments of Lev and Zarowin (1999). Assume that at least part of the 8% increase in Ballard's share price on March 10 was an abnormal return (i.e., firm-specific, not due to a market wide increase in the stock market).

b. How do Lev and Zarowin propose to improve the accounting for R&D but yet retain reasonable reliability? Explain how this proposal could affect R^2 and the ERC. Is complete reliability of accounting for R&D necessary for the Lev and Zarowin proposal? Explain.

c. Does Ballard's share price behaviour on March 10, 2000, suggest securities market efficiency or inefficiency? Explain. Continue the assumption that at least part of the March 10 increase in Ballard's share price was firm-specific.

12. Manulife Financial is a large Canadian-based insurance and financial services company, with operations in Canada, United States, and Asia. Like most such companies, Manulife's

profits are suffering from low interest rates and poor stock market returns following the 2007–2008 market meltdowns. These returns are less than the rates of return assumed by Manulife when setting pre-meltdown premiums for its insurance and other products. Much of the risk of a decline in interest rates and stock returns had not been hedged by Manulife. Subsequently, Manulife is increasing its hedging activity.

In its third quarter, 2012, Manulife reported a net loss under IFRS accounting standards of $227 million. The company also reported an alternate earnings number, which we interpret as persistent earnings, of $556 million for the quarter.

Persistent earnings are calculated as follows:

Net income per IASB standards		$(227)
Add back		
• Net fair value losses on unhedged items and longer-term assets and liabilities	$88	
• Actuarial adjustment to increase policy liability reserve due to low interest rates and reduced policy cancellations and lapses	1,006	
• limpairment of puchased goodwill due to low interest rates	200	
• Gains on hedged items and investments	(511)	783
Persistent earnings		$556

Required

a. Manulife management claims that their persistent earnings calculation gives a better picture of longer-term earnings. Do you agree? Explain.

b. Which earnings measure—IFRS or persistent earnings—best helps investors to predict Manulife's future earnings performance? Explain.

c. The Conceptual Framework includes reporting on manager stewardship as a goal of financial reporting. Which measure best reports on manager stewardship? Explain.

d. On November 8, 2012, the day of Manulife's earnings release, the company's share price fell 18 cents to $11.82, On the same day, the S&P/TSX Composite Index fell to 12,197.05, from its open at 12,227.85. Manulife's beta, per Reuters Finance at the time, was 1.48. Assume that the daily risk-free interest rate was effectively zero. Assume securities markets efficiency. Also assume that no other significant firm-specific information about Manulife became available on November 8. As evidenced by its share price performance, did the market approve or disapprove of Manulife's calculation of persistent earnings? Explain, and show calculations.

13. An economist suggests that the best measure of a firm's income is the change in the market value of that firm's shares over the period (adjusted for capital transactions). Furthermore, he argues, such a measure would avoid the reliability problems of attempting to fair-value individual assets and liabilities, particularly intangibles such as goodwill. In effect, he asks, why not fair-value the whole firm?

Required

a. How much information would net income calculated this way add to what the market already knows about the firm?

b. Note that measuring income as the change in the firm's market value is equivalent to fair-valuing all its assets and liabilities, including self-developed intangibles. Given that standard setters are attempting to extend fair value accounting to additional assets and liabilities, how far should fair value accounting be extended while still providing useful information to investors? In your answer, consider whether fair valuation of self-developed goodwill would be decision useful. Could valuing self-developed goodwill at value in use (i.e., at management's estimate of the present value of future abnormal earnings) be decision useful? Why or why not?

14. Refer to the sensitivity analysis of Husky Energy Inc. reproduced in Table 7.2. The analysis discloses the potential effects of changes in prices of oil and natural gas, and of changes in the Can./U.S. dollar exchange rate, on 2012 cash flows and earnings.

Required

a. Evaluate the relevance and reliability of this method of disclosing risk information.

b. The analysis indicates that the sensitivity of earnings to its oil and natural gas activities is before fair value gains and losses (Notes 3 and 8). Presumably, this is because price risks relating to these activities are effectively hedged. As an investor, would you find sensitivity information net of hedging, or before hedging, more useful? Explain.

c. Price risks arise from changes in the market prices of crude oil and natural gas, with associated foreign exchange risk because market prices are largely based on the U.S. dollar. Boards of directors of some companies limit hedging of future oil and gas price changes to only a portion of production or, at least, monitor the extent of hedging closely. That is, all production is not hedged. Why do boards impose such limitations on management's ability to manage risk? Give reasons based on corporate governance, cost, and investor diversification considerations.

15. Most large firms use derivative financial instruments to hedge their market risks.

Required

a. To obtain the benefits of hedge accounting for a derivative instrument under IFRS 9, the firm must designate the instrument as a hedge. What are the requirements for designation?

b. How are derivatives valued under IFRS 9?

c. What are the benefits to the firm of hedge accounting?

16. Vulture Ltd. is incorporated to invest in risky securities. On January 1, 2015, the company buys Volatile Ltd. bonds with a par value of $10,000. Vulture plans to hold these bonds until they mature in two years, on December 31, 2016. The bonds pay 5% interest, paid on December 31 of each year.

Volatile Ltd. is in financial distress, and payment of interest and principal on December 31, 2016, depends on whether Volatile Ltd. recovers from its financial problems. The probability that it will recover is 0.7 in which case Vulture Ltd. will receive full interest and principal. If Volatile does not recover, Vulture will receive no interest on December 31, 2016, and the bonds will be worth half of par value. Vulture finances the bond purchase by issuing common shares. The interest rate in the economy is 5%, which is also Vulture's cost of capital.

Required

Note: Assume ideal conditions of uncertainty for parts **a** and **b**. Part **b** contains a calculation not illustrated in the text.

a. How much did Vulture Ltd. pay for the Volatile Ltd. bonds?

b. In December 2015, it becomes apparent that Volatile Ltd. has recovered. Prepare a Vulture Ltd. balance sheet at the end of 2015 and an income statement for 2015.

c. Suppose instead that Vulture accounts for its bond investment under IFRS 9. Vulture's business model specifies that bond investments are intended to be held so as to collect interest and principal. Assuming that Vulture paid the amount for the bonds as calculated in part **a**, what would be its balance sheet valuation of its Volatile investment on December 31, 2015, and Vulture's net income for 2015?

d. Suppose now that Vulture's business model allows it to sell investments at any time. It contracts in December 2015 to sell its Volatile bond investment on January 1, 2016, for $9,600. Assume that Vulture accounts for its investments under IFRS 9. What would be the balance sheet valuation of its Volatile investment on December 31, 2015, and Vulture's net income for 2015?

17. As described in Section 1.3, the FASB introduced FIN 46 in 2003, expanding the requirements for consolidation of variable interest entities (VIEs) and requiring additional supplementary disclosure by firms with interests in VIEs. Many firms affected by FIN 46 avoided the new consolidation requirements through the creation of Expected Loss Notes (ELNs), under which an outside party became the primary VIE beneficiary.

Callahan, Smith, and Spencer (2012) studied firms affected by FIN 46 during the period 1998–2005. After controlling for other factors affecting cost of capital, they found that the cost of capital of firms affected by FIN 46 (and which thus had to either consolidate their VIEs or issue ELNs to avoid consolidation) increased on average after 2003, relative to a control sample of firms that were unaffected by FIN 46.

For those firms affected by FIN 46 that avoided consolidation through ELNs, the authors also found that their increase in cost of capital was less than the increase for those affected firms that did consolidate.

Required

a. Give an explanation for these results that is consistent with securities market efficiency.

b. Give an explanation that is consistent with behaviourially biased investors.

c. How did the FASB and IASB respond to the consolidation loophole of ELNs in FIN 46?

18. EnCana Corporation, a large Canadian oil and gas company, reported net income of US$393 million (EnCana reports in U.S. dollars) for its third quarter, 2004. This compares with net income of $290 million for the same quarter of 2003. However, third quarter, 2004, earnings would have been even higher but for a $321 million after tax unrealized loss on cash flow hedges of future oil and gas sales charged against operations. In accordance with Canadian GAAP at the time, and consistent with IFRS 9, EnCana accounted for these financial instruments at fair value, with unrealized gains and losses included in net income. The loss was due to the dramatic increase in oil prices during 2004, and illustrates that while hedging may protect the firm from losses if product prices decline, it also shuts them out of gains if prices increase.

Required

a. Explain why EnCana reported a loss on its hedging activities. Assume that IFRS 9 was in effect at the time.

b. Assuming that its hedges qualified for hedge accounting under IFRS 9 or SFAS 133 (now ASC 815), how would EnCana's unrealized hedging loss have been accounted for under these standards?

c. Give reasons why firms such as EnCana typically hedge at least part of its price risk of future anticipated sales.

19. In a press release dated April 23, 2005, Canadian Natural Resources Limited (CNRL) reported a loss of $679 million from cash flow hedges of its future crude oil and natural gas production, for the quarter ended March 31, 2005.

CNRL reported that the hedges in question did not meet the requirements for hedge accounting. Consequently, they had to be fair-valued at March 31 with the loss included in net income. The company indicated that fair value was determined by the hedges' market values at March 31.

Required

a. The purpose of hedging is to shield the firm from the impacts of changing prices. If so, explain how a loss on cash flow hedging can arise in net income.

b. Suppose that CNRL's hedges had met the requirements for hedge accounting laid down by accounting standards such as IFRS 9, and they were duly designated and accounted for by CNRL according to those standards. How would the $679 million loss be accounted for?

c. CNRL stated in its press release that the $679 million loss did not affect cash flows for the quarter ended March 31, 2005. As an investor in CNRL, do you find the information about the loss to be decision useful? Explain why or why not.

20. Refer to Theory in Practice vignette 7.4, describing how The Blackstone Group proposed to account for the carried interest to be received from future earnings of unconsolidated firms it has invested in.

Required

a. As a rational investor in the shares of Blackstone's initial public offering, would you find fair value accounting more or less decision useful than historical cost accounting for the value of Blackstone's carried interest? In your answer, consider issues of relevance, reliability, and full disclosure.

b. As an investor, would the increased volatility of Blackstone's earnings resulting from fair value accounting affect the amount you would be willing to pay for its shares? Explain your answer.

c. Why do you think that Blackstone changed its mind?

21. Swap contracts are a type of derivative that is often used to manage financing costs. To illustrate, suppose a firm has $200,000 of 10% bonds outstanding at December 31, 2010. Interest is payable semi-annually, and the bonds mature three (semi-annual) periods hence, on June 30, 2012.

The variable market interest rate on December 31, 2010, is also 10% per annum. However, the firm suspects that variable interest rates will decline, and it enters into a swap contract with a financial institution under which the firm receives $10,000 at the end of each period (i.e., equal to its 5% semi-annual fixed interest payments on its debt) and agrees to pay to the financial institution each period interest on its debt at the end-of-period variable rate (currently 5% per period).

On December 31, 2010, the fair value of this contract is zero, since the market variable interest rate equals the interest rate on the bonds. This is verified as

$$\text{Expected receipts at variable rate} = \frac{10,000}{1.05} + \frac{10,000}{1.05^2} + \frac{10,000}{1.05^3} = \$27,232$$

This amount is the same as the present value of the remaining fixed interest payments on the bonds. That is, the expected receipts and payments under the swap are equal. Note that it is assumed that the interest rate market is efficient, in which case the expected future variable rate equals the current variable rate.

Of course, the fair value of the swap will change over time as the variable rate varies. Suppose that at the end of the first period the variable rate is 8% per annum. Then the firm receives $10,000 as before and pays $8,000 per period under the swap contract.

The fair value of the firm's debt rises to $203,772. However, to compensate, the fair value of the swap rises from zero to $3,772:

$$\text{Fair value of swap} = \frac{2,000}{1.04} + \frac{2,000}{1.04^2} = 3,772$$

The $2,000 numerators represent the $10,000 payments to be received by the firm less the expected $8,000 payments out, over the remaining life of the contract. Thus the firm's net liability remains at $200,000 and its interest expense for the period is $8,000 ($10,000 interest paid on bonds less $2,000 net cash received under swap contract).

Now change the example. Specifically, assume that the firm is Country G, a member of the European Union (EU). EU rules include a requirement that member countries' ratio of deficit to gross domestic product cannot exceed 3%. Country G is concerned that its ratio will exceed 3%.

Country G enters into a swap contract with a financial institution on December 31, 2010, similar to the one described above, except that it will receive a payment of $15,000 each period, rather than $10,000. Since this payment greatly exceeds the country's expected variable rate payments of $10,000, the fair value of the swap contract increases from zero to $13,616.

The financial institution now pays Country G this fair value. Consequently, the swap contract disappears from Country G's financial statements. In return for the $5,000 increased payment to be received each period, Country G agrees to pay over to the institution the receipts from its airport landing fees and lottery proceeds for two years following the expiry of the swap contract.

EU rules allow the $13,613 payment to be credited to revenue, instead of being recorded as a liability. Country G thus avoids violating the 3% rule in 2010.

Note: I am indebted to a reviewer for the first part of this example.

Required
a. Verify that the fair value of Country G's swap contract on December 31, 2010, is $13,616.

b. From an accounting perspective, do you agree that the $13,616 payment of Country G is revenue, rather than a liability? Explain.

Notes

1. This valuation would be with respect to groups of assets and liabilities if they are used jointly.

2. Ideally, the discount rate is the firm's cost of capital.

3. A finance lease, called a capital lease under FASB rules, is a lease that transfers the significant risks and rewards of ownership to the lessee. In essence, the lessee has purchased the asset, financing it by means of the lease.

4. Under the exposure draft, the term of the lease contract includes periods covered by an option to extend the lease if the lessee has a "significant economic incentive" to exercise the option to extend. This would make it difficult to avoid lease capitalization by means of a series of one-year leases.

   Also, leased assets (more precisely, rights to use leased assets) are subject to an impairment test. The option to fair value non-financial assets (see Section 7.3.4) is also available for firms using IASB standards.

   The Exposure Draft also applies to lessors. For a Type A lease, the lessor derecognizes the leased asset, records the present value of the lease payments, and records profit on the "sale." For Type B, the lessor retains the asset on its books and records rental income each period.

5. The U.S. rule, however, is based on the lower of cost or current replacement cost, subject to the constraints that market value should not exceed net realizable value and should not be so low as to produce a greater-than-normal profit margin.

6. An effect of the two-step procedure is to avoid writedowns of assets that are only mildly impaired or for which the decline in fair value is viewed as temporary. For example, the undiscounted future direct net cash flows of an asset with book value of $100 might be estimated as $105, despite a fair value of $90. Then, the asset need not be written down. However, if undiscounted cash flows are, say, $95, the asset is written down to fair value.

7. This assumes the IASB firm does not use the revaluation option (Section 7.3.4). If this option is used, accounting for impairment losses is more complex.

8. These definitions are based on IAS 32, but omit some components of the full definitions contained in the accounting standard.

9. If the asset may also be sold under the business model, the IASB subsequently decided to require that the asset be valued at fair value, with unrealized gains and losses from periodic adjustments to fair value included in other comprehensive income. In effect, while the asset would be valued at fair value on the balance sheet, it would be valued on an amortized cost basis for income statement purposes, with OCI absorbing the difference.

10. Under the proprietorship view, the gain to shareholders would be included in net income. See Section 3.7.1 and Note 20 of Chapter 3.

11. The option to value a liability at fair value is only available when the liability is first recorded and is irrevocable. If the change in fair value increases a mismatch, it must be included in net income.

12. To simplify somewhat, short-term trade accounts receivable are to be valued net of lifetime expected credit losses, much like current bad debt accounting. For long-term receivables, the firm has the option to use this accounting.

13. Note the model's assumption of pure historical cost accounting, whereas accounting standards often include impairment tests. PSS also considered this situation. If market values are low, historical cost subject to impairment testing and fair value accounting produce similar effects on earnings. Then managers, and thus shareholders, are indifferent. However, since fair value accounting is still preferred to historical cost when market values are high, fair value accounting dominates historical cost with impairment tests.

14. The authors measure a stock's liquidity based on the ratio of return to trading volume. This measure will be higher the more a share's price varies (i.e., its return) relative to its trading volume. The intuition is that the greater is the change in share price for a given trading volume, the higher the impact of trade on price. The higher is this impact, the greater the transactions cost of buying or selling a share—that is, the lower the stock's liquidity.

15. Ng measured liquidity risk as the covariance between firm liquidity and market liquidity, a somewhat different measure than Lang and Maffett, who used the covariance between firm liquidity and the market return on the firm's shares. The intuition is similar, however. Investors value liquid stocks both if their liquidity holds up during market downturns (Lang and Maffett) and when the liquidity of the whole market declines (Ng).

16. In 2012, **investment entities** were excluded from the consolidation requirements. An investment entity is an entity that invests funds for capital gain, investment income, or both, and evaluates its investments on a fair value basis. Instead of consolidation, such firms value their investments on their balance sheets at fair value. The argument for this exception is that the fair values of investment entities' various investments are more decision useful than burying them in consolidated totals.

17. Consistent with the semi-strong version of market efficiency adopted in this book, the important question is not whether securities market prices prior to the meltdown were higher than their fundamental value (they were) but whether those prices reasonably reflected the information available at the time.

18. Examples of speculation using derivatives that resulted in bankruptcy or near bankruptcy include Orange County, California; Barings Bank; and Long-Term Capital Management. For accounts of these disasters, see Boyle & Boyle (2001), Chapter 8.

19. If the risk-free interest rate is greater than zero, the option fair value is more complex. Also, options are usually fair-valued by an equivalent approach, called a **replicating portfolio**. This is a portfolio consisting of an investment in the underlying share plus a short position in a risk-free asset, where the amounts of each security are determined each period so that the replicating portfolio yields the same return as the option for each possible end-of-period value of the option. Since the underlying share and the risk-free asset have readily available market values, and since the return on the option is the same as that of the replicating portfolio, arbitrage forces the fair value of the option to equal the value of the replicating portfolio. For details, see Boyle & Boyle (2001), Chapter 4.

20. Boyle & Boyle (2001), Chapter 5, p. 89, and the IASB, call this formula the Black-Scholes-Merton formula, due to important contributions by Robert Merton (1973).

21. If the option holder is not entitled to any dividends prior to exercise, the option value is also affected by expected dividends.

22. Note that risk goes both ways. That is, assets (and liabilities) may decrease or increase in value. Thus, if an asset is fully hedged against price risk, the firm will not suffer from a decline in asset value but will not enjoy an increase in value either. (See Problem 18 re EnCana Corporation.) This is a statistical notion of risk. Nevertheless, we will sometimes use the term *risk* in the sense of downside risk only. Credit risk, for example, is the risk of loss from the failure of the other party to a contract to fulfill its obligations.

23. Some standard setters disagree in principle with deferring unrealized gains and losses on cash flow hedges in other comprehensive income, arguing that instead these should be included in net income. The reason is that the hedged transactions have not yet occurred, so that an unrealized gain or loss on a cash flow hedge is not associated with the measurement of another existing asset or liability. In effect, the future hedged transactions depend on management intent and, as we suggested in Section 7.2.1, management intent is a shifting sand upon which to base a measurement approach. A counter argument, however, is that denying the anticipation of future transactions denies the going concern assumption. Note, in this regard, that IFRS 9 requires that the anticipated transactions be highly probable.

24. A firm cannot "overhedge" under IFRS 9. For example, if a firm buys twice as much hedging instrument as is needed to protect against losses on the hedged item, this implies speculation, not risk management.

25. The abnormal earnings installments could also be negative. This simply means that the firm is expected to earn less than its cost of capital—that is, it has "badwill."

26. Of course, this is not really "cash" income since it includes other accruals, such as sales on credit. It is not known where the term originated. Pro-forma income is discussed further in Section 11.6.2.

27. The company's preliminary net loss for the year was increased by further goodwill writedowns of $5.3 billion reported in its audited financial statements for the year.

28. Since research costs are expensed, R&D profitability can only be higher than its zero book value. Thus, this source of estimation risk is not diversifiable.

29. Management may not be willing to reveal this estimate, on grounds that it may reveal important information to competitors.

30. Canadian Tire reported purchased goodwill and other intangibles of $1,089.9 million in its 2012 Annual Report. However, only $376.9 million of this amount was purchased goodwill.

31. For further discussion of the possible use of the clean surplus model to account for goodwill, see AAA Financial Accounting Standards Committee (2001).

32. Reported in Boyd Erman and Tim Kiladze, "A call for long-term thinking," *The Globe and Mail* (October 19, 2010), p. B3.

Chapter 8

The Efficient Contracting Approach to Decision Usefulness

Figure 8.1 Organization of Chapter 8

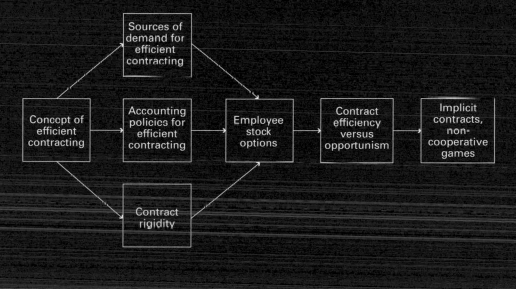

8.1 OVERVIEW

You may have noticed that there has been little reference to corporate management to this point. Yet, in Section 1.4 we suggested that aiding in efficient corporate governance, including efficient contracting and responsible manager performance, was an important role for financial reporting. This role contrasts with the decision usefulness approach of helping investors predict future firm performance that was the subject of Chapters 3 to 7. This chapter begins our study of financial reporting from management's perspective. As we shall see, issues of efficient contracting loom large.

Efficient contracting theory takes the view that firms[1] organize themselves in the most efficient manner, so as to maximize their prospects for survival.[2] Some firms are more decentralized than others, some firms conduct activities inside while other firms contract out the same activities, some firms finance more with debt than others, etc. The most efficient form of corporate governance for a particular firm depends on factors such as its legal and institutional environment, its technology, and the degree of competition in its industry.

Efficient contracting is a significant component of efficient corporate governance. Indeed, a firm can be largely defined by the contracts it enters into. To enhance corporate governance, these contracts must be efficient. That is, they must optimally balance contract benefits and costs.[3] Ultimately, the objective of the theory is to understand and predict managerial accounting policy choice in different circumstances and across different firms, and how financial accounting can contribute to contract efficiency.

The reason that financial accounting contributes to efficient contracting, hence to corporate governance, is that important contracts usually depend on accounting variables. For example, management compensation contracts typically depend on reported earnings, and debt contracts usually contain accounting-based covenants. As a result, managers have a crucial interest in accounting policies that affect compensation and covenant values. Note that, unlike efficient markets theory, this manager interest arises independently of whether different accounting policies affect cash flows.

The theory assumes that managers, like investors, are rational. Consequently, given that important contracts depend on accounting variables, managers may be tempted to bias or otherwise manage reported earnings and working capital valuations if they perceive this to be for their own benefit. This creates a demand for accounting policies to control such tendencies.

Controlling these tendencies is the efficient contracting and stewardship role of financial reporting. As explained in Sections 1.4 and 1.10, this book argues that motivation of responsible manager performance—that is, providing information to evaluate manager stewardship— is an equally important financial accounting role as providing useful information to investors.

Contract theory increases the stewardship role of the income statement relative to its role in helping investors predict future firm performance. This latter role was our main interest in Chapters 2-6. This stewardship role includes protecting debtholders and shareholders from opportunistic manager behaviour. Also, net income plays a **confirmatory role**—it can confirm, or disconfirm, announcements made by management during the year, such as earnings forecasts. This *ex post* checking up on information released by management motivates truthful announcements. Consistent with the fundamental problem (Section 1.10), we will see that some accounting policies recommended by contract theory differ from the investor-informing policies we have considered in previous chapters.

Efficient contracting theory helps accountants to understand why reporting on stewardship is important, and to appreciate the boundaries of legitimate management concern about accounting policy choice. This understanding is particularly important due to the extensive interaction between managers and accountants.

Management is an important constituency of financial accounting. However, as noted in Section 3.7, its role in financial reporting is largely "outside" the Conceptual Framework.[4] Thus, management's interests must be incorporated into accounting standards through due process or, equivalently, through a process of **conflict resolution**. In this chapter, we begin our study of how this conflict works out.

Figure 8.1 outlines the organization of this chapter.

8.2 WHAT IS EFFICIENT CONTRACTING THEORY?

Efficient contracting theory studies the role of financial accounting information in moderating information asymmetry between contracting parties, thereby contributing to efficient contracting and stewardship and efficient corporate governance.

Information asymmetry arises in contracting since management possesses inside information about the state of the firm, and may not necessarily share this with other contracting parties or, if they do share, may distort or exaggerate the information. Also, management's effort in operating the firm is not directly observable by outsiders. In both cases, outside contracting parties look to accounting information to help protect themselves from exploitation.

Recall from Section 1.2 that we defined corporate governance as those policies that align the firm's activities with the interests of its investors and society. Efficient contracting is an important component of this alignment. Firms enter into many contracts, such as with customers, suppliers, management, other employees, and lenders.[5] For good corporate governance, these contracts should be **efficient**. That is, they must attain an optimal tradeoff between the benefits and costs of contracting. For example, a firm may benefit from lower borrowing costs if it incurs costs to reassure lenders, such as pledging specific assets as security, or accepting a covenant to limit further borrowing that would water down the security of existing lenders.

Contracting is relevant to financial accounting since important contracts depend on accounting variables. Thus, debt contracts may contain covenants, such as maintaining a specified level of working capital, not exceeding a specified debt–equity ratio, or maintaining an agreed times interest earned ratio. Also, bonuses paid under managerial compensation contracts typically depend on net income, both directly and indirectly through the effect of reported earnings on share price.

Efficient contracting theory assumes that managers, like investors, are rational. As a result, managers cannot be assumed necessarily to maximize firm profits and, more generally, act in the best interests of investors. Rather, they will do so only if they perceive such behaviour to be in their own interests. Consequently, the interests of managers, lenders, and shareholders **conflict**. Efficient contracting theory studies how this conflict is resolved. In particular, it predicts how managers will react to new accounting standards, it helps us to understand why managers often object to new standards, and, through better understanding, it enables us to appreciate how efficient contract design can help to align the interests of managers with those of lenders and shareholders.

In addition to formal contracts such as those just discussed, the theory also envisages **implicit contracts**, which arise from continuing business relationships. For example, if a firm builds and maintains a reputation for high quality financial reporting, it generates the trust of customers, creditors, and investors that it will continue to operate with integrity. As a result, it may be able to charge higher product prices, and enjoy lower borrowing costs and cost of capital.

Finally, efficient contracting theory believes in markets. It asserts that, ideally, demands for financial accounting information should be met by market forces, with the role of standard setting being to provide general principles within which accounting practices can develop based on laws of supply and demand. Several information sources, in addition to the financial statements proper, are available to supply market information demands. For example, demand for future-oriented information can be met by management forecasts, analysts' forecasts and reports, superior MD&A, and notes to the financial statements. These information sources take some of the pressure off the financial statements proper to supply future-oriented information such as fair value accounting. Also, the financial statements play a confirmatory role by *ex post* checking up on the accuracy of forecasts, and forward-looking statements in MD&A.

8.3 SOURCES OF EFFICIENT CONTRACTING DEMAND FOR FINANCIAL ACCOUNTING INFORMATION

8.3.1 Lenders

Debt contracts are an important source of financing for most firms. While the ultimate security for lenders, like shareholders, is the firm's future performance, two aspects of debt contracts should be noted. First, it is management that has the best information about the state of the firm. Lenders are concerned about this information asymmetry because management may not share their information with them and, indeed, may choose accounting policies to hide performance that threatens lender interests. Lenders thus demand protection against this possibility.

Second, lenders face **payoff asymmetry**. Like equity investors, they stand to lose if the firm performs poorly. However, unlike equity investors, their gains are limited if the firm performs well. Consequently, lenders are crucially concerned about protecting themselves on the downside—that is, protection against financial distress. For this reason, they demand financial accounting policies that help prevent financial distress and provide an "early warning system" if distress threatens.[6]

8.3.2 Shareholders

An efficient contracting source of demand for accounting policies also arises from shareholders (and boards of directors operating on shareholders' behalf—see Note 1), to protect themselves from exploitation by management. To some extent, exploitation is controlled by basing manager compensation on some measure of manager performance, such as net income. Also, the confirmatory role of financial statements helps to prevent managers from overstating their inside information during the year, which could result in share price overvaluation by the market. However, since managers are assumed to act in their own interest, and since information asymmetry prevents shareholders from directly observing managers' efforts in running the firm (a moral hazard problem), managers may shirk on effort and cover up overstatements and lower profits through opportunistic behaviour such as overvaluation of assets and managing earnings upward. This creates a demand for financial accounting policies that encourage responsible manager efforts and limit opportunistic manager actions.

We now consider what accounting policies meet these lender and shareholder demands.

8.4 ACCOUNTING POLICIES FOR EFFICIENT CONTRACTING

8.4.1 Reliability

Payoff asymmetry shifts lenders' relevance–reliability tradeoffs toward greater concern for reliability relative to equity investors. That is, since lenders do not directly share in increases in firm value, they are less interested in good news future-oriented information, such as unrealized increases in fair values. However, they are very interested in bad news future-oriented information, since this may indicate that the firm is heading into financial distress. Thus, they demand reliable financial statement information that protects against opportunistic manager accounting policies that hide declines in value and overstate firm performance. Overstated performance reduces the protection provided by debt covenants.

To be reliable, accounting information for efficient contracting should be based on *realized* market transactions (i.e., transactions that have actually occurred), and be *verifiable* by third parties. Unrealized increases in fair value, for example, are regarded as unreliable since they are subject to error and possible manager bias, and may be difficult to verify. In Section 7.2.2, we pointed out that fair value accounting has a stewardship interpretation, since we can regard it as charging the manager with the opportunity cost of net assets used in the business. Stewardship is then evaluated by the manager's ability to earn a return on this opportunity cost. However, we also stated that this argument assumes that fair values can be determined with reasonable reliability. Thus, contract theory supports fair value only when this value can be determined reliably (e.g., Level 1 and perhaps Level 2 of the fair value hierarchy (Section 7.2.1)—the theory does not support Level 3).

Note that this increased concern for reliability implies that the best financial statements to inform lenders and protect against manager opportunism are not the same as the best ones to inform equity investors (who may find unrealized gains to be decision useful). This implication conflicts with the Conceptual Framework, which states that financial statements should provide useful information to investors *and* report on how efficiently and effectively management has used the firm's financial resources (see Section 3.7.1). The Framework implies that the same general purpose financial statements are useful for reporting to investors and reporting on manager stewardship.

In this regard, O'Brien (2009) questioned the dropping of the term "reliable" from the Conceptual Framework in favour of representational faithfulness. Recall, from Section 3.7.1, that representationally faithful information should be complete, free from material error, and neutral (i.e., without bias). In particular, O'Brien questioned dropping verifiability (a component of earlier FASB definitions of reliability) in the definition of representational faithfulness, and downgrading verifiability from a "fundamental" to an "enhancing" information characteristic. The standard setters' rationale for this, according to O'Brien, is to facilitate fair value accounting where, as is apparent from our discussion of Level 2 and 3 fair values in Section 7.2, verifiability can be problematic.

8.4.2 Conservatism

Payoff asymmetry also creates a demand for conditional conservatism (Section 6.11)—that is, for impairment tests. Lenders' demand for information about unrealized losses is greater than their demand for information about unrealized gains, since unrealized gains are believed to be less useful than unrealized losses in predicting financial distress.

While it is apparent from Chapter 7 that accounting standards contain numerous impairment tests, these tests are likely motivated by legal liability arising from the savings and loan debacle described in Section 6.11. A rationale for this legal liability is demonstrated in Section 6.12. There, conditions were shown under which risk averse investors who use financial statement information for consumption planning benefit from conditional conservatism, which also benefits accountants and auditors through reduced likelihood of their being sued.

However, the efficient contracting rationale for conditional conservatism extends beyond legal liability. As mentioned, it provides an early warning system of impending financial distress. Also, conditional conservatism, by creating a systematic understatement of net asset value, provides lenders with a lower bound on net assets to help them evaluate their loan security.

Evidence that lenders are a major source of demand for conditional conservative accounting is provided by Ball, Robin, and Sadka (2008). Based on a sample of 22 countries, these researchers reported evidence that several measures of a country's financial reporting quality, including conditional conservatism, were higher the greater the size of that country's debt market. No such relationship was found for the size of a country's equity market. The authors claimed that this result is consistent with the efficient contracting role of financial reporting since it supports an argument that it is the demand of lenders, not equity holders, that is a major driver of conditional conservatism.

Tan (2013) examined firms' accounting practices *after* a debt covenant violation. He pointed out that lenders then have significantly greater bargaining power over management (for an example of such power, see Theory in Practice 9.2 re Can West Global). Tan argued that lenders will use this power to force management to adopt increased (conditional) conservatism to further protect their interests. Based on a large sample of U.S. firms that reported a debt covenant violation during the period 1996–2007, he found a significant increase in conservatism during and after the quarter of violation, consistent with his argument. Tan conducted additional tests that reject two alternative explanations for the lower net income that results from increased conservatism—namely, reversal of earlier accruals made by management in an attempt to avoid covenant violation, and large writeoffs made by new management (covenant violations are often followed by replacement of management) to "clear the decks" of mistakes made by old management. Tan's findings thus support the lender demand for conservatism predicted by contract theory.

Conditional conservatism is also demanded by equity holders for stewardship purposes, since it is then more difficult for managers, who may wish to enhance their reputations and compensation, to include unrealized income-increasing gains in earnings and to cover up overstatements, such as optimistic forecasts, made during the year. Also, recording unrealized losses may motivate early manager action to correct operating policies that have led to such losses and, if not, alerting Boards of Directors to take timely steps to correct management's lack of action. Thus, in addition to its role in warning lenders, conditional conservatism also provides an early warning system of losing operating and investment policies.

Ramalingegowda and Yu (RY; 2012) studied the demand for conditional conservatism by institutional shareholders. Using the Basu measure of conservatism (Section 6.11), they found that reported earnings of firms with large dedicated institutional investors (institutions with large share holdings in the firm, long-term investment horizon, and independent of management) exhibited greater conservatism as the percentage ownership of these institutions increased, consistent with a demand for early warning of possible financial distress and protection from manager opportunism. No such relationship was found for other institutional investors using shorter-term investment strategies. Presumably, these shorter-term investors were less interested in firms' longer-term performance.

RY also reported that their findings were concentrated in firms with high information asymmetry and growth potential. Since large, powerful institutions have some ability to demand inside information from management, direct monitoring of management stewardship provides an alternative to conservatism in providing early warning of losing manager policies. However, firms with high information asymmetry and rapid growth are particularly hard to monitor in this manner. This latter result suggests that conditional conservatism provides an effective corporate governance vehicle to help protect against manager opportunism when direct monitoring is most difficult.

Chen, Chen, Lobo, and Wang (2010) studied the demand for conditional conservatism by borrowers in China. They pointed out that state-owned enterprises have lower default risk than non-state-owned enterprises, due to their government support. Using several measures of conservatism, they reported that non-state-owned enterprises exhibit greater accounting conservatism than state-owned enterprises, consistent with greater lender concern about downside risk when the borrower is not state-owned. They also reported that firms borrowing from non-state-owned banks exhibit greater conservatism than borrowers from state-owned banks. The reason, according to the authors, is that state-owned banks are less diligent in monitoring default risk on their loans; hence, borrowing firms respond with less conservatism.

Ball and Shivakumar (2006), in a study covering the period 1987–2003, found that the ability of earnings to predict future cash flows increases substantially for years in which the firm is performing poorly, compared to years of good performance. This suggests that accounting practice has moved toward increasing recognition of unrealized losses while avoiding recognition of unrealized gains. Their findings provide evidence of increasing conditional conservatism, consistent with the increasing number of impairment tests described in Chapter 7.

The extent to which lenders demand unconditional conservatism is less clear in efficient contracting theory. Arguably, valuing assets at less than expected value (and valuing liabilities at more) helps to retain assets in the business for the protection of lenders. Unconditional conservatism also benefits lenders to the extent that the fair value of some assets that are accounted for under unconditional conservatism, such as R&D, would fall in value or disappear if the firm becomes financially distressed, and hence provide little loan security. However, inconsistent with these arguments, Ball, Robin, and Sadka (2008), whose findings on conditional conservatism were outlined above, found no association between the size of a country's debt market and their measures of that country's unconditional conservatism.

8.5 CONTRACT RIGIDITY

Contracts, by their nature, can be hard to change. In other words, contracts are **rigid**. Also, many contracts, such as debt contracts, are long term. If long-term contracts depend on accounting variables, it is likely that accounting standards will change during the life of the contract. Such changes can adversely affect covenant values, increasing the likelihood of violation. For example, new standards for revenue recognition or early recognition of credit losses can reduce reported earnings, and hence increase the debt–equity ratio and reduce the times interest earned covenant ratio. Also, standards that increase earnings volatility, such as fair valuation of held-for-trading securities or undesignated derivatives, increase the probability of future covenant violation, even if they do not result in covenant violation currently. While it is possible that a contract could be renegotiated following an accounting standard change, such a process would be long and costly—lenders would be giving up the additional protection afforded by the original covenants, which are now more likely to be violated, and they would likely demand something in return such as a higher interest rate. Also, for public debt, agreement would be required from all, or a significant majority of, creditors.

Another possibility is to incorporate provisions into the contract itself to deal with unexpected events. However, as a practical matter, it is effectively impossible to anticipate all future events that can affect covenant values, particularly new accounting standards.

Yet another possibility is to "freeze" the accounting policies used to calculate covenant values at those in effect at the time the contract is signed. However, this would incur the cost and inconvenience of keeping track of the effect on the financial statements of all standard changes during the life of the contract.

Arguably, a more efficient way to deal with changes in GAAP is to allow the manager some *flexibility in accounting policy choice*, so that he/she can adapt to unexpected circumstances. Usually, the set of accounting policies from which the manager can choose is those allowed under GAAP. For example, suppose that a new accounting standard, such as expensing of ESOs, lowers reported the net income of a healthy, going concern firm to the point where possible violation of debt covenants is of concern. It may be less costly for management to increase reported net income by adjusting accruals, such as allowances for doubtful accounts, revenue recognition policy, amortization method, or length of useful life of capital assets, than to renegotiate the debt contract or suffer the costs of technical violation. If so, the manager's accounting policy changes are consistent with efficient contracting.

However, giving management discretion to choose from a set of accounting policies opens up the possibility of opportunistic behaviour. That is, given the available set, rational managers may choose accounting policies from the set for their own purposes, thereby reducing contract efficiency. For example, rather than being a healthy, going concern, suppose that the firm in the previous paragraph is approaching financial distress, and the new accounting standard will lead to violation of debt covenants. To avoid violation, and the resulting effects on compensation and reputation, the manager chooses the same income-increasing accounting policy changes. This action is opportunistic, since it hides the firm's financial distress from investors. While such policies may benefit the manager in the short run, they can harm lenders and shareholders. Theory in Practice 8.1 illustrates this type of opportunism.

Theory in Practice 8.1

To illustrate how serious consequences can arise from compensation contracts, consider Fannie Mae, established by the U.S. federal government in 1938, and converted to a public company in 1968. Its mandate is to facilitate home ownership by providing financing to mortgage lenders, including purchasing home mortgages from these institutions. Fannie Mae is one of the largest U.S. corporations in terms of assets. Its stability is essential to the U.S. housing market.

In 2004, the Office of Federal Housing Enterprise Oversight (OFHEO, now part of the Federal Housing Finance Agency) issued a report highly critical of Fannie Mae. OFHEO was an office of the U.S. government created to oversee the operations of Fannie Mae and a related organization (Freddie Mac). One concern was about the amortization of discount and premium on Fannie Mae's large mortgage portfolio, going back to 1998. In that year, falling interest rates led to a large volume of mortgage repayments,

as homeowners scrambled to refinance at lower rates. This created a need for Fannie Mae to accelerate amortization of discount and premium on these mortgages. For 1998, according to OFHEO, extra amortization expense of $400 million was required. However, Fannie Mae only recorded $200 million in that year, deferring the rest to 1999. This deferral did not affect operating cash flows. Nevertheless, the volatility of earnings was reduced and, of particular concern to OFHEO, management bonuses would not have been paid if the 1998 net income of Fannie Mae was reduced any further.

Another concern was with Fannie Mae's accounting for hedges. Fannie Mae claimed to account for these at fair value under SFAS 133 (now ASC 815) and, by the end of 2003, had about $12.2 billion of unrealized hedging losses accumulated in other comprehensive income. However, according to the OFHEO report, Fannie Mae did not properly designate its hedges and did not evaluate

Cont . . .

their effectiveness. Consequently, it did not qualify for the benefits of hedge accounting under SFAS 133 (recall, from Section 7.9.2, that one of these benefits is that unrealized gains and losses on hedging instruments are included in other comprehensive income rather than in net income). As a result, Fannie Mae's net income was overstated over several years. Furthermore, transfer of this amount back against net income threatened the adequacy of Fannie Mae's regulatory capital.

OFHEO obtained an agreement from Fannie Mae's board of directors to, among other things, bring its accounting into conformity with GAAP. In February 2006, a report commissioned by the board termed the company's accounting system at the time grossly inadequate, and accused the then-CFO of failing to provide adequate oversight of the system. The report also noted flawed accounting practices, including a drive to show smooth earnings growth and to report earnings that met analysts' forecasts. The SEC also weighed in, announcing that Fannie Mae should revise its earnings. Later, it fined the company $400 million for fraudulent accounting.

In December 2004, the Fannie May board dismissed its CEO and CFO, and announced a review of their bonus and severance payments. Fannie Mae's auditor was also dismissed. In December 2006, OFHEO revealed plans to sue Fannie Mae's former CEO and CFO to recover excess compensation, and Fannie Mae launched a $2 billion lawsuit against its former auditor.

Additional Fannie Mae reporting problems arose out of the 2007–2008 securities market meltdowns. In December 2011, the SEC launched civil lawsuits against three of its senior executives, including its CEO, for understating Fannie Mae's exposure to subprime mortgage loans. For example, in a 2007 public disclosure, the company reported that only 0.2%, approximately $4.8 billion, of its total holdings of single-family mortgages were subprime, omitting $43.4 billion of loans specifically targeted at borrowers with weaker credit histories. In addition, the company understated its exposure to reduced documentation loans. Recall, from Section 1.3, that lax mortgage lending practices bore much of the blame for the collapse of the asset-backed securities market. The result, according to the SEC, was to seriously mislead investors. Consistent with this misleading, Fannie Mae's share price had increased by more than 20% in the year prior to the meltdown.

During this period, the three executives received substantial and increasing incentive plan bonuses, which were tied to company and personal performance. In retrospect, their subprime understatements contributed substantially to reported performance, and thus to bonuses.

In 2008, Fannie Mae reported a loss of $2.3 billion, mainly due to losses on its higher risk assets. In the same year, the U.S. government took control of the company. The three senior officers were dismissed in 2008–2009.

Given contract rigidity, the firm faces a corporate governance tradeoff. The optimal set of accounting policies for the firm represents a compromise. On the one hand, tightly prescribing accounting policies beforehand will minimize opportunistic accounting policy choices by managers, but incur costs of lack of accounting flexibility to meet changing circumstances, such as new accounting standards that affect debt covenants and compensation. On the other hand, allowing the manager to choose from a broad array of accounting policies will reduce costs of contract rigidity but expose the firm to the costs of opportunistic manager behaviour.

Regardless of the amount of accounting policy choice available, it should be apparent that changes in accounting standards matter to the manager. If the manager has no flexibility, a new accounting standard that, say, reduces net income may result in the manager changing operating policies, such as cutting R&D or reducing maintenance. If the manager has flexibility, he/she may instead (or in addition) change accounting policies, such as lengthening the expected life of capital assets, or changing the timing of revenue recognition, so as to increase reported net income. In other cases, if a new standard, say, increases earnings volatility, the manager may compensate by increasing hedging activity. When managers change accounting policies and/or change operating decisions in response to a change in accounting standards, we say that the standard change creates **economic consequences**.

Economic consequences could be consistent with efficient contracting if they are the lowest-cost way to avoid costs of technical default on debt covenants when the economic state of the firm does not warrant default, or of preventing a competent manager from leaving the firm due to lower earnings-based compensation. However, economic consequences could also be opportunistic if their effect is to postpone investor awareness of financial distress, or if they are attempts by a poorly performing manager to preserve reputation and compensation. Distinguishing between these two possibilities is an important component of efficient contracting research. Some of this research is reviewed in Section 8.8.

Note that under efficient securities market theory described in Section 4.3, accounting standard changes do not have economic consequences if they are fully disclosed and do not have cash flow effects. Such changes should not matter to managers since an efficient market will see through the financial statement effects and not reward or penalize the firm, or its manager, for any changes in reported earnings that result. However, once we take efficient contracting into account, managers do care about accounting standard changes, cash flow effects or not, and, as just discussed, may change their accounting policies and/or operating actions to compensate. Thus, efficient contracting helps to explain what any accountant knows—accounting policies do matter to managers.

The study by Dichev and Skinner (DS; 2002) supports this argument that accounting policies matter. They studied a large sample of private[7] lending agreements, concentrating on agreements with covenants based on maintenance of a specified current ratio or a specified amount of net worth.

For each sample firm, DS calculated the *covenant slack* for each quarter during which the loan is outstanding. For example, for the current ratio, the covenant slack for a loan's first quarter is the difference between the firm's actual current ratio at the end of that quarter and the current ratio the firm is required to maintain under the lending agreement. This calculation was repeated for each sample firm for all quarters, for both current ratio and net worth covenants. To avoid covenant violation, managers will want to maintain zero or positive slack.

DS found in their sample that the number of quarters with zero or slightly positive slack is significantly greater than would be expected if firms were not managing their covenant ratios. Also, the number of quarters where slack is slightly negative is significantly less than expected. These results are consistent with economic consequence arguments since they suggest that managers choose accounting policies to maintain their covenant ratios so as to meet or exceed the levels required.

DS also found that this tendency to maintain zero or positive slack is particularly strong for quarters leading up to and including a *first* covenant violation. They pointed out that the costs of an initial violation are higher than for subsequent violations, since the lender will quickly take action to protect its interests, and much of the damage to manager and firm reputation occurs when a violation first occurs. Thus managers work particularly hard to manage covenant ratios so as to avoid an initial violation. This finding also supports the assumption that managers are rational—we would expect managers to work harder when the costs of failure are higher.

8.6 EMPLOYEE STOCK OPTIONS

We now examine an area where management concern about accounting policy was particularly apparent. This is the accounting for stock options issued to management and, in some cases, to other employees, giving them the right to buy company stock over some time period. We will refer to these options as **ESOs**.

Until about 2005, accounting for ESOs in the United States and elsewhere was based on the 1972 Opinion 25 of the Accounting Principles Board (APB 25). This standard required firms issuing fixed[8] ESOs to record an expense equal to the difference between the market value of the shares on the date the option was granted to the employee (the **grant date**) and the exercise, or strike, price of the option. This difference is called the **intrinsic value** of the option. Most firms granting ESOs set the exercise price equal to the grant date market value, so that the intrinsic value was zero. As a result, no expense for ESO compensation was recorded. For example, if the underlying share has a market value of $10 on the grant date, setting the exercise price at $10 triggered no expense recognition, whereas setting the exercise price at $8 would trigger an expense of $2 per ESO granted.

In the years following issuance of APB 25, this basis of accounting became widely recognized as inadequate. Even if there is no intrinsic value, an option has a fair value on the grant date, since the price of the underlying share may rise over the term to expiry (the **expiry date**) of the option. Failure to record an expense understates the firm's compensation cost and overstates its net income. Furthermore, a lack of earnings comparability across firms results, since different firms have different proportions of options in their total compensation packages. These problems worsened as a result of a dramatic increase in the use of ESO compensation since 1972, particularly for small, start-up, high-tech firms. These firms particularly liked the non-cash-requiring aspect of ESOs and their motivational impact on the workforce, as well as the higher reported profits that result compared to other forms of compensation.

Also during this period, executive compensation came under political scrutiny, due to the high amounts of compensation that top executives received. Firms were motivated to award seemingly excessive amounts of ESO compensation since such compensation was "free." Charging the fair value of ESOs to expense would, some felt, help investors to see the real cost to the firm of this component of compensation.

One of the reasons why the APB had not required fair value accounting for ESOs was the difficulty of establishing this value. This situation changed somewhat with the advent of the Black-Scholes option pricing formula. However, several aspects of ESOs are not captured by Black-Scholes. For example, their model assumes that options can be freely traded, whereas ESOs are likely non-transferrable and cannot be exercised until the **vesting date**, which is typically one or more years after they are granted. Also, if the employee leaves the firm prior to vesting the options are forfeited or, if exercised, there may be restrictions on the employee's ability to sell the acquired shares. In addition, the Black-Scholes formula assumes that the option cannot be exercised prior to expiry (a European option), whereas ESOs are an American option (can be exercised prior to expiry). Nevertheless, it was felt by many that Black-Scholes provided a reasonable basis for estimation of ESO fair value.

Consequently, in June 1993, the FASB issued an exposure draft of a proposed new standard. The exposure draft proposed that firms record compensation expense based on the fair value at the grant date (also called the *ex ante* value) of ESOs issued during the period. Fair value could be determined by Black-Scholes or other option pricing formula, with adjustment for the possibility of employee retirement prior to vesting and for the possibility of early exercise. Early exercise was dealt with by using the *expected* time to exercise, based, for example, on past experience, rather than the time to expiry, in the Black-Scholes formula.

The exposure draft attracted extreme opposition from business, which soon extended into the U.S. Congress. Concerns were expressed about the economic consequences of the lower reported profits that would result. These claimed consequences included lower share prices, higher cost of capital, a shortage of managerial talent, and inadequate manager and employee motivation. This would particularly disadvantage small start-up companies that, as mentioned, were heavy options users. To preserve their bottom lines, firms would be forced to reduce ESO usage, with negative effects on cash flows, motivation, and innovation. This, it was claimed, would threaten the competitive position of American industry. Business was also concerned that the draft proposal was politically motivated. If so, opponents of the proposal would feel justified in attacking it with every means at their disposal.

Another series of questions related to the ability of Black-Scholes to accurately and reliably measure ESO fair value. To see these concerns, we first need to consider just what the ESO costs are to the firm, since, unlike most costs, ESOs do not require a cash outlay. Essentially, the cost is borne by the firm's existing shareholders through dilution of their proportionate interests in the firm. Thus, if an ESO is exercised at a price of, say, $10 when the market value of the share is $30, the *ex post* cost to the firm and its shareholders is $20. This $20 is called the *ex post* cost since it is only after an ESO is exercised that its actual cost is known. We can also think of the $20 as an opportunity cost, since by admitting the new shareholder at $10, the firm forgoes the opportunity to issue the share at the market price of $30. That is, the $20 opportunity cost measures the dilution of the existing shareholders' interests.

The fair value of the ESO at the grant date, hence the *ex ante* cost to the firm, is the expected present value of the *ex post* cost.[9] Recognizing this cost as an expense increases relevance, since current shareholders will receive a less-than-proportionate share of future dividends. That is, future dividends per share will be reduced to the extent dividends are diluted over a larger number of shares. The reduction in earnings from expensing ESOs anticipates these lower dividends, thereby helping investors to better predict future cash flows from their investments.

But, this ESO expense is very difficult to measure reliably. As mentioned, the employee may exercise the option at any time after vesting up to expiry. The *ex post* cost to the firm will then depend on the difference between the market value of the share and the exercise price at that time. In order to know the fair value of the ESO it is necessary to know the employee's optimal exercise strategy.

This strategy was modelled by Huddart (1994). As Huddart pointed out, determining the employee's strategy requires knowledge of the process generating the firm's future stock price, the employee's wealth and utility function (in particular the degree of risk aversion), whether the employee holds or sells the acquired shares (many firms require senior officers to hold large amounts of company stock) and, if sold, what investment alternatives are available. Matters are further complicated if the firm pays dividends on its shares and if the motivational impact of the ESO affects share price.

By making some simplifying assumptions (including no dividends, no motivational impact), Huddart showed that the Black-Scholes formula, assuming ESOs are held to expiry date, does indeed overstate the fair value of an ESO at the grant date. To see why, we first note three option characteristics:

1. The expected return from holding an option exceeds the expected return on the underlying share. This is because the option cannot be worth less than zero, but the share price can fall below the option's exercise price. As a result, a risk-neutral employee would not normally exercise an ESO before maturity.

2. The "upside potential" of an American option (its propensity to increase in value) increases with the time to maturity. The longer the time, the greater the probability that during this interval the underlying share price will take off, making the option more valuable. Early exercise sacrifices some of this upside potential.

3. If an option is "deep in the money"—that is, if the value of the underlying share greatly exceeds the exercise price—the set of possible payoffs from holding the option and their probabilities closely resembles the set of payoffs and probabilities from holding the underlying share. This is because for a deep in the money option the probability of the share price falling below the exercise price is low. Then, every

realization of share price induces a similar realization in the option value. As a result, if the employee is required to hold the shares acquired, he or she might as well hold the option to maturity. The payoffs are the same and, due to the time value of money, paying the exercise price at expiry dominates paying it sooner.

The question then is, are there circumstances where the employee *will* exercise the option early? Huddart identifies two. First, if the ESO is only slightly in the money (substantial risk of zero payoff), the time to maturity is short (little sacrifice of upside potential), and the employee is required to hold the shares acquired, risk aversion can trigger early exercise. Since there is substantial risk of zero return, a risk-averse employee (who trades off risk and return) may feel that the reduction in risk from exercising the option now rather than continuing to hold it outweighs the lower expected return from holding the share.

The second circumstance occurs when the ESO is deep in the money, the time to expiry is short, and the employee can either hold the acquired share or sell it and invest the proceeds in a riskless asset. If the employee is sufficiently risk-averse, the riskless asset is preferred to the share. Because the option is deep in the money, the payoffs and their probabilities are similar for the share and ESO. Thus the employee is indifferent to holding the ESO or the share. Since holding the riskless asset is preferred to holding the share, it is also preferred to holding the option. Then, the employee will exercise the option, sell the share, and buy the riskless asset.

In a follow-up empirical study to test the early exercise predictions, Huddart and Lang (1996) examined the ESO exercise patterns of the employees of eight large U.S. corporations over a 10-year period. They found that early exercise was common, consistent with Huddart's risk aversion assumption. They also found that the variables that explained empirically the early exercises, such as time to expiration and extent to which the ESO was in the money, were "broadly consistent" with the predictions of the model.

The significance of early exercise is that the fair value of ESOs at grant date is less than the value determined by Black-Scholes, which, as mentioned, assumes the option is held to expiry. This is particularly apparent for the first early exercise scenario outlined above. If the ESO is barely in the money, the *ex post* cost of the option to the employer (share price less exercise price) is low. While the cost savings from the second circumstance are less, the cost to the employer is still less than Black-Scholes, as Huddart shows.

Subsequent research tended to confirm the tendency of Black-Scholes to overstate *ex post* ESO cost. Hall and Murphy (2002), using a different approach than Huddart, also demonstrated a substantial probability of early exercise, and showed that this significantly reduces the firm's ESO cost below Black-Scholes. Their analysis also suggested considerable variability in employees' exercise decisions.

Early exercise, presumably, is the reason the 1993 FASB exposure draft proposed using expected time to exercise, rather than expiry date, in the Black-Scholes formula.

However, as Huddart pointed out, use of expected time to exercise reduces the overstatement of ESO cost, but does not eliminate it, as also demonstrated by Hemmer,

Matsunaga, and Shevlin (HMS; 1994).[10] In an empirical study, Marquardt (2002) examined the accuracy of the Black-Scholes formula based on expected time to exercise. In a sample of 966 option grants by 57 large U.S. companies over the period 1963–1984, she found that Black-Scholes tended to produce positively biased estimates of *ex post* ESO cost, consistent with the analyses of Huddart and HMS. She also found that the accuracy of this estimated cost varied widely for different firms.

We conclude that ESO fair value estimates may be unreliable, due both to upward bias and possible error and bias in estimating the timing of employees' early exercise decisions in the face of wide variability of these decisions. Furthermore, other Black-Scholes model inputs, such as the share variability parameter, create additional reliability problems.

As one can imagine, theory and evidence suggesting that the exposure draft, if implemented, may not produce accurate estimates of ESO expense would be seized upon by critics, particularly if the estimates tended to be too high. As a result, in December 1994 the FASB announced that it was dropping the exposure draft, on the grounds that it did not have sufficient support. Instead, the FASB turned to supplementary disclosure. In SFAS 123, issued in 1995, it urged firms to use the fair value approach suggested in the exposure draft, but allowed the APB 25 intrinsic value approach provided the firm gave supplementary disclosure of ESO expense, determined by amortizing over their vesting periods the fair value of awarded ESOs based on expected time to exercise.

In the early 2000s, however, financial reporting scandals such as Enron and WorldCom led to increasing criticism of APB 25. In retrospect, it seems that manipulations of stock price by these and other companies were often driven by senior executives' tactics to increase the values of their ESOs.

Of course, such opportunistic behaviour to increase ESO value may be anticipated when the manager's remuneration contract is being negotiated, in which case the firm will price-protect itself by lowering the manager's formal remuneration by the expected amount of opportunism. That is, given competition in the labour market for managers, managers will be willing to work for a lower compensation from the company if they can augment their utility by means of opportunistic behaviour. As a result, given the remuneration contract, managers have an incentive to adopt opportunistic tactics to the extent they can do so.

One of these tactics was **pump and dump**, whereby managers would take actions to increase share value shortly before exercising options, then sell the shares (sometimes in a manner to disguise the transaction) before share price fell back and, presumably, invest the proceeds in less risky securities.

Bartov and Mohanram (2004) tested a sample of 1,218 U.S. companies with large ESO exercises by senior executives, during the period 1992–2001. They found a significant decrease in average abnormal share price and earnings in the two years following such exercises, relative to a control sample of similar firms with no large ESO exercises. They also showed evidence of abnormally large income-increasing accruals in the two years prior to exercise. The authors concluded that the senior managers in their test sample were aware of deteriorating profitability, and pumped up earnings and share price to delay the market's awareness of the deterioration. They then exercised their ESOs and, presumably, dumped the acquired shares immediately so as to maximize their cash proceeds. The lower earnings and share prices in the two years following exercise were driven by the reversal of the prior accruals and the market's belated awareness of the declining profitability.

Another tactic was reported by Aboody and Kasznik (AK; 2000), who studied the information release practices of CEOs around ESO grant dates. They reported evidence that CEOs of firms with scheduled grant dates (so that CEOs knew when the ESO award was coming)[11] used tactics (e.g., early announcement of bad news but not of good news) to lower share price, and thus ESO exercise price, leading up to award date. They also reported tactics to manage earnings upward after awards (e.g., influencing analysts' earnings forecasts).

Subsequently, Baker, Collins, and Reitenga (2009) investigated managers' discretion over accruals as a way to manage earnings (hence share price and ESO exercise price), downward during quarters when ESO awards were granted. They studied a large sample of U.S. firms over the period 1992–2003, reporting that when ESOs were a high proportion of CEO compensation (thus a high incentive to lower reported earnings during these quarters) or when the firm performed poorly in the prior quarter (thus an incentive to accrue large impairment test and other writedowns so as to relieve future quarters of fixed costs), CEOs, on average, did use accruals to manage grant-period reported earnings downward. However, this practice was observed only when ESO grant dates were unscheduled and thus could not be anticipated by investors. From this, the authors concluded that when investors *could* anticipate ESO grants they would realize managers' incentives and thus would tend to ignore lower reported earnings, in which case there was no point for managers to manage accruals. Note that this conclusion supports securities market efficiency and managers' acceptance of efficiency.

It also appears that some managers manipulated the ESO award date itself. This was investigated by Yermack (1997), who reported evidence that managers pressured compensation committees to grant unscheduled ESOs shortly before good earnings news (a tactic called **spring loading**). This gives the CEO a low exercise price and subsequent benefit as the share price rises in response to the GN.

Yet another tactic was **late timing,** an extreme case of award date manipulation. Late timing is the backdating of ESO awards to a date when the share price was lower than at the actual ESO grant date. This conferred an immediate benefit on the recipient, since, in effect, the ESO was in the money on the actual grant date; that is, intrinsic value was positive. While awarding ESOs that are in the money is not in itself illegal, backdating of ESO awards without full disclosure does violate GAAP. This is because, under APB 25, in effect when much of the late timing took place, an expense had to be recognized for ESOs awarded with positive intrinsic value. Late timing disguised this expense recognition. Discovery of late timing thus leads to restatement of prior years' earnings. If ESOs were expensed, earnings would still be overstated since, holding the share price constant, a decrease in the exercise price increases ESO fair value. The resulting increase in ESO expense would not be recognized under backdating. Other parameter inputs to Black-Scholes (Section 7.9.1) may also change. Lack of disclosure of the late timing also subjects those involved to liability under securities laws. SEC and company board investigations of late timing have led to a number of CEO and CFO firings and resignations, as illustrated by Theory in Practice 8.2.

The widespread abuse of late timing eroded investor confidence in management. Bernile and Jarrell (2009) investigated a sample of 129 firms identified as having engaged in backdating. They documented large negative abnormal stock returns for these firms in the days surrounding the backdating news. The authors argued that the firms' (as opposed to firm managers') various cash costs of being caught are relatively low, and presented evidence arguing that the declines in share value were instead due to increased estimation risk, as investors perceived managers as having behaved opportunistically.

Theory in Practice 8.2

On July 20, 2006, the SEC announced criminal and civil charges for securities fraud against the former CEO, vice-president human resources, and CFO of Brocade Communications Systems, Inc., a California-based developer of networking data storage products.

These were the first charges resulting from SEC investigations of numerous companies for late timing of ESO awards. The defendants, it was alleged, backdated employee ESO awards to a time when the company's share price was lower ($24.20) than at the real date of the award $36.56), thereby conferring an immediate benefit on the recipients by lowering the exercise price. In effect, the ESOs were issued in the money. Under APB 25, in effect at the time, an expense should have been recorded for in the money options, but this was disguised by the backdating.

In 2005, possibly in anticipation of forthcoming SEC charges, Brocade issued revised financial statements for the period 1999–2004 inclusive to correct for the APB 25 earnings overstatements. It increased compensation expense and decreased reported earnings by a total of $285 million. In July 2006, the company issued a statement indicating that the executives involved were no longer with the company, and reported a provision of $7 million for settlement of its own liability resulting from the actions of its former executives. In May 2007, the financial media reported that Brocade agreed to pay a $7 million penalty to settle the SEC charges. In June 2008, Brocade agreed to pay $160 million to settle a shareholder class-action lawsuit arising from the backdating.

In August 2007, the former Brocade CEO was found guilty by a jury in San Francisco on conspiracy and fraud charges for misleading investors. He was sentenced to 21 months in prison and ordered to pay a fine of $15 million. However, the verdict was later thrown out on appeal, on grounds that the prosecution had incorrectly told the jury that Brocade's finance department was unaware of the backdating. The court noted, however, that the prosecution's case was "relatively strong" and ordered a new trial. On retrial, the CEO was again convicted, sentenced to 18 months in prison, and fined $15 million.

More generally, Efendi, Files, Ouyang, and Swanson (2013) identified 141 firms with initial news of backdating during 2005 and 2006. After controlling for other factors, such as firm performance, that also affect executive turnover, they reported a significant positive relationship between backdating and CEO and CFO turnover, with the likelihood of a forced turnover twice as high as for a sample of control firms with no news of backdating. These executives were also significantly less likely to be hired in comparable positions with another firm.

The common theme of all these tactics is to increase the probability that ESOs will be deep in the money. This increases the likelihood of early exercise since, according to Huddart's analysis, deep in the money ESOs are more likely to be exercised early.

Obviously, managers would be unlikely to admit voluntarily to the behaviours just described. Nevertheless, if ESOs had to be expensed, their usage as a compensation device would decrease, thereby reducing the scope for manipulating ESO values for their own benefit. This undoubtedly added fuel to managers' economic consequences arguments against ESO expensing.

The combined effect of the above-described abuses, plus improved ability of accountants to model complexities such as early exercise,[12] enabled standard setters to overcome management opposition. SFAS 123R (2004), effective in 2005 (now ASC 718-10-30), requires expensing of *ex ante* ESO cost, as does IFRS 2 (2005) of the IASB.[13] These standards were implemented despite the raising by many managers of economic consequences and reliability concerns similar to those expressed over the 1993 exposure draft.

Indeed, management concern about ESO expensing does seem to have created some economic consequences. Choudhary (2011) compared the valuation of ESOs before and after SFAS 123R. For a sample of U.S. firms, he reported a significant downward bias in the average share return variability parameter input into the Black-Scholes model[14] (see Section 7.9.1) post-123R, relative to this input pre-123R. He found that the effect of lowering the variability parameter was to lower ESO fair value by about 7%, thus lowering ESO expense and increasing reported net income on average by 3.2% for his sample. Choudhary also reported some evidence that firms with an incentive to manage earnings upward biased the variability parameter even more. These results suggest that managers reacted to concerns about lower reported earnings by managing ESO expense downward.

Another economic consequence, as expected, was to greatly reduce the use of ESOs as a compensation device. For example, *The Economist* (2006) quoted an investment banker's estimate that the fair value of options granted by the top 500 U.S. firms fell from US$104 billion in 2000 to $30 billion in 2005. Consistent with this, Choudhary reported an average grant for his sample of 4.64 million ESOs before SFAS 123R, falling to 2.86 million ESOs after.

While, in this case, the standard setters ultimately "won," we may conclude that the accounting for ESOs is a prime illustration of management's interest in accounting policy, an interest that greatly complicates the setting of accounting standards. The intensity of management's objections to ESO expensing is particularly noteworthy given that the accounting policy for ESOs does not directly affect operating cash flows.

8.7 DISCUSSION AND SUMMARY OF ESO EXPENSING

The question then is: Why did management object to ESO expensing? Did they really believe that the result would be lower share prices, higher cost of capital, a shortage of managerial talent, and inadequate manager and employee motivation, as they claimed? One possibility that could explain this belief is that management did not accept securities market efficiency, believing that investors would react negatively to lower reported earnings regardless of the reason.

Other possibilities, though, arise from contracts. Lower reported earnings would increase the likelihood of debt covenant violation. Also, management compensation could decrease to the extent the compensation contract depended on reported earnings.

A further source of reduced compensation would arise as firms decreased ESO usage in compensation contracts. This would reduce a manager's ability to increase ESO value through opportunistic actions described above such as pump and dump, late timing, etc. In retrospect, it seems that compensation contracting was not very efficient, since it led to such tactics. This lack of efficiency is also borne out by the Enron, WorldCom, and 2007–2008 market meltdown disasters outlined in Chapter 1, where, as mentioned, suspicions arose that management's adoption of risky, even illegal, tactics to report high earnings was driven by a desire to increase ESO values. In Chapter 10, we will discuss some of the changes in manager compensation practices that have arisen in an attempt to increase contracting efficiency. For now, the important point to realize is that efficient contracting theory provides an explanation as to why accounting policy choice matters to managers.

Finally, note that management's concern about accounting policies does not contradict efficient securities market theory. Even if securities markets are efficient, and managers believe this, management concerns about the effects of accounting policies on contracts remain.

8.8 DISTINGUISHING EFFICIENCY AND OPPORTUNISM IN CONTRACTING

Despite the clear existence of opportunism illustrated by Theory in Practice 8.1 and 8.2, there is considerable empirical evidence of efficient contracting. Can it be that the various examples of opportunism outlined above are "the exceptions that prove the rule?" In this section, we consider some of the empirical studies that both support and question efficient contracting.

Mian and Smith (1990) provided a seminal study of efficient contracting. They examined the accounting policy choice of whether to consolidate a subsidiary company. They argued that the greater the interdependence between parent and subsidiary the more efficient it is (that is, the lower the contracting costs) to prepare consolidated financial statements. The reason is that the greater the interdependence the more desirable it is to evaluate the *joint* results of parent and subsidiary operations. Consolidated financial statements provide a basis for joint evaluation. Also, it is more efficient to monitor manager performance by use of consolidated financial statement-based performance measures than by performance measures based on separate parent and subsidiary financial statements when interdependence is high. Thus, Mian and Smith predicted that the greater the integration between parent and subsidiary, the more likely the parent will prepare consolidated statements. This argument can be extended to predict that if consolidated financial statements are prepared for internal monitoring of manager performance, it is less costly to also prepare consolidated statements for external reporting. Mian and Smith presented empirical evidence consistent with these predictions.

Dechow (1994) investigated whether managers use accruals opportunistically or efficiently. She argued that if accruals are largely the result of opportunistic manipulation of reported earnings, the market will reject them in favour of cash flows, in which case cash flows should be more highly associated with share returns than net income. Alternatively, if accruals reflect efficient contracting, net income should be more highly associated with share returns than cash flows. Her empirical tests found net income to be more highly associated with share returns than cash flows.

Dechow also argued that when accruals are relatively large (as, for example, in rapidly growing firms), net income should be even more highly associated with share returns, relative to cash flows, than when the firm is in a steady state (in which case cash flows and net income will be equal). Her empirical tests found this to be the case, adding further support to efficient contracting.

Bharath, Sunder, and Sunder (2008) investigated the effect of accounting quality on interest rates charged in public and private (i.e., banks) lending markets. They measured a firm's accounting quality by the magnitude of its operating accruals, on grounds that the higher accruals are, the greater will be the likelihood of opportunistic management manipulation of net income. They found that interest rates were significantly lower in public and private debt markets for firms with low accruals (i.e., high quality accounting), particularly in the public debt market. This is consistent with efficient contracting since it appears that lenders react favourably to accounting quality by rewarding the high quality firm with lower interest rates. The authors also found that firms with lower quality reporting tended to borrow from banks (i.e., a private debt market) while high quality firms tended to borrow in public markets. In effect, for high accounting quality firms, it is more efficient to borrow via public debt contracts, and vice versa for low accounting quality firms.[15]

Recall, from Section 8.4, that conditional conservatism is an important contributor to efficient debt contracting. This argument was tested by Wittenberg-Moerman (2008). She examined a large sample of borrowing firms in the U.S. syndicated loan market during the period 1998–2003, predicting that conditional conservatism reduces information asymmetry for persons buying and selling loans in that market, due to its early warning system characteristic, which reduces the likelihood that management will exploit its inside information to hide or delay the release of bad news.

Wittenberg-Moerman measured information asymmetry by the bid–ask spread (Chapter 1, Note 22) in the loan market. Sellers of loans (askers) possess inside information about the quality and future prospects of their loans on sale. However, buyers who do not possess this information will bid less than the asking price, one reason being fear that the seller may misrepresent loan quality. The greater the buyers' concerns, the wider the spread, other things being equal. As mentioned, these concerns, hence the spread, should be reduced to the extent that the financial statements of the borrowing firm exhibit conditional conservatism.

The extent of this conservatism was measured using the method of Basu (1997) described in Section 6.11. Wittenberg-Moerman found that, as expected, conditional conservatism and bid–ask spread were negatively associated. She did not find an association when firms recognized unrealized gains. These results are consistent with the efficient contracting prediction that lenders demand conditional conservatism.

It should be noted, though, that questions about conservative accounting in debt contracts were raised by Gigler, Kanodia, Sapra, and Venugopalan (2009). They pointed out that while conservative accounting may lower interest rates on debt, it carries a cost, since, by its nature, conservatism increases the likelihood of covenant violation when not warranted by the economic state of the firm. They demonstrated conditions under which this cost exceeds the benefits, in which case conservative accounting decreases contract efficiency.

In Section 8.2, we pointed out the importance of contract efficiency to corporate governance. **Income escalator clauses** are an interesting example of how clever contract design may improve efficiency. An income escalator clause increases the covenant level of net worth that the firm is required to maintain by a percentage of net income (e.g., 50%). Beatty, Weber, and Yu (2008) reported empirical evidence that firms with income escalator clauses in their debt covenants are more likely to choose conservative accounting policies. The reason, presumably, is that conservative accounting lowers reported net income, hence lowers the increase in the covenant net worth requirement. Since conservative accounting benefits lenders through asset retention and early warning of distress, the encouragement of conservatism created by income escalator clauses thus increases debtholder confidence, enabling a lower interest rate.

Many firms experience financial statement restatements, class-action lawsuits, and SEC investigations, which may suggest manager opportunistic behaviour. Armstrong, Jagolinzer, and Larcker (AJL; 2010) studied this issue. They examined a large sample of firms over 2001–2005 and, for each sample firm, estimated its CEO's temptation to behave opportunistically by his/her "portfolio delta"—that is, by the change in value of his/her holdings of company stock and options following a $1 change in the company's share price. Higher portfolio delta suggests that the manager has more to gain from opportunistic behaviour designed to increase the share price.

For each sample firm, AJL also identified another sample firm with similar size, complexity, leverage, and corporate governance characteristics, but with a differing CEO portfolio delta. This creates pairs of firms where firms in each pair have similar contracting environments but different portfolio deltas, hence different management temptations to behave opportunistically.

The question then is: Do firms with high portfolio delta CEOs exhibit more opportunistic CEO behaviour than similar firms with lower CEO portfolio deltas? That is, do high portfolio delta firms experience more restatements, lawsuits, or SEC investigations? AJL found no evidence of this. As they pointed out, this failure to find evidence suggests that firms are able to align CEO and shareholder interests, thereby supporting efficient contracting. That is, managers' holdings of company stock do not seem, by themselves, to lead to opportunistic behaviour.

Nevertheless, while the AJL study suggests that, on average, opportunistic manager behaviour is not driven by their holdings of company stock and options, the existence of restatements, lawsuits, and SEC investigations does suggest that such behaviour exists. Thus, it could be driven by other motivations. In this regard, Dechow and Shakespeare (2009) reported on a procedure that numerous firms use to manage their financial statements. The procedure is to securitize assets (Section 1.3), such as accounts receivable. Such transactions may be accounted for as secured borrowings. That is, the firm retains the securitized assets on its books and records a liability for the amount of cash received. However, under U.S. standards in effect at the time, firms could treat the securitization as a sale, thereby removing the assets off-balance sheet, if certain conditions were met. For example, the buyer must not have recourse to the firm if losses are incurred on the securitized assets. The sale treatment is preferred by many firms since debt–equity ratios are improved.

To increase the buyer's confidence in the quality of the securitized assets, the firm typically retains a portion of them, usually of lower quality. This retained portion is valued at fair value. Since there is no market value for these retained assets by definition, firms have considerable flexibility in their valuation.

These sales-treatment securitizations can result in a gain or loss. For example, a gain will result if the proceeds of sale plus the fair value assigned to the retained assets exceeds the book value of the securitized assets.

For a sample of 195 observations over the period 1987–2005, Dechow and Shakespeare examined the financial statement effects of sales-treatment securitizations. They found that a gain was generated for 171 of these 195 observations, of which 35 enabled the firm to report positive net income, rather than a loss, for the quarter. They also found that debt–equity ratios increased by an average of 42% over what they would have been had these securitizations been accounted for as secured borrowings.

Dechow and Shakespeare also examined the timing of these securitizations. They found that a significant percentage of the 35 firms that avoided reporting a loss entered into their securitization transactions during the last five days of the quarter. This suggests that managers, learning of an impending loss quarter, entered into sufficient profitable securitization transactions to enable a positive quarterly profit to be reported.

While at least some of these off-balance sheet securitizations could result from efficient contracting (i.e., a low-cost way to increase debt to equity, thereby avoiding covenant violation when the firm is not in a financially distressed state), the high proportion of them that avoided a loss, particularly in the last quarter, suggests opportunistic behaviour.

Further evidence of opportunistic behaviour is provided by Hope and Thomas (2008). They examined a sample of multinational firms that reported under SFAS 131.[16] This standard, effective in 1997, required firms to report supplementary information about their various domestic and foreign operations in a manner consistent with how it organizes its segment performance reporting internally. Prior to SFAS 131, firms were required to report sales, earnings, and total assets by geographic area. Under SFAS 131, disclosure of earnings by geographic area was made voluntary. Total foreign sales and earnings have to be disclosed, however.

Hope and Thomas reported that for those sample firms that did not disclose earnings by geographic area post-SFAS 131, total foreign sales increased but total foreign earnings decreased on average, relative to the period prior to SFAS 131, and relative to the post-SFAS 131 domestic earnings of those same firms. The share prices of these firms also fell, as investors became aware of lower foreign profitability. Once full disclosure of foreign earnings by geographic area was relaxed, it seems that managers may have exploited the reduced ability of investors to monitor their performance by increasing foreign sales at the expense of profits.

The authors attributed these results to "empire building," a form of moral hazard under which managers opportunistically increase firm size (higher foreign sales). Such behaviour is motivated by the increased reputation and compensation that accrues to managers of large, growing firms.

We conclude that both efficient contracting and opportunism exist in the real world of accounting. This puts accountants and auditors on notice that while the borderline between these two types of behaviour is imprecise, some manager accounting policy choice, even if within GAAP, may be opportunistic. This represents a failure of corporate governance. If managers cannot be dissuaded from such policy choices, the onus is on the accountant for full disclosure so that investors are not misled. Otherwise, the firm faces the likelihood of financial statement restatements, lawsuits, and possible securities commission investigation, all of which damage the reputations of the accountant as well as management.

8.9 SUMMARY OF EFFICIENT CONTRACTING FOR DEBT AND STEWARDSHIP

Efficient contracting theory studies the role of financial accounting information in moderating information asymmetry between contracting parties. It predicts that reporting to lenders and reporting on manager stewardship are important sources of demand for financial accounting information as a protection against managers' inside information advantage and possible shirking. At its most general level, the theory asserts that accounting policy choice is part of the firm's overall need to attain efficient contracting and corporate governance. To attain efficient contracting, financial information should be reliable and (conditionally) conservative.

A significant implication of efficient contracting theory is that accounting policies have economic consequences. That is, they matter to managers. To the extent that managers have flexibility to choose accounting policies, they may change these policies to offset the effect of new accounting standards on debt and compensation contracts. Lacking sufficient policy flexibility, they may change operating policies.

Firms face a tradeoff in the accounting policy flexibility granted to managers. Too little flexibility leads to contract inefficiency when accounting standards change. Too much flexibility opens up the possibility of manager opportunism. A reasonable compromise is to allow managers to choose accounting policies within GAAP.

Contract theory has led to a rich body of empirical literature. Some studies suggest manager opportunism. Others suggest efficient contracting. Accountants should be alert to the possibility of manager opportunism, since they are usually caught up in the lawsuits that follow.

8.10 IMPLICIT CONTRACTS

8.10.1 Definition and Empirical Evidence

In many situations, firms can realize the benefits of efficient contracting without actually entering into a formal contract. For example, a firm may consistently report smooth, growing profits, and/or build and maintain a reputation for a transparent information environment (i.e., high quality financial reporting). Consistent profitability, particularly if accompanied by a transparent information environment, creates the *trust* of customers, suppliers, and investors, who reward the firm with higher product prices, better terms for purchases, and lower cost of debt and equity capital than they would to firms with lower quality reporting. Such trust-based relationships are called **implicit contracts**. When a firm's past behaviour creates a valid expectation of outside parties that the firm will continue to behave with integrity, the implicit contract is also called a **constructive obligation**.

An early investigation of implicit contracting was conducted by Bowen, DuCharme, and Shores (BDS; 1995). They argued that firm reputation can be bolstered by high reported profits, which increase stakeholders' confidence that the manager will continue to meet contractual obligations. For example, they predicted that firms with relatively high cost of goods sold and notes payable (used as proxies for high continuing involvement with suppliers and short-term creditors, respectively) would be more likely to choose FIFO inventory and straight-line amortization accounting policies than LIFO[17] and accelerated amortization policies. FIFO and straight-line amortization are regarded as income-increasing since they tend to produce higher reported earnings over time than their LIFO and accelerated amortization counterparts.[18]

Based on a large sample of U.S. firms over the period 1981–1993, BDS found that firms with a high level of continuing involvement with stakeholders were more likely to choose FIFO and straight-line amortization policies than firms with lower levels of continuing involvement, consistent with their prediction. Graham, Harvey, and Rajgopal (2005), in a post-Enron survey of chief financial officers of U.S. public companies, supported BDS's findings. They reported that managers ranked relations with other stakeholders as an important reason to meet earnings targets.

More recently, the importance of implicit contracts was highlighted during the events leading up to the 2007–2008 market meltdowns (Section 1.3). As a way to credit-enhance securitizations, sponsoring firms often protected ABS purchasers against losses, even without a formal contractual commitment to do so. In this regard, Niu and Richardson (2006) reported evidence that the market valued a firm's shares as if the proceeds from off balance sheet ABSs issued by the firm were liabilities (see Chapter 1, Note 20) rather than sales. A major reason for this finding, they argued, is the prevalence of implicit guarantees under which issuing firms feel they have an obligation to "bail out" investors in securitized assets that lose value, thereby enhancing their reputations.

8.10.2 A Single-Period Non-Cooperative Game

Further consideration of implicit contracting, however, quickly involves us in the theory of **non-cooperative games**. A non-cooperative game models the competitive interaction of two or more rational players when there is no formal contract between them. In our context, we can think of the interaction between a firm manager and a potential investor as a non-cooperative game.

The essence of this interaction is that the investor is concerned about the manager's information advantage. The manager may exploit this advantage by not revealing all the information that the investor desires. The investor looks to the firm's financial statements to reduce this source of information asymmetry. However, the manager may behave opportunistically by, for example, omitting certain liabilities from the balance sheet, choosing accounting policies so as to manage reported profits, or recording excessive discretionary accruals. The investor, being aware of these possibilities, will take them into account when making an investment decision. The manager, in turn, will be aware of possible investor reaction when preparing the financial statements. Cooperative game theory provides a formal framework for studying this conflict situation and for predicting the decisions the parties will make.

We model this situation as a non-cooperative game since it is difficult to envisage a binding contract between manager and investor about what specific information is to be supplied. Such an agreement could be very costly, since similar contracts would have to be negotiated with all potential investors. But different investors have varied decision problems and hence different information needs, so that many different contracts would be needed. Even if such binding agreements were made, they would be difficult and costly to enforce, because each user would need to conduct, or hire, an audit investigation of the firm to monitor management compliance with the contract. In other contexts, binding agreements may be illegal, as when an oligopolistic industry enters into an agreement in restraint of trade.

To illustrate this implicit contract game between the manager and the investor, consider Example 8.1.

Example 8.1
Manager–Investor Relations as a Non-Cooperative Game

We assume the manager has two strategies, one of which must be chosen (see Table 8.1). We will call one of these "opportunistic" (O), which we can think of as engaging in one or more of the financial statement management devices outlined above. The other strategy is to choose "honest" (H), which we can think of as generating investor trust by maintaining a transparent information environment. The investor also has two strategies—to buy shares in the firm or to refuse to buy, denoted by B and R, respectively.

Table 8.1 Utility Payoffs in a Non-Cooperative Game

		Manager	
		HONEST (H)	**OPPORTUNISTIC (O)**
	BUY (B)	60, 40	20, 80
Investor			
	REFUSE TO BUY (R)	35, 20	35, 30

The numbers in Table 8.1 represent the utility payoffs to the investor and manager, respectively, for each possible strategy combination. Thus, if the manager chooses H and the investor B, the investor receives a utility of 60 and the manager receives 40, and so on for the other three pairs of numbers in the table. You should analyze the relationship between the payoffs to make sure they appear reasonable. For example, if the investor chooses B, a higher utility is attained by the investor when the manager is honest (60) than when the manager behaves opportunistically (20). Similarly, if the investor refuses to buy, the manager would prefer to choose O (if the manager behaves opportunistically, less money and effort is put into maintaining a transparent information environment).

It is important to emphasize the assumption in this example that each party has *complete information*. Thus, the investor knows the rules of the game, the strategies available to the manager, and the manager's payoffs, and vice versa. Common knowledge is also assumed—that is, each party knows that the other party has complete information, etc. Game theory can be extended to relax these assumptions, but this is beyond our scope. This completeness of information does not extend to choice of strategy, however. Each player in this example chooses his/her strategy without knowing the strategy choice of the other in this game but nevertheless anticipating that the other player is also behaving strategically.

What *strategy pair* will be chosen? The term means simply a statement of the strategy chosen by each player. Thus, BH is a strategy pair whereby the investor buys (B) and the manager is honest (H). Review Table 8.1 and make your own prediction before reading on.

We can rule out the RH and BO strategy pairs easily. If the manager were to choose H, the investor would reason that it would be better to choose B, because it yields a utility of 60 as opposed to one of 35 from R. Thus, RH would be unlikely to happen. Similarly, if the manager were to choose O, the investor would reason that it would be better to choose R, so BO would be unlikely.

Now consider the BH pair. If the investor were to choose B, the manager would then prefer O. Thus, it seems BH must be ruled out also. The only strategy pair not subject to this problem is RO. If the manager were to choose O, the investor would prefer R. Similarly, if the investor were to choose R, the manager would prefer O. RO is the only strategy pair such that *given* the strategy choice of the other player, each player is content with his or her strategy. Such a strategy pair is called a **Nash equilibrium**. Thus, RO is the predicted outcome of the game.

However, RO is not a completely satisfactory outcome of the game in Example 8.1. Notice that *both parties would be better off* if BH were chosen rather than RO. The strategy pair BH is called the **cooperative solution**. In our context, this is the efficient contracting outcome. But, as we have argued, if the investor were to choose B rather than R, he or she knows that the rational manager would then prefer O and the investor would end up with 20 rather than the 35 from choosing R. Consequently, the investor would not choose B. The Nash equilibrium outcome RO in this game is unfortunate, because it means, at least for payoff values assumed, that the market for the firm's securities would not work very well—no one would buy them.

It is interesting to speculate what might happen next. Perhaps the parties would get together and enter into a binding agreement to choose BH after all. However, each party would have to be convinced the agreement was in fact binding on the other and could be enforced. This could be difficult in a single-period contract.

Another approach would be to think of the game in a *long-run* perspective. If this game was repeated into infinity, or at least for an unknown number of periods, the investor and manager would realize that it was in their joint interest to always choose the cooperative solution (B, H) since, looking ahead, the payoff sequence of (60, 40) thus created gives the largest possible payoff for each (see Chapter 1, Note 23 re folk theorem). If the game continues for a known, finite number of periods, however, the game may or may not collapse to the Nash equilibrium. We will explore this possibility in the next section.

Even if we confine attention to the single-period game model of Example 8.1, it is not hard to see how it relates to the accounting and auditing scandals and resulting declines in stock markets in Canada and the United States in the early 2000s, and to the financial distress suffered by many financial institutions during 2007–2008. In Table 8.1, if we start with the players at the cooperative solution BH, certain managers, such as those at Enron and WorldCom, and many financial institutions (see Sections 1.2 and 1.3), moved to an opportunistic strategy O. They felt that the immediate payoff by departing from the cooperative solution outweighed the longer-run costs of investor and regulator reaction. This short-run strategy generated high payoffs for them. For example, the distortions and excessive risk taking they incorporated into their operations increased reported earnings and moved debt off-balance sheet. The resulting increase in share prices generated huge profits for them from bonuses and ESOs. When the market became aware of the financial statement distortions, investors immediately punished management by moving to R, and share price fell precipitously. However, management had already realized their bonuses and ESO profits.

Management appeared to have ignored, at its peril, another way to maintain the cooperative solution. This is for central authority, such as government, the courts, and standard setters, to attempt to restore investor confidence in financial reporting by changing the payoffs of the game through new regulations and/or increased penalties for distortion. The threat is credible to the extent that the regulations and penalties are enforced. In our example, an increase in penalties may lower the manager's payoffs for BO and RO to, say, zero. Then it can be verified that BH would be a Nash equilibrium.

In this regard, we have already mentioned the Sarbanes-Oxley Act in Section 1.2, which increased the cost of distortion for the manager. In addition, the Public Company Accounting Oversight Board in the United States and the Canadian Public Accountability Board were created (Section 1.2). These boards consist of prominent persons independent of the accounting and auditing profession whose role is to enforce tougher rules on auditors. Hopefully, any Enron- and WorldCom-style financial statement distortions will be deterred. To the extent these bodies succeed in their mission, the manager's payoff under strategy BO will be reduced to the point where the Nash equilibrium becomes BH. In effect, the change in payoffs increases investor confidence that the manager will not distort, with the result that the investors resume buying.

Note the essential difference between single-person decision theory and game theory approaches. In our earlier decision theory Example 3.1, Bill Cautious assessed probabilities of what would happen—he ended up with a 0.77 probability of the high payoff, and so on. The assumption in decision theory is that the high or low payoffs are generated by some random mechanism called nature. Thus, a decision theory problem is sometimes called a game against nature, because some impartial force (nature) is assumed to generate the high or low payoffs with the probabilities assessed. While we gave considerable attention to how investors might assess these probabilities and revise them as new information is obtained, we made an implicit assumption throughout Example 3.1 that the particular decision chosen by the investor would not affect what these probabilities were. That is, nature does not "think."

This assumption is fine for many decision problems. Indeed, as we outlined in Chapters 3, 4, and 5, much progress has been made in understanding the decision needs of users through study of the decision theory approach. However, the approach breaks down when the payoffs are generated by the actions of a thinking opponent rather than by nature. In Example 8.1, the manager will reason that if the investor buys, his/her best act is to act opportunistically, and the investor knows this. Thus, it is not correct for the investor to assign probabilities to the manager's action choice when the manager's action is not chosen probabilistically. Similarly, it would not be correct for the manager to assign probabilities to the investor's action.[19] Such behaviour, by either or both decision-makers, would be unlikely to lead to good decisions in the conflict situation.

While Example 8.1 spans only one period, we can use it to derive an important conclusion. Recall that in Chapter 3 we developed a considerable body of theory to enable us to understand the information needs of investors, and we suggested that major professional accounting standard-setting bodies have adopted the decision usefulness approach that follows from the theory. However, we did not consider management's role in accounting policy choice. That is, we did not consider whether firm management would be *willing* to adopt policies such as full disclosure and fair values proposed by standard setters. Example 8.1 suggests that managers are unwilling to sit idly by and adopt whatever accounting policies are suggested by the standard setters (representing the interests of investors). The efficient contracting assumption that managers are rational, leading to the possibility of opportunistic behaviour, makes it clear that management has *its own* interests at stake in accounting policy choice and cannot be assumed to necessarily adopt accounting policies solely on the ethical grounds that they will be useful to shareholders and other investors. This is shown in Example 8.1 by the utility of the manager being lower under H than under O. That is, the interests of the investor and manager constituencies may *conflict*.

Thus, any accounting body concerned about implementing a new standard must be concerned with the resulting payoffs to *both* investors and management. Only by ensuring that the payoffs to management are such that management will accept the new policy can a smooth implementation be assured.

Of course, any accountant with practical experience in choosing a firm's accounting policies will know about management's interest in and concern about these policies, without having to be convinced by a game theory example. Nevertheless, better understanding of this conflict situation by standard setters will result in more realistic accounting standard choices, which should help to avoid economic consequence disputes, such as those surrounding ESO expensing discussed in Section 8.6.

8.10.3 A Trust-Based Multi-Period Game[*]

As our discussion above of working out from under the unfortunate Nash equilibrium solution in Example 8.1 suggests, it is difficult to draw longer-run conclusions from a single-period game. In this section, we present a multi-period extension of the Example 8.1 game.

Recall from the previous section that if the single-period game is repeated for an indefinite number of periods (i.e., infinite horizon), the cooperative solution can be attained. If the game is repeated for a known, finite number of periods, a **trigger strategy** may also attain the cooperative solution if sufficient penalties can be credibly applied for any deviation. To illustrate, suppose that each player threatens that if the other player deviates from the cooperative solution, he/she will switch strategy the next time the game is played. Thus the deviating player will be punished by receiving only the non-cooperative Nash equilibrium payoff for the remainder of the game. This threat is credible because the Nash equilibrium *is* an equilibrium. For this to work, however, the players must not have too high a discount rate. For example, if the investor buys, the value to the manager of an immediate payoff of $80 may exceed the present value of the $10 reduction in each future period (i.e., $40 – $30) when the investor punishes the manager by switching to R.

The various government interventions following financial reporting disasters, outlined in the previous section, can be thought of in a trigger strategy context. The prospect of such interventions will hopefully deter short-run, opportunistic manager actions, even in a finite period context. However, since managers are adept at working around new rules, it seems that, for some managers at least, the prospect of immediate gain exceeded the expected present value of future penalties. This reminds us of the point made centuries ago by Hobbes (Section 1.5) that force and fear will not work because no set of rules can anticipate all human interaction, and that people must recognize that it is in

---

[*]This section can be omitted without loss of continuity.

their joint interests to cooperate. In this spirit, we now introduce a somewhat different approach, by introducing a measure of trust between the players.

Example 8.2
A Trust-Based Multi-Period Game[20]

Suppose that the game given in Table 8.1 is to be repeated for five periods. To simplify, assume that the players are risk neutral, and there is no discounting. Also assume that the play is sequential—in each period of the game the investor moves first. In period 1, the investor decides whether to invest (B) or not invest (R). The manager then decides whether to play honest (H) or opportunistic (O). In subsequent periods, the investor's decision is whether to hold the investment (B) or to sell it (R). The manager's decision continues to be H or O. If, in any period, the investor sells or the manager behaves opportunistically, the game ends. Otherwise, the game continues to the next play.

Figure 8.2 is a decision tree outlining the structure of the game. The bottom node represents the investor's first play, node 3 her second play, etc. Similarly, the second node represents the manager's first play, node 4 his second play, etc.

The payoffs to each player if the game ends are shown by the dark nodes, with the top number being the investor's payoff. Payoffs are easily calculated from Table 8.1. For example, if the investor plays R in period 1, the players receive the Nash equilibrium payoffs of the single-period game. If the game continues to the manager's decision in period 5 and the manager plays O, the investor receives 260 ($4 \times 60 + 20$) and the manager 240 ($4 \times 40 + 80$). If he plays H, payoffs are 300 and 200, respectively. Intermediate payoffs are calculated similarly.

To begin, consider period 5.[21] If the game were to continue to the manager's play in period 5, the payoff-maximizing manager will choose O, since the payoff of 240 exceeds the payoff of 200 from choosing H. But, anticipating this, the investor will choose R at the second last node, receiving payoff of 275 rather than 260. Thus, if the game proceeds to period 5, the investor will end the game. However, the game will not proceed to period 5 because in period 4 the manager, realizing that if he plays H the investor will end the game at the first of period 5, will instead choose O, receiving payoff of 200 rather than the 180 he would receive if he played H. Again, however, the investor at the fourth-from last node will anticipate this, and play R, ending the game at the beginning of period 4. This thinking continues into period 3, 2, etc., and the game unravels to the first node, where the investor ends the game and the players receive the Nash equilibrium payoffs of the single-period game of Example 8.1.

This result seems counterintuitive, however. Notice, reading from the dark nodes, that as the game continues the investor receives an additional payoff of 60 if she ends the game at her *next* play, rather than ending at her current play. Similarly, the manager receives an additional 40 if he ends the game at his *next* play. One might expect the players to realize this potential and continue playing, providing each has some trust that the other player will continue at his/her next turn.

To introduce some trust into this game, assume that, at each play, each player believes, correctly, that the other will continue with probability $p = \min(1, 0.5 + .01T)$ in the

Figure 8.2 A Trust-Based Multi-Period Game

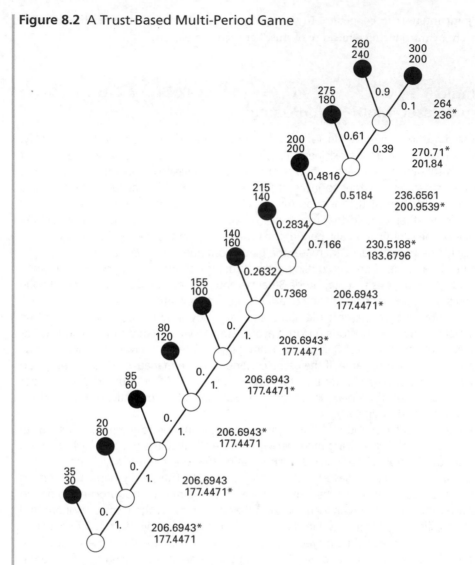

next play of the game, where T is the difference in that next play between that player's expected payoff from continuing and the payoff from ending the game. Note that if T ≥ 50, the player will continue with probability 1. If T ≤ −50, the player will end the game for sure. Thus, a player's probability of continuing is greater the more the expected payoff from continuing exceeds the payoff from ending the game—higher T implies more trust that the other player will continue. Nevertheless, trust is not complete since the complement of p measures the player's temptation to end the game. This temptation increases the lower is T—that is, as the excess payoff for continuing the game decreases.

Given this degree of trust, the investor believes the probability the manager plays H on his last play of the game is

$$p = 0.5 + .01(200 - 240) = 0.10$$

This probability, and its complement for O, are shown on the top branches of Figure 8.2. The expected payoff of each player at the time the manager makes his 5th period decision is thus

$$\text{Investor} \quad 0.10 \times 300 + 0.90 \times 260 = 264$$
$$\text{Manager} \quad 0.10 \times 200 + 0.90 \times 240 = 236$$

For the investor's last play, the manager believes the investor's probability of playing B is

$$p = 0.5 + .01(264 - 275) = 0.39$$

This yields expected payoffs of

$$\text{Investor} \quad 0.39 \times 264 + 0.61 \times 275 = 270.71$$
$$\text{Manager} \quad 0.39 \times 236 + 0.61 \times 180 = 201.84$$

These expected payoffs are entered opposite the related light-coloured nodes on Figure 8.2, with an asterisk denoting the expected payoff of the player whose turn it is at that node. Working down the tree, when it is the investor's decision in period 3 (node 5), the probability she chooses B is

$$p = 0.5 + .01(206.69 - 155) = 1.0169 > 1$$

Thus the investor will choose B with probability 1. Then, p remains at 1 for both players for all earlier nodes, yielding expected payoff of 206.69 and 177.45, respectively, for investor and manager at the beginning of the game.

Notice that, given the trust assumed, the game proceeds with probability 1 for the first five plays. After that, the game may end with the probabilities given. For example, for the 6th play, the manager chooses D with probability 0.2632. Thus, with probability 0.7368, the game continues to the next play, and so on.

Trust is particularly important in the last play of the game. In this play, the manager would be better off to choose O, for a payoff of 240 rather than the expected payoff of 236 from playing according to the probabilities given. If the investor feels the manager will play O for sure, she will choose R for a payoff of 275 rather than 260 from continuing. The game will unravel. For this not to happen, the investor must trust that the manager will in fact choose his final act with the probabilities shown. The manager may choose D due to a fear of legal liability if O is chosen,[22] and/or a desire to maintain a reputation. Also, many executive compensation plans require that the manager hold company stock for some time after retirement. For example, the Royal Bank compensation plan reviewed in Section 10.3 requires the CEO and CFO to hold company stock for two years after retirement. Even a very small probability that the manager (0.1 in this example) will do so is sufficient to prevent unravelling.

The question then is, how is trust maintained? One source of trust is a belief by the investor that the manager will be held liable for opportunism (see Note 22). However, fear of liability does not always deter cheating. Can accounting help to maintain investor trust? The answer is yes to the extent that GAAP, full disclosure, and an ethical audit profession prevent opportunism.

Nevertheless, it is quite possible for trust to be lost, at any point in the game. A major reporting failure by the manager of another firm could cause the investor to lose trust.

Arguably, revelation of accounting fraud by Enron and WorldCom (Section 1.2) caused investors to lose trust in all firms' financial reporting, thereby triggering the 2001 U.S. recession. From the manager's perspective, he may lose trust because of concern that the investor is likely to sell for portfolio reasons, or is unduly influenced by analyst forecasts, or is a noise trader.

Furthermore, if we replace trust with "bubble" or "bandwagon effect" in the model, we see that these forces could also motivate the players to proceed up the tree. Again, an event such as financial reporting failure could cause the bubble to burst, with the players heading for the nearest left node.

We conclude that, from an accounting perspective, the role of high quality financial reporting to maintain investor trust in managers is crucial. The example reinforces our argument (Section 4.7) that high quality reporting is essential to enable the investor trust that firms need if they are to raise investment capital.

8.10.4 Summary of Implicit Contracting

Non-cooperative game theory enables us to model the conflict situation that often exists between different constituencies of financial statement users. Even a very simple game-theoretic model shows that an accounting standard-setting body that fails to consider the interests of all constituencies affected by accounting policy choice is in danger of making policy recommendations that are difficult to implement.

8.11 SUMMARY OF EFFICIENT CONTRACTING

Efficient contracting raises two important questions for the Conceptual Framework. First, should the Framework give greater recognition to verifiability, such as moving it from an enhancing characteristic of financial statements to a component of representational faithfulness? As O'Brien argues (see Section 8.4.1), this would strengthen the role of reliability in the Framework, thus reducing investors' concern that managers may opportunistically manage earnings so as to avoid violation of debt covenants and to increase their reputation and compensation.

Second, to what extent should financial statements provide an early warning system to alert debtholders to possible firm financial distress? Conditional conservatism provides such an early warning system by recognizing unrealized losses. In fairness, accounting standards do recognize many unrealized losses through impairment tests. However, the motivation is likely due to a concern about legal liability rather than to an acceptance of contract theory.

Empirical research has reported evidence of both efficient contracting and opportunistic manager behaviour. While it is important for accountants to be aware of the possibility of manager opportunism, evidence of efficient contracting suggests that it is possible to align managers' interests with those of investors. In the next chapter, turn to a consideration of how this alignment may be achieved.

Questions and Problems

1. Debt contracts may contain covenants, such as maintaining a specified level of working capital, not exceeding a specified debt–equity ratio, or maintaining an agreed times interest earned ratio. Explain how these covenants help to generate the lenders' trust that is necessary if the firm is to borrow at reasonable cost. Do these covenants give lenders complete trust that their interest and principal will be paid? Explain.

2. Lenders are primarily concerned about poor firm performance, since this increases the likelihood that they will not receive their interest and principal. How do lenders benefit if the firm performs well? If lenders benefit when the firm does well, why are they primarily concerned about downside risk? Which accounting policies do lenders want to protect against downside risk? Explain how these policies decrease downside risk.

3. In his article "The Impact of Accounting Regulation on the Stock Market: The Case of Oil and Gas Companies," Lev (1979) examined the daily returns on a portfolio of oil and gas companies' common shares affected by the exposure draft of SFAS 19. This standard required firms to use the successful efforts method of accounting for the costs of oil and gas exploration. Under successful efforts, costs of drilling unsuccessful wells are written off when the well is determined to be unsuccessful. An alternative policy is full cost accounting, under which the costs of unsuccessful wells are capitalized into the costs of successful wells. For firms with an active exploration policy, successful efforts reports lower net income than full cost, and also increases earnings volatility. Under the proposed standard, firms that were using the full cost method would be required to switch to the successful efforts method. The new standard became effective in December 1977.

    SFAS 19 was objected to particularly strongly by small oil and gas firms, especially if they were actively exploring, who argued that successful efforts accounting would reduce their ability to raise capital, with consequent effects on oil and gas exploration and on the level of competition in the industry.

    Lev found that there was an average decline of 4.5% in the share prices of firms that would have to switch to the successful efforts method, during a three-day period following the release of the exposure draft (July 18, 1977). This study is one of the few that have detected a securities market reaction to an accounting policy change that would have no direct impact on cash flows.

    ### Required

    a. Why did Lev examine share returns around the date of the exposure draft (July 18, 1977) rather than the date SFAS 19 was issued (December 5, 1977)?
    b. Use contract theory and efficient securities market theory to explain why the stock market reacted as it did to the exposure draft of SFAS 19.
    c. Suppose that, pursuant to the theory and evidence described in Section 6.2, securities markets are not efficient. What reaction to SFAS 19 would you then expect? Explain.

4. Use contracting theory to explain why firms (i.e., Boards of Directors acting on shareholders' behalf) would prefer to allow managers a *set* of accounting policies (e.g., GAAP) from which to choose, rather than completely prescribe accounting policy choice so that managers have no flexibility to choose policies .

Use contracting theory to explain why managers may also prefer to have a choice of accounting policies.

5. A new accounting standard requires a firm to accrue major new liabilities for employee pensions and benefits. As a result, its debt–equity ratio rises to the point where technical violation of covenants in its borrowing agreements is threatened. Management knows that renegotiation of these covenants would be difficult and costly.

Suggest some accounting policy choices that could reduce the likelihood of technical violation. Ideally, any changes in policies should not violate GAAP, not affect the firm's real operations, and not reduce cash flows. Justify your suggestions.

6. Use contract theory to explain how conditionally conservative accounting can contribute to efficient contracting. Consider both debt and managerial compensation contracts.

7. *The Globe and Mail* (November 6, 2002, p. B1), reported "New accounting rules sow confusion about oil earnings." This refers to changes in Canadian accounting standards that required firms with monetary items denominated in a foreign currency to include, and disclose, gains and losses from translating these items into Canadian dollars in the current period's income statement. Previously, such gains and losses could be deferred and amortized over the life of the monetary item.

Many Canadian oil companies have long-term debt denominated in U.S. dollars. Under the new standard, fluctuations in the value of the Canadian dollar relative to the U.S. dollar increased the volatility of the reported earnings of Canadian oil companies. For example, according to the *Globe* article, EnCana Corp. reported an after-tax loss of $145 million on its foreign currency-denominated debt for its third quarter, 2002, reducing its reported earnings by about 40%. This loss followed a foreign currency conversion gain of approximately the same amount in its second quarter. The article went on to quote the managing director of research of a Calgary investment firm as saying that earnings are "going up and down like a toilet seat."

Required

a. In a follow-up article in the *Globe* on November 8, 2002 ("Accounting rule change burns big oil," p. B2), Deborah Yedlin reported the president and CEO of EnCana Corp. as commenting that the new accounting rules could deter companies from being able to lock in financing at the current low interest rates.

Evaluate this comment from the standpoint of efficient securities market theory.

b. Evaluate the comment in part a from the standpoint of contract theory.

8. Following the 1990 Iraqi invasion of Kuwait, the price of crude oil soared, as did retail gasoline prices. This led the major U.S. oil companies to try to hold down their reported earnings.

The oil companies were anxious to avoid a repeat of an earlier episode when crude oil and gasoline prices peaked during the 1970s, and earnings soared. At that time, the public outrage was so great that the U.S. Congress imposed an excess profits tax, taxing back several billion dollars of excess profits. Warnings of similar taxes were repeated in 1990.

To limit their 1990 profits, the major oil companies did exercise some price restraint to keep prices at the pump from rising as much as they otherwise would. They also engaged in a number of accounting practices, such as increased provisions for future environmental costs, increased maintenance, and large provisions for legal liabilities.

Required

a. What pricing and accounting policy choices are predicted by contract theory, in response to increasing crude oil prices? Explain.

b. For a U.S. company (see Note 17), what inventory accounting policy would be most effective in holding down profits? Explain.

c. Obviously, the major U.S. oil companies were concerned about political backlash. Do you think a strategy of holding down reported profits by means of accounting policy choice is effective in avoiding a backlash? Explain why or why not.

9. Many companies issue large numbers of stock options to executives and other employees. These companies frequently buy back some of their shares on the open market. For example, Microsoft Corp., which was a major issuer of ESOs, bought back over $20 billion of its shares over a five-year period up to 2003. In February 2005 ConocoPhillips, a large oil company based in Houston, Texas, announced a $1 billion buyback program over the next two years. ConocoPhillips was also a major ESO issuer.

Required

a. Why would firms with large ESO plans buy back their stock? Explain.

b. Normally, companies that buy back their shares do so over time, to avoid the increased demand bidding up share price, thus raising the cost of buying them back. As the shares are bought back, the company then records the reduction in outstanding shares and the cash payment. However, according to an article in *The Globe and Mail* (January 31, 2006, p. B13), "Watch out for the loophole: buybacks have hidden costs" (reproduced from *The Wall Street Journal*), many companies have engaged in "accelerated share repurchase." Under this tactic, firms recorded their *total planned* buyback all at once at their shares' current market price, even though they had not yet bought back the shares. This maximized the increase in current earnings per share. Would you, as a potential investor in firms using this tactic, be concerned? Why or why not?

10. For U.S. public corporations, SFAS 123R required expensing of ESOs. However, the exposure draft of this standard met considerable opposition, mostly from large technology companies. These companies formed an anti-expense lobby group, the International Employee Stock Options Coalition, to fight the proposal. As a result, several bills were introduced in the U.S. Congress to override or modify the FASB proposal. Suggested modifications included expensing only ESOs for the firm's top five executives, and setting share price variability to zero in the Black-Scholes formula.

The FASB's stand was strengthened, however, because numerous companies, including General Motors Corp., Microsoft Corp., and Exxon Mobil Corp., had already decided, voluntarily, to expense their ESOs. Also many firms reduced their ESO awards. For example, the Bank of Montreal reduced options issued as compensation by two-thirds, replacing them with increased cash bonuses and stock awards.

In October 2004, the FASB announced it was delaying implementation of its proposal for six months, to June 15, 2005. However, except for the implementation delay, it did not back down on this standard.

Required

a. Evaluate the relevance and reliability of Black-Scholes as a measure of the fair value of ESOs. Use the three components of representational faithfulness outlined in Section 3.7.1 in your answer.

b. Some critics of the proposed standard claim that the cost of ESOs is zero. Why? Explain to these critics why their claim is incorrect.

c. Why are managers of some firms strongly opposed to expensing ESOs?

d. Why would a firm voluntarily adopt expensing ESOs?

11. On October 25, 2002, *The Globe and Mail* (p. B2) reported "Former Big Bear head denies manipulation." The article described accusations against the former CEO of Big Bear Exploration Ltd. in a hearing before the Alberta Securities Commission. The accusations are that the former CEO fed the market gloomy news about Blue Range Resources Corp., a newly acquired subsidiary of Big Bear, in order to drive down Big Bear's stock price and benefit personally from a subsequent rebound in stock price when Blue Range sprang back from some financial difficulties that were revealed shortly after it was acquired by Big Bear.

Big Bear's former CEO strenuously denied these charges, which had not been proven at the time of the article.

Required

a. Assuming that the Big Bear CEO's compensation contract included regular grants of ESOs, are these accusations consistent with the findings of Aboody and Kasznik (2000)? Explain why or why not.

b. If, as a result of a rebound at Blue Range, Big Bear's CEO's options became deep in the money, what is the likely effect on the CEOs exercise decision?

12. Years prior to the 2007 meltdown in the market for asset-backed securities saw a significant increase in "covenant-lite" debt, under which debt contracts had few if any debt covenants. For example, a firm may issue such debt to finance a planned takeover. One estimate is that, in 2007, covenant-lite debt accounted for 35% of all debt issued in the United States.

Typically this debt was bought by financial institutions, such as banks. A bank would then combine this loan with other similar loans and slice the total up into tranches of similar credit quality. It would then sell these tranches to investors on a secondary loan market. The purchaser would receive his/her share of the interest and principal payments paid by the firms whose debt is in that tranche. Thus, the investor could buy interest-bearing debt with the level of default risk he/she desires, and pay accordingly. The effect, it was felt at the time, was to disperse credit risk through the economy. It was expected that even for a covenant-lite tranche of low quality there will be no more than a few defaulting firms, so that any credit losses are spread over all the investors in that tranche.

Furthermore, it was possible to increase the credit quality of a tranch by buying credit default swaps (CDSs). These are derivative instruments under which the issuer of the CDS, for a fee, agrees to compensate tranche investors for credit losses incurred by that tranche. If CDSs are bought to protect, say, 25% of the underlying debt in the tranche, the effect is to increase the credit quality of the tranche significantly. This further dispersed credit risk, since now at least part of the risk was borne by the CDS issuers.

Required

a. If you were an investor in interest-bearing securities, would you be willing to invest a substantial amount of your capital in tranches secured by covenant-lite debt? Explain why or why not. Consider both your evaluation of expected return and risk in your decision.

b. Concerns are sometimes expressed that issuing covenant-lite debt creates a moral hazard problem for the firms issuing such debt. What is the problem?

c. The ability to increase the credit quality of high-risk debt by means of CDSs seems almost "magical." However, based on experience from the 2007–2008 market melt-downs (Section 1.3), the increase in credit quality was not as great as expected. Why?

13. Beatty, Weber, and Yu (2008) (Section 8.8) analyzed a sample of U.S. firms with debt covenants that required the firm to maintain a specified level of net worth. Almost two-thirds of these covenants contained income escalators, whereby the required level of net worth to be maintained increased by a specified percentage (e.g., 50%) of positive net income. If net income was negative, the required level did not decrease.

The authors' findings included the following:

- Firms with high information asymmetry between the firm and its lenders (i.e., high estimation risk) were more likely to include income escalator clauses in their net worth covenants. The higher the information asymmetry, the greater are lenders' concerns that firm managers may behave opportunistically by, for example, paying excessive dividends and/or managing earnings upward to cover up or delay solvency concerns. Lender concerns can be measured by the spread between bid and ask price when bonds are traded (a higher spread suggests greater lender concerns), by the firm's credit rating, and by the magnitude of its accruals (high accruals suggest a volatile operating environment, which can lead to increased probability of covenant violation). All of these concerns increase with information asymmetry.

- Income escalator clauses and conservative accounting (including both conditional and unconditional conservatism) were positively associated. That is, firms with income escalator clauses in their net worth covenants were more likely to adopt conservative accounting policies. This finding was after allowing for other reasons for conservative accounting such as investor demand and concern about litigation (Sections 6.11 and 6.12). This finding is of interest because it implies that conservative accounting alone is not sufficient for efficient debt contracting. Rather, a combination of conservative accounting and sophisticated debt covenants may further increase contracting efficiency.

Required

a. Why do debt contracts often contain covenants requiring maintenance of a specified level of net worth?

b. Managers of firms with higher information asymmetry between the firm and its lenders have greater opportunities to opportunistically manage earnings upward. Why would such firms include income escalator clauses in their debt covenants?

c. Explain why income escalator clauses and conservative accounting work together to benefit investors. Give two examples of conservative accounting policies in your answer.

14. In the United States, SFAS 123 required firms to report employee stock option (ESO) expense either in its financial statements proper or in a financial statement note (Section 8.6). Many firms based their expense estimates on the Black-Scholes option pricing formula (Section 7.9.1). However, many of these firms included a management disavowal of the reliability of the ESO expense calculation in their financial statements.

Blacconiere, Frederickson, Johnson, and Lewis (BFJL; 2011) studied these reliability disavowals. Their interest was in whether the disavowals were informative about reliability or whether they indicated opportunistic behaviour by the managers involved. Informative disavowals would bring to investors' attention that management really believed ESO expense was unreliable. Opportunistic disavowals were not necessarily indicative of low reliability, but rather designed to benefit the manager. For example, the manager may wish to reduce political backlash to high ESO compensation by calling the value of that compensation into doubt.

Required

a. What are the problems of using the Black-Scholes option pricing model to estimate ESO expense?

b. Does a finding that management disavowals are associated with high unreliability of ESO estimates mean that reporting ESO expense is not decision useful for investors? Explain.

c. The authors found that firms with high implied share price variability were more likely to disavow than firms with low implied share price variability. The implied variability of share price applies to firms with *traded* stock options outstanding (i.e., options not issued as ESOs). Given the market price of the traded options, and estimates of the other inputs into the Black-Scholes formula (Section 7.9.1), the formula can be solved for the variability of share price implied by the model. This variability estimate is often regarded as a superior input to Black-Scholes than past share price variability for valuing ESOs since it is more forward looking. Does this finding suggest that management disavowals of reliability are informative or opportunistic? Explain.

d. Under SFAS 123, firms are required to disclose the values they use for the various inputs to the Black-Scholes formula, including the input for share price variability. For each firm in their sample, the authors compared this variability input with the firm's actual share price variability over a five-year period following the disavowal. They found that, on average, management's share price variability input exceeded actual variability following the disavowal. Does this finding suggest that management disavowals of reliability are informative or opportunistic? Explain.

15. Beatty, Liao, and Weber (2012) investigated **delegated monitoring** of public debt issues, under which holders of public debt delegate monitoring of the borrower's financial performance to a specialist, such as a bank. This tactic is common, particularly when a firm has several classes of debt outstanding. When there are several debt classes, holders of a class may leave it to holders of another class to monitor financial performance. If all debtholders feel this way, insufficient monitoring will be carried out. Alternatively, if holders of all debt classes do their own monitoring, total monitoring costs will be high. By hiring a monitoring specialist, these problems are reduced.

Knowing that its debt holders may delegate monitoring, the firm may include a **cross acceleration** covenant in its debt contracts. This is to overcome a problem that arises with multiple debt classes when some classes have greater security than others. For example, one class may have higher priority to receive debt repayments than another should the firm go into liquidation. Consequently, if the firm enters financial distress, the debt holders with priority may force liquidation even though the firm has a higher expected value if it continues operating. Cross acceleration relieves this problem because all debt classes are treated equally should debt repayments be accelerated because the firm has entered financial distress.

While, cross acceleration may treat all classes of debt equally, another problem remains—namely, inappropriate liquidation. To see why, note that most delegated monitors are banks, and it is likely that the bank has also loaned money to the firm in question. If so, and if the firm approaches financial distress, the bank may trigger liquidation to protect its own position, even though the firm's value as a going concern exceeds its liquidating value. This is of particular concern to debt holders if their debt is longer-term than the firm's bank debt.

Consequently, the firm faces a cost–benefit tradeoff when considering inclusion of a cross acceleration covenant in its debt contracts. Its borrowing costs will be reduced to the extent that debt investors feel more secure because of cross acceleration, but will be increased to the extent that investors are concerned about inappropriate liquidation.

Delegated monitoring and cross acceleration are of interest to accounting since, as mentioned, most delegated monitors are banks, which have usually loaned money to the borrowing firm. As the authors pointed out, bank lending agreements usually contain accounting based covenants, and the bank will base a decision to demand accelerated repayment, with resulting likelihood of forced liquidation, on these.

BLW studied 1,670 public debt issues from 515 firms over the period 1994–2007. They reported that 62% of their sample contained cross acceleration provisions. In their study of these contracts, the authors reported several findings, including the following:

i. Cross acceleration is less likely to the extent that the expected going concern value of the borrowing firm exceeds its expected liquidation value. The authors measured expected going concern value by the market value of total assets. They measured expected liquidation value by a proportion of the value of accounts receivable, inventory; property, plant and equipment; and cash.

ii. Cross acceleration is more likely as the number of covenants in the bank's lending contract increases.

iii. Cross acceleration is more likely as information asymmetry between the firm and investors increases. Information asymmetry is based on the discretionary accrual models of Dechow and Dichev (2002) (Section 5.4.1) and Jones (1991) (Section 11.3), with higher discretionary accruals implying lower earnings quality.

iv. The authors also found that interest rates paid by firms with a cross acceleration covenant in their lending agreements are higher on average the greater the level of discretionary accruals.

Required

Explain the likely reasons for each of the findings reported above.

16. The controversy over expensing of ESOs can be analyzed as a non-cooperative game. Let the two players be the standard setter and the large, powerful corporations that wish to prevent expensing. Each player faces two strategies. The "cooperate" strategy happens when one player accedes to the demands of the other, or, at least, expresses a willingness to compromise. (For example, one suggested compromise was to expense only ESOs granted to senior officers, with those granted to all other employees reported only as supplementary information. Another was to delay an expensing decision to give time to work out a compromise.) The "strong" strategy involves a player sticking to his/her own preferred policy and attempting to win support from business and government.

Hypothetical payoffs for each player are summarized in the following table.

		Standard setter	
		Cooperate	**Strong**
	Cooperate	30, 30	8, 40
Corporations			
	Strong	20, 10	12, 15

In each box, the first number represents the corporations' payoff and the second number the standard setter's payoff. Consider the lower left payoffs. Here, the corporations play strong; that is, they vigorously oppose expensing and proceed to gather support for their position from business and government. The standard setter backs down, as the FASB did in 1994, and allows all ESO expense to continue to be reported in the financial statement notes. The corporations' payoff is 20 in this case, because it is seen as the dominant player. However, because this strategy erodes their relationship with the standard setter, generates political controversy, and alienates other constituencies who feel that standard setting should be done in the private sector, its payoff is less than the 30 it would receive if both players had cooperated to reach a compromise solution. The standard setter receives a very low payoff of 10, because it is perceived as capitulating to the corporations' demands. If the corporations cooperate, however, and formulate a compromise, with payoffs of 30 each, the standard setter may seize on this as an expression of weakness and force through its preferred expensing option. Then, the standard setter's payoff is 40, since it is seen as the dominant player, and the corporations suffer an embarrassing defeat with payoff of only 8. If both parties play strong, no agreement is possible and the question of ESO expensing has to be settled by another authority, such as government. Here, both parties lose, with low payoffs as shown in the lower right of the table.

Required

a. Given the payoffs as shown, which strategy pair do you predict the players will choose in a single play of the game?

b. Is this strategy pair a Nash equilibrium? Explain.

c. Both parties would be better off if they cooperated. Explain why this strategy pair is unlikely to be chosen in a single play of the game.

17. The shareholders of X Ltd. will vote at the forthcoming annual meeting on a proposal to establish a bonus plan for X Ltd. management, based on firm earnings. Proponents of the plan argue that management will work harder under a bonus plan and that future cash flows will thereby increase. However, a dissident shareholder group argues that there is little point in granting a bonus plan, because management will bias or otherwise manage earnings to increase their bonus, rather than working harder.

   Upon investigation, you estimate that if the bonus plan is granted, expected future cash flows will be $150 if management does not manage earnings, and $140 if it does, *before* management remuneration in each case (cash flows are lower in the latter case because, rather than working harder, management uses earnings management to disguise shirking). Management remuneration, including the bonus, would be $50 if it does not manage earnings and $60 if it does. Assume that cash flows not paid as management remuneration will go to the shareholders. If the bonus plan is not granted, expected cash flows will be $140 before management remuneration if management does not manage earnings and $100 if it does. Management remuneration would be $30 in either case, with the balance of cash flows going to the shareholders.

   Required

   a. Prepare a payoff table for the above game between shareholders and management.

   b. Which strategy pair will be chosen? That is, identify a Nash equilibrium for the game. Assume both players are risk neutral.

   c. What is the main advantage of a game theory approach to modelling the management's decision whether to manage earnings, rather than modelling it as a single-person decision theory problem of the manager?

18. The following table depicts a non-cooperative game between an investor in a firm's shares and the firm's auditor.

		Auditor	
		Work for investor	**Work for manager**
	Invest	5, 4	2, 6
Investor			
	Do not invest	3, 1	3, 3

   The investor has two strategies: invest or not invest. The auditor can choose to work for the investor by ensuring that the firm's financial statements are free of opportunistic earnings management, or to work for the manager by allowing opportunistic earnings management, which may mislead the investor but benefit the manager.

The number pairs in the table represent the utility payoff to the investor and auditor, respectively, for each strategy combination. The rationale for these payoffs is as follows:

Invest, work for investor:	The investor receives high-quality information (generating utility of 5), but the auditor incurs high audit costs (generating utility of 4) due to time spent arguing with the manager and possible loss of audit engagement.
Invest, work for manager:	The investor receives low-quality information (utility of 2), but the auditor's costs are lower (utility of 6).
Do not invest, work for investor:	The investor buys lower-yielding securities (utility of 3). The firm's cost of capital rises due to lower demand for its shares. As a result, its earnings fall. Auditor incurs high audit costs, and absorbs lower audit fee due to lower firm earnings (utility of 1).
Do not invest, work for manager:	The investor buys lower-yielding securities. The auditor's audit costs are lower due to less arguing with manager but audit fee is still low due to lower firm earnings (utility of 3).

Required

a. Identify the Nash equilibrium of this game and explain why this is the predicted outcome of the game.

b. Identify the cooperative solution. Explain why it is unlikely to be attained in a single play of this game.

c. Outline three possible ways that the cooperative solution may be attained.

19. A problem with many games is that they can have multiple Nash equilibria. This makes it difficult to predict the outcome of the game.

As an illustration of a non-cooperative game with multiple equilibria, consider the following payoff table. The first number in each payoff pair is the payoff to country 2:

		Country 1	
		Keep	**Violate**
	Keep	100, 100	50, 200
Country 2			
	Violate	200, 50	50, 50

Required

a. Identify three Nash equilibria of this game.

b. Suppose that this game will be repeated a known, finite number of times. Suppose that the current equilibrium is in the lower left portion of the table. Describe an action by country 1 that would cause a shift to a new equilibrium.

c. Suppose that the game will be repeated an indefinite (i.e., infinite) number of times. What equilibrium would you then predict? Explain.

Notes

1. In the following discussion it will be helpful to distinguish between the firm and its manager. We can think of the firm as represented by the board of directors.

2. This is the "economic Darwinism" argument of Alchian (1950).

3. While the two concepts are related, contract efficiency should not be confused with securities market efficiency.

4. The Framework does recognize the importance of stewardship—it states that the financial reporting objective is to help investors in resource-providing decisions *and* assess whether management has made efficient and effective use of the firm's resources. However, this does not recognize the fundamental problem (Section 1.10) that the best income measure to inform investors is not necessarily the same as the best measure to motivate manager performance. Most accounting standards are devoted to the information needs of investors, not to the special needs of stewardship evaluation.

5. Efficient contracting theory, also referred to as **positive accounting theory**, refers to the firm as a "**nexus of contracts**." See Watts and Zimmerman (1986), page 196.

6. Important firm customers and suppliers have similar concerns. See Hui, Klasa, and Yeung (2012).

7. Private lending agreements are loans that are not publicly traded, in contrast to public lending agreements where investors can buy or sell bonds and other credit instruments on the market. The private lending agreements studied by Dichev and Skinner consisted of loans made by U.S. banks to large corporations. They reported that such loans are the main form of private lending.

8. A fixed ESO plan is one where the number of shares and the exercise price are known at the grant date. This contrasts with a variable plan, under which the number of shares the employee may acquire and/or the price to be paid are not determinable until some time after the grant date.

9. This assumes that the number of shares to be issued by means of options is not large enough to affect the market price of the firm's shares.

10. Concavity is the source of the overstatement. To see this, note first that the Black-Scholes value of an option is increasing in time to expiry, since the longer the time to expiry, the greater the probability that share price will take off. Also, recall that under APB 25, most ESOs were issued with exercise price equal to underlying share price at the grant date. When exercise price and grant date share price are equal, the Black-Scholes value may be an increasing, *concave* function of time to expiry, as argued by HMS. If so, the option value increases at a decreasing rate. The significance of concavity is that if an employee exercises his/her ESOs *before* expected time to exercise (note that expected time to exercise is an average across employees), the reduction in *ex post* cost to the firm is greater than the increase in cost if an employee exercises a similar time *after* expected time to exercise. That is, use of expected time to exercise in Black-Scholes upwardly biases ESO cost relative to *ex post* cost. When this upward bias is put together with the considerable variability of employees' exercise decisions, the bias can be significant. Using a procedure suggested by HMS to approximate the effects of this concavity, Marquardt (2002) found the tendency of Black-Scholes to bias ESO cost is reduced.

11. AK's argument assumed that investors do not know the scheduled date. If they did, they could discount the CEO's information release to adjust for manager biases. AK argued that there is considerable uncertainty that a firm will maintain its scheduled ESO grant dates, and whether or not it does is not known by the market until after the fact. Also, it would take several years before the market could identify that the firm was, in fact, adhering to a fixed schedule. AK presented evidence in support of their argument.

12. Instead of using the Black-Scholes model with expected exercise date, more elaborate versions of the binomial model illustrated in Figure 7.2 can incorporate the various early exercise possibilities directly into the model.

13. As discussed earlier, *ex ante* ESO cost is an estimate, based on an option pricing model applied at grant date. *Ex post* ESO cost is the actual cost, being the difference between the share price and exercise price at exercise date. SFAS 123R and IFRS2 do not require subsequent adjustment of ESO expense for any difference between *ex ante* and *ex post* cost.

14. Choudhary reported that 96% of the firms in his sample used the Black-Scholes model to measure ESO fair value.

15. The reason, according to the authors, is that banks can demand inside information, and tailor loan conditions such as maturity, collateral, and interest rate to the borrower's particular circumstances. They also have greater flexibility than bondholders to revise loan terms should the borrower enter financial distress. It is more difficult for public lenders to obtain and process inside information, and to change the terms of the debt contract. Consequently, the borrowing firm's accounting quality is the main variable that public lenders have in monitoring the safety of their investment.

16. SFAS 131 is discussed further in Section 12.10. This standard is now included in ASC 280-10.

17. LIFO inventory method uses the cost of the most recently acquired inventory as cost of sales, as opposed to FIFO, which uses the cost of the earliest inventory as cost of sales. On a rising market, LIFO produces a lower net income than FIFO. LIFO is allowed under FASB standards (ASC 330-10-30-9), but not under IASB standards (IAS 2).

18. This assumes that stakeholders do not unwind the earnings management. BDS argued that it is not cost effective for them to do so since it is difficult to isolate effects on reported income of continuing use of, for example, LIFO inventory or accelerated amortization, particularly since many stakeholders have limited ability to process information and may not have enough at stake to warrant careful evaluation of reported earnings.

19. The discussion here assumes only pure strategies—that is, strategies where one act is chosen with probability 1. It is possible to have mixed-strategy solutions, where players randomize between acts over which they are indifferent. Then this statement would need modification.

20. This example is based on a discussion in Friedman (1986), pp. 139–141. Friedman's discussion is, in turn, based on a model proposed by R.W. Rosenthal (1981).

21. The process of analyzing the game from the final play to the first is called **backwards induction**. It captures the forward-looking behaviour of rational players as they determine their first move.

22. Jeffrey Skilling, CEO of Enron, resigned in August 2001, prior to the disclosure of serious financial irregularities (Section 1.2). Nevertheless, he was subsequently found guilty of criminal behaviour, and was sentenced to a 24-year, 4-month prison term. In June 2010, the Supreme Court vacated part of Skilling's conviction and transferred the case back to the lower court for resentencing. During April 2011, a three-judge 5th Circuit Court panel ruled that the verdict would have been the same despite the legal issues being discussed, and Skilling's conviction was confirmed; however, the court ruled Skilling should be resentenced. Skilling appealed this new decision to the Supreme Court, but the appeal was denied. In 2013 the United States Department of Justice reached a deal with Skilling resulting in 10 years being cut from his sentence.

Chapter 9
An Analysis of Conflict

Figure 9.1 Organization of Chapter 9

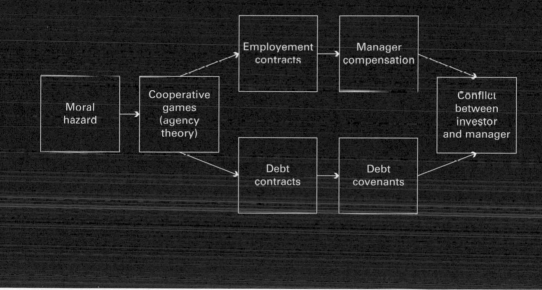

9.1 OVERVIEW

In this chapter, we consider agency theory, a branch of game theory, which studies the design of contracts between principal and agent that motivate the agent to work in the best interests of the principal. An efficient contract does this at lowest cost to the principal.

There are many principal–agent relationships in society, such as patient–doctor, client–lawyer, owner–hockey player. In each case, the principal wants the agent to work hard on his/her behalf. However, the interests of the principal and agent conflict, since working hard requires effort, and the principal may want more effort than the agent is willing to exert. In many cases, the nature of the agent's effort is too complex for the principal to observe it directly—it as hard for the patient to observe the doctor's effort, for example. This creates a moral hazard problem, and the agent may not work hard unless he/she is sufficiently motivated. While reputation and professional ethics contribute to motivation, it is often desirable to further motivate hard work by basing compensation on some observable measure of the agent's performance. Thus a hockey player's compensation may in large part depend on goals scored.

In our context, two important agency relationships are of interest. These are employment contracts between the firm (representing the firm owners) and its managers, and lending contracts between the firm and its lenders. Agency theory is relevant to accounting because both types of contracts often depend on the firm's reported earnings. Employment contracts frequently base managerial bonuses on net income, and, as noted in Chapter 8, lending contracts usually incorporate protection for the lenders in the form of covenants that, for example, bind the firm not to go below a stated times-interest-earned ratio, or not to pay dividends if working capital falls below a specified level.

As a result, accounting policies matter to managers, since their compensation, and ability to avoid debt covenant violation, are affected by these policies. As discussed in Section 8.5, economic consequences are created when accounting standards change during the term of compensation and debt contracts. Consequently, managers have a legitimate interest in the design of new accounting standards.

Reported net income has a different role in a managerial contracting context than in reporting to investors. Its role is to predict the ultimate payoff from current manager activities. In so doing, it monitors and motivates manager performance. For this, net income needs to be sensitive to manager effort and precise in its predictions of the payoff from that effort. The characteristics needed to best fulfil this role are not necessarily the same as those that provide the most useful information to investors, leading to the fundamental problem outlined in Section 1.10.

Finally, the contract-based role for financial statements that emerges from agency theory helps us to see how the theory of efficient securities markets is not inconsistent with economic consequences. Securities markets can be efficient and accounting policies can have economic consequences once the conflict implications for financial reporting are understood.

Figure 9.1 outlines the organization of this chapter.

9.2 AGENCY THEORY

9.2.1 Introduction

In the next few sections, we will illustrate two important types of contracts that have implications for financial accounting theory: employment contracts between the firm and its top manager and lending contracts between the firm manager and the lender. In these contracts, we can think of one of the parties as the principal and the other the agent. For example, in an employment contract, the firm owner is the principal and the top manager is the agent hired to run the firm on the owner's behalf.

> **Agency theory** is a branch of game theory that studies the design of contracts to motivate a rational agent to act on behalf of a principal when the agent's interests would otherwise conflict with those of the principal.

Agency theory contracts have characteristics of both cooperative and non-cooperative (see Section 8.10.2) games. They are non-cooperative in that both parties choose their actions non-cooperatively. The two parties do not specifically agree to take certain actions; rather, the actions are motivated by the contract itself. Nevertheless, each party must be able to commit to the contract—that is, to bind him/herself to cooperate, or to "play by the rules." For example, it is assumed that the manager in an employment contract will not grab the total firm profits and head for a foreign jurisdiction. Such commitment may be enforced by the legal system, by use of bonding or escrow arrangements, and by the ethical behaviour and reputations of the contracting parties. Consequently, for our discussion, we will regard them as cooperative games.

9.2.2 Agency Contracts Between Firm Owner and Manager

We begin with a single-period owner–manager contract example that introduces many of the concepts of agency theory and illustrates the basic moral hazard conflict between owner and manager. This section also illustrates how the owner can design an employment contract to control moral hazard.

It should be noted in our example that the use of two persons is a modelling device. The owner is a proxy for a large number of shareholders, whose interests conflict with those of managers. In effect, the firm exhibits a separation of ownership and control, captured by modelling the firm as two rational individuals with conflicting interests.

Example 9.1
A Firm Owner–Manager Agency Problem

Consider a simple firm consisting of a single owner (the principal) and a single manager (the agent). The contract is for a single period. Specifically, the owner hires the manager for one year. The firm faces risk: The payoff resulting from the manager's activities for the year will be $x_1 = \$100$ or $x_2 = \$55$.

We will think of the payoff here as the cash flows resulting from the manager's activities during the year. Many of these cash flows will be realized within the year. Activities aimed at cost control, for example, will generate cash savings with little delay. Advertising activities, if successful, will generate extra sales currently.

Other activities, such as R&D, however, may not pay off until next year, since it can take considerable time, if ever, for the results of current research to generate cash flow. In addition, current activities may generate future liabilities. Extraction of natural resources may generate environmental liabilities that may not be known for some time, for example. In effect, *the full payoff is not observable until after the current compensation contract has expired.*

It is this payoff that is the owner's ultimate interest. That is, the rational owner wishes to maximize the expected payoff, net of manager compensation.

Now assume that the owner does not operate the firm. This is the responsibility of the manager. Consistent with what we observe in real employment situations, the manager will be paid at year-end, despite the payoff not being observable at that time.

Assume also that, after being hired, the manager has two action choices: work hard, denoted by a_1, or shirk, denoted by a_2. The action choice of the manager will affect the probabilities of the payoffs. Let these probabilities be as follows:

■ If the manager works hard,

$$P(x_1|a_1) = 0.6$$
$$P(x_2|a_1) = \underline{0.4}$$
$$= \underline{\underline{1.0}}$$

■ If the manager shirks,

$$P(x_1|a_2) = 0.4$$
$$P(x_2|a_2) = \underline{0.6}$$
$$= \underline{\underline{1.0}}$$

Recall that x_1 represents the high payoff. If the manager works hard, the probability of x_1 is greater (0.6) than it would be under shirking (0.4). In statistical terms, the payoff distribution conditional on a_1 stochastically dominates (in the first degree) the distribution conditional on a_2. This is a critical point to realize—the action of the agent affects the probabilities of the payoffs. In particular, the greater the effort put into the operation of the firm by the manager, the higher the probability of the high payoff and the lower the complementary probability of the low payoff.

Of course, this is just what we would expect. Hard work by the manager increases the probability that the firm will do well. But, it is still possible for the low payoff to occur. In our example, there is a 40% probability that the payoff will be low even though the manager works hard, since hard work cannot always overcome the risks faced by the firm. Similarly, if the manager shirks, it is still possible for the high payoff to occur, since the shirking manager may be "bailed out" by good economic times. In our example, there is a 40% probability of the high payoff even though the manager shirks. In general, the harder the manager works, the lower the probability of the low payoff.

Finally, note that effort is interpreted quite broadly. Effort goes beyond a literal interpretation as the number of hours worked, and includes such factors as the care the manager takes in running the firm, longer-run planning, the diligence with which subordinates are motivated and supervised, the absence of perquisite-taking, and so on. In effect, effort is a modelling device that encompasses the whole range of activities undertaken by a manager during the year.

We summarize the example up to this point in Table 9.1. The dollar amounts in the table represent the payoffs under each of the four payoff–act combinations. The probabilities are conditional on the chosen act; that is, if a_1 is chosen by the manager the probability of x_1 is 0.6, whereas it is 0.4 if a_2 is chosen; and so on.[1]

As mentioned, the payoff is not observable until after the expiration of the current period. Figure 9.2 shows a timeline of the agency model.

Table 9.1 Payoffs for Agency Example

	Manager's Effort			
	a₁ (work hard)		**a₂ (shirk)**	
	Payoff	**Probability**	**Payoff**	**Probability**
x_1 (high payoff)	$100	0.6	$100	0.4
x_2 (low payoff)	55	0.4	55	0.6

Figure 9.2 Timeline for Agency Model

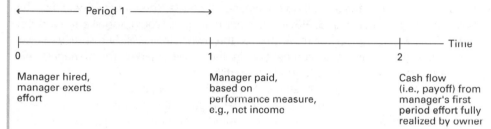

Now consider this problem from the standpoint of the owner of the firm. The owner wishes to hire the manager to operate the firm for the year; that is, the owner will have no direct control over the act taken. Indeed, it is unlikely that the owner can even observe which act the manager takes. Nevertheless, to maximize the expected payoff, the owner would like the manager to work hard—that is, to choose a_1, because the probability of the high payoff is higher conditional on a_1 than on a_2.

To illustrate this more formally, assume that the owner is risk neutral and that the owner's utility from a given payoff is equal to the dollar amount of that payoff. Assume also that the manager receives a fixed salary of $25 for the period. Then, the owner's expected utility conditional on each act is

$$EU_O(a_1) = 0.6(100 - 25) + 0.4(55 - 25)$$
$$= 0.6 \times 75 + 0.4 \times 30$$
$$= 45 + 12$$
$$= 57$$

$$EU_O(a_2) = 0.4(100 - 25) + 0.6(55 - 25)$$
$$= 0.4 \times 75 + 0.6 \times 30$$
$$= 30 + 18$$
$$= 48$$

where $EU_O(a_1)$ denotes the owner's expected utility given that the manager chooses a_1, and similarly for a_2. Just as in decision theory, we assume the players wish to maximize their expected utilities. Consequently, the owner wants the manager to choose a_1 because its expected utility to the owner is greater. It should be clear that this result will hold for any probabilities, such that the probability of x_1 given a_1 is greater than it is given a_2.

Now consider matters from the manager's standpoint. Let the manager be risk averse. Specifically, assume that his/her utility from remuneration equals the square root of the remuneration.

Will the manager *want* to work for the owner? Assume that there is a reasonably efficient **managerial labour market**. This market puts a value on the manager's services, where the value depends on the manager's ability, including training, experience, and reputation. If the manager is to be willing to work for the owner for the current period, the compensation offered must be sufficiently large that his/her expected utility is at least equal to its opportunity cost—that is, the utility that could be attained by the manager in the next best employment opportunity. This is the concept of **reservation utility**. We assume that the manager's reservation utility is 3. If the contract does not offer at least this amount, the manager will go elsewhere. Of course, the manager would prefer to receive a utility greater than 3. However, other managers would also like to work for this firm. If the manager asks for more than 3, the owner may well hire someone else. Consequently, given reasonable competition in the labour market for managers, we expect the manager to be willing to work for a utility of 3.

Now, given that the manager is hired, will a_1 in fact be chosen, as desired by the owner? First, it is important to remind ourselves again that in game theory, and in agency theory in particular, one player will not choose an act desired by another player just because that player says so. Rather, each player chooses the act that maximizes his or her own expected utility. This observation is consistent with contract theory, as discussed in Chapter 8.

Consequently, if the manager chooses a_1, it must be because the manager's expected utility is at least as great for a_1 as for a_2. Note that this assumption differs from much economic analysis, where it is simply *assumed* that firms act in a manner to maximize their profits. This expected utility-maximizing behaviour by all parties is one of the important and distinguishing characteristics of contract theory and the economic theory of games.

Next, assume that the manager is **effort averse**. This means that the manager dislikes effort and that the greater the level of effort the greater the dislike. In effect, the disutility of effort is subtracted from the utility of remuneration.

Consequently, we will assume

$$\text{Disutility of effort level } a_1 = 2.00$$
$$\text{Disutility of effort level } a_2 = 1.71$$

We can now calculate the manager's expected utility net of the disutility of effort for each act. Recall that the manager is offered a salary of \$25.

$$EU_m(a_1) = \sqrt{25} - 2.00 = 3$$
$$EU_m(a_2) = \sqrt{25} - 1.71 = 3.29$$

where $EU_m(a_1)$ denotes the expected utility of the manager, given that the manager chooses a_1, and similarly for a_2. The manager will choose a_2.[2]

This result is not very surprising. Most people, even managers, would prefer to take it easy, all other things being equal. Here, other things *are* equal, because the manager receives a salary of \$25 regardless. This tendency of an agent to shirk is an example of moral hazard.

Designing a Contract to Control Moral Hazard The question now is, what should the owner do in a situation such as that described in Example 9.1? One possibility is for the owner to refuse to hire the manager. But any other rational salaried manager would also choose a_2. Consequently, the owner could either go out of business or run the firm him/herself. These possibilities are unlikely, however. The running of an organization is a complex and specialized task for which the owner may not have the required skills, and, after all, we do witness a separation of ownership and management in all but the smallest organizations. In fact, our owner has a number of other options, which we will now consider.

Hire the manager and put up with a_2 The owner could proceed anyway, letting the manager get away with a_2 and putting up with a utility of 48 rather than 57. This also seems unlikely, however, since we will see that the owner can do better than this.

Direct monitoring If the owner could costlessly observe the manager's chosen act, this would solve the problem. Then, the contract could be amended to pay the manager a salary of $25 if a_1 was taken and, say, $12 otherwise. It is easy to verify that the manager would then choose a_1, because choosing a_2 would result in only $12 remuneration and expected utility of 1.75.

A contract where direct monitoring is possible is called **first-best**. It gives the owner the maximum attainable utility (57) and gives the agent his/her reservation utility (3). Under the assumptions of Example 9.1, no other contract can improve on this.

The first-best contract also has desirable **risk-sharing** properties. Note that under this contract the manager bears none of the firm's risk, because a fixed salary is received regardless of the payoff. Since the manager is risk averse, this is desirable. The owner bears all the risk of the random payoff. Since the owner is risk neutral, he or she does not mind bearing risk. Indeed, we could argue that a function of business ownership is to bear risk. If the owner was risk averse, rather than risk neutral, the first-best contract would involve the owner and manager sharing the risk. However, demonstration of this is beyond our scope.

Unfortunately, the first-best contract is frequently unattainable. This would seem to be the case in an owner–manager contract, because it is unlikely that the owner could monitor the agent's effort in a managerial setting. The nature of managerial effort is so complex that it would be effectively impossible for a remote owner to establish whether the manager was in fact "working hard." We thus have a case of information asymmetry: The manager knows the effort level, but the owner does not. As mentioned previously, this particular form of information asymmetry is called moral hazard.

Indirect monitoring Given that managerial effort is not directly observable, it may be possible under some conditions to impute the effort. To illustrate, let us change our example slightly. See Table 9.2. The only difference between this table and Table 9.1 is that the payoff for (x_2, a_2) is now $40 rather than $55. In agency theory terms, this is a case of **moving support**—that is, the set of possible payoffs is different (it moves) depending

Table 9.2 Payoffs for Agency Example

| | Manager's Effort | | | |
| | a$_1$ (work hard) | | a$_2$ (shirk) | |
	Payoff	Probability	Payoff	Probability
x$_1$ (high payoff)	$100	0.6	$100	0.4
x$_2$ (low payoff)	55	0.4	40	0.6

on which act is taken. Table 9.1 is a case of **fixed support**—the set of possible payoffs is fixed at (100, 55), regardless of the action choice.

It is apparent from Table 9.2 that if the owner observes a payoff of $40 it will be known that the manager chose a$_2$ even though effort is not directly observable. Then the owner could amend the contract to offer the manager a salary of $25 unless the payoff turns out to be $40, in which case the manager would be obligated to return $13 to the owner as a penalty, for a net salary of $12. It is easy to check that the manager would then choose a$_1$:

$$EU_m(a_1) = \sqrt{25} - 2 = 3$$
$$EU_m(a_2) = 0.4\sqrt{25} + 0.6\sqrt{12} - 1.71 = 2.37$$

The penalty of $13 if the $40 payoff happens is sufficient cause for the agent to choose a$_1$. This is also a first-best contract, since the agent works hard, bears no risk, and receives reservation utility, thereby maximizing the owner's expected payoff.

Indirect monitoring will *not* work for the fixed-support case of Table 9.1, however. The reason is that if a payoff of $55 is observed, this is consistent with either a$_1$ or a$_2$, and similarly for the $100 payoff. Thus, the owner cannot impute the act from the payoff.

It seems, then, that we cannot rely on indirect monitoring to ensure that the first-best contract will be attained. First, many contracting situations may be characterized by fixed support. For example, in many cases the payoff may be any positive or negative number. If the payoff is, say, a loss of $1 million, the owner cannot be certain whether this loss resulted from low manager effort or an unfortunate realization of the firm's risk.

Second, even if moving support holds, legal and institutional factors may prevent the owner from penalizing the manager sufficiently to force a$_1$. For example, it may be difficult for the owner to collect $13 from the manager after the current one-year contract has expired.

Owner rents firm to the manager At this point, the owner may well be tempted to say to the manager, "Okay, I give up—*you* take the firm and run it, taking 100% of the profits after paying me a fixed rental of $51." Then, the owner no longer cares what action the manager takes, since a rental of $51 is received regardless. This is referred to as **internalizing** the manager's decision problem.

Such arrangements do exist, or they have existed in the past, in the form of tenant farming. Tenant farming is usually regarded as inefficient, however, and it is easy to see why. The manager's expected utility under the two possible outcomes would be

$$EU_m(a_1) = 0.6\sqrt{100 - 51} + 0.4\sqrt{55 - 51} - 2$$
$$= 0.6 \times 7 + 0.4 \times 2 - 2$$
$$= 4.2 + 0.8 - 2$$
$$= 3.00$$

$$EU_m(a_2) = 0.4\sqrt{100 - 51} + 0.6\sqrt{55 - 51} - 1.71$$
$$= 0.4 \times 7 + 0.6 \times 2 - 1.71$$
$$= 2.80 + 1.20 - 1.71$$
$$= 2.29$$

Thus, the manager will choose a_1 and receive reservation utility of 3.

Note, however, that the owner receives a utility of 51 in this contract, compared to 57 in the first-best contract. Consequently, the owner is worse off. The reason is that this contracting arrangement has inefficient risk-sharing characteristics. The owner is risk neutral, and hence is willing to bear risk, but there is no risk for the owner because a fixed rent is received. The risk-averse manager, who dislikes risk, is forced to bear it all. The owner must lower the rent from $57 to $51 to enable the manager to receive reservation utility of 3, costing the owner 6 in lost utility. The 6 is called an **agency cost**, and is another component of contracting costs, which the owner will want to minimize.

Give the manager a share of the profits

Finally, we come to what is often the most efficient alternative if the first-best contract is not attainable. This is for the owner to give the manager a share of firm performance. However, the owner immediately runs into a problem. The payoff is not fully observable until next period. Yet the manager must be compensated at the end of the current period.

A solution to the problem is to base compensation on a **performance measure**—that is, on some jointly observable variable that reflects the manager's performance[3] and is available at the end of the first period. Net income is such a performance measure. Net income tells us *something* about manager performance, since much of manager effort shows up in current earnings. Effort devoted to cost control, maintenance, employee morale, and advertising, for example, will typically affect net income with little lag. We then say that net income is **informative** about manager effort.[4]

Unfortunately, net income is not *fully* informative about effort. One reason is poor corporate governance, such as weak internal controls, which allow random error or bias into net income. Recognition lag is another reason, since, as mentioned above, several components of manager effort may not fully pay off during the current period. R&D is a common example. While most R&D costs are written off currently, the realization of revenues from current R&D expenditures may be delayed until after the current period.

As a result, a random understatement of the ultimate payoff is introduced into net income. Alternatively, or in addition, current manager effort may have a side effect of creating environmental or legal liabilities that may not be known until next period, with the result that net income contains a random overstatement of the payoff.

Of course, through accruals, including fair valuations of assets and liabilities, net income anticipates at least some of the ultimate cash flows from current manager performance. This is consistent with the argument in the Conceptual Framework (Section 3.7.1) that earnings based on accrual accounting generally provide a better indicator of future cash flows than do current cash flows.

Nevertheless, since accruals are subject to error and bias, and fair values are volatile, net income does not tell the full story about current manager performance. That is, net income is noisy. Here, greater noise in net income means that it predicts the payoff from current manager effort less precisely. However, we assume in this section that despite net income not telling the full story, net income is unbiased. That is, while net income may be understated or overstated relative to the payoff, the expected value of the various understatements and overstatements is zero. This is equivalent to assuming that all assets and liabilities are fair valued.

In sum, in this section, we regard net income as a noisy, unbiased **message** about the payoff.

Example 9.2
Net Income as a Performance Measure

To illustrate the use of net income in compensation contracts, we extend Example 9.1. Recall from Table 9.1 that if the manager works hard (a_1) the probability of the high payoff ($100) is 0.6, with 0.4 probability of the low payoff ($55). If the manager shirks (a_2), the probabilities of the high and low payoffs are 0.4 and 0.6, respectively. As explained at the time, the reason why the payoff can be low even if the manager works hard, and vice versa, is because of the various risks faced by the firm. Despite hard work, bad economic times may result in the low payoff. Alternatively, good times may rescue the manager who shirks. These risks can be reduced by manager effort, but cannot be eliminated, as reflected in the 0.4 probability of low payoff given a_1 and the 0.4 probability of high payoff given a_2. In sum, while the manager can increase the probability of the high payoff by working hard, a high payoff cannot be guaranteed. Nor can it be guaranteed that shirking will result in a low payoff.

Furthermore, noisy net income introduces a second source of compensation risk for the manager: Given the ultimate payoff, compensation will still vary depending on which net income is realized. To reflect the noise in net income, assume the following:

- If the payoff is going to be $100, net income for the current period will be $115 with probability 0.8 and $40 with probability 0.2.
- If the payoff is going to be $55, net income for the current period will be $115 with probability 0.2 and $40 with probability 0.8.

There are thus two possible net income numbers. The manager who works hard requires a 0.3237 share of net income to attain reservation utility of 3. Once net income is reported, the manager's share could be paid in cash, paid by means of generous pension and other benefits, or paid by a combination of cash and benefits. Other methods of payment are considered in Chapter 10.

To verify that the manager does receive reservation utility with this share of net income, we have

$$EU_m(a_1) = 0.6[0.8\sqrt{0.3237 \times 115} + 0.2\sqrt{0.3237 \times 40}]$$
$$+ 0.4[0.2\sqrt{0.3237 \times 115} + 0.8\sqrt{0.3237 \times 40}] - 2$$
$$= 0.6[0.8\sqrt{37.2255} + 0.2\sqrt{12.9480}]$$
$$+ 0.4[0.2\sqrt{37.2255} + 0.8\sqrt{12.9480}] - 2$$
$$= 0.6 \times 5.6007 + 0.4 \times 4.0989 - 2$$
$$= 3.3604 + 1.6396 - 2$$
$$= 3.00$$

Recall that the manager's utility for money is given by the square root of the amount received and that the effort disutility of working hard is 2. The expression in the first set of square brackets is the expected utility of compensation given the high payoff. That is, if the payoff is going to be $100, net income will be $115 with probability 0.8 or $40 with probability 0.2. The result is then multiplied by the probability of the high payoff (0.6). A similar interpretation applies to the second expression, given the low payoff.

If the manager shirks, expected utility is 2.9896, net of effort disutility of 1.71, as follows:

$$EU_m(a_2) = 0.4 \times 5.6007 + 0.6 \times 4.0989 - 1.71$$
$$= 2.2403 + 2.4593 - 1.71$$
$$= 2.9896$$

Consequently, the manager will work hard.[5] As in Example 9.1, the owner is risk neutral, with utility equal to the dollar amount of the payoff, net of manager compensation. The owner's expected utility is now

$$EU_o(a_1) = 0.6[0.8(100 - (0.3237 \times 115)) + 0.2(100 - (0.3237 \times 40))]$$
$$+ 0.4[0.2(55 - (0.3237 \times 115)) + 0.8(55 - (0.3237 \times 40))]$$
$$= 0.6[0.8(100 - 37.2255) + 0.2(100 - 12.9480)]$$
$$+ 0.4[0.2(55 - 37.2255) + 0.8(55 - 12.9480)]$$
$$= 0.6 \times 67.6300 + 0.4 \times 37.1965$$
$$= 40.5780 + 14.8786$$
$$= 55.4566$$

The first expression in square brackets is the expected payoff net of manager compensation, given the high payoff. This is multiplied by the probability of the high payoff. A similar interpretation applies to the second expression given the low payoff.

Note that the owner's utility is greater than the utility of 51 under the rental contract. Thus the profit-sharing contract is more efficient. However, it is less efficient than the first-best contract of Example 9.1, where the owner's utility is 57. The agency cost is now $57 - 55.4566 = 1.5434$.

These differences in the owner's utility can also be explained in terms of the agent's compensation risk. In the first-best contract, the manager bears no risk, since a salary of $25 is expected regardless of the amount of net income (i.e., zero profit share). In the rental contract (i.e., a 100% profit share), the manager bears all of the risk. In Example 9.2, the manager bears only part of the risk (i.e., a 0.3237 profit share). Given the effort level, the more risk borne by the manager, the higher the profit share needed to overcome the manager's risk aversion and enable reservation utility to be attained.[6] The higher the profit share to the manager, the less there remains for the owner or, equivalently, the higher the agency cost. Thus, the agency costs are zero, 1.5434, and 6 for the first-best, profit sharing, and rental contracts, respectively. The most efficient contract short of first-best is called **second-best**.[7] Note that it is the *contract* that motivates the manager to work hard in this example. Given the terms of the contract, the manager *wants* to take a_1. This aspect of the contract is called **incentive-compatibility**, since the agent's incentive to take a_1 is compatible with the owner's best interests. (The first-best contract, if it is attainable, is also incentive-compatible, because the prospect of reduced remuneration following a_2 motivates the manager to take a_1.) We then say that the owner's and manager's interests are **aligned**, since they both want the firm to do well.

Agency costs are one of the costs of contracting that are part of contract theory. As discussed in Section 8.2, the firm will want to arrange its corporate governance efficiently, and we pointed out there that efficient contracts will depend on the firm's form of organization and its environment. Since the firm in Example 9.2 is organized with a separation of ownership and control, we would expect it to design and adopt profit-sharing contracts with the lowest agency costs. Such contracts impose the minimum compensation risk needed to motivate the manager to work hard.

This raises the question, can accountants improve the ability of net income to predict the payoff? This question is an important one for accountants. A less noisy (equivalently, more precise) net income will reduce compensation risk, enabling a lower profit-sharing proportion for the manager and increased contracting efficiency. This enhances the role of net income as a performance measure in managerial compensation plans.

Example 9.3
Less Noisy Net Income

A possible way to improve payoff prediction is to improve the accuracy of asset and liability measurement. To illustrate, suppose that improvements in techniques of estimation and valuation enable reduced noise in net income compared with Example 9.2, while retaining the unbiasedness assumption.

Assume that the lower noise in net income is as follows:

- If the payoff is going to be $100, net income for the current period will be $110 with probability 0.8462 and $45 with probability 0.1538.
- If the payoff is going to be $55, net income for the current period will be $110 with probability 0.1538 and $45 with probability 0.8462.

The differences from Example 9.2 are that net income, while still noisy and unbiased, is more precise. It falls within a narrower range of the ultimate payoffs and has a greater probability of reporting high when the payoff is going to be high, and a greater probability of reporting low when the payoff is going to be low. It can be verified that the manager now requires 0.3185 of profits to attain reservation utility, down from 0.3237 above (see problem 17). Also, the manager continues to work hard.

The owner's expected utility is now

$$
\begin{aligned}
EU_o(a_1) &= 0.6[0.8462(100 - (0.3185 \times 110)) + 0.1538(100 - (0.3185 \times 45))] \\
&\quad + 0.4[0.1538(55 - (0.3185 \times 110)) + 0.8462(55 - (0.3185 \times 45))] \\
&= 0.6[0.8462(100 - 35.0350) + 0.1538(100 - 14.3325)] \\
&\quad + 0.4[0.1538(55 - 35.0350) + 0.8462(55 - 14.3325)] \\
&= 0.6 \times 68.1491 + 0.4 \times 37.4834 \\
&= 40.8895 + 14.9934 \\
&= 55.8829
\end{aligned}
$$

The owner's expected utility is greater than that of the noisier contract of Example 9.2 (55.4566), reflecting reduced agency cost of $57 - 55.8829 = 1.1171$, in place of 1.5434 in Example 9.2. The improvement in accounting precision enables a more efficient compensation contract.

9.3 MANAGER'S INFORMATION ADVANTAGE

9.3.1 Earnings Management

In Section 9.2, we assumed that the payoff was not observable by the owner or the manager until the next period. Net income, which *is* observable currently by both parties, was viewed as a noisy, unbiased message about what the payoff will be.

Consequently, the manager had no reporting discretion in Section 9.2. Net income was viewed simply as a noisy number produced by an accounting system. The manager could not control or manage this number since the noise resulted from the characteristics of the system rather than from anything the manager does. Of course, as we showed in Example 9.3, even in the absence of earnings management, accountants can increase contracting efficiency by reducing the noise through improved measurement.

However, in reality, net income is not an unbiased payoff predictor. Despite movements toward fair value accounting described in Chapter 7, net income remains based on a mixed measurement model. Thus, as any accountant knows, managers frequently do engage in earnings management. Indeed, this is a prediction of contracting theory. To better understand the role of net income as a performance measure, we must allow for the possibility that the manager may bias or otherwise manage reported earnings.

There is a variety of forms that manager information advantage can take. One possibility is that the manager may have information about the payoff prior to signing the contract (called **pre-contract information**). For example, the manager may have information that the high payoff will occur, and, unless the owner can extract this information, may enter into the contract with the intention of shirking, taking advantage of the high payoff to generate high earnings and compensation. Alternatively, the manager may obtain payoff information after signing the contract but prior to choosing an act (**pre-decision information**). If the payoff information is sufficiently bad, the manager may resign unless this situation is allowed for in the contract. Yet another possibility is that the manager receives information after the act is chosen (**post-decision information**). For example, the manager may learn what net income is before reporting to the owner. If the owner cannot observe unmanaged net income, the manager may manage earnings so as to maximize compensation.

In Example 9.4, we will examine a case of post-decision information. Specifically, we extend Example 9.2 by adding an assumption that the owner cannot observe which of the two possible net income numbers is actually realized. Only the manager can observe this. What the owner does observe is an earnings number *reported by* the manager. This assumption seems reasonable since the manager has the ability to influence the accounting system, creating the possibility that reported net income may be biased for his/her own purposes.[8]

Example 9.4
Biased Reporting

Recall from Example 9.2 that there were two possible net income numbers. If the payoff is going to be $100, unmanaged net income will be $115 with probability 0.8 or $40 with probability 0.2. If the payoff is going to be $55, unmanaged net income will be $115 with probability 0.2 or $40 with probability 0.8. When the owner cannot observe which of these is actually realized, reporting may be delegated to the manager. Then, it is not hard to see how the manager will opportunistically exploit this information advantage in a single-period contract. Given that the manager bears no costs to manage earnings, and that the owner is committed by contract to pay the manager a portion of reported net income, the manager will shirk and bias net income upward to $115 regardless of what unmanaged net income is. More formally,

$$EU_m(a_1) = 0.6[0.8\sqrt{115k} + 0.2\sqrt{115k}] + 0.4[0.2\sqrt{115k} + 0.8\sqrt{115k}] - 2$$
$$= \sqrt{115k} - 2$$
$$EU_m(a_2) = 0.4[0.8\sqrt{115k} + 0.2\sqrt{115k}] + 0.6[0.2\sqrt{115k} + 0.8\sqrt{115k}] - 1.71$$
$$= \sqrt{115k} - 1.71$$

where k is the profit-sharing proportion. Obviously, the manager will choose a_2 for any k. To receive reservation utility, the manager now requires $k = 0.1929$, yielding compensation of $22.18:

$$
\begin{aligned}
EU_m(a_2) &= \sqrt{0.1929 \times 115} - 1.71 \\
&= \sqrt{22.1835} - 1.71 \\
&= 4.7099 - 1.71 \\
&= 3
\end{aligned}
$$

The owner's expected utility is now

$$
\begin{aligned}
EU_O(a_2) &= 0.4(100 - (0.1929 \times 115)) + 0.6(55 - (0.1929 \times 115)) \\
&= 0.4(100 - 22.1835) + 0.6(55 - 22.1835) \\
&= 0.4 \times 77.8165 + 0.6 \times 32.8165 \\
&= 31.1266 + 19.6899 \\
&= 50.8165
\end{aligned}
$$

This is less than the owner's utility in the contract of Example 9.2 (55.4566). The reduction arises because the manager can report the maximum net income regardless of effort. Consequently, the manager will shirk, and the owner's expected utility reflects the resulting lower expected payoff. Note also that the manager bears no risk, since the same compensation is received regardless of the payoff. We know from Example 9.2 that the manager must bear risk if the work-hard effort alternative is to be chosen.

9.3.2 The Revelation Principle[*]

While the owner's utility is lower in Example 9.4 than in Example 9.2, Example 9.4 more closely approximates the actual situation of a firm owner, since we would normally *expect* the manager to have an information advantage, possibly using it to manage earnings. Given separation of ownership and control, it is unlikely that the owner would be able to observe the detailed workings of the firm's accounting and reporting systems. Then, the question arises, can the owner do anything to control this obviously unsatisfactory situation? The answer is a qualified yes.

Example 9.5
The Revelation Principle

In Example 9.4, the manager does not report truthfully. Can truthful reporting be motivated? If so, this would at least eliminate earnings management, regardless of its effect

---

[*]This section can be omitted without loss of continuity.

on effect. To illustrate, suppose that the owner offers the following amended contract in Example 9.4:

If net income is reported as $115, k = 0.1929

If net income is reported as $40, k = 0.5546

Recall from Example 9.4 that k is the manager's profit-sharing proportion. It is easy to verify that the manager still receives compensation of $22.18 as in Example 9.4, regardless of what net income is reported (e.g., if net income of $40 is reported, compensation is $40 \times 0.5546 = 22.18$). Consequently, since no risk is borne, he/she will continue to shirk, receiving reservation utility of 3 as before. The owner continues to receive expected utility of 50.8165. What is different is that there is now no incentive for the manager to distort reported net income, since the same compensation is received regardless of what amount is reported.[9] This example illustrates the **revelation principle** (Myerson, 1979; see also Christensen, 1981, and Arya, Glover, and Sunder, 1998). For any contract under which the manager has an incentive to lie about his/her private information, an equivalent contract can be designed that motivates truth-telling.

The revelation principle raises an intriguing question. Why not design real compensation contracts to motivate truth-telling? Then, opportunistic earnings management would be a thing of the past. While managers would tend to shirk, the shirking would be no greater than what would take place without truth-telling, and the owner's expected utility would be the same. But, the firm would be worth more to prospective buyers, due to increased investor confidence that reported net income is free of manager distortion and bias.[10]

However, the revelation principle is not a panacea. There are several conditions that must be met if it is to hold. One such condition is that the owner must be able to commit that the truth will not be used against the manager. For example, if the manager anticipates that truthfully reporting net income of $40 in Example 9.5 may result in being fired by an angry owner, he/she is unlikely to report the truth.

A second condition is that there must be no restrictions on the form of contract. For example, many compensation contracts do not provide for a bonus unless performance exceeds some specified level, such as earnings greater than 10% of shareholders' equity. In addition, the amount of bonus may be capped so that no bonus is payable on earnings greater than, say, 25% of equity. When such restrictions exist, we cannot be sure that the contract that motivates truth-telling will meet these restrictions. For example, if no bonus is paid on earnings greater than 25% of equity, it is hard to say that the owner is not using the truth against the manager.

A third condition is that there be no restrictions on the manager's ability to communicate his/her information. Suppose, for example, that a manager has a forecast of next year's earnings, but that honest reporting of the forecast is potentially very costly to the manager personally, due to loss of reputation and possible legal liability if the forecast is not met. A contract to motivate truthful reporting of the forecast could impose so much risk on the manager that the level of compensation needed to attain reservation utility is more than the owner is willing to pay. Honest communication is effectively blocked. Consequently, the owner may allow the manager to report a biased forecast, or no forecast at all.

The impact of these restrictions is that we cannot rely on the revelation principle to assure us that the most efficient possible compensation contract involves truth telling. Under the assumptions of Example 9.4, a profit-sharing contract of 0.1929 of reported net income to the manager, with owner's utility of 50.8165, *is* the most efficient one available. If the revelation principle applies, we know from Example 9.5 that an equivalent contract involving reporting the truth yields the same utility to the owner. However, if the revelation principle does not apply, motivation of truthful reporting may require an increase in manager compensation, lowering the owner's expected utility below that of a contract that allows earnings management.

To illustrate, suppose that, pursuant to Example 9.5, net income is reported as $40 and the manager receives high compensation (i.e., $22.18) despite low reported earnings. Angry shareholders and media reports would likely adversely affect the manager's reputation. Suppose that the manager anticipates that these costs have a personal monetary equivalent of $2. Then, if he/she is to report this amount truthfully, a profit share of 0.6045 is needed, giving compensation of $0.6045 \times 40 = \$24.18$. Allowing for the reputation costs of $2, the manager's net compensation is $22.18, the same as before. However, paying the extra $2 of compensation lowers the owner's expected utility. The owner is better off to revert to the contract of Example 9.4, which allows earnings management, thereby saving $2 in compensation and restoring expected utility of 50.8165.

As a practical matter, it is unlikely that the revelation principle can eliminate earnings management.

9.3.3 Controlling Earnings Management

Example 9.4 illustrates how earnings management can lead to manager shirking. To control opportunistic earnings management, a response is to strengthen corporate governance. For example, audit and compensation committees of the Board may include independent and financially literate members, to monitor earnings management.

Indeed, GAAP itself, when accompanied by a competent audit, also fulfils a corporate governance role. While GAAP allows discretion in choosing among different accounting policies, it does limit the amount by which earnings can be managed. In Example 9.4, if unmanaged net income of, say, $40 is realized, could the manager really increase reported earnings to $115 without detection? Hopefully, accounting standards do not allow distortion of this magnitude, particularly when the financial statements are audited. By delegating some reporting discretion to the manager, but controlling through GAAP the magnitude of the resulting earnings management, we now illustrate how the manager's incentive to work hard can be restored and the owner made better off.

A way to control earnings management is to limit it by means of GAAP, to the point where the manager's incentive to work hard is restored. Consider the following example.

Example 9.6
Limiting the Bias in Net Income

Extend Example 9.4 to replace each possible net income number (i.e., $115, $40) with a $5 range. Thus, net income of $115 is replaced by the range [$111–$116]. Similarly, net income of $40 is replaced with the range [$36–$41].

This range assumption captures the quality of GAAP, which does allow some flexibility in accounting policy choice. Straight-line and declining-balance amortization of capital assets are both acceptable methods, for example. Consequently, net income will differ depending on which method is chosen. The assumption of a range for unmanaged net income is also consistent with our argument in Section 2.6 that true net income does not exist.

The payoff probabilities are assumed unchanged. For example, if the manager works hard, the probability of the high payoff is still 0.6. We assume that the owner knows the two possible earnings ranges, and knows which range has occurred. For example, if the manager reports $116, the owner knows that while the manager may have biased this number, at least GAAP net income is in the range [$111–$116]. This captures the fact that GAAP does impose some discipline on reported earnings. However, the owner does not know the actual unmanaged net income within that range.

To maximize compensation in a single-period contract, the rational manager will report the upper end of the appropriate range. For example, suppose that unmanaged net income is $112—that is, it is in the [$111–$116] range. Think of the $112 as the earnings number that results from the accounting policies and methods used by the firm *before any earnings management*. Given information advantage, however, the manager will engage in earnings management to bias reported earnings up to $116. This could be accomplished, within GAAP, in a number of ways. For example, the manager may accelerate revenue recognition or, as mentioned, switch from declining-balance to straight-line amortization. Note, however, unlike Example 9.4, that the manager cannot switch between ranges without violating GAAP. Thus, if unmanaged net income falls in the [$36–$41] range, reporting a net income of $116 would incur auditor qualification.

Knowing that the manager will report the upper end of the range, a compensation contract of 0.3193 of reported net income enables the manager to attain reservation utility. To verify, suppose a_1 is taken. Then, the manager's expected utility is

$$EU_m(a_1) = 0.6[0.8\sqrt{0.3193 \times 116} + 0.2\sqrt{0.3193 \times 41}]$$
$$+ 0.4[0.2\sqrt{0.3193 \times 116} + 0.8\sqrt{0.3193 \times 41}] - 2$$
$$= 0.6[0.8 \times 6.0860 + 0.2 \times 3.6182] + 0.4[0.2 \times 6.0860 + 0.8 \times 3.6182] - 2$$
$$= 0.6 \times 5.5924 + 0.4 \times 4.1118 - 2$$
$$= 3.3554 + 1.6447 - 2$$
$$= 3.00$$

The first quantity in square brackets is the manager's expected compensation if the high payoff occurs. Under the high payoff, net income is in the range [$111–$116] with probability 0.8 and [$36–$41] with probability 0.2. As mentioned, the manager will report the upper end of the range. This expected compensation is multiplied by the probability of the high payoff (0.6). A similar interpretation applies to the second quantity.

If act a_2 is taken,

$$EU_m(a_2) = 0.4[0.8\sqrt{0.3193 \times 116} + 0.2\sqrt{0.3193 \times 41}]$$
$$+ 0.6[0.2\sqrt{0.3193 \times 116} + 0.8\sqrt{0.3193 \times 41}] - 1.71$$
$$= 0.4 \times 5.5924 + 0.6 \times 4.1118 - 1.71$$
$$= 2.99$$

Thus the manager will now take a_1. The restrictions imposed by GAAP and auditing on the ability to misreport does not eliminate the manager's ability to exploit his/her information advantage, but reduces it to the point where hard work must be undertaken to attain reservation utility.

As might be expected, this limitation on the manager's ability to misreport benefits the owner. In fact, the owner's expected utility is now

$$EU_o(a_1) = 0.6[0.8(100 - (0.3193 \times 116)) + 0.2(100 - (0.3193 \times 41))]$$
$$+ 0.4[0.2(55 - (0.3193 \times 116)) + 0.8(55 - (0.3193 \times 41))]$$
$$= 0.6[0.8(100 - 37.0388) + 0.2(100 - 13.0913)]$$
$$+ 0.4[0.2(55 - 37.0388) + 0.8(55 - 13.0913)]$$
$$= 0.6(0.8 \times 62.9612 + 0.2 \times 86.9087) + 0.4(0.2 \times 17.9612 + 0.8 \times 41.9087)$$
$$= 0.6 \times 67.7507 + 0.4 \times 37.1192$$
$$= 40.6504 + 14.8477$$
$$= 55.4981$$

The owner is thus better off than under the contract of Example 9.4, where expected utility was 50.8165. This is because the limitation imposed by GAAP on the manager's ability to manage net income has enabled a contract that restores an incentive to work hard. Note, however, that the contract does allow for some earnings management since, unless unmanaged net income is at the upper end of its range, the manager will bias it upward.[11] Since the alternative is to revert to the contract in Example 9.5, this suggests that some degree of within-GAAP earnings management can be "good," even in a one-period contract. We will return to this point in Chapter 11.

9.3.4 Agency Theory with Psychological Norms[*]

In Section 6.6, we suggested that it is time for proponents of theories of rational and non-rational investor behaviour to consider moving the theories together. An interesting step in this direction was taken by Fischer and Huddart (FH; 2008). These authors pointed

---

[*]This section can be omitted without loss of continuity.

out psychological research suggesting that individual behaviour is affected by personal and social **norms**. A personal norm is an innate characteristic of an individual, such as a belief in hard work or a feeling that earnings management is bad. A social norm was defined by FH as the average behaviour of a peer group. For example, a manager may perceive that, on average, managers of similar firms regard earnings management as acceptable.

These norms influence individual behaviour. Thus, a manager with a strong work ethic and weak acceptance of a social norm that earnings management is acceptable will require a lower profit share to motivate hard work than a manager with a weak work ethic and strong acceptance of the social norm. This latter manager will be motivated to work less hard, perhaps substituting earnings management for the effort he/she would otherwise deliver. In effect, the personal and social norms interact to influence the manager's effort and earnings management incentives.

To analyze these interactions, FH developed an agency model, similar to the one we developed in Example 9.2, but which incorporates personal and social norms. We extend Example 9.2 with a simplified version of the FH model, to illustrate how norms can be incorporated.

Recall from Example 9.2 that the manager's compensation is based on net income with noise, as follows:

- If the payoff is going to be $100, net income for the current period will be $115 with probability 0.8 and $40 with probability 0.2.

- If the payoff is going to be $55, net income for the current period will be $115 with probability 0.2 and $40 with probability 0.8.

Recall also that if the manager works hard, the probabilities of the high and low payoffs, respectively, are 0.6 and 0.4. If the manager shirks, these probabilities are reversed. The manager's utility for money is the square root of the amount received, and disutility of effort is 2 if he/she works hard and 1.7 if he/she shirks. As shown in Example 9.2, a profit share of .3237 motivates hard work and yields the required reservation utility of 3.

Now, pursuant to the FH model, assume that the manager has a personal norm for hard work, so that disutility of effort is reduced from 2 to 1.5. If the manager shirks, effort disutility remains at 1.7. Assume that the manager can manage earnings upward by $25 without violating GAAP but, because of a feeling that earnings management is largely opportunistic, has a personal norm against earnings management, with disutility of 3. However, he/she is aware that his/her peer group accepts earnings management, reducing the personal disutility of earnings management by 2, to a net of 1.

The manager now has four possible decisions:

- Work hard, no earnings management $(a_1, 0)$
- Work hard, earnings management $(a_1, 25)$
- Shirk, no earnings management $(a_2, 0)$
- Shirk, earnings management $(a_2, 25)$

Assume that the owner prefers $(a_1, 0)$. The manager's expected utility for $(a_1, 0)$ is

$$EU_m(a_1, 0) = 0.6(0.8\sqrt{115k} + 0.2\sqrt{40k}) + 0.4(0.2\sqrt{115k} + 0.8\sqrt{40k}) - 1.5$$

$$= [(0.48 + 0.08)(10.7238) + (0.12 + 0.32)(6.3246)]\sqrt{k} - 1.5$$

$$= [(0.56 \times 10.7238) + (0.44 \times 6.3246)]\sqrt{k} - 1.5$$

$$= (6.0053 + 2.7828)\sqrt{k} - 1.5$$

$$= 8.7881\sqrt{k} - 1.5$$

where k is the manager's share of net income, and disutility of effort is now 1.5. Since the manager does not manage earnings, assume that the disutility of earnings management is zero.

To attain reservation utility of 3, we need

$$8.7881\sqrt{k} - 1.5 = 3$$

$$\sqrt{k} = \frac{4.5}{8.7881} = .5121$$

$$k = .2622$$

Since $(a_1, 0)$ is the owner's desired act, the owner offers the manager this profit share.

The manager's expected utility of working hard and managing earnings is

$$EU_m(a_1, 25) = 0.6(0.8\sqrt{140 \times .2622} + 0.2\sqrt{65 \times .2622})$$

$$+ 0.4(0.2\sqrt{140 \times .2622} + 0.8\sqrt{65 \times .2622}) - 1.5 - (3 - 2)$$

$$= (0.48 + 0.08) \times \sqrt{36.7080} + (0.12 + 0.32) \times \sqrt{17.0430} - 2.5$$

$$- 0.56 \times 6.0587 + 0.44 \times 4.1283 \quad 2.5$$

$$= 3.3929 + 1.8164 - 2.5$$

$$= 2.7093$$

Because of earnings management, net incomes are increased by 25. Since the manager manages earnings, the net disutility of managing earnings of 1 is now also subtracted.

It can also be shown that

■ $EU_m(a_2, 0) = 2.5297$

■ $EU_m(a_2, 25) = 2.2777$

Since these are all less than the reservation utility of 3, the manager will choose $(a_1, 0)$ and receive a .2622 profit share. The reduction in effort disutility due to a personal hard work norm reduces the profit share needed to motivate hard work relative to the .3237 share in Example 9.2. The manager's personal norm against earnings management reduces the incentive to manage earnings. The group norm increases the incentive to manage earnings but, in this example, is not strong enough to overcome the effect of the personal norm against earnings management.

9.4 DISCUSSION AND SUMMARY

We have studied a single-period agency model. This model illustrates several important aspects of agency theory:

1. Observability of an agent's effort seems unlikely in an owner–manager context, because of the separation of ownership and control that characterizes firms in a developed industrial society. This is an example of information asymmetry leading to moral hazard. The rational effort averse manager will, if possible, take advantage of the lack of effort observability to shirk. Agency theory, a branch of game theory, studies the problem of designing a contract to control moral hazard. The most efficient contract does so with the lowest possible agency cost.

2. The nature of the most efficient contract depends crucially on what can be jointly observed. Contracts can only be written in terms of performance measures that are jointly observable by both principal and agent:

   ■ If the agent's effort can be jointly observed, directly or indirectly, a fixed salary (subject to a penalty if the contracted-for effort level is not taken) is most efficient when the principal is risk neutral. This is called a first-best contract. There is no agency cost. Here, *effort* is the performance measure.

   ■ Unless the firm is of very short duration, it is unlikely that the payoff from the current period's manager effort can be observed until after the end of the current period. This is because the cash flows from certain types of manager effort, such as R&D, will not be realized until a subsequent period—that is, until after the current compensation contract has expired. Given that the manager must be paid periodically, compensation cannot be based on the payoff.

   ■ If the agent's effort cannot be jointly observed, but net income can, the most efficient contract may give the agent a share of net income. However, net income is a risky performance measure for the manager, both because the payoff is risky and because current period net income is a noisy measure of this payoff. Since the manager shares in net income, he/she bears compensation risk from both sources. Here, *net income* is the performance measure.

   ■ If effort, payoff, and net income are all unobservable, the optimal contract is a rental contract, whereby the principal rents the firm to the manager for a fixed rental fee, thus internalizing the agent's effort decision. Such contracts are inefficient because they impose all of the firm's risk on the agent, resulting in maximum agency cost. Here, there is *no* performance measure.

3. Since the agent is assumed risk averse, imposing compensation risk reduces his/her expected utility of compensation. This requires the principal to increase the share of net income so as to maintain the agent's reservation utility. The second-best contract is the contract that imposes the lowest amount of risk on the manager while maintaining reservation utility and the manager's incentive to work hard. Accountants

can improve the efficiency of compensation contracts by improving the precision of net income as a payoff predictor.

4. When net income is the performance measure, the manager has a further information advantage over the owner. This is because the manager controls the firm's accounting system, while the owner can observe only the net income number reported by the manager. This leads to the possibility of earnings management. In theory, it may be possible to design a compensation contract to motivate the manager to report unmanaged earnings (i.e., to completely eliminate earnings management), but this is unlikely in practice since it is costly. However, with efficient corporate governance, including responsible application of GAAP to limit the range over which earnings can be managed, accountants may be able to maintain the manager's incentive to work hard. This leads to a conclusion that some degree of earnings management can be "good."

5. Ethical behaviour by the manager, because of personal norms against shirking and/or earnings management, can lead to a more efficient contract, other things equal. However, to the extent the manager's peer group favours earnings management on average, motivation for earnings management is increased.

9.5 PROTECTING LENDERS FROM MANAGER INFORMATION ADVANTAGE

We now consider another moral hazard problem—namely, the possibility that the manager may act opportunistically against the best interests of lenders, thereby benefitting him/herself and/or the shareholders at lenders' expense. Since the financing decisions of most firms include borrowing, often in excess of the capital raised through share issues, it is important to control this agency problem if the firm is to borrow at reasonable cost. As referred to in Chapter 8, there are several ways that an opportunistic manager may compromise lender interests, for example by

■ Paying excessive dividends

■ Undertaking additional borrowing

■ Undertaking excessively risky projects, particularly if the firm is approaching financial distress

While concern about reputation may reduce the probability that the manager will act this way, reputation effects are unlikely to be strong enough to fully ease lender concerns. We now consider an agency theory approach to lender protection.

Example 9.7
A Lender–Manager Agency Problem

A risk-neutral lender (the principal) faces a choice of lending $100 to a firm or investing the $100 in risk-free government bonds yielding 10%. The firm offers 12% interest, contracting to repay the loan one year later—that is, to repay $112. However, unlike for

Table 9.3 Payoffs for Lender–Manager Contract

	a₁ (no dividends)		a₂ (high dividends)	
	Manager's Act			
	a₁ (no dividends)		**a₂ (high dividends)**	
	Payoff	**Probability**	**Payoff**	**Probability**
x_1 (interest paid)	$ 12	0.99	$ 12	0.9
x_2 (bankrupt)	−100	0.01	−100	0.1

the government bonds, there is credit risk—a possibility that the firm will go bankrupt, in which case the lender would lose both the principal and the interest.

The firm manager (the agent) can choose one of two acts. The first act, denoted by a_1, is to pay no dividends while the loan is outstanding. The second act, a_2, is to pay high dividends. If the manager chooses a_1, assume that the lender assesses the probability of bankruptcy as 0.01, so that there is a 0.99 probability of receiving repayment, including $12 interest. However, if a_2 is chosen, the lender assesses the probability of bankruptcy as 0.1, because the high dividends will reduce the firm's solvency. Thus, under a_2, the probability of repayment will be only 0.9.

Assume that the manager is paid by means of an incentive contract consisting of a bonus based on the firm's net income. Then, since dividends are not charged against income, the manager's remuneration is unaffected by the act chosen; that is, the manager is indifferent between the two acts. Thus, there is no compelling reason to assume that the manager will or will not take a_1, the lender's preferred act. After thinking about this, the lender assesses equal probabilities for each act of the manager; that is, the probability of a_1 is 0.5 and similarly for a_2. Table 9.3 summarizes this scenario.

The payoff amounts in the table exclude the $100 loaned. Thus, the lender either earns an interest income of $12 or loses the $100 investment. We could add $100 to each payoff to express returns gross of the $100 loaned without affecting the results.

Will the lender be willing to lend $100 to the firm? The alternative is to buy government bonds, with a return of 10% or $10 in total. The expected profit from investing in the firm is

$$ETR = 0.5(12 \times 0.99) - (100 \times 0.01) + 0.5(12 \times 0.9) - (100 \times 0.1)$$

$$= (0.5 \times 10.88) + (0.5 \times 0.80)$$

$$= 5.44 + 0.40$$

$$= 5.84$$

where ETR denotes expected total return.

The first term in brackets represents the lender's expected return conditional on a_1. There is a 0.5 probability that a_1 will be chosen. Similarly, the second term in brackets is the expected return conditional on a_2, also multiplied by the 0.5 probability that a_2 will be chosen.

Thus, the ETR is only $5.84 or 5.84% on the amount loaned. The reason, of course, is the probability of bankruptcy, particularly if a_2 is taken, which forces the expected return down to well below the nominal rate of 12%. Our lender, who can earn 10% elsewhere, will not make the loan.

What nominal rate would the firm have to offer in order to attract the lender? This can be calculated as follows:

$$10.00 = 0.5[0.99R - (100 \times 0.01)] + 0.5[0.9R - (100 \times 0.1)]$$

where R is the required nominal rate. The left side is the lender's required total return. Upon solving for R, we obtain

$$R = \frac{15.50}{0.945} = 16.40$$

Thus, the firm would have to offer a nominal rate of return of over 16% in order to attract the lender.

The 16% interest rate in Example 9.7 would probably seem too high to the manager, particularly if he or she shares in net income. Consequently, the manager may try to find some more efficient contractual arrangement that would lower the interest rate. One possibility is to increase the manager's commitment to take a_1. This could be done by writing covenants into the lending agreement. An example of a covenant would be to pay no dividends if the interest coverage ratio is below a specified level. Another example would be to not undertake any additional borrowing (which would dilute the security of existing lenders) if the debt equity ratio is above a specified level. Since covenants are a legally binding contract component, the lender will change the assessed probabilities of the acts. Assume the probability that the manager will take a_1 is now assessed by the lender as 1, and 0 for a_2. Thus, if the firm offers a nominal rate of 12%, then the lender's ETR is

$$ETR = 1[(12 \times 0.99) - (100 \times 0.01)] + 0[(12 \times 0.9) - (100 \times 0.1)] = 10.88$$

Since this exceeds the required $10, the lender would now make the loan.

Example 9.7 illustrates a moral hazard problem between lenders and firm managers—managers may act contrary to the best interests of the lenders. Rational lenders will anticipate this behaviour, however, and raise the interest rates they demand for their loans. As a result, the manager has an incentive to commit not to act in a manner that is against the lenders' interests. This can be done by inserting covenants into the lending agreement whereby the manager agrees to limit dividends or additional borrowing while the loan is outstanding. Consequently, the firm is able to borrow at lower rates. Empirical evidence that lenders lower interest rates as debt covenants are strengthened is reported by Beatty, Weber, and Yu (2008).

Of course, unlike in our example, debt covenants do not completely eliminate the possibility of firm financial distress and resulting non-payment of interest and principal. It is possible that an unfortunate state of nature realization could drive the firm into bankruptcy. Furthermore, as the firm approaches bankruptcy, the manager may attempt to cover up by earnings management, although GAAP and auditing will control opportunistic earnings management to some extent. Nevertheless, the manager still has considerable room to manage earnings within GAAP. Thus, to the extent debt covenants are based on accounting variables, lenders will still demand reliable and conservative (within GAAP) accounting policies, as discussed in Chapter 8. Agency theory helps us to understand why covenants are there in the first place.

Another way to protect lender interests is to require the manager to hold company debt. If a firm is approaching financial distress and the manager holds no debt, he/she may be tempted to adopt excessively risky projects. If they pay off, the distress is removed. If not, lenders bear much of the loss. Lenders will be aware of this possibility, again raising the interest rates they demand. By holding firm debt, the manager in effect becomes a lender and is thus motivated to protect lenders' interests by working to prevent financial distress.

Of course, this motivation could go too far, with the result that the manager adopts only very safe projects, against the interests of diversified shareholders. This suggests that manager compensation should include *both* equity and debt awards. The question then is, in what proportions?

This question was addressed by Edmans and Liu (2011). They analyzed an agency model in which the manager chooses between a safe and a risky project, and also can exert two types of effort.[12] One effort type is devoted to increasing expected firm value given that the firm remains solvent, which benefits shareholders. The other is to maximize expected recovery value if the firm becomes bankrupt, benefitting lenders. Thus, the model incorporates two agency problems—one between manager and shareholders and the other between manager and lenders. These problems are intertwined since the prospect of effort devoted to maximizing recovery values reassures investors, thereby benefitting shareholders through lower interest rates.

The authors showed that the optimal contract generally includes both manager compensation based on equity and compensation based on debt. The optimal proportion of compensation based on equity will be high when the firm has significant growth opportunities, since effort devoted to maximizing going-concern firm value then has a high expected payoff. Conversely, if the firm faces substantial risk of bankruptcy, the proportion of compensation based on debt will be high.

While incorporating firm debt into manager compensation may seem inconsistent with what we observe, Edmans and Liu argued that this is not really the case. Managers typically hold firm debt in the form of pensions and deferred compensation, both of which may be threatened should the firm become bankrupt. Indeed, deferred compensation, and clawbacks of compensation already paid, have increased significantly subsequent to the 2007–2008 market meltdowns. In effect, including debt and equity in compensation motivates the manager to maximize firm value, which is not necessarily the same as maximizing shareholder value. Theory in Practice 9.1 provides a further illustration of debt in compensation contracts.

9.6 IMPLICATIONS OF AGENCY THEORY FOR ACCOUNTING

9.6.1 Is Two Better Than One?

In a widely referenced paper, Holmström (1979) gave a rigorous extension of the agency model to allow more than one performance measure. We now review aspects of his model from an accounting perspective.

Holmström assumed that the agent's effort is unobservable by the principal but that the payoff is jointly observable at the end of the current period. This is contrary to our Examples 9.1 to 9.6. However, Feltham and Xie (1994) showed that Holmström's model carries over to the case of payoff unobservable, holding the set of possible manager acts constant. Consequently, for purposes of this discussion, we shall continue to assume the payoff is unobservable at the end of the current period.

Holmström showed formally that a contract based on an observable performance measure such as net income is less efficient than a first-best contract, consistent with Example 9.2. As in that example, the source of the efficiency loss is the necessity for the risk-averse agent to bear risk in order to overcome the tendency to shirk.

This raises the question of whether the second-best contract could be made more efficient by basing it on a second performance measure in addition to net income. For example, share price is also informative about manager performance. Rather than basing manager compensation solely on net income, would basing the contract on *both* net income and share price reduce the agency costs of the second-best contract?

Holmström showed that the answer to this question is yes, provided that the second measure is also observable and conveys some information about manager effort beyond that contained in the first measure.[13] This should be the case for share price, since it is jointly observable and based on more information than just accounting information. Granted, share price reflects the information content of net income (Sections 5.3 and 5.4). However, share price on an efficient securities market also reflects other information. For example, it reflects expected future benefits of R&D, and expected future environmental and legal liabilities, sooner than the accounting system. Furthermore, share price may be less subject to manager bias than is net income. Consequently, we would expect share price to reveal information about manager effort different from that in reported earnings. Share price, however, may be more subject than net income to volatility created by economy-wide events. Nevertheless, Holmström's analysis showed that no matter how noisy the second variable is, it can increase the efficiency of the second-best contract if it contains at least some additional effort information.[14] In effect, net income and share price together can better reflect current manager effort than either variable alone.

Example 9.8[*]
A Two-Variable Agency Contract

To illustrate this argument, we now add a second performance measure—share price—to Example 9.2.

Recall from Example 9.2 that the payoffs are $100 or $55. Continue the assumptions of that example. That is, net income is unbiased. Also, if the manager works hard, the probability of the high payoff is 0.6 and the probability of the low payoff is 0.4. If the manager shirks, the high and low payoff probabilities are 0.4 and 0.6, respectively. The payoff is not observable until after the manager's contract ends, and net income is used as a performance measure.

Now, however, share price is added to the contract as a second performance measure. Assume that share price at the end of period 1 can be high ($80) or low ($50). Let the joint probabilities of the performance measures be as follows in Table 9.4.

There are four possible net income–share price combinations. Like net income, share price anticipates the ultimate payoff. Thus, if the payoff is going to be high, the probability of a high share price (0.6 + 0.1 = 0.7) is greater than the probability of low share price (0.3). If the payoff is going to be low, these probabilities are reversed. However, the anticipation is not perfect since, for example, there is a (1 − 0.7) 0.3 probability of low share price if the payoff is going to be high. This is because of random economy-wide events (e.g., changes in interest rates) that affect share price.

Table 9.4 Joint Performance Measure Probabilities

		Payoff High Net Income		Payoff Low Net Income	
		High ($115)	Low ($40)	High ($115)	Low ($40)
Share Price	High ($80)	0.6	0.1	0.1	0.2
	Low ($50)	0.2	0.1	0.1	0.6

---
[*]This example can be omitted without loss of continuity.

A 0.308 share of net income and a 0.018 share of share price will motivate the manager to work hard (a_1). This is verified as follows:

$$EU_m(a_1) = 0.6[0.6\sqrt{115 \times 0.308 + 80 \times 0.018} + 0.1\sqrt{40 \times 0.308 + 80 \times 0.018}$$
$$+ 0.2\sqrt{115 \times 0.308 + 50 \times 0.018} + 0.1\sqrt{40 \times 0.308 + 50 \times 0.018}]$$
$$+ 0.4[0.1\sqrt{115 \times 0.308 + 80 \times 0.018} + 0.2\sqrt{40 \times 0.308 + 80 \times 0.018}$$
$$+ 0.1\sqrt{115 \times 0.308 + 50 \times 0.018} + 0.6\sqrt{40 \times 0.308 + 50 \times 0.018}] - 2$$
$$= 0.6[0.6\sqrt{36.860} + 0.1\sqrt{13.760} + 0.2\sqrt{36.320} + 0.1\sqrt{13.220}]$$
$$+ 0.4[0.1\sqrt{36.860} + 0.2\sqrt{13.760} + 0.1\sqrt{36.320} + 0.6\sqrt{13.220}] - 2$$
$$= 0.6[3.643 + 0.371 + 1.205 + 0.364] + 0.4[0.607 + 0.742 + 0.603 + 2.182] - 2$$
$$= 0.6 \times 5.583 + 0.4 \times 4.134 - 2$$
$$= 3.350 + 1.654 - 2$$
$$= 3.004$$
$$= 3.00 \; approx.$$

If the manager shirks (a_2),

$$EU_m(a_2) = 0.4 \times 5.583 + 0.6 \times 4.134 - 1.71$$
$$= 2.233 + 2.480 - 1.71$$
$$= 3.003$$
$$= 3.00 \; approx:$$

Thus the manager will choose a_1 and receive reservation utility of 3.

The owner's expected utility is

$$EU_o(a_1) = 0.6[0.6(100 - 36.86) + 0.1(100 - 13.76) + 0.2(100 - 36.32)$$
$$+ 0.1(100 - 13.22)] + 0.4[0.1(55 - 36.86) + 0.2(55 - 13.76)$$
$$+ 0.1(55 - 36.32) + 0.6(55 - 13.22)]$$
$$= 0.6 \times 67.922 + 0.4 \times 36.998$$
$$= 40.753 + 14.799$$
$$= 55.552$$

The owner's utility is higher than in Example 9.2 (55.4566). Thus, the two-performance-measure contract is more efficient, consistent with the analyses of Holmström, and Feltham and Xie. The greater efficiency arises because introduction of a second performance measure provides the manager with some diversification of compensation risk, enabling reservation utility to be attained with lower expected total compensation.[15] Lower compensation shows up as higher expected utility for the owner.

Given the potential for increased contracting efficiency from basing compensation on more than one performance measure, the question then becomes one of the relative *proportion* of compensation based on net income, versus based on share price, in compensation contracts.[16] Hopefully, from an accountant's standpoint, this proportion will be high.

Thus, an interesting implication of the Holmström model is that, just as net income competes with other information sources for investors under efficient securities market theory, it competes with other information sources for motivating managers under agency theory.

This raises the question of what characteristics a performance measure should have if it is to contribute to efficient compensation contracts. One important characteristic is its **sensitivity**. Sensitivity is the rate at which the expected value of a performance measure increases as the manager works harder, or decreases as the manager shirks. Sensitivity contributes to efficient compensation contracts by strengthening the connection between manager effort and the performance measure, thereby making it easier to motivate that effort.

If the performance measure is an unbiased payoff predictor, its expected value will increase at the same rate as the payoff. However, net income is generally a biased payoff predictor, since all assets and liabilities are not fair valued under the mixed measurement model. Then, net income does not capture all aspects of the manager's current effort. For example, if an increase in effort is devoted to R&D, current net income would include little, if any, of the payoff from this effort, in which case net income is low in sensitivity to effort. A move toward current value accounting for R&D can then be regarded as a way to increase earnings sensitivity. By recognizing changes in current value sooner (i.e., reducing recognition lag), more of the results of manager effort are captured in current income. Similarly, if the manager devotes more effort to decreasing future environmental liabilities, net income sensitivity will be low if the reduction in future liabilities is not recorded.

Another important characteristic of a performance measure is its **precision** in predicting the payoff from current manager effort. Precision is measured as the reciprocal of the variance of the noise in the performance measure. When a performance measure is precise, there is a relatively low probability that it will differ substantially from the payoff. Precision contributes to efficient compensation contracts, other things equal, by reducing the manager's compensation risk.

When net income is a biased predictor of the payoff, there is a tradeoff between sensitivity and precision. Attempts to increase sensitivity of net income by adopting current value accounting may reduce precision, since current value estimates tend to be imprecise unless there is a well-working market. For example, if accountants were to adopt fair value accounting for R&D, sensitivity of net income would increase, but precision of net income would decrease due to problems of estimating R&D fair value.

If we think of reserve recognition accounting (RRA) net income as a performance measure, RRA can also be viewed as an attempt to increase sensitivity, since RRA reflects manager effort devoted to proving oil and gas reserves sooner than historical cost accounting. However, RRA suffers from low precision. We saw this with a vengeance in Husky Energy's RRA income statement (Table 2.3), where changes in estimates dominated the income calculation. While Husky's RRA earnings may be relatively sensitive to current manager exploration and development efforts, they are an imprecise measure of these efforts since the ultimate payoff may differ considerably. The challenge for accountants to maintain and increase the role of net income as a manager performance measure is to produce a net income number that represents the best possible tradeoff between sensitivity and precision.

However, the characteristics needed by net income if it is to be a sensitive and precise performance measure are not necessarily the same as those needed if it is to be a useful input into investment decisions. This illustrates the fundamental problem of financial accounting theory introduced in Section 1.10. RRA, for example, may provide useful information to investors (if its relevance outweighs its low reliability) while it may not contribute to efficient compensation contracts (if its lack of precision outweighs its sensitivity).

9.6.2 Rigidity of Contracts

Agency theory assumes that the courts have authority to costlessly enforce contract provisions and adjudicate disputes. While the parties to a contract could agree among themselves to amend contract provisions following an unforeseen realization of the state of nature, this can be surprisingly difficult. As noted in Chapter 8, contracts tend to be *rigid* once signed. The reasons for this rigidity need some discussion. Otherwise, we might ask, if economic consequences have their roots in the contracts that managers enter into, why not just *renegotiate* the contracts following a change in GAAP, or other unforeseen state realization?

Since it is generally impossible to anticipate all contingencies when entering into a contract, it would be difficult to predict changes in GAAP that could affect the contract (unless the contract is of very short duration). In Example 9.7, the firm's ability to avoid debt covenant violation would be reduced if, say, a new accounting standard required fair valuing of long-term debt. Such a standard would affect both the levels and volatility of debt–equity ratios. Consequently, the probability of covenant violation is affected. It is unlikely that the contract could anticipate such GAAP changes.

Contracts that do not anticipate all possible state realizations are termed **incomplete**. The contracts in Examples 9.2 to 9.8 are complete. Thus, in Example 9.2, the only two possible state realizations lead to payoffs x_1 and x_2. While the set of possible state realizations could be expanded in the examples, in an actual contract the parties could not anticipate all possibilities.

If an unanticipated state realization happens, building a formal commitment for renegotiation into the contract *beforehand* is possible, but if the renegotiation is generous toward the manager (e.g., it may let the manager "off the hook" following an unfortunate state realization), the prospect of such renegotiation reduces the manager's effort incentive, which would not be in the owner's best interests.[17] In effect, a consequence of entering into contracts is just that—they are contracts, and hence tend toward rigidity. Thus, unforeseen state realizations impose costs on the firm and/or the manager. The manager who is unfavourably affected by a change of the accounting rules in midstream may be forced to take out his/her displeasure on the accountants who introduced the rule change rather than on the other parties to the contract. It is contract incompleteness that drives the economic consequences discussed in Chapter 8.

The severe consequences of contract incompleteness and rigidity are illustrated by numerous examples.

In its third quarter, 2002, report, Mosaic Group Inc., a large designer of marketing programs for major companies, reported an operating loss of over $395 million, after a writedown of goodwill of $347.6 million. The company had been hit by bad economic times and the loss of several major customers, state realizations that were unanticipated when its debt contracts were signed. The large loss put the firm into violation of its debt covenants. Its lenders were unwilling to waive the covenant requirements or amend the credit agreements.

Mosaic filed for bankruptcy protection in 2003. Its shares were delisted by the Toronto Stock Exchange in April 2004.

More recently, CanWest Global Communications Corp., a large Canadian media conglomerate, entered creditor protection in October 2009. The company was unable to meet its debt contract commitments due to a decline in revenue following the worldwide recession that resulted from the 2007–2008 financial markets meltdown. Much of its $3.9 billion debt arose from its purchase of a majority interest in Australian TV broadcaster Ten Network Holdings Ltd.

CanWest had attempted in vain to stave off filing for creditor protection by a series of negotiations with creditors, extensions of interest due dates, cost cutting moves, and sales of non-essential assets.

Following its creditor protection filing, a group of creditors extended a $175 million financial lifeline in return for majority ownership of CanWest shares. Other conditions included no payment of executive bonuses without creditor approval, and filing of a weekly cash flow report. The company also continued to sell off assets, including its Australian subsidiary. In addition, creditors were given authority to replace the CanWest CEO and to hire a senior executive to oversee financial restructuring.

Furthermore, contract rigidity has increased in recent years. The reason is that an increasing number of debtholders insure their holding using credit default swaps. Then, if the value of these holdings declines, say because of financial distress of the issuer, the value of the credit default swap increases. As a result, debtholders are less inclined to renegotiate the debt contract. This increased rigidity is illustrated by AbitibiBowater, a large Canadian-based newsprint and paper products company. In April 2009, the company filed for creditor protection. It was unable to meet its debt contract commitments due to declining revenue. Its attempts to renegotiate debt due in August 2009 by replacing it with longer-term debt with a higher interest rate did not receive majority bondholder approval. The reason, according to media reports at the time, was that some bondholders wished to force the company to file for creditor protection so that they would collect payments from their credit default swaps.

9.7 RECONCILIATION OF EFFICIENT SECURITIES MARKET THEORY WITH ECONOMIC CONSEQUENCES

We now see how firms are able to align manager and shareholder interests, consistent with efficient contracting. Agency theory demonstrates that the best attainable compensation contract usually bases manager compensation on one or more measures of performance. Then, managers have an incentive to maximize performance.

Since higher performance leads to higher expected payoff, this is a goal also desired by investors.

This alignment explains why accounting policies have economic consequences, despite the implications of efficient securities market theory. Under efficient securities market theory, only accounting policy choices that affect expected cash flows create economic consequences. The contracting-based argument we have given for economic consequences does not depend on accounting policy choices having direct cash flow effects. This argument is the same whether direct cash flow effects are present or not.

Rather, it is the rigidities produced by the signing of binding, incomplete contracts that create managers' concerns, and that lead to their intervention in the standard-setting process. These rigidities have nothing to do with whether accounting policy changes affect cash flows.

Thus, economic consequences and efficient securities markets are not necessarily inconsistent. Rather, they can be reconciled by contract theory, with normative support from agency theory that suggests *why* firms enter into employment and debt contracts that depend on accounting information. Nothing in the above arguments leading to managerial concern about accounting policies conflicts with securities market efficiency.

Similarly, nothing in the theory of efficient securities markets conflicts with managerial concern about accounting policies. Joint consideration of both theories, though, helps us to see that managers may well intervene in accounting policies, even though those policies would improve the decision usefulness of financial statements to investors. Thus, in the final analysis, the interaction between managers and investors is a game.

9.8 CONCLUSIONS ON THE ANALYSIS OF CONFLICT

The various conflict-based theories described in this chapter have important implications for financial accounting theory. These can be summarized as follows:

1. Conflict theories enable a reconciliation of efficient securities markets and economic consequences. Early applications of efficient market theory to financial accounting (as, for example, in Beaver's early article, discussed in Section 4.3) suggested that accountants concentrate on full disclosure of information useful for investors' decision needs. The form of disclosure and the particular accounting policies used did not matter, as the market would see through these to their ultimate cash flow implications.

    Certainly, accountants, including standard setters, have adopted the decision usefulness approach and its full-disclosure implications, and there is extensive empirical evidence that markets do respond to accounting information much as the theory predicts. Frequently, however, as is apparent in Chapter 8, management intervened in the standard-setting process. This was not predicted by efficient securities market theory, since under that theory the market value of a firm's securities should be independent of its accounting policies, unless cash flows were affected. Why would management care about accounting policies if these do not affect its cost of capital? An answer is that changes in accounting policies can affect provisions in contracts that firm managers have entered into, thereby affecting their expected utility and the welfare of the firm.

The reason why accounting policies can affect manager and firm welfare should be carefully considered. The basic problem is one of information asymmetry. In an owner–manager context, the manager knows his or her own effort in running the firm on the owner's behalf, but typically the owner cannot observe this effort. Knowing this, the manager faces a temptation to shirk, thereby reducing shareholder welfare. Thus, there is a moral hazard problem between owner and manager. To control moral hazard, the owner can offer the manager a share of reported net income. This profit sharing motivates the manager to work harder. However, it also means that the manager has a personal interest in how net income is measured. When managers enter into borrowing contracts with lenders, similar implications for manager and lender welfare occur. Borrowing contracts typically contain covenants that restrict the payment of dividends depending on the values of certain financial statement-based ratios, such as interest coverage. Since covenant violations can be costly to the firm, both the manager and the firm will have a personal interest in accounting policy changes that affect the probability of covenant violation, particularly if they share in firm profits.

Thus, economic consequences can be seen as a rational result of the rigidities introduced by entering into binding, incomplete contracts. The conflict situation between managers, who may object to accounting policies that have adverse economic consequences for them and their firms, and investors, who desire full disclosure, is an application of game theory.

2. An implication of agency theory is that net income has a role to play in motivating and monitoring manager performance. Arguably, this role is as important in society as facilitating the proper operation of capital markets by providing useful information to investors. The characteristics needed for net income to fulfil an important role in efficient contracting differ from those needed to provide useful information to investors. The ability of net income to fulfil a manager performance-enhancing role depends on its sensitivity and precision as a measure of the payoff from current manager effort, while its usefulness for investors depends on its ability to reliably provide relevant information about future firm performance.

3. Net income competes with other performance measures, such as share price. If accountants can improve the precision and sensitivity tradeoff needed for a good performance measure, they may expect to see an increase in the role of net income in manager compensation plans.

4. If carried to the extreme, earnings management allows manager shirking, with resulting low payoffs to owners. Complete elimination of earnings management is not cost effective. However, by controlling earnings management through GAAP, accountants can restore the manager's incentive to work hard, thereby increasing payoffs to owners.

For these various reasons, game theory is an important component of financial accounting theory. In addition to enabling a better understanding of the conflicting interests of various constituencies affected by financial reporting, it has encouraged research into executive compensation and earnings management. Chapters 10 and 11 will review some of this research.

Questions and Problems

1. Why is manager effort usually unobservable to the firm's owners? What problem of information asymmetry results? If the manager receives a straight salary, what is the effect of this information asymmetry on the manager's effort in a single-period contract?

2. Give some reasons why the payoff from the manager's current-period effort is typically not fully observable until a subsequent period. How do contracts respond to the need to pay managers currently, despite current unobservability of ultimate cash payoffs?

3. If net income is an unbiased and noisy measure of manager performance, less noise enables a more efficient compensation contract. Explain why. How can accountants reduce noise in net income when net income is an unbiased payoff predictor?

   Does the argument that less noise enables more efficient compensation contracting change if the assumption that net income is unbiased is dropped? Why?

4. Why do debt contracts typically impose covenants based on accounting information such as working capital, interest coverage, and the debt–equity ratio? Are debt covenants completely credible as a way to give lenders trust that managers will not take opportunistic actions that reduce their security? Explain.

5. Why is net income for the current period not fully informative about manager effort for that period?

6. Define the concepts of sensitivity and precision of a performance measure. How can accountants increase sensitivity? Precision? When do these two desirable qualities have to be traded off? Explain.

7. Suppose in Example 9.2 that net income turns out to be $25, despite the assumption that net income can only be one of $115 or $40. How could this happen, and what does it say about the completeness of the compensation contract in the example? How might the manager react to this lower net income number?

8. Haul-by-You, a "do-it-yourself" moving company, is doing a booming business these days. The reason is that some companies relocating employees are changing the way they reimburse moving expenses. Before the change, moves were very expensive, because the companies paid for everything. Now, the companies pay a fixed amount to the employee, who can keep any savings. Explain this change using agency theory concepts. Also, Haul-by-You offers to reimburse customers for the cost of oil used during the move, while customers have to pay for their own gasoline. Why?

9. Pierre's small business has grown to the point where he plans to hire a full-time manager. Pierre, an architect, has little inclination and ability to manage a medium-sized, fast-growing business himself. He plans to semi-retire, devoting his working hours to consulting on issues of design and project management. Pierre's accounting system is quite simple. There is no R&D or other recognition lags. Consequently, the firm's payoff and its net income for the year are equal.

Pierre is negotiating with Yvonne as a possible manager. He wants the manager to work hard, since his past experience is that hard work generates a net income (before any manager compensation) of $2,000 90% of the time and $900 10% of the time. Pierre's recent experience, when he has not worked hard, is that the $2,000 net income is generated only 10% of the time; otherwise, net income is $900.

During the negotiations, Pierre ascertains that Yvonne is both risk and effort averse. Her utility for money is equal to the square root of the amount of money received. Her disutility for effort is 4 if she works hard and 1.1 if she shirks. Her reservation utility is 11.

Pierre decides that Yvonne is ideal for the job. He quickly offers her a series of one-year contracts, with annual cash compensation of a $100 salary plus 10% of net income before manager compensation. Yvonne immediately accepts.

Required

Note: Take calculations to two decimals.
a. Show calculations to demonstrate why Yvonne accepts the position. Which act will she take?
b. After two years, Pierre is worried because net income has been $900 each year. He decides to change Yvonne's next year's compensation contract. After consulting a compensation specialist, he offers her a salary of $52.30 plus a profit share of 9.21% of net income before manager compensation. Yvonne hesitates, but decides to accept. Show calculations to demonstrate why she hesitates but accepts.
c. Pierre is risk neutral, with utility equal to the amount of profit received after manager compensation. Is Pierre's expected utility higher or lower under the new contract in part **b**, compared to the original contract in part **a**? Show calculations and explain why there is a difference.

10. Growth Ltd. is a high-tech firm whose owner does not have the required management expertise to run the firm. The owner wants to hire a manager with the required expertise. The continued success of Growth Ltd. depends crucially on how hard the new manager works.

If the manager works hard (a_1), firm net income will be $500 with probability 0.7 and $200 with probability 0.3. If the manager shirks (a_2), net income will be $500 with probability 0.2 and $200 with probability 0.8. In both cases, profits are before manager compensation.

The owner is interviewing a prospective manager, and finds out that she is risk averse, with utility for compensation equal to the square root of the dollar compensation received. Like most people, however, she is also effort averse. If she works hard, she suffers a disutility of effort of 2 units of utility. If she shirks, her effort disutility is zero.

Required

a. Growth Ltd. offers the manager a one-period contract with a salary of $41 per period plus 20% of net income before manager compensation. If she accepts the job, will the manager take a_1 or a_2? Show your calculations.

b. Instead, Growth offers the manager zero salary plus 30% of net income before manager compensation. Assuming the manager accepts, will she take a_1 or a_2? Show your calculations.

c. Does the manager's effort decision change between parts **a** and **b** above? Explain why or why not.

d. Many executive compensation contracts base the manager's compensation on *both* net income and share price performance. Explain an advantage of using two performance measures rather than one in compensation contracts.

11. Tom operates a small, fast-growing electronics business. His workload has expanded to the point where he decides to hire a full-time manager. He will then take one year off to travel, and on his return he will concentrate on the technical aspects of the business.

Tom is negotiating with Lily for the manager job. He ascertains that Lily is risk averse, with utility for money equal to the square root of the dollar compensation received.

Lily advises Tom that she already has a job offer, which yields her an expected utility of 6. She is not willing to work for less than this, but would accept an expected utility of 6 from Tom. Lily also advises that she is effort averse, with disutility of effort of 2 if she works hard, and 1 if she does not work hard.

Tom's business has, in previous years, earned net income (before manager compensation) of $725 75% of the time and net income of $0 25% of the time. Tom has always worked hard (a_1) and reckons that if he did not work hard, net income would have been $725 only 20% of the time and zero for 80% of the time. He expects this earnings pattern to continue into the future with a new manager. Tom realizes that he must motivate Lily to work hard, and he offers her a one-year contract, with compensation based on a proportion of reported net income before manager compensation.

Required

a. What proportion of net income must Tom offer Lily so that she will accept the position and work hard? Show calculations.

b. Assuming that Lily accepts Tom's offer, verify that she will in fact work hard.

c. Having accepted the position, Lily soon realizes that Tom cannot observe the firm's unmanaged net income—he can only observe the net income she reports. She is tempted to opportunistically manage earnings so as to *ensure* that net income of $725 is reported, even if she does not work hard. Calculate whether or not, in a one-year contract, Lily is better off to work hard and not manage earnings or to not work hard and manage earnings.

Note: Part **d** draws on an optional text section.

d. Concerned that Lily may manage earnings, Tom learns about the revelation principle. Design a contract that Lily will accept and, given that she shirks, will motivate her to report net income honestly—that is, will remove her motivation to manage net income. Note: If net income is reported as zero, Lily must receive a salary in order to attain reservation utility.

e. New GAAP rules make it impossible to manage earnings from $0 up to $725. In fact, if unmanaged net income is $725, net income can be managed only within a range [$700–$784]. If unmanaged net income is $0, net income can be managed in a range [$0–$9]. What proportion of net income must Tom offer Lily as compensation so that she will accept the position and work hard? Assume that whatever unmanaged net income is, Lily will manage it to the upper end of the appropriate range. Any further earnings management (i.e., beyond GAAP) will be immediately detected.

12. Feng is the owner of a small business. When Feng has worked hard (a_1) during the year, net income before manager compensation has been $1,600 60% of the time and $400 40% of the time.

   More recently, Feng has been ill and has had to shirk (a_2). Net income has been $1,600 only 30% of the time and $400 70% of the time.

   Feng realizes that he must hire a manager for one year while he devotes full time to his recovery. Feng is risk neutral, with utility equal to the amount of net income for the year after manager compensation.

   Feng is negotiating with Yuan for the manager job. He ascertains that Yuan is risk averse, with utility equal to the square root of the dollar compensation received.

   Yuan is willing to work for Feng providing she receives expected utility of at least 6. Yuan advises Feng that she is effort averse, with disutility of effort of 2 if she works hard, and 1 if she does not work hard.

   Required
   a. Feng suggests a salary of $64, Yuan immediately says that she would accept a salary of $64. Which act would she take?
   b. However, surprised by her quick acceptance, Feng consults you. You immediately advise against such an offer, suggesting instead a proportion of net income before manager compensation. Why do you advise against? What proportion of net income do you recommend? Show calculations.
   c. Show calculations to verify that Feng's expected utility is higher if he takes your advice instead of paying Yuan a salary. Why is his expected utility higher?
   d. Assuming that Yuan accepts Feng's new offer, verify that she will in fact work hard.

13. Mary is the owner–operator of a growing business. Until recently, she has worked hard (a_1), in which case annual net income (before manager compensation) was $10,000, 70% of the time and $1,600 30% of the time. More recently, Mary has found it difficult to work hard due to the increasing time devoted to her growing family. As a result, she has shirked on effort, and annual net income has been $10,000 only 30% of the time and $1,600 70% of the time. Mary decides to hire a manager on a trial basis for one year while she takes the year off. She expects the manager to work hard, thereby restoring net income probabilities to their earlier levels. Mary's utility of money is equal to her firm's annual net income after manager compensation.

   Mary is negotiating with Henry for the manager job. She ascertains that Henry is risk averse, with utility for money equal to the square root of the dollar compensation received.

   Henry is willing to work for Mary providing he receives expected utility of at least 12. Henry advises Mary that he is effort averse, with disutility of effort of 2 if he works hard, and 1 if he does not work hard.

   Required
   a. Mary realizes that if Henry is to work hard, his compensation must depend on his effort. She decides to offer him compensation based on net income. What proportion

of net income must Mary offer Henry if he accepts a one-year contract and works hard? Show calculations.

b. Verify that Henry will work hard based on the net income share you calculated in part **a**.

c. Net income for Mary's company has always been prepared based on a mixed measurement model. However, Mary hears that net income based on fair value accounting for certain assets and liabilities will better motivate a manager than net income based on a mixed measurement model. She consults Bill, an accounting theorist, who advises her that under fair value accounting and hard work by the manager, net income would be $11,025 70% of the time and $900 30% of the time. If the manager shirks, net income will be $11,025 30% of the time, and $900 70% of the time. Mary wonders why net income is both higher and lower under fair value accounting. Bill replies that, under fair value accounting, net income is volatile since more unrealized gains and losses are included in net income than is the case under the mixed measurement model.

Verify that net income is more sensitive and less precise under full fair value accounting than under the mixed measurement model.

Note: For sensitivity, calculate the expected values of net income under each effort alternative. For precision, calculate variances of net income assuming the manager works hard.

d. After some calculation, Bill advises Mary that if she adopts full fair value accounting, a .0288 share of net income will motivate Henry to work hard. Is this contract more or less efficient than the contract under mixed measurement calculated in part **a** (no calculations required). Explain your answer, using the concepts of performance measure sensitivity and precision.

14. Mr. K, a risk-neutral investor, is contemplating a one-year 8% loan of $500 to firm J. Mr. K demands at least a 6% expected return per annum on loans like this. K is concerned that the firm may not be able to pay the interest and/or principal at the end of the year. A further concern is that if he makes the loan, firm J may engage in additional borrowing. If so, K's security would be diluted and the firm would become more risky. Since firm J is growing rapidly, K is sure that the firm would engage in additional borrowing if he makes the loan.

K examines firm J's most recent annual report and calculates an interest coverage ratio (the ratio of net income before interest and taxes to interest expense) of 4, including his contemplated $500 loan.

Upon considering all of these matters, K assesses the following probabilities:

PAYOFF	PROBABILITY
θ_1: Interest and principal repaid	0.80
θ_2: Reorganization, principal repaid but not interest	0.18
θ_3: Bankruptcy, nothing repaid	0.02
	1.00

Required

a. Should Mr. K make the loan? Show calculations.

b. Firm J offers to add a covenant to its lending agreement with Mr. K, undertaking not to engage in any additional borrowing if its interest coverage ratio falls below 4 before the next year-end. Mr. K estimates that there is a 60% probability that the interest coverage ratio will fall below 4. If it does, there would be no dilution of his equity by additional borrowing under the firm J offer, and he feels the lower coverage ratio would still be adequate. He assesses that his payoff probabilities would then be

PAYOFF	PROBABILITY
θ_1	0.95
θ_2	0.04
θ_3	0.01
	1.00

If the coverage ratio does not fall below 4, the resulting additional borrowing and dilution of security would cause him to assess payoff probabilities as

PAYOFF	PROBABILITY
θ_1	0.87
θ_2	0.12
θ_3	0.01
	1.00

Should Mr. K now make the loan? Show calculations.

15. Toni Difelice is contemplating lending $10,000 to Tech Enterprises Ltd. Tech offers her 8% interest, with the principal to be repaid at the end of the year. Toni carefully examines the financial statements of Tech Enterprises and is concerned about its interest coverage ratio, which is currently at 1.8:1. She feels that there is a 25% chance that Tech will go bankrupt, in which case she would recover only $2,000 of her principal and no interest. She suggests a debt covenant in the lending contract, whereby Tech promises not to issue any more debt beyond what Toni invests if its interest coverage ratio falls below 1.8:1. With such covenant protection, Toni assesses only a 1% probability of bankruptcy and subsequent recovery of only $2,000.

The manager of Tech Enterprises agrees to this request, provided that Toni reduces her interest rate to 5%.

Toni is risk averse, with utility equal to the square root of the gross amount of her payoff.

Required

a. Which act should Toni take? Prepare a payoff table as part of your answer.

   a_1: 8% interest, no debt covenant
   a_2: 5% interest, debt covenant

b. Explain why the manager of Tech Enterprises would be concerned about new accounting standards that may come into effect after the lending contract with Toni is concluded. Consider both standards that will tend to lower reported net income and standards that will increase its volatility.

16. Arnold is the successful owner and operator of a small business. He plans to take a one-year vacation and is interviewing Minnie for the position of manager while he is away.

On the basis of extensive past experience, Arnold knows that if the manager works hard (a_1), the cash flow (payoff) from the year's operations will be $505 with probability 0.8 and $345 with probability 0.2. If the manager shirks (a_2), cash flow will be $505 with probability 0.2 and $345 with probability 0.8. Payoffs are *before* any manager compensation.

However, cash flow will not be known until some time after Arnold returns, since all sales are on long-term credit, and advertising costs incurred in the year continue to generate sales well after year-end. However, Minnie demands to be paid at year-end.

Arnold decides to base compensation on net income, a performance measure available at year-end. Due to random effects of states of nature, he knows that if the payoff is going to be $505, net income will be $625 with probability 0.7 and $225 with probability 0.3. If the payoff is going to be $345, net income will be $625 with probability 0.3 and $225 with probability 0.7. Net income is *before* any manager compensation.

Upon interviewing Minnie, Arnold finds that her reservation utility is 2.6, that her utility for money equals the square root of the amount of money received, and that her disutility of effort if she works hard is 8. If she shirks, her effort disutility is 7. Arnold decides to offer Minnie a one-year contract with compensation based on a percentage of audited net income before compensation. Minnie accepts.

Required
a. What percentage of net income before compensation did Arnold offer Minnie? Verify that Minnie will work hard.
b. Why did Arnold specify that net income be audited?
c. Suppose instead that if Minnie shirks, net income will be $625 with probability 0.3 and $400 with probability 0.7 (i.e., moving support). What contract would Arnold now offer Minnie so that she works hard? Explain.

17. Refer to Example 9.3. Show calculations to verify the statement in the example that with a profit share of 0.3185 the manager will work hard and receive reservation utility.

Explain why the contract in Example 9.3 is more efficient than the contract in Example 9.2. How can accountants contribute to this greater efficiency when net income is unbiased?

18. When an owner cannot observe unbiased net income, the manager is tempted to opportunistically manage reported net income upward, so as to increase current compensation. Suggest reasons why the manager may not yield to this temptation.

19. The owner of a medium-size electronics company is concerned about cash flow. The company operates in a growing industry and produces a product that is in high demand. The owner feels that cash flow should be higher than it has been lately and fears that the company manager may be shirking, despite receiving a generous salary.

Company shares are all held by the owner and are not traded. However, at the bank's insistence, audited financial statements are prepared annually in accordance with GAAP.

The owner has decided to replace the current manager and to hire a new manager under a one-year contract, with compensation paid at the end of the year. You are hired to recommend a contract that will align the manager's interests with those of the owner.

Upon reviewing the company's history of past performance, you determine that if the manager works hard (a_1), cash flows of $600 are generated with probability 0.7 and $200 with probability 0.3. If the manager shirks (a_2), the probability of $600 cash flow falls to 0.3, with the probability of $200 rising to 0.7.

You also note that while these cash flows result from the manager's effort during the year, they are not fully received until the end of the following year. This is because the company conducts R&D, and also incurs risks of legal liability, which do not fully pay off and come due for some time.

Your study of past financial statements reveals that net income is a noisy predictor of cash flows. Specifically, if cash flows are going to be $600, then net income for the year before any manager compensation is $725 with probability 0.8 and $100 with probability 0.2. If cash flows are going to be $200, net income for the year is $725 with probability 0.16 and $100 with probability 0.84. This is because of recognition lag—given the complex nature of R&D and legal liability, it is not possible to report a net income that perfectly predicts future cash flows.

You interview a prospective manager, and find that her reservation utility is 5. Also, she is risk averse, with utility of compensation equal to the square root of the dollar amount of compensation received. She is also effort averse, with disutility of effort of 2 units of utility if she works hard and 1 unit of utility if she shirks.

Required

a. You decide to recommend a compensation contract based on a percentage of audited annual net income before manager compensation. What percentage of net income should you recommend? Show calculations.

b. Why did you decide that net income should be audited to serve as a basis for payment of compensation?

c. Based on the percentage of net income that you recommend, verify that the manager will receive reservation utility and work hard. Show calculations.

d. Suppose that improvements to GAAP reduce the noise in net income, as follows. If cash flows are going to be $600, net income for the year is $650 with probability 0.9 and $150 with probability 0.1. If cash flows are going to be $200, net income for the year is $650 with probability 0.1 and $150 with probability 0.9. Will your recommended percentage of net income be higher or lower than the percentage you recommended in part **a**? Explain why. Calculations are not required.

20. The sensitivity of a performance measure is the rate at which the expected value of the performance measure increases as the manager works harder. Precision, or noise, is the reciprocal of the variance of the performance measure.

Required

Refer to Example 9.6. Calculate the percentage increase in the expected value of reported net income (i.e., its sensitivity) as the manager's effort increases from shirk (a_2) to work hard (a_1). Also calculate the precision of net income in this example, given that the manager works hard.

21. You are engaged by the owner of a small firm to recommend a one-year compensation contract for the firm's top manager. She is concerned about cash flow and feels that, in previous years, the manager may have been shirking.

You ascertain that if the manager works hard (a_1), the firm's ultimate cash flow from current year operations will be one of $225 or $100 (before manager compensation) with probability 0.6, 0.4, respectively. If the manager shirks (a_2), cash flow will be $225 or $100 with probability 0.2, 0.8, respectively. Cash flow, however, will not be known until after the manager's one-year contract has expired.

As an expert in GAAP, you know that if cash flow is going to be $225, net income for the year will be $300 with probability 0.7 and $50 with probability 0.3. If cash flow is going to be $100, net income will be $300 with probability 0.2 and $50 with probability 0.8. You recommend that the manager's contract be based on reported net income.

You interview the manager and find that he is rational, risk averse with utility for money equal to the square root of the amount of money received, and effort averse with disutility of effort of 2.5 if he works hard and 1.8 if he shirks. The manager's reservation utility is 4.

Required

a. What percentage of net income must the manager be offered so that he will accept the contract and work hard?

b. Suppose that all information given in the question is unchanged except that if the manager shirks, and cash flow is going to be $100, net income will be $300 with probability 0.3 and $30 with probability 0.7. What contract would you then recommend? Show calculations and explain your contract choice.

c. The owner is risk neutral, with utility equal to the dollar amount of the payoff, net of the manager's compensation. What is the agency cost of the contract in part **a**? Show calculations.

22. Cain, Denis, and Denis (CDD; 2011) studied a sample of acquisitions in the United States during the years 1994–2003. The target firms for most of these acquisitions were non-publicly traded companies. A problem faced in any acquisition, especially if the target company's shares are not publicly traded, is how much the acquirer company should pay. When there is disagreement between buyer and seller, a solution is to include an **earnout contract** in the acquisition agreement. In such contracts, the acquirer pays an additional amount to the vendors, contingent on the performance of the acquired company over a few years following the acquisition. Such contracts also help to retain and motivate key managers of the acquired company, since, to motivate them to work hard, an efficient contract should base compensation on a risky performance measure. The higher is the performance measure following acquisition, the greater is manager compensation.

As CDD pointed out, the performance measure in such contracts is usually based on some risky accounting variable, such as earnings or sales, although some contracts are based on risky non-financial variables, such as successful clinical trials or attainment of large contracts.

Required

a. CDD reported that earnout payments to the acquired firm (and hence to management) under the earnout contracts are positively related to the need to motivate acquired company management effort. Specifically, they found that earnout payments are larger the greater the riskiness of the acquired company's industry, measured as the variability of the share price of the average firm in that industry. They also found that earnout payments are greater the greater the growth options (i.e., prospects for future growth) of the acquired company's industry, where growth options are measured as the ratio of share market value to book value (this ratio is commonly known as **Tobin's Q**) of the average company in that industry. Are these findings consistent with agency theory concepts? Explain why of why not. In your answer, also explain why the ratio of share value to market value is commonly used as a measure of a firm's potential for future growth.

b. CDD reported that for 50% of their sample firms, the term of the earnout contract was between one and three years. They found that the contract term is greater the greater the riskiness of the acquired company. Is this latter finding consistent with agency theory concepts? Explain why or why not.

c. CDD reported that while the performance measure is earnings in many earnout contracts, sales is another common measure. They found that the relative likelihood of a sales-based earnout contract increases when the acquired firm is from an industry with higher risk and higher prospects for future growth. Is this finding consistent with agency theory contracts? Explain why or why not. Use concepts of sensitivity and precision of a performance measure in your answer.

Notes

1. There is an implicit assumption throughout Section 9.2 that principal and agent have the same state and payoff probabilities when the contract is being negotiated. This assumption is made in most agency models. See also Note 5.

2. For simplicity, we ignore here what might happen next. Given a reasonably efficient managerial labour market, other similar managers would also like to work for this firm. Once they see that the job promises more than reservation utility, they will offer to work for less. The resulting bidding process will drive the salary down to $22.18, so that the shirking manager earns only reservation utility, as follows:

$$EU_m(a_1) = \sqrt{22.18} - 2 = 2.71$$

$$EU_m(a_2) = \sqrt{22.18} - 1.71 = 3.00$$

Whether or not the owner opens the job up for bids, the important point is that the manager will prefer to choose a_2, contrary to the best interests of the owner.

3. If the payoff was observable at period end, it would also be a performance measure.

4. This use of the term *informative* is similar in concept to its earlier use in describing the information system (Section 3.3.2). Here, however, *informative* refers to the degree to which a performance measure informs the owner about manager effort, whereas in an information system context the term refers to the ability of current financial statement information to anticipate future firm performance.

5. The agency models in this section assume rational expectations. Thus, in equilibrium, the owner and manager know the possible payoffs and have the same net income and payoff probabilities (called **homogeneous probabilities**) for each manager effort level. This is equivalent to the owner and manager knowing the firm's production function. The owner also knows the manager's utility function and effort disutility, and can observe the firm's actual net income (i.e., net income is determined without any opportunistic earnings management or, equivalently, net income is a noisy, unbiased message about the future payoff from the manager's current-period actions). Without these assumptions, design of the contract becomes more complex. In Section 9.3, we relax one of these assumptions; namely, the assumption that the owner can observe actual net income. Since

investors (recall that the owner is a proxy for a typical investor) know which act the manager will take and know the firm's production function, reported net income and payoff reveal no new information about the manager's effort and ability. This justifies taking the agent's reservation utility R as a fixed constant in the single-period model—since net income and payoff resulting from current effort reveal no new information about the manager's performance, there is no effect on reputation.

This lack of market reaction to manager performance is obviously unrealistic, since if a manager does a good job (i.e., works hard), we would expect the manager's market value (i.e., his/her reservation utility) to increase. To generate an increase in reservation utility, we would require a more complex, multi-period agency model, which is beyond our scope here.

6. It is easy to verify what the manager's expected compensation is now:

$$
\begin{aligned}
\text{Expected comp.} &= 0.6[0.8(0.3237 \times 115) + 0.2(0.3237 \times 40)] \\
&\quad + 0.4[0.2(0.3237 \times 115) + 0.8(0.3237 \times 40)] \\
&= 0.6(0.8 \times 37.2255 + 0.2 \times 12.9480) + 0.4(0.2 \times 37.2255 + 0.8 \times 12.9480) \\
&= 0.6 \times 32.37 + 0.4 \times 17.80 \\
&= 19.44 + 7.12 \\
&= 26.56
\end{aligned}
$$

The manager's expected compensation has to be raised from $25 under the first-best contract to $26.56 under profit sharing to offset the compensation risk that the manager now bears and enable reservation utility to be attained. This increase in expected compensation accounts for the agency cost of 1.5434 now borne by the owner.

7. Agency theory seeks to find the contract with the lowest possible agency cost (i.e., the most efficient form of contract). We do not claim that the contract of Example 9.2, based on 0.3237 of net income, is necessarily the most efficient. In fact, it can be verified that a contract paying the manager a salary of $0.78 plus 0.3129 of net income (or, equivalently, 0.3197 of net income if net income is $115, and 0.3324 of net income if net income is $40) is slightly more efficient. This contract makes the manager indifferent between a_1 and a_2 (in which case it is assumed the agent will take a_1), and yields the owner expected utility of 55.6210, up from 55.4566 in our contract. The reason for the greater efficiency is that this contract places less risk on the manager, due both to the salary and the smaller profit share. This enables a lower risk premium for the agent to attain reservation utility. We use a straight profit share in the body of the text primarily for simplicity.

Note that both of the contracts here are linear in the performance measure. When there are more than two states of nature, it is possible that a non-linear contract would be more efficient. This is beyond our scope here.

8. This assumption may seem to violate our statement in Section 9.2.2 that contracts are based on variables that are jointly observable. However, this is really not the case. Reported net income (as opposed to unmanaged net income) is jointly observable. The question then is, does reported net income have sufficient credibility that parties are willing to contract on it? If not, other performance measures, such as share price, may take over. However, GAAP and auditing help to give the owner confidence in reported net income as a performance measure. Furthermore, as we will see in Chapter 10, actual compensation contracts are based, at least in part, on reported net income.

9. There is no incentive to report truthfully, either, since the manager receives the same utility regardless. The theory assumes that, if indifferent, the manager will report truthfully.

10. Offering the manager a straight salary in a single-period contract would also eliminate the incentive to report untruthfully. We base Example 9.5 on a proportion of reported net income for consistency with earlier examples.

11. The revelation principle could in turn be applied to this contract. The owner could simply agree to pay 0.3193 times the upper limit of the range that occurs, regardless of the amount of unmanaged net income reported within that range. The manager then has no incentive to manage earnings upward. However, paying the manager on the basis of a higher net income than reported may impose costs on the manager, since such compensation may be regarded as excessive in the media and by

regulators. In view of the restrictions on the revelation principle discussed in Section 9.3.2, we do not pursue this here.

12. Edmans and Liu assumed the manager is risk neutral. Since the manager then does not mind bearing risk, it is possible to motivate the manager to always work hard by imposing sufficient downside compensation risk (e.g., the manager may receive very high compensation if the firm does well, but be required to pay the firm if there is a loss). Then, there is no agency problem and a risk-neutral manager would work hard. In effect, the moral hazard problem disappears. To avoid this unrealistic outcome, risk-neutral models, including Edmans and Liu, assume limited liability of the manager. Then, it is not possible to impose sufficient downside risk so as to always drive hard work.

13. More precisely, for the second performance measure to reduce agency costs it must be false that the first measure is a sufficient statistic for the pair of variables (first performance measure, second performance measure) with respect to effort.

14. Holmström pointed out that if the contract with the manager is confined to a limited class, such as the linear contract with a straight profit share assumed in Example 9.2, this result may not hold.

15. The manager's expected compensation is

$$0.6[0.6 \times 36.86 + 0.1 \times 13.76 + 0.2 \times 36.32 + 0.1 \times 13.22] + 0.4[0.1 \times 36.86$$
$$+ 0.2 \times 13.76 + 0.1 \times 36.32 + 0.6 \times 13.22]$$
$$= 0.4 \times 36.86 + 0.14 \times 13.76 + 0.16 \times 36.32 + 0.3 \times 13.22$$
$$= \$26.45$$

The manager's expected compensation in Example 9.2, with only one performance measure, was calculated in Note 6 as $26.56. This example, with two performance measures reduces manager expected compensation, thus increasing the owner's expected utility.

16. Strictly speaking, our assumption that the firm has a share price is not consistent with the firm having a single owner. We make this assumption due to the prevalence of share price in real compensation contracts., as we shall see in the next chapter. Here, we could just as easily use a credit rating from an independent rating agency as a second performance measure. Even the weather could be a second performance measure. Obviously, the manager does not control the weather, but suppose that weather affects the probability that net income will be high or low (e.g., for a sporting goods manufacturer). Then, the weather tells us something about net income, which, in turn, tells us something about effort. For example, a high net income when weather is bad suggests higher manager effort than the same net income when weather is good. Then, net income as a performance measure should be interpreted conditional on the weather. This is known as the principle of **conditional controllability**. Even though a manager cannot control a variable, that variable can be informative about performance. This is an important point to notice, since managers often complain that their performance should *not* be evaluated on variables they cannot control.

17. Christensen, Demski, and Frimor (2002) presented a two-period agency model that allows contract renegotiation at the end of the first period but also allows the manager to underreport first period output (i.e., conservative accounting). Since accruals reverse, any underreporting of first period output must be added to second period reported output, however. This restores some of the agent's incentive to work hard since working hard in the first period leads to extra expected compensation in the second. This provides another argument that some degree of earnings management can be good. Further pursuit of contract renegotiation is beyond our scope.

Chapter 10
Executive Compensation

Figure 10.1 Organization of Chapter 10

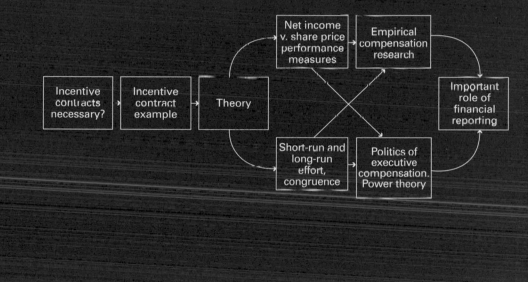

10.1 OVERVIEW

In this chapter we consider executive compensation plans. We will see that real incentive plans follow from the agency theory developed in Chapter 9, but they are more complex and detailed, and span multiple periods. They involve a delicate mix of incentive, risk, and decision horizon considerations.

> An **executive compensation plan** is an agency contract between the firm and its manager that attempts to align the interests of owners and manager by basing the manager's compensation on one or more measures of the manager's performance in operating the firm.

Many compensation plans are based on two performance measures: net income and share price. That is, the amounts of cash bonus, shares, options, and other components of executive pay that are awarded in a particular year depend on both net income and share price performance. The analyses of Holmström (1979) and Feltham and Xie (1994) outlined in Section 9.6.1 suggest that multiple performance measures increase contracting efficiency.

The role of net income in motivating manager performance is equally as important as its role in informing investors. This is because motivating responsible manager performance and improving the operation of managerial labour markets are desirable social goals. These goals are as important as the enabling of good investment decisions and securities market operation. Consequently, an understanding of the properties that net income needs in order to measure manager performance is important for accountants. Unless net income has desirable qualities of sensitivity and precision, it will not be informative about manager effort. That is, it will not measure performance efficiently and will not enable the market to properly value the manager's worth. It will also be "squeezed out" of efficient compensation plans.

Figure 10.1 outlines the organization of this chapter.

10.2 ARE INCENTIVE CONTRACTS NECESSARY?

Fama (1980) made the case that incentive contracts of the type studied in Section 9.2.2 are not necessary because the managerial labour market controls moral hazard. If a manager can establish a reputation for creating high payoffs for owners, that manager's market value (i.e., the compensation he/she can command) will increase. Conversely, a manager who shirks, thus reporting lower payoffs on average, will suffer a decline in market value. As a manager who is tempted to shirk looks ahead to future periods, the present value of reduced future compensation, Fama argued, will be equal to or greater than the immediate benefits of shirking. Thus, the manager will not shirk. This argument, of course, assumes an efficient managerial labour market that properly values the manager's reputation. Analogous to the case of a capital market, the operation of a managerial labour market is enhanced by full disclosure of the manager's performance.

Fama also argued that for lower-level managers, any shirking will be detected and reported by managers below them, who want to get ahead. That is, a process of "internal monitoring" operates to discipline managers who may be less subject to the discipline of the managerial labour market itself.

Since the owner knows which action the manager will take in the single-period models of Chapter 9, these models do not reveal any information about manager effort and ability.[1] Thus, they cannot deal directly with the multi-period horizon that is needed for reputation formation and internal monitoring. Recall that in the single-period model, the manager's market value enters only through the reservation utility constraint—the utility of the compensation of the next-best available position. In a one-period model, this utility is taken as a constant. Fama's argument is that if the manager contemplates the downward effect of current shirking on the reservation utility of future employment contracts, shirking will be deterred.

The agency model can be extended to deal with some of these considerations. With respect to internal monitoring, Arya, Fellingham, and Glover (AFG; 1997) designed a two-period model with one owner and two risk-averse managers. The managers' efforts produce a joint, observable payoff in each period. The owner cannot observe either manager's effort, but each manager knows the effort of the other. One way for the owner to motivate the managers to work hard is to offer each of them an incentive contract similar to the ones in Section 9.2.2, in each period. However, AFG showed that the owner could offer a more efficient contract by exploiting the ability of each manager to observe the other's effort. Since the payoff is a joint effort, shirking by either manager will reduce the payoff for both. Then, in the AFG contract, each manager threatens the other that he/she will shirk in the second period if the other shirks in the first.

If the contract is designed properly, the threat is credible and each manager works hard in both periods. The resulting two-period contract is more efficient because it imposes less risk than a sequence of two single-period contracts. As a result, managers can attain their reservation utility with lower expected compensation.

The important point for our purposes is that the contract continues to base manager compensation on some measure of the payoff. In effect, while exploitation of the ability of managers to monitor each other can *reduce* agency costs of moral hazard, it does not eliminate them. Thus, AFG's model suggests that an incentive contract for lower-level managers is still necessary.

With respect to the ability of manager reputation to control moral hazard, Fama's argument does not consider that the manager may be able to disguise the effects of shirking, at least in the short run, by managing the release of information. That is, the manager may try to "fool" the market by opportunistically managing earnings to cover up shirking. Since persons with a tendency to do this will be attracted to the opportunity, the managerial labour market is subject to adverse selection as well as moral hazard.

Of course, GAAP limits, to some extent, the manager's ability to cover up shirking even in a single period contract, as shown in Example 9.6. Also, since accruals reverse, multi-period shirking will eventually be discovered, in which case the manager's reputation will be destroyed. The question then is, are the expected costs of lost reputation strong enough to supply the missing effort motivation? If they are, then an incentive contract would not be necessary, Fama argued. The manager could be paid a straight salary, and the manager's reputation on the managerial labour market would prevent shirking.

In this regard, some empirical evidence on the market's ability to control the manager's incentive to shirk was presented by Wolfson (1985). He examined contracts of oil and gas limited partnerships in the United States. These are tax-advantaged contracts between a general partner (agent) and limited partners (principal) to drill for oil and gas. The general partner provides the expertise and pays some of the costs. The bulk of the capital is provided by the limited partners.

Such contracts are particularly subject to moral hazard and adverse selection problems, due to the highly technical nature of oil and gas exploration. For example, the general partner privately learns the results of the drilling. This leads to the "non-completion incentive problem." Once drilled, a well should be completed (i.e., brought into production) if its expected revenues—call them R—exceed the costs of completion. However, for tax reasons, completion costs are paid by the general partner. If the general partner receives, say, 40% of the revenues, then, from his/her perspective, it is worthwhile to complete only if 0.40R is greater than the completion costs. Given that only the general partner knows R, a well may not be completed (i.e., the manager covers up shirking by withholding information about R) unless R is very high.

Wolfson studied two types of well-drilling: exploratory wells and development wells. The non-completion problem is not as great for exploratory wells since, if an exploratory well does come in, the chances are that R will be high indeed.

Investors will be aware of this non-completion problem, of course, and will bid down the price they are willing to pay to buy in, possibly to the point where the general partner cannot attract limited partners at all. The question then is, can a general partner ease investor concerns by establishing a reputation, thereby increasing his/her market value and the amounts that investors are willing to pay?

To measure reputation, Wolfson collected information on the past performance of a sample of general partners over the period 1977–1980. The higher a general partner's past success in generating a return for limited partners, the higher that partner's reputation was taken to be. Wolfson found that the higher the reputation of a general partner, the more he/she received from limited partners to buy in, suggesting that investors were responding to the manager's reputation.

However, Wolfson also found that investors paid significantly less to buy into development wells than into exploratory wells. As mentioned, the undercompletion problem is greater for development wells.

Combination of these two findings suggests that while market forces can *reduce* the managers' moral hazard problem, *they do not eliminate it.* If reputation-building completely eliminated the undercompletion problem, we would not see investors paying less when the problem is greater.

While Wolfson's results apply only to a small sample of oil and gas contracts, they are of more general interest because of their implication that the managerial labour market is not completely effective in controlling moral hazard, contrary to Fama's argument. A manager's past success in generating payoffs for investors (i.e., a high manager reputation) does not fully convince investors that he/she will always "works hard."

This conclusion from Wolfson translates into a broader context relevant to accounting. Bushman, Engel, and Smith (BES; 2006) analyzed a large sample of firms over the period 1970–2000. They reported an average correlation of .34 between security market response to a firm's earnings and the change in its managers' cash compensation.[2, 3] As in Wolfson, this suggests that the managerial labour market is not completely effective in motivating the manager to work hard. That is, a positive association between market response and manager compensation suggests that the market interprets higher compensation as increased assurance that the manager is doing a good job—that is, working hard.[4] This assurance would not be needed if the manager's reputation on the labour market was completely effective in motivating effort.

We conclude that while internal and market forces may help control managers' tendencies to shirk, they do not eliminate them. It seems that effort incentives based on some measure of the payoff (e.g., net income) are desirable for efficient contracting. We now turn to an examination of an actual managerial compensation contract of a large corporation. As we will see, incentives loom large.

10.3 A MANAGERIAL COMPENSATION PLAN

Example 10.1
Executive Compensation Plan of Royal Bank of Canada

Royal Bank of Canada (RBC) is one of Canada's largest financial institutions, providing banking and related services throughout Canada and internationally. Its shares are traded on stock exchanges in Canada, the United States, and Switzerland.

The information below is mostly taken from RBC's *Notice of Annual Meeting of Common Shareholders, Management Proxy Circular* (2009). This 2009 circular retains interest since it describes some of the compensation plan changes resulting from the 2007–2008 market meltdowns. From this circular, RBC's executive compensation plan consists of four components:

- Salary, paid in cash
- Short-term incentive plan bonus awards paid in cash or, if the executive elects, in deferred share units, where deferred share units (also called restricted shares) are converted into RBC common shares after three years
- Mid-term incentive plan, awards paid in deferred share units
- Long-term incentive plan, awards paid in employee stock options (ESOs)

Total compensation is generally positioned relative to the median compensation of a peer group of similar large companies. However, total compensation, as well as that of individual executives, can vary substantially above or below the median depending on bank, segment, and individual performance. For example, if ROE is in the top third of peer group companies, total compensation is adjusted upward by 15%, and adjusted downward by 15% if in the bottom third.

For short-term incentives, for each business segment, RBC sets annual target levels of net income growth and return on equity (ROE). For an individual executive, bonus awards depend on both overall bank performance and segment performance, relative to targets. Payments are further adjusted for individual non-financial performance measures, namely performance relative to personal goals. These may include goals with respect to risk management, cost management, new revenue initiatives, financing, development of U.S. operations, etc. Finally, bonus awards may be adjusted up or down depending on ROE performance relative to the peer group.

For mid-term incentives, the number of deferred share units awarded depends on share price performance over the previous three years. Awards are further adjusted depending on share price performance relative to the peer group. However, if target ROE is not achieved, no deferred share unit awards are made.

For long-term incentives, the ESO exercise price is based on the RBC share price around the award date. That is, the intrinsic value is zero. ESOs have a term of 10 years, with vesting at the rate of 25% per year for the first four years. In addition, executives are required to hold minimum amounts of RBC common shares. For example, the President and CEO must hold shares worth eight times salary. This requirement extends for two years following retirement.

Note that bonus deferrals, vesting periods for deferred share units and ESOs, and required share holdings reduce executives' ability to form diversified investment portfolios. That is, they must bear firm-specific risk.

Despite the compensation plan provisions, the RBC Board, advised by its Compensation Committee, has the ultimate say in the amounts of salary and incentive awards. The compensation committee is a corporate governance device to deal with the fact that the RBC plan, like all real compensation contracts, is *incomplete*. (See the discussion of complete and incomplete contracts in Section 9.6.2.) While contracts tend to be rigid, the Board has discretion to deal with the effects on compensation of an unanticipated outcome. In this regard, with the exception of its legal capital ratio, RBC's performance target levels for 2008 were not attained. For example, ROE was 18%, short of the target of 20%. No doubt, this was largely due to the 2007–2008 market meltdowns. While the Board lowered 2008 incentive awards to below those of the previous year, it did award deferred share units under the mid-term incentive plan, even though the plan specifies that no such awards will be made if the ROE target is not met.

The incentive effects of RBC's compensation plan should be apparent. Annual bonus awards are based primarily on attainment of financial targets, such as earnings growth, ROE, and share price performance. Since the short-term and mid-term incentive awards depend largely on the current year's performance, this creates an incentive to maximize the current year's levels of earnings and ROE. Note, however, that maximizing current reported performance may be at the expense of the firm's longer-run interests, possibly leading to dysfunctional tactics such as opportunistic earnings management.

However, ESOs issued under the long-term incentive plan, and the requirement of substantial share ownership, are intended to give executives a longer-term interest in the success of the firm. Presumably, this reduces the temptation to engage in opportunistic practices to increase earnings in the short run. However, the decision horizon-lengthening effects of ESOs can be questioned in view of the 2007–2008 market meltdowns where, as noted in Section 1.3, it seems that instead of encouraging a longer-term decision horizon, ESOs encouraged short-run, risk-taking behaviour.

In this regard, proposed changes to RBC's compensation plan are worthy of note. In September 2009, RBC indicated that, for its capital markets division, deferral of bonus payments would be increased. Also, greater weight on individual non-financial performance measures relative to financial performance measures, and increases in required executive stock holdings, were announced. Also announced were provisions to claw back bonuses in cases of fraud or misconduct.[5] Presumably, these measures are intended to lengthen decision horizons from the somewhat short-term bias created by the short- and mid-term incentive components outlined above. No changes to ESOs were announced, however.

Even without these changes, it is apparent that the RBC plan imposes compensation risk on the manager. Economy- and industry-wide events, which may not be informative about the manager's effort, will affect both earnings and share price, hence the amounts of current and future incentive awards. This compensation risk is in addition to the firm-specific risk, mentioned above, arising from bonus deferrals, vesting periods for already-granted share-based awards, and requirements to hold company shares. Recall from our agency theory discussion in Chapter 9 that agents must bear risk if they are to work hard.

However, aspects of the RBC plan operate to limit compensation risk, since too much risk will require increased compensation for risk-averse managers, or generate opportunistic manager behaviour, such as excessive avoidance of risky projects. Base salary, of course, is relatively risk free. Also, the lower limit on incentive awards, including ESO value, is zero. This reduces downside risk since if earnings are negative, or share value falls below the ESO exercise price, the executive does not have to pay the firm. In addition, as mentioned, total compensation is adjusted relative to the median of the peer group. By setting total compensation in this way, an averaging effect is introduced, which would tend to make an RBC executive's total compensation less subject to variations in the performance of RBC itself.

In sum, the RBC compensation structure appears to be quite sophisticated in terms of its incentives, decision horizon, and risk properties. For our purposes, the most important point to note is that there are three main incentive components: short-term incentive awards based on earnings and individual achievement, long-term stock options whose value depends on share price performance, and mid-term awards whose value depends on both. Thus, both accounting and market-based performance incentives are embedded in the plan. These give management a vital interest in how net income is determined, both because earnings are a direct input into compensation and because, as we saw in Chapter 5, net income affects share price.

We now turn to a more general consideration of the compensation issues raised above.

10.4 THE THEORY OF EXECUTIVE COMPENSATION

10.4.1 The Relative Proportions of Net Income and Share Price in Evaluating Manager Performance

Much of the theory of executive compensation derives from the agency models developed in Chapter 9, despite their single-period orientation. In particular, the analysis of Holmström (Section 9.6.1) predicts that the efficiency of a compensation contract may be increased if it is based on two or more performance measures. The RBC contract discussed above is consistent with this prediction. The question then is, what determines the relative importance of net income and share price in evaluating manager performance? This is an important question for accountants, since motivation of manager performance is an important social goal. If financial reporting is to contribute to attainment of this goal, it must successfully complement other performance measures, such as share price. What determines the relative weights (i.e., the mix) of net income and share price in evaluating the manager's overall performance?

This question was studied by Banker and Datar (BD; 1989). BD demonstrated conditions under which the linear mix of performance measures depends on the product of the sensitivity and precision of those measures. These concepts were introduced in Section 9.6.1, where sensitivity was defined as the rate at which the expected value of the measure responds to manager effort, and precision as the reciprocal of the variance of the noise in the measure.[6] BD showed that the lower the noise (i.e., the greater the precision) in net income or the greater its sensitivity to manager effort, the greater should be the proportion of net income to share price in determining the manager's overall performance.

There are a number of ways that accountants can increase the sensitivity of net income. One possibility, raised in Section 9.6.1, is to reduce recognition lag by moving to current value accounting. Reduced recognition lag increases sensitivity since more of the future payoffs from manager effort show up in current net income.

However, current value accounting is a double-edged sword in this regard, since it tends to reduce precision. As mentioned above, BD show that lower precision reduces the optimal proportion of a performance measure in the contract. It is thus unclear whether adoption of current value accounting would result in a net gain in importance for net income.

Another approach to increasing sensitivity is through full disclosure, particularly of low-persistence items. Full disclosure increases sensitivity by enabling the compensation committee to better evaluate manager effort and ability, and thus to evaluate earnings persistence. Persistent earnings are a more sensitive measure of current manager effort than transitory or price-irrelevant earnings, which may arise independently of effort. Notice also that GAAP can reduce the scope for opportunistic earnings management, as illustrated in Example 9.6. Reduced earnings management increases sensitivity by reducing the manager's ability to disguise shirking.

With respect to share price, a major reason for its relatively low precision derives from the effects of economy-wide factors. For example, if interest rates increase, the expected effects on future firm performance will quickly show up in share price. These effects may say relatively little about current manager effort, however. As a result, they mainly add volatility to share price. Nevertheless, as we pointed out in Section 9.6.1, Holmström's analysis showed that share price could never be completely replaced as a performance measure as long as it contains some additional effort information. The sensitivity of share price is sufficiently great that it will always reveal additional payoff information beyond that contained in net income. Thus, we may expect both measures to coexist.

This coexistence, however, creates an opportunity for the compensation plan to influence the length of the manager's decision horizon. To explain, assume two types of manager effort—short run and long run. Efficient compensation plan design can adjust the relative proportions of earnings-based and share price-based compensation to exploit the fact that current net income aggregates the payoffs from only some manager activities in the current period. For example, to encourage more R&D (i.e., long-run effort), the owner can reduce the proportion of the manager's compensation based on net income and increase the proportion based on share price. Compensation will now rise more strongly due to securities market response to an increase in R&D, and there will be less compensation penalty from writing R&D costs off currently. Consequently, it will be in the manager's interest to increase R&D. More generally, firms with substantial investment opportunities will want to increase the proportion of share price-based compensation.[7]

Alternatively, suppose that the firm has to cut costs (short-run effort) due, for example, to an increase in competition or an increase in the domestic exchange rate. Net income will aggregate the favourable cash flow effects of cost cutting quickly and accurately, perhaps even more so than share price, particularly if the cost-cutting measures are complex or constitute inside information, or if the market is concerned about the longer-run effects of cost cutting. Also share price may not perfectly aggregate the cost-cutting information in the presence of noise trading or market inefficiencies. Then, the firm may wish to increase the weight of net income relative to share price in the manager's compensation.

In effect, when share price and net income differentially reflect the short- and long-run payoffs of current manager actions, the length of the manager's decision horizon can be influenced by the mix of share price-based and net income-based compensation—more share-based compensation produces a longer decision horizon and vice versa. This was demonstrated theoretically by Bushman and Indjejikian (1993). As we suggested in Section 10.3, the 2008 RBC compensation plan seems be tilted somewhat toward the short run (since both short- and mid-term awards depend on earnings, and the decision horizon-lengthening effect of ESOs can be questioned). However, the compensation committee has authority to adjust the mix; witness the 2008 payment of mid-term compensation even though target ROE was not achieved, and witness the 2009 changes that increase the long-term compensation component.

The mix of performance measures was further studied by Datar, Kulp, and Lambert (2001). Their analysis suggests that decision horizon must be traded off with the sensitivity and precision of performance measures. For example, an efficient compensation plan will increase the weight on a performance measure, even if this results in a manager decision horizon that is not exactly what the compensation committee wants, if that performance measure reflects an informative mix of sensitivity and precision. The reason is that such a performance measure "tells more" about effort, hence enables a more efficient contract. This greater efficiency is traded off against the benefits of controlling the manager's decision horizon. Consequently, sensitivity and precision remain as important characteristics in the presence of more than one type of managerial effort.

10.4.2 Short-Run Effort and Long-Run Effort*

Our discussion of agency theory in Chapter 9 assumed that manager effort is single-dimensional—a modelling device to encompass the whole range of managerial activities. Thus, we were interested in the *intensity* of effort, and envisaged two levels of intensity: "working hard" or "shirking." To enable us to better understand executive compensation, we now extend the agency model to regard effort as multi-dimensional. Specifically, we pursue the assumption in the previous section that effort consists of **short-run (SR) effort** and **long-run (LR) effort**. Now, however, we view these two effort components as separate manager decisions.

SR is effort devoted to activities such as cost control, maintenance, employee morale, advertising, and other day-to-day activities that generate net income mainly in the current period. LR is effort devoted to activities such as long-range planning, R&D, and acquisitions. While LR effort may generate some net income in the current period, most of the payoffs from these activities extend into future periods. Our development here is based on Feltham and Xie (1994).

The manager can either work hard or shirk along either or both effort dimensions. Then, we can regard current period net income (NI) as being generated by the following equation:

$$NI = \mu_1 SR + \mu_2 LR \pm \text{Random factors with expected value zero} \qquad (10.1)$$

where SR and LR are the quantities of short-run and long-run effort, respectively. There are now two sensitivities of NI rather than one. Thus μ_1 is the sensitivity of earnings to SR effort, and μ_2 is sensitivity to LR effort. The assumption that the random factors affecting NI have an expected value of zero implies that NI is an unbiased predictor of payoff (Section 9.2.2).

The firm's payoff, x, is also affected by these SR and LR activities. Thus, we can write the payoff as

$$x = b_1 SR + b_2 LR \pm \text{Random factors with expected value zero} \qquad (10.2)$$

where b_1 and b_2 are sensitivities of the payoff to SR and LR effort, respectively. We assume here that the manager exerts effort only in the first period, and that NI is reported at the end of this period. However, consistent with our assumption in Chapter 9, the payoff is not fully observable until the next period. That is, the full payoffs from the manager's SR and LR first-period effort decisions are not realized until that time. NI is a message that predicts what these payoffs will be. The manager is compensated based on first-period NI. The payoff, net of manager first period compensation, in the next period goes to the owner.

Recognition of effort as a set of activities introduces a new concept—the **congruency** of a performance measure. To illustrate congruency, consider the following example.

---

*This section can be omitted with little loss of continuity.

Example 10.2
A Congruent Performance Measure

Assume that the manager can work hard or shirk on both SR and LR effort, and that the NI and payoffs are as given in Table 10.1:

Table 10.1 Expected Net Incomes and Payoffs for Congruent Performance Measure

	Manager's Effort			
	Short-Run (SR) Effort		**Long-Run (LR) Effort**	
	Work Hard	Shirk	Work Hard	Shirk
Expected Net Income E(NI)	$4	$1.0	$3.0	$2
Expected Payoff E(x)	$6	$1.5	$4.5	$3

If the manager allocates all effort to SR and works hard, E(NI) is $4. However, some of this effort, such as cost control, may remain to benefit next period, assuming that at least some of the lower costs will persist. Let these future benefits amount to $2. Then the expected *payoff* from SR effort totals $6. If the manager works hard at LR effort, say, by devoting time to R&D, this generates E(NI) of $3 currently but is expected to create additional payoff of $1.5 next period, for a total of $4.5. Similar comments apply if the manager shirks.

From Table 10.1, the *increases* in expected payoffs if the manager works hard, compared to shirking, are given in Table 10.2:

Table 10.2 Increases in Net Incomes and Payoffs from Working Hard

	Manager's Effort	
	Short-Run (SR) Effort	**Long-Run (LR) Effort**
Expected Net Income E(NI)	$\mu_1 = \$3.0$	$\mu_2 = \$1.0$
Expected Payoff E(x)	$b_1 = \$4.5$	$b_2 = \$1.5$

The μ_1 and μ_2 in Table 10.2 are the sensitivities of NI to SR and LR effort, respectively—see Equation 10.1. Similarly, b_1 and b_2 are the sensitivities of the payoff to effort—see Equation 10.2. Note that b_1 is in the *same proportion* to μ_1 (4.5:3 = 3:2) as b_2 is to μ_2 (1.5:1 = 3:2). Then, NI is said to be **congruent** to the payoff. That is, an increase of E(NI) by, say, $1 will increase the expected payoff by $1.5 regardless of whether the increase in expected NI comes from LR or SR effort or any combination of the two.

This being the case, the owner can design a contract that compensates the manager on the basis of reported NI for the first period without worrying about how the manager allocates effort between short-run and long-run activities. Given the contract, the manager will choose an effort intensity and allocation to maximize his/her expected utility of compensation, net of effort disutility. This maximization process was implicit in Examples 9.2–9.6.

In sum, if there is more than one dimension to manager effort, and if NI is congruent to the payoff, the owner need not be concerned how the manager allocates effort across the dimensions. Each type of effort is equally effective in generating payoff.

Unfortunately, congruent NI is unlikely to be the case. Again, the reason derives from recognition lag. Consider Table 10.1 once more. While SR effort, such as cost control, may be an effective way to generate current NI, this is unlikely to be as effective in generating payoff in the next period, contrary to our assumption above. While some of the lower costs may persist, the cost-cutting nature of SR effort is likely to reduce employee morale and organization effectiveness in the next period, and this effect is not recognized in current NI. A more likely payoff from SR effort is, say, $2 if the manager works hard (i.e., the NI of $4 in the current period is reduced by $2 in the next, giving a net payoff of $2) and, say, $1.5 if he/she shirks. LR effort, however, is likely to have an opposite effect. Effort devoted to R&D, for example, will likely generate a high LR payoff, say $9 if the manager works hard and $4 if he/she shirks. Tables 10.3 and 10.4 summarize these assumptions:

Table 10.3   Expected Net Incomes and Payoffs for Non-congruent Performance Measure

	Manager's Effort			
	Short-Run (SR) Effort		Long-Run (LR) Effort	
	Work Hard	Shirk	Work Hard	Shirk
Expected Net Income E(NI)	$4	$1.0	$3	$2
Expected Payoff E(x)	$2	$1.5	$9	$4

Table 10.4   Increases in Net Incomes and Payoffs from Working Hard

	Manager's Effort	
	Short-Run (SR) Effort	Long-Run (LR) Effort
Expected Net Income E(NI)	$\mu_1 = \$3.0$	$\mu_2 = \$1$
Expected Payoff E(x)	$b_1 = \$0.5$	$b_2 = \$5$

Now, for SR effort, the proportion of b_1 to μ_1 is 0.5:3 = 1:6. For LR effort, the proportion is 5:1 = 5. Thus NI is **non-congruent** to the payoff—it *does* matter to the owner which type of effort generates NI. An increase of $1 in NI from SR effort will increase expected payoff by $1/6, whereas an increase in NI of $1 from LR effort will increase it by $5.

In our example, the owner will want high R&D, because of its high ultimate payoff (i.e., b_2 is greater than b_1 in Table 10.4). But the manager, whose compensation is based on first period net income, will tend toward a SR decision horizon since effort allocated to SR activities generates greater E(NI) and compensation (i.e., μ_1 is greater than μ_2 in Table 10.4). The compensation contract must now consider not only the intensity of manager effort but also the *allocation* of effort across activities. Raising the manager's profit share will not serve to lengthen the manager's decision horizon—it will simply encourage more SR effort. As a result, the owner settles for less LR effort than he/she would like.

The question then is, what might the owner do about this? Given that the manager's effort allocation cannot be directly observed by the owner, one possibility is to replace NI with a more congruent performance measure, such as share price. It is not hard to see that share price is more congruent with payoff than NI, since it is less subject to recognition lag. Then, favourable share price sensitivity to R&D will motivate the manager to increase LR effort. However, share price is less precise than net income. Consequently, it is not clear that basing compensation only on share price would increase contracting efficiency. This suggests once again basing compensation on both performance measures, so as to secure a tradeoff between congruity and precision, consistent with what we observe in real compensation contracts.

A second possibility is for the principal and manager to commit to a multi-period contract ending on a fixed date. Şabac (2008) modelled this scenario. The risk-averse manager is paid a salary plus a proportion of the period's net income. At the end of each period, the contract is renegotiated, based on the history of the manager's past earnings performance and changes over time in contract parameters such as the sensitivity of NI to effort. We can see this effect in the changes to the RBC compensation contract described in Section 10.3, where provision is made to claw back bonuses awarded in previous periods.

For present purposes, a significant aspect of Şabac's multi-period contract is that the manager knows that future compensation will include earnings from current LR effort, such as R&D and capital projects. Consequently, LR effort is not discouraged, since the desired balance between SR and LR effort is motivated by the contract itself.[8] Similarly, dysfunctional first-period SR effort, such as managing earnings upward, is discouraged.

10.4.3 The Role of Risk in Executive Compensation

We can also consider the manager's effort from a risk perspective since, as pointed out in Chapter 9, in the presence of moral hazard, the manager must bear some compensation risk if effort is to be motivated. Since managers, like other rational, risk-averse individuals, trade off risk and return, the more risk managers bear, the higher must be their *expected* compensation if reservation utility is to be attained. Thus, to motivate the manager at the lowest cost, designers of efficient incentive compensation plans try to get the most motivation for a given amount of risk imposed or, equivalently, the least risk for a given level of motivation.

It is important to realize that compensation risk affects how the manager operates the firm. If not enough risk is imposed, the firm suffers from low manager effort. If too much risk is imposed, the manager may underinvest in risky projects even though such projects would benefit diversified shareholders. Recall from our discussion of the RBC compensation plan that the plan takes steps to limit manager risk.

There are several ways to control compensation risk. Perhaps the most important of these from a theoretical perspective is **relative performance evaluation** (RPE). Here, instead of measuring performance by net income and/or share price, performance is measured by the *difference* between the firm's net income and/or share price performance and the average performance of a peer group of similar firms, such as other firms in the same economy or industry. The theory of RPE was developed by Baiman and Demski (1980) and Holmström (1982). By measuring the manager's performance relative to the average performance of similar firms, the systematic or common risks that the industry faces will be filtered out of the incentive plan, especially if the number of firms in the peer group is large. To see this, note that when there are noisy performance measures in the contract, there will be some risks that are common to all peer group firms. For example, at least some of the effects on share price and earnings of a downturn in the economy, such as a reduction in sales, will also affect other firms. RPE deducts the average earnings and share price performance of peer group firms from the manager's performance measures, leaving a net performance that more precisely reflects the manager's efforts in running the firm in question. Thus, under RPE, it is possible for a manager to do well even if the firm reports a loss and/or share price is down, providing the losses are lower than those of the average peer group firm.

If the RPE theory is valid, we would expect to observe manager compensation negatively related to average economy or industry performance. For example, when industry performance is low, high earnings and/or share price performance for the firm in question is even more impressive since it overcomes negative factors affecting the whole industry. Consequently, the compensation committee will award higher compensation. When industry performance is high, high earnings and/or share price for the firm in question is less impressive, so that lower compensation is awarded. The RBC plan exhibits some of this effect, since if RBC performs in the top 15% of the peer group, total compensation is increased, even if median peer group performance is low. Similarly, if RBC performs in the bottom 15%, total compensation is reduced even if median peer group performance is high.

However, despite RPE's theoretical appeal, strong statistical evidence that managers are compensated this way has been hard to come by. Antle and Smith (1986) found weak evidence for RPE, and, according to Pavlik, Scott, and Tiessen (1993), a survey of RPE articles shows that the ability of RPE to predict manager compensation is modest.[9]

Testing for RPE, however, is complicated by the need to identify a firm's appropriate peer group. Albuquerque (2009) argued that while a firm's industry is a good place to start, firm size must also be taken into account since different-size firms are affected differently by industry-wide events. For example, if demand for an industry's product falls, relatively small firms, with relatively low production volumes, may suffer more from fixed costs and/or financing problems than larger firms in the same industry that may enjoy economies of scale and greater financial flexibility.

Based on a large sample of firms over the period 1992–2005, Albuquerque found a significant negative relation between CEO total compensation and the average share price performance of a peer group of firms of similar size in the same industry, supporting the use of RPE.[10]

Nevertheless, it is possible that strategic factors work against finding empirical evidence of RPE. For example, Aggarwal and Samwick (AS; 1999) presented a model of firms in an oligopolistic industry, where the demand for a firm's product depends not only on its own product price but also on the prices of its competitors' products.[11] That is, the lower are competitors' prices, the lower is the demand for the product of the firm in question, and vice versa. This creates an incentive for managers to engage in cooperative pricing behaviour to "soften" competition, as AS put it. This raises profits for all firms in the industry. To encourage this cooperative behaviour, compensation plans put positive, not negative, weight on other firms' performance. Furthermore, the magnitude of this positive weight should be stronger the greater the degree of competition in the industry, since low profits from high competition increase the incentive of all firms in the industry to cooperate so as to increase industry profits.[12] AS reported empirical evidence consistent with this prediction.

The RBC plan has a similar characteristic of positive weight on other firms' performance, since total compensation is positioned relative to the median of that paid by a peer group of comparable companies. To the extent that profits, and thus compensation, of RBC's competitors are high, RBC's executive compensation will also rise. It thus seems that the RBC plan is a mixture of negative (increase or decrease in total compensation if RBC performance is extreme) and positive (total compensation positioned relative to peer group median) correlations. The difficulty of finding empirical support for RPE could be due to countervailing effects such as these.

Another way to control risk is through the bogey of the compensation plan. Consider the manager in Example 9.2 who receives compensation of 0.3237 of earnings. Suppose the firm loses $50 million. That is, earnings are negative, and so would be the manager's compensation. Instead of receiving compensation, the manager would have to pay the firm over $16 million! Under such a risky contract, the average level of compensation needed for the manager to attain reservation utility would be prohibitive. In other words, fear of personal bankruptcy is probably not the best way to motivate a manager to work hard. For this reason, compensation plans usually impose a **bogey**. That is, incentive compensation does not kick in until some level of financial performance—10% return on equity, for example—is reached. The effect is that if the bogey is not attained, the contract does not award any incentive compensation. However, an ancillary effect is that the manager does not have to pay the firm if there is a loss.[13]

If downside risk is limited, it seems reasonable for upside risk to be limited too; otherwise, the manager would have everything to gain and little to lose, which could encourage excessive risk taking. As a result, many plans impose a **cap**, whereby incentive compensation ceases beyond a certain level. For example, no bonus may be awarded for return on equity exceeding, say, 25%. Note that there is an implicit cap in the RBC plan, since compensation is tied to the median of the peer group.

Conservative accounting also controls upside risk by delaying recognition of unrealized gains and discouraging premature revenue recognition. Watts (2003a and b) argued that conservative accounting promotes contract efficiency by constraining the manager's ability to inflate current earnings, and hence compensation, by recording unrealized gains. However, basing compensation on conservative earnings gives the manager little incentive to invest in risky projects. No compensation will be received unless and until a project starts to generate realized profits. This creates a role for share-based compensation. Since share price will quickly reflect unrealized profits on long-term projects, managers can be encouraged to invest in such projects (equivalently, to incur upside risk) by basing compensation on share price performance. For example, ESOs provide this incentive since, if they succeed, they can become very valuable. Yet, if they do not succeed, the lowest the ESOs can be worth is zero.

Indeed, ESOs may be too effective in this regard. While they encourage upside risk, they impose little downside risk, and so may promote excessive risk taking. If so, a major potential cost to shareholders of ESOs, in addition to the dilution explained in Section 8.6, is that they may generate inefficient compensation contracts. Thus, ESOs seem to have been a driving force behind horror stories such as Enron and WorldCom, as described in Section 1.2, and also to have contributed to the 2007–2008 market meltdowns. It seems that manager effort was diverted away from value-increasing projects into opportunistic actions to increase share price, hence the value of their ESOs. In this regard, Efendi, Srivastava, and Swanson (2007) investigated a sample of 95 firms that announced financial statement restatements during 2001–2002, following which there were substantial declines in share prices of the restating firms. This suggests that, in retrospect, the shares of such firms were overvalued relative to fundamental value.[14] The authors found that CEOs of these firms had on average significantly larger ESO holdings, than CEOs of a control sample of firms that did not report restatements. They concluded that the larger the value of a CEO's ESO holdings, the greater his/her incentive to misstate the financial statements in order to support stock price.

Nevertheless, one should not necessarily conclude that ESOs should be eliminated from compensation plans. Rajgopal and Shevlin (RS; 2002), in a sample of oil and gas firms over the period 1992–1997, found that ESOs did motivate managers to increase firm risk. This increased risk showed up both in increased exploration risk and reduced hedging activity. RS also found, however, that the effect of ESOs in their sample firms was to encourage risk-averse managers to undertake risky projects when these projects were economically desirable, not to encourage excessive risk taking. In effect, their findings are consistent with efficient contracting.[15]

In sum, we arrive once again at a conclusion that a mix of performance measures is desirable. Compensation in the form of ESOs and/or company shares encourages upside risk and a longer-run decision horizon, while net income–based compensation, at least if deferred and subject to clawback, imposes some downside risk to discourage the excessive risk taking that pure share-based compensation may create.

Another approach to controlling risk is through the compensation committee of the Board. As we saw in the RBC plan, the Board has the ultimate responsibility to determine the amounts of cash and stock compensation, and it has the flexibility to take special

In a 2008 article "Make them pay," by William Scott. *The Economist* discussed what to do about bankers' compensation in the light of the 2007–2008 market meltdowns. The article quoted a U.S. survey showing the pre-meltdown average pay in investment banking as almost 10 times the national average.

The article pointed out a moral hazard problem that contributes to this high pay—bankers' compensation is not well aligned with the risks that their actions create. Bank compensation plans, the article claims, encourage managers to adopt risky strategies (e.g., excessive leverage) since, if the strategies pay off, short-run compensation awards are huge (high earnings generate high bonuses). However, compensation penalties are relatively small if the risky strategies do not pay off (e.q., bogey of the compensation plan, ESOs have minimum value of zero, bonuses tied to the average of a peer group, or Board approval of some bonus anyway).

To correct this imbalance, theory suggests lengthening the manager's decision horizon, by deferral of bonuses and increased compensation based on share price performance. Such compensation could be in the form of deferred share units and/or ESOs. These awards should be accompanied by longer vesting periods, to motivate managers to look to the longer run consequences of their actions, and reduce "pump and dump" and other dysfunctional practices outlined in Section 8.6.[16]

However, the article points out problems in practice with increasing manager share ownership:

- To the extent that share prices do not fully reflect the risk inherent in management strategies[17] (e.g., off balance sheet financing combined with poor disclosure), share values will be high relative to fundamental firm value, thereby continuing to encourage managers' excessive risk-taking behaviour.

- Most important firm decisions are made at the top. Then, lower-level managers will nevertheless suffer from the decline in share value if these decisions turn out badly. This possibility lowers the expected utility of their share compensation, possibly reducing effort incentive.

- Since deferral of compensation lowers its expected utility, managers, especially the most competent, may not attain their reservation utility, and will leave the firm. To prevent this, firms may have to reduce or reverse compensation deferral, thereby restoring the risk-taking incentives that deferral is intended to lower.

As a result, the ability of increased share holdings and compensation deferral to correct the excesses leading to the market meltdowns can be questioned. However, one suggestion of relevance to accountants is clear. This is to improve reporting on risk, so that share prices better reflect the firm's actual risk. Indeed, steps in this direction are being taken. In Section 7.8, we discussed new standards for derecognition and consolidation, including additional risk disclosures. Also, new SEC rules effective in 2010 increased risk disclosures in management proxy circulars, including disclosure of the relationship of compensation policies to risk management (so that investors can better detect excessive risk-taking incentives), and the Board's role in risk oversight.

circumstances into account. For example, if the firm reports a loss, or earnings below the bogey, it may award a bonus anyway, particularly if it feels that the loss is due to some low-persistence item. However, the committee must exercise some restraint in this regard. If it is overly generous in not penalizing the manager for state realizations that are not his/her "fault," this will destroy contract rigidity and reduce effort incentive.

Despite efforts to control compensation risk, it is essential that some risk remains. Thus, it is important that the manager not be able to work out from under this risk. The manager can shed compensation risk by, for example, selling shares and options acquired and investing the proceeds in a risk-free asset and/or a diversified portfolio. However, compensation plans typically constrain this possibility by restricting the manager's ability to dispose of shares and options. Thus the RBC plan requires executives to hold from two to eight times annual base salary in RBC shares. Also, stock options are not fully exercisable until four years after the grant date.

The manager can also shed risk by excessive hedging. Not only is hedging costly, but effort incentive will suffer if the manager works out from under risk this way. Consequently, the firm may limit hedging behaviour, as illustrated in Theory in Practice 10.2.

Theory in Practice 10.2

Suncor Energy Inc., in its 2006 annual report MD&A, described how it controls possible excess hedging in its oil and gas cash flow hedging program. Suncor's board restricted cash flow hedging to a maximum of 30% of crude oil production up to December 31, 2008.

Currently, Suncor does not report specific limits on hedging. It does, however, state in its 2011 MD&A that "Suncor's risk management activities are subject to periodic reviews by management to determine appropriate hedging requirements based on the company's tolerance for exposure to market volatility, as well as the need for stable cash flow to finance future growth."

10.5 EMPIRICAL COMPENSATION RESEARCH

The research of Rajgopal and Shevlin outlined above provides some evidence that on average real compensation plans are designed efficiently. In this section, we review other empirical studies bearing on the relation between compensation theory and practice, concentrating on studies that examine the role of accounting information.

An early study in this area was conducted by Lambert and Larcker (LL; 1987). Using a sample of 370 U.S. firms over the period 1970–1984 inclusive, LL investigated the relative ability of return on shares and return on equity (ROE) to explain managers' cash compensation (salary plus bonus). If, for example, compensation plans and compensation committees primarily use share return to motivate manager performance, then share return should be significantly related to cash compensation. Alternatively, if they primarily use net income as a motivator, ROE (a ratio based on net income) should be significantly related to cash compensation.

LL found that ROE was more highly related to cash compensation than was return on shares. Indeed, several other studies have found the same results. These results are consistent with RBC's short-term compensation incentives, where awards depend on net income growth and ROE. They support the decision horizon-controlling and risk-controlling roles for net income in compensation plans that were suggested in Sections 10.4.1 and 10.4.3.

LL also found that the relationship of these two payoff measures to cash compensation varied in systematic ways. For example, they found some evidence that the relationship between ROE and cash compensation strengthened when net income was less noisy relative to return on shares. They measured the relative noisiness of net income by the ratio of the variability of ROE over the period 1970–1984 to the variability of return on shares over the same period. The lower the noise in net income, the better it predicts the payoff, as illustrated in Example 9.3. This finding is also consistent with Banker and Datar's 1989 analysis outlined in Section 10.4.1.

LL also found that managerial compensation for growth firms' executives tended to have a lower relationship with ROE than average. This, too, is consistent with Banker and Datar, since, for growth firms, net income is relatively less sensitive to manager effort than it is for the average firm. Historical cost-based net income, which largely characterized accounting practice during the time of LL's analysis, tended particularly to lag behind the real economic performance of a growth firm, because this basis of accounting does not recognize value increases until they are realized. The market, however, would look through to real economic performance and growth opportunities and will value the shares accordingly. Thus, ROE should be related less to compensation than share return for such firms, which is consistent with what LL found.

Perhaps the most interesting finding of LL, however, was that for firms where the correlation between share return and ROE was low, there tended to be a higher weight on ROE in the compensation plan, and vice versa. In other words, when net income is relatively uninformative to investors (low correlation between share return and ROE) that same net income is relatively informative about manager effort (higher weight on ROE in the compensation plan). This provides empirical evidence on the impact of the fundamental problem (Section 1.10)—the investor-informing and the manager performance-motivating dimensions of usefulness must be traded off.

Further evidence of efficient compensation contracting was provided by Indjejikian and Nanda (IN; 2002). In a sample of 2,981 senior executives over the period 1988–1995, they found that, on average, the lower the variability of ROE the higher the target bonus relative to base salary. This suggests that firms substitute out of salary (riskless, but little incentive effect) into bonus (risky, but greater incentive) as firm risk is less. This is consistent with efficient contracting since, when firm risk is relatively low, the incentive benefits of a bonus can be attained with relatively low compensation risk loaded onto the manager. IN also found that target bonuses, especially for the CEOs in their sample, tended to increase, relative to base salary, with the volatility of return on shares. One interpretation is that firms in high-risk environments (hence, more volatile share prices) rely more on accounting-based performance measures relative to those based on stock price performance. Again, this is consistent with theory.

Bushman, Indjejikian, and Smith (1996) found that CEOs of growth firms, and of firms with long product development and life cycles, derived a greater proportion of their

Banker, Darrough, Huang, and Plehn-Dujowich (2013) studied the effect of manager ability on the optimal compensation contract. They measured ability by the past return on equity (ROE) generated by the manager. Based on a large sample of manager compensation data over the period 1993–2006, they found that manager salary was positively related to past ability to generate ROE. They also found, however, that manager bonus was *negatively* related to ability. The reason, according to the authors, is that the more able is the manager, the less the risk that needs to be imposed on the risk averse manager (i.e., lower risky bonus) to motivate effort. To enable the manager to attain reservation utility following a bonus reduction, higher risk-free compensation (i.e., salary) is awarded. In effect, by taking past evidence on manager ability into account, contract efficiency is increased, since less risk needs to be imposed to attain high effort.

compensation from *individual* performance measures relative to net income- and stock price-based measures. This is consistent with theory since net income, and perhaps even stock price, of such firms will be relatively uninformative about individual effort. Recall that RBC's compensation plan bases short-term incentive awards on attainment of individual goals in addition to earnings.

In Section 10.4.1, we suggested that full disclosure could improve the sensitivity of net income to manager effort by enabling identification of persistent earnings by the compensation committee. Evidence that suggests compensation committees do value persistent earnings more highly for compensation purposes than transitory or price-irrelevant earnings is provided by Baber, Kang, and Kumar (1999). In a sample of firms over the years 1992 and 1993, their results include a finding that the effect of earnings changes on compensation increases with the persistence of those earnings changes.

In sum, the above empirical results suggest that compensation committees, like investors, are on average quite sophisticated in their use of accounting and share price information. Just as full disclosure of value-relevant financial accounting information will increase investors' use of this information, full disclosure of "effort informative" stewardship information will increase its usage by compensation committees, thereby maintaining and increasing the role of net income in motivating responsible manager performance.

10.6 THE POLITICS OF EXECUTIVE COMPENSATION

The question of manager compensation is a longstanding one. Many have argued that top managers are overpaid.

In 1990, Jensen and Murphy (JM) published a controversial article about top manager compensation. They argued that CEOs were not overpaid but that their compensation was far too unrelated to performance, where performance was measured as the change in the firm's market value (that is, the change in shareholder wealth). They examined the salary plus bonus of the CEOs of the 250 largest U.S. corporations over the 15 years from 1974–1988. For each year, they added the current year's and next year's salary and bonus and found that on average the CEOs received an extra 6.7 cents compensation over the two years for every $1,000 increase in shareholder wealth. When they added in other compensation components, including stock options and direct share holdings, the CEOs still received only $2.59 per $1,000 increase in shareholder wealth.

Other aspects of JM's investigation were consistent with these findings. For example, the variability (as measured by the standard deviation) over time of CEOs' and regular workers' compensations were almost the same. JM concluded that CEOs did not bear enough risk to motivate good performance, and consequently they recommended larger stock holdings by managers. With respect to the RBC plan, note again that it includes deferred share units and ESOs, plus guidelines that require substantial stock holdings by executives. Also, RBC's 2009 move to defer bonus payments and increase executive stock holdings is consistent with an intent to increase manager risk.

However, some counterarguments can be made to JM.[18] First, we would *expect* the relationship between pay and performance to be low for large firms, simply because of a size effect. Suppose that a large corporation increased in value by billions of dollars last year (for example, RBC's 2012 net income was $7.39 billion). An increase of even a small proportion of this amount in the CEO's remuneration would likely attract media attention.

Second, for large corporations at least, it is difficult to put much downside risk on an executive, as we argued in Section 10.4.3. An executive whose pay is highly related to performance would have so much to lose from even a small decline in firm value that this would probably lead to excessive avoidance of risky projects. As a result, the compensation committee may, for example, exclude low-persistence losses when deciding on bonus awards, particularly if the loss is relatively uninformative about manager effort. Such losses do, however, lower company value and net income. Consequently, such exclusions lower the pay–performance relationship. If, in addition, upside risk is limited, the relationship is further lowered. Theory in Practice 10.4 illustrates the exclusion of low persistence items from compensation.

Theory in Practice 10.4

To illustrate the treatment of low persistence items in compensation practice, consider BCE Inc.'s accounting for the results of telecommunications deregulation in Canada during the 1990s. BCE is a large Canadian telecommunications firm.

In 1997, BCE Inc. reported a net loss of $1.536 billion, compared to net earnings of $1.152 billion for 1996. Nevertheless, 60,881 share units were awarded to six senior officers for 1997 under the short-term compensation plan in effect at that time, compared to 55,299 share units in 1996. Salaries were also up for 1997, as

were stock options awarded under the long-term incentive plan.

BCE's 1997 net loss resulted from a one-time item of $2.950 billion for "stranded costs." That is, increasing competition as a result of telecommunications deregulation resulted in BCE's inability to recover the full costs of certain assets from revenues. The $2.950 billion charge represented a writedown of these assets to estimated value in use, consistent with impairment test standards. BCE's 1997 earnings before this extraordinary item were $1.414 billion.

One could argue that deregulation of the telecommunications industry has little to do with manager effort, consistent with its one-time nature. In effect, the item is transitory, hence of low persistence. Low persistence supports a low weighting in determining compensation. Nevertheless, exclusion of the writedown for bonus purposes also supports an argument that a low pay–performance relationship is to be expected.

BCE's exclusion of a one-time loss, as just described, is consistent with the results of Gaver and Gaver (1998). For a sample of large U.S. firms over the years 1970–1996, these authors found that while low-persistence special item gains tended to be reflected in CEO cash compensation, special item losses were not. A possible explanation is that compensation committees feel that reducing manager bonus compensation for such losses imposes excessive downside risk on the manager, since the loss may be the result of a market downturn rather than manager shirking. Bertrand and Mullainathan (2001) found a similar result for ESO compensation, particularly for firms with weak corporate governance.

Of course, to the extent that special item losses *are* informative about manager effort, their exclusion from compensation awards is questionable, since the manager's anticipation that they will not affect compensation reduces effort incentive to avoid them.[19] While exclusion supports JM's argument that managers do not bear enough risk, it also supports a counterargument that it is difficult to impose much downside risk on managers. However, some more recent support for an argument that managers are not overpaid is provided by Gayle and Miller (GM; 2009). These researchers studied top-three executive compensation for two samples of North American corporations in aerospace, chemicals, and electronics industries. The first sample covered the period 1944–1978. The second covered the years 1993–2003. As we would expect, mean compensation increased greatly between the two sample periods. Also, there was a dramatic increase in firm size.

GM estimated the average salary their sample executives would require to attain reservation utility if they did not work hard (i.e., shirked), and bore no compensation risk. They found that this amount increased 2.3 times between the two samples. This increase is almost exactly the same as the increase in U.S. per capita average income over the same period. In terms of our agency theory discussion in Chapter 9, this implies that if managers bore no risk and did not incur the extra effort disutility of working hard (i.e., if they were paid only by a salary), their salary increase would not have been out of line with the average increase in income in society over this period.

GM then estimated the additional amount of compensation their managers would require if they were to work harder and bear increased compensation risk. They reported that this amount increased by up to 20 times between the two periods. Recall again from Chapter 9 that these compensation costs are necessary to overcome the moral hazard problem between manager and owner. That is, a hard-working, risk-averse manager's compensation contract must reimburse for these two elements if reservation utility is to be attained.

The question then is, why did these costs of moral hazard increase? After ruling out other factors that could account for the increase (e.g., an increase in manager risk aversion), the researchers attributed the increased cost to the increase in firm size and to an increase in the dispersion of firm returns between the two periods, hence of compensation.

The moral hazard problem increases with firm size due to increased complexity of corporate governance and increased opportunity for manager opportunistic behaviour. Greater dispersion reflects increased compensation risk.

These findings imply that the large increase in average executive compensation over time was not driven by managers securing higher compensation at the expense of the average wage-earner. Rather, it was driven by a dramatic increase in the costs of overcoming moral hazard in compensation contracts. The manager does not benefit from this compensation component since, in effect, it reimburses the manager for the utility costs of risk and effort. In this sense, the GM analysis suggests, as do JM, that managers are not overpaid.

Despite these counterarguments, however, compensation concerns continue to appear. For example, political attention grew in the 1990s and early 2000s with respect to ESOs. For CEOs of large U.S. corporations, the market value of these awards often ran into the hundreds of millions of dollars. This attention intensified as the proportion of compensation based on ESOs steadily increased during the 1990s. For example, according to Hall and Murphy (2002), option grants to CEOs of the S&P 500 industrial firms increased from 22% of median total compensation in 1992 to 56% in 1999. Furthermore, option grants continued to rise in the early 2000s, despite a severe decline in the stock market. However, fears that maintaining ESO value was a motivator of financial reporting frauds, such as Enron and WorldCom (Section 1.2), and revelations of management abuses of ESO compensation (Section 8.6), enabled standard setters to overcome management objections to expensing ESOs in 2004. Subsequently, some firms replaced or reduced their ESO compensation by issuing **restricted stock** (called deferred share units in the RBC plan), which was perceived as a more efficient compensation device. An advantage of restricted stock over ESOs is that it cannot be sold during a fixed period, so that the manager has less flexibility to opportunistically time its sale. This should reduce some of the ESO abuses, such as pump and dump and late timing.[20]

More recently, political opposition to manager compensation has further increased due to adverse public reaction to bonuses paid by financial institutions involved in the 2007–2008 market meltdowns. This reaction was particularly strong against firms that had received various forms of government assistance. For example, AIG Inc. sparked outrage by announcing bonuses totalling over $1 billion, despite receiving over $170 billion in U.S. government assistance and reporting a loss exceeding $60 billion in the fourth quarter of 2008. Episodes such as this led to various forms of government interference, such as bonus controls for bailed-out companies, prohibitions of bonuses and dividends for financial institutions whose legal capital falls below threshold, and, in the U.K. and France, a 50% surtax paid by the company on bonuses exceeding specified limits.

To fully understand the politics of executive compensation, however, it is important to realize that the value of a given amount of share-based compensation to a manager is lower than it might appear at first glance. For example, the cost of ESOs to the firm is usually based on an option pricing model such as Black-Scholes. This provides a reasonable measure of the *firm's* ESO cost, since this is the opportunity cost of issuing ESOs to managers (see Section 8.6). However, Black-Scholes assumes that options can be freely traded, whereas compensation plan ESOs usually vest over a period of several years (four years in the RBC plan). If a manager is forced to hold ESOs, he/she cannot diversify compensation risk by, for example, selling the acquired shares and buying a diversified portfolio. These restrictions reduce ESO value to the manager. The more risk averse the manager, and the less diversified the manager's other wealth, the greater the reduction.

This effect was studied by Hall and Murphy (2002), building on an earlier analysis by Lambert, Larcker, and Verrecchia (1991). They reported, for example, that the median 1999 total compensation of CEOs of S&P 500 industrial firms was US$5.695 million, of which 74% was in the form of ESOs and company stock (ESOs valued on a Black-Scholes basis). For a moderately risk-averse and diversified CEO, however, the cash-equivalent value of this compensation, after allowing for restrictions on disposal, was $3.420 million, a reduction of almost 40%. For a more risk-averse CEO, the reduction was almost 55%.[21] By ignoring an inability to diversify share-based compensation, media and politicians substantially overstate its value to the executive. An illustration of the effect of lack of diversifiability on the value of ESOs to the holder is provided by Theory in Practice 10.5.

The existence of "golden parachutes," under which the manager's compensation contract includes a component granting a substantial severance payment, regardless of the reason for leaving, is another source of media attention and political pressure on manager compensation. Severance pay is often viewed as rewarding poor performance. Theory in Practice 10.6 illustrates this attention.

However, Rau and Xu (RX; 2012) examined a 2004 sample of large U.S. firms, finding that 68% of their sample firms included severance pay in their managerial compensation contracts. Concentrating on new or revised compensation contracts offered to incumbent CEOs, they reported that the probability of a severance pay component in the

Theory in Practice 10.5

In January 2007, Zions Bancorporation announced that it had received SEC permission to use a market-based approach to valuation of its ESOs. Zions is a large U.S. financial services company that operates numerous banks in several U.S. states.

Zions's approach is to create special securities, called employee stock option appreciation rights securities (ESOARS), to be sold to outside investors. These give the holder the right to receive an amount equal to a portion of the gain realized by Zions's employees when they exercise their ESOs. Thus, the ESOARS are subject to all of the conditions attached to the ESOs. The fair value of the ESOs, Zions argued, can then be inferred from

the market value of the ESOARS. For example, if ESOARS give the holder an amount equal to 25% of the employees' ESO gains, the ESO fair value is four times the ESOARS' market value.

In May 2007, Zions announced a successful auction of ESOARS. There were 43 bidders, with an average price paid of $12.06. Thus, if the ESOARS entitle the holder to an amount equal to 25% of ESO gains, the underlying ESOs would be worth about $48.24. This implied ESO fair value was about one-half of the value estimated from an ESO valuation model, such as Black-Scholes. Zions indicated that it would use this implied fair value to measure its stock option expense under SFAS 123R.

compensation contract, and the magnitude of severance pay, increases as the incentive effect of the CEO's stock and ESO holdings falls. The incentive effect of stock and ESO holdings falls when the firm experiences a period of low stock price since, in addition to low value of his/her stock holdings, the CEO's ESOs are likely to be out of, or barely in, the money. In addition, poor stock price increases the likelihood that the CEO will be fired. As a result, the CEO is less inclined to adopt risky, longer-term projects,[22] since he/she may not be around to realize the benefits of the higher stock price that, hopefully, will result from these projects. In effect, even large stock and ESO holdings will not motivate risk taking when firm performance is low. RX then point out that the prospect of a substantial severance payment reduces the CEO's concerns about risk, thereby raising his/her willingness to adopt risky projects closer to the level desired by diversified shareholders.

RX also found that the likelihood and magnitude of severance pay increases for younger CEOs (who suffer more from loss of reputation and compensation than older CEOs), and with the probability that the firm will become financially distressed or taken over (both of which increase the likelihood of being fired).

These results suggest that severance pay is an important vehicle to control risk in managerial compensation contracts. The authors concluded that severance pay is consistent with efficient contracting.[23]

Nevertheless, political pressure on manager compensation continues. In this regard, "say on pay" votes, under which investors have a non-binding vote on the report of the compensation committee, further increase the influence of shareholders over compensation. Such votes are required in several countries, such as the United Kingdom and the United States. In other jurisdictions, such as Canada, many companies have voluntarily adopted say on pay.

To summarize, there is considerable evidence that executive compensation contracts and the administration of these contracts by compensation committees, are reasonably consistent with theory. Furthermore, despite the high absolute amounts of executive compensation, including golden handshakes, there is evidence that, on average, managers are not overpaid relative to shareholder value created. It seems that much of manager compensation is to compensate for the effort disutility and compensation risk the manager bears. Also, due to deferral of bonuses and requirements to hold share-based compensation for some time, managers bear firm-specific risk. As a result, the value of risky compensation received by the manager is less than the cost of this compensation to the firm. Nevertheless, sensitivity of shareholders, media, and politicians to perceived excessive compensation continues, reinforced by reaction to management abuses leading up to the 2007–2008 market meltdowns.

10.7 THE POWER THEORY OF EXECUTIVE COMPENSATION

Our discussion to this point has generally supported the efficient contracting view of executive compensation. Thus, we concluded in Section 10.5 that compensation committees are quite sophisticated in their use of accounting information and, in Section 10.6, that the utility of CEO compensation may be less than it seems at first glance. However, our discussion contained hints of another theory, the **power theory** of executive compensation. This theory suggests that executive compensation in practice is driven by manager opportunism, not efficient contracting.

The power theory was set forth by Bebchuk, Fried, and Walker (BFW; 2002). They argued that managers have sufficient power to influence their own compensation, and that they use this power to generate excessive pay, at the expense of shareholder value. If so, managers receive more than their reservation utility, contrary to our assumption in Chapter 9 that market forces prevent this. In effect, the power theory questions the efficient operation of the managerial labour market, much like behavioural finance questions efficient securities market theory (Section 6.2).[24]

The source of manager power, BFW argued, is the ability of the CEO to influence the board of directors, including the compensation committee. Even though a majority of the board may be nominally independent, the CEO can influence their appointment. Furthermore, once appointed, even an independent director may feel that if he/she blocks excessive CEO compensation awards, an anti-management reputation will quickly be acquired. Such a reputation will hamper his/her interaction with other directors and reduce the probability of appointment to other boards.

Revelations of late timing of ESO awards, discussed in Section 8.6, are an example of the power theory in action. Many firms, especially in the United States, backdated their ESO grant dates to create instant gains for the manager since the ESOs were, in effect, in the money when they were actually awarded.

The theory acknowledges that there are limits to the manager's power over compensation, namely "outrage." If compensation awards become too high, they attract negative publicity and at some point the board will have to step in to exercise its responsibility. However, as

BFW pointed out, there are ways to "camouflage" excessive compensation. One way is to hire a compensation consultant to add legitimacy to compensation awards. However, since the CEO also has influence over their appointments, compensation consultants may well feel that if they recommend a compensation plan that is unfavourable to the CEO, this will quickly get around and they will have difficulty obtaining other consulting engagements.

Another camouflage device is to tie total compensation to a peer group of similar companies. Recall that RBC adjusts total compensation relative to the median of its peer group. BFW pointed out that most companies do this. This creates pressure for total compensation to ratchet up over time as firms compete for competent personnel.

Also, since compensation consultants often do other work for their client firms, such as pensions and other benefit plans, concerns arise that to preserve their revenue from this work, consultants face a conflict of interest. That is, they may lack independence with respect to their compensation advice. However, Cadman, Carter, and Hillegeist (2010) (CCH), based on a sample of U.S. firms that employed a compensation consultant during 2006, found no evidence that firms whose consultants have greater conflicts of interest compensate their CEOs more highly than firms whose consultants have lower conflicts of interest. The authors suggested that consultants' concern for reputation and clients' corporate governance procedures control such tendencies.

In addition, there are other limits to manager power, such as the market for corporate control. Firms with managers that exercise excessive power may create shareholder discontent, to the point where the firm may be taken over, with resulting possibility of manager dismissal. In this regard, Armstrong, Balakrishnan, and Cohen (ABC; 2012) studied firms in those U.S. states that had passed "anti-takeover" laws to make it more difficult for firms incorporated in that state to be taken over. The effect of such laws is to decrease an important constraint on manager power and opportunism.

As ABC discuss, managers of firms that become less likely to be taken over may react in different ways. One possibility is "entrenchment," under which managers respond with lower quality financial reporting to camouflage lower effort. However, an alternative possibility is for the manager to improve financial reporting quality. This is because investors will realize that reducing the probability of a takeover increases the manager's temptation to shirk. This investor concern could affect share price, which is of particular concern if the manager intends to raise additional equity capital. To restore confidence, the manager responds with higher quality reporting.

ABC found, based on a version of the Ohlson clean surplus theory (Section 6.10), that the ability of book value and net income to explain share price increases following anti-takeover legislation, consistent with higher quality reporting and inconsistent with manager entrenchment. However, this increase in quality was concentrated in firms that planned to raise equity capital.

Despite the CCH and ABC studies, which suggest some constraints on manager power, the power theory raises several questions about the efficient contracting view of executive compensation. For example, BFW asked, why are ESO awards not adjusted downward for gains that are not under manager control? The results of Bertrand and

Mullainathan, referred to in Section 10.6, suggests that the answer may lie in weak corporate governance. Another question is why managers have so much freedom to control the exercise of ESOs. Recall from Section 8.6 that ESOs can be exercised any time between vesting date and expiry. Indeed, it is this exercise date flexibility that has complicated accountants' efforts to estimate the cost of ESO awards, since exercise date has to be estimated. Furthermore, after exercise, managers often have considerable freedom to sell the acquired shares. With stronger corporate governance, a manager's ability to manage compensation risk would be more constrained.

Additional support for the power theory is provided by Brown and Lee (2010). They investigated the equity compensation grants (ESOs plus restricted stock) of a large sample of U. S. corporations during the years 1998–2006, reporting a negative relation between corporate governance quality and excess equity grants, where excess grants were estimated after controlling for a variety of other factors, such as firm size and growth, that also affect compensation. This result is consistent with manager power being greater as corporate governance weakens.

Brown and Lee also divided their sample into pre- and post-Enron (Section 1.2) periods. Following Enron, outrage over CEO compensation increased, resulting in the 2002 Sarbanes-Oxley Act, and the 2004 SFAS 123R requiring expensing of ESO grants. Brown and Lee found that firms with weak corporate governance pre-Enron cut back on excessive equity grants post-Enron more than did firms with strong governance. Also, the negative relation between corporate governance and excess equity grants decreased post-Enron relative to pre-Enron. These results further support the power theory, at least pre-Enron, since if the theory was not operative, there would have been no excessive equity grants to cut back.

These various results suggest that while there are factors such as compensation consultant integrity and the takeover market that help to control manager power, the power theory does have some validity. The degree of validity seems to depend on the quality of corporate governance.

Accountants can assist the governance process, since managers may exploit their power through poor disclosure as well as through excessive compensation. Full disclosure enables better identification of earnings components with low persistence and informativeness. This helps compensation committees tie pay to performance, and, if they do not, improves the ability of investors and media to diagnose manager power, entrenchment, and excessive pay. Expensing of ESOs also plays a role, since an effect of expensing is to reduce the incentive for excessive ESO compensation, and encourage firms to move to possibly more efficient compensation vehicles such as restricted stock.

Of course, if the efficiency of compensation plans is to be controlled, politicians, media, and investors must know how much compensation the manager is receiving. In this regard, the SEC imposed regulations in 1992 to require firms to give more disclosure of their executive compensation, including a detailed explanation of the compensation of the five highest-paid executives and a report from the compensation committee justifying the pay levels. Similar requirements were adopted in Canada in 1993. These requirements were extended by the SEC in 2006 to include a Compensation Discussion and Analysis, a clear statement of total compensation received by five senior officers, and extensive disclosure of share-based compensation. Also required are disclosures of any late timing of ESO awards and of any golden parachutes. As mentioned in Theory in Practice 10.1, additional disclosures are required from 2010 to help investors evaluate the relationship between compensation policies and risk management. Presumably, the securities commissions feel that if investors have enough information to intelligently evaluate manager compensation levels, components, and risk-taking behaviour, they will take appropriate action if these appear excessive. Some evidence that full disclosure of compensation does have the desired effect was reported by Lo (2003). Lo studied the subsequent operating performance (measured by ROE and ROA) and share price performance of firms that had lobbied against the 1992 SEC disclosure regulations, relative to a control sample of similar firms that did not lobby. Note that if a firm's compensation contract is biased in the manager's favour so that the manager receives excess compensation, that firm's manager has an incentive to lobby against fuller disclosure of compensation plan details. Lo found that on average both the operating and share returns of the lobbying firms improved relative to the control firms subsequent to the new regulations. This improved performance is consistent with more efficient compensation contracts imposed on the lobbying managers as more compensation information became available.

A further attempt to control excessive pay is to limit the amount of manager compensation deductible for tax purposes. In the United States, compensation in excess of $1 million is not tax deductible, except for compensation based on achievement of performance targets set by the compensation committee. However, since ESOs are regarded as performance based (their value derives from share price performance), this exception may have been another contributor to the tremendous increase in ESO awards during the 1990s, rather than contributing to reduced total compensation. Surtaxes levied on firms that pay high bonuses in the United Kingdom and France are a more recent example of direct pay control.

We conclude that regulators and accountants have responded to the political pressures that result when managers exercise excessive power. To the extent these responses are successful, the operation of managerial labour markets is improved.

10.8 THE SOCIAL SIGNIFICANCE OF MANAGERIAL LABOUR MARKETS THAT WORK WELL

In a capitalist economy, manager performance contributes to social welfare. Welfare is increased to the extent managers "work hard"—that is, make good capital investment decisions and bring about high firm productivity.

Attainment of these desirable social goals is hampered to the extent that measures of manager performance are not fully informative. More informative performance measures enable more efficient compensation contracts, better reporting on stewardship, and better operation of the managerial labour market, resulting in higher firm productivity and social welfare. Accountants can contribute to informativeness both by an appropriate tradeoff between sensitivity and precision of net income and by full disclosure.

10.9 CONCLUSIONS ON EXECUTIVE COMPENSATION

Managerial labour markets undoubtedly reduce the severity of moral hazard. However, past manager performance is not an iron-clad indicator of future performance. Also, labour markets are subject to adverse selection problems such as earnings management to disguise shirking. Consequently, incentive contracts are still necessary even if managers' reputations on managerial labour markets fully reflect publicly available information.

Executive compensation contracts involve a delicate balancing of incentives, risk, and decision horizon. To properly align the interests of managers and shareholders, an efficient contract needs to achieve a high level of motivation while controlling compensation risk. Too little risk discourages manager effort. Too much risk may shorten a manager's decision horizon, encourage earnings-increasing tactics that are against the firm's longer-run interests, lead to avoidance of risky projects, and encourage excessive hedging. Managers are particularly sensitive to risk, because the compensation contract may restrict their ability to diversify it away, unlike shareholders.

To attain proper alignment, incentive plans usually feature a combination of salary, bonus, equity-based compensation such as restricted stock and options, and golden parachutes. These components of compensation are usually based on several performance measures—individual achievement, net income, and share price. We can think of these as noisy measures of the future payoff from current-period manager effort. Theory predicts that the relative proportion of each in the compensation plan depends on both their relative precision and sensitivity, and the length of manager decision horizon that the firm wants to motivate. Empirically, it appears that executive compensation is related to performance, although there is evidence suggesting that the strength of the relationship is low. However, for large firms at least, this low relationship is to be expected. Also, the relative proportion of net income-based and share price-based compensation components seems to vary as the theory predicts.

Executive compensation is surrounded by political controversy. Much of this controversy results from CEOs who exploit their power, using it to generate excessive compensation. Regulators have responded by expanding the information available to shareholders and others, on the assumption that they will take action to eliminate inefficient plans, or the managers and firms that have them. There is some evidence that expanded information is having the desired effect. However, politicians, media, and shareholders should realize that the utility of risky compensation to risk-averse managers may be less than it seems at first glance.

We conclude that financial reporting has an important role in motivating executive performance and controlling manager power. This role includes full disclosure, so that compensation committees and investors can better relate pay to performance. It also includes expensing stock option awards to help control their abuse and encourage more efficient compensation vehicles. As a result, responsible manager performance is motivated and the extent to which manager reputation is based on incomplete or biased information is reduced. This improves the operation of the managerial labour market, a goal equally important to society as promoting good investor decisions and improving the operation of securities markets.

Questions and Problems

1. Below is a portion of a 2013 proxy form sent to shareholders of Miracle-J Corporation. It reveals that Miracle-J has a bonus plan for its three senior executives that allocates them 10% of before-tax profits. Also, under the Employee Stock Option Plan, share options up to 12% of capitalization may be granted to directors or employees.

   Required

   a. Explain the reason for the bonus plan for senior executives. Are there any possible dysfunctional consequences of the bonus plan resulting from the apparent lack of a cap? Why is the bonus based on before-tax profits, rather than after-tax?

   b. Explain reasons for the Employee Stock Option Plan in addition to the bonus plan for senior executives. Why does the Plan apparently apply to all employees?

   c. To what extent would the bonus plan cause management to be concerned about accounting policies and changes in GAAP?

Miracle-J Corp.

Executive and Management Compensation

The Corporation's five executive officers were remunerated, in total, $440,000 by way of fees, salaries, and bonuses for the fiscal year ended May 31, 2013.

Included in the aforesaid sum was $280,000 paid to the three senior executive officers as full-time employees of the Corporation, pursuant to individual four-year Management Agreements made between the Corporation and those senior executive officers, effective June 1, 2011. Under the terms of the Agreements, the three senior executives are entitled to receive an aggregate bonus of 10% of before-tax profits earned by the company and their base salaries are to be increased 10% per year. For the 2013 fiscal year, the three senior executive officers waived their bonus entitlements to the extent that each received dividends on shares of the Corporation held by them which dividend was declared and paid for the fiscal year ended May 31, 2013.

It is to be noted that the Directors have adopted a form of Employee Stock Option Plan under which share options of up to 12% of the capitalization of the Corporation may be granted to Directors or employees. There are presently reserved, to that end, 930,000 common shares of the Corporation; but the Corporation has not granted any option to any Director or employees as of the date of this Information Circular.

---

2. Agency theory suggests that a way to motivate managers to act in the best interests of the owners/shareholders is to link managerial compensation to performance measures, such as net income or share price. However, such a linkage imposes risk on the manager.

   Required

   a. Why is it important to control the risk thus imposed on managers? Explain.

   b. Explain *two* methods by which risk imposed on the managers could be reduced. What happens if too much compensation risk is eliminated?

   c. Many managerial compensation packages impose restrictions on *when* managers can sell stock granted to them as a part of their compensation. For example, some compensation packages indicate that restricted stock awards may be forfeited unless the manager continues to work for the firm for a certain number of years after the granting of the award. Discuss the justification behind such restrictions.

   d. Inclusion of shares and options in managerial compensation packages has been attributed to the desire of the owners/shareholders to provide managers an incentive to undertake policies that benefit the firm's long-term rather than short-term interests. If this is true, why not compensate the manager only on the basis of share return (for example, only by stock options or restricted stock)? In other words, under these circumstances, what is the justification for having a cash or bonus element in the compensation package?

3. A proponent of ESOs argues that no expense should be recorded for ESOs issued to managers and other employees, since they do not cost the employer anything. On the contrary, the employer *receives* cash equal to the ESOs' exercise price.

   Do you agree that no expense should be recorded? Explain why or why not.

4. Explain why the value of ESOs and restricted stock to a manager is generally less than their fair values, such as Black-Scholes value for ESOs, or stock market value for restricted stock.

5. Explain why, for large corporations, a low pay–performance relationship is to be expected.

6. Firms A and B are roughly the same size, but operate in different industries. Firm A bases a high proportion of its executive compensation on net income and a relatively low proportion on share price performance. For firm B, these proportions are reversed. Yet, both firms appear to be well managed, consistently profitable, and growing. Use the concepts of sensitivity and precision of a performance measure to explain why both firms' compensation plans are efficient, despite the differing proportions.

7. In many compensation plans, short-term incentive awards are based on both earnings-based performance measures and non-financial measures such as attainment of personal goals. Why? Why might the weight placed on non-financial measures increase relative to the weight on earnings-based measures for lower-level executives?

8. Refer to Example 10.1. RBC requires that its executives hold substantial amounts of RBC shares. It also requires that they continue to hold these shares for two years past retirement. Why does RBC impose these requirements?

9. In 2002, Toronto-Dominion Bank (TD) announced that it would voluntarily expense ESOs, starting with its 2003 fiscal year beginning November 1, 2002. Accounting standards in Canada did not require ESO expensing until fiscal years beginning on or after January 1, 2004. In the MD&A section of its 2003 annual report, TD stated that it had charged to expense for 2003 an amount of $9 million for ESOs, using the fair value method.

   TD's reported net income for 2003 was $1.076 billion, compared to a net loss of $67 million for 2002.

   Suggest reasons why TD would voluntarily expense its ESOs.

10. In 2003, Microsoft Corp. discontinued its employees' stock option plan in favour of restricted stock, vesting over a five-year period. At that time, many of its already-granted ESOs were under water (i.e., exercise price greater than share market value).

   In 2003, no expense needed to be recorded for ESOs if they were granted with an intrinsic value of zero, since an FASB standard requiring expensing ESO fair value was not effective until fiscal years beginning after June 15, 2005. However, generally speaking, the fair value of restricted stock issued to employees *is* charged to expense.

For 2003, Microsoft reported earnings of $1.55 billion, after stock-based compensation expense of $2.17 billion. Analysts had expected net income, before stock-based compensation expense, of $3.28 billion.

Required

a. Give a reason why Microsoft's share price would be unaffected by the news of its reduction in reported earnings due to the 2003 stock-based compensation expense. Give reasons why stock price may fall.
b. Give reasons why Microsoft's share price might rise as a result of this news.
c. Why might Microsoft have eliminated ESOs in its compensation plan?

11. In its 2004 proxy statement to shareholders, the compensation committee of General Electric Company (GE) reported that in 2003 it had discontinued ESOs for its CEO, Jeffrey Immelt. In their place, GE awarded 250,000 restricted share units. One-half of these units entitled Mr. Immelt to one share each in 2008 if operating cash flow growth, adjusted for the effect of unusual events, increased at an average rate of 10% or more during 2003–2007. Otherwise, the share units would be cancelled. The other 125,000 units entitled him to one share each in 2008 if the total return on GE shares over the period 2003–2007 met or exceeded the return on the S&P 500 Index for the same period. Otherwise, the share units would be cancelled. GE's shares were trading for about US$30 at the time of this announcement.

For 2003, Mr. Immelt's compensation also included a base salary of $3 million plus a cash bonus of $4.325 million. The amounts of cash bonuses are determined by GE's compensation committee upon evaluation of an individual's performance for the year, including contribution to financial performance. According to the compensation committee, after taking into account cash bonus and restricted share units, more than 75% of Mr. Immelt's potential compensation for 2003 was at risk. GE also required that its CEO own six times salary in company shares.

Required

a. What balance between short-run and long-run CEO effort is the GE compensation plan likely to induce? Explain.
b. What are some of the dysfunctional effects for the firm of too much risk imposed on a risk-averse manager?
c. One-half of the restricted share units awarded to Mr. Immelt is based on meeting an operating cash flow target. Evaluate the relative precision and sensitivity of operating cash flow and net income as performance measures. Also, evaluate the effects on manager effort motivation of eliminating "unusual events" from the cash flow-based performance measure.
d. To what extent are the restricted share units awarded to Mr. Immelt based on shareholder return subject to the "pump and dump" behaviour that some managers seemed to adopt when their compensation was based on ESOs?

12. On November 18, 2002, *The Globe and Mail* (p. B4) reported "CEO assails pay disclosure rules." This referred to a speech by Claude Lamoureux, then CEO of Ontario Teachers Pension Plan Board. The Board is a major owner of and shareholder in numerous

companies, hence vitally interested in questions of executive motivation and compensation. Mr. Lamoureux's concern was with the OSC rules requiring firms to disclose and explain the compensation of their five most highly paid employees. He argues that the effect of these rules is simply to put upward pressure on pay levels, as executives demand raises to meet or exceed that of their peers in other companies.

In this regard, the RBC compensation plan (Example 10.1) states that an executive's total compensation is positioned relative to the median of what is paid by a group of similar companies.

Required

a. Explain the argument in favour of companies disclosing compensation information of their senior executives. Why do you think that Mr. Lamoureux, CEO of a very large and powerful institutional investor, rejected this argument?

b. How do you think the policy of RBC of relating its total executive compensation to the median of that paid by the comparable companies will affect the level of executive compensation in the banking industry over time?

13. Refer to Theory in Practice 10.5 re: Zions Bancorporation.

Required

a. Why would Zions Bancorporation use a market-based approach to estimating its stock option expense, instead of a model-based approach?

b. Why is the ESOARS-based ESO value so much lower than the model-based value? Assume that ESOARS purchasers are risk averse.

c. Do you agree with Zions's approach? Explain why or why not.

14. Grein, Hand, and Klassen (2005) studied the stock price reaction to repricing of ESOs. They examined a sample of 72 Canadian companies that repriced ESOs during the years 1994–2001. They found a 4.9% average positive abnormal share price reaction for their sample firms over a narrow window of three days surrounding the repricing announcement. Furthermore, the lower the stock market return on the firm's shares for the six-month period leading up to the repricing (and thus the greater the fall in value of employee ESOs), the more positive the stock market's reaction to the repricing.

They also found that the probability a firm would reprice its ESOs was greater when the CEO and the Board chair were the same person (their proxy for poor corporate governance).

Required

a. Explain reasons why firms may reprice their ESOs. Use efficient contracting and agency theory concepts in your answer where appropriate.

b. Which of the reasons you identified is most likely to predict the researchers' finding that share prices for their sample firms increased on average following ESO repricing? Does this finding support efficient securities market theory? Explain.

15. Aboody, Johnson, and Kasznik (AJK; 2010) examined a sample of 1364 firms over the years 1990–1996 that suffered a decrease in share price of 30% or more. Of these firms, 300 repriced their ESOs. They found that the earnings and cash flows of the repricing firms significantly exceeded, on average, those of the firms that did not reprice for up to five years after repricing. They also found that this improved operating performance was concentrated in firms with the greatest economic incentives to reprice. In addition, improved operating performance was concentrated in firms that repriced only for executives. Firms that extended repricing to all employees did not exhibit any additional improvement in performance.

Required

a. Why did operating performance of repricing firms for up to five years after repricing exceed that of non-repricing firms?

b. AJK found that improved operating performance was concentrated in firms with the greatest economic incentives to reprice. Suggest some of these economic incentives.

c. Suggest reasons why AJK found no additional operating performance improvement when repricing was extended beyond executives to all employees.

16. Ittner, Larcker, and Rajan (ILR; 1997) studied the relative weights placed on financial and non-financial performance measures in CEO bonus contracts for a sample of 317 U.S. firms across 48 industries for 1993–1994. Recall that RBC (Example 10.1) includes attainment of non-financial performance measures (i.e., personal goals) as a criterion for its short-term incentive awards. Non-financial performance measures in the RBC plan include goals with respect to risk management, cost management, new revenue initiatives, financing, and development of U.S. operations. Financial performance measures are net income growth and return on equity.

ILR found empirical support for the following hypotheses about the relative weights on financial and non-financial performance measures in compensation plans:

i. *Noise in net income.* The lower the correlation between manager effort and net income (measured by the correlation between stock market and accounting-based returns), the less the relative weight on financial performance measures.

ii. *Firm strategy.* "Prospector firms" (growth and innovation oriented, identify and adapt quickly to new product/service opportunities) will have greater relative weight on non-financial performance measures than "defender" firms (stable set of products/services, emphasis on increasing efficiency to reduce operating costs).

iii. *Product quality.* The greater the firm commitment to quality, the greater the relative weight on non-financial performance measures.

iv. *Regulation.* Regulated firms will have greater relative weight on non-financial performance measures than non-regulated firms.

Required

a. Give intuitive arguments to explain these four hypotheses.

b. Which of these four hypotheses might help explain the inclusion by RBC of non-financial performance measures in its short-term incentive awards?

17. Note: This question integrates several topics from earlier sections of the text.

UnitedHealth Group, Inc. is a large U.S. health insurance company. In a May 11, 2006, SEC filing, the company revealed a significant deficiency in its stock option granting practices, leading to a potential reduction of 2003, 2004, and 2005 reported earnings totalling about $286 million from correction of late timing of ESU grants. Of this amount, $150 million related to 2005, leading to a reduction in 2005 reported earnings of 4.5%. The company also disclosed that it would stop issuing ESOs to CEO William McGuire and other senior managers.

UnitedHealth shares fell $1.80 on May 11, closing at $44.37.

On October 15, 2006, Mr. McGuire resigned, following a report from a law firm engaged by the board that he had benefited from late timing of ESO grants and had not disclosed a conflict of interest with the chair of UnitedHealth's compensation committee.

On November 8, 2006, the company announced that it had agreed with Mr. McGuire to increase the exercise price of ESOs awarded to him from 1994 to 2002 to the highest share price for the year the ESOs were awarded, resulting in a material reduction in the value of the awards. Similar repricing applied to other senior officers. The company also announced that its financial statements from 1994 to 2005 could no longer be relied on, and that it would delay filing its financial results for third quarter, 2006, until the amounts of earnings restatements were fully determined. In December 2007, Mr. McGuire agreed to return about $468 million of ESOs and other benefits to the company.

Required

a. Use efficient contracting theory to explain why a company awards ESOs as compensation.
b. Use the power theory of compensation to explain why a company may engage in late timing of ESO awards.
c. UnitedHealth shares are listed on the New York Stock Exchange. On May 11, 2006, the Dow Jones Index fell by 141.92 points, a decline of 1.22%. UnitedHealth's stock beta at this time was 0.4, according to Reuters/business. The risk-free interest rate was 5%, or about 0.0001 per day. Calculate the abnormal return on UnitedHealth shares for May 11.
d. The company stated that there would be no effect on cash flows as a result of its reductions in reported earnings (presumably, it felt any effect on income tax would be negligible). If so, give reasons why its share price fell on May 11.
e. During the years of UnitedHealth's late timing, the rules of APB 25 applied (see Section 8.6). Explain why correcting the late timing resulted in an increase in compensation expense under APB 25.
f. What effect, if any, would late timing of ESOs have on their expected time to exercise? Explain.
g. In what other ways have CEOs manipulated the value of their ESO awards?

18. Refer to Theory in Practice 3.2, in Chapter 3.

Required

a. The Kmart CEO charged by the SEC was hired in May 2000 and fired in March 2002. Despite Kmart losses of $3.9 billion for the five quarters ended April 2002, the CEO received total compensation of almost $23 million during his tenure. Presumably, much of this compensation was in the form of Kmart shares and ESOs. Awarding manager compensation in the form of company shares and ESOs should, in theory, discourage the type of opportunistic behaviour charged against the Kmart executives. Explain why.
b. The theory seems to have broken down in Kmart's case. Explain why. Suggest an alternative, non-opportunistic strategy that management could have adopted to control the damage in response to Kmart's solvency problem.

19. In 1992, the SEC introduced regulations requiring U.S. firms to disclose to their shareholders information about the compensation of the firm's five highest paid executives. Due to

continuing public concern about high executive compensation levels, the SEC introduced further disclosure regulations in 2006 and 2010. These included requirements for a management discussion of its executive compensation policies, improved disclosure of executive stock option awards including the amount charged to expense during the year for such awards (recall that in 1992 stock option awards did not require expensing), golden parachutes, and increased risk disclosures. These regulations are briefly described in Section 10.7.

In Canada, the Canadian Securities Administrators introduced Form 51-102F6, effective December 2008, and amended July 2011. These requirements are substantially similar to current SEC requirements.

Required

a. What are the arguments in favour of giving shareholders more information about executive compensation, including its relationship to risk management?

b. Many of the disclosure requirements relate to longer-term incentive compensation, such as ESOs and/or restricted stock. What is the argument in favour of awarding compensation such as ESOs and/or restricted stock to senior executives?

c. What are the arguments against making executive pay too dependent on ESOs? Explain.

d. To what extent do you think that these disclosure requirements will improve the working of the managerial labour market? Explain. Include a definition of a well-working managerial labour market in your answer.

e. If the managerial labour market is fully efficient (that is, analogous to an efficient securities market), would manager incentive plans based on risky performance measures such as share price and reported net income be needed? Explain why or why not.

20. In May 2009, financial media reported that over 59% of shareholders of Royal Dutch Shell plc voted against the company's 2008 executive compensation report. The objection arose because of bonuses awarded to executives even though performance targets for the 2006–2008 period were not met.

While the vote was non-binding, Shell's Board chairman said the Board would "reflect carefully" on the vote and would consult with major shareholders.

In September 2009, the chair of Shell's compensation committee indicated that he would resign and leave the company. Another member resigned and moved to the audit committee.

Required

a. What are the advantages and disadvantages to the company and its shareholders of giving shareholders a non-binding say on pay?

b. Should non-binding say on pay be strengthened by making it binding on the company? Explain.

21. In Section 1.2, we noted a provision of the 2002 Sarbanes-Oxley Act (SOX)—namely, the requirement for the CEO and Chief Financial Officer (CFO) of public companies to certify the proper operation of their internal controls (ICs) over financial reporting, with deficiencies and their remediation to be publicly reported. Wang (2010) pointed out that the CFO is the senior executive primarily responsible for the quality of the firm's financial reporting, and thus that this reporting quality reflects the quality of the CFO's effort.

Wang compared the compensation of CFOs for a large sample of public companies before (1998–2001) and after (2002–2005) SOX, separately analyzing firms with weak ICs (one or more deficiencies reported post-SOX) and firms with strong ICs (no deficiencies reported). He found significant differences in CFO compensation post-SOX relative to pre-SOX, with average compensation of CFOs of weak IC firms lower, and that of CFOs of strong IC firms higher, than before. He also found a significant increase in the probability of a weak IC CFO being fired, relative to that of a strong CFO.

Required

a. Based on Wang's findings, what was the effect of SOX on the reservation utilities of CFOs? Explain your answer.

b. Wang also found that, for weak IC firms, when return on assets (ROA) increased post-SOX, executive bonuses, but not other compensation components, increased significantly. No such increase was found for strong IC firms. Does this imply an increase or decrease in the informativeness of net income (i.e., ROA) with respect to the quality of manager effort for weak IC firms? What does it imply about the sophistication of compensation committees in their use of accounting information?

c. Does the operation of the managerial labour market for CFOs appear to have improved post-SOX? Explain.

d. Why is the proper operation of the managerial labour market important for a market-oriented economy?

22. Refer to Theory in Practice 9.1, which describes UBS's plans to pay a substantial percentage of senior management bonuses by means of UBS bonds.

Required

Evaluate the effect of such a bonus plan, relative to a bonus plan paying all bonus in terms of company stock, on a senior manager's propensity to:

a. Adopt risky operating strategies

b. Adopt conditionally conservative accounting policies

c. Cover up the effects of shirking on effort by opportunistically managing reported earnings upward

Notes

1. See Chapter 9, Note 5.

2. This positive correlation is not predicted by the single-period agency models of Chapter 9. In those models, the agent's hard work is motivated by the contract and thus known in advance (see Chapter 9, Note 5). Thus, current earnings reveal nothing about the agent's performance and ability, so that we would not expect any relationship between market response to earnings and manager compensation—the correlation should be zero with a single-period contract. The BES study implicitly assumes a multi-period model, not considered in Chapter 9.

3. Cash compensation (i.e., salary plus bonus) tends to be based on accounting-based measures of performance, such as earnings. Earnings do not appear to explain other components of manager compensation, such as stock options, very well.

4. In a related study, Banker, Huang, and Natarajan (BHN; 2009) reported a high association between security market response to net income and cash flow, and manager compensation awards. They also demonstrated that as the informativeness of net income and cash flow for investors increases, so does their informativeness for compensation purposes.

Since both BES and BHN find a significant positive correlation between security market response to earnings and manager cash compensation, they helped to resolve the fundamental problem (Section 1.10), which asserts the difficulty of combining the investor-informing and manager-motivating roles of financial reporting. However, to fully resolve the fundamental problem, the association between security market response to earnings and manager compensation would have to be perfect. This is possible only under ideal conditions.

5. This latter change has also been adopted by other firms. For example, UBS AG, a large Switzerland-based multinational financial firm, will pay only one-third of bonuses in the current year, with the remainder placed in trust for two years and clawed back if there are subsequent losses or misconduct.

6. When there is more than one performance measure in the contract, the sensitivity concept becomes more complex. An increase, say, in effort increases the expected value of *all* the performance measures. In our context, an effort increase has a direct effect of increasing the expected value of net income. However, the expected value of share price also increases. To the extent that there is positive covariance between net income and share price, the increase in expected share price dilutes the ability of net income to convey information about effort, reducing its sensitivity and hence its weight in the mix of performance measures. A similar phenomenon reduces the sensitivity of share price.

   This argument can also be interpreted from a risk standpoint. Covariance between net income and share price measures the extent to which random factors affecting net income also affect share price—that is, the *common noise*. To avoid impacting the manager's compensation twice for the same noise, the weights on the performance measures are reduced by an amount that depends on the covariance between them.

7. For a methodology to estimate a firm's investment opportunities, and evidence that the proportion of share price-based compensation in firms' compensation contracts increases with investment opportunities, see Baber, Janakiraman, and Kang (1996).

8. Indeed, Şabac showed that anticipation of a longer-term payoff from current effort can be too effective. Since future compensation derived from current R&D and/or capital projects is risky, the manager must be paid a substantial risk premium if reservation utility is to be attained. To correct for this, the current period's proportion of net income to the manager is reduced somewhat in order to lower current period effort below what the manager would otherwise exert. Reducing effort reduces the manager's risk (lower effort means less R&D and fewer capital projects), thereby restoring an optimal tradeoff between the benefits of effort to the firm and the costs to the firm of the manager's risk aversion.

9. This is not to say that RPE does not operate in other contexts. For example, a doctor may be reimbursed by a medical plan based on the average time required for a procedure across the medical profession, and an auto repair shop may charge for a repair based on the average cost of the repair across similar vehicles.

10. Albuquerque also conducted a stronger RPE test, which estimates the past relationship between firm and peer group share price performance. With this relationship established, the *expected* level of peer group effect on CEO compensation can be estimated from share price performance for the current year. The question then is, is the actual level of CEO compensation in the current year significantly different from this expected amount? Albuquerque reported no significant difference, suggesting continuing use of RPE by her sample firms.

11. In economics, a situation where an oligopolist chooses product price is known as Bertrand competition. This is contrasted with Cournot competition, where the firm chooses the amount of production.

12. This argument should not be pushed too far. If a high degree of competition is due to numerous firms in the industry, it becomes more difficult to arrange cooperation, even implicitly. Also, the non-cooperative games illustrated in Section 8.10 suggest that cooperative strategies are subject to collapse.

13. In technical terms, compensation from plans that limit downside risk but not upside risk is a convex function of performance. Thus, plans with a bogey but no cap are convex, as are ESO plans.

14. This does not necessarily imply inefficient securities markets, since, under semi-strong efficiency, share prices reflect only publicly available information.

15. However, if the ESOs are deep in the money, the manager may avoid adopting risky projects to reduce the likelihood that share price, hence ESO value, will fall. That is, the expected payoff from holding a deep-in-the-money ESO is similar to that of holding the share, as pointed out in Section 8.6. This effect also applies to the manager's holdings of company stock. These possibilities illustrate the difficulties of evaluating the effects of compensation risk on managerial actions. These effects will vary depending not only on ESO holdings, but on the manager's risk aversion, on the extent to which the manager must hold an equity position in the company, on the manager's outside wealth, and on the extent to which the manager may be able to compensate for compensation risk by diversification and hedging.

16. RBC states in its proxy circular that it does not engage in late timing.

17. For firm-specific risk, share price would not reflect this risk to the extent investors can diversify it away. However, the market may not be aware of the extent of risk because of poor risk disclosure and off balance sheet activities. Also, if all firms in important industries (e.g., banking) adopt risky strategies, this risk quickly becomes economy-wide, as demonstrated by the 2007–2008 market meltdowns. Economy-wide risk is not diversifiable.

18. These arguments are based on R.A. Lambert and D.F. Larcker, "Firm Performance and the Compensation of Chief Executive Officers," working paper, January 1993.

19. Also, managers often claim that they do not control special item losses, hence they object to their deduction for compensation purposes. However, such losses can still be informative about effort, even if not under manager control (see Chapter 9, Note 16). However, it is inconsistent to reward managers for special item gains but not charge them with losses, as reported by Gaver and Gaver (1998).

20. From an optimal contracting perspective, whether restricted stock is a more efficient compensation device than ESOs depends on a number of other factors, such as employee risk aversion and the volatility of the firm's operations. Hall and Murphy (2002) analyzed this issue, arguing that if an increase in stock-based compensation is accompanied by a reduction in CEO cash compensation, as opposed to simply being added on to existing compensation (this is consistent with the manager not receiving more than reservation utility), the firm is better off to use restricted stock rather than ESOs with a positive strike price (restricted stock is similar to an ESO with zero strike price). The reason, according to Hall and Murphy, is that, other things equal, a share of restricted stock is preferred by the CEO to an ESO (since the ESO requires payment of the strike price while no payment is required for a share). Consequently, the CEO is willing to give up more cash compensation for restricted stock than for ESOs. Then, for a given reduction in cash compensation, the firm can issue more shares via restricted stock than via ESOs. Given that it is more difficult for the CEO to work out from under the risk imposed by restricted stock than under ESOs, the CEO's incentive to work hard is increased.

    If restricted stock can be a more efficient motivator than ESOs, why have ESOs been a more popular compensation vehicle? The answer seems to be that issuing restricted stock has always required expensing, whereas ESOs have required expensing only since 2004. Some firms were apparently willing to use a less-efficient compensation device (ESOs) in order to report higher net income. Once ESO expensing was required, this advantage disappeared. We would thus expect to see many firms moving toward more restricted stock compensation over time. Note that the RBC plan pays mid-term compensation, and possibly short-term compensation, in the form of restricted stock.

21. ESO recipients do not necessarily value their ESOs at their real value, however. A study by Farrell, Krische, and Sedatole (FKS; 2011) included a survey of ESO recipients who were asked to estimate the value of their ESOs. The estimates of 75% of these recipients were less than Black-Scholes value, with the remainder overestimating by as much as seven times Black-Scholes.

    To the extent recipients misvalue their ESOs, their effort incentives, and thus contract efficiency, are affected. While risk aversion would partially explain these underestimates, FKS regarded behavioural biases, such as limited attention, as a major contributor. The authors reported the results of an education session, which substantially increased recipients' value underestimates.

22. Recall from Section 10.4 that stock and ESO compensation are intended to lengthen the manager's decision horizon, thereby encouraging long-term effort. Long-term effort, such as R&D and major capital investments, is likely to be risky.

23. Severance pay does reduce the manager's effort incentive, since the manager must bear risk if effort is to be exerted. However, Rau and Xu pointed out that other compensation components can be adjusted to restore the desired effort level.

24. The power theory is particularly relevant to firms with dual-class common share structures. Such firms feature a separation of voting rights and rights to dividends. In effect, the holders of the high voting rights shares control the company with relatively few shares, while dividends are shared between the two classes. Thus, corporate power is concentrated in the hands of insiders. This type of share structure is common in Canada and several other countries.

Smart, Thirumalai, and Zutter (STZ; 2008) compared a sample of U.S. dual-class firms to a sample of single-class firms over a five-year period following an IPO. They reported lower market valuations on average for dual-class firms. However, they also reported that share returns for both types of companies are similar.

The question then is, *why* does the market put a lower value on dual-class firms? STZ reported similar earnings performance for both types, suggesting that anticipation of lower operating performance following the IPO is not the reason.

Rather, STZ looked to corporate governance. They found that CEO turnover is slightly lower for dual class than for single class, not inconsistent with a management entrenchment reason for lower share valuations. If so, the CEO compensation contracts for dual-class firms are less efficient than those of single-class firms, consistent with the power theory.

Chapter 11
Earnings Management

Figure 11.1 Organization of Chapter 11

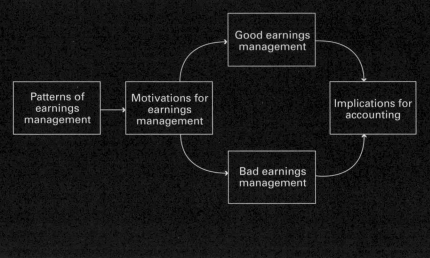

11.1 OVERVIEW

Earnings management can be viewed from both a financial reporting and a contracting perspective. From a financial reporting perspective, managers may use earnings management to avoid reporting losses or to meet analysts' earnings forecasts, thereby hoping to avoid the reputation damage and strong negative share price reaction that quickly follows a failure to meet investor expectations. Also, they may record excessive writeoffs or emphasize earnings constructs other than net income, such as "pro-forma" earnings. Some of these tactics suggest that managers do not fully accept securities market efficiency.

There is another view of earnings management, however. Management may use it to report a stream of smooth and growing earnings over time. Given securities market efficiency, this requires management to draw on its inside information. Thus, earnings management can be a vehicle for the communication of management's inside information to investors. Interpreted this way, income smoothing leads to the interesting, and perhaps surprising, conclusion that some earnings management can be useful from a financial reporting perspective.

From a contracting perspective, earnings management can be used as a way to protect the firm from the consequences of unforeseen events when contracts are rigid and incomplete. Also, as we saw in Chapter 9, when the manager controls the accounting system, compensation contracts that allow some earnings management can be more efficient than ones that do not. Too much earnings management, however, may reduce the usefulness of financial reports for investors. This is particularly so if opportunistic earnings management is not fully disclosed. Also, earnings management affects the manager's motivation to exert effort, because managers can use earnings management to smooth their compensation over time, thereby reducing compensation risk. But, we have seen that managers need to bear some risk if they are to work hard.

For whatever reason, it should be apparent that managers have a strong interest in the bottom line. Given that managers can choose accounting policies from a set of policies (for example, GAAP), it is natural to expect that they will choose policies that help achieve their objectives. They may also take real actions affecting earnings, such as cutting R&D. As mentioned, these choices can be motivated either by efficient markets and contracts, or by opportunism and rejection of market efficiency. Whatever the reason, this is called **earnings management**.

An understanding of earnings management is important to accountants, because it enables an improved understanding of the usefulness of net income, both for reporting to investors and for contracting. It may also assist accountants to avoid some of the serious legal and reputation consequences that arise when firms become financially distressed. Such distress is often preceded by serious abuse of earnings management.

> **Earnings management** *is the choice by a manager of accounting policies, or real actions, affecting earnings so as to achieve some specific reported earnings objective.*

Thus, earnings management includes both accounting policy choices and real actions.

It should be mentioned that choice of accounting policies is interpreted quite broadly. While the dividing line is not clear-cut, it is convenient to divide accounting policy choices into two categories. One is the choice of accounting policies per se, such as straight-line versus declining-balance amortization, or policies for revenue recognition. The other category is discretionary accruals, such as provisions for credit losses, warranty costs, inventory values, and timing and amounts of low-persistence special items such as writeoffs, and provisions for restructuring.

Regardless of its rationale, it is important to realize that there is an "iron law" surrounding accrual-based earnings management, which will be familiar from introductory accounting. This is that *accruals reverse*. Thus, a manager who manages earnings upward to an amount greater than can be sustained will find that the reversal of these accruals in subsequent periods will force future earnings downward just as surely as current earnings were raised.[1] Then, even more earnings management is needed if the reporting of losses is to be further postponed. In effect, if a firm is performing poorly, earnings management cannot indefinitely postpone the day of reckoning. Thus, the possibility that earnings management can be good should not be used to rationalize misleading or fraudulent reporting. The accountant treads a fine line between earnings management and earnings mismanagement. Ultimately, the location of this line must be determined by effective corporate governance, reinforced by securities and managerial labour markets, standard setters, securities commissions, and the courts.

The iron law of accruals reversal leads to an important aspect of earnings management. All the models of earnings management in Chapter 9 were single period. Even then, we showed that some earnings management could, in theory, be beneficial. However, to better understand earnings management, we need to think in terms of multiple periods. Then, further earnings management potential, such as income smoothing and "big bath," is revealed.

Yet, multi-period horizons also operate to inhibit earnings management. For example, to what extent is a manager's propensity to over- or understate reported net income reduced by the knowledge that accrual-based misstatements will inevitably reverse? To what extent do markets, such as the securities market and the manager's reputation on the managerial labour market, help to control opportunistic earnings management? We saw some evidence in Wolfson's (1985) study of oil and gas limited partnerships in Section 10.2 that reputation effects reduce but do not eliminate the moral hazard problem. While a multi-period horizon increases the potential for earnings management, it also operates to constrain the practice.

Another way to manage earnings is by means of *real* variables, such as advertising, R&D, maintenance, timing of purchases and disposals of capital assets, stuffing the channels, overproduction, etc. These devices may be costly, since they directly affect the firm's longer-run interests. Nevertheless, managers use them since the costs of managing earnings using accounting variables can also be high, due to reporting failures such as Enron and WorldCom and resulting legislation, notably Sarbanes-Oxley. Indeed, the survey of Graham, Harvey, and Rajgopal (2005), introduced in Section 8.10, found that most respondents indicated a willingness to manage real variables in order to meet earnings targets and/or smooth earnings, rather than risk the legal and reputation consequences of aggressive accounting policies. Use of accounting policy variables for earnings management purposes received relatively little support from the respondents. Note that earnings management by real variables manages cash flows as well as earnings.

Roychowdhury (2006) reported empirical evidence consistent with real earnings management. He found that firms with earnings close to zero opportunistically manage real variables, such as sales discounts, production levels, R&D and other discretionary expenditures, so as to increase reported earnings.

However, in the remainder of this chapter, we concentrate primarily on management of reported earnings based on accounting variables rather than real variables due to their historical importance, their relevance to accounting, and the probability that the lessons of Enron and WorldCom will grow dim over time.

Figure 11.1 outlines the organization of this chapter.

decks." Because of accrual reversal, this enhances the probability of future reported profits. In effect, the recording of large writeoffs puts future earnings "in the bank."

2. **Income minimization** This is similar to taking a bath, but less extreme. Such a pattern may be chosen by a politically visible firm during periods of high profitability, or when firms seek legislation to protect themselves from foreign competition. Policies that suggest income minimization include rapid writeoffs of capital assets and intangibles, and the expensing of advertising and R&D expenditures. Income tax considerations, such as use of LIFO inventory as currently allowed in the United States, provide another set of motivations for this pattern.

3. **Income maximization** From contract theory, managers may engage in a pattern of maximization of reported net income for bonus purposes, providing this does not put them above the cap. Firms that are close to debt covenant violations may also maximize income.

4. **Income smoothing** This is perhaps the most interesting earnings management pattern. From a contracting theory perspective, risk-averse managers prefer a less variable bonus stream, other things equal. Consequently, managers may smooth reported earnings over time so as to receive relatively constant compensation. Efficient compensation contracting may exploit this effect, and condone some income smoothing as a low-cost way to attain the manager's reservation utility.

We considered covenants in long-term lending agreements in Section 9.5. The more volatile the stream of reported net income, the higher the probability that covenant violation will occur. This provides another smoothing incentive—to reduce volatility of reported net income so as to smooth covenant ratios over time.

Managers may feel, with some justification, that they may be fired when reported earnings are low. Income smoothing can reduce the likelihood of reporting low earnings.

Finally, firms may smooth reported net income for external reporting purposes. If used responsibly, smoothing can convey inside information to the market by enabling the firm to credibly communicate its expected persistent earning power.

It should be apparent that these various earnings management patterns can be in conflict. Over time, the pattern chosen by a firm may vary due to changes in contracts, levels of profitability, and political visibility. Even at a given point in time, the firm may face conflicting needs, say, to reduce reported net income for political reasons, increase it to meet analysts' forecasts, or smooth it for contracting purposes.

11.3 EVIDENCE OF EARNINGS MANAGEMENT FOR BONUS PURPOSES

A paper by Healy (1985), entitled "The Effect of Bonus Schemes on Accounting Decisions," is a seminal investigation of a contractual motivation for earnings management. Healy observed that managers have inside information on the firm's net income before earnings management.[2] Since outside parties, including the board itself, may be unable to learn what this number is, he predicted that managers would manage net income so as to maximize their bonuses under their firms' compensation plans. By looking closely at the structure of bonus plans, Healy came up with specific predictions of how and under what circumstances managers will engage in this type of earnings management.

Healy's study was confined to firms whose compensation plans are based on current reported net income only. These will be called **bonus schemes** for the rest of this section. As we saw earlier, in Section 10.3, net income-based financial targets are a major input into short-term incentive awards. We also pointed out, in Section 10.4.3, reasons why bonus schemes may have bogeys and caps. For a bonus scheme with a cap, the incentive compensation ceases beyond a certain level. For a bonus scheme with a bogey, incentive compensation does not kick in until some specified level of financial performance, for example, 10% ROE, is reached. Figure 11.2 illustrates a typical bonus scheme.

In the figure, the bonus increases linearly (for example, 10% of net income) between the bogey and the cap. For net incomes equal to or below the bogey, bonus is zero. If there were no cap, the bonus would increase along the dotted line. Otherwise, the bonus becomes a constant for net income greater than the cap. Such bonus plans are called **piecewise linear**.

Consider the incentives to manage reported net income faced by a manager subject to such a scheme. If net income is low (that is, below the bogey), the manager has an

Figure 11.2 Typical Bonus Scheme

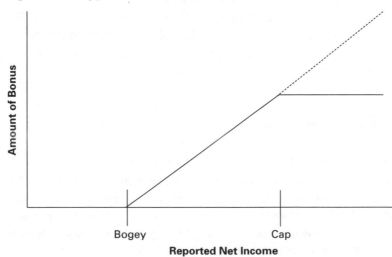

How does a manager manage net income? Healy assumed that managers use accruals. To illustrate how accruals may be used to manage earnings, we begin by repeating again the formula given in Sections 5.4.1 and 6.3:

$$\text{Net income} = \text{Cash flow from operations} \pm \text{Net accruals} \qquad (11.1)$$

This can be broken down into

$$\text{Net income} = \text{Cash flow from operations} \pm \text{Net non-discretionary accruals}$$
$$\pm \text{Net discretionary accruals}$$

Recall that discretionary accruals are accruals over which the manager can exercise some control. While it is easy for a researcher to estimate total accruals as the difference between net income and cash flow from operations, estimation of the discretionary component poses a major challenge.

To illustrate the interplay between discretionary and non-discretionary accruals, consider the hypothetical example in Table 11.1.

In the table, a positive sign for an accrual means that, for a given cash flow, it increases net income and vice versa. The information in the table could be taken from the statement of cash flows.[1] For simplicity, we have assumed that there is no income tax expense. Assume that explanations for the four accrual items are as follows:

■ **Amortization expense** Annual amortization expense is laid down by the firm's amortization policy and its estimates of assets' useful lives. Given this policy, amortization expense is a non-discretionary accrual. Of course, the firm might change its policy,

Table 11.1 Discretionary and Non-Discretionary Accruals

Cash flow, as per cash flow statement		$1,000
Less: Amortization expense	− 50	
Add: Increase in (net) accounts receivable during the year	+ 40	
Add: Increase in inventory during the year	+100	
Add: Decrease in accounts payable and accrued liabilities during the year	+ 30	120
Net income, as per income statement		$1,120

for example, by changing estimates of useful life, in which case amortization expense would contain a discretionary component.

- **Increase in net accounts receivable** Assume that this derives from a decrease in the allowance for doubtful accounts, resulting from a less conservative estimate than in previous years. This accrual is discretionary, since management has some flexibility to control the amount. Other reasons for the increase could include earlier revenue recognition, a more generous credit policy, keeping the books open beyond the year-end, or simply an increase in volume of business. The first three of these accruals are discretionary, the fourth is non-discretionary.

  Thus, we see that there can be several reasons for an increase in receivables. A researcher with access only to the comparative financial statements would find it difficult to know what particular reason or reasons accounted for the increase, or whether the increase was discretionary or non-discretionary or both. Nevertheless, it is clear that the manager who wishes to increase reported net income through accounts receivable accruals has several means available.

- **Increase in inventory** Assume that this derives from the firm manufacturing for stock during a period of excess manufacturing capacity. The result is to include fixed overhead costs in inventory rather than charging them off to expense as unfavourable volume variances. This accrual is discretionary, and illustrates the use of a real variable to manage earnings. However, non-discretionary reasons for the increase could be an inventory buildup in anticipation of a strike, or simply increased demand.

  While other reasons for the increase are possible, just as in the case of accounts receivable, discretionary income-increasing accruals are available for inventory as well.

- **Decrease in accounts payable and accrual liabilities** Assume that this derives from the firm being more optimistic about warranty claims on its products than it has been in previous years. Alternatively, or in addition, the decrease could be due to regarding certain borderline items as contingencies rather than accruals. Again, we see that there can be ample room for discretionary accruals in accounts payable.

The main point to note is that the manager has considerable discretion to manage reported net income. While it is easy to determine the change in account balances, the reasons for the change are typically unknown to the investor and researcher. Also, for many of these discretionary accruals, it would be difficult for the firm's auditors to discover the earnings management or, if they did discover it, to object, since all of the techniques mentioned, with the exception of holding the books open past the year-end, are within GAAP. A similar set of discretionary accruals to decrease reported net income is available to the manager, simply by reversing those described above.

Healy did not have access to the books and records of his sample firms, and was unable to determine the specific discretionary accruals made by those firms' managers. As a result, he had to take total accruals as a proxy for discretionary accruals. Thus, in our example, he would estimate discretionary accruals as +$120, instead of the +$170 that would be used if he had full information. The +$170 of discretionary accruals will raise between the bogey and cap. If his earnings management prediction is correct, total accruals should be income-increasing for the MID category and income-decreasing for the UPP and LOW categories.

For the 447 observations that had both a bogey and a cap, the results are summarized in Table 11.2. We see that 46% of the 281 observations in the MID portfolio had total accruals that were income-increasing. The average accrual of these 281 observations was +0.0021 of total assets (accruals were deflated by total assets so that they could be compared across firms of different sizes). For the observations in the LOW and UPP portfolios, the proportions with positive total accruals were much lower—only 9% and 10%, respectively. Also, the average accruals for these observations were negative (income-decreasing). These results are consistent with Healy's arguments that firm managers whose net incomes are below the bogey and above the cap will tend to adopt income-decreasing accruals and only managers with net income between the two will tend to adopt income-increasing accruals. Thus, Healy's predictions of earnings management by managers subject to bonus schemes were supported by the empirical results.

It should be emphasized that empirical earnings management studies face severe methodological problems. As mentioned earlier, a major difficulty is that discretionary

Table 11.2 Observations With Both a Bogey and a Cap

	Proportion of Firm Years with Income-Increasing and Income-Decreasing Accruals		Number of Observations	Average Accruals
	Income-Increasing	Income-Decreasing		
LOW	0.09	0.91	22	−0.0671
MID	0.46	0.54	281	+0.0021
UPP	0.10	0.90	144	−0.0536
			447	

Source: Data from P.M. Healy, "The Effect of Bonus Schemes on Accounting Decisions," *Journal of Accounting and Economics* (April 1985).

accruals cannot be directly observed. Consequently, some proxy must be used. Using total accruals, as Healy did, introduces measurement error into the discretionary accruals variable, making it more difficult to detect earnings management should it exist. For example, the amount of non-discretionary accruals is likely correlated with net income. As Kaplan (1985) pointed out, a firm with reported net income above the cap of its bonus plan may have low non-discretionary accruals if its high income is due to an unexpected increase in demand that runs down inventory. Then, the low total accruals that are used to infer earnings management are really due to the level of the firm's real economic activity and not to low discretionary accruals. Healy was aware of these problems and conducted additional tests to control for them, which he interpreted as confirming his findings.[5]

Subsequently, a more sophisticated procedure to estimate discretionary accruals was developed by Jones (1991), who studied the actions of firms to lower reported net income during import relief investigations. In the United States, trade legislation allows for the granting of assistance such as tariff protection to firms in industries that are unfairly affected by foreign competition. The International Trade Commission (ITC) is responsible for investigating whether there is injury. This investigation will consider economic factors such as sales and profits of affected firms. However, there is also a considerable political dimension to the granting of relief, since consumers will end up paying higher prices, and there may be retaliation by foreign countries. A determination of injury by the ITC goes initially to the president, who has 60 days to decide whether to grant relief. If relief is not granted, Congress may step in and override the president.

Thus, it is by no means clear that a deterioration of unmanaged profitability is sufficient for relief to be granted. As a result, affected firms have an incentive to choose accounting policies to lower their reported net income even more, so as to bolster their case. Of course, this incentive will be known to the ITC, politicians, and the public. However, as Jones pointed out, these constituencies may not have the motivation to adjust for any downward manipulation of earnings. For example, the effect of higher prices that would follow the granting of relief to an industry may not be sufficiently great for it to be cost effective for consumers to lobby against it. Even the ITC may not be fully motivated to adjust for manipulation of earnings if it was *a priori* sympathetic to the petitioning firms. These disincentives to unwind any earnings manipulation are strengthened if it is difficult to detect. As Jones noted, an effective way to reduce reported earnings in a hard-to-detect manner is to manipulate discretionary accruals.

Jones collected a sample of 23 firms from five industries involved in six import relief investigations by the ITC over the period 1980–1985 inclusive. As mentioned, it is easy to determine a firm's total accruals for the year, such as the difference between operating cash flows and net income. Jones used an alternate approach, taking the change in non-cash working capital for the year from the comparative balance sheets, plus amortization expense, as her measure of total accruals. Accruals are thus interpreted quite broadly here, being the net effect of all recorded operating events during the year other than cash flows. Changes in accounts receivable and payable are accruals, as are changes in inventories. Amortization expense is a negative accrual.

The question then is, how to decompose total accruals into discretionary and non-discretionary components? Jones's approach was to estimate the following regression equation for each firm j in her sample, over a period prior to the year of the ITC investigation:

$$TA_{jt} = \alpha_j + \beta_{1j} \Delta REV_{jt} + \beta_{2j} PPE_{jt} + \epsilon_{jt}$$

where

TA_{jt} = total accruals for firm j in year t. A positive TA_{jt} is income increasing, and vice versa

ΔREV_{jt} = revenues for firm j in year t less revenues for year $t - 1$

PPE_{jt} = gross property, plant, and equipment for firm j in year t

ϵ_{jt} = a residual term that captures all impacts on TA_{jt} other than those from ΔREV_{jt} and PPE_{jt}

The coefficients α_j, β_{1j}, and β_{2j} are simply constants to be estimated (in particular, β_{1j} and β_{2j} have nothing to do with a stock's beta discussed in Section 4.5.1). We expect β_{1j} to be positive, since the purpose of ΔREV_{jt} is to control for non-discretionary accruals of current assets and liabilities on the grounds that these depend on changes in business activity as measured by revenues—more business activity, more non-discretionary accruals. Also, PPE_{jt} controls for the non-discretionary component of amortization expense, on the grounds that this depends on the firm's investment in capital assets. Since amortization is income-reducing, β_{2j} is expected to be negative.

With this regression model estimated for each sample firm, Jones used it to predict non-discretionary accruals during the ITC investigation years. That is,

$$U_{jp} = TA_{jp} - (\alpha_j + \beta_{1j} \Delta REV_{jp} + \beta_{2j} PPE_{jp})$$

where p is the year of investigation, TA_{jp} is firm j's total accruals for this year, and the quantity in brackets is the predicted non-discretionary accruals for the year p from the regression model. The term U_{jp} is thus an estimate of discretionary accruals for year p for firm j.[7] If firms are recording discretionary accruals to lower reported net income, the U_{jp} should be negative across the sample firms.

Jones found evidence of the predicted behaviour. For almost all firms in the sample, discretionary accruals as measured above were significantly negative in the ITC investigation years. Significant negative accruals were not found in the years immediately preceding and following the investigations. These results, while perhaps not as strong as might be expected, suggest that affected firms were systematically choosing accrual policies so as to improve their case for import protection.

This procedure, called the **Jones model**, and modifications of it, has become a generally accepted way to estimate discretionary accruals.[8] For example, Holthausen, Larcker, and Sloan (HLS; 1995) used a version of the model to re-examine the Healy findings. They were able to obtain data on whether managers' annual earnings-based bonuses were in fact zero, greater than zero but less than the maximum bonus, or at the maximum.

These are substantially better data than Healy's, who had to estimate whether earnings before discretionary accruals were below bogey, between bogey and cap, or above cap on the basis of available descriptions of bonus contracts, and *assume* that if earnings were below the bogey the manager would not receive a bonus, etc.

For a sample of 443 firm-year observations over 1982–1990, HLS found that managers who received zero bonus did not use accruals to manage income downward, which differed from Healy's findings (row 1, Table 11.2). They concluded that methodological problems arising from Healy's procedures for estimating discretionary accruals explained why he appeared to find income-decreasing accruals for his low category.[9] However, HLS did find that managers who were at their bonus maxima managed accruals so as to lower reported earnings. This is consistent with Healy's results—see row 3 of Table 11.2.

We conclude that, despite methodological challenges to Healy's seminal study, there is significant evidence that, on average, managers use accruals to manage earnings so as to influence their bonuses, particularly when earnings are high.

11.4 OTHER MOTIVATIONS FOR EARNINGS MANAGEMENT

Healy's study applies to bonus contracts. However, managers may engage in earnings management for a variety of other reasons. Now, we will consider some of these.

11.4.1 Other Contracting Motivations

Debt contracts typically depend on accounting variables, arising from the moral hazard problem between manager and lender analyzed in Section 9.5. To control this problem, long-term lending contracts typically contain covenants to protect against actions by managers that are against the lenders' best interests, such as excessive dividends, additional borrowing, or letting working capital or shareholders' equity fall below specified levels, all of which dilute the security of existing lenders.

Earnings management for debt covenant purposes follows from efficient contracting theory. Given that covenant violations can impose heavy costs, firm managers will be expected to avoid them. These costs include not only direct costs imposed by the covenant, such as higher interest rates, but also indirect costs from impairment of continuing business relationships and reduced future ability to raise financing. Indeed, managers will even try to avoid being close to violation, because this will constrain their freedom of action in operating the firm. Thus, earnings management can arise as a device to reduce the probability of covenant violation in debt contracts.

Earnings management in a debt covenant context was investigated by Sweeney (1994). For a sample of firms that had defaulted on public and private debt contracts, Sweeney found significantly greater use of income-increasing accounting changes relative to a control sample, and she also found that defaulting firms tended to undertake early adoption of new accounting standards when these increased reported net income, and vice versa. Sweeney also found that most of the debt covenant violations in her sample were for private debt issues. The likely reason is that public debt contracts are much more difficult than private debt to renegotiate should the firm default. To compensate for the greater rigidity of public debt contracts, it seems that they contain less stringent covenants, relative to private debt.

DeFond and Jiambalvo (1994) also examined earnings management by firms disclosing a debt covenant violation during 1985–1988. They found evidence of the use of discretionary accruals to increase reported income in the year prior to and, to a lesser extent, in the year of the covenant violation.

Somewhat different results are reported by De Angelo, De Angelo, and Skinner (DDS; 1994). They studied a sample of 76 large, troubled firms. These were firms that had three or more consecutive loss years during 1980–1985 and had reduced dividends during the loss period. For 29 of these firms, the cut in dividends was forced by binding debt covenant constraints.

After controlling for the influence of declining sales and cash flows on accruals, DDS failed to find evidence that these 29 firms used accruals to manage earnings upward in years prior to the cut in dividends, relative to the remaining sample firms that did not face debt covenant constraints. Rather, all 29 firms exhibited large negative (that is, earnings-reducing) accruals extending for at least three years beyond the year of the dividend cut. DDS attribute this conservative behaviour in part to large, discretionary non-cash writeoffs. Apparently, these were to signal to lenders, shareholders, unions, and others that the firm was facing up to its troubles, and to prepare the ground for subsequent contract renegotiations that frequently took place.

It thus seems that when its troubles are profound, the firm's behaviour transcends debt covenant concerns and, instead, earnings management becomes part of the firm's (and its manager's) overall strategy for survival.

11.4.2 To Meet Investors' Earnings Expectations

Investors' earnings expectations can be formed in a variety of ways, such as earnings for the same period last year or on recent analyst or company forecasts.

Firms that report earnings greater than expected (i.e., positive earnings surprise) have typically enjoyed a share price increase, as investors revise upward their probabilities of good future performance. Conversely, firms with a negative earnings surprise suffer a significant share price decrease. Bartov, Givoly, and Hayn (2002), in a study over the years 1983–1997, documented significantly greater abnormal share returns for firms that exceeded their most recent analysts' earnings forecasts, relative to firms that failed to meet their forecasts. Skinner and Sloan (2002), in a study over 1984–1996, documented negative share returns for firms that failed to meet earnings expectations. These were significantly greater in magnitude than the positive returns for firms that exceeded expectations. This suggests that the market penalizes firms that fall short of expectations by more than it rewards firms that exceed them.[10]

As a result, managers have a strong incentive to ensure that earnings expectations are met, particularly if they hold ESOs or other share-related compensation. One way to do this is to manage earnings upward.[11] Rational investors will be aware of this incentive, of course. This makes meeting expectations all the more important for managers. If these are not met, the market will reason that if the manager could not find enough earnings management to avoid the shortfall, the firm's earnings outlook must be bleak indeed, and/or the firm is not well managed since it cannot predict its own future. This could explain the more severe market penalty for failure to meet expectations, particularly if the shortfall is small.

More recently, Keung, Lin, and Shih (2010), in a large sample of quarterly earnings surprises over the period 1992–2006, found that market reaction to a zero and even a small *positive* earnings surprise turned negative during 2002–2006, compared to a positive response during the earlier years of their sample. They suggested that investors' increasing skepticism during the years 1992–2001 that small earnings surprises are due to earnings management (thus not persistent) rather than to real factors is responsible. The authors reported evidence consistent with this interpretation.

Jackson and Liu (JL; 2010) studied the role of (unconditional) conservatism in earnings management. They selected a sample of firms with large accounts receivable balances over the period 1980–2004. For each sample firm year-end, they used accounts receivable writeoffs of the following year as a benchmark measure of what the allowance for bad debts on the year-end balance sheet should have been. They reported that, on average, bad debt allowances were much larger than the benchmark, with the excess increasing over time. This suggests considerable conservatism in accounts receivable valuation.

JL also reported that firms used these overstated allowances as an earnings management vehicle. If earnings before bad debt expense were close to not meeting analysts' earnings expectations, firms would draw down some of the excess to reduce bad debts expense of the current year, thus managing earnings upward to help meet expectations. Overall, the authors concluded that conservative bad debt accounting was a strategic process, with firms generally over-accruing bad debt expense to build up a large reserve, and drawing the reserve down when needed to bolster reported earnings.

Nevertheless, managers sometimes do fail to meet earnings expectations, and often offer explanations. Some explanations candidly face up to the firm's problems. Others, however, are simply excuses. For example, the weather may be blamed for disappointing results when the real reason is that the firm does not have adequate strategies to cope with the risks it faces. Barton and Mercer (2005) provided experimental evidence on analyst reaction to manager explanations for poor performance. They found that if an explanation is plausible, analysts will increase both their earnings forecasts and their opinion of management. However, if the explanation is not plausible, then earnings forecasts and analysts' opinion of management decrease. This latter finding is of interest since one might think that implausible information would simply be ignored.

Failure to meet investors' earnings expectations thus has serious consequences. There is a direct effect on the firm's share price and cost of capital as investors revise downward their probabilities of good future performance. There can also be an indirect effect through manager reputation, particularly if the shortfall is small and if manager explanations are perceived as excuses. Consequently, meeting earnings expectations and maintaining reputation are powerful earnings management incentives.

11.4.3 Stock Offerings

When a firm plans to issue new or additional shares to the public, management faces a temptation to manage earnings upward, so as to maximize the amount received from the share issue.

Cohen and Zarowin (2010) studied this possibility for a sample of firms making seasoned equity offerings (SEOs)[12] over the period 1987–2006. Consistent with several previous studies, they found, using a version of the Jones model (Section 11.3), that SEO firms recorded significantly positive discretionary accruals in the SEO year.

Cohen and Zarowin found that their sample firms also used real earnings management techniques to increase reported earnings. These were speeding up of sales recognition, overproduction,[13] and reduction of discretionary expenses such as R&D and advertising.

They also found that firms systematically substituted between these two approaches. For example, when costs of accrual management were relatively high (high net operating assets,[14] high prestige auditor, firm in a high litigation industry such as pharmaceuticals), real earnings management techniques were drawn on relatively more.

Cohen and Zarowin then examined their sample firms' performance over three years following their SEOs. They found that return on assets declined. This decline was due both to reversal of income-increasing accruals in the SEO year, and, presumably, to reduced future business following reduction of discretionary expenditures, with this latter possibility being the stronger of the two.

While firms seem to manage earnings upward in periods of share issuance, and thus report lower profitability later, the question arises whether the market is fooled by this earnings management. If it is fooled, we would expect abnormal share returns to fall in periods following the new issue as investors realize, from lower profitability, that they have overpaid.

However, an alternative, efficient markets possibility is that the market is not fooled, and that the SEO proceeds firms receive will be reduced due to investors' rational expectations that earnings management is taking place. Then, the manager might as well go ahead and manage earnings, since the market expects it. If so, there should be no abnormal negative share returns in subsequent periods. Shivakumar (2000) presented theory and empirical evidence consistent with this argument. Subsequently, Fan (2007), based on a sample of initial public offering (IPO) firms over 1987–1997, found, like Cohen and Zarowin, that managers do use discretionary accruals to manage earnings upward in IPO periods and that subsequent accrual reversals reduce future earnings. However, like Shivakumar, she did not find poorer subsequent abnormal share price performance for

Groupon Inc. is a large U.S.-based firm that sells discount coupons on the Internet for a wide range of food and merchandise. The coupons enable the purchaser to buy these products from local merchants with whom Groupon had negotiated the discount price. The company was created in 2008 and grew quickly, creating a large customer base.

From its beginnings, Groupon adopted aggressive accounting practices. For example, it recorded revenue as the full amount received from customers, despite its obligation to pay a significant portion to the merchants involved. In this way, it showed an impressive "top line" on its income statement. Recording revenue net of amounts owed to merchants would have reduced this top line by about 60%.

The company also emphasized "adjusted consolidated segment operating income (ACSOI)," a version of pro-forma income (Section 7.11.2) under which marketing costs were capitalized and amortized rather than deducted as expenses. Since the company was working hard to build up its customer base, it regarded these costs as an investment in its future rather than a current period expense. In this way, Groupon claimed to be profitable, despite substantial losses on a GAAP basis.

In November 2011, Groupon issued an IPO that attracted great interest from investors. Priced at US$20, the shares quickly exceeded $30 in early trading. However, the company's accounting issues returned. In April 2012, Groupon reported, in financial statements submitted to the SEC, a "material weakness" in internal controls (such reports are required by the Sarbanes-Oxley Act, see Section 1.2). This weakness had allowed a material understatement of expected refunds to customers (Groupon has a policy of refunding their money to customers who are not satisfied), and forced the company to restate its fourth quarter 2011 financial statements. Groupon had done nothing illegal—material weaknesses, for example, do not have to be reported in IPO prospectuses. Nevertheless, investors suspected that management must have known earlier about the underprovision and resulting profit overstatement but said nothing until forced to reveal it several months following the IPO. These suspicions added to already existing concerns about Groupon's accounting described above. Furthermore, additional concerns arose that Groupon may have been attempting to hide a decline in its customer base. As a result, the company's shares were trading below $5 in late December 2012 increasing to only $12 in December, 2013.

high-earnings management IPO firms. As suggested above, this is consistent with investors rationally anticipating the extent of an IPO firm's accruals-based earnings management and building this anticipation into the amount they pay for IPO shares. If so, no further share price decline takes place as firms report lower earnings in future.

Nevertheless, investors do not always fully anticipate IPO earnings management, as illustrated by Theory in Practice 11.1.

11.5 THE GOOD SIDE OF EARNINGS MANAGEMENT

In Section 11.1, we suggested that earnings management can be good. Here, we review these arguments, and outline theoretical and empirical evidence in their favour.

11.5.1 Blocked Communication

Our argument in favour of good earnings management is based on the **blocked communication** concept of Demski and Sappington (DS1; 1987). Frequently, agents obtain specialized information as part of their expertise, and this information can be prohibitively costly to communicate to the principal; that is, its communication is blocked. For example, it may be difficult for a physician to communicate to the patient exact details of an examination and diagnosis. Then, the physician's act (e.g., operating on the patient) must stand in not only for the physician's surgical skills but also for the information acquired during the diagnosis. DS1 showed that the presence of blocked communication can reduce the efficiency of agency contracts, since the agent may shirk on information acquisition and compensate by taking an act that, from the principal's standpoint, is sub-optimal—the physician may simply sew up a badly cut hand on the basis of a cursory examination that fails to check for possible tendon or nerve damage, for example. If so, the principal has an incentive to try to eliminate or reduce the blocked communication.

There is a variety of ways to reduce blockage. Gu and Li (2007) reported an increased positive market reaction to disclosures of business strategy by high-tech firms when the disclosures are preceded by a credible gesture of confidence in the firm by management, namely insider stock purchases. Hirst, Koonce, and Venkataraman (2007) reported, based on an experimental study, that *disaggregation* of a good news forecast (i.e., forecasting sales and expenses as well as net income) increases its credibility. They argued that disclosure of line items reduces the ability of managers to use earnings management to attain the forecast, thereby offsetting investor suspicions that the forecast may be biased upward.

In our context, earnings management can also be a device to reduce blockage. To illustrate, suppose that a manager desires to communicate the firm's expected long-run, persistent earnings potential. Assume that this amount is $1 million per annum. This earnings potential is complex inside information of the manager. If the manager simply announced it, the announcement would not be credible, since the market would find it prohibitively costly to verify. Suppose, however, that some low-persistence special item inflates earnings this period, such as a profit of $200,000 from the sale of a division. Suppose also that this item will increase current net income to $1,180,000, well above its sustainable level of $1 million. Rather than report a net income substantially higher than what is expected to persist in the long run, the manager decides to record a provision for restructuring of $180,000, thereby reducing current earnings to the $1 million the manager feels will persist.

This "unblocking" of the manager's inside information by means of large discretionary accruals to produce a desired result has credibility. The market knows that a manager (except one with a very short decision horizon) would be foolish to report higher earnings than can be sustained. One reason is the oversight and enforcement provided by security commissions, and even the firm's own audit committee. Of possibly greater importance to the manager, however, is that the inevitable reduction in future earnings would severely punish him/her through capital and labour market reaction. Notice that the market cannot unravel this earnings management, since it is based on inside information about sustainable earning power. However, the market can use the earnings management to infer what this inside information is.

The credibility of this unblocking is reinforced by the confirmatory role of net income, introduced in Section 8.1. There, we argued that net income plays a role of confirming inside information released by the manager during the period, thereby encouraging its honest communication. Here, the inside information is released at period end within the income statement (i.e., $1million in our example above), but the argument is the same. In effect, the income statement plays a dual role. In addition to informing investors about future expected earning power, reflecting inside information in the income statement serves to confirm its honesty to investors, since if this expected earning power information is misstated, this will be revealed in future income statements.

Arguments for good earnings management are strengthened by a further paper by Demski and Sappington (DS2; 1990), who showed conditions under which management's inside information can always be conveyed by means of earnings management, should management wish to do so. DS2 pointed out that operating cash flows, or some

Theory in Practice 11.2

General Electric Co. (GE) is a large conglomerate firm with world-wide operations spanning diverse industries. The company straddles so many industries that even analysts have difficulty in forecasting its earnings. Consequently, without some help from management, it is questionable whether even an efficient securities market could predict future earnings and thus properly value GE shares.

In this regard, GE was long regarded as a user of earnings management to unblock inside information about expected future earning power. By using a variety of earnings management devices, GE reported an impressive smooth and steadily growing earnings sequence (see Problem 9). This way of informing the market about future earnings potential is credible because management would be foolish to report earnings greater than what it expects will persist, since this will lead to earnings reductions in future years, with resulting negative stock market reaction. Consequently, until relatively recently, GE was often regarded as a practitioner of good earnings management.

In April 2008, GE reported sharply lower consolidated earnings for its quarter ended March 31. The drop in earnings resulted in large part from provisions for losses at GE's finance subsidiary, due to the 2007–2008 collapse of asset-backed security and related markets. Reported earnings were well short of analysts' estimates, and there had been no prior indications from GE management that earnings would be down.

When the market became aware of the lower earnings, GE's share price quickly fell by 13%. Furthermore, Jack Welch, the retired former CEO of GE, criticized current GE management for not delivering on its expected earnings. Mr. Welch was the architect of GE's previous policy of reporting steadily increasing earnings.

In response to the lower earnings and fall in share price, GE announced a $3 billion cost-cutting program and indicated it would increase its monitoring of subsidiaries.

other relatively unmanaged performance measure such as earnings before special items, convey some information about future firm performance. However, management typically has additional information about future performance, such as new firm strategies, planned restructurings, changes in firm characteristics, or changes in market conditions. While quite relevant, this information is likely to be sufficiently complex that its direct communication is blocked. Then, DS2 show that judicious choice and disclosure of discretionary accruals can reveal this information to investors.[15]

The above vignette 11.2 illustrates the above arguments for good earnings management, but it also illustrates how quickly good can turn into bad if management fails to incorporate lower future earnings expectations into its managed earnings.

We conclude that the possibility of good earnings management for financial reporting purposes is predicted by theory.

11.5.2 Empirical Evidence of Good Earnings Management

Notice that the empirical earnings management studies outlined in Section 11.4 generally do not distinguish between good and bad earnings management. For example, the findings of Sweeny (Section 11.4.1) that firms defaulting on debt covenants used high levels of income-increasing discretionary accruals can be interpreted as opportunistic or efficient, depending on whether insolvent firms were attempting to delay or hide their financial distress or whether firms that were basically solvent were attempting to avoid the effects on covenant ratios of a temporary downturn in economic activity. Also, the findings of Cohen and Zarowin (Section 11.4.3) that firms raising additional capital managed earnings upward can be interpreted as opportunistic or efficient depending on whether the manager is attempting to benefit existing shareholders at the expense of new ones, or whether the manager is reacting to investor rational expectations that the firm will manage earnings upward.

Yet, whether earnings management is good or bad is important to accountants since they are prominently involved in the techniques and implementation of earnings management, and will get drawn into the negative publicity and lawsuits that inevitably follow the revelation of bad earnings management practices. Also, to the extent that earnings management is good, excessive standard setting to overly limit accounting choice may not be desirable. In this section, we consider some empirical evidence consistent with good earnings management. Evidence of bad earnings management is considered in the following section.

Bowen, Rajgopal, and Venkatachalam (BRV; 2008) studied the relationship between corporate governance quality and manager accounting discretion for a 1990s sample of U.S. corporations. They found that weaker corporate governance[16] was positively associated with greater manager discretion (measured by the magnitude of discretionary accruals, by extent of income smoothing, and by the reporting of small positive abnormal earnings[17]). The question then is, how do managers use this discretion? If they use it opportunistically, future firm performance (measured by operating cash flows, by return on assets, and by share price performance) should be poor. For example, managers may be reporting artificially high earnings to increase their reputations and resulting compensation, at the expense of shareholders. If so, share price will fall in future as this earnings manipulation is revealed (i.e., accruals reverse).

To investigate this question, BRV examined the relationship between future firm performance and corporate governance quality. As just mentioned, if lower governance quality allows more accounting discretion and if this discretion is used opportunistically, the relationship should be negative. However, BRV found the relationship to be zero or mildly positive. They interpreted this finding as evidence of efficient contracting; that is, as evidence that managers use their accounting discretion to convey their expected future firm performance to the market.

Tucker and Zarowin (2006) (TZ) also examined the use of discretionary accruals to manage earnings. They argued that to the extent income smoothing increases investors' ability to predict future earnings (i.e., good earnings management), the response of share return to reported earnings (which we documented in Chapter 5) will increase, assuming securities market efficiency. Conversely, if smoothing makes it more difficult for investors to predict future earnings, this response will decrease.

The authors measured income smoothing by the correlation of changes in discretionary accruals with changes in pre-smoothed earnings (measured by reported earnings minus discretionary accruals). For example, if a smoothing firm's pre-smoothed earnings are up this year and the firm wishes to communicate its longer-run persistent earnings, we would expect it to adopt more income-decreasing discretionary accruals to reduce reported earnings, and vice versa. Thus, the correlation between pre-smoothed earnings and discretionary accruals should be negative, and a more negative correlation implies greater smoothing.

Based on a large sample of U.S. firms over the period 1993–2000, TZ report that greater smoothing behaviour is accompanied by increased share return, consistent with market efficiency and the good earnings management argument.

All these findings depend on the ability of the Jones model to separate accruals into discretionary and non-discretionary components in a manner consistent with how the market interprets them. Like any model, the validity of the Jones model has been extensively debated. This suggests that alternate approaches to studying the market's reaction to earnings management are desirable. For example, Liu, Ryan, and Wahlen (1997) (LRW) examined the quarterly loan loss accruals (a vehicle for earnings management) of a sample of 104 U.S. banks over the period 1984–1991. After separating these accruals into expected and unexpected components, they found a significantly positive share price reaction to unexpected increases in loan loss provisions for "at-risk" banks (banks with regulatory capital close to legal minimums), but only in the fourth quarter. For banks not at risk, share price reaction to unexpected loan loss provisions was negative. These results suggest that at-risk banks, by managing their earnings downward, credibly convey to the market that they are taking steps to resolve their problems, which should improve their future performance. This good news was strong enough to outweigh the bad news of the fact of the loan writedowns per se, particularly since the market may have already reacted to the banks being at risk. For banks not at risk, there is less need to take steps to resolve problems, with the result that the bad news component dominated the market's reaction. The reason why the at-risk banks' share prices rose only in the fourth quarter appears to be due to auditor involvement in that quarter. Presumably, management and investors take loan loss provisions more seriously when auditors are involved.

In addition to providing further evidence of how earnings management can convey inside information, LRW's results suggest considerable sophistication in the securities market's response, supporting the efficient market interpretation of the findings of TZ.

As described in Theory in Practice 11.2 (see also Problem 9), GE is, or at least was, a firm that practised good earnings management. For many years, it reported smooth and steadily increasing earnings, interrupted only by the 2007–2008 market meltdowns. Evidence reported by Das, Shroff, and Zhang (2009) suggests that earnings management such as this is quite common. They studied a large sample of firms over over the period 1988–2004 that exhibited earnings reversals—that is, firms that reported good news or bad news over their first three quarters but reported bad news or good news in the final quarter of their year. They found that 11.2% of reversals were of good news in the first three quarters followed by bad news in quarter 4. After ruling out alternative explanations for these good news–bad news reversals, the authors concluded that they were likely due to firms putting future earnings in the bank by smoothing annual earnings down to a number that would persist. They also reported that the fourth quarter earnings response coefficient (ERC) for such firms was significantly higher than for a control sample of similar firms that did not report earnings reversals. This higher ERC suggests that investors interpreted this good news–bad news pattern as good earnings management.

The studies reviewed above are generally consistent with securities market efficiency and average investor rationality. However, earnings management can also be evaluated from a behaviourial perspective. Koonce and Lipe (2010) drew on behavioural theory to predict that investors value **earnings consistency**, because consistent information over time (such as income smoothing) is easier to process and understand than inconsistent information (see our earlier outline of limited attention in Section 6.2.1). They conducted an experiment in which MBA student subjects were presented with several years of earnings information for four hypothetical firms. The total earnings of these firms over the whole period were held constant, but the earnings patterns varied. A consistent pattern was flat or increasing earnings each year (i.e., income smoothing). An inconsistent pattern was earnings that varied up or down. Earnings could also consistently meet analyst forecasts each year, or, inconsistently, miss forecast some years and meet or exceed it in others. The subjects were presented with various combinations of these patterns and asked for their judgments about firm value and desirability as an investment. As they predicted, Koonce and Lipe found that consistent earnings patterns led to more favourable judgments. The authors attributed this result, in part, to increased confidence in future firm performance and the integrity of management.

Another approach to whether discretionary accruals are perceived as good or bad is to use the Dechow and Dichev procedure described in Section 5.4.1 to determine accrual quality. Francis, LaFond, Olsson, and Schipper (FLOS; 2005) studied a large sample of U.S. firms over the period 1970–2001. For each firm, for each year, they used the Dechow and Dichev (DD) procedure to measure accrual quality residuals ϵ_t. They then estimated the portion of these residuals arising from "innate" firm characteristics such as the volatility of its environment. More volatile firms need to record larger accruals to meet earnings expectations and to smooth earnings for compensation and covenant reasons. FLOS then regarded the remaining portion of the DD residuals as discretionary, representing earnings management activities.

The question then is, how does the market react to these accrual quality components? FLOS reported a positive market reaction to the innate components. This is to be expected if accruals are doing their job. That is, it seems that larger innate accruals convey useful information to the market, despite the potential for greater estimation error in a more volatile environment.

FLOS also reported a positive market reaction to the discretionary accrual components, although less positive than to the innate components. From this, they argued that managers use discretionary accruals responsibly to convey useful information to investors. This finding, on balance, supports the good side of earnings management. However, to the extent the market reaction is less than to the innate accruals component, it seems that some bad earnings management is mixed in with the good.

Jayaraman (2008) examined the relationship between the volatility of earnings relative to the volatility of operating cash flows. For a large sample of U.S. firms over the period 1998–2005 he found that as earnings volatility increased relative to cash flow, the bid–ask spread on firms' shares increased on average. As relative earnings volatility declined, the bid–ask spread also increased. Jayaraman argued that when earnings volatility relative to cash flow is high or low (both high and low imply active use of accruals), investor concern about adverse selection increases, increasing estimation risk and driving up the bid–ask spread. This finding suggests bad earnings management, since investors suspect manager opportunism.

However, Jayaraman then examined those firms in his sample with the most extreme share returns. Firms with extreme share returns are likely experiencing major changes, which will show up as large discretionary accruals such as for impairment writedowns, restructurings, big baths, or lawsuits. For these firms, he found that bid–ask spread *decreased* for firms with high or low relative earnings volatility. A decrease in bid–ask spread suggests good earnings management—that is, increased investor trust that management is using large accruals responsibly.

We conclude that there is theory and evidence, from both rational and behavioural perspectives, that earnings management can be good, in the sense that it can inform investors, reduce estimation risk, and favourably affect share prices.

However, both the Francis, LaFond, Olsson, and Schipper and the Jayaraman studies suggest that bad (i, e., opportunistic) earnings management is mixed in with the good. We now look more closely at this bad side of earnings management.

11.6 THE BAD SIDE OF EARNINGS MANAGEMENT

11.6.1 Opportunistic Earnings Management

Despite theory and evidence of responsible use of earnings management, there is also evidence of bad earnings management. From a contracting perspective, this can result from opportunistic manager behaviour. The tendency of managers to use earnings management to maximize their bonuses, as documented by Healy, can be interpreted this way, for example.

Dechow, Ge, Larson, and Sloan (2011) examined a sample of firms charged by the SEC during the period 1982–2005 with financial statement misstatements. They reported that their sample firms were actively raising additional capital and had unusually high stock returns in periods leading up to and including the period of misstatement. The SEC misstatement charges suggest bad earnings management during these periods, to opportunistically maintain an overvalued share price and maximization of the proceeds of new share issues.

McInnis and Collins (MC; 2011) pointed out an increasing tendency of analysts to provide operating cash flow forecasts as well as earnings forecasts. Note that this, in effect, provides a forecast of operating accruals (i.e., Equation 11.1 can also be applied to forecasted net income), which can be compared with actual accruals when the financial statements become available. The result, as MC noted, is to increase the transparency of accruals-based earnings management since manager efforts to, say, meet analyst earnings forecasts by means of income-increasing accruals is more apparent when a forecast of accruals is available for comparison.

MC identified a sample of U.S. firms for which cash flow and earnings forecasts are available during the period 1993–2004. For each firm, they compared its earnings management behaviour before and after the first year for which a cash flow forecast was available. They reported an increase in accrual quality[18] following the availability of a cash flow forecast, suggesting less opportunistic earnings management.

However, they also found an increase in real earnings management and in attempts to "talk down" analysts whose earnings forecasts exceed the earnings expected by management, both of which make it easier to meet analyst forecasts.[19] Despite these tactics, however, MC found that the proportion of sample firms not meeting or exceeding analysts' earnings forecasts increased.

These findings are of significance since they suggest bad earnings management (i.e., low quality accruals) prior to the availability of cash flow forecasts and also that the availability of both analyst cash flow and earnings forecasts improves financial reporting quality. That is, despite switching to other tactics, management seems less able to manage earnings so as to meet analysts' forecasts. The authors concluded that the availability of both cash flow and earnings forecasts is a simple and cost-effective way to reduce bad earnings management and improve corporate governance.

Hanna (1999) discussed another type of earnings management. This is the frequent recording of excessive provisions for low-persistence special items such as writedowns under impairment test standards, and costs of restructuring. Hanna noted that manager bonuses are typically based on earnings before such special items. Furthermore, analysts' forecasts are typically of this earnings measure. If so, transitory provisions do not affect manager bonuses and do not take away from the ability to meet earnings forecasts. But, excessive provisions increase *future earnings*, by putting them in the bank through reduced future amortization charges and absorption of future costs that would otherwise be charged to operating expense when incurred. Then, the manager benefits both ways. Low-persistence special items do not affect bonuses or the ability to meet earnings forecasts, and the future expense reductions increase future operating earnings on which the manager *is* evaluated.

Furthermore, the upward effect on future earnings is very difficult to isolate, since reduced future amortization charges and other expense reductions are buried in larger totals. Burgstahler, Jiambalvo, and Shevlin (BJS; 2002), studied a large sample of firms for four quarters following their recording of negative (i.e., income-reducing) special items over the period 1982–1987. They reported that negative special items are followed by increased earnings in these four subsequent quarters. However, it is not clear whether these increases reflect the effects of excess provisions that concern Hanna (bad earnings management), or non-overstated provisions followed by increased efficiencies resulting from the restructurings or asset disposals (good earnings management), or a combination of both.

In this regard, Cready, Lopez, and Sisneros (2012) evaluated the performance of a sample of U.S. firms that reported negative special items during 2002–2009. They followed the subsequent performance of these firms for 16 quarters—substantially longer than BJS. They found that reported earnings of their sample firms increased over this period by 130% of the special item charges. Since the reversal of a special charge could not increase future earnings by more than 100% of that charge, this suggests that the firms experienced increased efficiencies on average. The authors concluded that a substantial portion of increased earnings following negative special charges is due to efficiency gains, consistent with good earnings management.

Nevertheless, the market appears to reflect the bad earnings management view. Elliott and Hanna (1996) found a significant ERC decline in quarters following the reporting of a large special item (usually, these were losses rather than gains). Furthermore, the ERC declined further if the firm reported numerous large special items over time. This latter evidence is consistent with the market interpreting the frequency of recording of special items as a proxy for their potential misuse. Of course, if accountants would disclose separately the effect on earnings of past special item writeoffs, a proxy such as this would not be needed.

Standard setters also appear to reflect the bad earnings management view. In the United States, to which the above studies relate, SFAS 146 (2002) (now ASC 420-10-25) prohibited recording a liability for restructuring until the liability was incurred. Previously, a provision could be recorded when the restructuring was announced. Also, restructuring liabilities should be measured at fair value, meaning that excess provisions are contrary to GAAP.

Internationally, IAS 37 (1999) defines a provision as a liability for which the timing or amount of future payments are uncertain. To be recorded, such payments must be probable (defined as more likely than not) and capable of reliable estimation. Like SFAS 146, such provisions must be fair-valued. IAS 37 specifically states that uncertainty does not justify excessive provisions. Also, provisions must be used only to absorb costs for which the provision was originally set up. According to IAS 1, restructuring expense and any reversals thereof must be shown separately on the income statement.

These standards undoubtedly constrain the extent of bad earnings management that concerned Hanna. However, they are unlikely to eliminate the practice completely. Note that management still controls the timing of a restructuring decision. Also, measuring the fair value of restructuring liabilities may require considerable estimation.

Theory in Practice 11.3 illustrates a particularly serious use of bad earnings management.

Theory in Practice 11.3

Olympus Corporation is a large Japanese multinational company, producing cameras and a range of electronic products. It is a world leader in medical diagnostic equipment. In October 2011, Olympus fired its president, after only six months on the job. He had become aware of an elaborate accounting scandal and had demanded the resignation of the company's Board.

Following his dismissal, the former president went public about the scandal, which had its roots in the 1980s when several of Olympus' investments began to fall in value. Over time, unrealized and unrecorded, losses of about US$1.7 billion had accumulated. In 2000, it became apparent that Japan was moving toward fair value accounting for financial investments, in which case a $1.7 billion writedown would be required. Olympus apparently felt that reporting this large loss would be highly embarrassing, and began an elaborate scheme to hide the losses.

A condensed and simplified reconstruction of the scheme is as follows:

■ Olympus transfers funds to an off balance sheet (i.e., not consolidated) subsidiary, which are used by the subsidiary to buy some small companies at their market values.

■ Olympus obtains a bank loan for $1.7 billion and buys the acquired small companies from its subsidiary at a grossly inflated price. Specifically, the price is inflated by $1.7 billion, the amount of the unrealized loss on investments which Olympus desires to hide. This creates purchased goodwill (Section 7.11.2) on Olympus' books, and a gain on the sale on the subsidiary's books, of $1.7 billion.

■ Since it owns the unconsolidated subsidiary, Olympus records the $1.7 billion gain in subsidiary book value on its books—debit investment in subsidiary—with the offsetting credit used to reduce the financial investments by the amount of their $1.7 billion unrealized loss. In effect, the unrealized loss on financial investments has "disappeared."

■ The subsidiary repays the $1.7 billion cash it has received for the purchase to Olympus as a dividend, which Olympus credits in its investment in subsidiary account. Olympus uses the cash to repay its bank loan.

The effect is to replace the $1.7 billion of overvalued investments with purchased goodwill on Olympus' books, which can now be amortized

Cont . . .

and written off over time. Presumably, the company felt that amortization and impairment of purchased goodwill, particularly since this could be reported in small amounts each year, would be easier to explain than a $1.7 billion writedown of investments.

This fraud continued until 2011 when, as mentioned, it was publicized by the fired president. Olympus' share price immediately declined by about 50%, with the decline falling to 80% by November 2011 (it has recovered significantly since). Questions arose about the company auditors, which had apparently failed to discover, or at least report on, the magnitude of the scandal. However, it appears, with the aid of the company's bankers, that the auditors were actually lied to.

Olympus was forced to restate five years of financial statements, which resulted in debt covenant violation. However, the company was confident that it could renegotiate the covenants with its bankers. In February 2012, seven persons, including the Chair of Olympus' Board and two other senior executives, were arrested in Japan on fraud charges. In September 2012, the three executives pleaded guilty. In December 2012, a former bank executive was arrested by U.S. authorities for his part in the scandal. As a result of these events, numerous concerns and calls for improvement in Japanese corporate governance have been raised.

Further investigation of bad earnings management was conducted by Leuz, Nanda, and Wysocki (LNW; 2003) in an international context. They evaluated the extent of earnings management in each of 31 countries during the period 1990–1999. One measure was based on the variability of operating income—lower variability implies income smoothing. Another measure was based on the correlation between accruals and cash flow—low correlation implies, for example, that firms in a country may be recognizing revenue well before it is received in cash. A third measure was the magnitude of total accruals—high total accruals contain high discretionary accruals, similar to the reasoning of Healy. Finally, drawing on the implication of prospect theory that small losses are more serious than small gains (Section 6.2.2), they calculated each country's ratio of small earnings losses to small gains. A low ratio suggests earnings management to avoid small losses.

LNW combined these measures into a score for each country. For example, the United States scored 2, Canada 5, Hong Kong 15.5, and Germany 21.5, where lower scores imply less earnings management. Then they related these scores to various country institutional characteristics, such as the level of investor protection. They found that lower investor protection was associated with more earnings management. This suggests that in countries with poor investor protection, opportunistic earnings management is more prevalent.

We conclude from these various results that both good and bad earnings management exist in practice. Accountants must scrutinize manager motivations with great care if they are to detect opportunistic earnings management.

11.6.2 Do Managers Accept Securities Market Efficiency?

The earnings management techniques just outlined are not necessarily inconsistent with securities market efficiency. They rely on poor disclosure to keep the extent of earnings management as inside information. Yet, other results question management's acceptance of efficiency itself.

Schrand and Walther (SW; 2000) reported yet another form of earnings management that questions managers' acceptance of market efficiency. They analyzed a sample of firms that reported a material, special item gain or loss on disposal of property, plant, and equipment in the *prior year*'s quarter, but no such gain or loss in the same quarter of the *current year*. In news releases that typically accompany earnings announcements, managers compare the current quarter's performance with the prior year's quarter. This is consistent with the survey results of Graham, Harvey, and Rajgopal (2005) (Section 11.1), who reported that same-quarter earnings of the previous year are a very important earnings benchmark for managers. The question then is, in these news releases, do managers remind investors of the low-persistence special item gain or loss in the prior quarter? SW found that the likelihood of such a reminder was significantly greater if the prior quarter's special item was a gain rather than a loss, thereby encouraging investors to ignore the prior quarter's gain. In this way, the lowest possible prior period benchmark was emphasized (i.e., managed), thereby showing the change in earnings from the prior quarter in the most favourable light.

Theory in Practice 11.4

In October 2009, Trump Hotels and Casino Resorts, Inc. (THCR) issued a press release stating that its net income for the third quarter of 2009 was $14 million, exceeding analysts' forecasts and net income for the same quarter of 2008. The company disclosed that this amount excluded a one-time charge of $81.4 million, but did not disclose that it included in revenue a one-time gain of $17.2 million. Excluding this gain and the one-time charge, the company's revenues and net income for the quarter were less than analysts' forecasts and less than those of its 2008 quarter. The company also created the impression in its announcement that the reported earnings increase arose from improved operating efficiencies when, in fact, operating improvements were negligible.

On the day of the earnings announcement, THCR's share price increased by 7.8%. However, analysts' soon figured out the existence of the one-time gain, and share price fell by 6% three days later. The company's quarterly report, filed two weeks later, reported the one-time gain in a financial statement note.

The SEC found that the press release, prepared by the company's Treasurer and CFO, was materially misleading. No fine was imposed, but THCR agreed to cease and desist from violations of relevant sections of the Exchange Act. The company also established a procedure by which future earnings announcements would be reviewed by the Audit Committee prior to issuance.

Pro-forma earnings were introduced in Section 7.11.2 (see also Problem 7.12). Managers who emphasize pro-forma earnings claim that this measure better portrays the firm's (and their own) performance than GAAP net income. However, since there are few rules to determine pro-forma earnings, managers may be tempted to disguise or omit revenue and expense items that contain useful information, in order to meet earnings targets, maximize compensation, and/or improve reputation. However, when the GAAP-based income statement becomes available, an efficient market would quickly adjust for decision useful items omitted from the pro-forma earnings announcement. Consequently, managers' emphasis on pro-forma earnings suggests they do not accept efficiency.

Investor reaction to pro-forma earnings was studied by Doyle, Lundholm, and Soliman (DLS; 2003). They obtained a large sample of firms that reported pro-forma quarterly earnings over the period 1988–1999 and, for each firm and quarter, calculated the difference from GAAP net income. They found, contrary to management's claim, that many special items excluded from GAAP net income (for example, provisions for restructuring) did have significant future effects on operating cash flows, persisting for up to three years from the dates of the quarterly announcements. Consequently, investors who look only at pro-forma earnings ignore useful information.

In 2002, the Sarbanes-Oxley Act (Section 1.2) directed the SEC to regulate pro-forma reporting. In 2003, new SEC rules included a requirement to reconcile pro-forma and GAAP earnings, and to explain why pro-forma earnings are decision useful.

Brown, Christensen, Elliott, and Mergenthaler (BCEM; 2012) examined managers' pro-forma reporting over the years 1998–2005. They reported a steady increase in the number of firms reporting pro-forma earnings, with only a temporary decline following the Sarbanes-Oxley Act. The authors' main interests were to determine if managers' pro-forma reporting is related to investor sentiment, and whether pro-forma reporting is informative to investors or whether it is due to opportunistic manager behaviour.

Behavioural research finds that when individuals are optimistic, they examine information less carefully than when they are pessimistic. Investor optimism can develop, for example, from behavioural characteristics such as limited attention and overconfidence (Section 6.2.1). It can also develop from real economic variables such as employment and industrial production. Whatever the reason, BCEM argued that if an optimistic investor takes relatively less care in examining managers' earnings announcements, it is easier to convince them that pro-forma earnings are a better measure of firm and manager performance than GAAP net income. After controlling for other factors affecting managers' pro-forma earnings disclosure decisions, BCEM reported significantly positive relationships between the level of investor sentiment[20] and both the number of firms reporting pro-forma and the total magnitude of items excluded from GAAP net income, consistent with their argument.

The question then is, is reporting of pro-forma earnings informative about future earnings or does it represent opportunistic behaviour by management? BCEM reported evidence consistent with opportunism. For example, they found that as investor sentiment increases, the average manager tends to exclude greater amounts of persistent expenses from the pro-forma earnings calculations. The effect is to raise pro-forma earnings above GAAP net income and, by omitting some persistent items, to reduce the usefulness of pro-forma earnings in predicting future firm performance. This finding became even stronger for those sample firms with managers who sell company shares after the earnings announcement.

In sum, the important point from the Schrand and Walters, DLS, and BCEM studies is that these earnings management policies make little sense if securities markets are efficient. Consequently, managers who engage in them must not fully accept efficiency. Furthermore, extending our argument in Chapter 9 that contracting variables create economic consequences, accounting policies without cash flow effects can matter to managers simply because they believe that the market will not see through them.

11.6.3 Analyzing Managers' Speech to Detect Bad Earnings Management

In Section 11.4.2, we referred to Barton and Mercer's 2005 study of analyst reaction to manager excuses for disappointing financial results. More recently, sophisticated computer programs are being used to analyze managers' written and spoken words for cues that may reveal their underlying beliefs about future firm performance and whether they are truthful in communicating these beliefs.

We have already seen examples of such large scale computer-based studies. In Theory in Practice 3.3, Li (2010) analyzed the "tone" of a large number of MD&As. He found that the tone of a firm's MD&A is useful in predicting future quarter's earnings. In Section 3.6.4 we reviewed the 2011 study of Brown and Tucker, who used computer software to analyze a large sample of MD&As for changes in wording from one year to the next. They reported a positive association between the extent of wording change and the firm's economic activity (e.g., earnings per share), and between this wording change and company share performance. These results suggest that less boilerplate implies better share performance.

Here, we outline another such study, by Hobson, Mayew, and Venkatachalam (HMV; 2012), oriented to detection of manager misstatements of financial performance during the conference calls that usually accompany the release of earnings information.

HMV's study is based on the behavioural theory of **cognitive dissonance**. Under this theory, dissonance arises when a person behaves in a manner contrary to that person's self-perception. For example, a manager may believe that he/she is an honest and responsible member of society. If that manager emphasizes during a conference call that the increase in current-quarter sales is expected to continue when in fact sales have been declining and the increase is due to forcing agents and distributors to accept more product than they need ("stuffing the channels"), that manager will feel guilty—that is, will experience cognitive dissonance.

The theory predicts that an individual subject to dissonance will try to reduce it. One way is to change his/her beliefs. Another is to back off somewhat from the dissonance-creating statement. Thus, if our manager is asked why sales will continue to increase, he/she may try to change his/her beliefs by giving convincing reasons, or may qualify the earlier statement by pointing out, for example, that it depends on market acceptance of new products. To the extent the manager's explanations provide clues such as these that he/she is suffering from cognitive dissonance, this makes the initial statement suspect. Sophisticated software is capable of scanning the manager's recorded speech to detect these clues.

HMV used such a program to analyze the manager's speech during the first five minutes of questions and answers[21] following 1,572 quarterly earnings presentations during 2007, obtaining a cognitive dissonance score for each manager. The question then is, does the dissonance score predict manager misreporting?

To answer this question, HMV checked future financial statements of each sample firm for evidence of an income-decreasing earnings adjustment. They reported that their dissonance score helped to predict those firms that made such adjustments.

It thus seems that analysis of manager's speech holds promise for the prediction of bad earnings management. Note, however, that once managers realize their speech is being analyzed, they will likely learn strategies to avoid revealing what they are trying to hide. The likely result is a sequence of increasingly sophisticated software in response to constantly improving manager counter-strategies.

11.6.4 Implications for Accountants

The implication for accountants who wish to reduce bad earnings management is not to reject market efficiency, but to improve disclosure. High-quality disclosure helps investors to evaluate the financial statements, thereby reducing investor susceptibility to behavioural biases, reduce managers' incentive to exploit poor corporate governance and market inefficiencies, and reduce management's ability to overstate performance during conference calls. For example, clear reporting of revenue recognition policies, and detailed descriptions of low-persistence items and major discretionary accruals, such as writedowns and provisions for reorganization, will bring earnings management into the open, reducing managers' ability to manipulate and bias the financial statements for their own advantage. Other ways to improve disclosure include reporting the effects on current earnings of all previous special item writeoffs and, in general, assisting investors and compensation committees to diagnose low-persistence items. Managers would then bear the full consequences of their actions and bad earnings management would decrease.

11.7 CONCLUSIONS ON EARNINGS MANAGEMENT

Earnings management is made possible by the fact that true net income does not exist (Section 2.6). Furthermore, GAAP do not completely constrain managers' choices of accounting policies and procedures. Such choices are much more complex and challenging than simply selecting those policies and procedures that best inform investors. Rather, managers' accounting policy choices are often motivated by strategic considerations, such as meeting earnings expectations, contracts that depend on financial accounting variables, new share issues, discouraging potential competition, and unblocking inside information. In effect, accounting policy choice has characteristics of a game. Economic consequences are created when changes in GAAP adversely affect managers' abilities to play the game. That is, managers will react against rule changes that reduce their flexibility of accounting choice. As a result, accountants need to be aware of the legitimate needs of management, as well as of investors, while at the same time being alert to opportunistic management strategies. Actual financial reporting represents a compromise between the needs and strategies of these two major constituencies.

Despite the reduction of reliability and sensitivity that often accompanies earnings management, strong arguments can be made that it is useful if kept within bounds. First, it gives managers flexibility to react to unanticipated state realizations when contracts are rigid and incomplete.

Second, earnings management can serve as a vehicle for the credible communication of inside information to investors.

Both of these arguments are consistent with efficient securities markets and the efficient contracting version of positive accounting theory.

Nevertheless, some managers may abuse the communications potential of GAAP by pushing earnings management too far, with the result that persistent earning power is overstated, at least temporarily. This behaviour can result from a failure to accept securities market efficiency or from an ability to hide bad earnings management behind poor disclosure, or both. Thus, whether earnings management is good or bad depends on how it is used. Accountants can reduce the extent of bad earnings management by bringing it out into the open. This can be accomplished by improved disclosure of low-persistence items and reporting the effect of previous writeoffs on current earnings. In addition to assisting share prices to more closely reflect fundamental firm value, improved disclosure assists corporate governance, since compensation committees and the managerial labour market can better reward good manager performance and discipline managers who shirk. The resulting improvements in allocation of scarce investment capital and firm productivity increase social welfare.

Questions and Problems

1. Explain why a firm's manager might both believe in securities market efficiency and engage in earnings management.

2. For an income management strategy of taking a bath, the probability of the manager receiving a bonus in a future year rises. Explain why. (CGA-Canada)

3. A manager increases reported earnings by $1,300 this year. This was done by reducing the allowance for credit losses by $500 below the expected amount and reducing the accrual for warranty costs expense to $800 below the expected amount. Explain why, other things equal, this will lower next year's earnings by $1,300.

4. You are a CEO operating under a bonus plan similar to the one assumed by Healy (Section 11.3). Explain whether you would react favourably or negatively to an exposure draft of a proposed change in GAAP that has the following effects on your financial statements and, as a result, on your bonuses. Treat each effect as independent of the others.

Required

a. The effect will be to increase liabilities. An example of such GAAP changes is expansion of requirements for lease capitalization (Section 7.3.2).

b. The effect will be to increase the volatility of reported net income. An example would be a standard that required unrealized gains and losses on capital assets and securities to be included in net income.

c. The effect will be to exert downward pressure on reported net income. Examples include the expensing of employee stock options (Section 8.6), impairment tests for property, plant, and equipment (Section 7.3.5), and purchased goodwill (Section 7.11.2).

d. The effect will be to eliminate alternative ways of accounting for the same thing. For example, a new standard might require fair value accounting for property, plant, and equipment, rather than optional at present under IAS 16 (Section 7.3.4).

5. The firms in Healy's study of earnings management (Section 11.3) would have been using the historical cost basis of accounting. Given that accounting standards have moved to increased use of fair value accounting for financial instruments, as described in Sections 7.4, 7.5, and 7.9, would this move to fair value increase or decrease the potential for opportunistic earnings management for bonus purposes? Explain.

6. The comparative balance sheet of JSA Ltd. at June 30, 2013, is as follows:

	June 30, 2013	June 30, 2012
	Assets	
Current assets:		
Accounts receivable (net)	$ 76	$ 60
Inventories	35	53
Prepaid expenses	2	1
	113	114
Capital assets (net)	37	39
Long-term investments	2	2
Prepaid development costs	40	39
	$192	$194
	Liabilities and Shareholders' Equity	
Current liabilities:		
Bank indebtedness	$ 18	$ 4
Accounts payable	64	71
Customer advances	13	8
Current portion of long-term debt	1	2
Current portion of future income taxes	2	1
	98	86
Long-term debt	5	3
Liability for future income taxes	0	6
Share capital	73	71
Retained earnings	16	28
	$192	$194

JSA Ltd.'s 2013 income statement is as follows:

Sales		$233
Expenses:		
Cost of sales	$184	
Administrative and selling	35	
Research and development	4	
Depreciation and amortization	14	
Interest	3	240
Loss before undernoted items		(7)
Income tax recovery		7
Provision for reorganization		(12)
Net loss for the year		$ (12)
Cash flow from operations for 2013 was $7.		

Required

a. Calculate the various accruals on an item-by-item basis. For each accrual indicate the extent to which that accrual may contain a discretionary component and briefly explain why.

b. Briefly describe two other ways that researchers have used to estimate discretionary accruals.

c. A manager, whose bonus is related to reported net income, finds that net income for the year (before bonus) is below the bogey of the incentive plan. What type of earnings management might the manager then engage in? Which of the accruals in part **a** would be most suitable for this purpose? Explain.

7. A common tactic to manage earnings is to "stuff the channels"—that is, to ship product prematurely to dealers and customers, thereby inflating sales for the period. A case in point is Bristol-Myers Squibb Co. (BMS), a multinational pharmaceutical company head-quartered in New York. In August 2004, the SEC announced a $150 million penalty levied against BMS. This was part of an agreement to settle charges by the SEC that the company had engaged in a fraudulent scheme to inflate sales and earnings in order to meet analysts' earnings forecasts.

The scheme involved recognition of revenue on pharmaceutical products shipped to its wholesalers in excess of the amounts demanded by them. These shipments amounted to US$1.5 billion during 2001–2002. To persuade its wholesalers to accept this excess inventory, BMS agreed to cover their carrying costs, amounting to millions of dollars per quarter. In addition, BMS understated its accruals for rebates and discounts allowed to its large customers.

According to the SEC, the company also engaged in "cookie jar" accounting. That is, it created phony reserves for disposals of unneeded plants and divisions during high-profit quarters. These would be transferred to reduce operating expenses in low-profit quarters when BMS's earnings still fell short of amounts needed to meet forecasts.

Required

a. Give reasons why managers would resort to earnings management tactics such as these.

b. Evaluate the effectiveness of stuffing the channels as an earnings management device. Consider both from the standpoint of a single year and over a series of years.

c. Evaluate the effectiveness of cookie jar accounting as an earnings management device. What earnings management pattern did BMS appear to be following by means of this tactic?

8. General Electric Company (GE) is a large U.S.-based conglomerate, with operations that included industrial equipment and services, healthcare, TV and entertainment, and commercial finance. The sheer complexity and industry diversity of GE made it particularly difficult for even financial analysts to fully understand the company, since it is unlikely, if not impossible, for anyone to be an expert in all the industries in which the company operated. As a result, it was very difficult for investors to predict GE's future performance. This put a strong onus on GE management to assist investors in this regard. (See Theory in Practice 11.2.)

Table 11.3 shows reported earnings for GE for the years indicated. What is striking is the steady increase in reported earnings until 2008. Only in 2005, when net income was pulled down by a large loss on discontinued operations, was there a small break in this impressive pattern of earnings growth.

Some of the techniques that GE is reported to have used to generate these smooth earnings are

- Changes to the expected rate of return on pension plan assets.

- Sales of divisions. Such sales generally lead to large special item gains.

- Restructuring charges. These are charges to current earnings to provide for expected costs of restructuring the operations of one or more of its many divisions. It is claimed that GE managed the amounts and timing of these charges so as to offset large special

Table 11.3 General Electric Company Reported Net Income 1993–2008, Incl.

Year	Reported Net Income	Year	Reported Net Income
2008	$17,335	2000	$12,735
2007	22,208	1999	10,717
2006	20,829	1998	9,296
2005	16,711	1997	8,203
2004	17,160	1996	7,280
2003	15,002	1995	6,573
2002	14,118	1994	4,726
2001	13,684	1993	4,315

Source: *Annual Reports*, General Electric Company.

item gains, such as from sales of divisions. The objective was to avoid reporting higher earnings than could be sustained in future years.

- Buying profitable businesses. GE was constantly acquiring new subsidiary companies. If needed to prevent reporting an earnings decrease, managing the timing and identity of such acquisitions can achieve an immediate contribution to consolidated reported earnings in the year of acquisition.

- Conservative accounting. Rapid amortization of, for example, leased aircraft by GE's commercial finance division enables large profits to be recorded when the aircraft are eventually sold. The timing of such sales can be managed by GE.

- Allocation of purchased goodwill upon acquisition of subsidiary companies. When GE acquires a subsidiary, it may decide, or be required, to dispose of segments of the acquired business. The flexibility under GAAP of allocation of the excess of amount paid for a subsidiary company over the fair value of assets acquired (i.e., purchased goodwill) enabled GE to record a gain on such dispositions, by allocating a relatively small amount of the excess amount paid to any subsidiary segments that it intended to dispose of.

The important point about the array of earnings management techniques available to GE is that they can be used in concert to report a smooth earnings sequence. Table 11.3 suggests that, until 2008, GE was quite successful in this regard.

Required
a. Evaluate restructuring charges as an earnings management device.
b. Under securities markets efficiency, share prices always fully reflect all public information about a firm's securities. In the absence of earnings management, would the share price of a complex firm like GE always have reflected all public information about GE? Explain why or why not. Given its earnings management during that time, would GE's share price have fully reflected all public information? Explain.
c. Was earnings management by GE during the period 1993–2007 good or bad? Explain.

9. Refer to Theory in Practice 11.2, concerning General Electric Co. (GE). In particular, consider the strong negative market reaction to lower reported earnings in April 2008.

Required
a. Why did GE's share price fall?
b. GE's previous policy of managing earnings so as to report a steady increase can be interpreted as "good" earnings management (see Problem 9). Outline the argument why earnings management by complex firms such as GE can provide useful and credible information to investors. Use the concept of blocked communication in your answer.
c. Suppose that GE had adopted Mr. Welch's urging to report increased earnings this quarter? Would this have been consistent with its reputation for good earnings management? Explain why or why not.

10. The 1997 *Annual Report* of Sunbeam Corp. reported net income of $109.4 million, with sales of $1.2 billion. According to CEO "chainsaw Al" Dunlap, "we had an amazing year." Mr. Dunlap was well known from his previous CEO positions for dramatic cost cutting, including firing much of senior management. Sunbeam's share price had risen from $12.50 when he took over in July 1996 to $53 in March 1998.

However, in May 1998, when Sunbeam reported its first quarter 1998 results, the market was shocked by a loss of $44.6 million, compared with a profit of $6.9 million for the first quarter of 1997. Sales were reported as $244.5 million, down $9 million from the first quarter of 1997—a decline of 3.6%. The company's share price quickly fell to $22.

Reasons for this sudden decline in performance were analyzed by Jonathan Laing, writing in *Barron's*. Laing claimed that Sunbeam's 1997 earnings were "largely manufactured." A revised summary of his analysis of the after-tax effect on 1997 net income of discretionary accruals is given in the following table.

Sunbeam Corp, 1997
Estimated Discretionary Accruals

	Effect on 1997 Net Income ($ millions) (Net of tax)	
	Increase	Decrease
Inventory written down to zero in 1996, sold at 50¢ on the dollar in 1997	$ 36.5	
Decline in prepaid expense from $40.4 in 1996 to $ 17.2 in 1997		$15
Decrease in other current liabilities ($18.1 before tax) and other long-term liabilities ($19 before tax), attributed mainly to reduction in product warranty provisions.	25	
Reduction in 1997 amortization, due to 1996 writedown of property, plant and equipment, and trademark	6	
Capitalization of product development, advertising, etc. into property, plant and equipment in 1997	10	
Decrease in allowance for doubtful accounts from $23.4 to $8.4 during 1997	10	
Manufacturing for stock in 1997, evidenced by 40% increase in inventories, thereby absorbing manufacturing overhead of about	10	
"Early buy" and "bill and hold" sales of $50: estimated profit from early revenue recognition	8	
	105.5	15
Less total of Decrease column	15	
Net income-increasing discretionary accruals	$ 90.5	

Required

a. Sunbeam reported that 1997 operating cash flow was −$8.2 million. Do you agree with Laing's statement that 1997 earnings "appear to be largely manufactured"? Explain why or why not.

b. Sunbeam had recently acquired several subsidiary companies, and had indicated that it would be recording a provision for restructuring of $390 million to integrate them into its operations. This suggests that Sunbeam still has scope to manage earnings. Use the earnings management tactics described by Hanna (Section 11.6.1) to explain how such a restructuring provision could be used to manage reported earnings.

c. Use the "iron law" of accruals reversal to help explain why there was a substantial first quarter 1998 loss.

11. Barton (2001) studied managers' use of derivatives and discretionary accruals to smooth reported earnings. As Barton pointed out, both of these devices have smoothing potential—since earnings can be expressed as the sum of operating cash flows and total accruals, smoothing can be accomplished through operating cash flows (which can be hedged by derivatives—a real earnings management device) and/or through accruals (by means of the discretionary portion).

From a sample of large U.S. firms during 1994–1996, inclusive, Barton found that managers trade off the use of derivatives and discretionary accruals in order to maintain (i.e., smooth) earnings volatility at a desired level. Specifically, firms that were heavy derivatives users tended to be low users of discretionary accruals, and vice versa. Other things equal, this suggests that managers are sensitive to the costs of smoothing earnings. That is, firms appear to use the combination of smoothing devices that are, for them, the least costly.

Required

a. Give reasons why managers may want to smooth earnings.

b. What are some of the costs of opportunistic smoothing of earnings? Why would managers trade off these two earnings smoothing devices, rather than use only one or the other?

c. Are Barton's results more consistent with opportunistic or efficient contracting? Why?

12. In April 2004, Nortel Networks Corp. announced that it had fired its CEO, Chief Financial Officer, and Controller. Its share price, over $11 prior to the announcement, fell to Can. $5.26. The company later announced that several more senior managers were also fired.

The events leading to these dismissals had their roots in the collapse of the technology boom in the early 2000s. This left many of Nortel's customers and subsidiary companies in financial distress. Conservative provisions were recorded by Nortel in 2001 and 2002 to provide for costs of contract cancellations, bad debts, layoffs, and plant closures. By mid-2002, about $5 billion of such provisions were on Nortel's balance sheet.

These provisions, together with reduced business activity following the collapse of the technology boom, resulted in Nortel reporting a series of losses totalling about $34 billion for 2000–2002 incl. As part of its attempts to stem these losses, Nortel instituted a system of "return to profitability" executive bonuses, which would be paid if quarterly pro-forma profits (Section 7.11.2) were earned. If one quarter was profitable, 20% of bonus would be paid, an additional 40% would be paid if the next quarter was profitable, and the final 40% paid if four consecutive quarters were profitable.

In the fourth quarter, 2002, it appeared that pro-forma earnings (but not GAAP earnings) for the quarter were going to be positive, which would trigger bonus payments. However, additional provisions were recorded by Nortel to ensure that pro-forma earnings were negative. These provisions were reversed in 2003, and Nortel reported positive pro-forma income in the first two quarters of 2003. Consequently, most employees received cash bonuses, including the CEO, who received $3.6 million.

However, the company issued restated 2000–2003 GAAP results in December 2003 in response to regulators' concerns, writing off some $900 million of excess reserves. These writeoffs were carried back to restate 2000–2002 earnings upward. However, earnings for the first two quarters of 2003 were revised downward to GAAP losses of $146 and $128 million, respectively, compared with an originally stated first quarter GAAP 2003 loss of $16 million and a second quarter profit of $40 million. This revision supported concerns expressed in the previous paragraph that management engaged in earnings management to enable bonus payments.

In February 2006, Nortel agreed to a US$2.7 billion settlement of two class-action lawsuits resulting from this incident. In March 2007, the SEC began civil proceedings against several former executives. These were settled with a payment of $35 million. In May 2007, Nortel agreed to pay $1 million to the Ontario Securities Commission to meet the costs of the Commission's investigation into this incident. No penalty was paid, although the company formally agreed that its 2002 and 2003 financial statements were not in compliance with GAAP.

In 2008, the three officers were charged with fraud in an Ontario court for deliberately misreporting Nortel's financial statements during 2000–2004. The prosecution claimed that the original financial statements and their 2003 revisions were materially misrepresented. Testimony at the trial, as reported in financial media, suggested that a reason for recording extra reserves in fourth quarter 2002 was that management felt paying executive bonuses when reported GAAP earnings for the quarter were negative would attract criticism. Also, management felt that a single pro-forma profitable quarter following huge losses would be ignored by a skeptical market. However, the prosecution claimed that the real motivation was that reversal of these 2002 reserves would enable Nortel to report successive profitable pro-forma quarters and pay greater bonuses in 2003.

In January 2013, the three executives were acquitted of fraud charges. Reasons for acquittal included immateriality of $900 million of reserve misstatements in relation to the $34 billion of losses Nortel had reported. Also, the judge concluded that since conservatism was well established in accounting practice, the overstatements of the original reserves (which enabled the subsequent management of excess reserves and earnings) were not fraudulent.

However, these events were part of a series of accounting misstatements, resulting in loss of investor confidence (see also Problem 14). This contributed to Nortel's filing for bankruptcy protection in 2009. The company has now sold its assets and is in the process of winding up.

Required

a. Which earnings management policy did Nortel appear to be using in its fourth quarter 2002? Why? Which policy did it appear to be using in the first two quarters of 2003? Why?

b. Outline accounting theory that supports the judge's conclusion that conservatism is a well-accepted accounting practice.

c. Discuss the possible impacts on manager effort of the Nortel compensation plan's tying of bonuses to a return to pro-forma profitability.

d. Assuming that the conservative special item accruals recorded by Nortel during 2000–2002 were justified by pessimistic economic conditions at the time, why was Nortel's senior management dismissed in 2004?

e. Given revisions to the reporting of special items under FASB and IASB GAAP (Section 11.6.1), could these events have happened if the special item revisions standards had been in effect during 2000–2003? Explain.

13. You are an expert on GAAP and the quality of financial reporting, with extensive experience in rational investing. You determine the current quality of financial reporting as summarized in the following information system:

		GN	BN
	High	0.9	0.1
State of Nature			
	Low	0.2	0.8

The states of nature refer to future firm performance. GN (good news) and BN (bad news) summarize the information content of current financial statements.

You are also a shareholder of HILO Ltd., which has just released its quarterly financial report, and are evaluating this report to decide whether to sell your shares now or hold them for another quarter.

Your prior probability of the high state is 0.7. The current market value (i.e., your payoff if you sell now) of your HILO Ltd. shares is $81. If HILO is in the high state, your payoff will be $100 if you sell at the end of the next quarter. If HILO is in the low state, your payoff will be $36 at the end of next quarter. You are risk averse, with utility equal to the square root of your payoff.

Required

a. HILO Ltd. has just reported its earnings, with net income before special items up 10% from the same quarter last year, and exactly equal to analysts' consensus forecast (assume that analyst forecasts are before special items). However, you notice a large, special item loss in net income that reduces net income to below the consensus forecast. Does the current financial report show GN or BN? Explain (no calculations required).

b. Based on rational decision theory, should you sell or hold your HILO shares? Show calculations.

c. Assume that HILO has reported steadily increasing quarterly earnings for several years, but that current earnings per share before special items are 2 cents below analysts' consensus forecast, otherwise it's the same scenario as in **a**. Would your evaluation of the GN or BN in earnings change? Explain why or why not (no calculations required).

14. On March 10, 2006, Nortel Networks Corp. announced that it would delay filing its 2005 financial reports with the SEC. The delay arose because Nortel and its auditors decided that certain revenue recognized in prior periods should have been deferred.

Nortel explained that these changes followed from Statements of Position issued by the AICPA (Nortel followed U.S. GAAP), which required that revenue from longer-term contracts involving "multiple deliverables," such as hardware, software, and services, should be deferred until delivery.

As a result, Nortel reduced its originally reported earnings for the first nine months of 2005 by $95 million, and for 2004 by $279 million.

On the same day, Nortel announced an estimated, unaudited, net loss from 2005 continuing operations of $2.421 billion. In addition to the reduction due to revenue deferral, this loss included an expense of $2.474 billion to settle shareholder litigation resulting from previous accounting restatements (see Problem 12). On March 10, 2006, Nortel's share price on the S&P TSX 500 Composite index fell 11 cents in heavy trading to C$3.50, for a return of −3.05% for the day. On the same day, the S&P TSX Composite index rose 68.28 points to 11,833.61, for a return of 0.58%. According to Reuters's website, Nortel's beta on the S&P TSX at this time was 1.96. The risk-free interest rate R_f was 4.5%, or 0.0001 per day.

Required

a. Evaluate the change in relevance and reliability of Nortel's 2005 revised financial statements, resulting from its revenue deferral.

b. What earnings management pattern did Nortel appear to be following for 2005? Why?

c. Calculate the abnormal return on Nortel's shares, relative to the return on the S&P TSX Composite index, for March 10, 2006. Do you feel that the abnormal return arose from the news of the revenue deferral or from the $2.474 billion shareholder litigation expense, or both? Explain.

Note: According to the market model and CAPM, $\alpha_j = R_f (1 - \beta_j)$.

15. In April 2005, the SEC announced settlement with Coca-Cola Company of charges of fraud and false and misleading financial reporting. The charges arose from "gallon pushing" at Coca-Cola's Japanese subsidiary during 1997 to 1999, whereby the subsidiary shipped more concentrate to its bottlers than needed to meet sales volumes.

According to the SEC, in the first quarter of 1997 over 3.3 million extra gallons were pushed, generating additional revenue for Coca-Cola of $46.2 million for the quarter. Amount pushed increased over the two years, reaching 10.1 million gallons in the fourth quarter of 1999, generating almost $209 million in extra revenue for that quarter. Coca-Cola granted extended credit terms to its bottlers to assist them in carrying the excess inventory.

The result of these activities was to increase Coca-Cola's quarterly earnings by 1 or 2 cents per share. This increase enabled Coca-Cola to meet analysts' earnings per share projections in eight of the 12 quarters under investigation. However, by the end of 1999, Japanese bottlers' inventories had risen to the point where additional gallonage could not be pushed. In January 2000, Coca-Cola announced a worldwide "inventory reduction" program to "optimum" levels. The company estimated that this would create a one-time reduction of earnings per share of 11 to 13 cents in the first two quarters of 2000, with about 5 cents of this reduction coming from Japan alone.

According to the SEC, Coca-Cola did not disclose the existence of the gallon-pushing program, its impact on earnings per share, or its likely impact on future reported earnings. The company was charged with violations of the U.S. Securities Act. Under the April 2005 settlement, Coca-Cola agreed, without admitting or denying liability, to remedial actions, including establishment of an Ethics and Compliance Office and a Disclosure Committee, close monitoring of any extended payment terms to customers, and adding an independent legal advisor experienced in securities law disclosure issues to its Audit Committee.

Required

a. Evaluate revenue recognition as an earnings management device. In your answer, consider both changes in the timing of revenue recognition to increase current revenue, and increasing current revenue by stuffing the channels. Give possible reasons why a firm may manage its reported earnings upward.

b. Explain why Coca-Cola had to increase the gallonage pushed over the 12 quarters in order to maintain a 1 to 2 cents per share increase of earnings per share each quarter.

c. Why did Coca-Cola undertake the "inventory reduction" program in 2000?

d. Coca-Cola Co. announced in December 2002 that it was discontinuing the provision of quarterly and annual earnings forecasts to analysts. Some other large public companies have taken similar action. Why would they do this?

16. Young and Yang (2011) examined managers' stock repurchase decisions, under which firms buy back outstanding shares on the market, for a sample of U.K. companies during 1998–2006. As the authors pointed out, stock repurchases are motivated by reducing dilution of shareholder interests created by exercise of ESOs, as a vehicle for earnings management, and for compensation purposes.

Required

a. Stock repurchases may or may not increase earnings per share (EPS). Suggest reasons why.

b. A manager claims in an interview that stock repurchases are a better way to manage earnings than by manipulation of accruals. Do you agree? Explain why or why not.

c. A compensation consultant claims that share buybacks are driven by provisions in managerial compensation contracts. Do you agree? Explain why or why not.

17. Note: This problem raises issues concerning replacement cost accounting that are not discussed in the text.

BP plc, a large British-based international oil and gas company, provides an interesting example of pro-forma earnings reporting. In its second quarter 2012 quarterly report, BP reported a net loss, based on IASB standards, of US$1,385 million. However, the company emphasized its "underlying replacement cost profits," which, it claimed, give a better picture of its operations. A summary of BP's determination of replacement cost profits is as follows:

Net loss based on IASB standards	($1,385)
Add back inventory holding losses, net of tax. This is the difference between cost of sales based on FIFO as per IASB, and cost of sales based on the average cost of inventory acquired during the quarter (regarded as an estimate of replacement cost of sales)	1,623
Add back non-operating item losses, consisting mainly of writeoffs of an offshore oil project off the coast of Alaska and abandonment of a solar power project, impairment test writedown of shale gas assets due to low gas prices, provisions for losses on planned sales of two U.S. refineries, and further provisions for losses arising from Gulf of Mexico oil spill; net of tax	3,447
Underlying Replacement Cost Profit	3,685
Interest and tax costs	2,214
Underlying Replacement Cost Profit before Interest and Tax costs	$5,899

Required

a. Under ideal conditions, what is the relationship between fair value of an asset (as defined by IFRS 13—see Section 7.2), and replacement cost? Explain why.

b. When conditions are not ideal, which measure, earnings as per IASB standards (based largely on fair value accounting) or replacement cost profit as defined by BP, best reports on and motivates manager performance? Discuss.

c. Which measure best informs investors about future firm performance? Discuss.

d. According to BP, underlying replacement cost profit is "closely tracked by management to evaluate operating performance and make financial, strategic, and operating decisions." Is underlying replacement cost profit a better way to evaluate company performance and make decisions than IASB-based earnings? Discuss.

18. Refer to Theory in Practice 11.1 re: Groupon Inc.

Required

a. Do you agree with Groupon's policy of capitalizing marketing costs for purposes of reporting its earnings to investors? Explain your answer.

b. Regardless of your answer to **a**, suggest a less aggressive way of accounting for revenue by Groupon.

c. Do you feel that Groupon's management accepted securities market efficiency? Explain.

d. To what extent is the share price behaviour of Groupon during and following its IPO consistent with securities market efficiency? Explain.

Notes

1. This assumes that the manager stays with the firm throughout the period required for the accruals to reverse. Should this not be the case, the manager may escape some of the accrual reversal consequences. Also, the accounting for ESOs (Section 8.6) provides an exception to the iron rule. ESO expense is estimated at the time ESOs are granted, and is not adjusted later for any difference between this estimate and actual expense.

2. This is a case of post-decision information. See Section 9.3.1.

3. Healy pointed out that if net income is just below the bogey, the manager might instead adopt policies to increase net income, so that at least some bonus would be received.

4. An alternative is to take changes in working capital items from the comparative balance sheets. However, Hribar and Collins (2002) cautioned that this may bias the accruals estimates. The reason is that many firms engage in acquisitions and divestitures. Then, working capital items are increased or decreased on the consolidated balance sheet, but these changes do not affect net income, and thus are not subject to earnings management. Changes in working capital items on the statement of cash flows do not include these non-earnings-related changes.

5. For further discussion of methodological issues in this area, see McNichols and Wilson (1988); Dechow, Sloan, and Sweeney (1995); and Bernard and Skinner (1996).

6. To standardize for firm size, Jones divides both sides of this equation by total assets.

7. This procedure will be recognized as conceptually related to the use of the CAPM to separate security returns into expected and abnormal components, as illustrated in Figure 5.2. The contexts in which the two models are applied are quite different, however.

8. Dechow, Hutton, Kim, and Sloan (DHKS; 2012) suggested a new approach to detecting earnings management by means of discretionary accruals. Their approach extends existing discretionary accrual models such as the Jones model. DHKS concentrated on detecting earnings management in working capital accruals, such as accounts receivable, inventory, accounts payable, etc. Non-discretionary working capital accruals generally reverse in the following one or two periods. However, assuming the firm is a going concern, these non-discretionary accruals are replaced by similar accruals in subsequent periods.

Consider, however, a discretionary income-increasing accrual in a particular period, such as an overstatement of net accounts receivable. A researcher, or an auditor, using the Jones model, finds that the model predicts earnings management. But, this is not conclusive evidence that earnings management has occurred, since such models are subject to error. However, like non-discretionary accruals, this accrual will also reverse in a following period when the overstatement is discovered and written off. Suppose that the researcher knows the period when the reversal takes place. He/she can use the Jones model to test for income-*decreasing* abnormal discretionary accruals in that period, resulting from the reversal of the earlier accrual. As mentioned, non-discretionary accruals tend to repeat in following periods, so that the new non-discretionary accrual cancels out the effect of the reversal of the earlier non-discretionary accrual. Consequently, if income-decreasing accruals are found in the following period, this reinforces a conclusion that earnings management was present in the earlier period. In effect, the DHKS procedure provides two chances of finding the earnings management rather than one. Based on extensive testing of this approach, the authors reported a significant improvement, relative to earlier models, in the ability to detect earnings management.

However, for this to work, the researcher must know the period when the reversal takes place. For some discretionary accruals, which may take a long time to reverse, this can be difficult. DHKS reported a substantial decline in the ability of their approach to detect earnings management when the reversal periods are misspecified.

9. Evidence for an alternative explanation of HLS's finding is provided by Abarbanell and Lehavy (2003). They argued that if managers are also compensated based on share price performance (recall that Healy studied only bonus plans, which are typically based on earnings), they will want to avoid the negative share price reaction that follows bad earnings news.

10. Skinner and Sloan studied growth firms (firms with a high ratio of market value to book value). They argued that investors overestimate the future performance of growth firms, due to behavioural factors such as self-attribution bias discussed in Section 6.2.1. Failure to meet earnings expectations brings investors "back to earth," resulting in a major share price decline.

11. Another way is to lower investors' expectations by "talking down" analysts, to the point where reported earnings meet or exceed the analysts' revised, lower forecasts. This was studied by Matsumoto (2002), who found that firms in her sample used both approaches. As Matsumoto pointed out, however, her study preceded regulation FD (an SEC regulation introduced in 2000 to prohibit firms from releasing material information only to analysts—see Section 13.4). Subsequent to 2000, the incidence of talking down analysts should decrease.

12. An SEO is a share offering by a firm that already has shares outstanding. This contrasts with an initial public offering (IPO), which is shares offered to the public for the first time.

13. Overproduction spreads fixed overheads over a larger number of units, thereby reducing cost of sales for the year.

14. Firms with high operating assets, the authors argued, were more likely to have "used up" accruals-based earnings management opportunities in previous years, and thus faced relatively high costs of finding additional income-increasing accruals in the SEO year.

15. As DS2 pointed out, the information conveyed by the financial statements in their model does not purport to fully convey the value of the firm. All that is claimed is that *some* value-relevant information is conveyed by net income. That is, their model does not get around our general observation that net income is well defined only under ideal conditions and our claim (Figure 4.2) that it is too costly to reveal all inside information.

16. BRV used several measures of corporate governance quality, including shareholder rights, whether the Board chair is also the CEO, number of Board meetings, and number of top firm executives on the Board.

17. Recall from Section 6.2.2 that Burgstahler and Dichev (1997) found that firms that would otherwise report a small loss tended to manage reported earnings upward so as to report a small profit.

18. The authors measured accrual quality two ways. One measure is based on a version of the Jones model (Section 11.3) to identify discretionary accruals. The other is based on the Dechow and Dichev procedure outlined in Section 5.4.1.

19. McInnis and Collins also compared these findings to those of a control sample of similar firms but for which cash flow forecasts were not available. These firms did not exhibit these changes in manager tactics. This makes it easier to argue that the documented changes in accrual quality result from the availability of both forecasts.

20. BCEM measure investor sentiment from the Baker and Wurgler (2006) sentiment index. This index measures sentiment based on industrial production, growth in employment, and several other economic indicators.

21. HMV argued that if evidence of cognitive dissonance is to occur, it is likely to do so in the early part of a discussion. They confined study to the question and answer portion of the presentation since this is when the manager has the greatest likelihood of revealing clues, such as reinforcing or qualifying his/her beliefs.

Chapter 12
Standard Setting: Economic Issues

Figure 12.1 Organization of Chapter 12

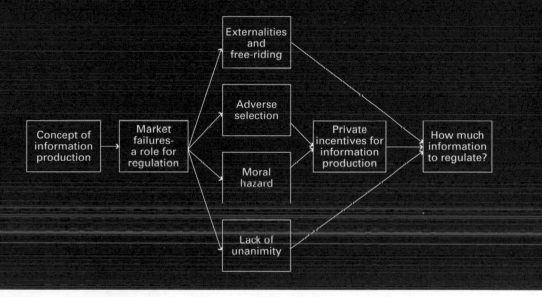

12.1 OVERVIEW

Standard setting is a form of regulation that is ultimately the responsibility of a country's government or legislature (we shall use the terms interchangeably). Governments typically delegate responsibility for standard setting in accounting to a specific agency, such as the securities commissions described in Section 1.12.5. In turn, these agencies may delegate standard-setting responsibility to semi-autonomous bodies such as the IASB, AcSB, and FASB. When it is not necessary to distinguish among them, we will often use the term **regulator** to refer to these various standard-setting bodies.

Recall that we view the standard setter as a mediator between the conflicting interests of investors and managers. The fundamental problem (Section 1.10) is how to conduct this mediation—that is, how to combine the financial reporting and efficient contracting roles of accounting information or, equivalently, how to determine the socially "right" amount of information.

This raises the question, what is the socially right amount of information? In theory, the economic answer is straightforward. This is the amount that equates the marginal social benefits of information to the marginal social costs. We shall call this the **first-best** amount of information production.

For many products, market forces are sufficient to drive production close to first-best with little regulation. However, while there are many market-based incentives for firms to produce information, first-best production of information is impossible to attain by market forces alone. A major reason is information asymmetry. Since financial accounting information has characteristics of a public good, suppliers of information do not always get paid for the information they produce. Consequently, they will under produce relative to first-best. As a result, information asymmetry, leading to adverse selection and moral hazard, is greater than is socially desirable. This market failure supports arguments for regulation of financial disclosure. However, due to the difficulty of measuring the complex benefits and costs of information, standard setters are unable to attain first-best either. Since regulation also has a cost, the question then becomes one of the *extent* of standard setting. Too little standard setting results in too much information asymmetry, as just mentioned. Too much standard setting imposes a greater cost on society than the benefits of lower information asymmetry.

In past years, many industries were deregulated, giving greater freedom to firms to make their own private decisions about prices, quantities, and product quality. Deregulation followed from a general belief that markets were superior to regulation as vehicles for producing goods and services. Airlines, trucking, financial services, telecommunications, and electric power generation are major examples of deregulation. This belief in markets suggests less regulation in accounting; that is, market forces can be relied on to motivate firms to produce "enough" financial information.

However, the Enron and WorldCom debacles (Section 1.2) and the 2007–2008 market meltdowns (Section 1.3) have resulted in severe criticism of the stability of unregulated markets. As a result, regulation has increased for some industries, such as financial services. Indeed, regulation in accounting has increased, as evidenced by the Sarbanes-Oxley Act, and new accounting standards, including financial instruments, derecognition, and consolidation, outlined in Chapter 7.

What happens as the extent of information-industry regulation changes? Does increased regulation smother competition and innovation? Is increased regulation cost-effective? Would deregulation cause information production to collapse into chaos? At present, the answers to these questions are not known. However, discussion of the pros and cons of standard setting helps us see the tradeoffs that are involved and appreciate the crucial role of information in society.

Accountants should not take the extent of regulation for granted. Regulation is an important component of the accounting environment, which is constantly changing. This affects much of what accountants do, their legal obligations, and their legal liabilities.

Figure 12.1 outlines the chapter organization.

12.2 REGULATION OF ECONOMIC ACTIVITY

There are numerous instances of regulation of economic activity in our economy. Firms that have a monopoly, such as electricity distribution, municipal water utilities, and local telephone service, are common examples. Here, regulation typically takes the form of regulation of rates, price caps, or the rate of return on invested capital. Public safety is an area subject to frequent regulation as, for example, in elevator inspection laws, compulsory use of seatbelts, standards for automobile tire construction, drinking water safety, and fire protection regulations. Communications is another area that, in many countries, is deemed sufficiently sensitive to attract regulation. Other sets of regulations affect financial institutions and securities markets. One reason for such regulation arises from the public-good nature of accounting information (Section 5.5), where the regulator tries to increase information production to compensate for the underproduction that arises for public goods. This is an example of an **externality**, where the actions of one party (e.g., underproduction) affect outside parties. Another reason for regulation is to protect individuals who are at an information disadvantage due to information asymmetry. If managerial actions and inside information were freely observable by all, there would be no need to protect individuals from the consequences of information disadvantage.

Externalities and information asymmetry are thus frequently used to justify regulations to protect investors. In addition to GAAP, we have insider trading rules, MD&A, executive compensation disclosures in management proxy circulars, public access to corporate conference calls, regulations of full disclosure in prospectuses, and laws to regulate accounting professions. As well as protecting ordinary investors, such regulations are also intended to improve the operation of capital and managerial labour markets by enhancing public confidence that these markets work well.

In this chapter, our primary concerns are the regulation of minimum disclosure requirements, generally accepted accounting and auditing standards, and the requirement that public companies have audits. We will use the term **standard setting** to denote the establishment of these various rules and regulations. Note that standard setting involves the regulation of firms' external information production decisions. Thus firms are not completely free to control the amount and timing of much of the information they produce about themselves. Rather, they must do so under a host of regulations that we will call standards, laid down by a regulator.

> **Standard setting** *is the regulation of firms' information production decisions by a regulator.*

In considering issues of information production, it is helpful to distinguish between two types of information that a manager may possess. The first type is **proprietary information**. This is information that, if released, would directly affect future cash flows of the firm. Examples are technical information about valuable patents, and plans for strategic initiatives such as takeover bids or mergers. The costs to the manager and firm of releasing proprietary information can be quite high.

The second type is **non-proprietary information**. This is information that, if released, does not directly affect firm cash flows.[1] It includes financial statement information, earnings forecasts, details of new financing, and so on. The audit is also included in non-proprietary information.

12.3 WAYS TO CHARACTERIZE INFORMATION PRODUCTION

While the term "production" of information may take some getting used to, we use it for two reasons. First, we want to think of information as a commodity that can be produced and sold. Then, it is natural to consider separately the costs and benefits of information, and whether the socially "right" amount is produced.

Second, we want a unified way of thinking about the various ways information production can be accomplished. Information is a complex commodity. Just what do we mean when we speak of the quantity of information produced? There are several ways to answer this question.

First, we can think of **finer information**. For example, a thermometer that tells you the temperature in degrees is a finer information system than one that only tells you if the temperature is above or below freezing—the first thermometer tells you everything that the second one does, and more. It enables a finer reading of the temperature. In an accounting context, a finer reporting system adds more detail to the existing financial statements. Examples of finer reporting include expanded note disclosure, additional line items on the financial statements, segment reporting, and so on.

In terms of our decision theory discussion of Chapter 3, finer information production means a better ability to discriminate between realizations of the states of nature. For example, in a decision problem where the relevant set of states of nature is the temperature, a thermometer that tells you degrees enables better discrimination between different temperature states than one that only tells you if the temperature is above or below freezing. In accounting, the concept of full disclosure suggests finer information production. Full disclosure increases the informativeness of the information system, enabling better discrimination between relevant states of the firm.

Second, we can think of **additional information**. For example, we might add a barometer to our thermometer. In an accounting context, additional information means the introduction of new information systems to report on matters not currently included. Examples would include informative extensions of current value accounting to additional assets and liabilities, future-oriented financial information included in MD&A, and expanded disclosures of firm risk. In decision theory terms, additional information means an expansion of the set of relevant states of nature upon which the firm's performance depends. Thus a thermometer–barometer reports on atmospheric pressure as well as temperature.

In accounting, reporting on firm risk implies an expansion of relevant states of nature, adding, say, risky or not risky to the high and low future performance states included in Example 3.1. Also, we argued in Section 7.2.2 that fair value accounting improves the ability of net income to report on manager stewardship. If so, this implies adding good or bad manager performance as additional relevant states of nature.

A third way to think about information production is in terms of its **credibility**. The essence of credibility is that the receiver knows that the supplier of information has an incentive to disclose truthfully. In our thermometer example, the purchaser knows that the manufacturer must produce an accurate product in order to stay in business. Thus, the purchaser accepts the thermometer as a credible representation of the temperature. In an accounting context, it is often suggested that a "Big Four" audit is more credible than a "non-Big Four" audit because a large audit firm has more to lose,[2] both in terms of reputation and "deep pockets"; hence it will maintain high audit standards. Also, the greater the penalties for managers who divulge false information, the more credibility investors attach to managers' disclosures.

In this chapter, we will not need to distinguish these different ways to produce information and will refer to them all, rather loosely, as **information production**. Note that however we think of its production, more information will require higher costs, some of which may be proprietary costs.

12.4 FIRST-BEST INFORMATION PRODUCTION

From society's standpoint, the socially right, or first-best, amount of information production is that amount that equates the marginal social benefits of information production to the marginal social costs of information production. This amount of information creates the largest possible "pie" of information benefits for society. Any additional production would cost more than the benefits generated. Similarly, if information production is less than this, society would benefit from producing more.[3]

Numerous benefits and costs of information production are discussed in this book. Benefits include better-informed investment decisions (Section 3.3.2), possible lower costs of capital for firms producing the information (Section 12.9), and better-working markets due to greater investor confidence resulting from lower adverse selection and moral hazard (Section 4.6.1). Other benefits of information production include reduction of monopoly power due to improved ability of potential entrants to an industry to identify profitable investment opportunities (Section 1.2), timely identification of failing firms (Section 8.4.2), reporting on stewardship (Section 10.5), and situations where information released by one firm generates information about others (Section 12.9.1).

Costs of information production[4] include the direct costs of preparing and releasing information, possible release of proprietary information (Section 12.3), and possible increased contracting costs resulting, for example, from greater earnings volatility produced by fair value accounting (Section 7.5.2).

For some competitive industries with a large number of firms and customers, such as agriculture and other commodities, market forces can generate equilibrium production quantities that approximate first best, with relatively little regulation.[5]

However, the characteristics of information and its various costs and benefits to society are so complex and varied that market forces alone are unlikely to attain first best.

12.5 MARKET FAILURES IN THE PRODUCTION OF INFORMATION

We now consider some of the market failures that prevent first-best information production.

12.5.1 Externalities and Free-Riding

We begin with two definitions:

> An **externality** is an action taken by a firm or individual that imposes costs or benefits on other firms or individuals for which the entity creating the externality is not charged or does not receive revenue.
>
> **Free-riding** is the receipt by a firm or individual of a benefit from an externality at little or no cost.

The crucial aspect of externalities and free-riding is that the costs and benefits of information production as perceived by the firm differ from the costs and benefits to society.

Anilowski, Feng, and Skinner (2007) examined the relationship between management's quarterly guidance about future earnings and aggregate stock market performance. If, for example, a large number of managers report that earnings are expected to increase, this creates an externality that conveys information about future performance of the economy, which would be quite useful to investors. If so, we should observe an increase in the stock market index following a lot of good news expected earnings guidance. The authors did find evidence of this effect[6] for "bellwether" firms, which are the largest 20 firms in their sample. However, they concluded that for most firms in their sample, issuance of earnings guidance *follows* the performance of the economy, rather than providing information about its future performance. That is, the number and timeliness of forecasts falls short of what is socially desirable. They suggested that if more firms would issue earnings guidance sooner, the externality effect would expand, benefiting society through better investment decisions.

With respect to free-riding, we noted in Section 5.5 that, due to the public-good nature of accounting information, its use by one individual does not destroy it for use by another. Then, other investors can "free-ride" on this information. Since all investors will realize this, no one has an incentive to pay. As a result, it is difficult for the firm to charge for producing accounting information, in which case it produces less information than is socially desirable.

In sum, the effects of externalities and free-riding are that since the firm cannot generate revenue or other benefits from all of its information production, it will produce less than it would otherwise. Thus externalities and free-riding are well-known reasons why market forces do not generate first-best information production. Then, the regulator steps in to try to restore the socially correct amount of production.

12.5.2 The Adverse Selection Problem

In our context, there are two versions of the adverse selection problem. First, we have the problem of insider trading, which was introduced in Chapter 4. If opportunities exist for insiders, including managers, to generate excessive profits by trading on the basis of their insider information, persons willing to do this will be attracted to the opportunity. Then, outside investors will not perceive the securities market as a level playing field. They reduce the amount they are willing to pay for all securities, or withdraw from the market completely. In effect, information production is not first-best since useful information is withheld from the market for insiders' benefit.

A second version of adverse selection arises when managers who are privy to bad news about the firm's future do not release that information, thereby avoiding, or at least postponing, the negative firm consequences. This lack of timeliness also constitutes a failure to produce information.

12.5.3 The Moral Hazard Problem

In Section 10.2, we noted the findings of Bushman, Engel, and Smith (2006), which suggested that net income is not completely informative about effort. A reason is that managers may be able to disguise shirking, and resulting low profitability, by opportunistic earnings management and/or by reducing voluntary disclosure. Thus, despite managerial labour markets and incentive contracts, investors will also be concerned about moral hazard and (bad) earnings management.

The 2007–2008 market meltdowns provide a recent example of moral hazard leading to market failure. Managers of financial institutions that were "too big to fail" knew that they would, if necessary, be rescued by the government. Consequently, they had an incentive to take on excessive risk (a form of shirking), which they disguised by, for example, avoiding consolidation of off balance sheet entities. This contributed to the severe market failures that are described in Section 1.3.

12.5.4 Unanimity

A characteristic of economies with markets that do not work well is a lack of **unanimity**, which derives from the effects of adverse selection and moral hazard just described. If markets work well, shareholders will be unanimously in favour of the manager maximizing the market value of the firm. When markets do not work well because of adverse selection and moral hazard, this need not be the case. Eckern and Wilson (1974) studied this problem with respect to the physical production of the firm—that is, the types and quantities of products to be produced—and showed that the manager's choice of production plan to maximize the market value of the firm would not in general be approved by all shareholders under certain market conditions.

A similar result applies to firms' production of information. Blazenko and Scott (1986) analyzed an economy where the information market does not work well, due to adverse selection. While the firm manager was motivated to choose an audit quality that would maximize firm market value (recall that an audit is a form of information production), all shareholders would prefer a higher-quality audit. The reason is that from the shareholders' perspective, there are two valuable functions of the audit. One is to add credibility to the firm's financial statements, as we have mentioned. This benefits both shareholders and manager. The other is that the audit provides a form of insurance. For example, it may force disclosure of information that the manager would prefer not to disclose, or it may discover inside information that the manager had intended to opportunistically suppress or distort. This role benefits only the shareholders. Consequently, the audit is of greater value to the shareholders, who will demand more information than the manager wishes to supply.

We conclude that market forces are unable to drive first-best information production. Thus some degree of regulation is to be expected in the information industry. However, due to the variety and complexity of the social costs and benefits of information, the regulator is unable to implement first-best either. It seems that some combination of regulation and private information production is needed if the information market is to work reasonably well.[7]

12.6 CONTRACTUAL INCENTIVES FOR INFORMATION PRODUCTION

12.6.1 Examples of Contractual Incentives

Despite the inability of regulation and/or market forces to generate first-best information production, there is a surprising number of incentives whereby firms want to produce information. One set of incentives arises from the contracts that firms enter into. As we saw in Chapter 9, information is necessary to monitor compliance with contracts. For example, if managerial effort is unobservable, this leads to an incentive contract, under which the manager's compensation is based on some observable measure of the firm's operations, such as net income. Also, an audit adds credibility to reported net income, so that both the owner and the manager of the firm are willing to accept reported net income as a measure of current managerial performance.

Similarly, when a firm issues debt, it typically includes covenants in the contract. Information is needed about the various ratios on which the covenants are based, so that the firm's adherence to its covenants can be monitored over the life of the debt issue. Again, an audit adds credibility to the covenant information.

Another contract-based reason for private information production arises when a privately owned firm goes public. This was modelled by Jensen and Meckling (1976). The owner–manager of a firm going public, after selling all or part interest, has a motivation to increase shirking. Prior to the IPO, the shirking problem was internalized—the owner–manager bore all the costs. The costs of shirking are the reduced profits that result.

Subsequent to the new issue, the owner–manager, assuming he/she continues to manage the firm, does not bear all the costs—the new investors will bear their proportionate share. Thus, shirking costs the owner–manager less after going public, so he or she will engage in more of it. Furthermore, the owner-manager now has an incentive to exploit inside information at the expense of the new investors. Thus the new investors face agency costs of both moral hazard and adverse selection.

Investors will be aware of these agency costs, however, and will bid down the amount they are willing to pay for the new issue by their expected amount. To reduce this penalty, the owner–manager has an incentive to commit to releasing high quality information. One possibility is to appoint a prestigious auditor. Another is to adopt (conditionally) conservative accounting, which will increase contract efficiency by reducing the manager's ability to recognize unrealized gains. Motivation to adopt such opportunistic actions arises from lack of alignment between manager and shareholder interests. LaFond and Roychowdhury (2008) reported evidence consistent with this argument. Based on a large sample of U.S. firms over the period 1994–2004, they reported a significant negative association between manager stock holdings and conservative financial reporting, consistent with conservative reporting counteracting the motivation of managers with low stock holdings (and thus low alignment) to overstate gains.

The key point here is that the firm has a private incentive to produce information in all of these contracting scenarios—no regulator is needed to force information production. The information production decision is internalized between the contracting parties.

12.6.2 The Coase Theorem

A key mechanism for the production of information for contracting was developed in a classic paper by Ronald Coase (1960). Coase showed conditions under which the problem of externalities can be internalized, thereby reducing the need for regulation. His demonstration has become known as the **Coase theorem**.

Coase used an illustration of two farms, side by side. One farmer raises cattle, the other grows crops. The externality is that the cattle stray into the crops, trampling them and reducing their value. One solution is regulation—farmers could be required to fence their properties. However, there is an alternative. Assume that a fence costs $100, and that the damage to crops totals $150. Suppose first that property rights belong to the cattle farmer—he/she has the right to let cattle stray onto the neighbour's field. Then, the crop farmer will erect a fence, since its cost is less than the crop damage. Alternatively, if the crop farmer has property rights, and thus the right to recover damages from the cattle farmer, the cattle farmer will erect a fence, since its cost is less than the damages that would have to be paid.

The important point of the Coase theorem is that regardless of how property rights are assigned, the fence will be built. This is socially desirable since the cost of the fence is less than the damage without it.[8] In effect, regulation is replaced by bargaining and contracting between the interested parties.

To translate the Coase theorem into an accounting context, consider a slightly extended example, in which a firm has information that, if released, will cost it $100. However, this information will benefit an investor, who values it at $150. Suppose that the investor has the right to demand that the information be released. The firm will release the information since this incurs costs of $100—less than the $150 cost of reimbursing the investor for damages if the information is not released.

A more reasonable assumption, however, is that the firm has the property rights to its information. That is, the firm has some monopoly power, since the investor is willing to pay up to $150 for information that if released will cost the firm only $100. What happens next depends on the parties' relative bargaining power. If, for example, they are evenly matched, a reasonable contract could be that the investor pays $125 for the information.

Regardless of the outcome, however, the information will be released without regulation. This is socially desirable since the benefits of the information total $150 whereas the costs of releasing it are $100.

In principle, the Coase contractual motivation for information production can be extended to any group of contracting parties.[9,10] However, different investors will, in general, want different amounts of information about the firm. One investor, adept at financial analysis, might demand a very fine projection of future operations, from which to prepare an estimate of future cash flows and returns on investment. Another investor may simply want information about the firm's dividend policy. A very risk-averse investor might demand a very credible and high cost audit, while another investor would prefer the least costly audit available. Other investors may not demand any information at all, particularly if their investment portfolios are well diversified. Instead, they might rely on market efficiency to price-protect them.

If the manager were to attempt to negotiate a contract for information production with every potential investor, the negotiation costs alone would be prohibitive. In addition, to the extent that different investors want different information, the firm's costs of information production would also be prohibitive. If, as an alternative, the manager attempted to negotiate a single contract with all investors, these investors would have to agree on what information they wanted. Again, given the disparate information needs of different investors, this process would be extremely time-consuming and costly if, indeed, it was possible at all. Hence, the contracting approach seems feasible only when there are a few parties involved.

Even if contracting parties do reach an information production agreement, another problem arises. Unless the agreement can be enforced (as in a cooperative game), parties to the agreement may be tempted to violate it for their own short-run benefit. For example, suppose that a managerial compensation contract provides for a year-end audit. Knowing this, the manager works hard during the year. Then, since the manager's effort has already been exerted, the principal (i.e., the shareholder or investor) would benefit from cancelling the audit, thereby saving the audit costs. But cancelling the audit this year will reduce the incentive for the manager to work hard next year.

It should now be apparent that while direct contracting for information production may be good in principle, it will not always work in practice. Indeed, Coase himself recognized that when a large number of people are involved, the costs of bargaining may be high. Thus, while contracts are an important source of private information production, we cannot rely on them completely for the information needs of society.

12.7 MARKET-BASED INCENTIVES FOR INFORMATION PRODUCTION

Accordingly, we now turn to a second set of private incentives for firms' information production. We will call these **market-based incentives**. Several markets are involved.

The *managerial labour market* constantly evaluates manager performance. As a result, managers who release false, incomplete, or biased information will suffer damage to their reputations. While reputation considerations do not completely remove the need for incentive contracts, as discussed in Section 10.2, they do reduce the amount of incentives needed. In terms of Example 9.2, where the manager received a 32.37% profit share, a profit share of, say, 20% may be sufficient when reputation considerations are taken into account.[11] With a lower proportion of compensation at risk, the (risk-averse) manager is less concerned about releasing information that affects firm value. Thus, the managerial labour market provides important incentives for information production.

Similar incentives are provided by *capital markets*. Managers are motivated by reputation and contracting considerations to increase firm value. This creates an incentive to release information to the market. The reason is that more information, by reducing expected losses from adverse selection and estimation risk (Section 4.6.3), increases investor confidence in the firm. If so, the market prices of the firm's securities may rise or, equivalently, its cost of capital will fall. This will show up in enhanced firm profitability and value, hence enhanced reservation utility and compensation for the manager.

Another market that disciplines managers is the *takeover market*, also called the market for corporate control. If the manager does not increase firm value, the firm may be subject to a takeover bid, which, if successful, frequently results in replacement of the manager. The more disgruntled the shareholders are, the more likely that such a takeover bid will be successful. Consequently, the takeover market also motivates managers to increase firm value, with implications for information production similar to those of the managerial labour and capital markets.

12.8 A CLOSER LOOK AT MARKET-BASED INCENTIVES

12.8.1 The Disclosure Principle

A simple argument can be made that suggests that a manager will release all information, good or bad. This is known as the **disclosure principle**.[12] If rational investors know that the manager has some decision-useful information, but do not know what it is, they will assume that if it was favourable the manager would release it. Thus, if investors do not observe the manager releasing it, they will assume the worst and bid down the market value of the firm's shares accordingly. For example, suppose that all investors know that a manager possesses a forecast of next year's earnings, but they do not know what the forecast is. The manager may as well release it, as failure to do so would be interpreted by the market as the lowest possible forecast.

This argument is reinforced by the manager's incentive to keep the firm's share price from falling. As mentioned earlier, a fall in share price will harm the manager through lower remuneration and/or through lower value on the labour market for managers. Since the market will assume the worst if the information is not released, any release of credible information will prevent share price and market value from falling as low as it would otherwise.

Undoubtedly, the disclosure principle operates in many situations—see Theory in Practice 12.1. However, it does not always work. This was examined by Verrecchia (1983), who sought to reconcile the disclosure principle with the empirical observation that managers do not always fully disclose. Verrecchia assumed that, if disclosure is made, it is truthful. He also assumed that there is a cost to disclosure. The cost is constant, independent of the nature of the information. For example, there may be a proprietary cost of releasing valuable patent information. He assumed that investors know that the manager has the news, and know its cost of disclosure, but do not know what the news is.

Theory in Practice 12.1

General Electric Corporation (GE) is a large and complex U.S.-based conglomerate, with operations extending from industrial and medical equipment to aircraft leasing and mortgage lending. Its share price fell considerably during 2000–2002, following the Enron scandal and resulting stock market collapse and economic recession. This fall occurred despite there being no evidence that GE had engaged in any irregular accounting practices, and reflected the general decline of public confidence in financial reporting at that time.

GE adopted a number of strategies to halt and reverse its share price decline. Several of these strategies involved increased disclosure. GE's CEO was quoted as saying "If the annual report ... has to be the size of the New York City phone book, that's life." For example, GE's 2001 annual report, issued in March, 2002, disclosed separate revenue and operating profits for 26 of its business segments, up from 12 segments previously. The company also provided extensive discussion of its off balance sheet entities, in view of the abuses of these entities by Enron. It disclosed that none of its off balance sheet entities was allowed to hold GE stock, and that none of them engaged in speculative activities, or were used to hedge any of GE's operations. Furthermore, GE employees were not allowed to invest in any of them.

Also, the CEO reaffirmed the firm's 2002 earnings forecast, and GE began providing quarterly conference calls and webcasts, available to analysts and investors, to answer questions and provide additional information about its earnings announcements.

GE also announced in 2002 that it would voluntarily begin to record options to employees (ESOs) as an expense. (An FASB standard requiring expensing of ESOs did not come into effect until 2005.)

If we rank the nature of the news on a continuum from bad to good, Verrecchia showed that for a given disclosure cost there is a threshold level of disclosure. The manager, who is assumed to maximize firm value, will disclose the information only if it exceeds the threshold. Then, the disclosure principle fails. The lower the disclosure cost, the lower the threshold, and if disclosure cost is zero, the disclosure principle is reinstated.

Also, as shown by Dye (1985), the disclosure principle can break down due to a conflict between information desired by investors and information needed for contracting purposes. Recall from our discussion in Chapter 10 that manager compensation is based, at least in part, on share price performance. Suppose that the firm has incurred costs to prepare a forecast of net income. The market knows the forecast exists but does not know the amount. If reported, the forecast will affect share price. This reduces the ability of share price to reflect manager effort, since this ability is swamped by the impact of the forecast on price. In effect, release of the forecast incurs an agency cost that reduces the efficiency of the manager's compensation contract. Thus, it may be desirable to discourage the reporting of forecasts even though a forecast provides useful information to investors. The best information for contracting may not be the best information for investor decision-making, and the investor information may not be reported for contracting reasons. This suggests that, like a securities market, a managerial labour market does not guarantee that information release is complete. Dye's model provides a supplement to legal liability as an expected cost of forecasting.

It seems that while the disclosure principle is a simple and compelling argument for the release of inside information, it may break down, and hence cannot be relied upon to ensure that firms always release full information. The following section reviews other conditions under which the disclosure principle may fail.

12.8.2 Empirical Disclosure Principle Research[*]

Note that, consistent with the disclosure principle, Verrecchia assumed that the market knows that the manager has the information. What if the market is unsure about this? Is there still an incentive for the manager to voluntarily release information? Also, what if the firm has more than one item of information? Under what conditions will the manager reveal all items, some of them, or none? What if the information is non-proprietary?

Pae (2005) considered these questions. Consider, for example, a forecast of earnings and a cash flow forecast. It is costly for a firm to develop these two items of non-proprietary information. Consequently, investors do not know whether the firm has internally generated the information or not. Pae assumed that investors assess probabilities that the firm

---

[*]This section can be omitted with little loss of continuity.

has no forecasts, only one forecast, or both. While forecasts are costly to develop, Pae assumed that there is no cost to release them (i.e., non-proprietary information). If a disclosure is made, it is assumed truthful.[13]

Pae showed that if the firm has developed both forecasts, the manager who wants to maximize firm value will disclose them if they are both sufficiently favourable to exceed disclosure thresholds, especially if the items tend to confirm each other (high forecast earnings and high cash flows tend to go together, for example). However, if one forecast is below a threshold and the other above, only the one above will be disclosed. If both are below thresholds, neither will be disclosed.

If the firm has developed one forecast, it will disclose it if it exceeds a threshold. Otherwise, it discloses nothing.

If the firm has not developed either forecast, it will obviously disclose nothing. Note that if a firm discloses nothing, investors do not know whether the firm has developed both forecasts but they are both below their thresholds, developed one but it is below its threshold, or has developed neither. This is what prevents the disclosure principle from operating to force full disclosure—recall that this principle requires that investors know the firm has the information.[14]

Pae's threshold results seem similar to those of Verrecchia. The difference, however, is that the information is non-proprietary, and the manager's motivation to release it derives from its effect on investor uncertainty and firm value. In Verrecchia's model, disclosure must also overcome the proprietary cost of releasing the information. Nevertheless, the general impression from both models is that the better the news, the more likely it is to be disclosed voluntarily.

Einhorn (2007) examined a scenario where the market is unsure about the manager's reporting objective. Some managers may want to maximize firm value to enhance their reputation, to increase the value of shares and ESOs they own, and/or to protect against a possible takeover bid. Other managers, however, may want to minimize firm value. For example, we saw in Section 8.6 that some managers manipulate share price downward prior to ESO awards. Also, as discussed in Section 11.3, managers may want to lower ne income for bonus purposes or for political reasons.

Suppose that a manager has inside information about firm value. Suppose also that the market feels that most managers want to maximize firm value. Consistent with the disclosure principle, the manager who wants to maximize firm value will disclose this information unless the news is very bad.

However, in Einhorn's model, managers who want to lower firm value can exploit the disclosure policy of value-maximizing managers. Since the market knows that value-minimizing managers are rare, their failure to disclose is almost as effective in lowering their firm value as it is for value-maximizing managers. Unless the value-minimizing manager's information is very bad, non-disclosure will result in a value lower than what would result from disclosure. Then, the value-minimizing manager will not disclose, and the disclosure principle fails.

The above models implicitly assume that all investors react the same way to the lack of disclosure, and the firm knows this. What if the firm is unsure of investor reaction? This scenario was modelled by Suijs (2007). In his model, a rational investor can allocate investment between the firm in question, to another firm, or to a risk-free asset. The goal of the firm is to attract as much of this investment as feasible. The firm knows its profitability but investors do not. However, the firm does not know the profitability of the other firm. Consequently, it is unsure of investor reaction. For example, if it discloses its profitability and this is less than the profitability of the other firm, it will attract no investment,

Obviously, if the firm's profitability is less than the risk-free rate, it will not want to disclose. However, even if the firm's profitability is higher than the risk-free rate, it may not disclose either, since there is a risk that the profitability of the other firm is even higher, in which case, as mentioned, the firm will attract no investment if it discloses. If the firm expects that this risk outweighs the benefit of reporting its profitability, it will not disclose and the disclosure principle fails.

In sum, when the requirements of the disclosure principle are not fully met, all of the above models predict zero or partial disclosure. That is, while the capital market encourages voluntary release, it by no means ensures that all information will be released. As a result, a role for regulation remains.[15]

In this regard, Einhorn (2005) showed that voluntary disclosure depends on the quality of regulated disclosure. To illustrate, suppose that an oil and gas company, whose manager wants to maximize firm value, has two segments. A production segment explores for and sells crude oil and natural gas. Due to high energy prices, this segment is currently very profitable. The other segment refines and markets oil products. Traditionally, this segment has low profit margins. The firm is concerned about reporting high profits because this creates the possibility of proprietary costs such as an excess profits tax or other political costs.

Assume initially that GAAP is of low quality. Specifically, separate reporting of segments is not required. Consequently, to reduce political costs, the firm disguises the high profits of the production segment by combining them with the refining segment.

Now suppose that the firm has accurate inside information about the level of crude oil and gas prices next period. Should it release this information even though not required to do so? The higher the expected prices, the higher will be share price, other things equal, since investors will respond positively to higher expected future product prices. However, if high expected product prices are reported, political costs will increase since the market will then figure out the excessive profits of the production segment.

Einhorn showed that there is a threshold level of next-period prices above which the forecast information will be disclosed. That is, if the expected prices are high enough, the positive effect on firm value of high future prices outweighs the negative effect of increased political costs. Furthermore, the higher the current reported net income, the higher the disclosure threshold for the forecast—since high reported earnings operate to increase the prospect of political costs, the firm can less "afford" to make matters worse by reporting the favourable forecast. If the forecast is not reported, the disclosure principle fails.

Now suppose that GAAP quality improves. Specifically, the earnings of each firm segment must now be disclosed. Then, everyone knows the high past profitability of the production segment. Reporting the high forecast would further add to the prospect of political costs. Einhorn showed that the firm would prefer to disclose bad news, not good news. That is, the disclosure threshold switches so that only expected prices *below* a threshold will be voluntarily reported.[16]

The above studies assume that information released under the disclosure principle is credible. That is, the market must know that the manager has an incentive to reveal it truthfully. Obviously, if a manager lies about next year's forecast of net income, it can hardly be said that information is being disclosed. Information that is subject to verification after the event, such as a forecast, will be credible to the extent that misstatement can be proved and penalties applied. Another way to secure credibility is to have released information attested to by a third party, such as an auditor. However, since much inside information is not verifiable even after the fact, or subject to audit, truthful disclosure cannot always be attained.

The need for truthful disclosure is relaxed somewhat by Newman and Sansing (1993) (NS). They analyzed a two-period model consisting of an incumbent firm, a representative shareholder, and a potential entrant to the industry. The firm manager, who is assumed to act in the shareholder's best interests, knows the firm value exactly. If it were not for the potential entrant, the shareholder's best interests would be served if the firm committed to publicly disclosing this value, since the shareholder could then optimally plan consumption and investment over the two periods. However, full disclosure of firm value may trigger entry, in which case the incumbent firm will suffer a loss of profits and value. How should the firm report?

The answer depends on the costs to the entrant should it decide to enter the industry, and the resulting loss of profits to the incumbent. For example, if entry costs are high and there is substantial loss of profits upon entry, the incumbent firm may disclose imprecise information about its value. That is, instead of an exact disclosure, it will disclose an interval within which its value lies. If it reported its value exactly, its disclosures would not be credible, since everyone knows it has an incentive to deter entry.[17]

Disclosure in the NS model is truthful in the sense that the firm credibly reveals an interval within which its value lies, that is, a range estimate. Nevertheless, the firm does not fully report the truth since it does not report its value exactly. Interestingly, Cotter, Tuna, and Wysocki (2006), in an empirical study of management's quarterly public earnings forecasts, reported that range estimates are the most common form of forecast in their sample.[18]

12.8.3 Signalling

It frequently happens that firms differ in quality. For example, a firm may have better investment opportunities than other firms. Alternatively, a firm may conduct superior R&D, leading to potentially valuable patents. Such information would be of considerable usefulness to investors. Yet, voluntary disclosure of the details of high-quality projects and technology may reveal valuable proprietary information. Furthermore, even if the manager did disclose the details, he/she may not be believed by a skeptical marketplace. How can the manager credibly reveal the firm's **type**, as these underlying quality differences are called, without incurring the excessive costs?

This problem of separating firms of different types has been extensively considered by means of signalling models.

> A **signal** is an action taken by a high-type manager that would not be rational if that manager was low type.

A necessary requirement for a signal is that it be less costly for a high-type manager than for a low type. This is what gives a signal its credibility, since it is then irrational for a low type to mimic a high type, and the market knows this.

Spence (1973) was the first to formally model signalling equilibria. He did so in the context of a job market. Given that it is less costly (i.e., less effort needed) to a high-type job applicant to obtain a specified level of education than to a low type, Spence showed that equilibria exist where employers can rely on the applicant's chosen level of education as a credible signal of that person's underlying competence.

A number of signals have been suggested that are relevant to accounting. Leland and Pyle (1977) showed that for an entrepreneur/manager making an initial public offering (IPO), the proportion of equity retained is a signal, because it would not be rational for a bad-news manager to retain a high-equity position—he/she would find this too costly. Also, audit quality can be a signal of the value of a new securities issue. A rational manager would be unlikely to retain a high-quality (and high-cost) auditor when the firm is a low type—why pay more to credibly reveal poor prospects? Similar arguments relate to the choice of underwriter for a new stock issue. Titman and Trueman (1986) and Datar, Feltham, and Hughes (1991) developed models where audit quality is a signal.

A forecast can be a signal. For example, it is less costly for a high-type firm to release a high-quality, good-news forecast—a low-type firm would be unlikely to meet a good-news forecast and its high quality would only increase investor backlash. In MD&A (Section 3.6), information about future firm prospects (a type of forecast) is required. However, there is sufficient latitude in the MD&A requirements that firms can signal by means of their forecast quality. For example, we concluded in Section 3.6.3 that forward-looking information in Canadian Tire's MD&A went beyond minimal requirements. As a result, its disclosure has a signalling component, since in addition to the information in the disclosure itself, the firm's willingness to choose high-quality disclosure reveals inside information that management has a confident and well-planned view of its future, thereby adding credibility to the forecast.

A firm's capital structure has signalling properties. There is evidence, for example, that the market value of existing common shares falls when the firm issues new shares. While dilution of existing shareholders' equity is one possibility, another explanation is the market's concern that the new shares may be issued by a low-type firm—a high-type firm would be more likely to issue bonds or finance internally. One reason for issuing debt is that the high profitability of a high-type firm would then accrue to existing shareholders. Another reason is that a high-type firm would assess its probability of bankruptcy as low (thus, the probability that the shareholders would have to hand the firm over to the bondholders is low).

Dividend policy can also be a signal. A high payout ratio may signal a firm as having a confident future. However, a high payout ratio could also mean that the firm sees little prospect for profitable projects that could be financed internally through retained earnings. Thus, dividend policy may not be as effective a signal as others.

Accounting policy choice also has signalling properties. For example, a firm may adopt a number of conservative accounting policies. A high-type firm can do this and still report profits, while a low-type firm would report losses. Thus, conservative accounting policies can also signal a manager's confident view of the firm's future.

Firms may also use multiple signals. Fan (2007) modelled a high-type firm whose entrepreneur/manager is issuing an IPO, and used both reported earnings and ownership retention as signals. There are costs to the firm of managing earnings (e.g., possible litigation if the earnings management is discovered and/or the costs of real earnings management such as cutting R&D). There is no cost to the firm of ownership retention. Fan predicted that the high-type manager will nevertheless use reported earnings as a signal. Specifically, he/she will manage reported earnings upward so as to raise the expected forecasting costs of a low-type firm that may wish to mimic the high-type's reported earnings. However, since there is no cost of ownership retention, the high-type firm manager will also use this second signal to attain the most efficient signalling combination. Fan reported empirical evidence consistent with these predictions.

Note that for signals to be applicable, the manager must have a *choice*. Indeed, Spence (1973) showed that for a viable signalling equilibrium to exist, there must be a sufficient number of signal levels available to the manager. For example, if a regulator imposed a uniform level of audit quality on all firms, audit quality would not be available as a signal. Furthermore, reducing the latitude to choose level of forecasting quality in MD&A would reduce its signalling content.

This argument, that standards to enforce uniform accounting destroy managers' abilities to signal, is important for standard setting. In Section 2.5.1 we suggested that a problem with historical cost accounting is that there is no unique way to match costs with revenues, implying that diversity in reporting practices is undesirable because of reduced comparability of financial statements. This implication is correct as far as it goes. Diversity in reporting practices imposes costs on investors who want to compare the performance of different entities, because it is necessary to restate their financial statements to a common basis before valid comparisons can be made.

However, if we reconsider this implication in the light of signalling theory, we see that diversity may not be as bad as first suggested. To the extent that firms' choices of accounting policies signal credible information about those firms, diversity of reporting practices is desirable. This argument is reinforced by our discussion of earnings management in Chapter 11. We argued there that some earnings management can be good since it can serve as a vehicle for the release of inside information. For example, earnings management to reveal blocked inside information about persistent earning power can be interpreted as a signal since it can be very costly for a low-type manager to report higher earnings than can be maintained (since accruals reverse). Obviously, earnings management by means of accounting policy choice is feasible only if there is a sufficiently rich set of accounting policies within GAAP from which to choose. Signalling theory serves as a counterargument to the continual refinement of GAAP so as to eliminate accounting policy choice.

12.8.4 Private Information Search

To this point, our investigation of market-based incentives for release of information has centred on the manager. The argument has been that a high level of information release may improve the manager's reputation, lower investors' estimation risk, and reduce the firm's cost of capital to the firm's and manager's benefit. Thus, the onus is on the manager to release information.

Implicit in this line of reasoning is that investors are passive. They merely react to whatever information the manager releases in deciding on their demand for the firm's securities. In effect, they are price-protected by the market. It may be, however, that many investors will be active in seeking out information, particularly in the presence of noise traders or securities market inefficiencies. For example, they may conduct their own investigations and analyses of fundamental firm value, or hire financial analysts, mutual fund managers, and other experts to assist them. They may watch closely persons who they suspect have inside information and mimic their actions.

Thus, there is a variety of ways that investors or their representatives can conduct a **private information search**. Bill Cautious, in Example 3.1, did so by analysis of the annual report, using Bayes' theorem to process the resulting information, thereby updating his prior knowledge of the state of the firm. Other investors will also become informed, or perhaps buy the information from Bill. To the extent that such activities are successful, private inside information is very quickly transferred into public information. By limiting the time available to insiders to capitalize on inside information, the severity of the adverse selection problem is reduced.

Unfortunately, private information search can be quite costly from society's perspective, since more than one investor incurs costs to discover the same information. It would be cheaper, in terms of total resources used to generate information, if the firm produced the information only once, making the information public. Then, each investor would not have to rediscover it.

Hirshleifer's (1971) analysis is a classic in the area of private information search. Hirshleifer considered an exchange economy—that is, an economy without production of goods and services. Then, Hirshleifer's analysis implied that the social value of costly information search is negative, even though individual investors may perceive it as valuable. The reason is that, without production, the amount of goods and services in the economy is fixed. Then, even if the information is made public, its release just redistributes wealth, it does not create wealth. Since information production has a cost, the net social effect is negative.

Hirshleifer also considered a production economy. Costly information search to predict state realization is still perceived as valuable by the individual investor, but does not benefit society because the insider's gain is offset by losses suffered by those not possessing that information. Thus, when developing this inside information is costly, the net social effect is negative. To the extent that this information finds its way into the public domain, however, investors will redirect their investments to those firms best able to take advantage of the state realization, thereby increasing production in society. Then, society benefits from private information search. However, the costs of developing and publicizing this information create a drag on these benefits.

12.9 ARE FIRMS REWARDED FOR SUPERIOR DISCLOSURE?

12.9.1 Theory

If market forces are to motivate superior disclosure, firms should benefit through higher share price and lower cost of capital. There are several ways that these benefits can be achieved.

One way is to improve the ability of investors to diversify. Merton (1987) presented a model where information asymmetry is modelled as only a subset of investors knowing about each firm. As a result, investors cannot fully diversify to eliminate their idiosyncratic risk (Section 3.5). And as a result of this additional risk, the firm's cost of capital is greater than that given by the CAPM (Section 4.5). If the firm can increase the size of its subset of investors, say, by superior disclosure, its cost of capital will fall and its market value rise, other things equal. In effect, idiosyncratic risk is reduced through better diversification.

A second way for the firm to benefit from information production is to improve liquidity.[19] In the model of Diamond and Verrecchia (1991), credible[20] voluntary disclosure reduces information asymmetry between the firm and the market, thereby increasing liquidity of trading in its shares. This attracts large institutional investors who, if they have to do so in future, can then sell large blocks of the firm's shares without the risk of lowering the price they receive. The firm's share price increases as a result of this greater demand.

A third approach to lowering cost of capital is to reduce investor estimation risk. Easley and O'Hara (EO; 2004) presented a model with inside and outside information. They showed that investors demand a higher expected return (i.e., higher than the CAPM) the greater the ratio of inside information to outside. The reason is that insiders can make better investment decisions than outsiders due to their information advantage. Outside investors know this but, due to noise trading, are unable to fully infer from share price what this inside information is—it could be good or bad. Thus, outsiders face estimation risk, which cannot be fully diversified away if the number of investors and securities is finite (which EO assumed). Consequently, investors demand a higher expected return to compensate. The more inside information there is relative to outside, the stronger this effect is. If so, firms can reduce their costs of capital and increase market value by reducing inside information through superior disclosure.

The EO model, however, has been criticized by several authors. In addition to assuming a finite number of investors, EO assumed that returns on firms' shares are independent. Thus, there is no role for covariances between returns in their model. Yet, the CAPM tells us that covariances, through beta, are a crucial component of cost of capital. This leads to a related way to reduce cost of capital—namely, to reduce market synchronicity; that is, to reduce the extent to which share prices move together (see Chapter 4, Note 6). This will be accomplished to the extent that high quality disclosure enables share prices to reflect firm-specific information, which could be good or bad.

In this regard, Lambert, Leuz, and Verrecchia (2007) showed conditions under which lower syncronicity reduces cost of capital. They pointed out that information about one firm often affects the market's expectations about other firms. For example, consider a large firm such as General Electric Corporation (GE). If GE improves the informativeness of its reporting, for example by increased disclosure of its various divisions' operations, the market is better able to predict GE's future performance. However, due to GE's size and diversity, its performance also provides investors with information about the future performance of other firms, so that the market is better able to predict the future performance and share price of these firms. Then, since each firm's share price better reflects that firm's firm-specific performance, the market exhibits less synchronicity. That is, with more informative reporting by GE, investors' assessed covariances of GE's share performance with other firms decreases. Since a stock's beta is essentially the covariance between its return and the return of other firms in the market (Section 4.5), GE's beta falls, reducing its cost of capital.

More generally, if a firm reduces information asymmetry about itself through higher quality disclosure, its share price then reflects more information about itself relative to the effects of economy-wide events. As a result, investors' assessment of its share price covariance with other firms in the market falls. Thus, other things equal, its cost of capital falls. As Lambert, Leuz, and Verrecchia pointed out, estimation risk in financial reporting cannot be diversified away when reporting quality affects the covariance terms, since these terms increase greatly in number as the number of firms in the investor's portfolio increases.[21]

A variety of other models also investigate superior disclosure. For example, non-cooperative game theory models (Section 8.10) are used to study disclosure decisions. In an early study, Darrough and Stoughton (DS; 1990) analyzed a game between a monopolistic firm (the incumbent) and a potential entrant to the industry (the entrant). The incumbent needs to raise equity capital for a new project. It has inside information about itself that can be either favourable or unfavourable about its future prospects. If the information is favourable, its disclosure will lower the incumbent's cost of capital for its new equity issue. However, the entrant will revise upward its prior probability of good future prospects in the industry upon seeing the favourable disclosure. This will encourage the entrant to enter. If the information is unfavourable, its disclosure[22] will deter the entrant but raise cost of capital. What should the incumbent do—disclose or not disclose?

The answer depends on how profitable the incumbent is. If existing monopoly profits are high and the need for equity capital is moderate, the dominant consideration for the incumbent is to deter entry. Then, DS showed that if the entrant has high prior probability that the incumbent's inside information is favourable and/or the costs of entry to the industry are low (i.e., the threat of entry is high), the incumbent firm will fully disclose its inside information, favourable or unfavourable. If the incumbent's inside information is unfavourable, its loss of profits if the entrant enters outweighs the higher cost of capital, so the incumbent will disclose so as to discourage entry. If its inside information is favourable, the incumbent will disclose even if this attracts entry since profits will still be satisfactory, particularly in view of the lower cost of capital following the favourable disclosure.

Other outcomes are possible, however. DS showed that if the entrant has low prior probability that the incumbent's inside information is favourable (low threat of entry), the incumbent will not disclose favourable or unfavourable information. Even the incumbent with favourable news will be better off not disclosing if the higher profits from discouraging entry outweigh the higher cost of capital that results.

These conclusions are of interest, because they suggest that the question of full disclosure extends into industry structure. In the DS model, the greater the competition in an industry (measured by the threat of entry), the better the disclosure.

DS also reinforced the claim of Merino and Neimark (Section 1.2) that, prior to the creation of the SEC in 1933, the primary role of full disclosure was to enable potential entrants to identify high-profit industries. Presumably, the higher an incumbent firm's monopoly profits the more incentive it had to deter entry by means of distorted or incomplete financial reporting.

Arya and Mittendorf (2005) also modelled a firm's voluntary disclosure (assumed truthful). When third parties (e.g., analysts, credit rating agencies) follow a firm, their information-gathering activities will generate information, which is then available to a competitor. But, by voluntarily releasing some information, the firm may be able to "herd" the third parties to accept the firm's information, thereby pre-empting third parties' own information-gathering activities. While revealing inside information will reduce firm profits by giving competitive advantage to the competitor, the reduction may be less than what would be revealed if the third parties pursued their other information-gathering activities. If so, the firm will disclose voluntarily.

12.9.2 Empirical Tests of Measures of Reporting Quality

Despite the theoretical models just described, the extent to which firms benefit from high-quality disclosure is ultimately an empirical question. Botosan (1997) conducted an early test of reporting quality, using a self-developed disclosure quality scale. She was the first to empirically document an association between superior disclosure and lower cost of capital, at least for firms followed by relatively few analysts. However, Francis, Nanda, and Olsson (2008), using a different self-developed disclosure quality scale than Botosan, found that their measure of voluntary disclosure had little or no effect on cost of capital over and above other measures of earnings quality. A possible explanation is that self-developed disclosure quality scales are highly subjective, and different scales may capture different dimensions of disclosure.

The Merton model was tested by Lehavy and Sloan (2008), based on a large sample of firms over the period 1982–2004. They used the number of wealthy investors holding a stock as a proxy for the number who "know about" that stock. After allowing for other factors that affect stock returns, they found that when the number of investors knowing about a stock increased, future returns on that stock fell (i.e., lower cost of capital), consistent with Merton's prediction. They also found that this effect strengthened as idiosyncratic risk increased. That is, when investors were poorly diversified, firm-specific risk decreased rapidly as more stocks were added to their portfolios.

Hail and Leuz (2009) pointed out that foreign firms that crosslist their shares in the United States face both increased disclosure obligations and, since they become subject to SEC regulatory enforcement, the opportunity to benefit from increased disclosure. They studied a large sample of foreign firms during the period 1990–2005, analyzing the effect on the cost of capital for those firms that chose to crosslist. They found a significant and sustained reduction in the cost of capital for firms that crosslisted on U.S. exchanges, consistent with reduced investor concern about inside information. Their results are also consistent with the Merton model, since crosslisting enlarges the set of investors who know about the firm.

Healy, Hutton, and Palepu (1999) tested implications of the Diamond and Verrecchia model. They used financial analysts' ratings of disclosure quality, based on evaluations of firms' quarterly and annual reports and investor relations, and found that firms with improved disclosure ratings were associated with a significantly improved share price in the year following the rating increase, compared to other firms in their same industry. They also found a significant increase in institutional ownership. Both of these results were predicted by Diamond and Verrecchia.

Welker (1995) investigated the effect of disclosure quality on the bid-ask spread component of liquidity. Since the bid–ask spread is a measure of information asymmetry, the greater are prospective buyers' concerns about inside information the less they will pay relative to amounts asked by sellers. Welker predicted that shares of firms with better disclosure policies would have lower spreads. After controlling for other factors that also affect spread, such as trading volume,[23] Welker found a significant negative relationship between disclosure quality (as measured by analysts' disclosure quality ratings) and the bid–ask spread. Again, this result is consistent with the Diamond and Verrecchia model.

Sengupta (1998) investigated the impact of disclosure quality on the cost of debt. He found that, on average, his sample firms enjoyed a 0.02% reduction in interest cost for every 1% increase in their disclosure quality as rated by financial analysts over the period 1987–1991. He also found that this result strengthened for riskier firms, where a firm's riskiness was measured by the standard deviation of the return on its shares. The reason for this favourable impact, according to Sengupta, was that lenders assigned lower credit risk to firms with superior disclosure policies.

Barth, Konchitchki, and Landsman (2013) examined the relationship between earnings transparency and cost of capital. They defined earnings transparency as the relationship between a firm's earnings and stock returns for the year. A stronger relationship implies that net income captures more of the firm-specific economic events that currently affect the firm's share price[24]—that is, less synchronicity.

The question then is, is greater transparency associated with lower cost of capital? If so, this would provide an incentive for firms to reduce recognition lag by, for example, greater use of fair value accounting (assuming the increased relevance outweighs reduced reliability). Based on a large sample of U.S. firms over the period 1974–2000, the authors reported significantly lower cost of capital for firms with high earnings transparency. This result is after controlling for other factors affecting cost of capital (e.g., beta, growth, ERCs).

In a test of the Lambert, Leuz, and Verrecchia (LLV 2007) model outlined in Section 12.9.1, Ashbaugh-Skaife, Collins, Kinney, and Lafond (ACKL; 2009) examined the effects of internal control deficiencies reported under Section 404 of the Sarbanes-Oxley Act (Section 1.2). Recall that under the Act, managers and auditors must report on the state of the firm's internal controls (an important component of corporate governance). ACKL found that firms reporting internal control deficiencies (i.e., low quality reporting) exhibited higher betas, estimation risk, and cost of capital than firms without such deficiencies. This is consistent with the LLV prediction of the effects of estimation risk on beta and cost of capital. ACKL also reported significant declines in cost of capital once the deficiencies were remedied.

Riedl and Serafeim (2011) also tested the 2007 LLV model. They pointed out that estimation risk surrounding the fair value of financial instruments increases as valuation moves from Level 1 to Level 2 to Level 3 (see Section 7.2.1), because more manager judgment is required as the level gets higher. The LLV 2007 model predicts that a firm with primarily Level 1 financial instruments, and thus relatively low estimation risk, should have a lower beta[25] than a similar firm whose financial instruments are primarily Level 3, with Level 2 betas in between. The authors studied a sample of U.S. financial institutions during 2007–2008. Their estimates of firms' betas were based on the market model version of the CAPM (see Equation 4.4). They found that betas increased as the fair valuation level moved from Levels 1 to 3, consistent with LLV.

Riedl and Serafeim then divided their sample into firms with high and with low quality information environments,[26] where a high quality environment implies more investors

In March, 2004, Canadian Superior Energy Inc. (now Sonde Resources Corp.) held a conference call concerning the abandonment of its Mariner E-85 exploration well off the coast of Nova Scotia. The company's CEO explained that the well was a success but that its partner, El Paso Corp., had decided not to invest more money into it. The CEO indicated his optimism that a new partner could be lined up, but refused to answer any questions from the audience.

Previously, in January 2004, Canadian Superior had issued favourable press releases about the Mariner well. However, its CEO had sold $4.3 million of his holdings of company stock in the same month. Following the news of well abandonment in March and the CEO's refusal to answer questions, the company's shares lost half their value. Class action lawsuits were initiated on behalf of U.S. investors (Canadian Superior shares were traded in the United States as well as in Canada), claiming that investors had been misled. In 2006, these lawsuits were settled by a settlement fund of $2.15 million.

"knowing about" the firm. They found that the difference between Level 3 and Levels 1 and 2 betas was lower for high information quality firms than for low information quality firms. This result is also consistent with the Merton (1987) model.

The market response to *lack of* disclosure quality is also worth noting. Kravet and Shevlin (2010) studied a sample of firms that reported financial statement restatements due to accounting irregularities during the period 1997–2002. They reported an increase in cost of capital of restatement firms, with increased estimation risk a significant contributor to the increase. They measured estimation risk using the Dechow and Dichev accrual quality model (Section 5.4.1): Lower accrual quality implies more estimation risk, and vice versa. A related result was reported by Dechow, Sloan, and Sweeney (1996), who studied firms under investigation by the SEC for violations of GAAP. They found an average drop of 9% in share price on the day the investigation is announced.

The collapses of Enron Corp. and WorldCom Inc., outlined in Section 1.2, provide dramatic examples of the consequence of poor disclosure. The loss of investor confidence was so severe that these firms' costs of capital effectively became infinite.

Theory in Practice 12.3 illustrates another consequence of poor disclosure.

12.9.3 Is Estimation Risk Diversifiable?*

The theory and evidence outlined in the previous two sections demonstrates that firms can benefit from superior disclosure. However, some investor uncertainty about the extent of a firm's inside information and possible manager shirking remains (see Chapter 4, Note 8). The question then is, are these sources of estimation risk diversifiable? If so,

---

*This section can be omitted with little loss of continuity.

investor concerns about estimation risk, hence the beneficial effects of superior disclosure on cost of capital, are reduced.

The model of Dechow and Dichev (2002), outlined in Section 5.4.1, predicts that lower accrual quality implies lower informativeness of earnings, thus higher estimation risk and cost of capital. As we noted at the time, this interpretation is supported by the empirical studies of Francis, LaFond, Olsson, and Schipper (2005), and others who reported that lower accrual quality is accompanied by higher cost of capital. This interpretation is disputed by Core, Guay, and Verdi (2008), who, following extensive empirical tests, found little evidence supporting it. However, subsequently, Ogneva (2012) found that when the effect on cost of capital estimates of changes in the market's expectations of future firm cash flows (i.e., cash flow shocks) are adjusted for, there *is* a significant negative relationship between accrual quality and cost of capital.[27]

Mohanram and Rajgopal (MR; 2009) used yet another measure of estimation risk—namely, the proportion of total buy and sell orders for a stock that come from informed investors (called the stock's PIN). Proponents of PIN argue that the higher this proportion, the greater is the concern of outside investors about adverse selection. Based on a large sample of firms with shares traded on U.S. exchanges over the period 1984–2002, MR found little evidence that PIN affects cost of capital, suggesting that estimation risk, at least as measured by PIN, can be diversified away.

However, Hwang, Lee, Lim, and Park (2013), based on a sample of large firms traded on the Korea Stock Exchange over the years 2000–2004, did find a significant positive relation between PIN and cost of capital, with the relationship stronger for firms with poor information environments (e.g., smaller firms, fewer shareholders). They estimated cost of capital by backing it out of versions of the clean surplus model described in Section 6.10. The authors attributed their results to a more accurate estimate of PIN based on stock trading data in the Korean Stock Exchange relative to that from U.S. exchanges, and to adjusting for stock liquidity—another component of PIN.

A partial explanation of these opposing results is differences in methodology. For example, accrual quality is measured in several ways, including the Dechow and Dichev procedure (Section 5.4.1), the Jones model (Section 11.3), or simply total accruals (Section 11.6.1). PIN as a measure of estimation risk is accompanied by measurement problems, such as identifying informed investors.

Also, estimation of cost of capital itself is subject to problems of methodology. While the CAPM is a place to start, estimation is complicated by other factors, such as book-to-market and firm size (Section 6.2.3), and behavioural biases (e.g., Section 6.2.1), not to mention the need to use actual market returns as a proxy for expected returns and the CAPM's failure to include complications due to liquidity, rational expectations, and common knowledge (Section 4.5.2). Another approach, backing implied cost of capital out of the clean surplus model (Section 6.10.4), requires accurate estimates of investors' future earnings expectations.[28]

A different explanation for these opposing results is suggested by the study of Lambert, Leuz, and Verrecchia (LLV 2012), who pointed out that if the number of a firm's shareholders is sufficiently large, no individual investor, including insiders, can influence the firm's share price and cost of capital through their buying and selling activity (i.e., investors are price takers or, equivalently, the firm's shares are highly liquid). Thus, from the standpoint of a price-taking investor, if some other investor buys or sells a firm's shares, share price will not be affected by that transaction, regardless of whether that other investor has inside information. If insider trades do not affect share price there is less need to be worried about inside information. Consequently, the threat of insider trading will not affect cost of capital.

However, if the number of investors in the firm is sufficiently small that they are no longer price takers, their buying and selling activities *will* affect cost of capital. The reason is that if investors observe another investor, such as an insider, buying or selling the firm's shares when estimation risk is present, they will reason that this investor may have some information that they do not,[29] and that this buying or selling activity will affect share price. They will follow that investor with their own buying and selling, thereby increasing the effect on share price and cost of capital of the original trade. The greater the degree of estimation risk, the stronger is this effect. If so, estimation risk *will* affect cost of capital.

Thus, in the LLV 2012 model, whether or not estimation risk affects a firm's cost of capital depends on whether or not investors are price takers with respect to that firm's shares.

Armstrong, Core, Taylor, and Verrecchia (ACTV; 2011) tested this argument based on a large sample of publicly traded shares over the period 1976–2005. For each sample firm, they measured estimation risk several ways, including bid–ask spread and accrual quality. They measured a firm's cost of capital by means of an extended version of the CAPM discussed in Section 4.5. After extensive tests to rule out other explanations for their findings, ACTV reported that increased estimation risk had no effect on cost of capital for those sample firms in the top 20% of number of shareholders, where the price taking assumption is most likely to apply. However, for those sample firms in the smallest 20% of number of shareholders, almost all of their measures of information asymmetry showed significantly lower cost of capital for high earnings quality firms. This result is consistent with the LLV 2012 model.

ACTV's findings suggest that questions about the diversifiability of estimation risk are primarily concentrated in firms with relatively few shareholders (which could still be a large number).

12.9.4 Conclusions

From an accounting perspective, it seems difficult to argue that firms do not benefit from superior disclosure and reduced estimation risk. Indeed, the existence of such benefits is suggested by considerable theory and empirical evidence.

However, conclusive proof is difficult. The basic problem is that the information system probabilities introduced in Section 3.3.2 are unobservable, meaning that researchers have to develop proxies for disclosure quality, as well as for information asymmetry and cost of capital. While some proxy measures support the cost of capital-lowering properties of superior disclosure, others seem not to.

We conclude that while much theory and evidence supports benefits of superior disclosure, the sources and extent of these benefits are not yet fully understood.

12.10 DECENTRALIZED REGULATION

To return to the extent of regulation, we concluded in Section 12.5 that market failures in information production are sufficiently serious that some extent of regulation is needed. However, given regulation, one can ask if the *efficiency* of regulation can be improved. One possibility is to give management some flexibility in reporting.

We call this flexible approach **decentralized regulation** (also called a "management approach") since compliance is decentralized to the internal decisions of management. While comparability across firms is reduced, decentralization improves the relevance of reporting since it is adapted to the particular firm's circumstances.

Segment reporting is an example of decentralized regulation. Information about firm segments is potentially useful to investors, since, in evaluating the performance of large and complex firms, relevant information, such as differing risks, rates of return, and opportunities for growth, may be buried in consolidated totals. Furthermore, firms vary considerably in the extent and bases of segmentation, so that segment information should better enable investors to value individual firms.

While segment reporting increases relevance, reliability is threatened to the extent that management acts opportunistically in choosing the basis and degree of aggregation of segment reporting. Theory predicts two motives for opportunism. One is that reporting on segment performance may reveal information to competitors, thus incurring proprietary costs. The second is that management wants to cover up poor performance by including poorly performing segments in larger totals. These issues were examined by Bens, Berger, and Monahan (2011). Based on a sample of U.S. firms over the period 1987–1997, they found that a segment of a multi-segment firm is less likely to be disclosed separately to the extent its gross profit remains above the industry average. Since above-average profits attract competition, this supports the proprietary cost motive. They also found that a segment is less likely to be disclosed separately to the extent that it receives financing from head office. Since such segments are likely to be poorly performing, this supports the motive of covering up poor performance.

The question then is, how should segment information be regulated? Should it be on the basis of product, industry, geography, or some combination of these and other possible bases?

IFRS 8 (2006) regulates segment reporting. A similar standard, ASC 280-10 (formerly SFAS 131 (1997)), is in effect in the United States. Of interest is the basis of segmentation in these standards. They require that the firm normally report segment information on the same basis as it organizes its segments internally for top management decision making and performance evaluation. For our purposes, two aspects of this requirement are of interest. First, of the various bases of segmentation that are possible, reporting on a basis consistent with the firm's business model, and thus its internal organization, is potentially of greatest usefulness to investors, since it is management that knows best how to organize the business, given the products and services it produces and the risks, returns, and growth opportunities it faces. Thus, reporting externally on the same basis as internally will give investors the most relevant insights into the firm's operations.

Second, the cost of opportunism in segment reporting will be high, since, under the standards just described, it would require the firm to change its internal organization if it desires to change its segment reporting format. However, some evidence of opportunism was suggested by Hope and Thomas (2008), whose findings were outlined in Section 8.8. They concluded that by dropping a previous requirement to report segment information by geographic area, SFAS 131 encourages "empire-building," under which the reduced ability of investors to monitor managers' foreign performance encourages managers to increase foreign sales at the expense of profitability. Obviously, to the extent it encourages opportunism, the usefulness of segment reporting is impaired.

However, some evidence of usefulness of segment reporting was provided by Berger and Hann (BH; 2007), who compared the segment disclosure of a sample of U.S. firms in 1997 (first year of SFAS 131) with the segment disclosure of the same firms in 1996. SFAS 131 resulted in an increase in the number of reported segments. Of interest are the characteristics of these new segments.

BH divided their sample into firms with a motive to avoid separate reporting of abnormally profitable segments (assumed to be firms with an excess of return on sales over industry average), and firms with a motive to conceal the results of poorly performing segments (assumed to be firms with an excess of capital investment over cash flow). With respect to the sample firms with a motive to conceal low-profit segments, they found that the average profitability of the newly reported segments was less than the average profitability of segments not newly reported. This suggests that pre-SFAS 131, managers were burying poorly performing segments in larger totals. It thus seems that SFAS 131 improved the ability of investors to identify the non-profitable components of multi-segment firm performance.

With respect to the sample firms with a motive to conceal very profitable segments, BH failed to find significantly higher profits of newly reported segments relative to segments not newly reported. This suggests little ability of SFAS 131 to improve the ability of investors to identify abnormally profitable segments.

Another example of decentralized reporting is the financial instrument risk disclosure required by IFRS 7, requiring reporting of summary quantitative risk data to be based on the information provided internally to key management personnel. Presumably, the best way to report on risk is in a manner consistent with the firm's internal risk management procedures.

Standards allowing the fair value option (Section 7.5.3) are also decentralized, since management is given a choice. Note that standards that allow a choice, unlike rigid standards, give management some ability to signal through its choice of reporting methods.

We conclude that decentralized standards have potential to generate decision useful information, despite reduced comparability across firms that results from a decentralized approach.

12.11 HOW MUCH INFORMATION IS ENOUGH?

Despite market failures in information production, however, we must not assume that ever-increasing regulation is necessarily socially desirable. This is because regulation carries with it substantial costs. These include direct costs of the bureaucracy needed to establish and administer the regulations, and compliance costs imposed on firms. Of possibly greater magnitude are indirect costs. One such cost arises when standards to enforce uniform accounting and reporting reduce managers' opportunity to signal. Uniform audit standards for all firms and stricter forecasting requirements are examples of possible standards that would reduce signalling potential.

A second indirect cost arises because, as concluded in Section 12.5.4, the regulator, in practice, is unable to calculate the socially optimal amount of information to require. This is because information is such a complex commodity, because private information production supplements regulation in complex ways, because there are conflicts between decision usefulness and contracting needs for information, and because different investors have different decision needs. Since information regulations affect firms' financing, investment, and production decisions, the indirect costs of any "wrong" amount of information production can be large indeed.

Given these complex cost–benefit considerations, we simply do not know how much regulation is enough. It is safe to say that complete deregulation would not be socially desirable. The uncontrolled impacts of information asymmetry, externalities, and moral hazard would be sufficiently serious to cause markets probably to cease to function. Nor is complete regulation desirable, since the costs to completely eliminate accounting policy and disclosure choice would be astronomic. However, this leaves a considerable range over which to debate the extent of regulation.

Indeed, we may never know the socially correct extent of regulation. This argument derives from the **theorem of the second best** by Lipsey and Lancaster (1956–1957). The authors showed that adding or removing a constraint to the economic system, such as an accounting standard, creates ripples throughout the economy, making it difficult, if not impossible, to determine whether the new standard is beneficial or harmful.[30]

This book contains several illustrations of the theorem of the second best in action. For example, in Chapter 9 we gave a series of illustrations showing that accounting standards with an appropriate tradeoff between sensitivity and precision improved the efficiency of managerial compensation contracts. Clearly, greater efficiency benefits the firm's shareholders. What we did not consider, however, were the ancillary ripples.

Thus, to the extent managers are motivated to work harder, organizations that rely on volunteers may suffer, not to mention the reduced demand for leisure clothing and golf clubs. To determine whether or not new standards to improve contracting efficiency are socially valuable, it would be necessary to determine whether or not the increased wealth of shareholders is greater or less than the ancillary consequences.

The Sarbanes-Oxley Act (Section 1.2) provides another illustration of the complexity of regulation. This Act was intended to increase social welfare by reducing the ability of managers to act opportunistically. The effects of Sarbanes-Oxley were studied by Hochberg, Sapienza, and Vissing-Jørgensen (HSV-J; 2009). They examined the lobbying behaviour of managers, investors, and other interested parties who were affected by the Act. HSV-J found that, on average, investors were in favour of the Act while managers were opposed. They also found that firms whose managers lobbied against the Act suffered from potentially opportunistic manager behaviour and relatively poor corporate governance. Consistent with these findings, over a 24-week period leading up to the passage of Sarbanes-Oxley, share returns demanded of these firms by the market were on average 7% higher than for a control sample of similar firms that did not lobby. All of these findings suggest that investors felt that the benefits of the Act would exceed costs of implementation, with the main benefits being better governance and less opportunistic manager behaviour. The authors also reported that following the implementation of the Act the returns of firms that lobbied were similar to the returns of a control sample. This suggests that investors' favourable expectations were realized, since if the Act was not effective, share returns demanded of lobbying firms would revert to a higher level over time.

These results imply that the net benefits of Sarbanes-Oxley to investors are positive. However, as HSV-J pointed out, we cannot infer that the *social* benefits are necessarily positive, since benefits to investors must be reduced by any lower utilities of managers and other insiders, and possible reductions in the number of firms offering securities to the public so as to avoid costs of conforming to the Act.

Deng, Melumad, and Shibano (2012) further questioned the social benefits of Sarbanes-Oxley. They argued that increased audit responsibilities under the Act lead auditors to be more conservative in valuation decisions, so as to reduce the possibility of legal liability. For example, auditors may insist on more frequent and larger impairment writedowns (conditional conservatism). The authors showed conditions under which such lower valuations lead to increased cost of capital, resulting in reduced investment.[31]

While the HSV-J study suggests that at least investors may benefit from increased regulation, other studies question even this finding. Ely and Waymire (EW; 1999) studied the period 1927–1993. For each year in this period, they estimated the share price response to net income for a sample of 100 firms, similar to the procedure used by Lev (1989) outlined in Section 6.9. EW found an average R^2 of 0.185 over this period, suggesting a "market share" of slightly over 18% for net income information in explaining share price change during this time.

The researchers then examined separately four sub-periods. The first was 1927–1939. This was prior to the creation of the Committee on Accounting Procedure (CAP) of the AICPA. CAP was the first professional accounting standard-setting body in the United States. Subsequent periods examined coincided with major reorganizations of U.S. standard-setting bodies. For example, the fourth period began in 1973 with the creation of the FASB. In sum, in the 1927–1939 period there were no accounting standards. In the three subsequent periods, the number of standards increased steadily, with the FASB being the latest and most active.

If these new accounting standards were socially desirable, EW argued, the value relevance of net income should increase in the later periods, relative to the 1927–1939 period, and there should be further increases in each successive standard-setting regime. However, using a variety of tests, no significant increases were found.

Theory in Practice 12.4

Jamal, Maier, and Sunder (JMS; 2003) examined the privacy policies and practices of the website industry. In the United States, this industry is largely unregulated. Consequently, there is an adverse selection problem that websites will abuse the privacy of visitors to the site, such as bombarding them with unsolicited e-mails, including from third parties to whom the site may have sold private information.

As JMS suggested, market forces constrain such acts—websites may feel that it is in their long-run interests to protect the privacy of their customers. They can do so, for example, by establishing and following privacy policies that enable site visitors to opt out of receiving subsequent advertising messages. These policies can be reinforced by voluntarily hiring an assurance service. Several such services exist, including WebTrust offered by the AICPA and CICA, which includes a full audit of clients' privacy policies.

With these considerations in mind, JMS evaluated 100 high-traffic websites. Of these, 34 had some form of assurance service and all 34 posted an easily accessible privacy policy on their sites. However, of the 66 sites without an assurance service, 63 also posted a privacy policy. This suggests that most websites were at least aware of the benefits of protecting users' privacy.

To evaluate whether the sites actually followed their posted policy, JMS registered at each site twice, under separate identities. In one identity, they opted to allow their identity information to be shared with others. In the other, they did not. They then kept track of subsequent e-mails received by each identity for 26 weeks. For those registrations for which they had opted to allow identity sharing, 15,143 e-mails were received. Most of these were generated by five sites, none of which used an assurance service. For those registrations for which they opted out, only 501 messages were received. It seems that even without regulation, almost all websites respect the privacy wishes of registrants.

JMS concluded that market forces can drive substantial voluntary use of assurance services to signal integrity, and can drive substantial respect for the interests of consumers. However, they caution that the website industry and the accounting industry differ. For example, they are at different stages of development. Nevertheless, their findings question whether constantly increasing regulation of accounting—also intended to secure integrity and protect customers (investors)—should be taken for granted.

12.12 CONCLUSIONS ON STANDARD SETTING RELATED TO ECONOMIC ISSUES

The question of the extent to which standards for information production should be imposed is a complex and important one for accountants, since standards largely determine the environment in which the accountant operates. The extent of standard setting is also important for a market economy. At present, we witness substantial regulation of firms' information production decisions. These regulations include insider trading laws and laws to regulate full disclosure. They also include laws to establish accounting and auditing professions. These professions, in turn, may form bodies empowered to establish GAAP, such as the IASB, AcSB and FASB. However, whether the extent of standard setting imposed by these regulators is socially desirable is open to debate, since there are numerous incentives for firms to produce information, even beyond minimal regulated amounts.

Indeed, theory suggests a number of reasons why firms would voluntarily produce information. These derive from the information needs of contracts, and from market forces. Parties to contracts will want information to motivate effort and to reward accomplishment. Managerial labour markets and takeover markets interact with securities markets to motivate managers to release information so as to increase market value. Signalling is an important vehicle for credible information release.

Such private forces undoubtedly result in much information production. Theory also suggests, however, that the amount produced by private forces alone may fall short of society's demands. The reason can be seen by means of a two-stage argument. First, contracts for information production break down when a large number of persons are involved. Consequently, we cannot rely on contracts for all of society's information needs.

Second, when contracts break down, market prices (for managerial services and for securities) must take over as motivators of voluntary information production. However, market forces may not motivate full information release in the presence of information asymmetries. Also, there are costs of releasing information and firms will trade off the costs with the benefits. As a result, some inside information remains, creating a fundamental lack of unanimity between managers' information production decisions and information demanded by investors. Investors may then demand regulation to remedy the perceived deficiency.

However, it is important to realize that private forces need not completely eliminate market failures to preclude regulation. This is because regulation also has costs. These include direct costs, such as a bureaucracy to set and enforce the standards, and compliance costs imposed on firms. Costs also include indirect costs imposed on society if the regulator mandates the wrong amount of information. Since information is such a complex commodity, this can happen. Given the impact of information on firms' production, financing, and investment decisions, and the ripples it sends through the economy, the costs to society here can be significant.

The question of standard setting then boils down to a cost–benefit tradeoff. The costs of regulation include not only the enforcement costs, but also the costs of any wrong decisions made by the regulator. The benefits lie in reduced market failures that persist after private market forces have done their best. At present, the extent to which the benefits of regulation exceed the costs is not known, and may never be fully known, although giving firms some flexibility in how they meet reporting standards may be worthwhile.

Finally, it should be noted that this chapter concentrated on the total benefits of information to society, without considering how these benefits are distributed. However, lack of unanimity leads directly to questions about the fairness of the distribution of information. That is, standard setting must draw on politics as well as economics. We will explore this topic in Chapter 13.

Questions and Problems

Note: several of these problems draw significantly on material from earlier chapters.

1. Information has both costs and benefits to a firm. What are the costs and benefits of information production to a firm? How much information should the firm produce? Is this amount necessarily socially optimal?

2. "Contracting internalizes the problem of information production." Explain what this statement means. (CGA-Canada)

3. To what extent do (i) security market forces and (ii) managerial labour market forces operate to motivate managers to work hard—that is, to operate their firms in the best interests of the shareholders? Do these forces eliminate the need for incentive compensation contracts? Explain.

4. The notion of a market for information, unlike markets for agricultural commodities, transportation services, and so on, may be unfamiliar to most people. A main reason for this is that information is a very complex commodity.

    Give three ways that we can think about the quantity of information, and explain each briefly.

5. An adverse selection problem can arise from information asymmetry between firm insiders and ordinary investors.

    Required

    a. Explain what the adverse selection problem is in this context.
    b. How can financial accounting information reduce the adverse selection problem?
    c. Can financial accounting information eliminate the problem completely? Explain.
    d. What other ways operate to reduce the problem of inside information?

    Note: Part **b** of question 6 draws in part from Section 12.8.2 (optional section).

6. The failure of managers to release bad news is a version of the adverse selection problem. Such failure indicates that the securities market is not working well.

Required

a. Why might a manager withhold bad news?

b. When will the disclosure principle operate to motivate the manager to report bad news? Under what conditions is the disclosure principle subject to failure?

7. Hollander, Pronk, and Roelofsen (2010) described a conference call during which executives of Apple, Inc. presented the company's third quarter 2008 financial results.

   In response to a question about the health of Apple CEO Steve Jobs, Apple executives answered, "Steve's health is a private matter." Apple's earnings for the quarter had reached an all-time high, yet Apple's share price fell 2.6% on the day of the conference call.

   Why did Apple's share price fall?

8. Explain why the adverse selection problem is a source of market failure in the production of information. Do the same for the moral hazard problem.

9. On September 15, 2004, the Dow Jones Industrial Index suffered its largest fall in a month, dropping by 0.8% or 86.8 points. The Standard & Poor's 100, 400, and 500 indices also dropped by similar amounts.

   According to media reports, the market declines were triggered by The Coca-Cola Company and Xilinx Inc. (a large producer of computer logic chips and related products). These companies announced that sales and profits for the third quarter 2004 would be less than analysts' estimates.

Required

a. Why did the whole market decline?

b. What market failure does this episode illustrate? Use the concept of externalities to explain why this is a failure.

10. Behavioural factors and noise trading can distort a firm's share price. As a result, managers of some firms may find their firms undervalued by the capital market relative to their inside information. The question then is, how can they best signal the real value of the firm?

    Healy and Palepu (HP; 1993) provided an illustration of what managers might do in response to this question. Patten Corporation[32] acquires large undeveloped tracts of land, subdivides them into lots, and sells them, with up to 90% of the financing supplied by Patten. Revenue is recognized upon sale—that is, when at least 10% of the purchase price has been received and collection of the balance is reasonably assured. This creates a potential problem of bad debt losses. However, in its 1986 financial statements, Patten provided a bad debt allowance of only $10,000 on accounts receivable of $29.4 million. The firm claimed that this low amount was justified by past experience and a low current delinquency rate.

    However, concern appeared in the financial media that Patten's bad debt allowance was too low. Specifically, the fear was expressed that past delinquency rates may not be representative of future delinquency. Patten's share price plunged following the publication of these concerns, as investors quickly revised their beliefs about Patten's future performance.

    Patten's management reviewed its procedures for estimating doubtful accounts and concluded that the $10,000 allowance was reasonable. As a result, management felt that the media article resulted in substantial undervaluation of the company's shares.

Required

a. Suggest three signals that management could use to convince the market of this undervaluation. For each signal, explain why the signal is credible.

b. Which of your three signals would you recommend to Patten's management? Explain why. Your recommendation criteria should include incurring the lowest cost of releasing proprietary information.

11. Refer to Theory in Practice 12.3 concerning Canadian Superior Energy, Inc.

Required

a. Obviously, the news of well abandonment was a major factor contributing to Canadian Superior's share price decline in March. However, other reasons for the decline can also be suggested. Give two other reasons.

b. What well-known problem of information asymmetry is suggested by the CEO's sale of stock in January 2004? Explain.

c. Assuming that the market's concerns about the information asymmetry problem you identified in part **b** are well founded, what is the likely effect of these concerns on the share prices of all Canadian oil and gas companies? Why?

d. Suppose that given the CEO's optimism about the ultimate success of the well, the company believes that its share price is undervalued by the market. Suggest three credible signals that the company and/or its CEO could give to increase its share price. Explain why the signals you suggest are credible.

12. Imax Corporation is a large entertainment technology company, with headquarters in New York and Toronto, and theatres worldwide. Its share price, which was as high as Can.$13.89 on the Toronto Stock Exchange in 2003, had fallen to a low of $5.50 following its reporting of a loss, in accordance with U.S. GAAP, of US$896,000 for the first quarter of 2004. This compared with a profit of over $2.4 million for the same quarter of 2003.

On May 14, 2004 (i.e., after reporting the first-quarter loss), *The Globe and Mail* reported that a group of senior Imax executives had bought about US$1 million of Imax shares on the open market. The company's share price immediately rose by Can.$1.17 to $7.20.

Imax later reported earnings for the second quarter of 2004 of US$1.552 million. However, its problems were not over. In March 2007, the company announced that it was expanding a probe into its accounting for the previous six years, following SEC and OSC investigations into its revenue recognition practices. The company also indicated that it had misclassified some expenses as capital. Imax shares were threatened with delisting by NASDAQ, the exchange on which its shares traded in the United States, since the probe delayed the filing of its financial statements. The filing delay also violated the covenants on its long-term debt. Imax shares fell by over 6% to Can.$5.79 on the Toronto Stock Exchange on the day following its announcement.

Required

a. What apparent information was conveyed to the market by the executive share purchase? Did the share repurchase constitute a credible signal at the time? Explain why or why not.

b. What market failures are revealed by the subsequent probes into Imax's accounting policies? Explain.

c. Why would the Imax executives have bought shares when they must have known about the opportunistic management of its reported earnings?

13. In February 1998, Newbridge Networks Corporation, a telecommunications equipment maker based in Kanata, Ontario, announced that its revenues and profits for the quarter ending on February 1, 1998, would be substantially below analysts' estimates. Its share price immediately fell by 23% on the Toronto and New York stock exchanges.

    The sale, in December 1997, of over $5 million of the company's shares by an inside director of Newbridge was widely reported in the financial media during February 1998. Details of sales by other Newbridge insiders, including its CEO, during previous months were also reported. The implication of these media reports was that these persons had taken advantage of inside information about disappointing sales of a new product line.

    ### Required

    a. Which source of market failure is implied by these media reports of insider trading?
    b. What effects on investors, and on the liquidity of Newbridge shares, would media reports of such insider sales be expected to create?
    c. Suppose that Newbridge's management felt that its share price was undervalued by the market after the February earnings announcement. Describe some signals that management and directors could engage in to counter the public impression of lower-than-expected profitability.

14. On May 16, 2002, Toronto-Dominion Bank (TD) announced that it would voluntarily begin expensing its executive stock options (ESOs), effective for its fiscal year beginning November 1, 2002. This announcement coincided with the release of its earnings for the quarter ended April 30, 2002. Net income was $132 million, down substantially from earnings of $359 million for the same quarter of 2001. While profits in TD's retail banking division were down somewhat, the main component of the earnings decrease came from writeoffs of problem loans and massive provisions for further loan losses.

    ### Required

    a. Given its sharply reduced earnings, why would the bank make matters worse by expensing its ESOs?
    b. Canadian accounting standards required expensing of ESOs beginning in 2004, with IASB and FASB standards following in 2005. Previously, ESO fair value was reported in the financial statement notes. TD was one of numerous firms that voluntarily decided to expense their ESOs prior to these standards coming into effect. Given this voluntary expensing, the question arises as to whether a standard is needed. Explain some of the costs and benefits of a standard requiring ESOs to be expensed.

15. XYZ Ltd. is an owner-managed retail grocery store that went public on January 1, 2010. Afterward, Tom Jones, the fun-loving owner–manager, held 40% of the common stock and remained the chief executive of the company.

    ### Required

    a. Why is it likely that Tom Jones will shirk more after going public relative to the time he was the owner–manager of the company prior to January 1, 2010? Will this affect the amount that Tom receives for his new share issue? Explain.
    b. What steps can Tom Jones take to convince potential shareholders that he will not engage in excessive shirking?

16. In *The Wall Street Journal* dated June 30, 1997, Suzanne McGee described why institutional investors, such as mutual fund managers, search for highly liquid stocks to invest in. If the stock is not liquid, these large investors will have to pay a higher price to buy in and receive a lower price if they sell out, simply because the quantities they deal in are large enough to affect share price. These concerns are heightened, according to McGee, because many large investors adopt a strategy of selling out at the first sign of trouble and buying back in at the first sign of recovery.

McGee points out that liquidity has a favourable effect on share price. For example, highly liquid stocks such as Coca-Cola are selling at 46 times earnings, whereas the Standard & Poor's 500-stock index trades at 22 times earnings. In effect, McGee argues, the market pays a premium for liquidity.

Required

a. Given its size and number of shares outstanding, how can a firm increase the liquidity of its shares? Consider depth, bid–ask spread, and synchronicity in your answer.

b. What are some of the costs to a firm of higher quality reporting?

17. In November 2006, the financial media reported a 12-year jail sentence to Sanjay Kumar, ex-CEO of Computer Associates International, a large computer software company (now called CA Technologies Inc.). In addition, Mr. Kumar was ordered to pay $8 million in fines and restitution. Six other senior executives of the company were also sentenced.

Established in 1976, Computer Associates had grown rapidly during the 1980s and 1990s. During this period of rapid growth, the company issued large amounts of debt, leading to difficulties in avoiding debt covenant violations.

The defendants were found guilty of a massive fraud during 1998–2000. Tactics used were to hold the books open after period end and to backdate sales contracts to the current period, to meet Wall Street's expectations. In 2004, Computer Associates restated its revenue in the amount of $2.2 billion, the amount of sales fraudulently booked.

Mr. Kumar joined Computer Associates in 1987, and, through a combination of brilliance and hard work, rose through the ranks to become CEO in 2000. He resigned in 2004, when the magnitude of revenue misstatement had become apparent.

Mr. Kumar apologized to the court for his conduct, for which he accepted full responsibility.

Required

a. Would the revenue overstatements carried out by Mr. Kumar have affected Computer Associates's total net income over a period of several years? Explain why or why not.

b. Would an accounting standard mandating more conservative revenue recognition policies have prevented the revenue misstatements? Why or why not?

c. Give reasons why a manager would overstate current period revenue and earnings.

d. What source of market failure is most likely at work here? Outline the effects of this failure on investors and on the operation of securities markets.

18. A number of firms, such as BCE Inc., Coca Cola, and McDonald's, have discontinued their practice of issuing quarterly earnings forecasts, thereby lowering their disclosure quality. Often, a reason given is that the severe negative consequences of not meeting quarterly targets gives management a short-run focus, distracting it from the attainment of longer-term goals. Consequently, the firm is better off not to issue a forecast in the first place.

These and other possible reasons were examined by Chen, Matsumoto, and Rajgopal (2011), who identified a sample of firms that discontinued quarterly earnings guidance over the period 2000–2006. They reported that firms that are losing long-term investors are relatively likely to discontinue quarterly forecasts. They also found that firms that stop forecasts tend to have poor share returns leading up to the stopping announcement, and past difficulty in meeting analyst earnings forecasts. These findings suggest another reason for discontinuing forecasts.

Required

a. Use the disclosure principle to explain why management may issue quarterly earnings forecasts.

b. Outline some of the costs to firms of issuing quarterly earnings forecasts.

c. Chen, Matsumoto, and Rajgopal (2011) also found that stopping firms suffer an average negative share return during a short window around the date of the stopping announcement. Are these negative share returns consistent with the authors' other findings described above? Why?

d. The stopping announcements suggest a failure of the disclosure principle. Use the models of Verrecchia (1983) and Dye (1985) to explain why firms may discontinue earnings forecasts.

19. Refer to Theory in Practice 12.1.

Required

a. Give reasons why GE's share price fell during 2001–2002. Give reasons why increased disclosure exerts upward influence on a firm's share price.

b. Despite GE's increased segment disclosure, numerous analysts and investors were concerned that the company's increased disclosure did not extend to reporting how much of its consolidated earnings came from the earnings of new subsidiaries and how much from previously acquired ones. The source of these concerns appeared to be GE's practice of "buying earnings" by acquiring profitable companies whose earnings exceeded the cost of financing the acquisitions. To what extent will GE's increased segment disclosures reduce investor concerns about low transparency of GE's financial reporting?

20. In December 2006, after a lengthy hearing, the Alberta Securities Commission found that former officers and directors of Blue Range Resources Corp. had "failed to make fair, accurate, public disclosure of material information during 1997 and 1998." Blue Range was an Alberta corporation engaged in exploring for and selling natural gas.

The defendants were found to have overstated physical quantities of reserves and production volumes. This was accomplished by adding a "heat adjustment" to actual volumes, on the grounds that the company's natural gas had greater-than-average energy content. These practices were not disclosed and appeared to depart from industry practice.

The company had also announced a 30% increase in new natural gas production, without disclosing that its 1999 total production volume was expected to decline by 20%. A related charge was that the company over-contracted to deliver natural gas, but did not disclose the risks resulting from having to buy natural gas on the open market to meet its commitments.

Note: For an earlier episode involving Blue Range, see Chapter 8, Problem 11.

Required

a. This episode contributed to the adoption of increased regulation of disclosures of oil and gas reserves in Canada (National Instrument 51-101 of the Canadian Securities Administrators, 2003). The new regulations went considerably beyond the reserve recognition requirements in the United States at that time (see Chapter 2, Problem 28 and Section 2.4.2). What are the costs and benefits of increased regulation of oil and gas disclosures?

b. The new disclosure regulations allow firms to seek an exemption from the new regulations and instead report in accordance with U.S. reserve recognition accounting. Many large companies have applied for and received such exemption. Why would these companies do this?

c. In 2008, Suncor Energy Inc., a large integrated Canadian oil and gas company with extensive operations in Alberta, reported reserves information under National Instrument 51-101 in place of its previous policy of reporting under U.S. reserve recognition accounting rules. Suggest reasons for this change in policy. Use the disclosure principle and signalling theory in your answer.

21. Linck, Netter, and Yang (2008) documented an increase over the 1990–2004 period in the proportion of outside directors on the Boards of U.S. corporations, where they defined outside directors of a firm as those who are not executives of that firm. For example, for large firms in their sample, the average proportion of outsiders on the Board had risen to about 76% by 2004, with only slightly lower averages for medium- and small-size firms. While changes in Board structure may be due in part to the 2002 Sarbanes-Oxley Act (Section 1.2), the authors documented that this trend was underway well before Sarbanes-Oxley.

    Outside directors, however, since they are more independent of management than inside directors, are particularly likely to be at an information disadvantage. Managers may exploit this information disadvantage through, for example, bias and lack of timeliness of inside information given to the Board. In particular, while management is likely to convey good news, it may be less likely to convey bad news. Yet, directors need high quality information to carry out their monitoring and advisory duties.

    Required

    a. Outline policies and procedures under which managers can credibly supply high quality inside information to the Board.

    b. Outside directors can also receive relevant firm information from public sources, such as published financial statements. Outline reasons why public financial statements may be more credible to such directors than information supplied by management.

    c. Improvements over time in the quality of inside and public information available to Board members are a possible explanation for the increase in outside directors. Explain this argument.

22. Gao (2011) studied the reaction to the 2002 Sarbanes-Oxley Act by non–U.S. firms issuing bonds in the U.S. bond market (called the Yankee market). Foreign firms issuing bonds in this market are subject to Sarbanes-Oxley requirements. However, other non–U.S. markets are also available for a firm that wishes to issue U.S.-denominated debt.

After controlling for other factors that affect a firm's choice of debt market, Gao found a significant reduction in the likelihood of foreign firms choosing the Yankee market.

Required

a. Sarbanes-Oxley introduced new, more stringent requirements for corporate governance and financial reporting (see Section 1.2), designed to strengthen the alignment between firm managers and shareholders. Use contract theory (Chapter 8) to explain why Sarbanes-Oxley may have increased the concerns of bondholders, thereby contributing to the reluctance of firms, including foreign firms, to issue bonds in the Yankee market.

b. Despite the overall decrease in Yankee bond issues, Gao found that use of the Yankee market, relative to use of other non–U.S. bond markets, *increased* for foreign firms that already had listed their shares in the United States, and for foreign firms that had adopted IFRS in place of their local GAAP. Explain the likely reasons for these increases.

c. Gao also found that large firms, with large bond issues, also increased their relative use of the Yankee market. Explain why. Draw on the theory of Diamond and Verrechia (1991) (Section 12.9.1) in your answer.

Notes

1. The dividing line between proprietary and non-proprietary information is somewhat ambiguous. For example, the release of information that may seem non-proprietary (such as a favourable financial forecast) could reduce future cash flows if it attracts entry to the industry. Nevertheless, the distinction is a useful one. For further discussion of the interrelationships between proprietary and non-proprietary information, see Dye (1986).

2. See, for example, L. De Angelo (1981).

3. In economic terms, this condition is known as **Pareto optimality**, after Vilfredo Pareto, an Italian economist and philosopher. Under this condition, no one in society can be made better off without making someone else worse off. Our criterion of equating the marginal costs and benefits of information is Pareto optimal because it creates the largest possible pie of information benefits, in which case if one person receives a larger piece of the pie, someone else must receive a smaller piece. Further discussion of Pareto optimality is given in Section 13.4.

4. We assume throughout that the firm incurs the direct and indirect costs of producing its own information, both voluntary and regulated. A theoretical alternative is for the government to reimburse the firm for the social value of the information it produces. However, due to the difficulties of measuring benefits of information production, such an alternative seems infeasible as a practical matter.

5. Precise conditions for market forces to generate a socially first-best outcome are laid down in the fundamental theorems of welfare economics. See, for example, Takayama (1985, pp. 185–201.)

6. Note that management's earnings guidance is subject to blockage, as discussed in Section 11.5.1. To the extent that a large number of managers report similar earnings guidance, this is another way to overcome blockage.

7. For an analysis of what this combination might be in the context of fair value accounting, see Demski, Lin, and Sappington (2008).

8. This assumes that the $100 cost of the fence is not so high that the paying farmer is better off to go out of business.

9. Note that free riding does not arise in our example since we have assumed that there is only one investor. To the extent that other investors benefit from the information without paying, the social benefits will increase but the incentive for the investor in the example to bargain for information release may be affected.

10. Strictly speaking, this analysis ignores the fixed costs of providing information to society. These fixed costs include firms' fixed costs of getting ready to produce information and any proprietary costs. Coase (1960 and references therein) pointed out that, in general, we cannot be sure that individual consumers are willing to pay the fixed costs that are necessary in order to produce a product. In our context, perhaps society would be better off if firms produced no information at all. However, complete deregulation of firms' information production would likely lead to social chaos. If so, we can safely assume that the benefits of information production are sufficiently great so as to outweigh the fixed costs.

11. It would be necessary to top up the manager's contract with, say, increased salary to meet the manager's reservation utility requirement.

12. The disclosure principle is attributed to Grossman (1981) and Milgrom (1981).

13. A similar model, with one information item, was developed by Penno (1997).

14. These thresholds have to be consistent with each other. In Pae's model, investors have rational expectations; consequently, they know the various thresholds (which depend, among other things, on investors' probabilities that the firm has developed the information). If thresholds differ depending on whether the firm has developed one or both forecasts, investors would know how many forecasts the firm has developed, and the disclosure principle would operate to force their release regardless of whether they are above or below their thresholds.

15. Since the undisclosed information is usually bad news, regulation to require conditional conservatism is supported in theory, since it forces bad news disclosure. This is consistent with what we observe in practice—see the accounting standards that impose impairment tests described in Chapter 7.

16. Refer to Chapter 8, Question 8, pertaining to the 1990 Iraqi invasion of Kuwait, for an illustration of how oil companies found themselves in a situation somewhat similar to that envisaged by Einhorn.

17. This type of game is called a **cheap talk game**, since, unlike the signalling models to be discussed next, there is no *direct* cost of disclosure to the manager. However, there is an indirect disclosure cost. This is because the reporting of imprecise interval information to deter entry reduces the ability of the shareholder to optimally plan consumption. It is this tension between deterring entry and reporting accurately to the shareholder that drives the reporting of imprecise information. Such games were first modelled by Crawford and Sobel (1982).

18. Rather than preventing entry of competitors, the authors attribute the issuance of a forecast to management's attempt to "talk down" overly optimistic analyst forecasts to levels the firm can meet.

19. As noted in Chapter 1, Note 22, the liquidity of a security is the extent to which investors can quickly buy and sell large quantities of that security at the market price with reasonable transaction costs and with little or no effect on the market price.

20. Devices to attain credibility include lawsuits, audits, and stock exchange or country of listing. Hiring a higher-quality auditor implies a commitment to greater information release. Also, a manager could commit to a higher level of information production by moving the firm to an exchange, possibly in a different country with higher information standards.

21. The number of covariance terms is $n(n-1)/2$ for a portfolio of n securities. Due to the squared tern, this number increases more rapidly than n.

22. Darrough and Stoughton assumed that if disclosure is made, it is honest. See Note 20.

23. Lee, Mucklow, and Ready (1993) found that a share's spread increases when its trading volume is unusually high. They suggest that the market interprets the high volume as due to insiders or other traders with superior information trading on the basis of this information. Without knowing what this information is, the market becomes more uncertain about the share's future return prospects, and increases the spread to protect itself. Other components of the spread are costs to process buy and sell orders, dealers' costs of holding shares in inventory to meet orders promptly, and the degree of competition among dealers—more competition, less spread. The reported market price of a stock is the midpoint of the spread.

24. In terms of our information system discussion in Section 3.3.2, a higher relationship implies higher main diagonal probabilities of the information system or, equivalently, greater decision usefulness of net income.

25. As explained in our discussion of the Lambert, Leuz, and Verrecchia model in Section 12.9.1, lower investor concerns about insider trading is another way of saying that more firm-specific information is incorporated into share prices, that is, there is lower synchronicity in the market. Lower synchronicity means less co-movement of share prices—that is, lower betas.

26. The authors used four measures of information environment. Firms with above-median analyst following, above-median market value, below-median analyst earnings forecast error, and below-median analyst forecast dispersion were deemed to be of high information quality.

27. Recall that the CAPM (Section 4.5.1) requires the expected return on the market portfolio as an input into its estimate of cost of capital. Since this expected return is unobservable, researchers have often used recent actual market returns as a proxy for expected returns, on the assumption that actual returns are an unbiased estimate of expected returns. However, if firms with low accrual quality are subject to negative cash flow shocks, as Ogneva documents, this produces a downward bias in actual returns, lowering the cost of capital estimate. This offsets any increased cost of capital resulting from low accrual quality, and is a possible explanation for the failure of Core, Guay, and Verdi to find a cost of capital effect of accrual quality.

28. It should be noted, however, that, in a specific study, researchers often measure information asymmetry and cost of capital several ways. To the extent that similar results are obtained, their conclusions are strengthened.

29. This argument follows from the partially informative nature of share price in noisy rational expectations models. See our discussion in Section 4.4.1.

30. In technical terms, maximizing social welfare can be modelled as a mathematical programming problem, subject to constraints such as wealth, production capacity, and, in our case, accounting standards for information production. The first-order conditions for the constrained maximum give a Pareto optimal solution to the social welfare problem, and the Lagrangian multipliers on the various constraints represent the social costs of those constraints. Lipsey and Lancaster showed that if a constraint is changed, for example by a new accounting standard, all the multipliers change, not just the multiplier for the accounting standards. This means that to determine if the new standard increases or decreases welfare, its effects throughout the whole economy must be evaluated, a task of incredible complexity. In particular, we cannot be sure that a standard that increases the quality of the information system necessarily increases social welfare, even though it may benefit the share price and corporate governance of affected firms. From an accounting perspective, this result is not as bleak as it may seem, however. It suggests that the need for professional expertise and judgment in the design and implementation of accounting standards will be with us for a long time to come.

31. In this regard, the 2012 U.S. Jobs Act reduced some adverse consequences of Sarbanes-Oxley by reducing several information requirements for small business. In particular, "emerging growth companies"—that is, companies planning an initial public offering and with revenues less than $1 billion—were relieved of the obligation under Section 404 of Sarbanes-Oxley to have an independent auditor report on the adequacy of the company's internal controls over financial reporting. (See also Chapter 13, Problem15.)

32. For further discussion, see Healy and Palepu (1993). Data on Patten Corp. are from Harvard Business School case #9-188-027.

Chapter 13
Standard Setting: Political Issues

Figure 13.1 Organization of Chapter 13

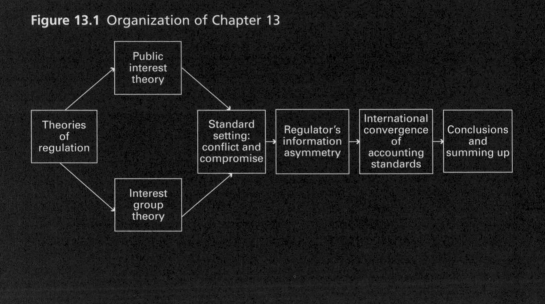

13.1 OVERVIEW

In Chapter 12 we saw that, from an economics perspective, the question of extent of regulation of accounting and reporting standards is unsettled. While we can suggest a number of contractual and market-based incentives for private information production in the absence of regulation, we simply do not know whether decreased market failures that would follow from expanded accounting standards would be of greater benefit to society than the various costs of the standard-setting process. It does appear, however, that the problem of market failure is quite fundamental. Information asymmetry (and the resulting problems of moral hazard and adverse selection), which creates the demand for information production by firms, also creates a demand for regulation of that information production. This is because of the problem of unanimity—the amount of information that firms would privately produce need not, and in general will not, equal the amount that investors want. As a result, investors may push for regulation to remedy the perceived deficiency.

Chapter 12 is primarily concerned with the *size* (net of costs) of the information "pie"—the larger the pie, whether generated by market forces or regulation or both, the better for society. However, the *distribution* of the benefits of information production among constituencies further complicates standard setting, since constituency interests often conflict. In setting standards, the interests of managers, small investors, large investors, and others must be traded off. Value judgments about these tradeoffs are difficult to make.

These considerations suggest that standard setting is fundamentally as much a political process as an economic one. Such a viewpoint is consistent with the concept of constituencies of accounting, with the game theoretic and agency theoretic views of constituency conflict in Chapters 8 and 9, and with attempts by governments to influence standard setters during the 2007–2008 security market meltdowns. It seems natural to expect that the various accounting constituencies would appeal to the political process when their conflicting interests cannot be resolved by contractual or market forces.

Our first objective in this chapter is to review two theories of regulation. The first, the **public interest theory**, takes the view that regulation should maximize social welfare. This was the viewpoint of Chapter 12. The second, the **interest group theory** of regulation, suggests that individuals form coalitions, or constituencies, to protect and promote their interests by lobbying the government. These coalitions are viewed as being in conflict with each other to obtain their share of benefits from regulation.

Our second objective is to consider the criteria that standard setters need to consider if their standards are to be acceptable. While decision usefulness and reduction of information asymmetry are necessary for any standard, we shall see that much more is needed. Specifically, the standard must be acceptable to its various constituencies. This requires a careful attention to due process by the standard setter.

Information asymmetry between regulator and regulated is yet another regulatory complication, which was also largely ignored in Chapter 12. The regulator faces information asymmetry, since the manager has the best knowledge of the firm's own costs, sources of demand, and information environment. In effect, the firm is a monopoly producer of information about itself—it cannot be assumed that the manager will willingly and truthfully reveal this information to the regulator. The regulator must then decide whether to set accounting standards using the best information about firms' costs and benefits of information production that it can obtain, or to allow the firm at least some authority and discretion, thereby relying on contracting and market forces to drive the firm's information production.

Finally, we shall consider the additional challenges to financial reporting and standard setting resulting from global integration of capital markets and international convergence of accounting standards.

Figure 13.1 outlines the organization of this chapter.

13.2 TWO THEORIES OF REGULATION

13.2.1 The Public Interest Theory

The public interest theory of regulation was implicit in our examination of standard setting in Chapter 12. This theory suggests that regulation is a response to public demand for correction of market failures. In this theory, the regulator is assumed to have the best interests of society at heart. It does its best to maximize social welfare—that is, to attain a first-best amount of information production. Consequently, regulation is thought of as a tradeoff between its costs and its social benefits in the form of improved operation of markets. Chapter 12 addressed these various costs and benefits.

While this view represents an ideal of how regulation should be carried out, there are problems with its implementation. One problem is the very complex task of deciding on the correct amount of regulation. This is particularly true for a commodity like information, where, as Chapter 12 makes clear, it is effectively impossible to please everyone. Then, the door is left open for other theories of how the amount of regulation is determined. An equally serious problem, however, lies in the motivation of the regulator. Due to the regulator's information disadvantage and the complexities of measuring social costs and benefits, it is difficult for the government to monitor the regulator's operations, even if the regulator is an agency of government. Costly and lengthy hearings would be needed to know whether the regulator is doing a good job. This creates a moral hazard problem—the possibility that the regulator will operate on its own behalf rather than on behalf of the public. This problem is more difficult than monitoring the manager in our agency theory discussion of Example 9.1, where the manager was motivated to shirk because his/her action was unobservable to the owner. The regulator faces fewer constraints on shirking since there is no capital market to help motivate his/her actions. This leads directly to another theory.

13.2.2 The Interest Group Theory

The interest group theory of regulation was introduced into economics by Stigler (1971). Subsequently, Posner (1974), Peltzman (1976), and Becker (1983) made contributions to the theory, which takes the view that an industry operates in the presence of a number of interest groups (or constituencies, as we have used the term in earlier chapters). Consider any manufacturing industry as an example. The firms in the industry comprise an obvious interest group, as do the firms' customers, and organized labour. Another interest group would be environmentalists, who would be concerned about the industry's social responsibility. These various interest groups will lobby the regulator for various amounts and types of regulation. For example, the industry itself, and organized labour, may demand regulation to protect against foreign competition or against encroachments on operations by other industries. Customers may form groups to lobby for better product labelling, high-quality standards or price controls. Environmentalists may lobby for emission control regulations and greater disclosure of environmental performance. These various constituencies can be thought of as demanders of regulation.

Constituencies may also lobby *against* regulation. For example, firms may lobby against price controls if customers are lobbying for them, and managers may lobby against new accounting standards.

For our purposes, the most relevant version of the interest group theory is that of Becker, which we can view as an application of the Coase theorem (Section 12.6.2) when there are bargaining costs. Coase points out that if bargaining costs are too high for parties to contract, an appeal to government to step in is possible.

Becker views interest groups as competing for and against regulation. The outcome depends on which group is relatively most effective in applying pressure on the regulator. Of course, the ability of interest groups to pursue their own interests is constrained somewhat by laws, the courts, the media, and public opinion. Nevertheless, pressure can take forms such as forming a lobbying organization, making political donations, carrying out subjective analyses of costs and benefits, and promoting the group's position in the media.

Interest groups are assumed rational, and will thus not throw good money after bad. If a group sees that its pressure will not prevail, it will cut its losses by discontinuing its efforts, or may not even bother to organize in the first place. Failure to organize may result if a group is widely dispersed, or if its members are likely to free-ride on the efforts of others.

Which interest group will get what it wants? This depends on the pressure exerted by each group, which requires organization and expenditure. However, the pressures of competing groups offset one another: All groups could spend heavily to no avail to the extent that their various expenditures cancel each other out. Thus, while the winner will be determined by how much it spends and the effectiveness of its organization, each group must take the expenditures of the other groups into account. In effect, the pressure decision is a game, similar to the non-cooperative games described in Section 8.10.

In our context, the interest group theory makes several predictions:

- *Creation of standard-setting bodies.* It would be very costly to organize a group as large and diverse as investors to act as a cohesive interest group to negotiate with management or lobby for its own interests. In addition to communication and organization costs, other costs include fund raising and overcoming a tendency for many investors to free-ride. As a result, investors would support creation of standard-setting bodies, with representatives thereon to act on their behalf. While the costs of operating these bodies may be considerable, they are surely lower than the costs of organizing investors themselves.

- *Activities subject to market failure.* These are more likely to be regulated, due to demand from groups adversely affected. As described in Section 12.5, market failures in the production of information are common, due to adverse selection and moral hazard. In the Becker theory, market failures increase the potential benefits of regulation for investors. To the extent management is the source of these market failures, we expect to observe considerable regulation of their information disclosures.

- *Due process.* Obviously, if they are to play the game, interested groups must have a seat at the table. Thus, we expect management to be involved in standards development through, for example, reaction to exposure drafts, and standards board representation.

The public interest theory makes none of these predictions. Under public interest theory, implementing a new standard requires only that the regulator evaluate its social costs and benefits. If the benefits exceed the costs, the standard will be implemented, and vice versa. No interest group involvement is needed.

Interest group theory was extended by Bertomeu and Magee (2011) (BM), who considered how the extent of regulation varies over the business cycle, such as the sequence of events leading up to and following the market meltdowns described in Section 1.3. Their model includes managers who finance their projects initially with bank loans. The quality of these projects, known only to managers, can be high or low. Banks supply the loans. The standard setter chooses standards that balance the lobbying demands of these two constituencies.

Then, managers report on the progress of their projects according to the chosen reporting standards. The higher the quality of these standards, the greater the probability that low quality projects will be publicly revealed to be of low quality. Projects revealed to be of low quality are then liquidated. Managers sell the equity (net of bank loan) of the remaining projects on a securities market.[1] Note that, unless the reporting standards are perfect, the unliquidated projects consist of a mixture of high and low quality. Then, the market prices of both equity and loan securities reflect a discount due to quality uncertainty (lemons problem). As the authors showed, the higher the reporting standards, the lower the discount.

The question then is, what reporting quality does the standard setter set? Suppose first that the economy is in expansionary mode. Then, most projects are of high quality, and their managers lobby for high-quality financial reporting to validate this quality. The standard setter responds with high-quality standards. If economic conditions start to deteriorate, the number of low quality projects increases, leading more managers to lobby strongly for lower quality standards to disguise this low quality. The standard setter, under the interest group theory, responds with lower standards.[2] As it does, banks know that they hold more low quality loans, since managers are then better able to disguise real project quality. Also, the probability that this low quality will be reported decreases. Banks raise interest rates in response, and also begin to support low quality reporting to disguise the deteriorating value of their loans. If the economy proceeds toward a recession, interest rates will have become so high and the proportion of low quality projects becomes so high that the credit market is threatened with collapse. Then, managers begin to lobby for higher quality reporting to prevent collapse, and to lower interest rates. The standard setter responds with higher quality standards.

The model suggests, then, that standard setting is a dynamic process, influenced by demands of managers, bankers and, as a result, governments. These demands can change over time depending on the state of the economy. The demands of banks for relaxation of fair value accounting during the 2007–2008 market meltdowns and the flurry of new accounting standards that followed illustrates this process. While the standard setters must keep the interests of investors in mind, the model emphasizes that other powerful constituencies are also involved.

13.2.3 Which Theory of Regulation Applies to Standard Setting?

It should be apparent that the public interest theory is difficult to implement. The sources of market failure in the production of information discussed in Chapter 12 imply that market forces cannot always be relied upon to generate the socially right accounting standards and procedures. Yet, the complexities arising from the diverse information needs and interests of investors and managers make it effectively impossible for standard setters to calculate the right accounting standards either. We simply do not know how to calculate the best tradeoff between the conflicting uses of information by investors and managers that is required by the public interest theory of regulation. This is why the choice of accounting standards is better regarded as a conflict between constituencies than as a process of calculation. Standard setters are players in a complex game where affected constituencies choose strategies of lobbying for or against a proposed new standard.

Consistent with this game-theoretic view, we saw in Section 1.12.5 that major constituencies with an interest in financial reporting are represented on the standard-setting bodies. Also, there are due process provisions for public hearings, exposure drafts, and, generally, for openness, as well as requirements for super-majority votes in favour before new standards are issued. If the players of the game are to accept the outcome (e.g., a new standard), they must feel that the process was fair, their views were heard, and their strategy at least had a chance of working. This explains the attention to due process as a way of moderating the inherent constituency conflicts in standard setting.

These considerations suggest that the interest group theory of regulation is a better predictor of new standards than the public interest theory, since the interest group theory formally recognizes the existence of conflicting constituencies. To pursue this question further, we next consider a specific accounting standard-related conflict.

13.3 CONFLICT AND COMPROMISE: AN EXAMPLE OF CONSTITUENCY CONFLICT

In November 2009, during debate in the U.S. Congress of the Financial Stability Improvement Act, two members of the House of Representatives introduced an amendment entitled "Prudential Oversight of Accounting Principles and Standards that Pose Systemic Risk." The amendment would shift oversight of the FASB from the SEC to a Financial Services Oversight Council, comprising representatives of the U.S. Treasury, U.S. banking regulators, the SEC, and several other regulatory agencies. If any Council member felt that an accounting principle or standard threatened the stability of the U.S. financial system, the Council would investigate and, if approved by majority vote, force the SEC to take "corrective action" that could include modification or cancellation of the standard.

The American Bankers' Association, an important and powerful constituency concerned about bank accounting, supported the amendment, presumably due to its concerns over the effects of fair value accounting for financial instruments on legal capital ratios during the 2007–2008 market meltdowns (Section 1.3), and concerns over new FASB standards that included expanded requirements for consolidation of off balance sheet activities.

Following strong objections by other constituencies, including investor protection groups, the U.S. Chamber of Commerce, the chair of the SEC, and the American Accounting Association, the amendment was withdrawn and replaced with one requiring Financial Services Oversight Council members to "review and comment" on accounting standards. Since the SEC already had this power, the new amendment substantially weakened the original proposal.

The bottom line of conflicts such as these between the standard setter and affected constituencies is that standards cannot be set in a vacuum. If important constituencies cannot obtain what they want, they will appeal to the political process.

13.4 DISTRIBUTION OF THE BENEFITS OF INFORMATION, REGULATION FD

As should be apparent from our discussion to this point, a complication of standard setting is the *distribution* of the benefits of information production among interest groups. Questions of the distribution of economic benefits are difficult, since they also involve value judgments of fairness among affected parties. To illustrate, hold total information production constant and consider two scenarios. In the first, 80% of the benefits of information go to the wealthiest 10% of investors; that is, the "big guys." In the second, the benefits are distributed equally across all investors. Most people would not feel that the two scenarios were equivalent.

Consequently, maximizing the pie is not the only consideration that standard setters face. For example, while the Coase theorem demonstrates how bargaining and contracts can overcome some problems of externalities, the distribution of property rights determines who pays for the fence. How is this distribution decided?

Value judgments about who is entitled to property rights arise because individual utilities cannot in general be aggregated into a social preference ordering (see our discussion in Section 1.2). Thus, we cannot add up the losses in utility if benefits are taken from one individual or group, compare it with the gains in utility if these benefits are transferred to another individual or group, and claim that society is better off if the utility gains exceed the losses. Instead, economists usually impose a criterion of Pareto optimality, in which society is deemed to be best off if no redistribution of wealth can make one individual better off without making another worse off (see Chapter 12, Note 3). This is a relatively weak criterion since, in the final analysis, we cannot know if the *utility* gain of the individual who receives an increase in wealth (and is thus better off) is greater than the utility loss of the individual who suffers a decrease in wealth. In the face of these difficulties, society leaves the resolution of distributional issues to bargaining, contracting, and/or market forces, with regulation stepping in when these appear to fail.

To illustrate a regulation intended to improve fairness of information distribution, consider SEC Regulation FD, adopted in 2000, which prohibits companies from selectively disclosing information, for example to analysts. Regulation FD arose from a concern that "big guys" may have more resources, either directly or from privileged access to analysts, to find and analyze information. Also, the big guys may have enough bargaining power to receive privileged inside information directly from management. As a result, small investors were at an information disadvantage. Requiring firms to release information to everyone, the SEC felt, would enhance public confidence in a fair marketplace and contribute to market liquidity.[3]

The introduction of Regulation FD was surrounded by considerable constituency conflict, however. One prediction was that abnormal share returns between earnings announcement dates would become more volatile, since new information would be released by firms directly to the market, rather than being filtered through analysts (i.e., prior to FD, analysts might downplay or smooth out the significance of new information in return for the favour of receiving it in advance). Note that volatility of share returns is a measure of new information coming to the market (i.e., new information leads to price changes). Thus, more volatility between earnings announcements implies that the market receives more information sooner—investors do not have to wait until earnings are announced. From a small investor standpoint, this is desirable, since there is then less time available for insiders and big guys to take advantage of inside information. But critics of FD, presumably representing analyst and large-investor interest groups, claimed that, to reduce the share price volatility just mentioned, firms would reduce the amount of information they released between earnings announcements. This would show up as an increased number of earnings surprises, leading to increased abnormal share return volatility around earnings announcement dates.

Francis, Nanda, and Wang (2006) examined a sample of firms spanning six quarters prior to and six quarters following the implementation of Regulation FD. They found no increase in abnormal share returns, either between or surrounding earnings announcement dates, implying that Regulation FD had little effect on improving the amount or timing of information coming to the market.

They did find, post-FD, lower abnormal share returns around the dates analysts released their earnings forecasts, suggesting that analysts' forecasts became less informative. This conclusion is strengthened by Kross and Suk (2012), who examined analysts' earnings forecasts following managers' public information disclosures (earnings announcements, earnings forecasts, and conference calls). For a four-year period surrounding the implementation of Regulation FD, they found, post-FD, that analysts revised their earnings more quickly in response to managers' information disclosures than pre-FD and that the magnitude of their forecast revisions increased. They also found that the accuracy of forecasts increased and that forecast dispersion decreased. They found no change in these analyst forecast characteristics for a sample of foreign firms with shares traded in the United States that were not subject to Regulation FD. These findings suggest greater analyst reliance on public information post FD—that is, a decline in their inside information advantage.

Eleswarapu, Thompson, and Venkataraman (2004) examined a sample of firms over a 16-month period surrounding Regulation FD implementation. They found that the average bid–ask spread of their sample firms fell post-FD, implying less investor concern about adverse selection and resulting estimation risk. They also found that spread decreased on the day that firms released their quarterly earnings. Typically, spread increases at this time, due to increased concern by the market about insider trading around earnings announcements. A finding that spread decreased suggests increased investor confidence in a fair market place.

Subsequently, Sidhu, Smith, Whaley, and Willis (2008) pointed out that the bid–ask spread consists of components other than fear of adverse selection (see Chapter 12, Note 23), and that these components could also be affected by Regulation FD. After controlling for changes in these components, the authors found, in a large sample of U.S. firms surrounding the effective date of FD, that the adverse selection component of the spread actually increased. This finding contrasts with that of Eleswarapu, Thompson, and Venkataraman just outlined. The authors attributed this implication of increased adverse selection to a tendency of firms post-FD to hold on to information longer, thereby increasing the potential for insider trading. In response to this potential, the bid–ask spread increases.

We conclude that the extent to which Regulation FD has benefited small investors seems unclear. Only one of its goals (decline in analysts' information advantage) seems to have been met.

Whether or not FD's goals are met, notice that by attempting to improve the fairness of the distribution of information, the SEC's introduction of this regulation is consistent with the public interest theory, even though the constituency conflict preceding Regulation FD indicates that the interest group theory was also operative. That is, the two theories are intertwined. With this in mind, we now suggest criteria for standard setting.

13.5 CRITERIA FOR STANDARD SETTING

We have seen that there are a number of factors that affect the process of standard setting. Standards should be decision useful, but they should also be acceptable to other constituencies—in particular, management. This puts the standard setter in a conflict situation and it is difficult to predict what an acceptable resolution of this conflict will be. Nevertheless, we now suggest some criteria that should be kept in mind when trying to understand standard setting.

13.5.1 Decision Usefulness

The criterion of decision usefulness underlies the empirical value relevance studies described in Chapter 5. Recall that the more informative about future firm performance an information system is, the stronger will be investor reaction to information produced by the system, other things equal. Thus, empirical evidence that security prices respond to accounting information suggests that investors find accounting information useful.

This suggests that a necessary condition for the success of a new standard is that it be decision useful. Of course, this can be hard to assess beforehand, since the market has not yet had a chance to respond to the standard. Nevertheless, the theory of rational investor decision making can be used to predict decision usefulness. For example, Bandyopadhyay (1994) predicted that oil and gas companies' earnings reported under successful efforts were more informative than under full-cost accounting,[4] and provided evidence to this effect. Also, as argued in Chapter 6, the incorporation of current values into financial reporting will increase investor decision usefulness to the extent that this tightens up the linkage between current and future performance.

However, while decision usefulness may be a necessary criterion for a successful standard, it is not sufficient to ensure success. We saw in Section 5.5 that, because of certain public good characteristics of accounting information, we cannot be sure that the standard that has the greatest decision usefulness is best for society. Since investors do not directly pay for accounting information, they may "overuse" it. Thus, a standard could appear to be decision useful, yet society would be worse off because the costs of producing the information were not taken into account (in this regard, see Problem 15). Furthermore, changes in standards can impose contracting costs on firms and their managers. In effect, as implied by the fundamental problem (Section 1.10), standard setters must consider criteria other than decision usefulness.

13.5.2 Reduction of Information Asymmetry

We saw in Section 12.7 that market forces operate to motivate management and investors to generate information. Standard setters should be aware of these forces and take advantage of them, to the extent possible, to reduce the need for standards. Unfortunately, market forces alone cannot ensure that the right amount of information is produced. As we saw in Section 12.5, one of the reasons for this is information asymmetry. Consequently, standard setters should use reduction of information asymmetry in capital and managerial labour markets as a criterion for new standards.

While the public good characteristics of accounting information complicate the ability of decision usefulness to guide standard setters, as just pointed out, these same characteristics mean that standards can be quite effective in reducing information asymmetry. That is, since the use of financial accounting information by one individual does not destroy it for use by another, expanding disclosure by means of standards works toward a fair distribution of the benefits of information to all investors. These benefits are available *directly* to those who are willing and able to use the expanded information (as in the case of Bill Cautious in Example 3.1), or *indirectly* to other investors through the price-protection mechanism of efficient securities markets (Section 4.3.1). Consequently, reduction of information asymmetry improves the operation of markets, since investors will perceive investing as more of a level playing field. This will reduce investor concern about information asymmetry and resulting estimation risks, reduce the bid–ask spread and expand market liquidity, and generally produce social benefits from better-working markets.

However, reduction of information asymmetry as a criterion is again a necessary condition for a successful standard but not a sufficient one. Just as decision useful information has a cost, so does reduction of information asymmetry. Consequently, it is hard to know when standards to reduce information asymmetry cease to be cost effective.

13.5.3 Economic Consequences of New Standards

One of the costs of a new standard is the cost imposed on firms and managers to meet that standard. This goes beyond the out-of-pocket costs of producing the newly mandated information. Costs are also created by contract rigidities, as in an increased probability of violating debt covenants and effects on the level and volatility of managers' future bonus streams. These costs can affect managers' operating and financial policies. Furthermore, to the extent that new standards require the release of proprietary information, firms' future profitability can be affected by the reduction of competitive advantage.

The reduction in managers' freedom to choose from different accounting policies that frequently results when a new standard is implemented is also a source of economic consequences. We argued in Section 12.8.3 that firms can signal inside information by accounting policy choice. Also, responsible earnings management can reveal inside information, as discussed in Section 11.5. Obviously, if accounting policy choice is constrained, there is a reduction in the extent to which these private forces for information production can operate.

Finally, the Darrough and Stoughton model in Section 12.9.1 suggests that the greater the degree of competition in an industry, the better the disclosure, other things equal. As a result, there may be less need for accounting standards in some industries than in others.

These considerations suggest that standard setters should weigh the possible economic consequences of new standards as an important source of cost that will affect both the need for the standard and the willingness of constituencies to accept it. Of course, it may be that the economic consequences of a new standard will be overstated during the debate leading to the standard. For example, would banks really stop long-term lending if their long-term investments have to be fully marked to market? Probably not, but the costs to banks of long-term lending would increase and, as a result, the charges to borrowers would likely rise.

13.5.4 Consensus

Economic consequences lead directly to our last criterion, deriving from the political aspects of standard setting. Standard setters, in effect, must engineer a consensus sufficiently strong that even a constituency that does not like a new standard will nevertheless go along with it. As should be apparent from Section 1.12.5, the structure and due process of standard-setting bodies is designed to encourage such a consensus. But, as described in Section 13.3, if constituency conflict is severe, even due process cannot always forestall appeal to the political process.

We concluded earlier that the standard-setting process seems most consistent with the interest group theory of regulation. Certainly, technical, and even theoretical, correctness is not sufficient to ensure the success of a standard. As we argued in Section 8.6, failure to record an expense for employee stock options (ESOs) overstates net income and reduces the comparability of reported earnings across firms. Yet the FASB's 1993 exposure draft proposing fair value accounting for ESOs met with such resistance that it had to be withdrawn, and its 2005 expensing standard encountered similar resistance (see Problem 4). While careful attention to due process may be time consuming, such attention seems essential if costly and embarrassing retractions are to be minimized. Too many of these will threaten the existence of the standard-setting body itself.

13.5.5 Summary

Accounting standard setters can be guided by decision usefulness and reduction of information asymmetry. However, while these criteria are necessary, they are not sufficient to ensure successful standard setting. It is also necessary to consider the legitimate interests of management and other constituencies, and to pay careful attention to due process.

In this regard, the IAS implemented a **post-implementation review** process in 2008. Its purpose is to review any contentious issues that arose during the development of standards and to consider any subsequent costs or implementation problems. Normally, the review would begin two years following the date of the standard.

We conclude that because of the fundamental problem, the actual process of standard setting is better described by the interest group theory of regulation than by the public interest theory.

13.6 THE REGULATOR'S INFORMATION ASYMMETRY*

More recently, the theory of regulation has formally recognized that, like everybody else, the regulator faces information asymmetry—much of the information needed by the regulator, such as financial information, is in the hands of firm managers who are, in effect, monopolistic producers of information about their firm. Furthermore, the regulator is unable to observe manager effort. Thus, the regulator faces both adverse selection and moral hazard problems. To illustrate how regulation theory may proceed under information asymmetry, we adapt a model from Section 2.7 of Laffont and Tirole (LT; 1993) to an accounting context.

Consider an economy with information demanded by investors and supplied by managers. Let q be the quality of information released by a firm. If the firm is unregulated, the manager chooses q. If it is regulated, q is set by the regulator. Higher q benefits investors, who reward the firm with lower cost of capital, which we denote by p.

---

*This section can be omitted without loss of continuity.

Firms differ with respect to the amount of their inside information. For example, inside information of large, complex firms with high R&D will be relatively high. Let β be a firm-specific parameter, with lower β implying more inside information. We assume that the lower β is, the "easier" it is—that is, less costly—for the firm to release a given information quality. A large, complex firm will typically be low-β. It will thus, for example, have more scope to signal, thereby releasing information without incurring proprietary costs. Also, such firms may receive high media attention, and enjoy economies of scale in information production.

Managers, however, find it personally costly to release information. To do so, they must exert effort. Let e denote the information-related effort devoted by the firm manager. Components of e include designing and monitoring financial reporting systems, conference calls with analysts and investors, dealing with auditors, costs of signalling, etc. Managers are assumed rational, risk neutral, and effort averse. Let the manager's effort aversion be $\Psi(e)$, where Ψ is an increasing, convex function of effort.

Managers must be compensated for their effort. As a minimum, the manager must receive $\Psi(e)$ if he/she is to attain reservation utility. However, if the inside information parameter β is private information of the manager, he/she may secure additional compensation and utility through opportunistic behaviour, such as bad earnings management (Section 11.6), manipulating the value of option awards (Section 8.6), or extra compensation procured under the power theory (Section 10.7). Denote this excess compensation by X. The manager's total compensation[5] t is then

$$t = X + \Psi(e)$$

Profit π from the firm's information activities is thus

$$\pi = pq - C - t$$

where pq is the benefit to the firm from producing information of quality q at cost of capital p. The cost to producing information of quality q is C, where

$$C = (\beta - e)q.$$

The lower β is (i.e., more inside information), the lower C is, as specified above. Also, greater manager effort e devoted to producing information q lowers its cost of production. This effort could include signalling costs, good earnings management, choice of accounting policies to reduce the probability of debt-covenant violation, as well as adoption of improved information technology.

Now, without regulation, the rational manager will choose q so as to take advantage of inside information β to maximize excess compensation X, at the expense of investors through lower firm profit. This sets up a case for regulation.

Assume that the regulator follows the public interest theory of regulation. Then, the regulator's goal is to maximize the social benefits of information—that is, the sum of the benefit to investors of information plus the manager's compensation. (Managers, like investors, are entitled to receive compensation for their services.)

Assume first that all investor and firm parameters, including inside information β, are known to the regulator. That is, there is no information asymmetry. Thus, the regulator knows the determinants of the firm's cost of capital p (e.g., CAPM), knows costs C (firm files annual information form with the regulator), knows total manager compensation (compensation information in annual proxy form), and knows the manager's effort aversion. Given that the regulator also knows β, it can prevent the manager exploiting this information to generate excess compensation. Thus the regulator has enough information to set q so that firm profit is zero[6] and the manager earns no excess compensation. Given q as set by the regulator, the manager chooses e. LT show that under these conditions,

$$\frac{\partial \psi(e)}{\partial e} = q$$

That is, the manager's marginal disutility of effort equals the marginal benefit of information to investors. This result is firm specific, since different managers will have different effort disutility and firms will have different βs and different costs of capital. Nevertheless, for each firm, this constitutes a socially first-best regulatory outcome.

Now, introduce information asymmetry by assuming that the regulator does not know the firm's β. Instead, the regulator assesses probabilities of the various possible values of β. The regulator can still observe *total* information costs, C, and other components of firm profit, so it can regulate firm profits to zero. But, it cannot observe the $(\beta - e)$ components of C, and so cannot prevent the manager from exploiting inside information β to earn excess compensation. Thus firm profits now include a deduction for excess compensation. The optimal regulation is the information quality that maximizes the expectation over β of the social benefits of information under these conditions. LT show that the manager chooses effort so that

$$\frac{\partial \psi(e)}{\partial e} = q - a\ positive\ constant$$

where q is the information quality without information asymmetry, as above. Thus, under information asymmetry, regulated information quality is lower than q. Since the manager is effort averse, this implies that the manager works less hard to produce information than under first-best conditions, thereby increasing C and reducing firm profits. But since firm profits, which now contain a deduction for excess compensation, are constrained to be zero by the regulator, the amount of excess compensation the manager can receive is reduced. In effect, under this model of information asymmetry, the optimal regulation limits socially undesirable manager excess compensation, at the cost of reducing somewhat the quality of information to investors.

From an accounting perspective, we draw three conclusions from this model:

- If the standard setter follows the public interest theory, the socially optimal extent of standard setting allows for some reduction in earnings quality so as to limit the manager's ability to receive more compensation than is required to attain reservation utility.

- To the extent that the accountant can reduce the amount of inside information, the problem of excess manager compensation is reduced. Of course, this reduction cannot be complete since the costs to the firm of eliminating all inside information are prohibitive.

- The optimal regulation is firm specific, since firm and manager characteristics differ. This suggests that instead of laying down omnibus standards that apply to all firms, the regulator should allow flexibility in reporting quality. This supports a principles-based approach to standard setting (Section 1.6), where reliance is placed on accountant and auditor judgment to tailor general standards to specific situations. Decentralized regulation, as discussed in Section 12.10, is also supported.

Of course, the assumptions of the model just outlined are restrictive. A major limitation is that we have considered only the firm's information-related activities. A more elaborate model would recognize that cost of capital affects the firm's product decisions as well, and thus models the effects of information regulation on a broader spectrum of firm activities. Another limitation is that the model assumes the public interest theory of regulation, whereas we concluded above that the interest group theory better applies to regulation in accounting. Consequently, while the LT model provides some insights, it does not contradict our conclusion in Section 12.11 that it is effectively impossible to calculate the socially correct extent of regulation. Additional theoretical research is needed if we are to better understand the standard-setting process.

To illustrate how such research may proceed, we now outline a model of regulation that moves somewhat closer to the interest group theory.

Specifically, we consider the research of Dessein (2002), who modelled the outcome of a strategic reporting game between regulator and manager, looking more closely at how the regulator may extract the manager's inside information than in the analysis above. We adapt Dessein's model to a financial reporting context.

Assume that the regulator is a securities commission, charged by the government with primary responsibility for protecting the interests of investors. The commission faces a decision about the extent of standard setting. That is, should it lay down high-quality accounting standards, or reduce standards quality by allowing firm managers at least some accounting policy flexibility?

If the regulator adopts the first alternative, it needs information about the most useful accounting policies for the firm in question. However, the manager who knows the most useful policies may not fully communicate them to the regulator. We can think of these most useful policies as those that generate unmanaged net income, or perhaps net income after "good" smoothing to reveal persistent earning power (Section 11.5). Lacking this inside knowledge, the regulator must then attempt to set standards based on the best information it can obtain. The regulator will have some prior information about what the most useful policies are, since it knows current economic conditions, the firm's industry, its capital structure, stock options outstanding, etc. However, it will not know them precisely.

If the regulator adopts the second alternative, it is unlikely that the manager will release as much information to investors as is socially desirable—market failures in the production of information were discussed in Section 12.5. Thus, the manager may use discretionary accruals and other accounting policy choices to manage reported earnings.

The regulator then has two options.[7] Under a communication option, it requires the manager to submit an information return, including an earnings statement and MD&A. Upon examining the return, the regulator revises its prior probabilities of what the firm's best accounting policies are, and then lays down standards to require the firm to report according to them. Alternatively, under a delegation option, it can reduce the extent of standard setting by delegating the reporting decision to the manager, in effect allowing the possibility of a biased earnings report, but relying on market forces to at least control the amount of the bias.

If the communication option is chosen, Dessein showed that the manager reports to the regulator a *range* within which its unmanaged net income lies. If the manager reported a single number, it would not be credible since the regulator knows the manager is biased—the regulator would simply adjust the reported number by the amount of bias it contains and implement accounting standards that would correct the bias. Reporting a noisy earnings number (i.e., a range) reduces the ability of the regulator to infer unmanaged net income and hence design the best accounting policies, while giving the regulator *some* credible information.[8] This range can be created by the manager in several ways. For example, poor disclosure of low-persistence items complicates the regulator's ability to infer continuing earnings. Also, less-than-full information in notes and MD&A about risks, hedging, contingent liabilities, and off balance sheet activities complicate the regulator's ability to estimate the effect on net income of various contingencies.

Which option will the regulator choose? This depends on the regulator's prior information about what the firm's most useful accounting policies should be. If this prior information is poor, the regulator's posterior information is also poor since the manager reports noisy information. Then, the regulator will favour the delegation option—the loss of decision usefulness to investors from allowing the manager to report relatively unregulated net income is less than the loss if the regulator lays down reporting standards based on its poor information about what the best accounting policies should be.

However, if prior information is sufficiently high, the communication option is favoured, since the regulator's posterior information is then also high. Then, the regulator is better able to set standards for decision useful reporting since the possible loss of decision usefulness to investors from the manager reporting unregulated information exceeds the loss from laying down imperfect accounting standards.

In our context, we would expect the regulator setter to have considerable prior information, due to its experience, research, and financial expertise. Then, theory predicts standard setting rather than unregulated reporting.

Nevertheless, some loss of decision usefulness remains since, as mentioned, the regulator cannot set perfect standards in the absence of perfect information about what accounting policies are socially most useful.

However, Dessein showed conditions under which this loss of decision usefulness can be reduced if the regulator brings in an **intermediary** to communicate with the manager and set standards. A key condition for bringing in an intermediary is that it be biased toward management, but less biased than the manager. (If the intermediary is unbiased, like the regulator, there is no point in bringing it in in the first place; nor is there any point in bringing in the intermediary if it simply reflects management's views.)

In our context, this condition seems reasonable. It may be politically unwise for a government securities commission, charged with responsibility for protecting investors' interests, to be seen consulting with management. However, the intermediary standard setter, by following due process, takes management's views as well as investors' interests into account in their deliberations. Consequently, some bias toward management is introduced. The result of this bias is that the intermediary communicates "better" with the manager, resulting in better knowledge than the regulator of what standards are best. Consequently, expected loss of decision usefulness is reduced by bringing in the intermediary.

The Dessein model further enhances our understanding of the standard-setting process. While this model assumes that the objective of the securities commission is to maximize usefulness of financial reporting to investors (the public interest theory), the commission's decision about the extent of standard setting takes place in the presence of conflict between regulator and managers (the interest group theory). Furthermore, the analysis shows conditions for delegation of standard setting by the securities commission to an intermediate body, consistent with what we observe in practice. By showing the social benefits of communication between the intermediary and management, it supports due process, and also our contention (Section 11.7) that responsible management has a legitimate interest in financial reporting.

13.7 INTERNATIONAL INTEGRATION OF CAPITAL MARKETS

13.7.1 Convergence of Accounting Standards

Accounting, in any country, takes place within the social, political, legal, and economic institutions of that country. In this book, we have taken North American market-oriented institutions largely for granted. However, as capital markets become more integrated worldwide, investors are increasingly investing in firms in foreign countries, whose customs, institutions, and accounting standards may differ from those of the investor's home country. Arguably, integration leads to better-working capital markets, lower costs of capital and increased investment, and more efficient contracting across the integrated markets. Consequently, any evaluation of the political aspects of standard setting must now take international integration into account.

One response to capital markets integration is to pursue a common set of international accounting standards. Indeed, as noted in Section 1.12.5, this is the basic objective of the IASB. To the extent that a common set of standards becomes acceptable to securities regulators as a substitute for local GAAP, costs of multiple stock exchange listings will fall. This should lower firms' financial statement preparation costs. It may also lower their costs of capital, as they are better able to tap more liquid sources of financing. Also, a common set of international standards should decrease **network externalities**. That is, increased financial statement comparability may decrease costs for analysts and other financial statement users, who do not then have to familiarize themselves with more than one set of GAAP. Consequently, the working of securities markets, and cross-border investment, should improve.

Empirical evidence supports this argument. Covrig, DeFond, and Hung (2007) studied stock holdings of mutual funds for a large sample of firms from 29 countries, excluding the United States and Canada. They found that foreign mutual funds (i.e., funds not located in the same country as a sample firm) included in their portfolios a significantly higher number of shares of firms that had voluntarily adopted IASB standards, relative to firms using their local GAAP. Also, Tan, Wang, and Welker (2011) studied 25 countries that adopted IFRS standards during 1988–2007, finding that the number of foreign analysts (i.e., analysts located in a country other than the IFRS-adopting country) following firms in the adopting country increased. They also found that the earnings forecast accuracy of foreign analysts increased. The increase in accuracy was greater as the difference between IFRS and previous home-country (i.e., local) GAAP increased, and also as the difference between IFRS and analyst local GAAP decreased. These results suggest an increase in financial statement comparability from IFRS adoption.

However, U.S. accounting standards have worldwide influence too, particularly for foreign firms that wish to raise capital in the United States. The convergence question then becomes, should convergence be to IASB or FASB standards? A response is to converge these two sets of standards to each other.

In this regard, the 2002 Norwalk Agreement[9] between the FASB and IASB commits the two bodies to work toward a common set of high-quality standards. Some progress has been made toward IASB/FASB standards convergence. For example, IFRS 2 requires expensing of ESOs, as does ASC 718-10-30 (Section 8.6). IFRS 3 requires the purchase method of accounting for purchased goodwill. Goodwill is not amortized but is subject to an impairment test. These requirements are similar to SFAS 142 (now ASC 350-20-35) (see Section 7.11.2). Both IASB and FASB standards now require other comprehensive income (Section 1.10) to immediately follow net income in a single statement of comprehensive income, or in a separate statement immediately following the net income statement. Also, the derecognition provisions of IFRS 9 are converged with ASC 860-20 (Section 7.8).

Yet, differences remain. For example, IASB standards do not allow the LIFO inventory method,[10] IAS 16 allows upward revaluation of property, plant, and equipment, whereas historical cost is generally used in the United States and Canada. Development costs may be capitalized under IAS 38, while in the United States, almost all R&D is expensed. At present, standards on financial instruments and loan loss provisioning are not converged (Section 7.5.2). See also Theory in Practice 13.1. Given the differences that remain, further progress on standards convergence will take some time and will likely require further development of the Conceptual Framework (Section 3.7.1).

In its 2011 Annual Report, Manulife Financial Corporation reported net income under IFRS of Can.$245 million. The company also reported that under U.S. accounting standards, its net income would be Can.$3.765 billion. The company attributed the difference as due primarily to differences in the extent of fair value accounting for variable annuity guarantee liabilities and related hedging. Presumably, differences such as these will be reduced when a new converged insurance accounting standard, currently in process, becomes effective.

13.7.2 Effects of Customs and Institutions on Financial Reporting

As mentioned, financial reporting is affected by local customs and institutions. The legal environment in a country is an important example. Ball, Kothari, and Robin (BKR; 2000), in a study spanning 1985–1995, compared the quality of financial reporting in several common law countries (Australia, Canada, United Kingdom, United States) to reporting quality in code law countries (France, Germany, Japan). In common law countries, accounting standards are set, in varying degrees, in the private sector, and are oriented primarily to investors. In contrast, standards in code law countries were set primarily by governments, hence subject to more political influence than under common law. As a result, additional constituencies are represented *within* the corporate governance structure under code law, such as banks, business associations, and labour unions. In effect, BKR pointed out, there is less information asymmetry in code law countries, since important constituencies are insiders rather than outsiders.

If so, insiders will quickly learn, for example, about major gains and losses. Consequently, there is less need for timeliness in conveying this information outside the company. Thus BKR predicted that financial reporting has greater recognition lag in code law countries relative to common law countries.

BKR also predicted that financial reporting will be less conservative in code law countries. Since influential insiders will already be aware of major losses, they can rapidly bring pressure to bear on management to forestall and correct them, without waiting for the pressure to arise from violation of debt covenants and capital market reaction to public disclosure of bad news. Consequently, there is less need for conservative standards, such as impairment tests, relative to common law countries. In effect, the agency costs of contracting between managers and owners are lower under code law.

To test their predictions, BKR studied a large sample of firm year ends from the countries involved. They measured economic income by the change in a firm's share value over the year (adjusted for capital transactions). Recognition lag was then evaluated by the association between net income and economic income—lower association indicates greater recognition lag between the occurrence of an economic gain or loss and its incorporation into the financial statements. Their empirical results showed significantly lower associations for code law countries, consistent with their prediction.

To test for conservative reporting, BKR used a technique similar to that used by Basu (1997) (see Section 6.11). They evaluated the association between economic income and reported net income separately for firms with negative and positive economic incomes. Recall that an efficient market will bid up share prices of firms with good economic news and bid down the prices of firms with bad news. Under conservative accounting, recognition lag is less for bad news (i.e., negative economic income) than for good news. Consequently, the association between bad economic news and net income will be higher than the association between good economic news and net income. BKR's empirical results were broadly consistent with their prediction of less conservative accounting under code law.

High recognition lag and less conservative accounting suggest that financial reporting in code law countries is of lower quality than under common law. However, this does not imply that financial reporting under code law is necessarily more opportunistic than under common law. Rather, these differences reflect underlying differences in institutions, agency costs, and corporate governance structures.

By and large, the countries in the BKR study did not at the time use international accounting standards. For example, IASB standards had not yet been adopted by the European Union (EU). We might then be tempted to conclude that if all countries adopted international standards, the higher costs to investors of interpreting and analyzing financial statements of foreign firms in the face of differences such as timeliness and conservatism would disappear. However, one must be careful about such a conclusion. Even high-quality accounting standards are flexible—they allow considerable judgment and discretion in the application of accounting policies.

In this regard, Ball, Robin, and Wu (BRW; 2003) studied a sample of firm year-ends over 1984–1996 from Hong Kong, Singapore, Malaysia, and Thailand. All of these countries had adopted high-quality standards, such as IASB, which have their origins in common law countries. However, institutional characteristics in the four countries are typical of code law, namely greater family and bank influence and more private debt. These reduce the agency costs of managerial and debt contracts, since information needed for monitoring and corrective action can be communicated among insiders rather than through financial disclosure. This reduces the need for timely and conservative reporting, as in the BKR study. BRW found that financial reporting in these countries, as measured by recognition lag and conservatism, was similar to the lower-quality of code law countries even though they used high-quality standards similar to those of common law countries. This suggests that we cannot take for granted that high-quality standards will, by themselves, improve financial reporting.

An additional complication of international accounting standards is that governments may influence financial reporting. In some countries, firms may be allowed, or even encouraged, to cover up large losses so as to avoid bankruptcy, which would embarrass the government. Indeed, poorly performing firms themselves have an incentive to smooth recognition of losses and accelerate recognition of gains if they fear the government may take over in the national interest. Alternatively, large gains may be smoothed so as to forestall racial tensions within the country. Smoothing of large losses and gains increases recognition lag since, instead of reporting them currently, their recognition is deferred over future periods. Also, smoothing of large losses reduces conservatism.

These issues were examined by Bushman and Piotroski (2006), who studied a sample of 38 countries during the period 1992–2001. They found that in countries with substantial state involvement in the economy, recognition lag for good news firms was relatively low, while the lag for bad news was relatively high. This tendency to maximize reported earnings through faster recognition of good news and smoothing of losses suggests that a desire to reduce the possibility of further state involvement dominates any concerns firms may have about lower-quality financial reporting and possible racial tensions.

13.7.3 Enforcement of Accounting Standards

Accounting standards must be enforced if they are to contribute to higher-quality financial reporting. Enforcement of IASB standards is of particular concern since, as pointed out in Section 1.12.5, IOSCO does not have formal enforcement powers. Enforcement is up to the jurisdictions that adopt IASB standards. Should this enforcement be less than adequate, we cannot be sure that high-quality standards are applied in practice. Investors may face serious exposure to estimation risk arising from adverse selection and moral hazard, if legal systems, stock exchanges, and securities regulators do not reinforce the application of accounting standards to provide a stable environment for high-quality financial reporting. Furthermore, markets that do not work well reduce incentives for voluntary disclosure, since firms' share prices will be less rewarded for quality reporting.

A related enforcement issue is the protection of small investors. In many countries, firms are controlled by families, large institutions, or governments. Minority shareholders in firms with highly concentrated ownership may suffer at the hands of the controlling interest. This creates a different type of agency problem than the manager–owner conflict studied in this book. While concentrated ownership may reduce the moral hazard problem between managers and owners, the problem now shifts to one between controlling shareholders and minority shareholders. Minority investors will be wary of this moral hazard, and will not invest, or will demand a high return. If so, capital markets will not work well, constraining productivity and growth in the economy.

For individual firms, the adverse effects of this reluctance of minority investors to invest will increase as firms' ownership concentration increases. Consequently, high ownership concentration firms may have an incentive to adopt policies to signal to outside investors that their interests will be protected. One such policy is to hire a high-quality auditor.

Auditing is an important enforcement mechanism. A well-functioning audit contributes to investor confidence and efficient contracting. In particular, full disclosure protects small minority investors by making it more difficult for controlling interests to expropriate firm value through, for example, excessive compensation, perquisites, and related party transactions. In this regard, Fan and Wong (2005) studied the audit hiring practices of a sample of firms from several East Asian countries during 1994–1996. They reported that firms with high ownership concentration were significantly more likely than low ownership concentration firms to hire a big, prestigious auditor, particularly for firms that frequently raised outside equity capital. This latter result suggests that the entrenched owners of such high ownership concentration firms perceived the benefits of higher share price to be greater than the costs of reduced perquisites and other insider benefits, implying that a high-quality audit is effective in reducing the agency problem between inside and outside owners.

Guedhami and Pittman (2006) also studied the relationship between the audit and ownership concentration. With a sample of firms drawn from countries worldwide (excluding Canada, the United States, and the United Kingdom), they, like Fan and Wong, used ownership concentration as a proxy for the extent of the agency problem between controlling interests and small investors. They found that ownership concentration was lower in countries with strong laws enforcing auditor liability. It appears that auditors do a better job on behalf of outside investors when they are more under the threat of legal liability. Small investors are then less wary of investing, reducing ownership concentration.

In a related study, Francis and Wang (2008) analyzed the investor protection environment of 42 countries over the period 1994–2004. Based on a sample of firms from each country, they found that earnings quality (based on two measures: Abnormal accruals and the likelihood of reporting a loss) increased with the strength of investor protection, but only for firms with Big Four auditors. They also found a positive association between investor protection and conservative accounting, but again only for firms with Big Four auditors.

These results suggest that big audit firms, facing the possibility of lawsuits and reputation loss, tailor their audit quality and use of impairment tests to the regulatory environment of the company under audit.

From a professional standpoint, this seems unfortunate, since we would hope that ethical behaviour would drive audit performance, regardless of audit liability. However, it does reinforce our argument in Section 1.5 that reputation considerations, such as avoiding legal liability, can drive behaviour that is, in effect, ethical.

13.7.4 Benefits of Adopting High-Quality Accounting Standards

Despite the problems just discussed, adoption of high-quality accounting standards is potentially worthwhile, since economies with relatively weak regulatory environments may benefit from higher-quality reporting and consequent strengthening of their capital and managerial labour markets. To the extent that adoption of IASB standards improves capital market liquidity and synchronicity, the models of Diamond and Verrecchia (1991) and Lambert, Leuz, and Verrecchia (2007) discussed in Section 12.9.1, predict lower costs of capital and better working capital markets. The question then is, are these benefits realized upon adoption of IASB standards?

Daske, Hail, Leuz, and Verdi (DHLV; 2008) examined the effects of mandatory adoption of IASB standards on firms' share liquidity and cost of capital for 26 countries. Most of these countries belonged to the European Union, which adopted IASB in 2005. DHLV reported a significant increase in market liquidity, concentrated in countries with large differences between domestic and IASB GAAP, and with strong regulations and institutions to encourage quality reporting. These findings suggest a decrease in information asymmetry and estimation risk following the switch from domestic GAAP. DHLV also reported some evidence of lower cost of capital. However, the authors qualified their findings by pointing out that part of these results could be driven by increases in disclosure regulation, which often accompanied IASB adoption, and thus are not attributable solely to IASB standards.

More recently, Byard, Li, and Yu (BLY; 2011) studied the effects of the European Union's adoption of IASB standards on the quality of analysts' earnings forecasts. To the extent forecast quality improves, this is consistent with an improvement in financial reporting quality, since analysts then have better data to work from. BYU analyzed a sample of firms from the 27 countries then in the European Union. They found, on average, no improvement in the accuracy of analysts' earnings forecasts, or in forecast dispersion, over a two-year period following mandatory IASB adoption.[11] However, they went on to identify sample firms located in EU countries with both relatively strong law enforcement and previous accounting standards (i.e., local GAAP) that differed significantly from IASB. After controlling for other factors that may affect analyst forecast quality, they reported a significant increase in forecast accuracy for these firms, and reduced forecast dispersion. In further analysis, BLY identified those firms in their sample with both relatively *weak* law enforcement and significantly different previous accounting standards, *and* with strong incentives for voluntary quality reporting (e.g., high-quality auditor, dispersed shareholders, high growth rate). Again, they found a significant increase in analyst forecast quality. The authors concluded that mandatory IASB adoption improves analyst forecasts only when previous local GAAP differed significantly from IASB, and laws are rigorously enforced. Furthermore, when enforcement is weak, this increases the role of voluntary reporting incentives.

Landsman, Maydew, and Thornock (LMT; 2012) studied the information content of earnings for a sample of firms from 16 countries that had adopted IASB standards during the 2002–2007 period; relative to a control sample of firms from 11 countries that had not adopted IASB during the same period—that is, firms that continued to use their local GAAP.

LMT's measures of the information content of a company's earnings included a measure based on the variability of share returns over a three-day window surrounding the date of earnings announcement—greater variability implies greater information content. They reported that the average information content of earnings of IASB-adopting firms increased following adoption, relative to the control sample. This increase was particularly strong for companies in those adopting countries with strong legal environments. The authors concluded that adoption of IASB standards leads to higher information content of earnings—that is, decreased market synchronicity.

High-quality standards can also improve the efficiency of managerial compensation contracts. Ozkan, Singer, and You (2012) studied a sample of firms from 15 continental European countries that adopted IASB standards as a result of their adoption by the European Union in 2005. They reported a significant average increase in the weight of net income in compensation contracts for those countries with large differences between IASB standards and their former local GAAP (but not for countries with small differences). They also reported a significant increase in the inclusion of foreign firms in the peer groups used for relative performance evaluation (RPE—see Section 10.4.3). The authors concluded that the adoption of IASB standards increased compensation committees' perceptions of earnings quality and comparability.[12]

Daske, Hail, Leuz, and Verdi (DHLV; 2013) analyzed a sample of firms across 30 countries that claimed to have voluntarily adopted IASB standards during the period 1990–2005. They divided their sample into "serious" and "label" adopters. Serious adopters were viewed as firms that adopted IASB as part of a strategy to commit to high-quality reporting. DHLV measured this commitment by a series of firm-specific variables such as financing needs, diversity of ownership, ratio of accruals to cash flows, and number of analysts following the firm. Higher values of these variables (except lower for accruals to cash flow) suggest a higher motivation for the firm to commit to quality reporting. Firms with above-average increases in these variables following IASB adoption were thus classified as serious adopters, who would then use the flexibility of IASB standards[13] to improve reporting quality over the quality of their previous reporting under local GAAP.

Firms with lower than average changes in these variables were classified as label adopters. DHLV argued that such firms adopt IASB for other reasons than higher quality reporting, such as the prestige and wide acceptance of IASB standards, and would use the flexibility of IASB GAAP to make only minimal changes to the accounting policies they were already using under their local GAAP.[14]

A question then is, do the economic consequences of IASB adoption (measured by liquidity of trading in the firm's shares, bid–ask spread, and cost of capital) differ between serious and label adopters? DHLV predicted that the shares of serious adopters will enjoy higher liquidity, lower bid–ask spread, and lower cost of capital than label adopters following IASB adoption. Their empirical results are consistent with this prediction. The authors also tested this prediction on a sample of firms under mandatory FASB adoption, with similar results.

A major implication of the DHLV study is that the average benefits of IASB adoption outlined earlier are not due only to IASB adoption as such. Rather, the benefits depend on how adopting firms use the flexibility of GAAP. Only if IASB GAAP are used to increase reporting quality will these benefits be realized. It should also be noted that the results of this study suggest considerable investor rationality and securities markets efficiency across 30 countries, in that investors are apparently able to distinguish between serious and label adopters.

We conclude that a shift from local GAAP to IASB GAAP can benefit the economies involved, particularly when the local and IASB GAAP differ significantly, and when there is a strong legal and institutional regime to enforce and encourage investor protection and quality financial reporting. However, the extent of these benefits also seems to depend on how the flexibility of GAAP is used.

13.7.5 The Relative Quality of IASB and FASB GAAP

While the evidence just cited suggests that a shift from local GAAP to IASB GAAP can benefit the economies involved, a related question is the relative quality of IASB and United States GAAP. This question is important since the SEC allows foreign firms under its jurisdiction to report using IASB standards without reconciliation to FASB standards. In this regard, Leuz (2003) examined the liquidity of shares traded on the former German New Market. This market allowed its listed firms to report under either IASB or FASB standards. Leuz measured a share's liquidity by its bid–ask spread and turnover, where share turnover is a proxy for market depth—see Chapter 1, Note 22. He found no significant differences between IASB and FASB standards for these measures, and concluded that there is little difference in information asymmetries between firms reporting under the two sets of standards.

However, Barth, Landsman, Lang, and Williams (BLLW; 2012) examined a sample of firms from 27 countries, including Canada, that had switched to IASB standards, relative to a sample of similar U.S. firms. Their interest was in assessing the comparability of financial statements under IASB and FASB standards.[15]

BLLW measured comparability two ways. First, if statements are comparable, they should lead to similar estimates of share price. Second, comparable financial statements should have similar ERCs (Section 5.4).

After allowing for other factors that affect share price and ERCs, the authors reported a significant lack of comparability, on average, between IASB and FASB financial statements. However, comparability has increased more recently (2007–2009 versus 2005–2006), which the authors attributed in part to the increasing convergence between IASB and FASB standards. In addition, comparability between the two sets of standards was greater than average for firms located in common law countries, and for firms located in countries with strong law enforcement.

Note that a comparability gap does not in itself mean that one set of standards is better than another. However, BLLW also compared accounting quality for firms using IASB and FASB standards. Their measures of quality included recognition lag (less lag, higher quality) and the accruals-based quality measure of DeChow and Dichev (2002) (Section 5.4.1). They found that, on average, the accounting quality of FASB standards exceeded that of IASB. However, for sample firms located in common law countries, IASB standards exhibited higher quality than FASB on some quality measures and less on others.

We conclude that there is mixed evidence about the relative quality of IFRS and FASB GAAP. However, the comparability and quality of the two sets of standards will move together over time if standards convergence progresses.

13.7.6 Should Standard Setters Compete?

An alternative to standards convergence is for each country to allow firms in its jurisdiction to use either domestic accounting standards or IASB standards (or any other set of standards, for that matter). In particular, as mentioned above, suppose that the SEC were to allow all firms in its jurisdiction to use, without reconciliation, either U.S. GAAP or IASB GAAP.

Competition in regulated industries (such as standard setting) is considered by Armstrong and Sappington (AS; 2006). They concluded that there is no "one size fits all" answer to the question of competition. Rather, any introduction of competition will be a long and complex process, and must be tailored to the industry in question. They also pointed out that if the regulator could fully implement the public interest theory of regulation there is little point in introducing competition, since social welfare would be maximized by definition. However, in view of our conclusion in Section 12.11 that the standard-setting industry is too complex to calculate the socially best extent of standard setting, and in Section 13.2.3 that the interest group theory better describes actual standard setting, the question of competition between standard setters is worthy of consideration.

Despite the lack of a unique answer to competition among standard setters, AS did offer some general conclusions. For example, there are potential gains to competition when economies of scale are low. This would seem to be the case in standard setting since it is unlikely that the FASB's unit costs per standard would increase substantially if it was in competition with the IASB. Also, since both standard-setting bodies have roughly similar organizational structures, it seems unlikely that lower costs of one of them would drive the other out of business. AS also concluded that there are potential gains to competition when the regulator is at an information disadvantage relative to the regulated firms. This would seem to be the case in standard setting. Despite the standard setter's resources and sophistication, it is likely that the firm has better information than the standard setter about its optimal accounting policies. Then, as discussed in Section 13.6 (optional section), the regulator acts to limit the ability of the manager to exploit his/her information advantage, but at the cost of reducing the regulated quality of information. This gives the firm greater flexibility to choose its own accounting policies. If so, perhaps competition among standard setters, by enabling individual firms to choose the GAAP best tailored to its particular information environment, would increase the average quality of financial reporting.

Thus, there seem to be potential benefits to competition. But, there would also be increased costs to the extent that U.S. investors would have to support two standard setters rather than one (i.e., increased network externalities). We then have the familiar question: Do the potential benefits outweigh the increased costs?

The question of introducing competition into the standard-setting process was discussed by Dye and Sunder (2001). One possible effect, they suggested, is a "race to the bottom," whereby each standard setter lowers its standards so as to attract firms and their managers away from the other. As a result, the potential for bad earnings management is increased. This outcome is analogous to the Nash equilibrium outcome of the game discussed in Example 8.1.

However, as Dye and Sunder discussed, there are forces to control such a tendency. There would be investor reaction to a firm that chooses low-quality accounting standards. Also, we suggested in Section 12.9.2 that market forces reward managers who release full and timely information. Furthermore, a race to the bottom is inconsistent with the objectives of the IASB and FASB, which include high-quality accounting standards.

In addition, firms themselves have incentives to adopt high-quality reporting, such as the lower cost of capital resulting from increased share liquidity and lower investor estimation risk. While firms can always voluntarily exceed the reporting requirements laid down by any GAAP, choosing the higher of two available GAAP qualities serves as a signal of commitment by the firm to high reporting quality. In the extreme, a "race to the top" could develop as standard setters compete to attract such firms by implementing high-quality standards (see Problem 8).

However, competition would limit both of these tendencies. If a race to the bottom develops, more and more firms would wish to signal their commitment to higher reporting quality, and the lower-quality standard setter would "lose customers." If a race to the top develops, more and more firms would be unwilling to bear the increasing costs of higher quality reporting, and the higher quality standard setter would lose customers. Given the impossibility of calculating the socially correct extent of standard setting, competition would, hopefully, move standard setting *toward* a socially correct level. At the least, competition should reduce the tendency of a monopoly standard setter, as predicted by the interest group theory of regulation, to push the extent of standard setting beyond a social optimum.

As mentioned above, network externalities would increase if firms could choose between different GAAPs. However, Dye and Sunder suggested that these costs would be relatively low. For example, analysts and other experts could specialize in interpreting a particular set of standards. Given reasonable securities market efficiency, the results of their analyses would quickly be incorporated into share market values, thereby price-protecting ordinary investors.

In sum, the social benefits of competition lie in the potential to move the extent of standard setting toward a socially correct level. However, these benefits have to be traded off against the costs of maintaining two sets of standards. Whether the benefits exceed the costs is not known at the present time.

13.7.7 Should the United States Adopt IASB Standards?

An alternative to competition is for the United States, like many other countries, to adopt IASB standards. In 2010, the SEC initiated a work plan to evaluate the impact on U.S. securities markets of eventual adoption of IASB standards. Subsequently, a 2012 SEC Staff Report examined the adoption of IASB standards in detail. Based on this Report, it seems that a one-time "big bang" adoption of IASB standards, as took place in Canada, is unlikely. What seems more likely is a gradual process, aided by increasing standards convergence. The Report reflects some skepticism that the more principles-based IASB standards are suitable for many U.S. applications, and suggests a need for the FASB to retain significant influence in ensuring that any IASB standards are adapted to U.S. needs.

This caution toward IASB standards adoption is consistent with much of the international accounting research outlined earlier in this section, where we saw that most of the benefits of IASB adoption occur in countries with local GAAP much different from IASB, and with relatively weak capital markets regulations and enforcement. In the United States, IASB and FASB GAAP have much in common, and enforcement through the legal and regulatory systems is strong. Furthermore, as standards convergence progresses, differences between the two sets of standards will continue to decline. Also, a strong auditing profession is present in the United States. As a result, there may be little to gain in terms of better operation of capital markets if IASB standards were adopted.

However, there is some evidence that IFRS adoption can benefit even countries with strong capital markets regulations and enforcement. For example, Chalmers, Clinch, and Godfrey (2011) documented an increase in the value relevance and persistence of earnings following IFRS adoption in Australia.

Nevertheless, the capital market benefits of IFRS adoption by the United States are unclear. The question then is, are there other benefits to convergence? One such benefit would be lower financial statement preparation costs for U.S.-based multinational corporations. Many of the subsidiaries of these corporations are in countries that have adopted IASB standards. Thus it is necessary for these subsidiaries to prepare IASB statements for local authorities, but they then have to be translated to FASB standards for purposes of consolidation with the parent. Another possible benefit is that the greater flexibility and principles-based orientation of IASB standards relative to rules-based FASB standards would enable firms that wish to do so to adopt high-quality financial reporting, better suited to their individual characteristics. However, since there seems to be little difference in the overall quality of the two sets of standards (Section 13.7.5), any such benefits would be small.

There would also be costs of adopting IASB standards. These include one-time transition costs of financial statement preparation, increased audit fees, and contracting costs arising from effects on accounting variables used in existing contracts. As mentioned, additional costs would also arise since domestic U.S. investors would have to become familiar with IASB standards, and how these standards would fare in the face of the U.S. legal system.

Overall, the most likely result is that any adoption will be gradual, aided by continuing standards convergence. Whether this convergence process will continue to the point where differences between the two sets of standards are minimal remains to be seen. However, even if adoption should be worthwhile from an economic perspective, it is likely that U.S. political and institutional constituencies will lobby in favour of U.S. standard setters retaining significant influence over U.S. accounting standards.

In this regard, it is interesting to note that in its 2013 Conceptual Framework Discussion Paper (see Section 3.7.1), the IASB states that its Conceptual Framework project is no longer being conducted jointly with the FASB, despite the joint release of Chapters 1 and 3 of the project. Possibly, the IASB may now recognize that U.S. adoption of IFRS is unlikely, and is beginning to go its own way. Note that to the extent that the two bodies adopt different conceptual frameworks, future standards convergence is also threatened.

13.7.8 Summary of Accounting for International Capital Markets Integration

It should be emphasized that financial reporting that seems to be of lower quality than that of North America is not necessarily opportunistic, but may instead efficiently reflect differences in customs, institutional structures, government involvement, and enforcement. Nevertheless, capital markets worldwide are becoming increasingly integrated. Better-working capital markets can contribute to social welfare through increased market liquidity, lower cost of capital, increased foreign investment, and increased contracting efficiency.

High-quality financial reporting standards have a role to play in bringing about better-working markets, with resulting increased social welfare. Indeed, empirical studies suggest that adoption of IASB standards is accompanied by higher market liquidity, financial statement comparability, earnings quality, and increased foreign investment. However, adoption of IASB standards does not by itself guarantee higher quality reporting, since any set of GAAP allows considerable discretion in accounting policy choice. Application of standards needs to be enforced by a strong regulatory environment and auditor liability. Even then, investors and standard setters need to be aware that different customs and institutional structures continue to affect actual reporting. If investors who invest in another country on the strength of IASB standards suffer losses arising from reporting failures, they may react by blaming the standards rather than their failure to realize the impact of country-specific factors on reporting quality. Since it is even more difficult to change customs and institutions than accounting standards, differences in foreign environments will likely persist for many years. As a result, complete integration of accounting standards, including U.S. adoption of IASB standards, will take some time if, indeed, it is desirable at all. In the meantime, some ability of firms to choose between competing sets of accounting standards should not be ruled out.

13.8 CONCLUSIONS AND SUMMING UP

In a sense, this whole book comes to a focus on standard setting. We saw, in Chapter 2, that under ideal conditions accounting and reporting standards are not needed, since there is only one way to account, on the basis of the present values of firms' future cash flows. Indeed, under ideal conditions one can question whether financial accounting is needed at all. Fortunately, in view of our conclusion in Section 2.6 that accountants would not be needed under ideal conditions, such conditions do not exist. As a result, financial accounting becomes much more challenging. Information asymmetry is a major source of this challenge.

We have seen two major types of information asymmetry, both of which create estimation risk. The first is adverse selection. That is, managers and other insiders typically know more than outside investors about the state and prospects of the firm. Here, the accounting challenge is to convey information from inside to outside the firm, thereby improving investor decision making, limiting the ability of insiders to exploit their information advantage, and enhancing the operation of capital markets.

The second type of information asymmetry is moral hazard. That is, the effort exerted by a manager is unobservable to shareholders and lenders in all but the smallest firms. Here, the accounting challenge is to provide an informative measure of managerial performance. Such a measure enables efficient incentive contracts to motivate manager effort, protect lenders and shareholders from manager opportunism, and inform the managerial labour market.

It is important to realize that the accounting system that best meets the first challenge is unlikely to best meet the second, so that actual financial reporting represents a compromise between the two. Specifically, investors need decision-relevant information to help them predict future firm performance. This implies current value-based information since current values are generally the best predictors of future values. However, problems of volatility and possible low reliability of fair values reduce the informativeness of net income about manager performance. It can then be argued that reliable and conservative accounting better motivates manager performance. Consequently, despite standard setters' preference for current value accounting, current value- and efficient contracting-based accounting information must be traded off.

It is this need for financial reporting to fulfil the dual role of meeting investors' information needs and the needs of efficient contracting that creates the fundamental problem of financial accounting theory. Investors, including securities commissions acting on their behalf, push for additional information, including current value information. Management pushes the other way when they perceive that proposed standards will affect their flexibility under the contracts they have entered into, inhibit their ability to credibly communicate with the market through accounting policy choice, or reduce their ability to hide poor performance through opportunistic earnings management or to choose a tradeoff between full disclosure to investors and the agency costs that are thus created. As mentioned, the standard setter must then seek a compromise between these conflicting interests. The structure of standard-setting bodies is designed to facilitate such a compromise.

With the increasing globalization of commerce, including securities markets, the need for international accounting standards will continue to expand. However, the difficulties of standard setting will also increase. In addition to investor–manager conflict, new constituencies arise representing different levels of economic development, different business practices, and different cultures. Standard-setting bodies and investors will have to adapt to take these additional challenges into account.

Questions and Problems

1. Contrast the public interest and interest group theories of regulation with respect to
   a. the role of the regulatory body
   b. their implications for the amount of the regulated commodity or service (here, information) to be supplied

2. The interest group theory of regulation predicts constituency conflict surrounding the design and implementation of new accounting standards.

   Required

   a. Describe how the structure of standard setting is designed to facilitate the resolution of constituency conflicts surrounding new accounting standards.
   b. Explain why a super-majority vote (Section 1.12.5) by IASB members is required to pass a new standard.

3. Numerous countries, including Canada, have adopted, in whole or in part, IASB accounting standards. What are some of the benefits and costs to a country of adopting IASB standards?

4. In March 2004, the FASB issued an exposure draft of a standard proposing the expensing of ESOs. However, the proposal faced powerful opponents. These included large corporations such as Texas Instruments, Cisco Systems Inc., Intel Corporation, and Sun Microsystems, Inc., all of which were heavy ESO users. Also, bills were introduced in the U.S. Congress to override or water down the expensing requirement. For example, one such bill would have limited ESO expensing to the firm's top five officers. These bills were of concern, since Congress has the power to override the FASB.

   Objections to the proposed standard were similar to those raised when the FASB attempted to implement a similar standard in 1994. These include the confusing of investors, damage to job creation and innovation, damage to the competitive position of U.S. industry, and unreliability of fair value ESO measures.

   The proposed standard also had powerful proponents, including some congressional leaders and then-Chairman Greenspan of the Federal Reserve. Also, despite the opposing arguments, by early 2004 almost 500 U.S. corporations had voluntarily decided to expense their ESOs.

   Required

   a. In theory, what are the advantages of ESOs as a compensation device?
   b. In practice, during the period leading up to the 2007–2008 market meltdowns, what were the claimed negative effects of ESOs on financial institution managers' incentives and actions?
   c. Are ESOs an expense? Explain why or why not.
   d. With what theory of regulation are the claims of opponents of the proposed standard most consistent? With what theory are the FASB's actions in implementing the new standard most consistent? Explain your answers.
   e. Suppose that you are a member of the FASB. Evaluate a proposal to expense ESOs in relation to the four criteria suggested in Section 13.5.

5. Refer to Section 13.3 concerning the debate in the U.S. Congress of the Financial Stability Improvement Act.

Required

a. Is this sequence of events most consistent with the public interest theory or the interest group theory of regulation? Explain.

b. Evaluate the extent to which the bankers' objections to fair value accounting for financial instruments have merit, since fair value accounting may be subject to liquidity pricing, under which fair values are less than value in use.

c. Investor protection groups opposed the original amendment. Evaluate the costs of moving standard setting for financial instruments to the SEC. Is there a possible benefit?

6. Suppose that the standard-setting body in a country has decided to adopt IASB standards for publicly traded companies. Explain this decision from the perspective of the public interest theory of regulation. Can you explain it from the interest group theory perspective?

7. IAS 39, *Financial Instruments: Recognition and Measurement*, first adopted in 1999, required companies using IASB standards to fair-value many financial instruments including derivatives. This standard moved the IASB accounting for financial instruments into substantial agreement with financial instrument standards in the United States. It is an example of the ongoing movement toward international harmonization of accounting standards.

However, IAS 39 met substantial opposition from the European Union, which required its members to adopt IASB standards effective in 2005. The opposition arose from concerns of European banks and insurance companies, which claimed that fair value accounting would introduce volatility into their financial statements. As a result, the European Union carved out the fair value option and hedging provisions of IAS 39, leaving it up to member states and individual firms to decide if they wanted to adopt them. The European Union was concerned about artificial volatility of earnings resulting from fair value accounting and the strict hedging provisions of IAS 39. It also felt that the IASB was following FASB standards too closely and thus ignoring the "Europeness" of risk management.

More recently, the European Union delayed acceptance of IFRS 9 following objections from certain banks and insurance companies that its relaxation of fair value accounting did not go far enough.

Required

a. Why would EU banks and insurance companies be concerned about financial statement volatility introduced by fair value accounting? Consider both the balance sheet and income statement in your answer.

b. As international harmonization of accounting standards has progressed, there have been suggestions for the SEC to accept either FASB or IASB standards for firms, including domestic firms, under its jurisdiction. What would the costs and benefits to firms and investors be if the SEC were to accept either FASB or IASB standards?

c. How might the EU carve-outs of IAS 39 and its delay in accepting IFRS 9 affect the likelihood that the SEC will allow U.S. companies to use either FASB or IASB standards?

8. In 2007, the SEC cancelled its requirement that foreign companies whose shares are traded in the United States and whose financial statements are prepared according to IASB accounting standards reconcile their reported net income to U.S. GAAP. At the same time, the SEC was considering allowing U.S. companies to prepare financial statements in accordance with IASB GAAP. If so, companies would be able to choose between two sets of GAAP, resulting in a degree of competition between IASB and FASB standard-setting bodies.

Competition creates the possibility of a race to the bottom, discussed by Dye and Sunder (2001) and outlined in Section 13.7.6. However, competition between the two standard-setting bodies also raises an alternate possibility of a "race to the top."

Required

a. What is meant by a "race to the top" in this context?

b. Assuming that standard-setting bodies wish to maximize the number of firms using their standards, why might a race to the top, rather than a race to the bottom, result?

c. Given the SEC's dropping of its reconciliation requirement, what difficulties are created for investors who wish to use financial statements for investment decisions?

9. In its report to shareholders for its quarter ended April 30, 2007, TD Bank Financial Group reported the following items ($ million) in other comprehensive income:

– Change in unrealized gains and losses on available-for-sale securities, net of cash flow hedges	$87
– Reclassification to earnings in respect of available-for-sale securities	(26)
– Change in gains and losses on derivative instruments designated as cash flow hedges	13

At the time, Canadian accounting standards with respect to financial instruments were similar to current IASB standards (Section 7.5.2).

Required

a. Explain the nature of each of these three items.

b. What is the purpose of other comprehensive income?

c. Outline the two alternative formats for reporting other comprehensive income under current IASB and FASB standards. TD, like most firms, included other comprehensive income items in a statement of changes in equity rather than immediately following the net income statement. This alternative reporting of other comprehensive income was acceptable prior to the current IASB and FASB standards under U.S. and Canadian GAAP. Why would TD choose to report the changes in equity rather than report them immediately following the income statement?

d. As an investor, which earnings measure, net income or comprehensive income, is most useful to you in deciding whether to buy, hold, or sell TD shares? Explain.

e. As a member of the Compensation Committee of TD's Board of Directors, which performance measure, net income or comprehensive income, is most useful to you in deciding on the amount of cash bonuses for senior officers for 2007? Explain.

10. In its 1999 annual report, Scotiabank's auditors qualified their audit report. The problem was with the bank's provision for credit losses. During 1999, Scotiabank decided to increase its general provision for credit losses on loans receivable by $700 million. This was in addition to a specific provision for loan losses on identified problem loans. The general provision applied to loans that had not as yet been specifically identified as in arrears.

Under GAAP, the $700 million increase in the general provision should be charged as an expense of the year. However, Scotiabank obtained permission from the Superintendent of

Financial Institutions of Canada (OSFI) to charge $550 million of this amount ($314 million after tax) directly to retained earnings.

As a result, Scotiabank reported net income for 1999 of $1,551 million. Net incomes for 1998 and 1997 were $1,394 million and $1,514 million, respectively.

This direct charge to retained earnings was criticized in the financial media. For example, Eric Reguly, in *The Globe and Mail*, December 7, 1999, called it "an accounting sleight-of-hand that has never been used by the Big Five Canadian banks." Reguly described the objections of the OSC, which, however, could do nothing because the federal Bank Act (administered by OSFI) overrides the Ontario Securities Act. OSFI permitted the direct charge, according to Reguly, because it wanted banks to have a "thicker safety cushion."

Required

a. Use the public interest theory of regulation to justify OSFI's permission for the direct charge to retained earnings.
b. Use the interest group theory of regulation to explain OSFI's permission for the direct charge.
c. Given that the treatment was fully disclosed in the notes to Scotiabank's annual report, in the auditors' report, and in the media, how do you think the securities market would respond to this treatment?

11. IFRS 9 allows financial assets with a predictable cash flow to be measured at amortized cost, subject to an impairment test, if the firm's business model is to hold them to collect cash flows from interest and principal payments. Given that reliance on manager intent is a shifting sand upon which to base a measurement approach (Section 7.2.1), and that management determines the firm's business model, why would a standard setter who wishes to minimize opportunistic manager actions allow the accounting to depend on the firm's business model?

12. Regulation FD of the SEC was intended to reduce small investor concerns about analysts' information advantage and increase their confidence in a fair marketplace. However, during the period leading up to Regulation FD, critics complained that this regulation would result in firms releasing less public information between earnings announcements, leading to increased abnormal share return volatility at earnings announcement dates.

Required

a. Explain the reasoning that led to this concern. Was it confirmed by empirical evidence?
b. To what extent does regulation FD appear to have attained its goals? Base your answer on empirical evidence.

13. Regulation FD of the SEC came into effect in 2000. This standard requires firms that release material information that may affect their share price to release it to all investors simultaneously. The purpose is to stop "selective disclosure," whereby managers release information, such as changes in earnings forecasts, to a select group of analysts and institutional investors, relying on these persons to convey the information to the market.

Required

a. Explain the market failure that has led to this new standard.
b. Describe the effects on market liquidity of selective disclosure. Why is liquidity important if securities markets are to work well?

c. While research suggests that Regulation FD has been at least partially effective in levelling the playing field for outside investors, it is unclear whether or not its benefits outweigh its costs. Describe and explain sources of increased cost to firms and/or society resulting from this regulation.

14. On October 7, 2000, *The Globe and* Mail reported that Air Canada had slashed its third- and fourth-quarter 2000 earnings forecasts. The company had revealed this information by phone calls to a select group of analysts. Air Canada's share price dropped by 12% on the day it revealed this information to analysts, and by another 3% on the next trading day.

    The selective disclosure to certain analysts immediately produced strong negative reactions by angry investors and media, and led to calls for investigation by the Ontario Securities Commission and the Toronto Stock Exchange.

    This episode was particularly embarrassing to Canadian securities regulators since, a few weeks previously, the SEC had passed Regulation FD in the United States. This is a fair disclosure regulation that prohibits material information from being revealed only to investment analysts. Canadian regulators said at the time that a similar regulation was not needed in Canada because Canadian laws already prohibited such selective disclosure.

    Air Canada defended its disclosure policy by claiming that the information underlying the lower earnings forecasts (e.g., higher fuel prices and increased payments to pilots) was already in the public domain. It was attempting to remind analysts that they had not properly incorporated this information into their earnings forecasts.

    Subsequently, Air Canada agreed to pay a fine of $1,080,000 in settlement of charges levied against it over this incident.

    Required

    a. Why would Air Canada want to disclose information about lower-than-expected earnings prior to the actual release of its quarterly income statements?
    b. Give two reasons why share price fell in the day following the selective disclosure.
    c. Explain the impact of selective disclosure practices on the operation of the securities market.
    d. *The Globe and Mail* also reported that a huge block of Air Canada shares had traded on the day prior to the selective disclosure. What problem of information asymmetry is suggested by this trade? Explain.
    e. Canadian securities legislation prohibits use for personal gain of such material information by the analysts to whom it is given. Assuming that the analysts did not use the information for personal gain, do you think that Air Canada should have been charged and fined? Explain why or why not.

15. The Sarbanes-Oxley Act was passed by the U.S. Congress in 2002, following financial reporting disasters of Enron Corp. and WorldCom Inc. (Section 1.2). Section 404 of the Act required that senior management and an independent auditor certify the proper operation of a public company's controls over financial reporting.

    Undoubtedly, Sarbanes-Oxley has benefited investors and contributed to restoration of investor confidence in capital markets, since it reduces investors' concerns about information asymmetry and resulting estimation risk. That is, the Act reduced investor concerns that investment values would suddenly disappear due, for example, to opportunistic manager behaviour covered up for a time by misleading financial reporting.

However, Section 404 drew increasing criticism from companies, due to the costs of implementing the section. These costs were estimated to average as high as US$4.36 million per firm for 2004, and up to US$10 million for very large firms. Section 404 was particularly onerous for small companies since the costs of establishing, evaluating, and auditing internal controls over financial reporting contain a significant fixed cost component—they do not decrease in proportion to lower firm size. Also, then U.S. Treasury Secretary Henry Paulson, in a November 2006 speech, stated that excessive regulation stifles innovation, and that a significant portion of management time, energy, and expense devoted to Section 404 might have been better spent on more direct business matters.

Furthermore, it appeared that U.S. capital markets were losing market share to foreign capital markets such as those in London and Hong Kong. Foreign firms that had been previously attracted to listing their shares on U.S. capital markets because of the availability of large amounts of capital and a share price premium due to lower investor concerns about information asymmetry and estimation risk on well-regulated markets were going elsewhere in increasing numbers.

These concerns led to the creation in the United States of the Committee on Capital Markets Regulation, an independent panel of business and academic leaders. The Committee's first report, issued in December 2006, identified reasons for lower market share. These included foreign companies' fear of lawsuits, perceived overzealous regulation by agencies such as the SEC, and costs imposed by Section 404 of Sarbanes-Oxley. Among the Committee's recommendations were easing of Section 404 and measures to reduce the number of prosecutions and lawsuits. Also, foreign companies should be exempt from some Sarbanes-Oxley requirements if they meet similar regulations in their home countries.

In 2007, the SEC announced some relaxation of Section 404. Managers were given some flexibility to identify and test only the most critical financial reporting risks, and the audit requirements were reduced.

In Canada, NI 52-109 of the CSA proposes similar requirements to Section 404, but does not require auditor certification.

Required

a. While certifying the adequacy of companies' controls over their financial reporting is a form of information production (increased credibility), it is difficult for a regulator to determine the socially correct amount of information to require. What is the socially correct amount of information? Did Section 404 of the Sarbanes-Oxley Act require more or less than the socially correct amount? In your answer, outline both costs and benefits of Section 404.

b. The 2012 U.S. Jobs Act is referenced in Chapter 12, Note 31. For convenience, this note is repeated here:

> ... the 2012 U.S. Jobs Act reduced some adverse consequences of Sarbanes-Oxley by reducing several information requirements for small business. In particular, 'emerging growth companies,' that is, companies planning an initial public offering and with revenues less than $1 billion, were relieved of the obligation under Section 404 of Sarbanes-Oxley to have an independent auditor report on the adequacy of the company's internal controls over financial reporting.

Outline the favourable and unfavourable effects of this relaxation on social welfare.

   c. The Committee report criticized the SEC, recommending that it should adopt a principles-based approach focused on establishing general rules of behaviour for capital market participants, and monitoring the operation of these rules to ensure they were accomplishing their desired effect of protecting investors (this is somewhat ironic since the SEC has urged accounting standard setters to become more principles based—see Section 1.6). The Committee felt that the SEC was too rules-oriented—issuing too many detailed rules and regulations, the enforcement of which sidetracked it into securing settlements and convictions for violations with relatively little attention to whether the rules and regulations were cost effective in improving the operation of capital markets.

     Is a principles-based approach to regulation of financial accounting and reporting feasible in the complex environment in which securities commissions, auditors, and accountants operate? Justify your answer.

16. Numerous countries, including Canada, have adopted IASB accounting standards.

Required

   a. Explain the benefits of a common set of high-quality global accounting standards.
   b. Outline the role of a country's auditing profession in implementing a set of high-quality global accounting standards in that country.
   c. Will high-quality global accounting standards and a strong audit profession lead to a uniform high quality of financial reporting across countries? Explain why or why not.

17. Suppose that a foreign company plans to crosslist its shares on a U.S. securities exchange. The company currently uses local GAAP. Before applying for crosslisting, it plans to switch its current and future financial statements to IASB GAAP for reporting in its home country to improve the likelihood that its application will be approved. The company is based in a country with weak institutional structures, but wishes to signal its commitment to high-quality reporting and high corporate governance standards.

Required

   a. Explain why crosslisting is a credible signal of this commitment.
   b. What are the higher costs that a company from a country with weak institutional structures to support capital markets and protect investors would face if it switches to IASB GAAP for reporting in its home country?

18. This problem illustrates the Becker (1983) interest group theory of regulation, under which affected groups compete for the extent of regulation they desire.

     Assume two groups, investors and managers, and, to simplify somewhat, that the pressure applied by each group can be measured by the amount of money it spends. Suppose that investors desire higher-quality accounting standards. Managers, however, object to higher-quality standards. Each group must decide to exert pressure for their desired extent of regulation or not to exert pressure.

     Costs to managers of higher-quality standards include greater difficulty in using earnings management to disguise shirking (Section 9.3.1), release of proprietary information (Section 12.2), and/or concern about increased earnings volatility, leading to debt covenant violation (Section 8.5) and increased compensation risk. Assume that managers perceive these costs as totalling 100.

But the benefits to investors may be much greater than the costs to managers, since more information production reduces adverse selection, leading to better investment decisions, and reduces moral hazard, leading to more efficient corporate governance and contracting. Suppose that investors perceive these benefits as 125.

If neither party brings pressure to bear, nothing happens—no new standard. However, to bring pressure to bear, a group must organize. Suppose that the cost of investors to organize is 25. Assume that costs for managers to organize and oppose the standards are only 10, since an industry interest group is already in place. Given that they organize, investors are willing to spend an additional 100 to lobby for the standard. Given that management organizes, it is willing to spend an additional 100 on lobbying against it.

Required

a. Prepare a payoff table for this game, similar in format to Table 8.1. Note that in the Table 8.1 game, payoffs were in terms of benefits. Here, payoffs are in terms of costs.
b. Identify the Nash equilibrium of this game, and explain why it is the predicted outcome.
c. Suppose that the benefits of the proposed standard to investors are now 90. Organization costs remain at 25. Other assumptions are unchanged. What is the predicted outcome of the game now? Explain.

19. In 1997, SFAS 130, Reporting **Comprehensive Income**, was issued by the FASB (now included in ASC 220). We introduced other comprehensive income, including the related IASB standard, in Section 1.10. Comprehensive income is defined as all changes in equity during the period except those resulting from investments by or distributions to owners. Thus, in addition to net income as calculated under GAAP, comprehensive income includes **other comprehensive income**—namely, items such as unrealized translation gains and losses resulting from consolidation of foreign subsidiaries, some unrealized fair value gains and losses on financial assets (Section 7.5.2), and unrealized gains and losses on cash flow hedges (Section 7.9.2). A reason for the creation of other comprehensive income is that management objects to the inclusion of unrealized items in net income, on the grounds that they are volatile, uncontrollable, and uninformative about their effort.

Under both IASB and FASB standards, other comprehensive income items can be reported following net income in a combined comprehensive income statement or, if shown separately, in a statement beginning with net income and reported immediately following the net income statement. Either way, comprehensive income is the sum of net income and other comprehensive income. In most cases, as unrealized gains and losses are realized (e.g., by selling fair-valued securities), the now-realized gain or loss is transferred from other comprehensive income to net income.

Required

a. Assuming that the goal of standard setters is to ultimately value all assets and liabilities at fair value, is the inclusion of unrealized gains and losses in other comprehensive income most consistent with the public interest or the interest group theory of regulation? Explain.
b. Under the original 1997 FASB accounting standard (SFAS 130), other comprehensive income could be reported either in a combined comprehensive income statement or as part of a statement of changes in shareholders' equity. This latter option shows

other comprehensive income *apart* from net income. Most U.S. firms choose this latter option. Why?

c. Is inclusion of other comprehensive income in a separate statement of changes in shareholders' equity consistent with managers' acceptance of efficient securities market theory? Explain.

20. Insurance companies have developed a product called **finite insurance**. Under finite insurance, a client firm enters into an insurance contract under which it pays annual premiums to the insurer that sum to an amount equal to or close to the policy coverage. For example, a firm may take out a three-year policy to protect itself against natural disasters, with coverage of, say, $1,500. It pays an annual premium of $500, or $1,500 over the policy term. If a loss occurs, the insurer pays up to the $1,500 coverage. If no loss occurs, the $1,500 of premiums are returned to the firm. The insurance company will charge a fee for this service.

Note that the firm taking out the insurance bears the risk, not the insurer, since the firm does not recover its premiums paid to the extent there are policy claims. Why would a firm pay a fee for a policy such as this? A reason is that the policy acts as an income smoothing device. The firm may not be concerned about its ability to withstand the loss financially, but may be concerned about the "hit" to reported earnings in the event a major loss takes place. By taking out the finite insurance policy, the loss is recorded as an insurance expense over the term of the policy. (If there is no loss, the return of premiums paid will result in a large credit to earnings; however, the firm may be more concerned about avoiding a large loss than reporting a large gain.)

From the insurer's standpoint, the question arises whether the premiums received from the client represent premium income or simply a loan from the client. In this regard, the insurance industry has a 10/10 rule: The insurer should face at a minimum a 10% chance of losing 10% of the policy coverage if the premiums are to be regarded as income. Under this rule, if the total premiums to be paid are equal to or less than 90% of the policy coverage, and if there is at least a 10% chance of loss, the insurer is deemed to be bearing enough risk that premiums are regarded as income.

General Re Corporation is a large U.S. insurance company that had issued a large number of finite insurance contracts to various clients. American International Group (AIG) is a large multinational insurance company also based in the United States, with shares traded on the New York Stock Exchange. During 2000–2001, AIG took over $500 million of finite insurance contracts from General Re Corp. General Re paid over the $500 million of premiums it had collected for these policies to AIG. Thus, AIG was now in the role of insurer, instead of General Re. AIG paid General Re a $5 million fee for taking over these finite insurance contracts.

At first glance, this deal seems illogical for AIG. When the finite insurance contracts expire, AIG would have to repay the $500 million received from General Re to the various firms that had taken out the finite insurance, less any claims it may have paid. Consequently, its net cash flows would be zero. Why would AIG pay a $5 million fee (instead of receiving a fee) for taking over the contracts when it had nothing to gain?

On closer scrutiny, however, it turned out that investors had been concerned that AIG did not have sufficient reserves (insurance companies are required to create reserves to help ensure they can meet policy claims). AIG credited the $500 million received from

General Re to revenue, then transferred the same amount from earnings to reserves. It was thus able to increase its reserves by $500 million, with only a $5 million reduction in earnings.

In February 2005, AIG received subpoenas from the Office of the Attorney General of the State of New York and the SEC relating to its accounting for this transaction. Its stock price plummeted, costing shareholders over $544 million. In March 2005, AIG's directors dismissed CEO Maurice "Hank" Greenberg and CFO Howard I. Smith. AIG also issued a statement that due to the lack of risk transfer, the payment from General Re should have been accounted for as a loan rather than revenue. Financial statements for five years ending with 2004 were subsequently restated. Earnings over this period were reduced by 10%, about $3.9 billion, as a result of this and other accounting manipulations.

In 2006, AIG paid $1.64 billion to settle fraud claims, including the General Re transaction. The company also made changes to its corporate governance process. Greenberg and Smith also faced lawsuits of their own. In 2013, they agreed to pay a total of $115 million to settle shareholder claims. They still face a trial for fraud that could prevent them from serving in management or Board positions or in the securities industry, and that could result in repaying performance-based compensation.

Required

a. From the standpoint of a firm that takes out a finite insurance policy, evaluate finite insurance as an income smoothing device.

b. A firm has just suffered a large special item, low-persistence uninsured loss. The firm is concerned about securities market reaction to lower reported net income this quarter if the loss is charged to current operations. The firm approaches an insurance company with a request to *retroactively* sell it a finite insurance policy with face value equal to the amount of the loss. Under such a policy, the firm would immediately receive a payment from the insurer equal to its loss, which would be credited to current net income. The firm would then pay the policy premium quarterly, over a five-year period, with each payment charged to insurance expense for that quarter. The insurance company agrees to this arrangement.

You are the firm's auditor and are debating whether or not to qualify your report. Should you? If you did qualify, what would be your basis for qualification?

c. Do you agree that the $500 million received by AIG from General Re should have been accounted for as a loan rather than as income? Explain.

d. Should a new accounting standard to prevent the use of finite insurance contracts be implemented? In your answer, draw on the question of rules-based versus principles-based accounting standards.

21. Satyam Computer Services (now called Mahindra Satyam)[16] was formed by Ramalinga Rau in 1987, in India. The company expanded rapidly, specializing in information technology and computer software, and became an important outsourcer of computer systems and customer services worldwide. While the company remained under family control, its shares were listed in India in 1981, and subsequently on U.S. and European stock exchanges. The company received several awards for corporate governance and accountability.

In October 2008, a financial analyst expressed concern about large cash balances held by Satyam in non-interest bearing bank accounts. However, it seems that this concern was ignored by investors. Markets did become concerned, however, in December 2009 when it became public that Satyam planned to buy two companies to, it claimed, diversify its operations. The plan had been approved by Satyam's Board of Directors. However, the two target companies were controlled by members of Mr. Rau's family, and it was feared that the purchases were really a way for Satyam to transfer money into the hands of family members (presumably, by overpaying for the acquisitions). Satyam's share price fell and four of five independent directors resigned. The company reversed these transactions, but sustained a major drop in its reputation. Numerous analyst sell recommendations followed and its share price continued to fall. Satyam hired Merrill Lynch, a leading financial management and advisory firm, to advise it how to recover. However, Merrill Lynch soon resigned from its engagement, citing suspicion of fraud.

In January 2009, Mr. Rau admitted that he had been overstating the company's financial performance for years to meet analyst earnings expectations. This was done by creating fictitious non-interest bearing bank accounts on company books, and by reporting fictitious interest earned on these accounts. Fictitious invoices were also created to inflate reported revenue, and liabilities were underreported. Other tactics included adding fictitious employees to the company's payroll, diverting the cash paid for their salaries to other family-owned companies. The total overstatement amounted to about US$1.47 billion. Satyam shares quickly lost 82% of their remaining market value. As in the case of Enron and WorldCom (Section 1.2), the whole Indian stock market fell by about 13%, suggesting that investors were losing faith in Indian financial reporting in general.

Mr. Rau, his brother (a managing director), the firm's head of internal audit, and its CFO were quickly arrested by Indian authorities and charged with fraud. Several company auditors were also arrested. It appeared that the auditors were paid about twice the fee that other audit firms would have charged.

Serious questions were raised about why the company's Big Four auditor and Board of Directors had apparently not discovered the fraud, and about the quality of corporate governance in India.

To prevent even more serious collapse of confidence, the Indian government moved to put Satyam up for auction. The successful buyer paid only about one-third of the company's pre-crisis market value. The rescue was successful, and both Satyam and Indian stock markets have since recovered.

Since Satyam securities were traded in the United States, the SEC became involved. In April 2011, the SEC charged five India-based affiliates of Satyam's Big Four auditor with audit failures. They were also censured by the PCAOB (Section 1.2). The auditors were fined $6 million, required to take training, and prohibited from accepting any new U.S.-based clients for six months. Satyam was fined $10 million on related charges.

Required

a. To what extent did family control of Satyam contribute to the fraud? What agency problem increases when control of a publicly traded firm is concentrated in a small group of insiders, such as a family? Explain one signal that a firm with concentrated ownership can adopt to reduce this increased agency problem. Did the signal work in this case?

b. Satyam's Board of Directors apparently did not discover, or did not question, these fraudulent transactions, despite including five prestigious independent directors.

Explain why it is difficult for a firm with an entrenched and powerful management to obtain directors who are truly independent.

c. In fairness to the independent directors, they may have been at an information disadvantage. Explain why. Does information disadvantage fully explain the independent directors' apparent failure to discover the fraud? Explain.

See also Chapter 12, Problem 21 re: independent directors.

d. Satyam's financial statements were prepared under Indian accounting standards, which differ in many ways from IASB standards. Outline potential benefits to a country from adopting IASB standards in place of its local GAAP. What factors in the adopting country reduce these benefits? Would this fraud have occurred if Satyam had reported under IASB GAAP?

Notes

1. In the BM model, investors who buy these projects are price protected by an efficient market that reflects the average quality of the projects. Consequently, they are not directly affected by financial reporting quality and do not lobby. Standards quality in the model is determined entirely by the demands of managers and banks.

2. The authors pointed out that we do not observe an actual decrease in standards. Rather, the source of lower standards is the ingenuity of managers who find ways to circumvent current standards. The creation of expected loss notes to enable off balance sheet liabilities, as outlined in Section 1.3, illustrates this point. Until standard setters design and implement new standards to close such loopholes, standards quality, in effect, will decline.

3. In Canada, the Ontario Securities Act, for example, prohibits companies from releasing information to selected individuals before releasing it to the general public.

4. Successful efforts is a form of historical cost accounting under which the costs of successful oil and gas wells are capitalized and costs of unsuccessful drilling are written off. Under full cost accounting, costs of both successful and unsuccessful wells are capitalized, on grounds that costs of finding successful wells include the costs of unsuccessful ones.

5. In economic terms, X is a rent.

6. That is, the regulator knows all the components of firm profit π. Thus, by regulating that profits and excess compensation are zero, the manager is forced to exert a level of effort that produces this result. Note that, in economics, zero profit allows for a normal return on investment.

7. A third option might be for the regulator and manager to contract to use the most decision useful accounting policies. However, in Section 9.3, we discussed the revelation principle, which could potentially be applied to extract these policies from the manager. But, as we concluded there, this principle cannot be applied when the regulator is unable to commit not to use the truth against the manager. Here, by extracting the truth (i.e., the most decision useful accounting policies) and implementing standards to require the manager to use them, the regulator is using the truth against the manager, who may prefer other policies. As a result, from the regulator's perspective, the firm's accounting policy communication is "soft." The regulator cannot verify that the accounting policies communicated by the regulator are the best ones. Thus, they cannot be contracted upon.

8. Dessein's analysis is based on the "cheap talk" model of Crawford and Sobel (1982). See also (optional) Section 12.8.2 and Note 17 of Chapter 12. Dessein also showed that the higher or lower is unmanaged net income, the wider will be the reported range. This reflects the fact that if a manager is known to want to bias-report earnings, the more extreme the amount of unmanaged income the more suspicious it is. To cloud this suspicion, the manager reports a wider range.

9. This agreement was reaffirmed in 2006, followed by a 2008 progress report and timetable for completion. However, the 2007–2008 market meltdowns resulted in some accounting policy differences with

respect, for example, to accounting for financial instruments and loan loss provisioning. Nevertheless, in February 2010, the SEC announced its continuing support of IASB/FASB standards convergence.

10. In the United States, LIFO is currently allowed for tax purposes, providing it is also used in the firm's financial statements. It is possible that LIFO will be disallowed for tax purposes in the United States, presumably to help lower the budget deficit. If so, convergence of FASB inventory standards with those of the IASB would be facilitated.

11. BLY's findings are relative to a control sample of firms that had voluntarily adopted IASB standards at least two years previously.

12. Note, however, that an increase of earnings quality for managerial contracting is not necessarily the same as an increase in quality for investors, since earnings quality for investors is affected by the tradeoff between relevance and reliability, while earnings quality for compensation plan contracting depends on the tradeoff between sensitivity and precision. These different tradeoffs are a consequence of the fundamental problem (Section 1.10).

13. Any set of GAAP has flexibility. It is sometimes claimed that IASB standards have somewhat greater flexibility than other GAAPs. One reason is that FASB GAAP has to adapt to a wide variety of different economies and institutional structures. For example, IASB GAAP allows greater flexibility to adopt current value accounting than FASB GAAP, as illustrated by IAS 16, which allows a revaluation option for property, plant, and equipment (Section 7.3.4).

14. DHVL pointed out that this does not necessarily imply that the financial reporting of label firms was of low quality before FASB adoption. All that is implied is that there was little change in their motivation to increase reporting quality following FASB adoption.

15. BLLW used a simplified version of the clean surplus model (Section 6.10) to estimate the share prices of their sample firms. Recall that in this model, share price is based on net book value plus expected future abnormal earnings. They estimated the average relationship between share price and these two accounting variables for all U.S. firms in their sample (i.e., firms using FASB GAAP). They did the same for all IASB firms in their sample.

    With these two relationships established, they could then estimate share price for all U.S. firms in their sample *as if* those firms used IASB standards, and similarly for all IASB firms. For each firm, the difference between the two share price estimates is a measure of the comparability of that firm's financial statements between IASB and FASB GAAP—a greater difference implies less comparability. The average difference across all sample firms was then taken as a measure of the comparability of IASB and FASB GAAP.

16. The narrative in this problem has drawn heavily on the 2010 Briefing Paper of David Winkler, "India's Satyam Accounting Scandal," published by the University of Iowa Center for International Finance and Development.

Bibliography

ABARBANELL, J.S. and B.J. BUSHEE, "Fundamental Analysis, Future Earnings, and Stock Prices," *Journal of Accounting Research* (Spring 1997), pp. 1–24.

ABARBANELL, J.S., W.N. LANEN, and R.E. VERRECCHIA, "Analysts' Forecasts as Proxies for Investor Beliefs in Empirical Research," *Journal of Accounting and Economics* (July 1995), pp. 31–60.

ABARBANELL, J. and R. LEHAVY, "Can Stock Recommendations Predict Earnings Management and Analysts' Earnings Forecast Errors?" *Journal of Accounting Research* (March 2003), pp. 1–31.

ABOODY, D., N.B. JOHNSON, and R. KASZNIK, "Employee Stock Options and Future Firm Performance: Evidence from Option Pricing," *Journal of Accounting and Economics* (May 2010), pp. 74–92.

ABOODY, D. and R. KASZNIK, "CEO Stock Option Awards and the Timing of Corporate Voluntary Disclosures," *Journal of Accounting and Economics* (February 2000), pp. 73–100.

ACHARYA, V.J. and L.H. PEDERSEN, "Asset Pricing with Liquidity Risk," *Journal of Financial Economics* (August 2005), pp. 375–410.

AGGARWAL, R.K. and A.A. SAMWICK, "Executive Compensation, Strategic Competition, and Relative Performance Evaluation: Theory and Evidence," *The Journal of Finance* (December 1999), pp. 1999–2043.

AHMED, A.S., E. KILIC, and G.J. LOBO, "Does Recognition versus Disclosure Matter? Evidence from Value-relevance of Banks' Recognized and Disclosed Derivative Financial Instruments," *The Accounting Review* (May 2006), pp. 567–588.

AHMED, A.S., E. KILIC, and G.J. LOBO, "Effects of SFAS 133 on the Risk Relevance of Accounting Measures of Banks' Derivatives Exposures" *The Accounting Review* (May 2011), pp. 769–804.

AKERLOF, G.A., "The Market for 'Lemons': Quality Uncertainty and the Market Mechanism," *Quarterly Journal of Economics* (August 1970), pp. 488–500.

ALBUQUERQUE, A., "Peer Firms in Relative Performance Evaluation," *Journal of Accounting and Economics* (October 2009), pp. 69–89.

ALCHIAN, A., "Uncertainty, Evolution and Economic Theory," *Journal of Political Economy* (June 1950), pp. 211–221.

ALI, A., S. KLASA, and O.Z. LI, "Institutional Stakeholdings and Better-Informed Traders at Earnings Announcements," *Journal of Accounting and Economics* (September 2008), pp. 47–61.

ALLEN, F. and E. CARLETTI, "Mark-to-Market Accounting and Liquidity Pricing," *Journal of Accounting and Economics* (August, 2008), pp. 358–378.

ALLEN. F., S. MORRIS, and H.S. SHIN, "Beauty Contests and Iterated Expectations in Asset Markets" *The Review of Financial Studies* (2006), pp. 720–752.

AMERICAN ACCOUNTING ASSOCIATION COMMITTEE TO PREPARE A STATEMENT OF BASIC ACCOUNTING THEORY, "*A Statement of Basic Accounting Theory*" (American Accounting Association, 1966).

AMERICAN ACCOUNTING ASSOCIATION FINANCIAL ACCOUNTING STANDARDS COMMITTEE, "*Response to FASB's Invitation to Comment on the Proposed Statement of Financial Accounting Standards on Business Combinations and Intangible Assets— Accounting for Goodwill*" (American Accounting Association, 2001).

AMERICAN INSTITUTE OF CERTIFIED PUBLIC ACCOUNTANTS STUDY GROUP ON THE OBJECTIVES OF FINANCIAL STATEMENTS, *Objectives of Financial Statements* (New York, NY: AICPA, 1973).

ANILOWSKI, C., MEI FENG, and D.J. SKINNER, "Does Earnings Guidance Affect Market Returns? The Nature and Information Content of Aggregate Earnings Guidance," *Journal of Accounting and Economics* (September 2007), pp. 36–63.

ANTLE, R. and A. SMITH, "An Empirical Examination of the Relative Performance Evaluation of Corporate Executives," *Journal of Accounting Research* (Spring 1986), pp. 1–39.

ARMSTRONG, C.S., K. BALAKRISHNAN, and D. COHEN, "Corporate Governance and the Information Environment: Evidence from State Antitakeover Laws," *Journal of Accounting and Economics* (April 2012), pp. 185–204.

ARMSTRONG, C.S., J.E. CORE, D.J.TAYLOR, and R.E. VERRECCHIA, "When Does Information Asymmetry Affect the Cost of Capital?" *Journal of Accounting Research* March 2011), pp. 1–40.

ARMSTRONG, C.S., A.D. JAGOLINZER, and D.F. LARCKER, "Chief Executive Officer Equity Incentives and Accounting Irregularities," *Journal of Accounting Research* (May 2010), pp. 225–271.

ARMSTRONG, M. and D.E.M. SAPPINGTON, "Regulation, Competition, and Liberalization," *Journal of Economic Literature* (June 2006), pp. 325–366.

ARROW, K.J., *Social Choice and Individual Values*, Cowles Foundation Monograph (New York, NY: John Wiley, 1963).

ARYA, A., J. FELLINGHAM, and J. GLOVER, "Teams, Repeated Tasks and Implicit Incentives," *Journal of Accounting and Economics* (May 1997), pp. 7–30.

ARYA, A., J. GLOVER, and S. SUNDER, "Earnings Management and the Revelation Principle," *Review of Accounting Studies* (1998), pp. 7–34.

ARYA, A. and B. MITTENDORF, "Using Disclosure to Influence Herd Behavior and Alter Competition," *Journal of Accounting and Economics* (December 2005), pp. 231–246.

ASHBAUGH-SKAIFE, H., D.W.COLLINS. W.R. KINNEY, Jr., and R. LAFOND, "The Effect of SOX Internal Control Deficiencies on Firm Risk and Cost of Equity," *Journal of Accounting Research* (March 2009), pp. 1–43.

AUMANN, R.J., "War and Peace," Nobel Prize Lecture (December 8, 2005), available at http://nobelprize.org/nobel_prizes/economics/ laureates/2005/aumann-lecture.html

AYERS, B.J., O.Z. LI, and P.E. YEUNG, "Investor Trading and the Post-Earnings-Announcement Drift, *The Accounting Review* (March 2011), pp. 385–416.

BABER, W.R., S. JANAKIRAMAN, and S-H. KANG, "Investment Opportunities and the Structure of Executive Compensation," *Journal of Accounting and Economics* (June 1996), pp. 297–318.

BABER, W.R., S-H. KANG, and K.R. KUMAR, "The Explanatory Power of Earnings Levels vs. Earnings Changes in the Context of Executive Compensation," *The Accounting Review* (October 1999), pp. 459–472.

BADERTSCHER, B.A., J.J. BURKS, and P.D. EASTON, "A Convenient Scapegoat: Fair Value Accounting by Commercial Banks during the Financial Crisis, *"The Accounting Review* (January 2012), pp. 59–90.

BAIMAN, S. and J.S. DEMSKI, "Economically Optimal Performance Evaluation and Control Systems," *Journal of Accounting Research* (Supplement 1980), pp. 184–220.

BAKER, M. and J. WURGLER, "Investor Sentiment and the Cross-Section of Stock Returns," *Journal of Finance* (August 2006), pp. 1645–1680.

BAKER, T.A., D.L. COLLINS, and A.L. REITENGA, "Incentives and Opportunities to Manage Earnings around Option Grants, *"Contemporary Accounting Research* (Fall 2009), pp. 649–672.

BALL, R., "Market and Political/Regulatory Perspectives on the Recent Accounting Scandals," *Journal of Accounting Research* (May 2009), pp. 277–323.

BALL, R. and E. BARTOV, "How Naive Is the Stock Market's Use of Earnings Information?" *Journal of Accounting and Economics* (June 1996), pp. 319–337.

BALL, R. and P. BROWN, "An Empirical Evaluation of Accounting Income Numbers,"

Journal of Accounting Research (Autumn 1968), pp. 159–178.

BALL, R. and S.P. KOTHARI, "Nonstationary Expected Returns: Implications for Tests of Market Efficiency and Serial Correlation in Returns," *Journal of Financial Economics* (1989), pp. 51–74.

BALL, R., S.P. KOTHARI, and A. ROBIN, "The Effect of International Institutional Factors on Properties of Accounting Earnings," *Journal of Accounting and Economics* (February 2000), pp. 1–51.

BALL, R., A. ROBIN, and G. SADKA, "Is Financial Reporting Shaped by Equity Markets or by Debt Markets? An International Study of Timeliness and Conservatism," *Review of Accounting Studies* (September 2008), pp. 168–205.

BALL, R., A. ROBIN, and J.S. WU, "Incentives versus Standards: Properties of Accounting Income in Four East Asian Companies," *Journal of Accounting and Economics* (December 2003), pp. 235–270.

BALL, R., G. SADKA, and R. SADKA, "Aggregate Earnings and Asset Prices," *Journal of Accounting Research* (December 2009), pp. 1097–1133.

BALL, R. and L. SHIVAKUMAR, "The Role of Accruals in Asymmetrically Timely Gain and Loss Recognition," *Journal of Accounting Research* (May 2006), pp. 207–242.

BALL, R. and L. SHIVAKUMAR, "How Much New Information Is There in Earnings? *Journal of Accounting Research* (December 2008), pp. 975–1016.

BALL, R.T., Does Anticipated Information Impose a Cost on Risk-Averse Investors? A Test of the Hirshleifer Effect," *Journal of Accounting Research* (March 2013), pp. 31–66.

BANDYOPADHYAY, S., "Market Reaction to Earnings Announcements of SE and FC Firms in the Oil and Gas Industry," *The Accounting Review* (October 1994), pp. 657–674.

BANDYOPADHYAY, S., C. CHEN, A. HUANG, and R. JHA, "Accounting Conservatism and the Temporal Trends in Current Earnings' Ability to Predict Future Cash Flows versus Future Earnings: Evidence on the Trade-off between Relevance and Reliability," *Contemporary Accounting Research* (Summer 2010), pp. 413–460.

BANKER, R.D., M.N. DARROUGH, R. HUANG, and J.M. PLEHN-DUJOWICH, "The Relation between CEO Compensation and Past Performance, *The Accounting Review* (January 2013), pp. 1–30.

BANKER, R.D. and S. DATAR, "Sensitivity, Precision, and Linear Aggregation of Signals for Performance Evaluation," *Journal of Accounting Research* (Spring 1989), pp. 21–39.

BANKER, R.D., R. HUANG, and R. NATARAJAN, "Incentive Contracting and Value Relevance," *Journal of Accounting Research* (June 2009), pp. 647–678.

BARBERIS, N., A. SHLEIFER, and R. VISHNY, "A Model of Investor Sentiment," *Journal of Financial Economics* (1998), pp. 307–343.

BARRON, O., J. PRATT, and J.D. STICE, "Misstatement Direction, Litigation Risk, and Planned Audit Investment," *Journal of Accounting Research* (December 2001), pp. 449–462.

BARTH, M.E., L.D. HODDER and S.R. STUBBEN, "Fair Value Accounting for Liabilities and Own Credit Risk," *The Accounting Review* (May 2008), pp. 629–664.

BARTH, M.E., Y. KONCHITCHKI, W.R. LANDSMAN, "Cost of Capital and Earnings Transparency," *Journal of Accounting and Economics* (April 2013), pp. 206–224.

BARTH, M.E., R. LANDSMAN, M. LANG, and C. WILLIAMS, "Are IFRS-Based and U.S. GAAP-Based Accounting Amounts Comparable?" *Journal of Accounting and Economics* (September 2012), pp. 68–93.

BARTON, J., "Does the Use of Financial Derivatives Affect Earnings Management Decisions?" The Accounting Review (January 2001), pp. 1–26.

BARTON, J. and M. MERCER, "To Blame or Not to Blame: Analysts' Reactions to External Explanations for Poor Financial Performance," *Journal of Accounting and Economics* (September 2005), pp. 509–533.

BARTOV, E., D. GIVOLY, and C. HAYN, "The Rewards to Meeting or Beating Earnings Expectations," *Journal of Accounting and Economics* (June 2002), pp. 173–204.

BARTOV, E. and P. MOHANRAM, "Private Information, Earnings Manipulation, and Executive Stock Option Exercise," *The Accounting Review* (October 2004), pp. 889–920.

BARTOV, E., S. RADHAKRISHNAN, and S. KRINSKY, "Investor Sophistication and Patterns in Stock Returns after Earnings Announcements," *The Accounting Review* (January 2000), pp. 43–63.

BASU, S., "The Conservation Principle and the Asymmetric Timeliness of Earnings," *Journal of Accounting and Economics* (December 1997), pp. 3–37.

BATTALIO, R.H., A. LERMAN, J. LIVNAT, and R.R. MENDENHALL," Who, if Anyone, Reacts to Accrual Information?" *Journal of Accounting and Economics* (April 2012), pp. 205–224.

BCE INC., *1997 Annual Report* (Montreal, QC: BCE Inc., 1997).

BEATTY, A., S. LIAO, and J. WEBER, "Evidence on the Determinants and Economic Consequences of Delegated Monitoring," *Journal of Accounting and Economics* (June, 2012), pp. 555–576.

BEATTY, A., J. WEBER, and J.J. YU, "Conservatism and Debt," *Journal of Accounting and Economics* (August 2008), pp. 154–174.

BEAVER, W.H., "The Information Content of Annual Earnings Announcements," *Journal of Accounting Research* (Supplement, 1968), pp. 67–92.

BEAVER, W.H., "What Should be the FASB's Objectives?" *The Journal of Accountancy* (August 1973), pp. 49–56.

BEAVER, W.H., *Financial Reporting: An Accounting Revolution* (Englewood Cliffs, NJ: Prentice Hall, 1981).

BEAVER, W.H., R. CLARKE, and W.F. WRIGHT, "The Association Between Unsystematic Security Returns and the Magnitude of Earnings Forecast Errors," *Journal of Accounting Research* (Autumn 1979), pp. 316–340.

BEAVER, W.H. and J. DEMSKI, "The Nature of Income Measurement," *The Accounting Review* (January 1979), pp. 38–46.

BEAVER, W.H., P. KETTLER, and M. SCHOLES, "The Association Between Market-Determined and Accounting-Determined Risk Measures," *The Accounting Review* (October 1970), pp. 654–682.

BEBCHUK, L.A., J.M. FRIED, and D.I. WALKER, "Managerial Power and Rent Extraction in the Design of Executive Compensation," *The University of Chicago Law Review* (2002), pp. 751–846.

BECKER, G.S., "A Theory of Competition among Pressure Groups for Political Influence," The Quarterly Journal of Economics (August 1983), pp. 371–400.

BEGLEY, J. and G.A. FELTHAM, "The Relation between Market Values, Earnings Forecasts, and Reported Earnings," *Contemporary Accounting Research* (Spring 2002), pp. 1–48.

BENS, D.A., P.G. BERGER, and S.J. MONAHAN, "Discretionary Disclosure in Financial Reporting: An Examination Comparing Internal Firm Data to Externally Reported Segment Data," *The Accounting Review* (March 2011), pp. 417–449.

BENSTON, G.J., "Required Disclosure and the Stock Market: An Evaluation of the Securities Exchange Act of 1934," *American Economic Review* (March 1973), pp. 132–155.

BERGER, P.G. and R.N. HANN, "Segment Profitability and Agency Costs of Disclosure," *The Accounting Review* (July 2007), pp. 869–906.

BERNARD, V.L. and D.J. SKINNER, "What Motivates Managers' Choice of Discretionary Accruals?" *Journal of Accounting and Economics* (August–December 1996), pp. 313–325.

BERNARD, V.L. and J. THOMAS, "Post-Earnings Announcement Drift: Delayed Price Reaction or Risk Premium?" *Journal of Accounting Research* (Supplement, 1989), pp. 1–36.

BERNILE, G. and G.A. JARRELL, "The Impact of the Options Backdating Scandal on Shareholders," *Journal of Accounting and Economics* (March 2009), pp. 2–26.

BERTOMEU, J. and R.P. MAGEE, "From Low-Quality reporting to Financial Crisis: Politics of Disclosure Regulation along the Economic Cycle,"

Journal of Accounting and Economics (November 2011), pp. 209–227.

BERTRAND, M. and S. MALLAINATHAN, "Are CEOs Rewarded for Luck?: The Ones Without Principles Are," *Quarterly Journal of Economics* (2001), pp. 901–929.

BHARATH, S.T., J. SUNDER, and S.V. SUNDER, "Accounting Quality and Debt Contracting," *The Accounting Review* (January 2008), pp. 1–28.

BHAT, G., R. FRANKEL, and X. MARTIN, "Panacea, Pandora's Box, or Placebo: Feedback in Banks' Mortgage-Backed Security Holdings and Fair Value Accounting, *Journal of Accounting and Economics* (November 2011), pp. 153–173.

BIDDLE, G.C., G. HILARY, and R.S. VERDI, "How Does Financial Reporting Quality Relate to Investment Efficiency?" *Journal of Accounting and Economics* (December 2009), pp. 112–131.

BITTI, M.T., "Enhancing Audit Quality," *CA Magazine* (March 2013), pp. 22–28.

BLACCONIERE, J.R., J.R. FREDERICKSON, M.F. JOHNSON, and M.F. LEWIS, "Are Voluntary Disclosures that Disavow the Reliability of Mandated Fair Value Information Informative or Opportunistic? *Journal of Accounting and Economics* (November 2011), pp. 235–251.

BLACK, F. and M. SCHOLES, "The Pricing of Options and Corporate Liabilities," *Journal of Political Economy* (May/June 1973), pp. 637–654.

BLAZENKO, G. and W.R. SCOTT, "A Model of Standard Setting in Auditing," *Contemporary Accounting Research* (Fall 1986), pp. 68–92.

BOONE, J.P., "Revisiting the Reportedly Weak Value Relevance of Oil and Gas Asset Present Values: The Role of Measurement Error, Model Misspecification, and Time Period Idiosyncrasy," *The Accounting Review* (January 2002), pp. 73–106.

BOTOSAN, C.A., "Disclosure Level and the Cost of Equity Capital," *The Accounting Review* (July 1997), pp. 323–349.

BOWEN, R.M., L. DUCHARME, and D. SHORES, "Stakeholders' Implicit Claims and Accounting Method Choice," *Journal of Accounting and Economics* (December 1995), pp. 255–295.

BOWEN, R.M., S. RAJGOPAL, and M. VENKATACHALAM, "Accounting Discretion, Corporate Governance, and Firm Performance," *Contemporary Accounting Research* (Summer 2008), pp. 351–405.

BOYLE, P. and P. BOYLE, *Derivatives: The Tools That Changed Finance* (London: Risk Books, 2001).

BRAV, A. and J.B. HEATON, "Competing Theories of Financial Anomalies," *The Review of Financial Studies* (2002), pp. 575–606.

BROWN, L.D., R.L. HAGERMAN, P.A. GRIFFIN, and M. ZMIJEWSKI, "Security Analyst Superiority Relative to Univariate Time-Series Models in Forecasting Quarterly Earnings," *Journal of Accounting and Economics* (April 1987), pp. 61–87.

BROWN, L.D. and Y.-J. LEE, "The Relation Between Corporate Governance and CEOs' Equity Grants, *Journal of Accounting and Public Policy* (November 2010), pp. 533–558.

BROWN, N.C., T.E. CHRISTENSEN, W.B. ELLIOTT, and R.D. MERGENTHALER, "Investor Sentiment and Pro-Forma Earnings Disclosures," *Journal of Accounting Research* (March 2012), pp. 1–40.

BROWN, R.G. and K.S. JOHNSTON, *Paciolo on Accounting* (New York, NY: McGraw-Hill, 1963).

BROWN, S.J. and J.B. WARNER, "Measuring Security Price Performance," *Journal of Financial Economics* (September 1980), pp. 205–258.

BROWN, S.V. and J.W. TUCKER, "Large-Sample Evidence on Firms' Year-Over-Year MD&A Modifications," *Journal of Accounting Research* (May 2011), pp. 309–346.

BURGSTAHLER, D. and I. DICHEV, "Earnings Management to Avoid Earnings Decreases and Losses," *Journal of Accounting and Economics* (December 1997), pp. 99–126.

BURGSTAHLER, D., J. JIAMBALVO, and T. SHEVLIN, "Do Stock Prices Fully Reflect the Implications of Special items for Future Earnings? *Journal of Accounting Research* (June 2002), pp. 561–612.

BUSHMAN, R.M., E. ENGEL, and A. SMITH, "An Analysis of the Relation between the

Stewardship and Valuation Roles of Earnings," *Journal of Accounting Research* (March 2006), pp. 53–83.

BUSHMAN, R.M. and R.J. INDJEJIKIAN, "Accounting Income, Stock Price and Managerial Compensation," *Journal of Accounting and Economics* (January/April/July 1993), pp. 3–23.

BUSHMAN, R.M., R.J. INDJEJIKIAN, and A. SMITH, "CEO Compensation: The Role of Individual Performance Evaluation," *Journal of Accounting and Economics* (April 1996), pp. 161–193.

BUSHMAN, R.M. and J.D. PIOTROSKI, "Financial Reporting Incentives for Conservative Accounting: The Influence of Legal and Political Institutions," *Journal of Accounting and Economics* (October 2006), pp. 107–148.

BUSHMAN, R.M. and C.D. WILLIAMS, "Accounting Discretion, Loan Loss Provisioning, and Discipline of Banks' Risk-Taking," *Journal of Accounting and Economics* (August 2012), pp. 1–18.

BYARD, D., Y. LI, and Y. YU, "The Effect of Mandatory IFRS Adoption on Financial Analysts" Information Environment," *Journal of Accounting Research* (March 2011), pp. 69–96.

CADMAN, B., M.E. CARTER, and HILLEGEIST, 'The Incentives of Compensation Consultants and CEO Pay, " *Journal of Accounting and Economics* (April 2010), pp. 263–280.

CAIN, M.D., D.J. DENIS, and D.K. DENIS, "Earnouts: A Study of Financial Contracting in Acquisition Agreements," *Journal, of Accounting and Economics* (February 2011), pp. 151–170.

CALLAHAN, C.M., R.E.SMITH, and A.W. SPENCER, "An Examination of the Cost of Capital Implications of FIN 46," *The Accounting Review* (July 2012), pp. 1105–134.

CALLEN, J.L., M. KHAN, and H.LU, "Accounting Quality, Stock Price Delay, and Future Stock Returns," *Contemporary Accounting Research* (Spring 2013), pp. 269–295.

CANADIAN ACCOUNTING STANDARDS BOARD, Accounting Guideline AcG-15 Consolidation of Variable Interest Entities, (Toronto, ON: AcSB, 2004).

CANADIAN SECURITIES ADMINISTRATORS, *National Instrument 51-101. Standards of Disclosure for Oil and Gas Activities* (Montreal, QC: CSA, 2003).

CANADIAN SECURITIES ADMINISTRATORS, *National Instrument 52-107, Acceptable Accounting Principles, Auditing Standards and Reporting Currency* (Montreal, QC: CSA, 2004).

CANADIAN SECURITIES ADMINISTRATORS, *National Instrument 51-102F6. Statement of Executive Compensation* (Montreal, QC: CSA, 2008).

CANADIAN SECURITIES ADMINISTRATORS, *National Instrument 52-109, Certification of Disclosure in Issuers' Annual and Interim Filings* (Montreal, QC: CSA, 2008).

CANADIAN SECURITIES ADMINISTRATORS, *National Instrument 51-102, Continuous Disclosure Obligations* (Montreal, QC: CSA, 2011).

CAO, S.S. and G.S. NARAYANAMOORTHY, "Earnings Volatility, Post-Earnings Announcement Drift, and Trading Frictions," *Journal of Accounting Research* (March 2012), pp. 41–74.

CHALMERS, K., G. CLINCH, and J.M. GODFREY, "Changes in Value Relevance of Accounting Information upon IFRS Adoption: Evidence from Australia," *Australian Journal of Management* (August 2011), pp. 151–173.

CHEN, H., J.Z. CHEN, G.J. LOBO, and Y. WANG, "Association between Borrower and Lender State Ownership and Accounting Conservatism," *Journal of Accounting Research* (December 2010), pp. 973–1014.

CHEN, S., D. MATSUMOTO, and S. RAJGOPAL, "Is Silence Golden? An Empirical Analysis of Firms that Stop Giving Quarterly Earnings Guidance," *Journal of Accounting and Economics* (February 2011), pp. 134–150.

CHENG, M., D.S. DHALIWAL, and M. NEAMTIU, "Asset Securitization, Securitization Recourse, and Information Uncertainty," *The Accounting Review* (March 2011), pp. 541–568.

CHORDIA, T. and l. SHIVAKUMAR, "Inflation Illusion and Post-Earnings-Announcement Drift," *Journal of Accounting Research* (September 2005), pp. 521–556.

CHOUDHARY, P., "Evidence on Differences Between Recognition and Disclosure: A Comparison of Inputs to Estimate Fair Values of Employee Stock Options,"*Journal of Accounting and Economics* (February 2011), pp. 77–94.

CHRISTENSEN, J., "Communication in Agencies," *The Bell Journal of Economics* (Autumn 1981), pp. 661–674.

CHRISTENSEN, P.O., J.S. DEMSKI, and H. FRIMOR, "Accounting Policies in Agencies with Moral Hazard," *Journal of Accounting Research* (September 2002), pp. 1071–1090.

CHUNG, D.Y., and K. HRAZDIL, "Market Efficiency and the Post-Earnings Announcement Drift," *Contemporary Accounting Research* (Fall 2011), pp. 926–956.

COASE, R.H., "The Problem of Social Cost," *The Journal of Law and Economics* (October 1960), pp. 1–44.

COHEN, D.A. and P. ZAROWIN, "Accrual-Based and Real Earnings Management Activities around Seasoned Equity Offerings," *Journal of Accounting and Economics* (May 2010), pp. 2–19.

COLLINS, D.W. and S.P. KOTHARI, "An Analysis of the Intertemporal and Cross-Sectional Determinants of Earnings Response Coefficients," *Journal of Accounting and Economics* (July 1989), pp. 143–181.

CORE, J.E., W.R. GUAY, and R. VERDI, "Is Accruals Quality a Priced Risk Factor?" Journal of Accounting and Economics (September 2008), pp. 2–22.

COTTER, J., I. TUNA, and P.D. WYSOCKI, "Expectations Management and Beatable Targets: How Do Analysts React to Explicit Earnings Guidance?" *Contemporary Accounting Research* (Fall 2006), pp. 593–624.

COURTEAU, L., J. KAO, and G.D. RICHARDSON, "Equity Valuation Employing the Ideal versus Ad Hoc Terminal Value Expression," *Contemporary Accounting Research* (Winter 2001), pp. 625–661.

COVRIG, V.M., M.L. DEFOND, and M. HUNG, "Home Bias, Foreign Mutual Fund Holdings, and the Voluntary Adoption of International Accounting Standards," *Journal of Accounting Research* (March 2007), pp. 41–70.

CRANDALL, R.H., "Government Intervention—the PIP Grant Accounting Controversy," *Cost and Management* (September/October 1983), pp. 57–59.

CRAWFORD, V.P. and J. SOBEL, "Strategic Information Transmission," *Econometrica* (November 1982), pp. 1431–1451.

CREADY, W.H., T.J. LOPEZ, and C.A. SISNEROS, "Negative Special Items and Future Earnings: Expense Transfer or Real Improvements? *The Accounting Review* (July 2012), pp. 1165–1195.

DANIEL, K.D., D. HIRSHLEIFER, and A. SUBRAHMANYAM, "Investor Psychology and Security Market Investor Under- and Over-Reactions," *Journal of Finance* (December 1998), pp. 1839–1885.

DANIEL, K.D., D. HIRSHLEIFER, and A. SUBRAHMANYAM, "Overconfidence, Arbitrage, and Equilibrium Asset Pricing," *The Journal of Finance* (2001), pp. 921–965.

DANIEL, K.D. and S. TITMAN, "Market Efficiency in an Irrational World," *Financial Analysts' Journal* (1999), pp. 28–40.

DARROUGH, M.N. and N.M. STOUGHTON, "Financial Disclosure Policy in an Entry Game," *Journal of Accounting and Economics* (January 1990), pp. 219–243.

DAS, S., P.K. SHROFF, and H. ZHANG, "Quarterly Earnings Patterns and Earnings Management," *Contemporary Accounting Research* (Fall 2009), pp. 797–831.

DASKE, H., L. HAIL, C. LEUZ, and R. VERDI, "Mandatory IFRS Reporting around the World: Early Evidence on the Economic Consequences," *Journal of Accounting Research* (December 2008), pp. 1085–1142.

DASKE, H., L. HAIL, C. LEUZ, and R. VERDI, "Adopting a Label: Heterogeneity in the Economic Consequences around IAS/IFRS Adoption," *Journal of Accounting Research* (June 2013), pp. 495–547.

DATAR, S.M., G.A. FELTHAM, and J.S. HUGHES, "The Role of Audits and Audit Quality in Valuing New Issues," *Journal of Accounting and Economics* (March 1991), pp. 3–49.

DATAR, S.M., S.C. KULP, and R.A. LAMBERT, "Balancing Performance Measures, *Journal of Accounting Research* (June 2001), pp. 75–92.

DE ANGELO, H., L.E. DE ANGELO, and D.J. SKINNER, "Accounting Choice in Troubled Companies," *Journal of Accounting and Economics* (January 1994), pp. 113–143.

DE ANGELO, L.E., "Auditor Size and Auditor Quality," *Journal of Accounting and Economics* (December 1981), pp. 183–199.

DE BONDT, W.F.M. and R. THALER, "Does the Stock Market Overreact?" *The Journal of Finance* (July 1985), pp. 793–805.

DECHOW, P.M., "Accounting Earnings and Cash Flows as Measures of Firm Performance: The Role of Accounting Accruals," *Journal of Accounting and Economics* (July 1994), pp. 3–42.

DECHOW, P.M. and I. DICHEV, "The Quality of Accruals and Earnings: The Role of Accrual Estimation Errors," *The Accounting Review* (Supplement, 2002), pp. 35–59.

DECHOW, P.M., W. GE, C.R. LARSON, and R.G., SLOAN, "Predicting Material Accounting Misstatements," *Contemporary Accounting Research* (Spring 2011), pp. 17–82.

DECHOW, P.M., A.P. HUTTON, J.H. KIM, and R.G.SLOAN, "Detecting Earnings Management: A New Approach," *Journal of Accounting Research* (May 2012), pp. 275–334.

DECHOW, P.M., and C. SHAKESPEARE, "Do Managers Time Securitization Transactions to Obtain Accounting Benefits? *The Accounting Review* (January 2009). pp. 99–132.

DECHOW, P.M., R.G. SLOAN, and A.P. SWEENEY, "Detecting Earnings Management," *The Accounting Review* (April 1995), pp. 193–225.

DECHOW, P.M., R.G. SLOAN, and A.P. SWEENEY, "Causes and Consequences of Earnings Manipulation: An Analysis of Firms Subject to Enforcement Actions by the SEC," *Contemporary Accounting Research* (Spring 1996), pp. 1–36.

DEFOND, M.L. and J. JIAMBALVO, "Debt Covenant Violation and Manipulation of Accruals," *Journal of Accounting and Economics* (January 1994), pp. 145–176.

DEFRANCO, G., F. WONG, and Y. ZHOU, "Accounting Adjustments and the Valuation of Financial Statement Note Information in 10-K Filings," *The Accounting Review* (September 2011), pp. 1577–1604.

DELONG, J.B., A. SHLEIFER, L. SUMMERS, and R.J. WALDMANN, "Positive Feedback Investment Strategies and Destabilizing Rational Speculation," *Journal of Finance* (June 1990), pp. 375–395.

DEMSKI, J., *Information Analysis* (Reading, MA: Addison-Wesley, 1972).

DEMSKI, J., H. LIN, and D.E.M. SAPPINGTON, "Asset Revaluation Regulation with Multiple Information Sources," *The Accounting Review* (July 2008), pp. 869–891.

DEMSKI, J. and D.E.M. SAPPINGTON, "Delegated Expertise," *Journal of Accounting Research* (Spring 1987), pp. 68–89.

DEMSKI, J. and D.E.M. SAPPINGTON, "Fully Revealing Income Measurement," *The Accounting Review* (April 1990), pp. 363–383.

DENG, M., N. MELUMAD, and T. SHIBANO, "Auditors' Liability, Investments, and Capital Markets: A Potential Unintended Consequence of the Sarbanes-Oxley Act," *Journal of Accounting Research* (December 2012), pp. 1179–1215.

DESSEIN, W. "Authority and Communication in Organizations," *Review of Economic Studies*, 69 (2002), pp. 811–838.

DHALIWAL, D.S., K.J. LEE, and N.L. FARGHER, "The Association Between Unexpected Earnings and Abnormal Security Returns in the Presence of Financial Leverage," *Contemporary Accounting Research* (Fall 1991), pp. 20–41.

DIAMOND, D.W. and R.E. VERRECCHIA, "Disclosure, Liquidity, and the Cost of Capital," *The Journal of Finance* (September 1991), pp. 1325–1359.

DICHEV, I.D. and D.J. SKINNER, "Large-Sample Evidence on the Debt Covenant Hypothesis," *Journal of Accounting Research* (September 2002), pp. 1091–1123.

DICHEV, I.D. and V.W. TANG, "Matching and the Changing Properties of Accounting Earnings over the Last 40 Years," *The Accounting Review* (November 2008), pp. 1425–1460.

DOPUCH, N. and S. SUNDER, "FASB's Statements on Objectives and Elements of Financial Accounting: A Review," *The Accounting Review* (1980), pp. 1–21.

DORAN, B.M., D.W. COLLINS, and D.S. DHALIWAL, "The Information Content of Historical Cost Earnings Relative to Supplemental Reserve-Based Accounting Data in the Extractive Petroleum Industry," *The Accounting Review* (July 1988), pp. 389–413.

DOYLE, J.T., R.J. LUNDHOLM, and M.T. SOLIMAN, "The Predictive Value of Expenses Excluded from Pro Forma Earnings," *Review of Accounting Studies* (2003), pp. 145–174.

DURNEV, A., R. MORCK, B. YEUNG and P. ZAROWIN, "Does Greater Firm-Specific Return Variation Mean More or Less Informed Stock Pricing?" *Journal of Accounting Research* (December 2003), pp. 797–836.

DURTSCHI, C. and P. EASTON, "Earnings Management? Erroneous Inferences Based on Earnings Frequency Distributions," *Journal of Accounting Research* (December 2009), pp. 1249–1281.

DYE, R.A., "Disclosure of Nonproprietary Information," *Journal of Accounting Research* (Spring 1985), pp. 123–145.

DYE, R.A., "Proprietary and Nonproprietary Disclosures," *Journal of Business* (April 1986), pp. 331–366.

DYE, R.A. and S. SUNDER, "Why Not Allow FASB and IASB Standards to Compete in the U.S.?" *Accounting Horizons* (September 2001), pp. 257–271.

EASLEY, D. and M. O'HARA, "Information and the Cost of Capital," *The Journal of Finance* (August 2004), pp. 1553–1583.

EASTON, P.D. and T.S. HARRIS, "Earnings as an Explanatory Variable for Returns," *Journal of Accounting Research* (Spring 1991), pp. 19–36.

EASTON, P.D., T.S. HARRIS, and J.A. OHLSON, "Aggregate Accounting Earnings Can Explain Most of Security Returns," *Journal of Accounting and Economics* (June/September 1992), pp. 119–142.

EASTON, P.D. and G.A. SOMMERS, "Effect of Analysts' Optimism on Estimates of the Expected Rate of Return Implied by Earnings Forecasts," *Journal of Accounting Research* (December 2007), pp. 983–1015.

EASTON, P.D. and M.E. ZMIJEWSKI, "Cross-Sectional Variation in the Stock-Market Response to Accounting Earnings Announcements," *Journal of Accounting and Economics* (July 1989), pp. 117–141.

ECKER, F., J. FRANCIS, I. KIM, P.M. OLSSON, and K. SCHIPPER, "A Returns-Based Representation of Earnings Quality," *The Accounting Review* (July 2006), pp. 749–780.

ECKERN, S. and R. WILSON, "On the Theory of the Firm in an Economy with Incomplete Markets," *The Bell Journal of Economics and Management Science* (Spring 1974), pp. 171–180.

EDMANS, A. and Q. LIU, "Inside Debt," *Review of Finance* (January 2011), pp. 75–102.

EFENDI, J., R. FILES, B. OUYANG, and E.P. SWANSON, Executive Turnover Following Option Backdating Allegations," *The Accounting Review* (January 2013), pp. 75–105.

EFENDI, J., A. SRIVASTAVA, and E.P. SWANSON, "Why Do Corporate Managers Misstate Financial Statements? The Role of Option Compensation and Other Factors, "*Journal of Financial Economics* 85 (2007), pp. 667–708.

EINHORN, E., "The Nature of the Interaction between Mandatory and Voluntary Disclosures," *Journal of Accounting Research* (September 2005), pp. 593–621.

EINHORN, E., "Voluntary Disclosure under Uncertainty about the Reporting Objective," *Journal of Accounting and Economics* (July 2007), pp. 245–274.

ELESWARAPU, V.R., R. THOMPSON, and K. VENKATARAMAN, "Measuring the Fairness of Regulation Fair Disclosure through its Impact on Trading Costs and Information Asymmetry," *Journal of Financial and Quantitative Analysis* (2004), pp. 209–25

ELLIOTT, J.A. and J.D. HANNA, "Repeated Accounting Write-Offs and the Information Content of Earnings," *Journal of Accounting Research* (Supplement, 1996), pp. 135–169.

ELLIOTT, W.B., S.B. KRISCHE, and M.E. PEECHER, "Expected Mispricing: The Joint Influence of Accounting Transparency and Investor Base" *Journal of Accounting Research* (May 2010), pp. 343–381.

ELY K. and G. WAYMIRE, "Accounting Standard-Setting Organizations and Earnings Relevance: Longitudinal Evidence from *NYSE* Common Stocks, 1927–93," *Journal of Accounting Research* (Autumn 1999), pp. 293–317.

ERMAN, BOYD and TIM KILADZE, " A call for long-term thinking," *The Globe and Mail* (October 19, 2010), p. B3.

FAMA, E.F., "Efficient Capital Markets: A Review of Theory and Empirical Work," *Journal of Finance* (May 1970), pp. 383–417.

FAMA, E.F., "Agency Problems and the Theory of the Firm," *Journal of Political Economy* (April 1980), pp. 288–307.

FAMA, E.F., "Market Efficiency, Long-Term Returns and Behavioral Finance," *Journal of Financial Economics* (September 1998), pp. 283–306.

FAMA, E.F. and K.R. FRENCH, "The Cross-Section of Expected Stock Returns," *The Journal of Finance* (1992), pp. 427–465.

FAN, J.P.H. and T.J. WONG, "Do External Auditors Perform a Corporate Governance Role in Emerging Markets? Evidence from East Asia," *Journal of Accounting Research* (March 2005), pp. 35–72.

FAN, Q., "Earnings Management and Ownership Retention for Initial Public Offering Firms: Theory and Evidence," *The Accounting Review* (January 2007), pp. 27–64.

FANNIE MAE BOARD OF DIRECTORS, *Report to the Special Review Committee* (Washington: Fannie Mae, February 2006).

FARRELL, A.M., S.D. KRISCHE, and K.L. SEDATOLE, "Employees' Subjective Valuations of their Stock Options: Evidence on the Distribution of Valuations and the Use of Simple Anchors," *Contemporary Accounting Research* (Fall 2011), pp. 747–793.

FELTHAM, G.A. and J.A. OHLSON, "Valuation and Clean Surplus Accounting for Operating and Financial Activities," *Contemporary Accounting Research* (Spring 1995), pp. 689–731.

FELTHAM, G.A. and J.A. OHLSON, "Uncertainty Resolution and the Theory of Depreciation Measurement," *Journal of Accounting Research* (Autumn 1996), pp. 209–234.

FELTHAM, G.A. and J. XIE, "Performance Measure Congruity and Diversity in Multi-Task Principal/Agent Relations," *The Accounting Review* (July 1994), pp. 429–453.

FINANCIAL ACCOUNTING STANDARDS BOARD, *Accounting Standards Codification* (ASC), (Norwalk, CT: FASB, 2009).

FINANCIAL ACCOUNTING STANDARDS BOARD, Interpretation 46(R), *Consolidation of Variable Interest Entities (revised December 2003— an interpretation of ARB 51* (Norwalk, CT, FASB, December 2003).

FINANCIAL ACCOUNTING STANDARDS BOARD, *Proposal for a Principles-based Approach to U.S. Standard-setting* (Norwalk, CT: FASB, 2002).

FINANCIAL ACCOUNTING STANDARDS BOARD, *Statement of Financial Accounting Concepts No. 1, Objectives of Financial Reporting by Business Enterprises* (Norwalk, CT: FASB, 1978).

FINANCIAL ACCOUNTING STANDARDS BOARD, *Statement of Financial Accounting Standards No. 33, Financial Reporting and Changing Prices* (Norwalk, CT: FASB, 1979)

FINANCIAL ACCOUNTING STANDARDS BOARD, *Statement of Financial Accounting Standards No. 106, Employers' Accounting for*

Postretirement Benefits Other Than Pensions (Norwalk, CT: FASB, 1990).

FINANCIAL ACCOUNTING STANDARDS BOARD, *Statement of Financial Accounting Standards No. 123, Accounting for Stock-based Compensation* (Norwalk, CT: FASB, 1995).

FINANCIAL ACCOUNTING STANDARDS BOARD, *Statement of Financial Accounting Standards No. 123R, Share-Based Payment* (Norwalk, CT: FASB, 2004).

FINANCIAL ACCOUNTING STANDARDS BOARD, *Statement of Financial Accounting Standards No. 130, Reporting Comprehensive Income* (Norwalk, CT: FASB, 1997).

FINANCIAL ACCOUNTING STANDARDS BOARD, *Statement of Financial Accounting Standards No. 131, Financial Reporting for Segments of a Business Enterprise* (Norwalk, CT: FASB, 1997).

FINANCIAL ACCOUNTING STANDARDS BOARD, *Statement of Financial Accounting Standards No. 133, Accounting for Derivative Instruments and Hedging Activities* (Norwalk, CT: FASB, 1998).

FINANCIAL ACCOUNTING STANDARDS BOARD, *Statement of Financial Accounting Standards No. 141, Business Combinations* (Norwalk, CT: FASB, 2001).

FINANCIAL ACCOUNTING STANDARDS BOARD, *Statement of Financial Accounting Standards No. 142, Goodwill and Other Intangible Assets* (Norwalk, CT: FASB, 2001).

FINANCIAL ACCOUNTING STANDARDS BOARD, *Statement of Financial Accounting Standards No. 146, Accounting for Costs Associated with Exit or Disposal Activities* (Norwalk, CT: FASB, 2002).

FINANCIAL ACCOUNTING STANDARDS BOARD, *Statement of Financial Accounting Standards No. 157, Fair Value Measurements* (Norwalk, CT: FASB, 2006).

FISCHER, P. and S. HUDDART, "Optimal Contracting with Endogenous Social Norms," *American Economic Review* (September 2008), pp. 1459–1475.

FRANCIS, J., R. LAFOND, P. OLSSON and K. SCHIPPER, "The Market Pricing of Accruals Quality," *Journal of Accounting and Economics* (June 2005), pp. 295–327.

FRANCIS, J., D. NANDA, and X. WANG, "Re-examining the Effects of Regulation Fair Disclosure using Foreign Listed Firms to Control for Concurrent Shocks," *Journal of Accounting and Economics* (September 2006), pp. 271–292.

FRANCIS, J., D. NANDA, and P. OLSSON, "Voluntary Disclosure, Earnings Quality, and Cost of Capital," *Journal of Accounting Research* (March 2008), pp. 53–99.

FRANCIS, J., K. SCHIPPER and L. VINCENT, "Expanded Disclosures and the Increased Usefulness of Earnings Announcements," *The Accounting Review* (July 2002), pp. 515–546.

FRANCIS, J.R., S. HUANG, I.K. KHURANA, and R. PEREIRA, "Does Corporate Transparency Contribute to Efficient Resource Allocation?" *Journal of Accounting Research* (September 2009), pp. 943–989.

FRANCIS, J.R. and D. WANG, "The Joint Effect of Investor Protection and Big 4 Audits on Investor Protection around the World," *Contemporary Accounting Research* (Spring 2008), pp. 157–191.

FRANKEL, R. and C.M.C. LEE, "Accounting Valuation, Market Expectation, and Cross-Sectional Stock Returns," *Journal of Accounting and Economics* (June 1998), pp. 283–319.

FRIEDMAN, J.W., *Game Theory with Applications to Economics* (New York, NY: Oxford University Press, 1986).

GAO, P., "Keynesian Beauty Contest, Accounting Disclosure, and Market Efficiency," *Journal of Accounting Research* (September 2008), pp. 785–807.

GAO, Y., "The Sarbanes-Oxley Act and the Choice of Bond Market by Foreign Firms," *Journal of Accounting Research* (September 2011), pp. 933–968.

GAYLE, G.-L. and R.A. MILLER, "Has Moral Hazard Become a More Important Factor in Managerial Compensation?" *American Economic Review* (December 2009), pp. 1740–1769.

GAVER, J.J. and K.M. GAVER, "The Relation Between Nonrecurring Accounting Transactions and CEO Cash Compensation," *The Accounting Review* (April 1998), pp. 235–253.

GIGLER, F., C. KANODIA, H. SAPRA, and R. VENUGOPALAN, "Accounting Conservatism and the Efficiency of Debt Contracts," *Journal of Accounting research* (June 2009), pp. 767–797.

GJESDAL, F., "Accounting for Stewardship," *Journal of Accounting Research* (Spring 1981), pp. 208–231.

GONEDES, N. and N. DOPUCH, "Capital Market Equilibrium, Information Production, and Selected Accounting Techniques: Theoretical Framework and Review of Empirical Work," *Journal of Accounting Research* (Supplement, 1974), pp. 48–129.

GRAHAM, J.R., C.R. HARVEY and S. RAJGOPAL, "The Economic Implications of Corporate Financial Reporting," *Journal of Accounting and Economics* (December 2005), pp. 3–73.

GREIN, B.M., J.R.M. HAND, and K.J. KLASSEN, "Stock Price Reactions to the Repricing of Employee Stock Options." *Contemporary Accounting Research* (Winter 2005), pp. 701–828.

GREEN, J., J.R.M. HAND, and M.T. SOLIMAN, "Going, Going, Gone? The Apparent Demise of the Accruals Anomaly," *Management Science* (May 2011), pp. 797–816.

GROSSMAN, S., "On the Efficiency of Competitive Stock Markets Where Traders Have Diverse Information," *The Journal of Finance* (May 1976), pp. 573–585.

GROSSMAN, S., "The Informational Role of Warranties and Private Disclosure about Product Quality," *Journal of Law and Economics* (December 1981), pp. 461–484.

GU, F. and J.Q. LI, "The Credibility of Voluntary Disclosure and Insider Stock Transactions," *Journal of Accounting Research* (September 2007), pp. 171–810.

GUAY, W.R. and S.P. KOTHARI, "How Much do Firms Hedge with Derivatives?" *Journal of Financial Economics* (December 2003), pp. 423–461.

GUEDHAMI, O. and J. PITTMAN, "Ownership Concentration in Privatized Firms: The Role of Disclosure Standards, Auditor Choice, and Auditing Infrastructure," *Journal of Accounting Research* (December 2006), pp. 889–929.

F. GUERRERA, "Citi Ends SIV Foray as Last $17.4bn is Returned," *Financial Times* (November 19, 2008).

HAIL, H. and C. LEUZ, Cost of Capital Effects and Changes to Growth Expectations around U.S. Cross-Listings, *Journal of Financial Economics* (September 2009), pp. 428–454.

HALES, J., "Directional Preferences, Information Processing, and Investors' Forecasts of Earnings," *Journal of Accounting Research* (June 2007), pp. 607–628.

HALL, B.J. and K.J. MURPHY, "Stock Options for Undiversified Executives," *Journal of Accounting and Economics* (February 2002), pp. 3–42.

HAMADA, R., "The Effect of the Firm's Capital Structure on the Systematic Risk of Common Stocks," *Journal of Finance* (May 1972), pp. 435–452.

HAN, J. and H.-T. TAN, "Investor Reaction to Management Earnings Guidance: The Joint Effect of Investment Position, News Valence, and Guidance Form," *Journal of Accounting Research* (June 2010), pp. 81–104.

HANNA, J.D., "Never Say Never," *CA Magazine* (August 1999), pp. 35–39.

HATFIELD, H.R., *Accounting* (New York, NY: Appleton-Century-Crofts, Inc., 1927).

HEALY, P.M., "The Effect of Bonus Schemes on Accounting Decisions," *Journal of Accounting and Economics* (April 1985), pp. 85–107.

HEALY, P.M., A.P. HUTTON, and K.G. PALEPU, "Stock Performance and Intermediation Changes Surrounding Sustained Increases in Disclosure," *Contemporary Accounting Research* (Fall 1999), pp. 485–520.

HEALY, P.M. and K.G. PALEPU, "The Effect of Firms' Financial Disclosure Strategies on Stock Prices," *Accounting Horizons* (March 1993), pp. 1–11.

HEALY, P.M. and K.G. PALEPU, "The Fall of Enron," *Journal of Economic Perspectives* (Spring 2003), pp. 3–26.

HEFLIN, F. and C. HSU, "The Impact of the SEC's Regulation of Non-GAAP Disclosures," *Journal of Accounting and Economics* (December 2008), pp. 349–365.

HEMMER, T.S., S. MATSUNAGA, and T. SHEVLIN, "Estimating the 'Fair Value' of Employee Stock Options with Expected Early Exercise," *Accounting Horizons* (December 1994), pp. 23–42.

HIRSHLEIFER, D., "Investor Psychology and Asset Pricing," *Journal of Finance* (August 2001), pp. 1533–1597.

HIRSHLEIFER, D. and S.H. TEOH, "Limited Attention, Information Disclosure, and Financial Reporting," *Journal of Accounting and Economics* (December 2003), pp. 337–386.

HIRSHLEIFER, J., "The Private and Social Value of Information and the Reward to Inventive Activity," *American Economic Review* (September 1971), pp. 561–573.

HIRST, D.E. and P.E. HOPKINS, "Comprehensive Income Reporting and Analysts' Valuation Judgments," *Journal of Accounting Research* (Supplement, 1998), pp. 47–75.

HIRST, D.E., L. KOONCE, and S. VENKATARAMAN, "How Disaggregation Enhances the Credibility of Management Forecasts," *Journal of Accounting Research* (September 2007), pp. 811–837.

HOBBES, T., *Leviathan*, ed. C.B.Macpherson (Hammondsworth, England: Penguin Books, 1968).

HOBSON, J.L., W.J. MAYEW, and M. VENKATACHALAM, "Analyzing Speech to Detect Financial Misreporting," *Journal of Accounting Research* (May 2012), pp. 349–392.

HOCHBERG, Y.V., P. SAPIENZA, and A. VISSING-JØRGENSEN, "A Lobbying Approach to Evaluating the Sarbanes-Oxley Act of 2002," *Journal of Accounting Research* (May 2009), pp. 519–583.

HODDER, L.D., P.E. HOPKINS, and J.W. WHALEN, "Risk-Relevance of Fair-Value Income Measures for Commercial Banks," *The Accounting Review* (March 2006), pp. 335–337.

HOLLANDER, S., M. PRONK, and E. ROELFOSEN, "Does Silence Speak? An Empirical Analysis of Disclosure Choices During Conference Calls," *Journal of Accounting Research* (June 2010), pp. 531–563.

HOLMSTRÖM, B., "Moral Hazard and Observability," *The Bell Journal of Economics* (Spring 1979), pp. 74–91.

HOLMSTRÖM, B., "Moral Hazard in Teams," *The Bell Journal of Economics* (Autumn 1982), pp. 324–340.

HOLTHAUSEN, R.W., D.F. LARCKER, and R.G. SLOAN, "Annual Bonus Schemes and the Manipulation of Earnings," *Journal of Accounting and Economics* (February 1995), pp. 29–74.

HOPE, O.-K. and W.B. THOMAS, "Managerial Empire Building and Firm Disclosures," *Journal of Accounting Research* (June 2008), pp. 591–626.

HOSSAIN, T. and J. LIST, "The Behaviorialist Visits the Factory: Increasing Productivity Using Simple Framing Manipulations, " NBER Working Paper No. W15623 (December 2009).

HOU, K., M.A. van DIJK, and Y. ZHANG, "The Implied Cost of Capital: A New Approach," *Journal of Accounting and Economics* (June 2012), pp. 504–526.

HRIBAR, P. and D. W. COLLINS, "Errors in Estimating Accruals," *Journal of Accounting Research* (March 2002), pp. 105–134.

HUANG, C-F, and R.H. LITZENBERGER, *Foundations for Financial Economics* (Englewood Cliffs, N.J., Prentice-Hall, Inc., 1988).

HUDDART, S., "Employee Stock Options," *Journal of Accounting and Economics* (September 1994), pp. 207–231.

HUDDART, S., "Employee Stock Options," *Journal of Accounting and Economics* (September 1994), pp. 207–231.

HUDDART, S. and M. LANG, "Employee Stock Option Exercises: An Empirical Analysis," *Journal of Accounting and Economics* (February 1996), pp. 5–43.

HUI, K. W., S. KLASA, and P.E. YEUNG, "Corporate Suppliers and Customers and Accounting Conservatism, *Journal of Accounting and Economics* (April 2012), pp. 115–135.

INDJEJIKIAN, R. J. and D. NANDA, "Executive Bonuses and What They Imply about Performance Standards," *The Accounting Review* (October 2002), pp. 793–819.

INTERNATIONAL ACCOUNTING STANDARDS BOARD, *The Conceptual Framework for Financial Reporting* (joint with FASB, Chapters 1 and 3, London: IASB, September 2010).

INTERNATIONAL ACCOUNTING STANDARDS BOARD, *Consolidation—Special Purpose Entities* (London: IASB SIC Interpretation 12, 2008).

INTERNATIONAL ACCOUNTING STANDARDS BOARD, *Discussion Paper, Preliminary Views on Financial Statement Presentation* (London: IASB, October 2008).

INTERNATIONAL ACCOUNTING STANDARDS BOARD, *Discussion Paper, A Review of the Conceptual Framework for Financial Reporting* (London: IASB, July 2013).

INTERNATIONAL ACCOUNTING STANDARDS BOARD, *Exposure Draft, Revenue from Contracts with Customers* (London: IASB, November 2011).

INTERNATIONAL ACCOUNTING STANDARDS BOARD, *Exposure Draft, Financial Instruments: Expected Credit Losses,* (London: IASB, March 2013).

INTERNATIONAL ACCOUNTING STANDARDS BOARD, *Exposure Draft, Joint with FASB, Leases* (London: IASB, May 2013).

INTERNATIONAL ACCOUNTING STANDARDS BOARD, *International Accounting Standard IAS 1, Presentation of Financial Statements* (London: IASB, 2007).

INTERNATIONAL ACCOUNTING STANDARDS BOARD, *International Accounting Standard IAS 2, Inventories* (London: IASB, 2005).

INTERNATIONAL ACCOUNTING STANDARDS BOARD, *International Accounting Standard IAS 16, Property, Plant & Equipment* (London: IASB, 2005).

INTERNATIONAL ACCOUNTING STANDARDS BOARD, *International Accounting Standard IAS 17, Leases* (London: IASB, 2005).

INTERNATIONAL ACCOUNTING STANDARDS BOARD, *International Accounting Standard IAS 18, Revenue* (London: IASB, 1995).

INTERNATIONAL ACCOUNTING STANDARDS BOARD, *International Accounting Standard IAS 32 Financial Instruments: Presentation* (London: IASB, 2005).

INTERNATIONAL ACCOUNTING STANDARDS BOARD, *International Accounting Standard IAS 36, Impairment of Assets* (London: IASB, 2004).

INTERNATIONAL ACCOUNTING STANDARDS BOARD, *International Accounting Standard IAS 37, Provisions, Contingent Liabilities, and Contingent Assets* (London: IASB, 1999).

INTERNATIONAL ACCOUNTING STANDARDS BOARD, *International Accounting Standard IAS 38, Intangible Assets* (London: IASB, 2004).

INTERNATIONAL ACCOUNTING STANDARDS BOARD, *International Accounting Standard IAS 39, Financial Instruments: Recognition and Measurement* (London: IASB, 1999).

INTERNATIONAL ACCOUNTING STANDARDS BOARD, *International Financial Reporting Standard IFRS 1, First-Time Adoption of International Financial Reporting Standards* (London: IASB, 2003).

INTERNATIONAL ACCOUNTING STANDARDS BOARD, *International Financial Reporting Standard IFRS 2, Share-based Payment* (London: IASB, 2005).

INTERNATIONAL ACCOUNTING STANDARDS BOARD, *International Financial Reporting Standard IFRS 3, Business Combinations* (London: IASB, 2004).

INTERNATIONAL ACCOUNTING STANDARDS BOARD, *International Financial Reporting Standard IFRS 7, Financial Instruments: Disclosures* (London: IASB, 2007).

INTERNATIONAL ACCOUNTING STANDARDS BOARD, *International Financial Reporting Standard IFRS 8, Operating Segments* (London, IASB, 2006).

INTERNATIONAL ACCOUNTING STANDARDS BOARD, *Financial Instruments IFRS 9* (London, IASB, 2010).

INTERNATIONAL ACCOUNTING STANDARDS BOARD, *Consolidated Financial Statements IFRS 10* (London, IASB, 2011).

INTERNATIONAL ACCOUNTING STANDARDS BOARD, *Disclosure of Interests in Other Entities IFRS 12* (London, IASB, 2011).

INTERNATIONAL ACCOUNTING STANDARDS BOARD, *International Financial Reporting Standard IFRS 13, Fair Value Measurement* (London: IASB, 2013).

INTERNATIONAL ACCOUNTING STANDARDS BOARD, *Management Commentary*, (London: IASB, December 2010).

INTERNATIONAL ACCOUNTING STANDARDS BOARD, STANDING INTERPRETATIONS COMMITTEE, *Interpretation 12, (SIC 12) "Consolidation-Special Purpose Entities"* (London: IASB, 1998).

INTERNATIONAL ORGANIZATION OF SECURITIES COMMISSIONS, "Multilateral Memorandum of Understanding Concerning Consultation and Cooperation and the Exchange of Information" (Madrid: IOSCO, May 2002).

ITTNER, C.D., D.F. LARCKER, and M.V. RAJAN, "The Choice of Performance Measures in Annual Bonus Contracts," *The Accounting Review* (April 1997), pp. 231–255.

JACKSON, DALE, "Dividends rise and shine during recession," *The Globe and Mail* (Toronto, November 6, 2009).

JACKSON, S.B. and X.T. LIU, "The Allowance for Uncollectible Accounts, Conservatism, and Earnings Management," *Journal of Accounting Research* (June 2010), pp. 565–601.

JAGOLINZER, A.D., D.F. LARCKER, and D.J. TAYLOR, "Corporate Governance and the Information Content of Inside Trades, "*Journal of Accounting Research* (December 2011), pp. 1249–1273.

JAMAL, K., M. MAIER, and S. SUNDER, "Privacy in E-Commerce: Development of Reporting Standards, Disclosure, and Assurance Services in an Unregulated Market," *Journal of Accounting Research* (May 2003), pp. 285–309.

JAYARAMAN, S., "Earnings Volatility, Cash Flow Volatility, and Informed Trading,"*Journal of Accounting Research* (September 2008), pp. 809–851.

JENSEN, M.C. and W.H. MECKLING, "Theory of the Firm: Managerial Behavior, Agency Costs and Ownership Structure," *Journal of Financial Economics* (October 1976), pp. 305–360.

JENSEN, M.C. and K.J. MURPHY, "CEO Incentives—It's Not How Much You Pay, But How," *Harvard Business Review* (May/June 1990), pp. 138–149.

JONES, D.A., and K.J. SMITH, "Comparing the Value Relevance, Predictive Value, and Persistence of Other Comprehensive Income and Special items," *The Accounting Review* (November 2011), pp. 2047–2073.

JONES, J., "Earnings Management During Import Relief Investigations," *Journal of Accounting Research* (Autumn 1991), pp. 193–228.

KAHNEMAN, D. and A. TVERSKY, "Prospect Theory: An Analysis of Decision Under Risk," *Econometrica* (March 1979), pp. 263–291.

KANODIA, C., R. SINGH, and A. SPERO, "Imprecision in Accounting Measurement" *Journal of Accounting Research* (June 2005), pp. 487–519.

KAPLAN, R.S., "Comments on Paul Healy," *Journal of Accounting and Economics* (April 1985), pp. 109–113.

KE, B. and S. RAMALINGEGOWDA, "Do Institutional Investors Exploit the Post-Earnings Announcement Drift?" *Journal of Accounting and Economics* (February 2005), pp. 25–53.

KEUNG, E., Z-X LIN, and M. SHIH, "Does the Stock Market See a Zero or a Small Positive Earnings Surprise as a Red Flag?" *Journal of Accounting Research* (March 2010), pp. 105–135.

KIM, M. and W. KROSS, "The Ability of Earnings to Predict Future Operating Cash Flows Has Been Increasing—Not Decreasing," *Journal of Accounting Research* (December 2005), pp. 753–780.

KIM, O. and R.E. VERRECCHIA, "Pre-announcement and Event-period Private Information," *Journal of Accounting and Economics* (1997), pp. 395–419.

KNETSCH, J.L., "The Endowment Effect and Evidence of Nonreversible Indifference Curves," *The American Economic Review* (December 1989), pp. 1277–1284.

KOLASINSKI, A.C., "Mark-to-Market Regulatory Accounting when Securities Markets are Stressed: Lessons from the Financial Crisis of 2007–2009, *Journal of Accounting and Economics* (November 2011), pp. 174–177.

KOONCE, L. and M.G. LIPE, "Earnings Trend and Performance Relative to Benchmarks: How Consistency Influences Their Joint Use," *Journal of Accounting Research* (September 2010), pp. 859–884.

KORMENDI, R.C. and R. LIPE, "Earnings Innovations, Earnings Persistence, and Stock Returns," *Journal of Business* (July 1987), pp. 323–346.

KOTHARI, S.P., J. SHANKEN, and R. SLOAN, "Another Look at the Cross-Section of Expected Returns," *Journal of Finance* (March 1995), pp. 185–224.

KRAVET, T. and T. SHEVLIN, "Accounting Restatements and Information Risk," *Review of Accounting Studies* (2010), pp. 264–294.

KROSS, W.J. and I. SUK, "Does regulation FD Work? Evidence from Analysts' Reliance on Public Disclosure," *Journal of Accounting and Economics* (February/April 2012), pp. 21–33.

KURZ, M., ed., *Endogenous Economic Fluctuations* (New York, NY: Springer-Verlag, 1997a).

KURZ, M., "Endogenous Uncertainty: A Unified View of Market Volatility," working paper, Stanford University (September 1997b).

LAFFONT, J.J., *The Economics of Uncertainty and Information* (Cambridge, MA: MIT Press, 1989).

LAFFONT, J.J. and J. TIROLE, *A Theory of Incentives in Procurement and Regulation* (Cambridge, MA: MIT Press, 1993).

LAFOND, R. and S. ROYCHOWDHURY, "Managerial Ownership and Accounting Conservatism," *Journal of Accounting Research* (March 2008), pp. 101–135.

LAING, J., "Dangerous Games," *Barron's* (June 8, 1998).

LAMBERT, R.A. and D.F. LARCKER, "An Analysis of the Use of Accounting and Market Measures of Performance in Executive Compensation Contracts," *Journal of Accounting Research* (Supplement, 1987), pp. 85–125.

LAMBERT, R.A. and D.F. LARCKER, "Firm Performance and the Compensation of Chief Executive Officers," working paper (January 1993).

LAMBERT, R.A., D.F. LARCKER, and R.E. VERRECCHIA, "Portfolio Considerations in Valuing Executive Compensation," *Journal of Accounting Research* (Spring 1991), pp. 129–149.

LAMBERT, R.A., C. LEUZ, and R.E. VERRECCHIA, "Accounting Information, Disclosure, and the Cost of Capital," *Journal of Accounting Research* (May 2007), pp. 385–420.

LAMBERT, R.A., C. LEUZ, and R.E. VERRECCHIA, "Information Asymmetry, Information Precision, and Cost of Capital," *Review of Finance* (January 2012), pp. 1–29

LANDSMAN, W.R. and E.L. MAYDEW, "Has the Information Content of Quarterly Earnings Announcements Declined in the Past Three Decades?" *Journal of Accounting Research* (June 2002), pp. 797–808.

LANDSMAN, W.R, K.V. PEASNELL, and C. SHAKESPEARE, "Are Asset Securitizations Sales or Loans?" *The Accounting Review* (September 2008), pp. 1251–1272.

LANDSMAN, W.R., E.L. MAYDEW, and J.R. THORNOCK, "The Information Content of Annual Earnings Announcements and Mandatory Adoption of IFRS," *Journal of Accounting and Economics* (April 2012), pp. 34–54.

LANG, M. and M. MAFFETT, "Transparency and Liquidity Uncertainty in Crisis Periods," *Journal of Accounting and Economics* (November 2011), pp. 101–125.

LEE, C.M.C., "Measuring Wealth," *C.A. Magazine* (April 1996), pp. 32–37.

LEE, C.M.C., "Market Efficiency and Accounting Research: A Discussion of 'Capital Market Research in Accounting' by S.P. Kothari," *Journal of Accounting and Economics* (September 2001), pp. 233–253.

LEE, C.M.C., B. MUCKLOW, and M.J. READY, "Spreads, Depths, and the Impact of Earnings Information: An Intraday Analysis," *The Review of Financial Studies* (1993), pp. 345–374.

LEHAVY, R. and R.G. SLOAN, "Investor Recognition and Stock Returns," *Review of Accounting Studies* vol. 13 (2008), pp. 327–361.

LELAND, H.E. and D.H. PYLE, "Information Asymmetries, Financial Structure, and Financial Intermediation," *The Journal of Finance* (May 1977), pp. 371–387.

LEUZ, C., "IAS Versus U.S GAAP: Information Asymmetry–Based Evidence from Germany's New Market," *Journal of Accounting Research* (June 2003), pp. 445–472.

LEUZ, C., D. NANDA, and P. WYSOCKI, "Earnings Management and Investor Protection: An International Comparison," *Journal of Financial Economics* (September 2003), pp. 505–527.

LEV, B., "On the Association Between Operating Leverage and Risk," *Journal of Financial and Quantitative Analysis* (September 1974), pp. 627–640.

LEV, B., "The Impact of Accounting Regulation on the Stock Market: The Case of Oil and Gas Companies," *The Accounting Review* (July 1979), pp. 485–503.

LEV, B., "On the Usefulness of Earnings: Lessons and Directions from Two Decades of Empirical Research," *Journal of Accounting Research* (Supplement, 1989), pp. 153–192.

LEV, B., and D. NISSIM, "The Persistence of the Accruals Anomaly," *Contemporary Accounting Research* (Spring 2006), pp. 193–226.

LEV, B. and S.R. THIAGARAJAN, "Fundamental Information Analysis," *Journal of Accounting Research* (Autumn 1993), pp. 190–215.

LEV, B., and P. ZAROWIN, "The Boundaries of Financial Reporting and How to Extend Them," *Journal of Accounting Research* (Autumn 1999), pp. 353–385.

LI, F., "The Information Content of Forward-Looking Statements in Corporate Filings- A Naïve Bayesian Machine Learning Approach, *Journal of Accounting Research* (December 2010), pp. 1049–1102.

LI, F., "Earnings Quality Based on Corporate Investment Decisions," *Journal of Accounting Research* (June 2011), pp. 721–752.

LINCK, J., J. NETTER, and T. YANG, "The Determinants of Board Structure," *Journal of Financial Economics* (February 2008), pp. 308–328.

LINTNER, J., "The Valuation of Risky Assets and the Selection of Risky Investments in Stock Portfolios and Capital Budgets," *Review of Economics and Statistics* (February 1965), pp. 13–37.

LIPSEY, R.G., and K. LANCASTER, "The General Theory of Second Best," *The Review of Economic Studies* vol. 24 (1956–1957), pp. 11–32.

LIST, J.A., "Does Market Experience Eliminate Market Anomalies?" *The Quarterly Journal of Economics* (February 2003), pp. 41–71.

LIU, C.-C., S.G. RYAN, and H. TAN, "How Banks' Value-at-Risk Disclosures Predict their Total and Priced Risk: Effects of Banks' Technical Sophistication and Learning over Time," *Review of Accounting Studies* (2004), pp. 265–294.

LIU, C.-C., S.G. RYAN, and J.M. WAHLEN, "Differential Valuation Implications of Loan Loss Provisions Across Banks and Fiscal Quarters," *The Accounting Review* (January 1997), pp. 133–146.

LIVNAT, J. and R.R. MENDENHALL, "Comparing the Post-Earnings Announcement Drift for Surprises Calculated from Analyst and Time Series Forecasts," *Journal of Accounting Research* (March 2006), pp. 177–205.

LO, A., "The Adaptive Markets Hypothesis," *Journal of Portfolio Management* 30 (2004), pp. 15–29.

LO, K., "Economic Consequences of Regulated Changes in Disclosure: the Case of Executive Compensation," *Journal of Accounting and Economics* (August 2003), pp. 285–314.

LOBO, G.J. and J. ZHOU, "Did Conservatism in Financial Accounting Increase after the Sarbanes-Oxley Act? Initial Evidence," *Accounting Horizons* (March 2006), pp. 57–73.

MAFFETT, M., "Financial Reporting Opacity and Informed Trading by International Institutional Investors," *Journal of Accounting and Economics* (December 2012), pp. 201–220.

MAGLIOLO, J., "Capital Market Analysis of Reserve Recognition Accounting," *Journal of Accounting Research* (Supplement, 1986), pp. 69–108.

MALKIEL, B.G., *A Random Walk Down Wall Street* (New York, NY, W.W. Norton, 1973).

MARQUARDT, C.A., "The Cost of Employee Stock Option Grants: An Empirical Analysis," *Journal of Accounting Research* (September 2002), pp. 1191–1217.

MASHRUWALA, C., S. RAJGOPAL, and T. SHEVLIN, "Why Is the Accrual Anomaly not Arbitraged Away? The Role of Idiosyncratic Risk and Transactions Costs," *Journal of Accounting and Economics* (October 2006), pp. 3–33.

MATSUMOTO, D.A., "Management's Incentives to Avoid Negative Earnings Surprises," *The Accounting Review* (July 2002), pp. 483–514.

MAY, George O., "Financial Accounting: A Distillation of Experience," (New York, NY: The Macmillan Company, 1943).

McINNIS, J., and D.W. COLLINS, "The Effect of Cash Flow Forecasts on Accrual Quality and Benchmark Beating," *Journal of Accounting and Economics* (April 2011), pp. 219–239.

McNICHOLS, M. and G.P. WILSON, "Evidence of Earnings Management from the Provision for Bad Debts," *Journal of Accounting Research* (Supplement, 1988), pp. 1–31.

McVAY, S.E., "Earnings Management Using Classification Shifting: An Examination of Core Earnings and Special Items," *The Accounting Review* (May 2006), pp. 501–531.

MENDENHALL, R.R., "Arbitrage Risk and Post-Earnings Announcement Drift," *Journal of Business* (2004), pp. 875–894.

MERINO, D.B. and M.D. NEIMARK, "Disclosure Regulation and Public Policy: A Sociohistorical Reappraisal," *Journal of Accounting and Public Policy* (Fall 1982), pp. 33–57.

MERTON, R.C., "Theory of Rational Option Pricing," *Bell Journal of Economics and Management Science* (Spring 1973), pp. 141–183.

MERTON, R.C., "A Simple Model of Capital Market Equilibrium with Incomplete Markets," *The Journal of Finance* (July 1987), pp. 483–510.

MIAN, S.L. and C.W. SMITH, JR., "Incentives for Unconsolidated Financial Reporting," *Journal of Accounting and Economics* (January 1990), pp. 141–171.

MICROSOFT CORPORATION, *Annual Report 2012* (Washington: Microsoft Corporation, 2012).

MILGROM, P., "Good News and Bad News: Representation Theorems and Applications," *Bell Journal of Economics* (Autumn 1981), pp. 380–391.

MODIGLIANI, F. and R.A. COHN, "Inflation, Rational Valuation and the Market," *Financial Analysts' Journal* (1979), pp. 24–44.

MOHANRAM, P. and S. RAJGOPAL, "Is PIN Priced Risk?" *Journal of Accounting and Economics* (June 2009), pp. 192–2007.

MONTGOMERY, R.H., *Auditing Theory and Practice* (New York, NY: The Ronald Press Company, 1912).

MULLER, KARL A., NEAMTIU, MONICA, AND RIEDL, EDWARD J., "Do Managers Benefit from Delayed Goodwill Impairments?" (July 31, 2012). Available at http://ssrn.com/abstract=1429615 or http://dx.doi.org/10.2139/ssrn.1429615

MYERSON, R.B., "Incentive Compatibility and the Bargaining Problem," *Econometrica* (1979), pp. 61–74.

NARAYANAMOORTHY, N., "Conservatism and Cross-Sectional Variation in the Post-Earnings Announcement Drift," *Journal of Accounting Research* (September 2006), pp. 763–789.

NEWMAN, P. and R. SANSING, "Disclosure Policies with Multiple Users," *Journal of Accounting Research* (Spring 1993), pp. 92–112.

NG, J., "The Effect of Information Quality on Liquidity Risk," *Journal of Accounting and Economics* (November 2011), pp. 126–143.

NG, J., T.O. RUSTICUS, and R.S. VERDI "Implications of Transactions Costs for Post-Announcement Drift," *Journal of Accounting Research* (June 2008), pp. 661–696.

NIU, F.F. and G.D. RICHARDSON, "Are Securitizations in Substance Sales or Secured Borrowings? Capital-market evidence, *Contemporary Accounting Research* (Winter 2006), pp. 1105–1133.

O'BRIEN, P.C., "Analysts' Forecasts as Earnings Expectations," *Journal of Accounting and Economics* (January 1988), pp. 53–83.

O'BRIEN, P.C., "Changing the Concepts to Justify the Standards," *Accounting Perspectives* vol. 8, no. 4 (2009), pp. 263–275.

OGNEVA, M., "" Accrual Quality, Realized Returns, and Expected Returns: The Importance of Controlling for Cash Flow Shocks," *The Accounting Review* (July 2012), pp. 1415–1444.

OHLSON, J.A., "On the Nature of Income Measurement: The Basic Results," *Contemporary Accounting Research* (Fall 1987), pp. 1–15.

ONTARIO SECURITIES COMMISSION, National Instrument 51–102, "Continuous Disclosure Obligations" (Ontario Securities Commission: March 2004).

OZKAN, N., Z. SINGER, and H. YOU, "Mandatory IFRS Adoption and the Contractual Usefulness of Accounting Information in Executive Compensation," *Journal of Accounting Research* (September 2012), pp. 1077–1107.

PAE, J., D.B. THORNTON, and M. WELKER, "The Link between Earnings Conservatism and the Price-to-Book Ratio," *Contemporary Accounting Research* (Fall 2005), pp. 693–717.

PAE, S., "Selective Disclosure in the Presence of Uncertainty about Information Endowment," *Journal of Accounting and Economics* (September 2005), pp. 383–409.

PALMROSE, Z.-V., SCHOLZ, S., "The circumstances and legal consequences of non-GAAP reporting: evidence from restatements," Contemporary Accounting Research (Spring 2004), pp. 139–180.

PATON, W.A. and A.C. LITTLETON, *An Introduction to Corporate Accounting Standards* (Ubana, IL: American Accounting Association, 1940).

PAVLIK, E.L., T.W. SCOTT, and P. TIESSEN, "Executive Compensation: Issues and Research," *Journal of Accounting Literature* (1993), pp. 131–189.

PELTZMAN, S., "Toward a More General Theory of Regulation," *The Journal of Law and Economics* (August 1976), pp. 211–240.

PENNO, M.C., "Information Quality and Voluntary Disclosure," *The Accounting Review* (April 1997), pp. 275–284.

PLANTIN, G, H. SAPRA, and H. S. SHIN, "Marking-to-Market: Panacea or Pandora's Box?" *Journal of Accounting Research* (May 2008), pp. 435–460.

POSNER, R.A., "Theories of Economic Regulation," *Bell Journal of Economics and Management Science* (Autumn 1974), pp. 335–358.

PRATT, J.W., "Risk Aversion in the Small and in the Large," *Econometrica* (January–April 1964), pp. 122–136.

RAIFFA, H., *Decision Analysis: Introductory Lectures on Choices Under Uncertainty* (Reading, MA: Addison-Wesley, 1968).

RAJGOPAL, S. and T. SHEVLIN, "Empirical Evidence on the Relation between Stock Option Compensation and Risk Taking," *Journal of Accounting and Economics* (June 2002), pp. 145–171.

RAMAKRISHNAN, R.T.S. and J.K. THOMAS, "Valuation of Permanent, Transitory and Price-Irrelevant Components of Reported Earnings," working paper, Columbia University Business School (July 1991).

RAMALINGEGOWDA, S and Y. YU, "Institutional Ownership and Conservatism," *Journal of Accounting and Economics* (April 2012), pp. 98–114.

RAU, P.R., and JIN XU, "How do ex-ante Severance Contracts fit into Executive Incentive Schemes?" (Working paper, September 2012, forthcoming in *Journal of Accounting Research*).

RICHARDSON, S.A., R.G.SLOAN, M.T. SOLIMAN, and I. TUNA, "Accrual Reliability, Earnings Persistence, and Stock Prices, *Journal of Accounting and Economics* September 2005), pp. 437–485.

RICHARDSON, S., I. TUNA, and P. WYSOCKI, "Accounting Anomalies and Fundamental Analysis: A Review of Recent Research Advances," *Journal of Accounting and Economics* (December 2010), pp. 410–454.

RIEDL, E.J., and G. SERAFEIM, "Information Risk and Fair Values: An Examination of Equity Betas," *Journal of Accounting Research* (September 2011), pp. 1083–1122.

ROLL, R., "R^2," *Journal of Finance* (July 1988), pp. 541–566.

ROSENTHAL, R.W., "Games of Perfect Information, Predatory Pricing and the Chain-Store Paradox," *Journal of Economic Theory* (1981), pp. 92–100.

ROYAL BANK OF CANADA, "Notice of Annual Meeting of Common Shareholders, Management Proxy Circular" (Toronto, Ontario: February 26, 2009), pp. 22–31.

ROYCHOWDHURY, S., "Earnings Management through Real Activities Manipulation," *Journal of Accounting and Economics* (December 2006), pp. 335–370.

ROYCHOWDHURY, S. and R.L. WATTS, "Asymmetric Timeliness of Earnings, Market-to-Book and Conservatism in Financial Reporting," *Journal of Accounting and Economics* (September 2007), pp. 2–31.

RYAN, S.G., "A Survey of Research Relating Accounting Numbers to Systematic Equity Risk, with Implications for Risk Disclosure Policy and Future Research," *Accounting Horizons* (June 1997), pp. 82–95.

ŞABAC, F., "Dynamic Incentives and Retirement," *Journal of Accounting and Economics* (September, 2008), pp. 172–200.

SAMUELSON, P.A., "Proof That Properly Anticipated Prices Fluctuate Randomly," *Industrial Management Review* (Spring 1965), pp. 41–49.

SAPRA, H., "Do Accounting Measurement Regimes Matter? A Discussion of Mark-to-Market Accounting and Liquidity Pricing," *Journal of Accounting and Economics* (August 2008), pp. 379–387.

SAVAGE, L.J., *The Foundations of Statistics* (NY: Wiley, 1954).

SCHRAND, C.M. and B.R. WALTHER, "Strategic Benchmarks in Earnings Announcements: The Selective Disclosure of Prior-Period Earnings Components," *The Accounting Review* (April 2000), pp. 151–177.

SCOTT, W.R., "Auditor's Loss Functions Implicit in Consumption-Investment Models," *Journal of Accounting Research* (Supplement, 1975), pp. 98–117.

SECURITIES AND EXCHANGE COMMISSION, *Selective Disclosure and Insider Trading. Release Nos. 33-7881, 34-43154* (Washington, DC: SEC, 2000), (Regulation FD).

SECURITIES AND EXCHANGE COMMISSION, *Study Pursuant to Section 108(d) of the Sarbanes-Oxley Act of 2002 on the Adoption by the United States Financial Reporting System of a Principles-Based Accounting System* (Washington, DC: SEC, 2003).

SECURITIES AND EXCHANGE COMMISSION, *Work Plan for the Incorporation of International Financial Reporting Standards into the Financial reporting system for U.S. Issuers: Final Report* (Washington DC: SEC, July 13, 2012).

SENGUPTA, P., "Corporate Disclosure Quality and the Cost of Debt," *The Accounting Review* (October 1998), pp. 459–474.

SERAFEIM, G., "Consequences and Institutional Determinants of Unregulated Corporate Financial Statements: Evidence from Embedded Value Reporting," *Journal of Accounting Research* (May 2011), pp. 529–571.

SHARPE, W.F., "Capital Asset Prices: A Theory of Market Equilibrium Under Conditions of Risk," *The Journal of Finance* (September 1964), pp. 425–442.

SHEFRIN, H. and M. STATMAN, "The Disposition to Sell Winners Too Early and Ride Losers Too Long," *Journal of Finance* (July 1985), pp. 777–790.

SHILLER, R.J., "Do Stock Prices Move Too Much to be Justified by Subsequent Changes in Dividends?" *The American Economic Review* (June 1981), pp. 421–436.

SHILLER, R.J., *Irrational Exuberance* (New York, NY: Broadway Books, 2000).

SHIVAKUMAR, L., "Do Firms Mislead Investors by Overstating Earnings Before Seasoned Equity Offerings?" *Journal of Accounting and Economics* (June 2000), pp. 339–371.

SHROFF, P.K., R. VENKATARAMAN, and S. ZHANG, "The Conservatism Principle and the Asymmetric Timeliness of Earnings: An Event-Based Approach," *Contemporary Accounting Research* (Spring 2013), pp. 215–241.

SIDHU, B., T. SMITH, R.E. WHALEY, and R.H. WILLIS, "Regulation Fair Disclosure and the Cost of Adverse Selection," *Journal of Accounting Research* (June 2008), pp. 697–728.

SIMON, H.A., "A Behavioural Model of Rational Choice," *The Quarterly Journal of Economics* (February 1955), pp. 99–118.

SKINNER, D.J., "Earnings Disclosure and Stockholder Lawsuits," *Journal of Accounting and Economics* (1997), pp. 249–282.

SKINNER, D.J. and R.G. SLOAN, "Earnings Surprises, Growth Expectations, and Stock Returns or Don't Let an Earnings Torpedo Sink Your Portfolio," *Review of Accounting Studies* (2002), pp. 289–312.

SLOAN, R.G., "Do Stock Prices Fully Reflect Information in Accruals and Cash Flows About Future Earnings?" *The Accounting Review* (July 1996), pp. 289–315.

SMART, S.B., R.S. THIRUMALAI, and C.J. ZUTTER, "What's in a Vote? The Short- and Long-run Impact of Dual-Class Equity on Firm Values," *Journal of Accounting and Economics* (March 2008), pp. 94–115.

SONG, C.J., W.B. THOMAS, and H. YI, "Value Relevance of FAS No. 157 Fair Value Hierarchy Information and the Impact of Corporate Governance Mechanisms," *The Accounting Review* (July 2010), pp. 1375–1410.

SPENCE, M., "Job Market Signalling," *Quarterly Journal of Economics* (August 1973), pp. 355–374.

SPENCE, M., "Competitive and Optimal Responses to Signals: An Analysis of Efficiency and Distribution," *Journal of Economic Theory* (March 1974), pp. 296–332.

STIGLER, G.J., "The Theory of Economic Regulation," *The Bell Journal of Economics and Management Science* (Spring 1971), pp. 3–21.

STOREY, R.K. and S. STOREY, *The Framework of Financial Accounting Concepts and Standards* (Norwalk, CT: Financial Accounting Standards Board, 1998).

STUDY GROUP ON THE OBJECTIVES OF FINANCIAL STATEMENTS, *Objectives of Financial Statements* (New York, NY: American Institute of Certified Public Accountants, 1973). (Also called the Trueblood Committee Report.)

SUIJS, J. "Voluntary Disclosure of Information when Firms are Uncertain of Investor Response, "*Journal of Accounting and Economics* (July 2007), pp. 391–410.

SUROWIECKI, JAMES, *The Wisdom of Crowds* (New York, NY: Doubleday Division of Random House Inc., 2004).

SWEENEY, A.P., "Debt-covenant Violations and Managers' Accounting Responses," *Journal of Accounting and Economics* (May 1994), pp. 281–308.

TAKAYAMA, A., *Mathematical Economics, Second edition* (Cambridge: Cambridge University Press, 1985).

TAN, H., S. WANG, and M. WELKER, "Analyst Following and Forecast Accuracy after Mandated IFRS Adoption," *Journal of Accounting Research* (December 2011), pp. 1307–1357.

TAN, L. "Creditor Control Rights, State of Nature Verification, and Financial Reporting Conservatism," *Journal of Accounting and Economics* (February 2013), pp. 1–22.

The Economist, "Getting the goat," (February 20, 1999), p. 72.

The Economist, "Executive share options: Dates from hell," (July 20, 2006), pp. 59–60.

The Economist, "Make Them Pay: Bankers; pay is an easy target. Is it the right one?" Special report: International banking (May 15, 2008). Available online at http://www.economist.com/node/11325420,

The Economist, "All's fair: the crisis and fair value accounting," (September 18, 2008).

The Globe and Mail, "CEO assails pay disclosure rules," (November 18, 2002), p. B4.

TITMAN, S. and B. TRUEMAN, "Information Quality and the Valuation of New Issues," *Journal of Accounting and Economics* (June 1986), pp. 159–172.

TUCKER, J.W. and P.A. ZAROWIN, "Does Income Smoothing Improve Earnings Informativeness?" *The Accounting Review* (January 2006), pp. 251–270.

VALUKIS, A.R., "Report, in re Lehman Brothers Holdings Inc., et al," *United States Bankruptcy Court Southern District of New York, Chapter 11, Case no.08-13555 (JMP)* (New York, NY: Jenner & Block, LLP, March 11, 2010).

UNITED STATES CONGRESS SPECIAL COMMITTEE ON BANKING, HOUSING, AND URBAN AFFAIRS, *The OFHEO Report of the Special Examination of Fannie Mae* (Washington: BiblioBazzar, 2010).

VASSALOU, M., "News Related to Future GDP Growth as a Risk Factor in Equity Returns," *Journal of Financial Economics* (2003), pp. 47–73.

VERRECCHIA, R.E., "Discretionary Disclosure," *Journal of Accounting and Economics* (December 1983), pp. 179–194.

WANG, X., Increased Disclosure Requirements and Corporate Governance Decisions: Evidence from Chief Financial Officers in the Pre- and Post-Sarbanes-Oxley Periods," *Journal of Accounting Research* (September 2010), pp. 885–920.

WARFIELD, T.D. and J.J. WILD, "Accounting Recognition and the Relevance of Earnings as an Explanatory Variable for Returns," *The Accounting Review* (October 1992), pp. 821–842.

WATTS, R.L., "Conservatism in Accounting Part I: Explanations and Implications" *Accounting Horizons* (September 2003a), pp. 207–221.

WATTS, R.L., "Conservatism in Accounting Part II: Evidence and Research Opportunities," *Accounting Horizons* (December 2003b), pp. 287–301.

WATTS, R.L. and J.L. ZIMMERMAN, *Positive Accounting Theory* (Englewood Cliffs, N.J.: Prentice-Hall, 1986).

WELKER, M., "Disclosure Policy, Information Asymmetry, and Liquidity in Equity Markets," *Contemporary Accounting Research* (Spring 1995), pp. 801–827.

WINKLER, D., "India's Satyam Accounting Scandal," *The University of Iowa Center for International Finance and Development* (Briefing Paper, February 1, 2010).

WITTENBERG-MOERMAN, R., "The Role of Information Asymmetry and Financial Reporting Quality in Debt Trading: Evidence from the Secondary Loan Market," *Journal of Accounting and Economics* (December 2008), pp. 240–260.

WOLFSON, M.A., "Empirical Evidence of Incentive Problems and their Mitigation in Oil and Gas Tax Shelter Programs," in J.W. Pratt and R.J. Zeckhauser, eds., *Principals and Agents: The Structure of Business* (Boston, MA: The President and Fellows of Harvard College, 1985), pp. 101–125.

WONG, M.H.F., "The Association between SFAS 119 Derivative Disclosures and the Foreign Exchange Risk Exposure of Manufacturing Firms," *Journal of Accounting Research* (Autumn 2000), pp. 387–417.

WURGLER, J., "Financial Markets and the Allocation of Capital," *Journal of Financial Economics*, vol. 58 (2000), pp. 187–214.

YEDLIN, DEBORAH, "Accounting rule change burns big oil," *The Globe and Mail* (November 8, 2002), p. B2.

YERMACK, D., "Good Timing: CEO Stock Option Awards and Company News Announcements," *Journal of Finance* (1997), pp. 449–476.

YOUNG, S. and J. YANG, "Stock Repurchase and Executive Compensation Contract Design: The Role of Earnings per Share Performance Conditions," *The Accounting Review* (March 2011), pp. 703–733.

ZEFF, S.A., "How the U.S. Accounting Profession Got Where it is Today: Part II," *Accounting Horizons* (December 2003), pp. 267–286.

ZHANG, JIEYING, "The Contracting Benefits of Accounting Conservatism to Lenders and Borrowers," *Journal of Accounting and Economics* (March 2008), pp. 27–54.

ZHANG, LI, "The Effect of *Ex Ante* Management Forecast Accuracy on the Post-Earnings-Announcement Drift," *The Accounting Review* (September 2012), pp. 1791–1818.

ZHANG, X.F., "Accruals, Investment, and the Accrual Anomaly," *The Accounting Review* (October 2007), pp. 1333–1363.

ZHANG, YUAN., "Revenue Recognition Timing and Attributes of Reported Revenue: The Case of Software Industry's Adoption of SOP 91–1," *Journal of Accounting and Economics* (September 2005), pp. 535–561.

ZHANG, YUAN., "Analyst Responsiveness and the Post-Earnings Announcement Drift," *Journal of Accounting and Economics* (September 2008), pp. 201–215.

INDEX

rational decision-making
    theory, 6
  single-person, 74–78
decision tree, 76
decision useful, 6
decision usefulness
    see also decision theory
    approach, described, 73–74
    concept of, 72
    conclusions, 107
    described, 6, 22, 28
    efficient contracting. See effi-
        cient contracting theory
    measurement approach. See
        measurement approach
    overview, 72–73
    portfolio diversification,
        85–87
    professional accounting bodies
        and, 102–107
    standard setting, 538–539
    vs. stewardship, 73
"deep in the money," 324–325, 329,
    442n
delegated monitoring, 350n–351n
Deloitte and Touche, 234
depth (market), 35n, 143
derecognition, 271–275
deregulation, 488
derivative instruments
    characteristics of, 275–277
    fair value, 276–278
    as financial assets, 259
    hedge accounting, 278–281
    leverage aspect, 276
    option pricing model,
        276–278, 277f
    settlement in cash, 275–276
    speculation with, 292, 309n
    swap contracts, 306n
    underlying variables, 257
Deutsche Bank, 260
development costs, 547
direct monitoring, 363
disclosure
    see also full disclosure
    changing prices, effects of, 5
    disclosure principle, 497–503
    ERC findings, 169–170
    expanded, 24
    of fair value, 261
    financial statements
        proper, 71n
    golden parachutes, 431
    internal control effective-
        ness, 31
    late timing, ESO awards, 431
    of management compensa-
        tion, 16
    notes to statements, 35n
    partial, 501

present value, 49
quality, tests for, 509–511
regulations controlling, 3
selective, 563n, 564n
sensitivity, 294, 295t
superior, 506–511
voluntary, 3, 131, 501, 508
disclosure principle, 497–503
discount rate, 308n
discretionary accruals, 166, 445,
    449t, 484n–485n
disposition effect, 194–195
diversification, 85–87, 207–208
dividend irrelevancy, 39–40, 221
dividend payout ratio, 290
dividend policy, 504
double entry system, 1–2
Dow Jones Industrial Average, 156,
    159, 521n
dual-class common share struc-
    tures, 443n
due process, 29, 533
dynamic provisioning, 300n

E

earnings
    abnormal, 44–45, 187n, 222,
        225–226, 249n
    actual, 229
    future, 232, 462–463, 466
    gains training, 233, 268
    investor expectations, 168
    management. See earnings
        management
    persistence, 164–166,
        169–170
    pro-forma, 444, 470–471
    quality, 164–167
    quarterly seasonal earnings
        changes, 203–204
    and recognition lag, 162
    terminal value, 231–232
    unexpected, 45
    use of term, 33n
    variability of, 199–200
    volatility, 247n
earnings dynamic, 225–226
earnings management
    and accruals reversal, 445
    bad side of, 465–472
    biased reporting, 370–371
    blocked communication,
        459–461
    for bonus purposes, 448–454
    conclusions, 472–473
    contracting motivations,
        454–455
    controlling, 373–375
    debt covenants, 454–455
    defined, 445
    described, 369–370

empirical evidence, 461–464
good side of, 458–464
implications for accoun-
    tants, 472
income maximization, 447
income minimization, 447
income smoothing, 447
international context, 468
investors' expectations, 455–
    457
managers' speech, 471–472
market efficiency, 469–471
motivations for, 454–458
multi-period horizons, 446
net income, limiting bias
    in, 374–375
opportunistic, 465–468
overview, 444–446
patterns of, 447
pro-forma earnings, 444,
    470–471
real variables, 446
reputation, 446, 457
revelation principle, 371–373
stock offerings, 457–458
taking a bath, 447
earnings persistence, 164–166,
    188n, 225–227
earnings quality, 79, 164–167
earnings response coefficients (ERC),
    163–172
    calculation of, 163
    described, 163
    differential marketing
        response, 163–169
    earnings expectations, measur-
        ing, 170–171
    market value ERCs, 187n
    research and, 169–170
earnout contract, 399n
economic consequences
    accounting policies, 334
    defined, 321
    efficient securities mar-
        kets, 321, 388–389
    ESO expensing, 329
    of IASB adoption, 553
    incomplete contracts, 390
    new standards, 321, 358, 540
    overview, 321–322
    standard changes, 321, 358
economic profit, 245n
Economist, The, 260, 329, 419, 427
economy-wide factors, 86, 118n
effective interest rate, 256
efficiency, 121–123, 126
efficient contracting theory
    accounting policies, 315–318
    conservatism, 316–318
    contract rigidity, 318–322
    debt and stewardship, 334–335